Changdeokgung

1 The 'Palace of Illustrious Virtue' (p45; pictured below) was built in the early 15th century as a secondary palace to Gyeongbukgung, though these days this Unesco World Heritage–listed property exceeds Gyeongbukgung in beauty and grace – partly because so many of its buildings were actually lived in by members of the royal family well into the 20th century. The most charming section is the Huwon, a 'secret garden' that is a royal horticultural idyll. Book well ahead to snag one of the limited tickets to view this special palace on a moonlight tour.

Winter Sports

2 They say third time's a charm, and so Pyeongchang (p142) won the chance to host the Winter Olympics with its third bid. In 2018 the Games were held at the Alpensia and Yongpyong ski resorts, as well as the Gangneung coastal area. Located near each other, Alpensia and Yongpyong have dozens of runs, including slopes for families and beginners, views of the East Sea (Sea of Japan) on clear days and some new and first-rate accommodation and leisure facilities.

JAIONE_GARCIA / SHUTTERSTOCK ©

2

RICHARD NEBESKY / GETTY IMAGES ©

3

YOCHIKA PHOTOGRAPHER / SHUTTERSTOCK ©

4

BOB AND TESSA / SHUTTERSTOCK ©

Boryeong Mud Festival

3 Every July, thousands of people converge on the welcoming seaside town of Boryeong and proceed to jump into gigantic vats of mud. Welcome to the Boryeong Mud Festival (p293; pictured top). The official line is that the mud has restorative properties, but one look around and it's clear that no one really cares for much except having a slippery, sloshin', messy good time. Mud aside, this foreigner-friendly and high-profile festival also features concerts, raves and fireworks. A tip: don't wear anything you want to keep!

Hwaseong Fortress

4 Built as an act of filial devotion and heavily damaged during the colonisation period of the early 20th century and again in the Korean War, the restoration of this Unesco World Heritage site began in the 1970s and is now almost finished. A detailed 1801 record of its construction has allowed the 5.52km-long wall and the Hwaseong Haenggung (p101; pictured above), a palace for the king to stay in during his visits to Suwon, to be rebuilt with great historical accuracy. A walk around the wall takes you through four grand gates.

5

ESCAN / SHUTTERSTOCK ©

6

YEONGSIK IM / SHUTTERSTOCK ©

Island Hiking

5 The dramatic volcanic landscape of Jeju-do, the largest of South Korea's islands, is best seen on foot. The Jeju Olle Trail (p250; pictured top) is a network of 26 half- to full-day hiking routes that meander around the island's coast, part of the hinterland and three other islands. Spending a day following all or part of a trail is a wonderful way to soak up Jeju's unique charms and beautiful surroundings. The summit of Halla-san, the country's highest peak, is also very achievable and, in good weather, provides spectacular views.

Hanok Delights

6 Jeonju's version of a traditional village (p269; pictured above) is impressive although many of the buildings are new. The slate-roof houses are home to traditional arts – artisans craft fans, hand-make paper and brew *soju* (local vodka). Foodies will be pleased that the birthplace of bibimbap offers the definitive version of this dish. If you decide to stay (and you will), you'll find plenty of traditional guesthouses, where visitors sleep on a *yo* (padded quilt) in an *ondol* (underfloor heating) room. There's even one run by the grandson of King Gojong.

CJ NATTANAI / SHUTTERSTOCK ©

South Korea's Second City

7 Mountains, beaches, street food and a cosmopolitan vibe make Busan (p182), Korea's second-largest metropolis, one of the country's most enjoyable cities to hang out. Its top attraction is the atmospheric Jagalchi Fish Market, where you can buy and eat the freshest of seafood. Also, don't miss sunrise on Haeundae beach (p183; pictured above); the Busan Cinema Center, an architecturally dazzling structure; strolling the lanes of Gamcheon Culture Village; sampling the local dessert *sulbing;* and knocking back shots of *soju* in a tent bar.

Gwangjang Market

8 Secondhand clothes, fabrics and eats can be found during the day, but it's at night that Gwangjang (p75; pictured top right) comes into its own, when diners are drawn to the aroma of street food that fills some of the market's alleys (pictured above right). Stewed pigs' trotters and snouts, *gimbap* (rice, vegies and Spam wrapped in rice and rolled in sheets of seaweed) and *bindaet-tok* (plate-sized crispy pancakes of crushed mung beans and vegies fried on a skillet) are all washed down with copious amounts of *makgeolli* (rice wine) and *soju* (local liquors).

Bulguk-sa

9 It's hard to choose just one standout treasure in and around magnificent Gyeongju, but this Unesco World Heritage cultural site is most likely to take the honour, not least because it contains seven Korean 'national treasures' within its walls. The high point of the so-called golden age of Silla architecture, this sophisticated yet wonderfully subtle temple complex (p162; pictured bottom right), with its pagodas, white stone sets of stairs and gorgeous, undulating scenery, is a monument to the skill of its carpenters, painters, craftsmen and architects.

8

9

ISARINT SANGMANEE / SHUTTERSTOCK ©

Templestay

10 A bell rings and you wake at 3.30am to prepare for a morning meditation session. Breakfast is an austere meal, taken in silence so you can contemplate the ache in your bones from bowing 108 times in front of a Buddha image. Later, you'll have more meditation time to contemplate the surrender of your body and mind in the search for inner peace. A templestay is the perfect antidote to fast-paced modern Korea, and while the country is awash with temples, the impressive fortress-like compound of Guin-sa (p307; pictured top) is among the finest.

Hahoe Folk Village

11 The closest thing Korea has to a time machine, the charming Hahoe Folk Village (p176; pictured above) is a truly wonderful experience for anyone wanting to get a sense of how Korea looked, felt, sounded and smelt before the 20th century changed the country forever. More than 200 people continue to live here, maintaining traditional ways and customs and even inviting people to spend the night in their *minbak* (private homes with rooms for rent). At the village heart rises an ancient spirit tree, the focus of local rituals and prayers.

Cheong-gye-cheon

12 A raised highway was demolished to allow reconstruction of this buried stream (p42; pictured top). The effort transformed central Seoul, creating a riverside park and walking course that provides respite from the surrounding hubbub. Public art is dots the banks of the stream and many events are held here, including a spectacular lantern festival in November, when thousands of giant glowing paper sculptures are floated in the water. There's also a good museum where you can learn about the history of the Cheong-gye-cheon (the name means 'Clear Stream').

Seeing the Border

13 It's known as the Demilitarized Zone (DMZ; p96; pictured above). But this 4km-wide, 250km-long heavily mined and guarded buffer, splitting North from South Korea, is anything but. An enduring Cold War symbol, the DMZ is a surreal tourist draw, on both sides of the border. The tension is most palpable in the Joint Security Area, the neutral area built after the 1953 Armistice for the holding of peace talks, which can only be visited on an organised tour. Seven observations points along the South Korean side of the DMZ allow visitors to peer into the secretive North.

Need to Know

For more information, see Survival Guide (p385)

Currency

Korean won (₩)

Language

Korean

Visas

Many visitors don't need a visa, but if your country is not on the permit-on-arrival list, you will need one.

Money

The South Korean unit of currency is the won (₩), with ₩10, ₩50, ₩100 and ₩500 coins. Notes come in denominations of ₩1000, ₩5000, ₩10,000 and ₩50,000.

Mobile Phones

Most networks in South Korea use the WCDMA 2100 MHz network, as well as one of five different 4G LTE bands. Most unlocked recent smartphones will work with a Korean SIM. Mobile phones and portable wi-fi eggs can be hired.

Time

Korea Standard Time (GMT/UCT plus nine hours)

When to Go

High Season (Jun–Sep)

- Be prepared for sweltering heat and a very heavy rainy season through July across the peninsula.

Shoulder (May, Oct)

- Late spring sees the country bathed first in blossoms – cherry trees, azaleas – then fresh, abundant greenery as the weather warms.
- In autumn the heat of summer has ebbed and things are cool, comfortable and crisp.

Low Season (Nov–Apr)

- Snow falls and temperatures plummet.
- Best time for skiing and visiting museums and galleries, while winter photographers will be in seventh heaven.

Useful Websites

Everyday Korea (www.everydaykorea.com) Info on a whole range of Korean topics.

Korea Tourism Organization (KTO; www.visitkorea.or.kr) Official government-run site.

Korea4Expats (www.korea4expats.com) Covers many aspects of Korean life.

Korea.net (www.korea.net) A treasure trove of background detail on the Republic of Korea (ROK).

Lonely Planet (www.lonelyplanet.com/south-korea) Destination information, hotel bookings, traveller forum and more.

Important Numbers

Ambulance & Fire (English translators available)	☎119
Emergency medical information (English available)	☎1339
Police	☎112
South Korea country code	☎82
Tourist information (English-speaking)	☎1330

Exchange Rates

Australia	A$1	₩800
Canada	C$1	₩865
Euro zone	€1	₩1305
Japan	¥100	₩1010
UK	UK£1	₩1470
US	US$1	₩1130

For current exchange rates, see www.xe.com.

Daily Costs

Budget: Less than ₩100,000

- Dorm bed: ₩20,000
- Street food: ₩1000–5000
- Hiking: free
- Entry to National Museum of Korea: free
- Subway ticket: ₩1300

Midrange: ₩100,000–300,000

- *Hanok* guesthouse: ₩70,000
- Entry to Gyeongbokgung (Palace of Shining Happiness): ₩3000
- Barbecued pork meal: ₩40,000
- Theatre ticket: ₩40,000

Top end: More than ₩300,000

- High-end hotel: ₩200,000
- Royal Korean banquet: ₩80,000
- Scrub and massage at a *jjimjilbang* (luxury sauna): ₩60,000
- Demilitarized Zone (DMZ) tour: ₩100,000

Opening Hours

Banks 9am to 4pm Monday to Friday, ATMs 7am to 11pm (or 24 hours)

Bars 6pm to 1am, longer hours Friday and Saturday

Cafes 7am to 10pm

Restaurants 11am to 10pm

Shops 10am to 8pm

Arriving in South Korea

Incheon Airport (Seoul) Express trains (₩9000, 43 minutes from Terminal 1, 51 minutes from Terminal 2) every 30 minutes to Seoul; also all-stop trains ₩4150 from Terminal 1 (55 minutes), ₩4950 from Terminal 2 (one hour). Buses (from ₩9000) and taxis (around ₩65,000) to city-centre hotels take an hour or more.

Gimpo Airport (Seoul) Express trains (₩1450, 24 minutes) run regularly to Seoul station; or catch the subway (₩1450, 35 minutes). Limo buses (₩7000) and taxis (around ₩35,000) take 40 minutes to one hour to the city centre or Gangnam.

Gimhae Airport (Busan) Limo buses (₩6000 to ₩7000, one hour) and regular 'town' buses (₩1300, one hour) to Busan every 20 minutes; or light rail line to Sasang subway station (₩2800, one hour). Taxis (around ₩40,000) take 30 minutes to one hour to the city.

Getting Around

Air There are dozens of local airports and reasonable fares, thanks to competition from budget airlines.

Bus Cheaper and slower than trains but serving every corner of the country.

Car Not recommended for first-time visitors. You must be over 21 and have an international driving permit.

Ferry Connecting the mainland to hundreds of islands.

Train Clean, comfortable and punctual but not comprehensive. A KR Pass is useful, even for something as straightforward as a return Seoul–Busan train.

For much more on **getting around**, see p395

First Time Korea

For more information, see Survival Guide (p385)

Checklist

- Check the validity of your passport
- If you plan to hire a car, bring a current international driving permit
- Check airline baggage restrictions
- Check government travel websites
- Call banks and credit-card providers and tell them your travel dates
- Organise travel insurance
- Check whether your mobile phone is compatible with Korea's WCDMA digital standard. See p16 for more.

What to Pack

- Phrasebook, mini dictionary
- Travel plug
- Insect repellent
- WCDMA-enabled phone
- Painkillers
- Padlock
- Small backpack for day hikes
- Slip-on shoes (for taking off and putting on quickly when entering and exiting abodes)
- Medical kit
- Sunscreen

Top Tips for Your Trip

- It's worth investing in a KR Pass even if you make only one longish trip on a fast train, such as Seoul to Busan return.
- Save money on public-transport fares (and also pay for taxis) using a touch-and-go T-Money Card (or Cash Bee Card).
- Check with local tourist offices about free guided tours with students and other citizens who speak English and other languages.
- Spend over ₩30,000 at shops participating in the Global Refund scheme and you can claim VAT back on leaving the country.
- Hops from Seoul to Jeju-do on budget airlines may seem cheap, but check on baggage restrictions and extra costs before deciding – flying with Korean Air or Asiana may work out a better deal.

What to Wear

The vast majority of Koreans wear western-style dress these days, although you'll sometimes see people in *hanbok* (Korean clothing). The best version of this type of clothing – in fine silks and organza – are usually worn by women, and sometimes men, for formal occasions. More casual pyjama-style *hanbok* are made from cotton and are very comfortable for everyday wear.

For business, Koreans are quite formal and wear suits and ties. Out on the hiking trails or golf courses you'll see locals kitted out in the latest high-tech performance gear as if they were about to scale Everest or compete in the Masters.

Sleeping

In general you don't need to worry about where to stay – hotels and motels are so numerous there's usually little need to book ahead.

Motels The most common form of accommodation. Most offer plain, if well-equipped rooms. Some can be fancy, particularly rent-by-the-hour love motels.

Hanok guesthouses Often only have a few rooms, so advance booking is advised.

Hostels and guesthouses Common in cities, and the best place to meet fellow travellers and English-speaking Koreans.

Advance Planning

Three months before Check your passport validity; start learning *hangeul* (written Korean), a straightforward alphabet. Book ahead for super-popular tours.

One month before Book *hanok* (traditional house) rooms, as these have only three or four guest rooms in total, and templestays. Book the Koridoor Tours trip, run by the USO (p98), to the Demilitarized Zone (DMZ).

Two weeks ahead If you are travelling over any of Korea's major holidays, book all internal transport well ahead of time. Book tables at sell-out restaurants.

Bargaining

Try bargaining (with a smile) if you're prepared to pay in cash and buy in bulk at markets, from street and subway vendors and even, occasionally, for big-ticket items in department stores.

Tipping

Tipping is generally not expected.

Restaurants No need to tip; only top-end hotel restaurants will add a service charge.

Guides Not expected; a small gift will be appreciated, though.

Taxis No need to tip; fares are metered or agreed before you get in.

Hotels Only in the most luxurious do you need to tip bellhops etc, and only if service is good.

Language

Korean is the common language. It's relatively easy to find English-speakers in the big cities, but not so easy in smaller towns and the countryside. Learning the writing system, *hangeul,* and a few key phrases will help you enormously in being able to decode street signs, menus and timetables. In big cities, nearly all the street signs are in Korean and English.

Etiquette

There are several social rules that Koreans stick to, although foreigners are generally given some slack.

Meetings and greetings A quick, short bow is most respectful for meetings and departures. Use both hands to give or receive business cards (an essential feature of doing business in Korea), money or gifts. Receive money crossing one hand over the receiving arm.

Shoes Remove your shoes on entering a Korean home, guesthouse, temple or Korean-style restaurant. Some temples indicate a side entrance for nonmonks.

Eating and drinking Pour drinks for others and use both hands when pouring or receiving. Use chopsticks or a spoon to touch food and don't leave either sticking up in a bowl of rice.

Loss of face A mishandled remark should be smoothed over quickly, and if you sense someone trying to change the subject, go with the flow. Arguing is best avoided, even if you are in the right.

Eating

Dining options range from casual bites at a market stall to elaborate multicourse meals at lavish restaurants. While the basic building blocks of the cuisine are recognisably Asian (garlic, ginger, green onion, black pepper, vinegar and sesame oil), Korean food combines them with three essential sauces: *ganjang* (soy sauce), *doenjang* (fermented soybean paste) and *gochujang* (hot red-pepper paste). The main course is nearly always served with *bap* (boiled rice), soup, kimchi and a procession of *banchan* (side dishes).

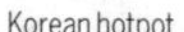

Korean hotpot

BOONTOOM SAE-KOR / SHUTTERSTOCK ©

If You Like...

Top Tastes

Busan Sink your teeth into a twitching squid tentacle at Jagalchi Fish Market (p182; pictured top right), or snack on the nether parts of chickens in tent bars.

Jeonju Eat bibimbap, Korea's most famous culinary export (after kimchi, of course), at its birthplace. (p269)

Boseong Try the green-tea ice cream, green-tea noodles and green-tea biscuits close by tea plantations. (p225)

Chuncheon Along Dakgalbi Geori there are 20-plus restaurants serving the town's famous spicy chicken dish, *dakgalbi*. (p120)

Gwangjang Market Sample supertasty and cheap street food in one of Seoul's massive covered markets. (p75)

Sokcho Platters of raw fish and other seafood delights at this east-coast port. (p127)

Sansawon Brewery & Museum Unlimited tastings during the tour of this producer of traditional Korean liquors. (p102)

Traditional Architecture

Changdeokgung The most attractive of Seoul's palaces, this World Heritage–listed site also has a 'secret garden'. (p45)

Bukchon Hanok Village Around 900 *hanok* (traditional wooden houses) make this Seoul's largest neighbourhood of traditional homes. (p44)

Seokbul-sa Hidden in the mountains of Busan, this temple perches daintily among enormous cliff-like boulders. (p186)

Jeonju Hanok Maeul Jeonju's sprawling *hanok* village is a charming nod to Korea's low-slung architectural style. (p269)

Hahoe Folk Village People still live in the rustic homes in this beautiful riverside village complex. (p176)

Haein-sa This delightful temple houses the *Tripitaka Koreana*: 81,258 wooden printing blocks containing Buddhist scriptures. (p155)

Dosan Seowon Lovely arrangement of traditional halls at this scenically located Confucian academy in the hills north of Andong. (p174)

World Heritage Sites

Jongmyo The royal ancestral shrine set in peaceful wooded grounds is just one of several World Heritage sites in Seoul. (p48)

Namhansanseong Hike beside 17th-century fortress walls surrounded by beautiful pine and oak forests and wildflowers. (p105)

Hwaseong Suwon's impressive fortress walls have been meticulously reconstructed with great historical accuracy. (p99)

Gochang Thousands of Bronze Age tombs known as dolmen dot the hills around this small village. (p276)

Gyeongju Sublime ancient burial mounds undulate parts of town into gorgeous, grass-covered hillocks. (p158)

Jeju-do The dormant volcanoes, Halla-san and Seongsan Ilchulbong, and a network of lava-tube caves are all World Heritage worthy. (p237)

Haein-sa This serene and beautifully situated Buddhist temple is the repository for the priceless *Triptaka Koreana*. (p155)

Outdoor Activities

Jeju Olle Trail Discover Jeju-do's byways on this excellent series of hiking routes around the volcanic island. (p250)

Cycle along the Han River Pedal the cycle lanes linking the parks strung along Seoul's major waterway. (p65)

Wolchulsan National Park Hike through Korea's smallest national park over a vertigo-inducing 52m-high bridge spanning two ridges. (p234)

Seogwipo Korea's best scuba-diving destination, with colourful corals, kelp forests and dolphins. (p259)

Top: Jagalchi Fish Market (p182), Busan, South Korea

Bottom: Seoul City Hall (p51), Seoul, South Korea

High1 Ski Resort Check out the ski season at this resort in the mountains west of Taebaek. (p143)

Seoul City Wall Hike beside and upon these ancient walls as they snake over the capital's four guardian mountains. (p57)

Saryangdo Tackle jagged ridges, 400m peaks, ropes and ladders on the hike around this beautiful island. (p202)

Seoraksan National Park Hike from temple to temple, past waterfalls, fortress remains, peaks and valleys in a sublime landscape. (p123)

Contemporary Buildings

Dongdaemun Design Plaza & Park Zaha Hadid's sleek building is straight out of a sci-fi fantasy. (p56)

Seoul City Hall This giant glass wave is a modern reinterpretation of traditional Korean design. (p51; pictured bottom left)

Busan Cinema Center Architecturally dazzling structure with the biggest screen in the country. (p195)

Songdo International City Marvel at this model urban development in the bay off Incheon. (p107)

Glass House Stunning glass, concrete and steel structure on Jeju-do, designed by Japanese architect Ando Tadao. (p252)

Museums & Galleries

National Museum of Korea Packed with national treasures spanning the centuries. (p55)

Leeum Samsung Museum of Art Three top architect-designed buildings and a dazzling collection of art from ancient to contemporary. (p55)

National Museum of Modern and Contemporary Art Make the trek out to Seoul Grand Park to see this classy art museum. (p107)

Asian Culture Complex Collection of galleries and performance spaces on the main site of Gwangju's May 18 uprising. (p215)

Arario Museum A quartet of renovated buildings in Jeju-si house showcase an outstanding collection of contemporary art. (p240)

Gyeongju National Museum Houses a superb collection of artefacts from the Silla dynasty and beyond. (p158)

Daegu National Museum One of Korea's best regional museums, packed with everything from armour to Buddhist relics. (p148)

Offbeat Experiences

Dragon Hill Spa & Resort Strip down for a communal steam and full-body scrub at this fancy *jjimjilbang* (upmarket sauna) in Seoul. (p59)

Chamsori Gramophone & Edison Museum If you love music and the spirit of invention, don't miss this astounding collection of vintage machines. (p135)

Haesindang Park Admire phallic sculptures in this park in the fishing village of Sinnam. (p140)

Jeju's Sex Museums Gain a very adult education at Jeju-do's trio of nookie-obsessed exhibitions. (p265)

Kumsusan Memorial Palace of the Sun Pay your respects to the embalmed body of Great Leader Kim Il-sung in his former palace. (p312)

Mr Toilet House Hilarious poo-related exhibits and more serious sanitation issues at this toilet-shaped museum in Suwon. (p101)

Unification Park Climb aboard a captured North Korean submarine at this east-coast seafront park. (p138)

Early Printing Museum Being rained upon by countless *hanja* (Chinese characters) at an interactive display at this fascinating Cheongju museum. (p299)

Scenic Spots

Suncheon-man Rich mud beneath the rustling reeds attracts migratory birds and, in turn, scores of tourists. (p221)

Paekdusan One of the best reasons to visit the Democratic People's Republic of Korea (DPRK; North Korea) is this stunning and fabled mountain. (p322)

Bukhansan National Park Sweeping mountaintop vistas, maple leaves and rushing streams all within easy reach of Seoul. (p99)

Ji-dong Mural Village Outside Suwon's city walls, this labyrinth of grungy alleyways bursts with vibrant wall murals. (p102)

Changpyeong Slow City Enjoy the slow life in this village of centuries-old stone walls, homesteads and heritage houses. (p219)

Jikji-sa Popular templestay in a postcard-pretty temple in a quiet forest. (p156)

Geumgang Park Cable Car Providing breathtaking views of Busan's mountains, harbour and cityscape. (p186)

Seoullo 7017 This elevated park on a disused highway overpass looks out onto views of central Seoul. (p49)

Island Life

Namhaedo You'll blink several times and think you've been transported to southern France on this gorgeous island. (p206)

Ulleungdo This East Sea island offers mist-shrouded volcanic cliffs, traditional harbour towns and a breathtaking jagged coastline. (p169)

Udo Admire the Seongsan Ilchulbong tuff cone volcano from the white coral-sand beach on this lovely island. (p253)

So-Muuido Stroll around this car-free island at the southeastern tip of lovely Muuido. (p112)

Sapsido Offers undeveloped beaches, bucolic villages surrounded by rice paddies, and the salty smell of fish. (p294)

Namiseom Island Spot deer, ostriches and waterfowl on this wooded, lake-bound island southwest of Chuncheon. (p120)

Crafts & Shopping

Namdaemun Market Open round the clock, with more than 10,000 stores dealing in everything from seaweed to spectacles. (p49)

Shinsegae Centum City Shop till you drop in Busan at the world's largest department store. (p197)

Icheon Ceramic Village See traditional kilns and buy beautiful pots directly from their makers. (p105)

Goryeo Celadon Museum Before you buy, watch celadon (green-glazed pottery) being crafted and kiln-fired here. (p227)

Daegu's Herbal Medicine Market Stock up on anything from cheap ginseng to reindeer horns at this fascinating market. (p149)

Damyang Long famed for its bamboo products, this town holds a bamboo crafts festival in May. (p219)

Daein-sijang Fifty-plus artists have studios beside regular stalls at this traditional market in Gwangju. (p214)

Month by Month

TOP EVENTS

Lotus Lantern Festival, May

Jongmyo Daeje, May

Boryeong Mud Festival, July

Busan International Film Festival, October

Gwangju Biennale September to November

January

Freezing temperatures and snow across much of the country.

Taebaeksan Snow Festival

Enjoy sledding fun and marvel at giant ice sculptures at this winter celebration in Taebaeksan Provincial Park. (p139)

February

Local religious holidays and festivals follow the lunar calendar, while the rest follow the Gregorian (western) calendar.

Seollal (Lunar New Year)

Koreans visit relatives, honour ancestors and eat traditional foods over this three-day national holiday. For more information see www.visitseoul.net or www.visitkorea.or.kr. In 2019 Seollal begins on 5 February, in 2020 on 25 January and in 2021 on 12 February.

April

Bring your raincoat and warm clothes as the weather can still be wintry and wet. Early April is cherry-blossom season.

Chinese Day Cultural Festival

This event is held in Incheon's Jayu Park and around Chinatown in September as well as April.

Yeongdeungpo Yeouido Spring Flower Festival

Masses of cherry blossoms around Seoul draw the biggest crowds, but you can also see the flowers on Namsan and at Ewha Womans University. (p60)

Samcheok Maengbang Canola Flower Festival

Head down to the beach at Maengbang outside Samcheok to tiptoe through the bright-yellow rapeseed flowers, celebrated in this floral festival.

GIC Biennale

Running into May, the world's largest biennale specialising in ceramics (www.kocef.org) is for people potty about pottery. It's held in odd-numbered years in Incheon.

Pyongyang Marathon

Held on the nearest Sunday to 15 April (Kim Il-sung's birthday), this event (www.pyongyangmarathon.com) is a unique chance to run through the North Korean capital.

May

One of the most pleasant months to visit, with good weather and fewer accommodation issues.

Jongmyo Daeje

Held on the first Sunday of the month, this ceremony honours Korea's royal ancestors and involves a solemn, costumed parade through central Seoul to the royal shrine at Jongmyo, where spectators can enjoy traditional music and an all-day ritual. (p60)

Lotus Lantern Festival

The weekend preceding Buddha's birthday, Seoul celebrates with a huge daytime street festival and evening lantern parade – the largest in South Korea. (p60)

Buddha's Birthday

Brings a kaleidoscope of light and colour, as rows of

paper lanterns are strung down main thoroughfares and in temple courtyards across Korea (celebrated on 12 May 2019, 30 April 2020 and 19 May 2021).

Chuncheon International Mime Festival

The lakeside city hosts street performers, magicians, acrobats and quirky shows such as a soap-bubble opera at this festival. (p122)

June

Warmer weather makes this an excellent time to enjoy the outdoors on hiking trips and at the beach.

Gangneung Danoje Festival

Recognised by Unesco as a Masterpiece of the Oral and Intangible Heritage of Humanity, this festival is held according to the lunar calendar and features shamanist rituals, mask dances and market stalls. (p135)

July

It rains a lot during July; make sure you have the gear and arrange your travel plans accordingly.

Ansan Valley Rock Festival

One of Korea's premier summer music festivals (www.valleyrockfestival.com), with a stellar line-up of international headliners as well quality K-Indie bands.

Boryeong Mud Festival

Head to Daecheon Beach to wallow in mud pools and take part in stacks of muddy fun and games. (p293)

August

Head for coastal areas and the mountains to find some relief from the sweltering heat of summer.

Chungju World Martial Arts Festival

This festival is held in the World Martial Arts Park, where you'll see all sorts of unusual martial arts with teams participating from across the world. (p302)

September

Book ahead for transport around Chuseok, when many Koreans visit family and friends.

Chuseok

The three-day Harvest Moon Festival is a major holiday when families gather, visit their ancestors' graves and perform *sebae* (a ritual bow). Begins on 12 September in 2019, 30 September 2020 and 20 September 2021.

Gwangju Biennale

Held from September until November in even-numbered years, Korea's leading international art show is a two-month carnival of the avant-garde. (p215)

Mask Dance Festival

This 10-day festival in Andong, held at the end of the month and running into October, brings together more than 20 traditional dance troupes. (p174)

Korea International Art Fair

Held at Seoul's COEX Mall, KIAF (http://kiaf.org) is one of the region's top art fairs and a good opportunity to get a jump on the country's hot new artists.

October

This is the season when the mountains display a palate of rustic colours.

Busan International Film Festival

Korea's top international film festival, held in the architecturally stunning Busan Cinema Center, attracts stars from across Asia and beyond. (p188)

Seoul International Fireworks Festival

Best viewed from Yeouido Hangang Park, this festival sees dazzling fireworks displays staged by both Korean and international teams. (p60)

Baekje Cultural Festival

This major festival, packed with events, is held in Buyeo in even-numbered years and in Gongju in odd-numbered years. (p288)

Gwangju World Kimchi Culture Festival

Join the celebrations for Korea's most famous contribution to the culinary arts. For details see http://kimchi.gwangju.go.kr.

Incheon Bupyeong Pungmul Festival

Dance along to traditional folk-music performances and experience other aspects of Korean culture; see www.icbp.go.kr/open_content/foreign/eng/festival.jsp for details.

Itineraries

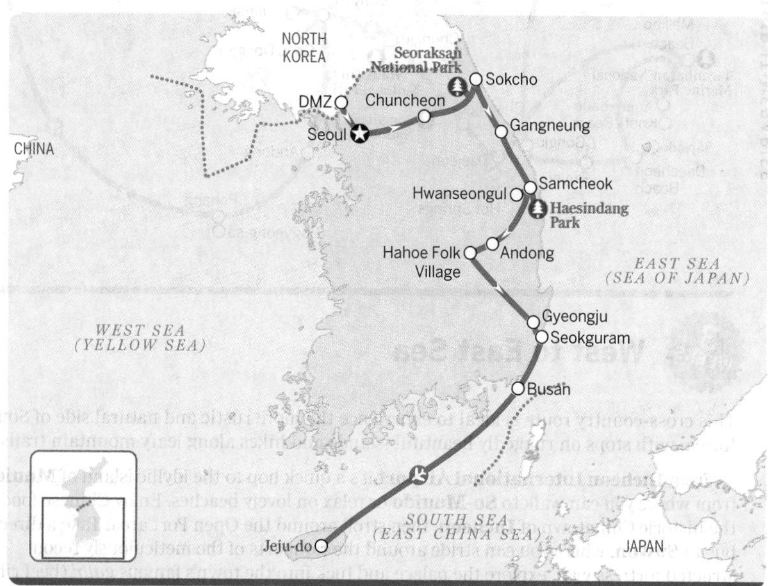

2 WEEKS

South Korea's Highlights

Enjoy the best of Korea on this trip lassoing in the dynamic capital Seoul, the bustling southern port of Busan, lost-in-time country towns and offbeat sights before finishing on the beautiful island of Jeju-do.

Spend four or five days exploring **Seoul**, including a day trip north to the **DMZ**. Next head east to **Chuncheon**, to cycle alongside Uiam Lake and sample the town's famous chicken dish, *dakgalbi*.

Dine on fresh seafood in **Sokcho**, then hike around the sublime peaks and waterfalls of **Seoraksan National Park**. Follow the coast south to **Gangneung** to discover well-preserved Joseon-era buildings before continuing to **Samcheok** to set foot in the huge **Hwanseongul** cave, as well as **Haesindang Park**, packed with phallic sculptures. Hunt down the pagodas, temples and sights in and around **Andong** before delving into Korea's thatched past at serene **Hahoe Folk Village**. Continue to **Gyeongju**, ancient capital of the Silla kingdom, where the town's royal tombs, excellent museum and the World Heritage–listed grotto at **Seokguram** will need several days.

Busan, with its fish market, beaches and urban buzz, is worth a few days. From here fly to **Jeju-do**, where amazing volcanic scenery accompanies leisurely hikes.

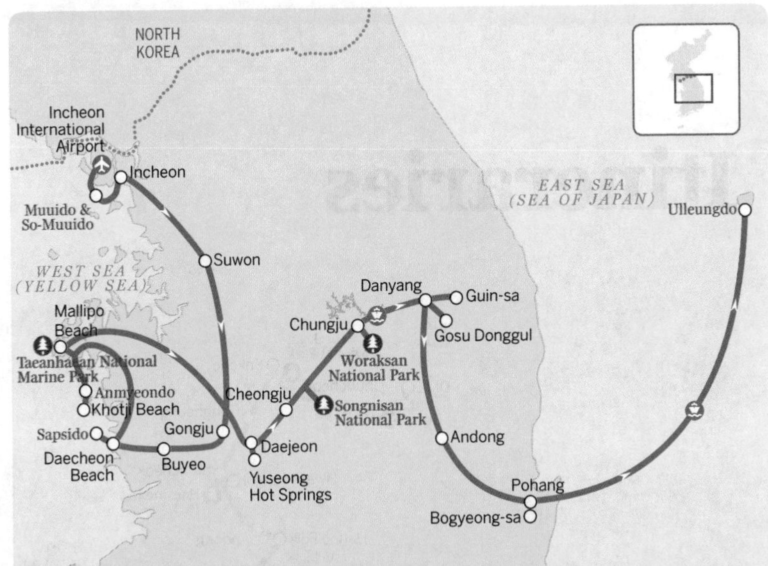

West to East Sea

This cross-country route is ideal to experience the more rustic and natural side of South Korea, with stops on ruggedly beautiful islands and hikes along leafy mountain trails.

From **Incheon International Airport** it's a quick hop to the idyllic island of **Muuido**, from where you can walk to **So-Muuido** or relax on lovely beaches. Enjoy Chinese food in the historic Chinatown of **Incheon**, then stroll around the Open Port area. Take a direct bus to **Suwon**, where you can stride around the ramparts of the meticulously reconstructed fortress wall, explore the palace and tuck into the town's famous *galbi* (beef ribs).

Gongju and **Buyeo**, the ancient capitals of the Baekje kingdom, are next: hillside tombs, a fortress and a museum will give you insights into Korea's oldest dynasty. After enjoying the mud skincare spa of **Daecheon Beach**, sail to the serene island of **Sapsido** for the night, before returning to Daecheon and continuing north by bus to **Anmyeondo**, the largest island in the **Taeanhaean National Marine Park**. Work on your tan at either **Khotji Beach** or **Mallipo Beach**, or hike some of the trails in the park.

Travel inland to **Daejeon** to soak at **Yuseong Hot Springs**. Continue to **Cheongju**, learn about the world's oldest printed book then move on to **Songnisan National Park**, covering central Korea's finest scenic area and a temple that is home to a rare and handsome five-storey wooden pagoda. **Chungju** is the gateway to lovely **Woraksan National Park** and two-hour scenic ferry trips across Chungju-ho towards sleepy **Danyang**, a restaurant-rich small town with a lovely waterside perch and hilly backdrop. Explore the limestone caves at nearby **Gosu Donggul** and the stately temple complex of **Guin-sa** within Sobaeksan National Park.

Use **Andong** as a base for exploring the surrounding area packed with attractive river and lakeside villages – it's also famous for its *soju* (Korean-style vodka). It's only a couple of hours by bus from here to **Pohang**. From Pohang visit **Bogyeong-sa** temple in a gorgeous valley with 12 waterfalls, then board the ferry to **Ulleungdo**, a sparsely inhabited, volcanic island.

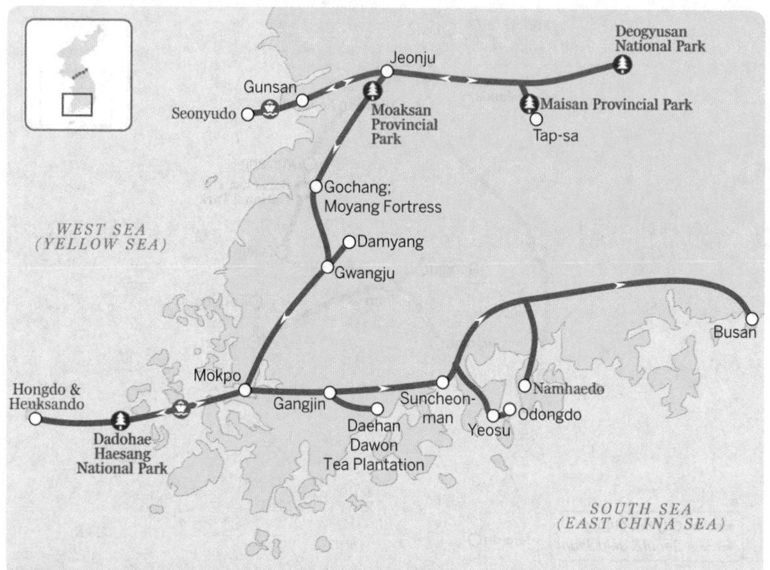

The Deep South Trail

This 850km route around Korea's least industrialised region offers the opportunity to stop by rural islands, dine in seafood restaurants and dig deep within artistic traditions.

Jeonju has a fascinating village crammed with traditional *hanok* (wooden homes) and buildings. It's also the birthplace of the classic rice dish bibimbap and a place to enjoy the milky rice wine *makgeolli*. Visit the 6th-century Geumsan-sa temple in **Moaksan Provincial Park** and don't miss **Maisan Provincial Park**, where you can hike between 'horse ear' mountains and encounter a garden of stone pinnacles piled up by a Buddhist mystic at **Tap-sa**. Alternatively, go hiking or skiing in beautiful **Deogyusan National Park**.

The industrial port city of **Gunsan** boasts Korea's largest collection of Japanese-colonial-period buildings. From here hop on a ferry to the relaxing island of **Seonyudo**, situated amid 60 mostly uninhabited small islands. When the tide is in and the sun is out, the views are unbelievably beautiful. Bronze and Iron Age tombs dot the lush green hills around the small village of **Gochang**, where you can also explore the 15th-century, ivy-covered **Moyang Fortress**.

Further south, **Gwangju** is home to several intriguing historical sites, museums and a major arts complex. Make a day trip to **Damyang** to stroll the sandy trails through its Juknokwon bamboo grove. Move on to the port of **Mokpo** to board boats to the remote havens of **Heuksando** and **Hongdo** in the **Dadohae Haesang National Park**. Admire Korea's centuries-old tradition of pottery at **Gangjin** and taste food and drinks made from healthy green tea at the beautiful **Daehan Dawon Tea Plantation** in Boseong.

Go bird-spotting in the Ramsar-listed wetlands of **Suncheon-man** then continue to **Yeosu**, site of Expo 2012, and head to the small bamboo- and camellia-tree-clad island of **Odongdo** to wander its paths. For a final island experience, take in terraced rice paddies and misty temples on picturesque **Namhaedo**. The trail finishes at Korea's second-largest city, **Busan**.

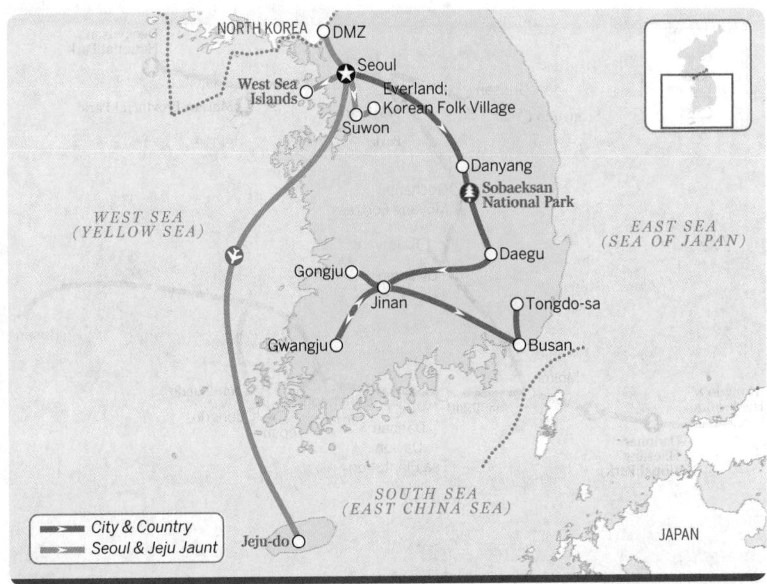

City & Country

Some of South Korea's top temples feature on this route linking its two main cities.

In **Seoul** attend a Templestay program at Jogye-sa or Bongeun-sa.

Danyang is the transit point for **Sobaeksan National Park**, where you'll find modern Guin-sa, headquarters of the Cheontae order.

Daegu (home to some tremendous heritage architecture, including an early-19th-century cathedral) is the base for trips to sublimely situated Haein-sa, and houses a World Heritage–listed library of more than 80,000 14th-century woodblocks.

From **Jinan**, you can reach **Gongju**, one-time capital of Korea's Baekje dynasty, to visit remote Magok-sa, with a hall of 1000 pintsized disciples, each one slightly different. From Jinan you can also go to **Gwangju**, to reach Unju-sa, with its fine collection of stone pagodas and unusual twin and reclining Buddhas.

Finish just outside of **Busan** at **Tongdo-sa**, home to an excellent Buddhist art museum containing 30,000 artefacts.

Seoul & Jeju Jaunt

This two-centre itinerary is well suited to parents travelling with kids.

Seoul's many parks, interactive museums and, in summer, outdoor swimming pools are ideal for family fun. Older kids will most likely be happy cruising the capital's vast shopping malls and department stores looking for souvenirs of Korea's pervasive pop culture.

Day trips include the beaches of the **West Sea Islands**, such as Deokjeokdo; Korea's biggest amusement park, **Everland**; and the **Korean Folk Village**. The latter two can just as easily be visited from **Suwon**, where it's fun to walk around the walls of an 18th-century fortress. North of Seoul, gain closer proximity to North Korea with a trip to the **DMZ**.

Hop on a flight to **Jeju-do**, blessed with a fascinating volcanic landscape and dozens of sandy beaches. Amusement and water parks, cycle and skate hire and a whole raft of adventure activities, from quad biking to scuba diving, are possible on this fun-packed island with plenty of world-class resorts.

Plan Your Trip
Outdoor Activities

Hiking & Rock Climbing

Hiking is Korea's number-one leisure activity. There are 21 national parks and scores more provincial parks, threaded with thousands of trails – everything from leisurely half-day walks, such as those along the Jeju Olle Trail, to strenuous mountain-ridge treks. Basic shelters are available, but expect a full house during holidays, summer months and autumn weekends. If you're planning a major overnight mountain trek, make reservations for shelters two weeks in advance. About a quarter of the trails may be closed at any one time to allow areas to regenerate.

Korea National Park Service (www.knps.or.kr) For trail information and online reservations for park accommodation.

Hike Korea (www.hikekorea.com) Learn about Korean mountain culture as well as many of the country's best trails. The site's author, Roger Shepherd, is one of the authors of *Bakedu-Daegu Trail*, a book that details the 1400km-long 'White Head Great Ridge' down the southern Korean Peninsula.

Hiking Hub Korea (www.hikinghubkorea.com/about-hiking-hub.html) Downloadable PDFs of English-language hiking guides for many of Korea's mountains.

Adventure Korea (www.adventurekorea.com) As well as running hiking trips, this expat-focused

Activity Tips

Top Five Outdoor Activities

Climb Halla-san, Jeju-do

Dive Seogwipo, Jeju-do

Ski at Alpensia, Pyeongchang

Cycle around Seonyudo

Hike through Jirisan National Park

Responsible Outdoors

- Pay any entrance fees required by park authorities.
- Obtain reliable information about route conditions and only tackle trails within your realm of experience and fitness level. Do not hike closed trails.
- Be aware of local laws, regulations and etiquette about wildlife and the environment.
- Be aware that the weather can change quickly and seasonal changes will influence how you dress and the equipment you need to carry.
- Don't litter and don't bring back souvenirs such as seashells or flowers.
- Be aware that, during the dry season, many national parks have strict fire prevention policies; some areas can be shut to regenerate.

operator offers other adventurous activities, including cycling and rafting trips.

Korea on the Rocks (www.koreaontherocks.com) Details on rock and ice climbing across Korea.

Cycling

To hire a bike, some form of ID is usually required. A helmet or lock is almost never included unless you ask.

In major cities it's possible to rent bikes, including electric bicycles – Seoul has great bicycle trails along the Han River. Seoul has its own city bike scheme, Seoul Bike (www.bikeseoul.com), which visitors can use.

Resorts with water frontage and hordes of tourists are sure to have a stand where bikes can be hired. Most bike paths are geared towards leisure riders, with couples and families in mind, so expect well-marked, paved, flat trails designed for pleasure rather than intense cross-country exhilaration.

The 200km pedal around Jeju-do, Korea's largest island, takes from three to five days, depending on your level of fitness and how quickly you wish to take it. Hwy 1132 runs around the entire island and has bicycle lanes on either side. Udo, the island off Jeju-do, is a much easier one-day joyride.

Another lovely island to cycle around is Seonyudo at the centre of the Gogunsan Archipelago, off the coast of Jeollabuk-do.

Single Tracks (www.singletracks.com) lists good mountain-bike trails.

Skiing & Snowboarding

In 2018 Pyeongchang (p142) county in Gangwon-do hosted the Winter Olympic Games, with Alpensia (p142) serving as the main resort and the larger Yongpyong (p143) nearby hosting the slalom events.

Korea's snow season runs from December to March. Lift tickets cost about ₩75,000 and equipment rentals about ₩35,000 per day. Package deals from

KOREA'S TOP PARKS

National Parks

PARK	AREA (SQ KM)	FEATURES & ACTIVITIES
Bukhansan	78	Great hiking, subway access from Seoul
Dadohae Haesang	2344 (2004 sq km marine)	A marine park of scattered, unspoilt islands
Deogyusan	219	Ski resort, a fortress and a magical valley walk
Gyeongju	138	A historic park strewn with ancient Silla and Buddhist relics
Hallasan	149	An extinct volcano; Korea's highest peak
Jirisan	440	Straddling two provinces; high peaks popular with serious hikers
Seoraksan	373	Korea's most beautiful park
Sobaeksan	320	Limestone caves and Guin-sa, an impressive temple complex, to explore

Provincial Parks

PARK	AREA (SQ KM)	FEATURES & ACTIVITIES
Daedunsan	38	Granite cliffs, great views, hot-spring bath
Gajisan	104	Scenic views; famous Tongdo-sa
Mudeungsan	30	Near Gwangju, with an art gallery and a green-tea plantation
Taebaeksan	17	Visit the Coal Museum, hike to Dangun's altar

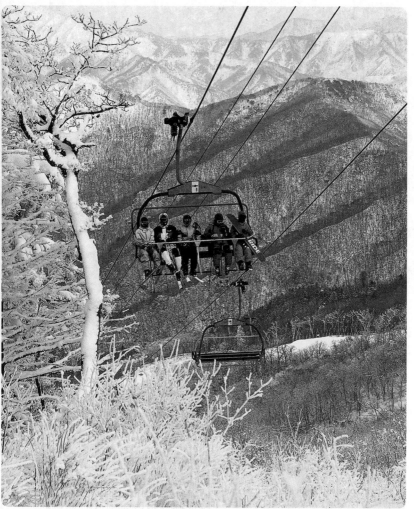

Top: Muju Deogyusan Resort, Deogyusan National Park (p275), South Korea

Bottom: Cycling along the Han River (p65), Seoul, South Korea

GW NAM / GETTY IMAGES ©

Rafting, northwest Gangwon

travel agents include transport, tickets, rentals and, if required, lessons and accommodation. Overnight packages vary from ₩60,000 for a night in a *minbak* (private room in a home) or basic hotel, to upwards of ₩300,000 for apartments and upmarket suites. Weekends are often very crowded, especially at resorts near Seoul. Skiers and snowboarders alike are catered for; boarding is especially popular with Koreans.

Many resorts run dedicated shuttle buses to/from pick-up points in Seoul, making for a long, but easy, day on the slopes.

Gangwon-do

High1 Ski Resort (p143) Modern ski resort with among the best facilities and snow in Korea. Set in the mountains west of Taebaek and boasting 18 slopes, five lifts and four gondolas, this is also home to Korea's first ski school for the disabled.

Yongpyong (p143) Korea's oldest and biggest resort, with slopes ranging from bunny options to advanced runs.

Alpensia (p142) The 2018 Winter Games host resort. Its compact size makes it a good place for families and anyone learning to ski.

Elysian Gangchon (p96) Small, slick ski resort reachable by the Seoul subway.

Jeollabuk-do

Muju Deogyusan (p275) The only ski area inside a national park, its 26 slopes are set in a village containing an Austrian-themed hotel.

North Korea

Masik-Ryong (p320) A pet project of Kim Jong-un, offering several runs (one over 5km long), bunny slopes, Ski-Doos, skating and the luxurious Masik Ryong Hotel.

Ice Skating

Indoor ice skating is available year-round at Seoul's Lotte World (p57). In winter there's an outdoor rink (p59) outside City Hall, and the Grand Hyatt (p66) and Sheraton Walkerhill hotels have temporary outdoor rinks. The vast, new Gangneung Ice Arena that was the venue for figure-skating and speed-skating events at the 2018 Winter Olympics is planned to be converted for local use.

Surfing

Haeundae (p183) and Songjeong beaches in Busan are among the best places to experience South Korea's surf. However, you'll need to suit up as the best time for surf is winter, when waves are whipped up by strong winds from the north. Water temperatures at these times dip to 3°C, but could be as high as 10°C. If that's too chilly for you, head to balmy **Jungmun Beach** (중문해수욕장; kayak/boogie board per 2hr ₩15,000/5000) off Jeju-do's south coast.

Diving

Korea has an active scuba-diving scene. The top dive site is just off Seogwipo on Jeju-do's south coast, with walls of colourful soft coral, 18m-high kelp forests (March to May), schools of fish and the occasional inquisitive dolphin. Diving here is a mixture of tropical and temperate – rather like diving in Norway and the Red Sea at the same time. Visibility is best from September to November, when it can be up to 30m (it's around 10m at other times) and water temperature varies from 15°C to 28°C.

Other good underwater sites on the east coast are Hongdo, off the south coast; Pohang, Ulleungdo and Dragon Head, off Sokcho; and a wreck dive off Gangneung. The west coast has some dive operators – at Daecheon beach, for instance – but visibility can be poor.

Golf

In 1998 Se Ri Pak put South Korea onto the golf map by winning the US Women's Open. Today, Korean women dominate the American LPGA Tour and golf is a national pastime, with hundreds of courses dotting the country.

One of the most popular golfing destination is Jeju-do, where courses include **Jungmun Beach Golf Club** (중문골프클럽; ☎064-735 7241, reservations 064-736 1202; www.jungmunbeachgolfclub.com; 60 Jungmungwangwang-ro 72beon-gil; green fees ₩46,000-128,000, cart & caddy extra; ⏲sunrise-sunset) and **Pinx Golf Club** (☎064-792 8000; www.thepinx.co.kr; 62-3 Sangcheon-ri, Andeok-myeon; 9 holes weekday/weekend ₩76,000/96,000, caddy & cart extra).

Playing on a course in Korea isn't cheap. An average 18-hole round of golf may set you back ₩200,000, and you may have to book months in advance. But for virtual golf, there are thousands of golf cafes around the country, so you'll find one in just about any city. A round of virtual golf at chains such as Golfzon (www.golfzongolf.com) costs about ₩30,000. Also common are golf practice ranges.

Birdwatching

With some of the widest and most extensive tidal flats in the world, the Korean Peninsula is a natural magnet for birds. More than 500 species have been spotted in Korea, including 34 threatened species. Most are on their migratory route between Siberia and Manchuria in the north, Southeast Asia, Australia and New Zealand in the south.

Birds Korea (www.birdskorea.org) has photos of Korean birds and lots of info for bird lovers.

Popular birding spots:

Suncheon Bay This wetland park on Jeollanam-do's south coast is where the hooded crane winters.

Demilitarized Zone (DMZ) A preferred stop for migrating birds because it's been uninhabited for 65 years. The southern section is promoted through a nature tour as the Peace and Life Zone (PLZ).

Bamseom Island Bird Sanctuary This pair of islets in Seoul's Han River is off limits to humans, but birds – including mandarins, spotbills, great egrets and mallards – can be spotted from an observation platform in Yeouido's Han River Park.

Kayaking, Canoeing & Rafting

Gangwon-do's northwest is the hot spot for kayaking, canoeing and rafting from mid-April to October. Adventure Korea (www.adventurekorea.com) and **Koridoor** (☎02-6383 2570; www.koridoor.co.kr; 251 Hangangdae-ro, Yongsan-gu , Seoul; ⓢLine 1 to Namyeong, Exit 1) also offer white-water rafting trips.

Regions at a Glance

Seoul

History
Food
Shopping

Historic Landmarks

Given how thoroughly it was trashed during the Korean War, it's no small miracle that so many of Seoul's historic landmarks remain. A number of them are meticulous reconstructions, but that doesn't diminish their significance or impact.

Food & Drink

Seoul is the best place to sample the full range of Korean culinary delights – from hot kimchi (pickled vegetable) stews and sizzling street snacks to the delicate morsels that make up a royal banquet.

Shoppers' Delight

At all times of day or night there's always somewhere to shop in Seoul. The teeming markets of Dongdaemun and Namdaemun are must-do experiences, as is cruising the boutiques and department stores of Myeong-dong or ritzy Apgujeong and Cheongdam.

p38

Around Seoul

Islands
History
Art

Island Escapes

Scores of islands flaking off like crumbs into the West Sea make for perfect escapes from the urban grip of Seoul and Incheon. Try historic Ganghwado or laid-back Deokjeokdo, which has a gorgeous crescent-shaped beach.

Historic Sites

The Demilitarized Zone (DMZ) splitting North and South Korea is a must-see, as are the Unesco World Heritage–listed fortress walls surrounding the inner core of Suwon.

Artistic Places

The pottery town of Incheon draws in ceramics lovers, and Heyri near the DMZ border is a village packed with small galleries. See something different in the exhibitions at Incheon Art Platform or the sculptures of Anyang Art Park.

p93

Gangwon-do

Hiking
Skiing
Quirky

Misty Mountains

Seoraksan National Park abounds with gorgeous vistas of mist-shrouded crags that rarely fail to stun. The valleys are loaded with quiet temples, hot springs, hiking trails and quietude.

Hit the Slopes

Host of the 2018 Winter Olympics, Pyeongchang's Yongpyong and Alpensia ski resorts aren't the biggest in the world but they pack in lots of family-friendly options such as sledding and inner tubing.

Priapic Park

Take the bus down from Samcheok to Haesindang Park and wander through a parkland decorated with an almost-surreal assortment of penile statues to a backdrop of beautiful marine views.

p118

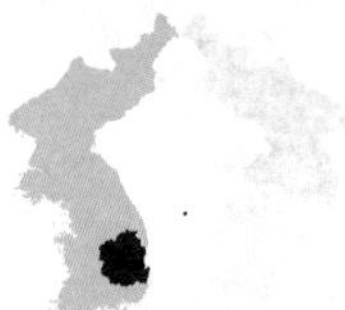

Gyeongsangbuk-do

Temples
History
City Life

Idyllic Retreats

Secreted away among the misty mountains are ancient esoteric temples, buffered from the neon-drenched cities of Gyeongsangbuk-do by isolation and dense woodland.

Historic Sites

Head to Gyeongju, the 'museum without walls', for a rich display of Silla history, from hill-shaped tumuli to riveting finds on display at the excellent National Museum, ancient temple remains and a Unesco World Heritage site outside town.

Discover Daegu

The huge city of Daegu is not just a great stop for some superb cuisine, craft beer and a youthful, buzzing atmosphere – it's home to tremendous cultural heritage too and some terrific museums.

p146

Busan & Gyeongsangnam-do

Food
Beaches
Islands

Fresh Fish

You'd have to go fishing to get your hands on seafood fresher than the produce at Busan's Jagalchi Fish Market. Pick your creature from a tank and it'll be your next meal within minutes.

Sand-Castling

Sure, Haeundae beach can be overcrowded and overhyped, but it's the nation's most loved for good reason. Kick back in the sand, frolic in the waves and snack on savoury barbecued shellfish in Cheongsapo, a short taxi ride from the beach.

Island-Hopping

The crumbly coastline has myriad islands to explore, but Namhaedo, one of the largest, is stunningly beautiful, with mountain-top temples and terraced rice paddies sloping down to the sea.

p180

Jeollanam-do

Arts & Culture
Islands
Quirky

Ceramics & Contemporary Art

From Gangjin's ancient celadon (green-tinged pottery) kilns to Gwangju's new Asian Culture Complex, Jeollanam-do has a long history of supporting the arts. Visit in September for the Gwangju Biennale.

Islands Galore

The rolling hills lead down to the coastline, where you can hop on a boat to explore hundreds of islands. Don't forget to sample the local catch of the day: fish, abalone or even live octopus.

Eclectic Excursions

Hunting for murals in a traditional market (in Gwangju), getting steamy in a seawater sauna (in Hampyeong), gawking at sunken treasures (in Mokpo)... just some of the quirky sights and activities possible in this region.

p212

Jeju-do

Hiking
Art & Culture
Food

Hiking Trails

Discover the island the slow way, following one or more of the 26 routes on the Jeju Olle Trail. Alternatively, take one of four routes to the top of Halla-san (1950m), South Korea's tallest mountain.

Arty Stones & Sexy Art

Jeju-do is packed with all manner of galleries and museums, from the impressive Jeju Stone Park and stunning photos at Kim Young Gap Gallery Dumoak, to a trio of quirky sex museums.

Local Delicacies

Jeju's separately developed island culture reveals itself in a distinct cuisine, heavy on seafood but also with cuts of black pig and horse on the menu.

p237

Jeollabuk-do

Hiking
Food
History

Head for the Hills

For a small province, Jeollabuk-do has an impressive amount of parkland. Choose from a number of national and provincial parks and join the droves of outdoor enthusiasts in exploring Korea's natural beauty.

Glorious Food

In the middle of an agricultural heartland, Jeonju is Korea's favourite foodie destination, home of the rice dish bibimbap and a lively street-food culture. After hours it's all about the *makgeolli* (milky rice wine).

Go Back in Time

History is celebrated in Jeonju's *hanok* (traditional wooden homes) village and its clusters of artisans. Other engaging reminders of the past include the Gochang fortress and the former colonial port of Gunsan.

p267

Chungcheongnam-do

Beaches
Festivals
History

Sunbath Fun

There are opportunities galore to work on that tan at Korea's most popular beaches. Whether you like packed summer scenes or intimate small strips of sand, you'll find it here.

Mud Rollicking

Possibly Korea's most famous (some say infamous) festival, the Boryeong Mud Festival is a messy extravaganza that's hugely popular with foreigners.

Baekje History

The twin sleepy towns of Gongju and Buyeo were once the seat of power of Korea's earliest dynasty, the long-running Baekje dynasty. Festivals, fortresses, tombs and museums pay tribute to its legacy.

p280

Chungcheongbuk-do

Temples
Gentle Activities
History

Discover Inner Peace

Some of Korea's most intriguing and impressive temples are here. The hillside Guin-sa complex and its hiking opportunities are alluring, and find time for the rare five-storey wooden pagoda at Beopju-sa.

Slow it Down

This landlocked region offers a chance for exploration of Korea's heartland. Take a meandering cruise along Chungju-ho or soak in an *oncheon* (hot-spring spa) at Suanbo.

Footnotes in History

The world's first book printed by movable metal type was created in Cheongju, and is celebrated in a museum on the site of the temple that oversaw its production. The book's legacy is perhaps the greatest cultural treasure to emerge from Korea.

p297

North Korea

Politics
Quirky
Scenery

Monuments & Propaganda

Any trip to North Korea is shot with politics, from the ubiquitous propaganda to the museums, monuments and art. Coming here is a fascinating chance to see things from a different perspective.

Mind-Bogglers

Whether visiting an exhibition of Kim Jong-il's gifts housed in a mountainside warehouse, or taking a trip on the world's most secretive metro system, there's no trip weirder than a tour of the Democratic People's Republic of Korea (DPRK).

Spectacular Scenery

Beyond its unique political situation, North Korea is rich in natural beauty, with soaring mountains, sandy beaches and crystal-clear lakes, making it a great place for nature lovers.

p309

On the Road

Seoul

02 / POP 10.17 MILLION

Includes ➡

Best Places to Eat

- Jungsik (p76)
- Noryangjin Fish Market (p51)
- Congdu (p70)
- Samwon Garden (p77)
- Gwangjang Market (p75)
- Onion (p75)

Best Places to Stay

- Hide & Seek Guesthouse (p61)
- Park Hyatt Seoul (p67)
- Small House Big Door (p61)
- Itaewon G Guest House (p64)
- K-Grand Hostel Dongsaemun (p66)

Why Go?

Fashion- and technology-forward but also deeply traditional, this dynamic city mashes up palaces, temples, cutting-edge design and mountain trails, all to a nonstop K-Pop beat.

Over the last decade, Seoul has also worked to soften its industrial hard edges into an appealing urban ideal of parks, culture and relaxed spaces. But whatever you want, at any time of day or night, this city can provide. An early-morning temple visit could lead to a palace tour followed by tea sipping in Bukchon and gallery-hopping in Samcheong-dong. *Soju* (local vodka) and snacks in a street-tent bar will fuel you for shopping at the buzzing Dongdaemun or Namdaemun night markets, partying in Hongdae or Itaewon, or singing in a self-service karaoke *noraebang*. Follow this with steaming, soaking and snoozing in a *jjimjilbang* (sauna and spa). By the time you look at your watch, it will be dawn again.

When to Go

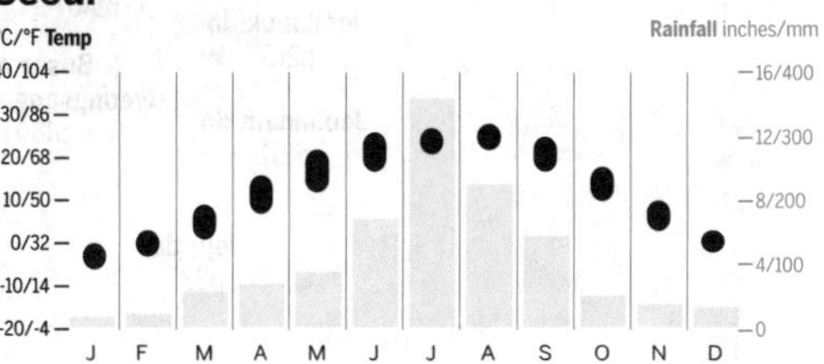

Apr–May Blossoming flowers and festivals like Buddha's Birthday and the Lotus Lantern Festival.

Oct Go hiking in rustic-coloured mountains and enjoy Seoul Fireworks Festival and KIAF art fair.

Nov–Jan Wrap up for Seoul Lantern Festival, then hit the ice rink or warm up in a sauna.

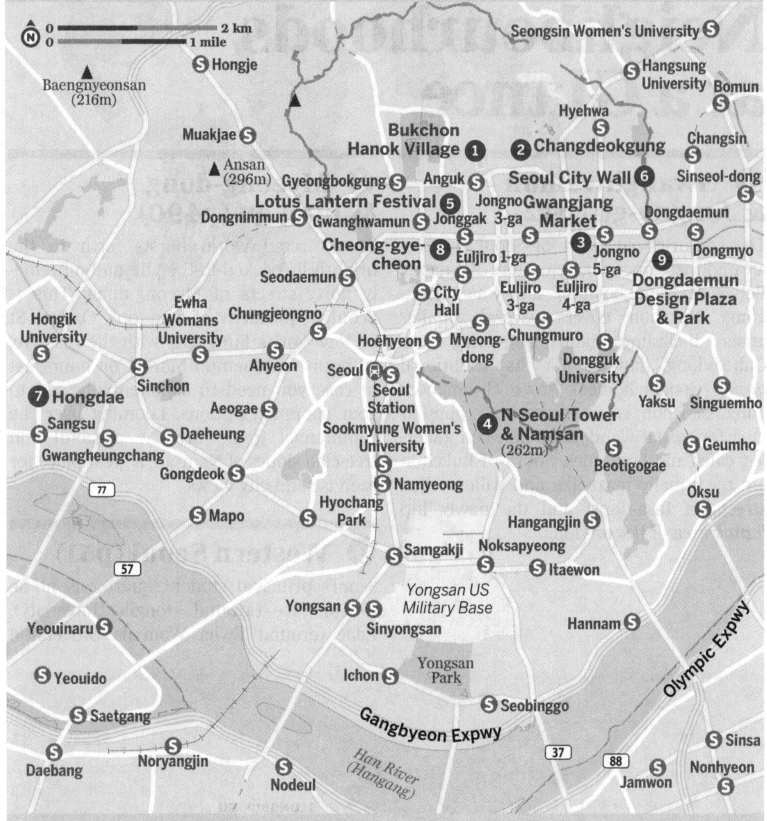

Seoul Highlights

❶ **Bukchon Hanok Village** (p44) Enjoying skyline views from the labyrinthine streets of this historic village.

❷ **Changdeokgung** (p45) Soaking up the serenity of the Secret Garden at this World Heritage–listed palace.

❸ **Gwangjang Market** (p75) Digging for fashion finds and gobbling down street eats at one of the city's best markets.

❹ **N Seoul Tower & Namsan** (p49) Hiking the city's guardian mountain and ascending its striking tower for immense city views.

❺ **Lotus Lantern Festival** (p60) Celebrating the Buddha's birthday in lantern-clad temples.

❻ **Seoul City Wall Museum** (p57) Uncovering six centuries of history along these ancient fortifications.

❼ **Hongdae** (p40) Partying the night away in hip bars and indie-music clubs in this university district.

❽ **Cheong-gye-cheon** (p42) Taking a break from the city with a stroll beside this reclaimed urban river.

❾ **Dongdaemun Design Plaza & Park** (p56) Marvelling at the space-age architecture of this the Zaha Hadid–designed plaza.

History

The mighty walls of Korea's modern capital rose in 1394, when King Taejo, founder of the Joseon dynasty, settled the government seat in the valley of Hanyang (later to become Seoul) and ordered the building of Gyeongbokgung, the Palace of Shining Happiness, at the foot of Bukaksan. But while the city's roots stretch back many centuries before that,

continued on p42

Neighbourhoods at a Glance

❶ Gwanghwamun & Jongno-gu (p42)

The centuries-old heart of Seoul revolves around these once-regal quarters of palaces. Between Gyeongbokgung and Changdeokgung, Bukchon covers several smaller areas, including Samcheong-dong, and Gahoe-dong, famous for its traditional *hanok* (wooden homes). West of Gyeongbokgung, Seochon is an increasingly popular area for casual wanderings between galleries, cafes and boutiques. South of Bukchon are the equally maze-like and gallery-filled streets of Insa-dong, and the newly hip *hanok* area of Ikseon-dong.

❷ Myeong-dong & Jung-gu (p490)

Seoul's retail world bursts forth in the brightly lit, packed-to-the-gills and supremely noisy streets of Myeong-dong. This is Seoul's equivalent of London's Oxford St or New York's Fifth Ave, with the massive, 24-hour Namdaemun Market on hand just in case you need to exponentially add to your shopping options. Looming over the commercial frenzy are the peaceful and tree-clad slopes of Namsan, a great place for exercise and city views.

❸ Western Seoul (p51)

Seoul's principal student quarter is home to Hongdae (around Hongik University), Edae (around Ewha Womans University)

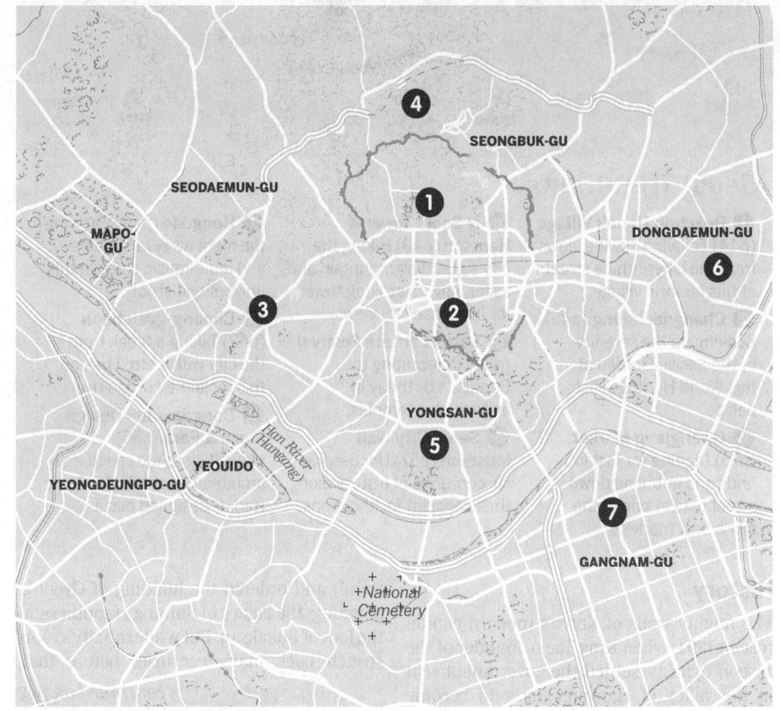

and Sinchon (between Yonsei and Sogang Universities). These are youthful, creative districts short on traditional sights but big on modern-day diversions and sybaritic entertainments. South of Hongdae across the Han River, the island of Yeouido has several places of interest, all easily visited if you hire a bike at its riverside or central park.

❹ Northern Seoul (p54)

Some of Seoul's most charming neighbourhoods are clustered in an arc across three of the city's guardian mountains. To the east, beside Naksan, you'll find the student and performing-arts hub of Daehangno. Moving anticlockwise across to Bukaksan is Seongbuk-dong, an affluent residential district with excellent museums. Buam-dong further west is the starting point for hikes along the scenic Seoul City Wall, while the slopes of Inwangsan are home to the city's most famous shamanist shrine. Continuing south there's a park dedicated to the country's independence at Seodaemun.

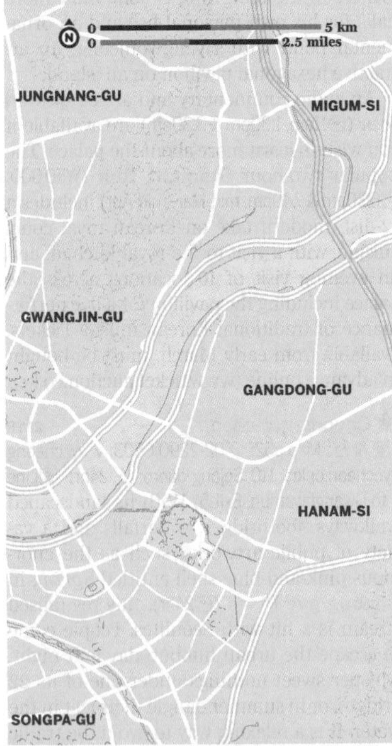

❺ Itaewon & Yongsan-gu (p55)

Defined by the off-limits US army base that eats up a great chunk of Yongsan-gu, this area has long been Seoul's 'foreign' hang-out for hamburgers, hookers and everything else. Nowadays Itaewon (and adjacent 'hoods Hannam-dong, Haebangchon and Gyeongridan) boasts one of the most dynamic restaurant scenes in Asia, with a new global food trend seemingly emerging every five minutes. This diversity extends to the nightlife, with craft beer, underground clubs and something for every sexual persuasion. In daylight hours the area has several major museums you won't want to miss.

❻ Dongdaemun & Eastern Seoul (p56)

Home to high-rise malls and labyrinthine covered markets, the 24-hour retail frenzy that is Dongdaemun attracts suitcase-wheeling shoppers from all over Asia. It's mostly clothing and fabrics, but you can also find Seoul's busiest street-food arcades within Gwangjang Market. Further east the couture gives way to antiques, flea-market goods and herbal medicines. Dramatic contemporary architecture is provided by Zaha Hadid's Dongdaemun Plaza & Park, while up-and-coming Seongsu-dong, an old shoemaking district being touted as Seoul's answer to Brooklyn, is awash with industrial-chic cafes and hip boutiques.

❼ Gangnam & Southern Seoul (p57)

Gangnam (meaning South of the River) is booming with new luxury high-rises bisected by broad highways. Expansive areas of greenery figure, too, in the shape of Olympic Park, the strip of recreation areas along the Han River, and Seonjeongneung Park, home to royal tombs. Luxury label boutiques are clustered in Apgujeong and Cheongdam. You'll also find several major performance-arts centres across the district.

continued from p39

its development in recent times into an economic powerhouse and the second-largest metropolitan area in the world has been breathtaking.

During the 20th century the city suffered first under Japanese colonial rule and then during the Korean War when it was almost entirely destroyed. Rebuilt from the 1960s, Seoul today is the country's centre of cultural, economic and political centre.

Park Won-soon, a former human rights lawyer and independent candidate, was re-elected for his third term as Seoul's mayor in June 2018. Under previous mayors, construction-led growth resulted in flashy, expensive projects. By contrast, Park's popularity has been stoked by policies like the building of pavements and pedestrian-only zones, a bicycle-sharing scheme and expansion of the subway.

Sights

Gwanghwamun & Jongno-gu

★Gyeongbokgung PALACE

(경복궁, Palace of Shining Happiness; Map p52; www.royalpalace.go.kr; 161 Sajik-ro; adult/child ₩3000/1500; ⏲9am-5pm Wed-Mon Nov-Feb, to 6pm Mar-May, Sep & Oct, to 6.30pm Jun-Aug; ⓈLine 3 to Gyeongbokgung, Exit 5) Like a phoenix, Seoul's premier palace has risen several times from the ashes of destruction. Hordes of tourists have replaced the thousands of government officials, scholars, eunuchs, concubines, soldiers and servants who once lived here. Watch the changing of the guard ceremonies at the main entrance **Gwanghwamun** (광화문; Map p52), then set aside at least half a day to do justice to the compound, which includes a couple of museums, ornamental gardens and some of Seoul's grandest architectural sights.

Originally built by King Taejo, the founder of the Joseon dynasty, Gyeongbokgung served as the principal palace until 1592, when it was burnt down during the Japanese invasions. It lay in ruins for nearly 300 years until Heungseon Daewongun, regent and father of King Gojong, started to rebuild it in 1865. King Gojong moved in during 1868, but the expensive rebuilding project virtually bankrupted the government.

Altogether the palace consisted of 330 buildings and had up to 3000 staff, including 140 eunuchs, all serving the royal family. During Japanese colonial rule, most of the palace was again destroyed – much of what you see today is accurate recent reconstructions.

Once beyond the landmark Gwanghwamun, flanked by a pair of protecting, giant *haetae,* mythical lion-like creatures, head straight for the flagstone courtyard fronting the ornate two-storey Geunjeongjeon, the main palace building. This highly impressive building, with its double-tiered stone platform and surrounding open-sided corridors, is where kings were crowned, met foreign envoys and conducted affairs of state.

West of Geunjeongjeon is the spectacular Gyeonghoeru, a large raised pavilion resting on 48 stone pillars and overlooking an artificial lake with two small islands. State banquets were held inside and kings went boating on the pond.

A series of smaller meeting halls precede the king's living quarters, Gangyeongjeon, behind which are Gyotaejeon, the queen's chambers. Behind that is a terraced garden, Amisan; the brick chimneys decorated with longevity symbols on the garden's top terrace are to release the smoke from the palace's ondol (underfloor heating) system.

On the eastern side of the grounds is Donggun, the living quarters for the Crown Prince. To the rear, King Gojong built more halls for his own personal use and an ornamental pond with Hyangwonjeong, an attractive hexagonal pavilion on an island.

An audio commentary and a **free guided tour** (⏲11am, 1.30pm & 3.30pm) are available if you wish to learn more about the palace. The popular two-hour **Starlight Tour** (₩50,000; ⏲6.30pm & 7.40pm; mid-Mar–mid-Apr) includes a 12-dish modern take on Korean royal court cuisine, with a visit to the royal kitchen, and an evening visit of 10 locations across the palace including the pavilion for a live performance of traditional Korean music. Tickets, available from early March, must be bought in advance online (www.ticket.auction.co.kr).

★Cheong-gye-cheon RIVER

(청계천; Map p52; ☎02-2290 6803; www.cheonggyecheon.or.kr; 110 Sejong-daero; ⏲24hr; ⓈLine 5 to Gwanghwamun, Exit 5) With its landscaped walkways, footbridges, waterfalls and a variety of public artworks, such as the enormous pink-and-blue shell entitled *Spring* in **Cheong-gye Plaza** (⏲24hr), this revitalised stream is a hit with Seoulites. People come to escape the urban hubbub day and night, whisper sweet nothings under one of its 22 bridges, or in summer dangle their feet in the water. It is a relaxing way to avoid the traffic

SEOUL IN...

Two Days

Stroll around Bukchon Hanok Village (p44), then attend the changing of the palace guard at Gyeongbokgung (p42) or join the day's last tour of Changdeokgung (p45). Enjoy dinner and dazzling lights in Namdaemun Market (p49).

On day two, visit the National Museum of Korea (p55), followed by the splendid Leeum Samsung Museum of Art (p55). In the afternoon, hike up Namsan to N Seoul Tower (p49) to watch the sunset before dinner in Itaewon. Finish off the evening with a steam in the saunas and a soak in the tubs at the Dragon Hill Spa & Resort (p59).

Four Days

On day four visit Seodaemun Prison History Hall (p55) and hike up Inwangsan (p59) along Seoul City Wall for fabulous views. Continue the hike to Bukaksan with a tea break at Gilsang-sa (p55) temple. In the evening, head to Dongdaemun Design Plaza & Park (p56) for 21st-century architecture and night-market shopping and eats.

Fill your final morning with contemporary art and panoramic views at 63 Sky Art Gallery (p54) on Yeouido and cycling in Hangang Riverside Park. Then head to Sangsu-dong and Yeonnam-dong in Hongdae to relax in hip cafes like Channel 1969 (p80). After dinner, pitch up at the Banpo Hangang Park by 9pm to see the day's last floodlit flourish of the **Banpo Bridge Rainbow Fountain** (반포대교 달빛무지개분수; Map p84; 22-404, 22-405, 405 or 740, S Line 3, 7 or 9 to Express Bus Terminal, Exit 8-1) FREE.

while traversing the downtown area, passing near places of interest such as Gwangjang Market (p75), Dongdaemun and Insa-dong.

Jogye-sa TEMPLE

(조계사; Map p81; 02-768 8600; www.jogyesa.kr/user/english; 55-Ujeongguk-ro; 24hr; S Line 3 to Anguk, Exit 6) The focus of Jogye-sa is the grand wooden hall Daeungjeon, Seoul's largest Buddhist worship hall and the epicentre of Korean Buddhism. Completed in 1938, its design followed the Joseon-dynasty style. The exterior is decorated with scenes from Buddha's life and carved floral latticework, while inside are three giant Buddha statues: on the left is Amitabha, Buddha of the Western Paradise; in the centre is the historical Buddha, who lived in India and achieved enlightenment; and on the right is the Bhaisaiya or Medicine Buddha, holding a medicine bowl.

On the right as you enter Daeungjeon, the small 15th-century Buddha in the glass case was the main Buddha statue before he was replaced by the much larger triad in 2006. Also on the right-hand side is a guardian altar with lots of fierce-looking guardians in the painting behind, and on the left side is the altar used for memorial services.

Believers who enter the temple, which is the headquarters of the Jogye Order of Korean Buddhism, bow three times, touching their forehead to the ground – once for Buddha, once for the *dharma* (teaching) and once for the *sangha* (monks) who serve in this temple. Outside there are candles (like Buddha they light up the world, dispelling darkness and ignorance) and incense sticks (the smoke sends wishes up to heaven).

Behind the main shrine is the modern Amitabha Buddha Hall, where funeral services are held. On the left side of the compound is the octagonal 10-storey stupa in which is enshrined a relic of Buddha brought to Korea in 1913 by a Sri Lankan monk.

The Beomjongru (Brahma Bell Pavilion) houses a drum to summon earthbound animals, a wooden fish-shaped gong to summon aquatic beings, a metal cloud-shaped gong to summon birds and a large bronze bell to summon underground creatures. The bell is struck 28 times at 4am and 33 times at 6pm.

The **Central Buddhist Museum** (02-2011 1960; 9am-6pm Tue-Sun) FREE has three galleries of antique woodblocks, symbol-filled paintings and other Buddhist artefacts.

Near the main entrance gate is the **Information Centre for Foreigners** (02-732 5292; 10am-5pm), staffed by English-speaking Buddhist guides. Drop by here to make a booking for the **Temple Life program** (₩30,000; 1-4pm Sat), which includes a temple tour, meditation practice, lotus-lantern and prayer-bead making, woodblock printing, painting and a tea ceremony. An

continued on p48

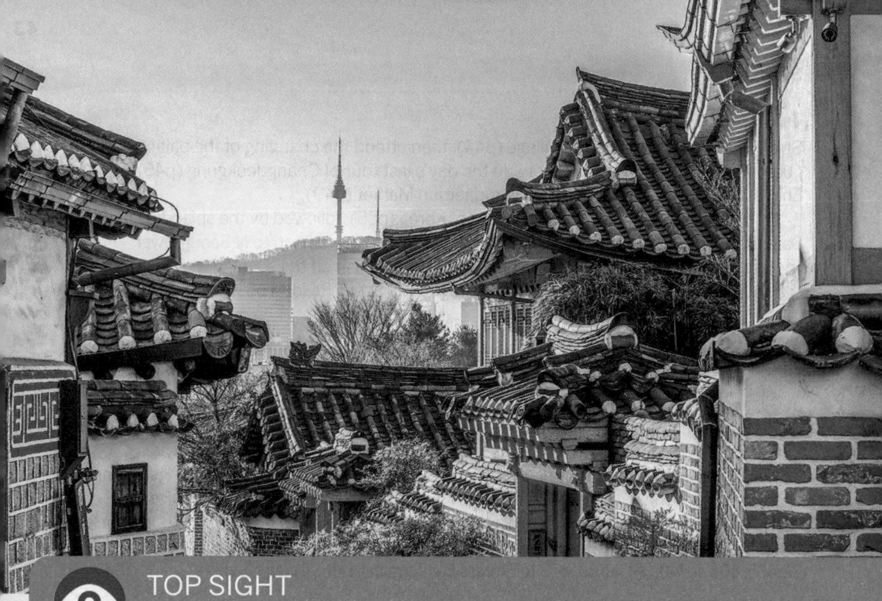

TOP SIGHT
BUKCHON HANOK VILLAGE

Bukchon (North Village), covering the area between Gyeongbokgung and Changdeokgung, is home to around 900 *hanok*, Seoul's largest concentration of these traditional Korean homes. Although supertouristy in parts, the streets here are a pleasure to aimlessly wander and get lost in, admiring the buildings' patterned walls and tiled roofs contrasting with the modern city in the distance.

Despite being a residential area, several *hanok* are open to the public. Simsimheon (p49), meaning 'House Where the Heart is Found', was rebuilt using traditional methods. Entry includes tea, sipped overlooking the internal garden. It's also possible to stay in a family home turned guesthouse. Avoid crowds of tour groups by visiting early in the morning or later in the evening, rather than midday.

Don't miss **Gahoe Minhwa Workshop** (가회민화공방; ☎02-741 0466; www.gahoemuseum.org; 17 Bukchon-ro 8-gil; adult/child ₩2000/1000; ⏲10.30am-6pm Tue-Sun, to 5pm Dec-Feb; Ⓢ Line 3 to Anguk, Exit 2), a *hanok* museum and cultural centre with a treasure trove of amulets and folk paintings. **Dong-Lim Knot Workshop** (www.shimyoungmi.com; 10 Bukchon-ro 12-gil; classes ₩7000-10,000; ⏲10am-6pm Tue-Sun; Ⓢ Line 3 to Anguk, Exit 2) offers classes on making traditional knotted ornaments.

Housed in a *hanok*, **Bukchon Traditional Culture Center** (북촌문화센터; ☎02-2171 2459; http://bukchon.seoul.go.kr/eng/exp/center1_1.jsp; 37 Gyedong-gil; ⏲9am-6pm Mon-Sat) FREE has a small exhibition. **Seoul City Walking Tours** (☎02-6925 0777; http://dobo.visitseoul.net) offer free guided tours with three days' advance notice. **Bukchon Tourist Information Center** (☎02-2148 4161; cnr Bukchon-ro & Bukchon-ro 4-gil; ⏲9am-6pm) has free maps and leaflets.

DON'T MISS

- Bukchon Traditional Culture Center
- Simsimheon
- Gahoe Minhwa Workshop
- Dong-Lim Knot Workshop

PRACTICALITIES

- 북촌한옥마을
- Map p52
- http://hanok.seoul.go.kr
- Bukchon-ro
- ⏲24hr
- Ⓢ Line 3 to Anguk, Exit 3

TOP TIP

The area is quite a maze. Set aside time to get blissfully lost. There are roving tourist information officials dressed in red with useful maps.

JULIE MAYFENG / SHUTTERSTOCK ©

TOP SIGHT
CHANGDEOKGUNG

The most beautiful of Seoul's four main palaces, World Heritage–listed Changdeokgung was originally built in the early 15th century as a secondary palace to Gyeongbokgung. Following the destruction of both palaces during the Japanese invasion in the 1590s, Changdeokgung was rebuilt and became the primary royal residence until 1872. It remained in use well into the 20th century.

Enter through the imposing gate Donhwamun (1608), turn right and cross over the stone bridge (1414) with guardian animals carved on its sides. On the left is the beautiful main building, Injeongjeon. It sits in harmony with the paved courtyard, open corridors and trees.

Next door are the government office buildings, including one with a blue-tiled roof. Further on are the private living quarters of the royal family. Peering inside the partially furnished rooms, you can feel what these Joseon palaces were like in their heyday – a bustling beehive buzzing round the king, full of gossip and intrigue.

Round the back is a terraced garden with decorative *ondol* chimneys. Over on the right is something completely different – Nakseonjae, built by King Heonjong (r 1834–49) in an austere Confucian style using unpainted wood. Royal descendants lived here until 1989.

Walk through the dense woodland and suddenly you come across a serene glade. The **Huwon** (Secret Garden; www.eng.cdg.go.kr) is a beautiful vista of pavilions on the edge of a square lily pond, with other halls and a two-storey library. The board out the front, written by King Jeongjo, means 'Gather the Universe'. Joseon kings relaxed, studied and wrote poems in this tranquil setting.

DON'T MISS

- Huwon
- Injeongjeon
- Nakseonjae

PRACTICALITIES

- 창덕궁
- Map p52
- http://eng.cdg.go.kr/main/main.htm
- 99 Yulgok-ro
- adult/child ₩3000/1500, incl Huwon ₩8000/4000
- 9am-6pm Tue-Sun Feb-May, Sep & Oct, to 6.30pm Jun-Aug, to 5.30pm Nov-Jan, Huwon closes 1hr earlier
- S Line 3 to Anguk, Exit 3

Greater Seoul

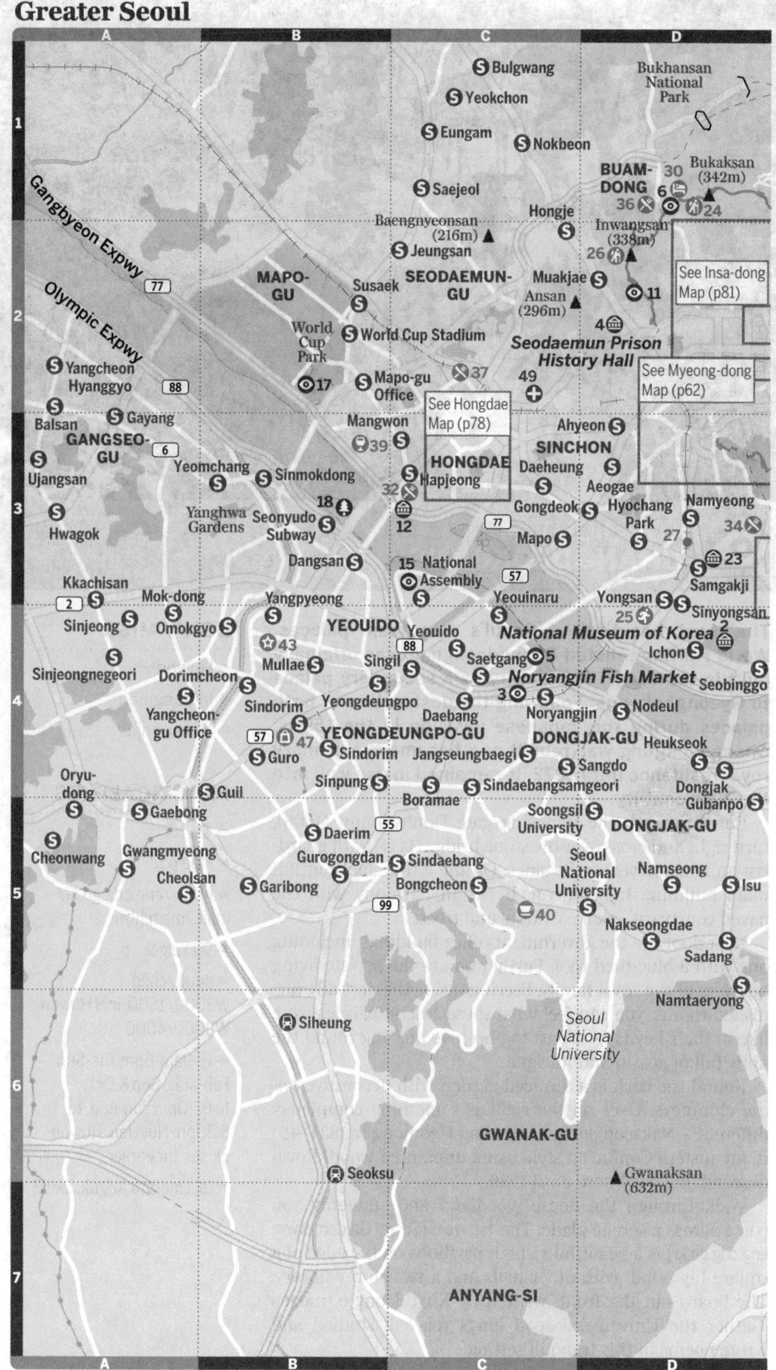

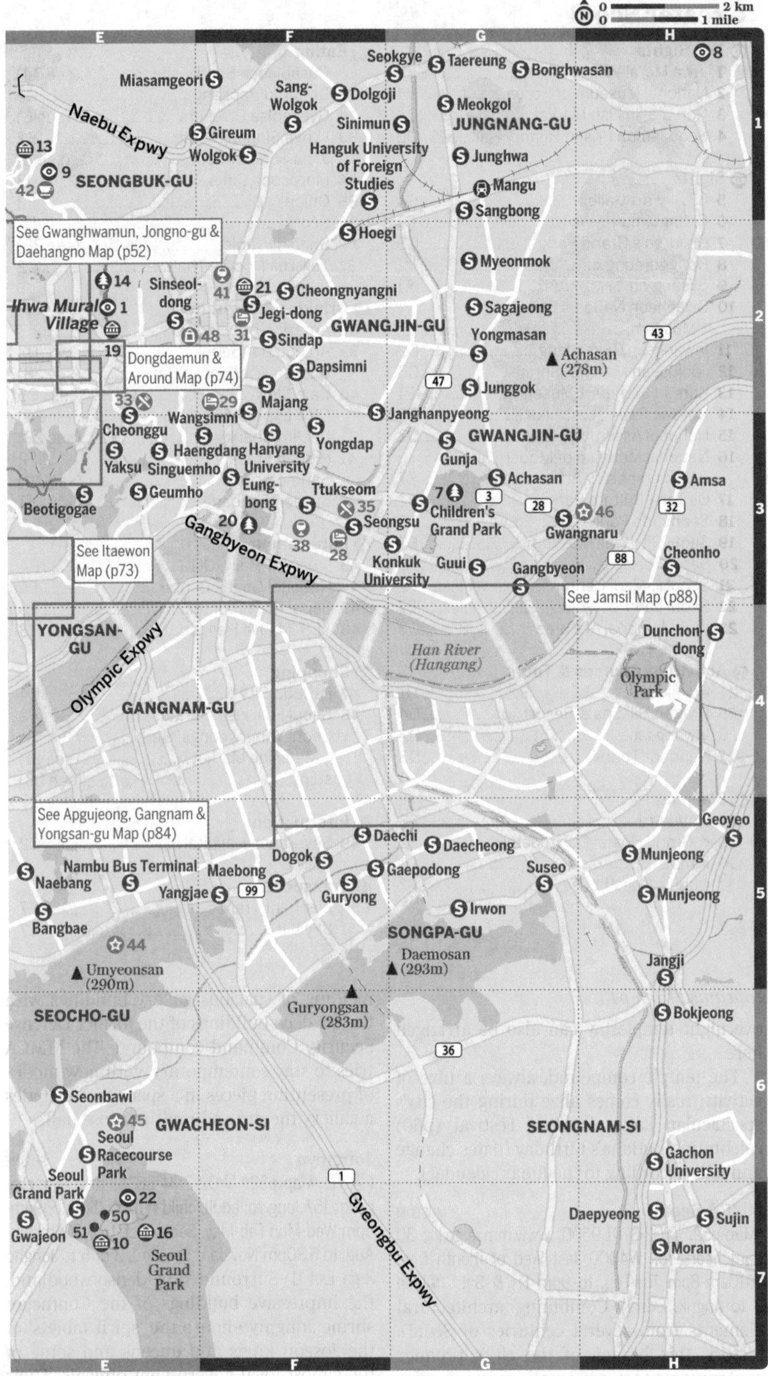

0 2 km
0 1 mile
E
F
G
H
Seokgye
Taereung
Bonghwasan
Miasamgeori
Sang-Wolgok
Dolgoji
Meokgol
Naebu Expwy
Gireum
Sinimun
JUNGNANG-GU
13
Wolgok
Hanguk University of Foreign Studies
Junghwa
9
SEONGBUK-GU
Mangu
42
Sangbong
See Gwanghwamun, Jongno-gu & Daehangno Map (p52)
Hoegi
Myeonmok
14
Sinseol-dong
41
21
Cheongnyangni
Ihwa Mural Village
1
Jegi-dong
Sagajeong
48
31
Sindap
GWANGJIN-GU
Yongmasan
43
19
Dongdaemun & Around Map (p74)
Dapsimni
Achasan (278m)
47
Junggok
33
29
Majang
Janghanpyeong
Cheonggu
Wangsimni
GWANGJIN-GU
Haengdang
Hanyang University
Yongdap
Gunja
Yaksu
Singuemho
Achasan
Amsa
Geumho
Eung-bong
Ttukseom
7
3
35
Children's Grand Park
28
46
32
Beotigogae
20
Seongsu
Gwangnaru
38
28
Gangbyeon Expwy
See Itaewon Map (p73)
Konkuk University
Guui
Gangbyeon
88
Cheonho
See Jamsil Map (p88)
YONGSAN-GU
Olympic Expwy
Dunchon-dong
Han River (Hangang)
Olympic Park
GANGNAM-GU
See Apgujeong, Gangnam & Yongsan-gu Map (p84)
Geoyeo
Daechi
Daecheong
Munjeong
Dogok
Nambu Bus Terminal
Maebong
Gaepodong
Suseo
Naebang
Yangjae
99
Guryong
Munjeong
Irwon
Bangbae
SONGPA-GU
44
Daemosan (293m)
Umyeonsan (290m)
Jangji
SEOCHO-GU
Guryongsan (283m)
Bokjeong
36
Seonbawi
45
GWACHEON-SI
SEONGNAM-SI
Seoul Racecourse Park
Gachon University
Seoul Grand Park
1
22
Daepyeong
Sujin
50
Gwajeon
51
16
10
Moran
Seoul Grand Park
Gyeongbu Expwy
SEOUL

Greater Seoul

Top Sights
1 Ihwa Mural Village E2
2 National Museum of Korea D4
3 Noryangjin Fish Market C4
4 Seodaemun Prison History Hall D2

Sights
5 63 Sky Art Gallery C4
6 Changuimun D1
7 Children's Grand Park G3
8 Donggureung H1
9 Gilsang-sa E1
10 Gwacheon National Science Museum E7
11 Inwangsan Guksadang D2
12 Jeoldusan Martyrs' Shrine C3
13 Korean Stone Art Museum E1
14 Naksan Park E2
15 National Assembly C3
16 National Museum of Modern and Contemporary Art E7
17 Oil Tank Culture Park B2
18 Seonyudo Park B3
19 Seoul City Wall Museum E2
20 Seoul Forest F3
21 Seoul K-Medi Center F2
22 Seoul Land E7
23 War Memorial of Korea D3

Activities, Courses & Tours
24 Bukaksan D1
25 Dragon Hill Spa & Resort D4
26 Inwangsan D2
27 Koridoor Tours D3

Sleeping
28 Hotel Atti F3
29 K-Grand Hostel Dongdaemun F2
30 Kims D1
31 Uhbu's Guesthouse F2

Eating
Casablanca Sandwicherie .... (see 34)
32 Dongmu Bapsang C3
Gyeyeolsa Chicken .... (see 6)
33 I Love Sindangdong E2
Jaha Sonmandoo .... (see 6)
34 Morococo Cafe D3
35 Onion F3
36 Scoff D1
Share D Table .... (see 28)
37 Tuk Tuk Noodle Thai C2

Drinking & Nightlife
38 Amazing Brewing Co F3
39 Arcade Bar Seoul B3
Baesan Warehouse Cafe .... (see 28)
40 Cafe More C5
Club Espresso .... (see 6)
Daelim Changgo .... (see 28)
41 Hidden Track F2
Sanmotoonge .... (see 30)
42 Suyeon Sanbang E1

Entertainment
43 Indie Art-Hall GONG B4
44 National Gugak Center E5
45 Seoul Racecourse E6
46 YES 24 Live Hall H3

Shopping
47 D-Cube City B4
48 Seoul Folk Flea Market E2
Seoul Yangnyeongsi Herb Medicine Market .... (see 21)
su;py .... (see 28)

Information
49 Severance Hospital C2

Transport
50 Elephant Tram Car E7
51 Sky Lift E7

continued from p43

overnight templestay can also be arranged here.

The temple compound, always a hive of activity, really comes alive during the city's spectacular Lotus Lantern Festival (p60) celebrating Buddha's birthday (dates change annually according to the lunar calendar).

MMCA Seoul MUSEUM

(Map p52; ☎02-3701 9500; www.mmca.go.kr; 30 Samcheong-ro; ₩4000, last Wed of month free; ⏲10am-6pm Tue-Thu, to 9pm Fri & Sat; Ⓢ Line 3 to Anguk, Exit 1) Combining architectural elements from several centuries of Seoul's history, this branch of the city's premier contemporary-art museum is an impressive melding of spacious gallery buildings with the art deco buildings of the former Defense Security Command compound. The MMCA tries to stay contemporary, with new modes of presenting pieces in a space that includes a gallery theatre and multipurpose hall.

Jongmyo SHRINE

(종묘; Map p52; ☎02-2174 3636; http://jm.cha.go.kr; 157 Jong-ro; adult/child ₩1000/500; ⏲9am-5pm Wed-Mon Feb-May, Sep & Oct, to 6.30pm Jun-Aug, to 5.30pm Nov-Jan; Ⓢ Line 1, 3 or 5 to Jongno 3-ga, Exit 11) Surrounded by dense woodland, the impressive buildings of the Confucian shrine Jongmyo house the 'spirit tablets' of the Joseon kings and queens and some of their most loyal government officials. Their

spirits are believed to reside in a special hole bored into the wooden tablets.

For its architecture and the special ceremonies that take place here, the shrine has been awarded World Heritage status: the most famous ceremony is the Jongmyo Daeje (p60) in early May.

National Folk Museum of Korea MUSEUM
(국립민속박물관; Map p52; ☎02-3704 3114; www.nfm.go.kr; 37 Samcheong-ro; free with Gyeongbokgung; ⊙9am-6pm Wed-Mon Mar-Oct, to 5pm Wed-Mon Nov-Feb; SLine 3 to Anguk, Exit 1) FREE Give yourself at least an hour to do justice to this excellent museum. It has three main exhibition halls, covering the history of the Korean people, the agricultural way of life and the life of *yangban* (aristocrats) during the Joseon era. Among the many interesting exhibits is an amazingly colourful funeral bier (it looks like a fantasy Noah's Ark) – these were used to give the deceased a great send-off.

Simsimheon ARCHITECTURE
(심심헌; Map p52; ☎02-763 3393; www.simsimheon.com; 47 Bukchon-ro 11-gil; ₩15,000; ⊙9am-6.30pm Mon-Sat; SLine 3 to Anguk, Exit 2) This modern *hanok* was rebuilt using traditional methods on the site of two older ones to create a home with museumlike grandeur, which gives a rare opportunity to see inside a (splendid) residential property in the heart of Bukchon. Entry includes tea, which is sipped overlooking the internal garden. The private body National Trust of Korea manages Simsimheon, meaning 'House Where the Heart is Found'. Reservations required.

Another Way of Seeing GALLERY
(우리들의 눈; Map p52; ☎02-733 1996; http://artblind.or.kr; 19 Bukchon-ro 5na-gil; ⊙10-11am & 1-6pm Mon-Sat; SLine 3 to Anguk, Exit 1) FREE Running a program to support art education and activities for the blind, Another Way of Seeing is a gallery where the thought-provoking exhibitions frequently play on senses other than sight, such as smell, touch and sound.

Myeong-dong & Jung-gu

★N Seoul Tower & Namsan TOWER
(Map p62; ☎02-3455 9277; www.nseoultower.com; Namsan; adult/child ₩10,000/8000; ⊙10am-11pm Sun-Fri, to midnight Sat; shuttle bus 2, 3 or 5) The iconic N Seoul tower (236m), atop the city's guardian mountain Namsan, offers panoramic views of this immense metropolis from its observation deck. Come at sunset and you can watch the city morph into a galaxy of twinkling stars. Up top is the upmarket **N.Grill** (☎02-3455 9297; set lunch/dinner from ₩50,000/95,000; ⊙11am-2pm & 5-11pm; SLine 4 to Myeongdong, Exit 3 then cable car) and a cafe. The tower has become a hot date spot with the railings around it festooned with locks inscribed with lovers' names.

Walking up Namsan isn't difficult, but riding the **cable car** (www.cablecar.co.kr; 1-way/return adult ₩6000/8500, child ₩3500/5500; ⊙10am-11pm) is popular for more good views.

Shuttle buses run from 7.30am to 11.30pm from various subway stations around the mountain (such as Myeong-dong Exit 3, Chungmuro Exit 2 and Seoul Exit 9); normal bus fares apply.

★Deoksugung PALACE
(덕수궁; Map p62; www.deoksugung.go.kr; 99 Sejong-daero; adult/child/under 7yr ₩1000/500/free; ⊙9am-9pm Tue-Sun; SLine 1 or 2 to City Hall, Exit 2) One of Seoul's five grand palaces built during the Joseon dynasty, Deoksugung (meaning Palace of Virtuous Longevity) is the only one you can visit in the evening and see the buildings illuminated. It first served as a palace in 1593 and is a fascinating mix of traditional Korean and western-style neoclassical structures. The palace's main gate is the scene of the entertaining changing of the guard ceremony at 11am, 2pm and 3.30pm. Free one-hour guided tours in English start at 10.45am and 1.30pm.

★Namdaemun Market MARKET
(Map p62; www.namdaemunmarket.co.kr; 21 Namdaemun-sijang 4-gil; ⊙24hr; SLine 4 to Hoehyeon, Exit 5) You could spend all day in this swarming night-and-day market. The largest market in Korea, each section has hundreds of stalls, from clothing to handicrafts and accessories. Its market food, though, is the biggest highlight, with dozens of stalls selling *sujebi* (dough and shellfish soup), homemade *kalguksu* noodles, bibimbap (mixed rice, meat and vegetables) and an alley dedicated to fish dishes. Restaurant Alley has a huge range of Korean food – all with plastic replicas outside to make choosing easy.

Seoullo 7017 PARK
(서울로7017; Map p62; http://seoullo7017.seoul.go.kr; 432 Cheongpa-ro; ⊙24hr; SLine 4 to Hoehyeon, Exit 5) FREE This overpass-turned-park is a green space in the heart of the city. About 24,000 plants are grown here, including various types of flowers and trees, all labelled. Seoullo 7017 provides an interesting, airy (though sun-exposed) view of the city centre, its highways and architecture.

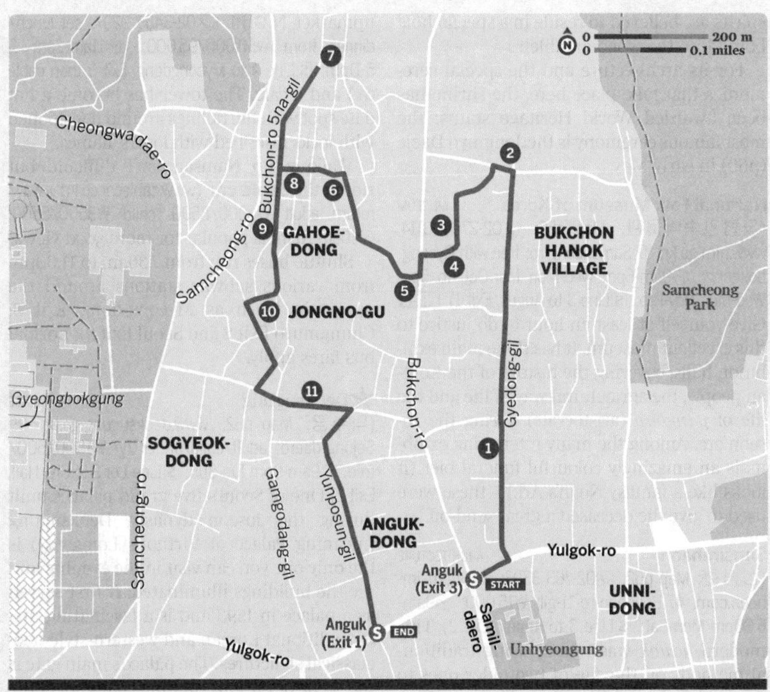

City Walk
Bukchon Views

START ANGUK STATION, EXIT 3
END ANGUK STATION, EXIT 1
LENGTH 3KM; TWO HOURS

Take in views across Bukchon's tiled *hanok* roofs on this walk around the area between Gyeongbokgung and Changdeokgung. Don't worry if you get a little lost in the maze of streets – that's part of the pleasure. This walk is best done in the early morning or early evening (or even on a moonlit night) to avoid the daytime crowds.

From the Anguk station subway exit turn left at the first junction and walk 200m to **1 Bukchon Traditional Culture Center** (p44) where you can learn about the area's architecture. Continue to head north up Gyedong-gil, an appealing street lined with cafes, boutiques and *hanok* guesthouses; at the T-junction at the top of the hill is the entrance to **2 Choong Ang High School**, an attractive early-20th-century educational complex that featured as a location in the hit Korean TV drama *Winter Sonata*. Wind you way back downhill from here past the **3 Gahoe Minhwa Workshop** (p44) and the **4 Dong-Lim Knot Workshop** (p44) to emerge on the major road Bukchon-ro. Cross over and locate the start of **5 Bukchon-ro 11-gil**; follow this narrow street uphill towards the parallel set of picturesque streets lined with *hanok* in Gahoe-dong. To see inside one of the *hanok* pause at **6 Simsimheon** (p49).

Turn left and go a few blocks west towards the chimney stack to Bukchon-ro 5na-gil; to the right is a **7 viewing spot** across Samcheong-dong. Head south down the hill, perhaps pausing for tea at **8 Cha Masineun Tteul** (p77). Further downhill is **9 Another Way of Seeing** (p49), an art gallery with interesting exhibitions by the vision impaired.

Turn left after the **10 World Jewellery Museum** and then right at the junction; on the corner by a tourist information booth, walk up to **11 Jeongdok Public Library**, where the small, quiet park in front of the building is a prime spot for viewing cherry blossoms in spring and the yellowing leaves of ginkgo trees in autumn. Return to the subway station via Yunposeon-gil.

Cross-country locomotives snake across a web of train tracks, then at night the old Seoul Station glows and the overpass itself is lit up in moody colours.

The overpass was built in 1970, but in 2014 it was deemed unfit for automobiles and the 17m-high road was refitted as a green space for pedestrians based on the High Line in New York. Seoullo (sounding like 'Seoul Road' in English) opened in 2017, giving meaning to the numbers 7017 alongside the original build year. A handful of cafes and galleries are located along its length and there are sometimes art exhibitions, concerts, and activities for kids, including trampolines. Free day and night walking tours of the park are provided by the Seoul city government; reserve at www.visitseoul.net.

Seoullo 7017 can be entered from various points, starting on Toegye-ro at Nomdaemun Market gate 5 (which is also Hoehyeon station, Exit 5), where there is a dedicated **information booth** (Map p62; ☎02-312 9575; http://seoullo7017.seoul.go.kr; 281 Namdaemun-ro 5-ga; ⏰10am-10pm) with maps. The midpoint entrance is at Seoul Station Exit 8 and the overpass ends just after Cheongpa-ro.

Namsangol Hanok Village CULTURAL CENTRE
(남산골한옥마을; Map p62; ☎02-2264 4412; www.hanokmaeul.or.kr; 28 Toegye-ro 34-gil; ⏰9am-9pm Tue-Sun, to 8pm Nov-Mar; Ⓢ Line 3 or 4 to Chungmuro, Exit 4) FREE Located in a park at the foot of Namsan, this peaceful village is a wonderful spot to encounter traditional Korean culture. It features five differing *yangban* (upper class) houses from the Joseon era, all relocated here from different parts of Seoul. Also here is a traditional theatre; **Seoul Namsan Gugakdang** (☎02-2261 0512; tickets from ₩20,000; ⏰closed Tue). On the right of the entrance gate is an office that provides free hour-long guided tours around the village in English (noon Thursday to Sunday, and 2pm Tuesday, Wednesday, Saturday and Sunday).

Seoul City Hall ARCHITECTURE
(서울시청사; Map p62; http://english.seoul.go.kr; 110 Sejong-daero; ⏰7.30am-6pm Mon-Fri, from 9am Sat & Sun; Ⓢ Line 1 or 2 to City Hall, Exit 5) FREE Looking like a tsunami made of glass and steel, Seoul City Hall was completely redeveloped in 2013 and now is a major architectural attraction of the city. It is a modern reinterpretation of traditional Korean design; the cresting wave provides shade (like the curved eaves found on palaces and temple roofs in Korea) over the handsome old City Hall, which was built from stone in 1926, now a **library** (http://lib.seoul.go.kr; ⏰9am-9pm Mon-Fri, to 6pm Sat & Sun) FREE.

Western Seoul

★Noryangjin Fish Market MARKET
(노량진수산시장; Map p46; ☎02-2254 8003; www.susansijang.co.kr; 674 Nodeul-ro; ⏰24hr; Ⓟ; Ⓢ Line 1 to Noryangjin, Exit 1) Providing terrific photo opportunities, Korea's largest fish market supplies every kind of aquatic life form to restaurants, fish shops and the public. Originally established in 1927 and relocated here in 1971, the current multistorey, state-of-the-art complex opened its revamped doors in 2016 and now is the home of 700 stalls and numerous restaurants.

★Gyeongui Line Forest Park PARK
(경의선숲길, YeontralPark; Map p78; www.gyeonguiline.org; 27 Susaek-ro; 🚸🐾; Ⓢ Line 2 to Hongik University, Exit 3) This 6.3km park, named for the former Gyeongui Line (on which it was built), is a narrow, long green space that runs along the discarded railroad tracks above Gajwa Station to Hyochang Park station. Within are nooks for reading, grassy picnic areas, exercise equipment and more.

The Gyeongui Line was built by the Japanese in 1905 and abandoned in the early 1950s. Since the park opened in 2016, many restaurants, cafes and bars in its bordering regions have surfaced. Parts of the park are themed; eg Yeonnam-dong (next to Hongik University Station Exit 3), nicknamed Yeontral Park because of its Central Park–like atmosphere, is popular for picnics (albeit on uncomfortable artificial grass) and is also a great place to grab a beer (available at several nearby craft-beer marts), people-watch and enjoy the warm weather on a nice day or night. The area between Hongik University station and Sinchon is known as **Gyeongui Line Book Street** (경의선책거리; Map p78; www.gbookst.or.kr; 50-4, Wausan-ro 35-gil; ⏰bookshops 11am-8pm; Ⓢ Line 2 to Hongik University, Exit 6) FREE, with train-carriage-like bookshops.

KT&G SangsangMadang ARCHITECTURE
(KT&G 상상마당; Map p78; ☎02-330 6200; www.sangsangmadang.com/main/HD; 65 Eoulmadang-ro; ⏰shop noon-11pm, gallery 1-10pm; Ⓢ Line 2 to Hongik University, Exit 5) Funded by Korea's top tobacco company, this visually striking building is home to an art-house cinema, a concert space (hosting top indie bands) and galleries that focus on experimental, fringe exhibitions. There's also a great design shop for gifts on the ground floor. The architect,

Gwanghwamun, Jongno-gu & Daehangno

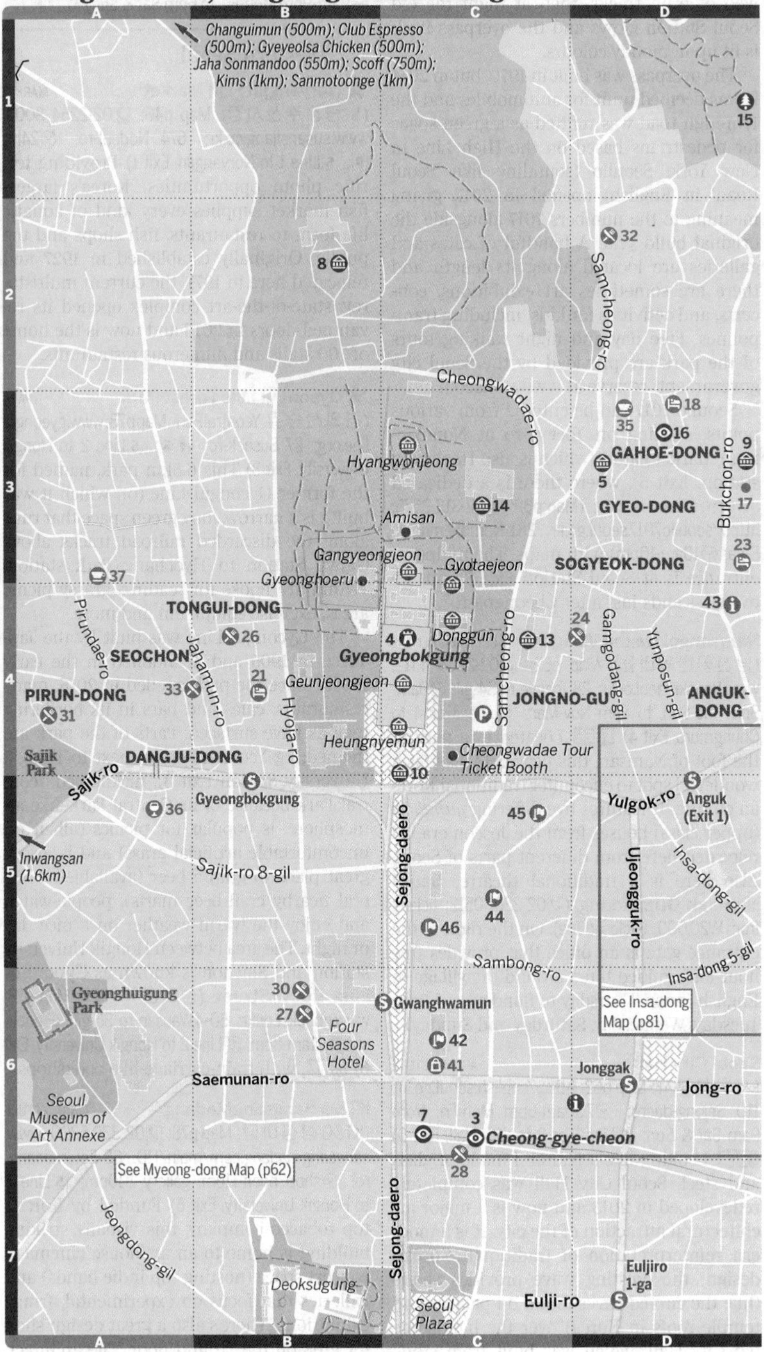
Changuimun (500m); Club Espresso (500m); Gyeyeolsa Chicken (500m); Jaha Sonmandoo (550m); Scoff (750m); Kims (1km); Sanmotoonge (1km)
15
8
32
Samcheong-ro
Cheongwadae-ro
35
18
16
GAHOE-DONG
9
Bukchon-ro
5
Hyangwonjeong
14
GYEO-DONG
17
Amisan
23
Gangyeongjeon
Gyotaejeon
SOGYEOK-DONG
37
Gyeonghoeru
43
TONGUI-DONG
24
Pirundae-ro
26
Gamgodang-gil
Yunposun-gil
4
Donggun
13
SEOCHON
Jahamun-ro
Gyeongbokgung
Samcheong-ro
21
Geunjeongjeon
PIRUN-DONG
33
Hyoja-ro
JONGNO-GU
ANGUK-DONG
31
Heungnyemun
Cheongwadae Tour Ticket Booth
Sajik Park
DANGJU-DONG
Sajik-ro
10
Gyeongbokgung
Yulgok-ro
Anguk (Exit 1)
36
45
Inwangsan (1.6km)
Sajik-ro 8-gil
Sejong-daero
Ujeongguk-ro
Insa-dong-gil
44
46
Sambong-ro
Insa-dong 5-gil
Gyeonghuigung Park
30
Gwanghwamun
See Insa-dong Map (p81)
27
Four Seasons Hotel
42
41
Jonggak
Jong-ro
Saemunan-ro
Seoul Museum of Art Annexe
7
3
Cheong-gye-cheon
28
See Myeong-dong Map (p62)
Jeongdong-gil
Sejong-daero
Euljiro 1-ga
Deoksugung
Eulji-ro
Seoul Plaza
A
B
C
D
1
2
3
4
5
6
7

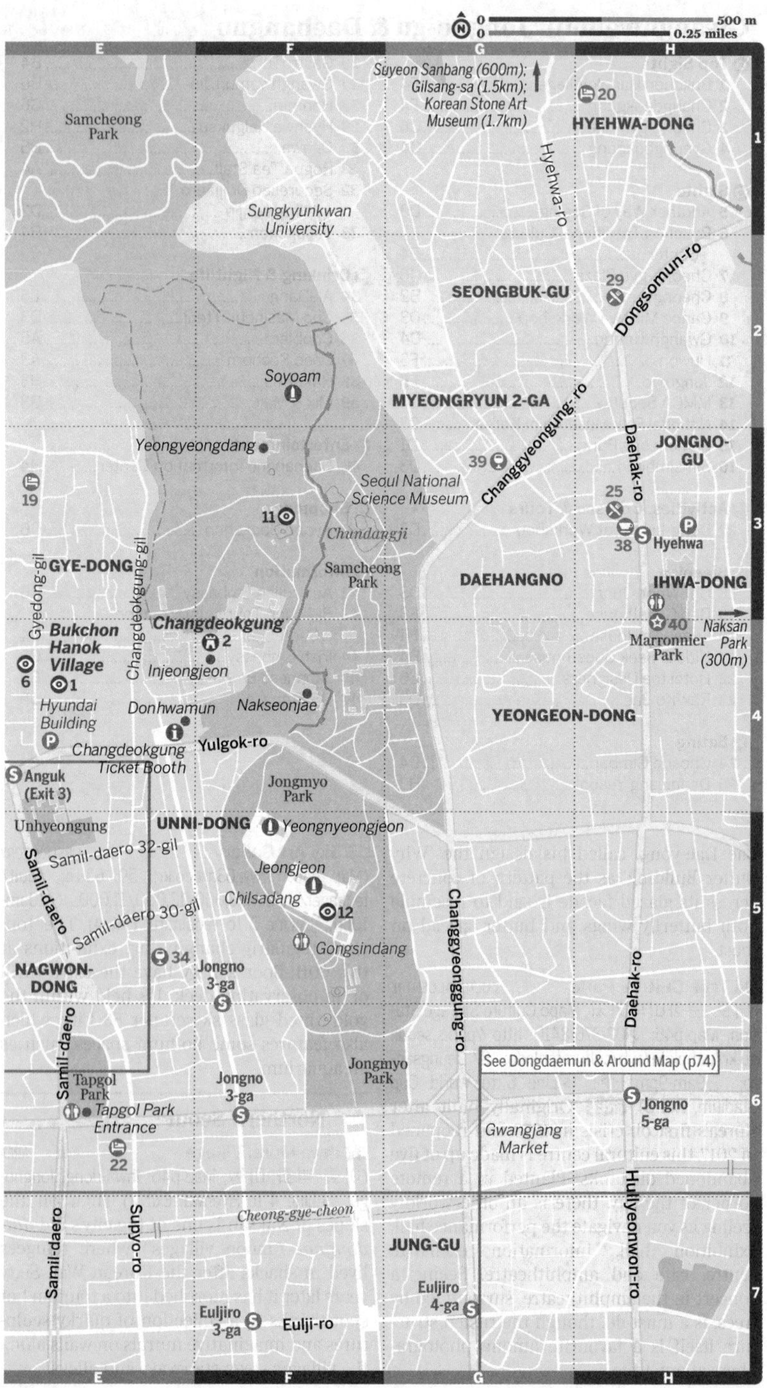

0 500 m
0 0.25 miles
Suyeon Sanbang (600m); Gilsang-sa (1.5km); Korean Stone Art Museum (1.7km)
20
HYEHWA-DONG
Samcheong Park
Hyehwa-ro
Sungkyunkwan University
Dongsomun-ro
29
SEONGBUK-GU
Soyoam
MYEONGRYUN 2-GA
Changgyeonggung-ro
Yeongyeongdang
Daehak-ro
JONGNO-GU
39
Seoul National Science Museum
19
25
11
Chundangji
38
Hyehwa
Samcheong Park
GYE-DONG
Gyedong-gil
DAEHANGNO
IHWA-DONG
Changdeokgung-gil
Changdeokgung
40
Naksan Park (300m)
Bukchon Hanok Village
2
Marronnier Park
Injeongjeon
6
1
Hyundai Building
Donhwamun
Nakseonjae
YEONGEON-DONG
Changdeokgung Ticket Booth
Yulgok-ro
Anguk (Exit 3)
Jongmyo Park
Unhyeongung
UNNI-DONG
Yeongnyeongjeon
Samil-daero 32-gil
Samil-daero
Jeongjeon
Chilsadang
12
Samil-daero 30-gil
Changgyeonggung-ro
Gongsindang
34
Jongno 3-ga
NAGWON-DONG
Daehak-ro
Samil-daero
Jongmyo Park
See Dongdaemun & Around Map (p74)
Tapgol Park
Jongno 3-ga
Jongno 5-ga
Tapgol Park Entrance
Gwangjang Market
22
Hullyeonwon-ro
Cheong-gye-cheon
Samil-daero
Supyo-ro
JUNG-GU
Euljiro 4-ga
Euljiro 3-ga
Eulji-ro
E
F
G
H
1
2
3
4
5
6
7
SEOUL

Gwanghwamun, Jongno-gu & Daehangno

Top Sights
1 Bukchon Hanok Village E4
2 Changdeokgung F4
3 Cheong-gye-cheon C6
4 Gyeongbokgung C4

Sights
5 Another Way of Seeing D3
6 Bukchon Traditional Culture Center E4
7 Cheong-gye Plaza C6
8 Cheongwadae B2
9 Gahoe Minhwa Workshop D3
10 Gwanghwamun C4
11 Huwon F3
12 Jongmyo F5
13 MMCA Seoul C4
14 National Folk Museum of Korea C3
15 Samcheong Park D1
16 Simsimheon D3

Activities, Courses & Tours
17 Dong-Lim Knot Workshop D3

Sleeping
18 Chi-Woon-Jung D3
19 Doo Guesthouse E3
20 Eugene's House H1
21 Hide & Seek Guesthouse B4
22 Hotel the Designers E6
23 Rak-Ko-Jae D3

Eating
24 Chosun Gimbap D4
25 Deongjang Yesool H3
26 GastroTong B4
27 Gwanghwamun Jip B6
28 Hanmiri C6
29 Hyehwa Kalguksu H2
30 Ogawa B6
31 Rogpa Tea Stall A4
32 Seoureseo Duljjaero Jalhaneunjip D2
33 Tosokchon B4

Drinking & Nightlife
34 AleDang E5
35 Cha Masineun Tteul D3
36 Cobbler A5
37 Daeo Sochom A3
38 Hakrim H3
39 Mix & Malt G3

Entertainment
40 Daehangno Information Center H4

Shopping
41 Kyobo Bookshop C6

Information
42 Australian Embassy C6
43 Bukchon Tourist Information Center D4
44 Irish Embassy C5
45 Japanese Embassy C5
46 US Embassy C5

Bae Dae-yong, called his design the 'Why Butter Building' as the pattern of concrete across its glazed facade is said to resemble both butterfly wings and butter spread on toast.

Oil Tank Culture Park CULTURAL CENTRE
(마포 문화비축기지, Mapo Culture Storage Station; Map p46; ☎02-376 8410; http://parks.seoul.go.kr/template/sub/culturetank.do; 87 Jeungsan-ro; ⏰9am-9pm; P; S Line 6 to World Cup Stadium, Exit 3) FREE Originally built after Korea's first oil crisis in 1973 and reopened in 2017, this cultural centre is made up of five abandoned oil tanks. Planted in a remote corner of the city, there is an otherworldly feeling as you navigate the performance hall, exhibition hall, information exchange centre, cafe and amphitheatre. Seeing a concert in the amphitheatre, surrounded by trees, is a must-do, though the rusted structure itself is a favourite among photographers at any time.

63 Sky Art Gallery OBSERVATORY
(Map p46; www.63art.co.kr; 50, 63-ro; adult/teenager/child ₩13,000/12,000/11,000; ⏰10am-10pm; S Line 5 to Yeouinaru, Exit 4) The top-class, regularly changing art exhibitions at this 60th-floor gallery have the extra thrill of an observation deck. It's held within the gold-tinted glass skyscraper 63 City, which also features some ho-hum spaces, such as an aquarium.

Northern Seoul

★ **Ihwa Mural Village** AREA
(이화 벽화 마을; Map p46; Ihwa-dong, Jongno-gu; S Line 4 to Hyehwa, Exit 2) High on the slopes of Naksan is one of the city's old *daldongnae* ('moon villages') where refugees lived in shacks after the Korean War. Sixty years later it has morphed into a tourism hot spot thanks to a collection of quirky sculptures and imaginative murals on walls along the village's steep stairways and alleys.

★ Seodaemun Prison History Hall MUSEUM
(서대문형무소역사관; Map p46; www.sscmc.or.kr/culture2/foreign/eng/eng01.html; 251 Tongil-ro; adult/youth/child ₩3000/1500/1000; ⊙9.30am-6pm Tue-Sun Mar-Oct, to 5pm Tue-Sun Nov-Feb; SLine 3 to Dongnimmun, Exit 5) Built in 1908, this former prison is a potent symbol of Korean suffering at the hands of Japan during colonial occupation in the early 20th century. However, it was also used by Korea's various postwar dictators up until its closure in 1987. You can tour the original cell blocks where independence fighters and democracy campaigners were held, as well as the nightmarish interrogation and torture rooms. An execution block dating from 1923 features a concealed tunnel to remove the dead.

Korean Stone Art Museum MUSEUM
(우리옛돌박물관; Map p46; www.koreanstonemuseum.com; 66 Daesagwan-ro 13-gil; adult/youth/child ₩7000/5000/3000; ⊙10am-6pm Tue-Sun; SLine 4 to Hansung University, Exit 6) A score of centuries-old stone sentinels stands guard on the hillside at this terrific museum overlooking Seongbuk-dong. A road winds through sculpted gardens revealing collections of various stone figures as you go. You'll learn to tell your *muninseok* from your *dongjaseok* (the former wear the hats of government officials while the latter have double-knot hairdos); there's also the more crudely carved *beoksu* – totems placed at the entrance to Korean villages to protect against evil spirits and illnesses.

Gilsang-sa TEMPLE
(길상사; Map p46; ☎02-3672 5945; www.kilsangsa.info; 68 Seonjam-ro 5-gil, Seongbuk-gu; ⊙10am-6pm Mon-Sat; SLine 4 to Hansung University, Exit 6) FREE This modern hillside temple is a pleasure to visit at any time of the year, but particularly in May when the grounds are festooned with lanterns for Buddha's birthday. The buildings once housed the elite restaurant Daewongak, where *gisaeng* (female entertainers accomplished in traditional arts) performed. In 1997 the property was donated by its owner, a former *gisaeng*, to a Buddhist monk to be turned into a temple. From the subway take bus 2; it stops right outside the temple entrance.

★ Inwangsan Guksadang SHRINE
(인왕산국사당; Map p46; Inwangsan, Seodaemun-gu; SLine 3 to Dongnimmun, Exit 2) This ornate shrine atop Inwangsan is one of Seoul's most important sites for shamanism, Korea's ancient, highly ritualised and somewhat taboo folk religion. If you're lucky, you might witness a *gut* (service) performed by female *mudang* (shamans), invoking the spirits to bless a marriage, bring good fortune or cure illness. The Japanese demolished the original shrine on Namsan in 1925, and it was rebuilt here.

Itaewon & Yongsan-gu

★ Leeum Samsung Museum of Art GALLERY
(Map p73; www.leeum.org; 60-16 Itaewon-ro 55-gil; adult/child ₩10,000/5000; ⊙10.30am-6pm Tue-Sun; SLine 6 to Hangangjin, Exit 1) Amid the celebrity-owned apartments on the leafy southern slope of Namsan is Korea's premier art gallery. Beautifully designed and laid-out, it balances modern and contemporary art with traditional Korean art across its three distinct areas. The big draw is Museum 2, a rusted stainless-steel structure designed by French architect Jean Nouvel, showcasing early- and mid-century paintings, sculptures and installations by esteemed Korean and international artists, including Nam June Paik, Damien Hirst, Andy Warhol and Jeff Koons.

★ National Museum of Korea MUSEUM
(국립중앙박물관; Map p46; www.museum.go.kr; 137 Seobinggo-ro; ⊙10am-6pm, to 9pm Sat, to 7pm Sun; SLine 1 or 4 to Ichon, Exit 2) FREE This vast and imposing concrete slab of a museum takes visitors on a fascinating journey through Korea's past from prehistory all the way to the Korean Empire period (1897–1910). If you're short on time, prioritise the Joseon Dynasty gallery (1392–1897). Among the must-see exhibits in the ground-floor galleries are the Baekje Incense Burner, an extraordinary example of the artistry of the 6th- to 7th-century Baekje Kingdom; and the Golden Treasures from the Great Tomb of Hwangham.

War Memorial of Korea MUSEUM
(전쟁 기념관; Map p46; www.warmemo.or.kr; 29 Itaewon-ro; ⊙9.30am-6pm Tue-Sun; SLine 4 or 6 to Samgakji, Exit 12) FREE This huge museum documents the history of the Korean War (1950–53) using multimedia exhibits and black-and-white documentary footage, along with artefacts like weapons, uniforms and maps. Outside, a sombre memorial walkway is inscribed with the names of every casualty from the allied forces. There are plenty of tanks, helicopters and planes too, and just to remind you that the war remains unresolved, you can clamber aboard

SEOUL FOR FAMILIES

Seoul is a safe city with lots of child-friendly museums (including several devoted to kids themselves), as well as amusement parks, playgrounds and fun events that will appeal to all age groups.

Korean Culture

The National Museum of Korea (p55) and the National Folk Museum (p49) have fun, hands-on children's sections, and the War Memorial of Korea (p55) has outdoor warplanes and tanks that make for a popular playground. Various events, some involving dressing up in traditional costumes or having a go at taekwondo, happen at Namsangol Hanok Village (p51). Older kids and teenagers will likely want to visit places such as the **Seoul Animation Center** (서울애니메이션센터; Map p62; www.ani.seoul.kr; 126 Sopa-ro; ⏲9am-5.50pm Tue-Sun; **S** Line 4 to Myeongdong, Exit 1 or 3) FREE to learn more about local animated TV series and films, or **Samsung D'Light** (Map p84; www.samsungdlight.com; Samsung Electronics Bldg, 11 Seochodae-ro 74-gil; ⏲10am-7pm Mon-Sat; **S** Line 2 to Gangnam, Exit 8) FREE to play with the latest digital technology. Nonverbal shows such as Nanta (p85) and Jump (p86) are great family entertainment.

Thanks to the global appeal of local pop culture, little ones are likely to be more au fait with contemporary Korean pop culture than their parents. Be prepared to search out shops stocking BTS or Big Bang posters, DVDs of Korean TV soap operas, or *manhwa* (Korean comics and graphic novels). Kyobo Bookshop (p86) is a good place to start.

Getting Active

At theme parks like Lotte World (p57) and Everland (p104), family entertainment comes in mega-sized portions. Easier on the wallet are the scores of free open spaces that constitute Seoul's wealth of city-managed parks – places such as Olympic Park (p57), **Seoul Forest** (서울숲; Map p46; 685 Seongsu 1-ga 1-dong, Seongdong-gu; ⏲24hr; 👪; **S** Bundang Line 2 to Seoul Forest, Exit 2) FREE; **Children's Grand Park** (서울 어린이대공원; Map p46; ☎02-450 9311; www.childrenpark.or.kr; 216 Neungdong-ro, Gwangjin-gu; amusement park rides ₩4000; ⏲5am-10pm, amusement-park 10am-6.30pm, zoo 9.30am-5.30pm; 👪; **S** Line 5 or 7 to Children's Grand Park, Exit 1) FREE, and the string of bicycle-lane-connected parks that hug the Han River's banks (p65). Each summer six big outdoor-pool complexes open in the Han River parks too.

a replica of the patrol boat sunk by North Korean forces in 2002.

Stairway Flea Market MARKET
(Map p73; Usadan-ro) Held on the last Saturday of each month, this market attracts hundreds of shoppers to Usadan-ro on top of Itaewon Hill, where local artists sell their works on the stairs, and set up stalls along the street, which is lined with artist studios, galleries, pop-up shops and cool hole-in-the-wall bars and eateries.

Dongdaemun & Eastern Seoul

★Dongdaemun Design Plaza & Park CULTURAL CENTRE
(동대문디자인플라자, DDP; Map p74; ☎02-2153 0408; www.ddp.or.kr; 28 Eulji-ro, Jung-gu; ⏲10am-7pm Tue, Thu, Sat & Sun, to 9pm Wed & Fri; **S** Lines 2, 4 or 5 to Dongdaemun History & Culture Park, Exit 1) FREE Designed by the late Zaha Hadid, this neofuturistic cultural complex was commissioned to replace the Dongdaemun Stadium, built during Japanese rule in the 1920s. Dubbed the 'largest three-dimensional atypical structure in the world', the undulating concrete and aluminium landmark comprises galleries, event spaces, shops and lawns that rise to its roof. The attached Dongdaemun History & Culture Park includes museums that highlight past uses of this area, such as a 16th-century military camp.

During the site's excavation, major archaeological remains from the Joseon dynasty were uncovered, including original sections of the Seoul City Wall. The ruins have been incorporated into the park and include the arched floodgate Yigansumun. The **Dongdaemun History Museum** (⏲10am-7pm Tue-Sun) FREE imaginatively displays the pick of the 575 artefacts from the site and provides historical background to the ancient foundations preserved outside. The **Dongdaemun Stadium Memorial** (⏲10am-7pm

Tue-Sun) FREE relives key moments from the stadium's history and includes video clips.

★Seoul K-Medi Center MUSEUM

(서울한방진흥센터, Seoul Yangnyeongsi Herb Medicine Museum; Map p46; http://kmedi.ddm.go.kr; 26 Yangnyeongjungang-ro; museum entry ₩1000, foot bath or machine massage ₩5000; ⊙10am-6pm Tue-Sun; SLine 1 to Jegi-dong, Exit 2) Learn about the history and practice of traditional Korean medicine at this impressive facility styled to resemble Bojewon, a clinic from the early Joseon Dynasty strategically located here outside the City Walls to prevent the spread of infection. There's an array of natural ingredients on show (the Korean word for medicine is *boncho*: literally 'roots and grasses'), and after you can treat your feet with a herbal bath on the upstairs terrace.

Seoul City Wall Museum MUSEUM

(한양도성박물관; Map p46; ☎02-724 0243; 283 Yulgok-ro, Jongno-gu; ⊙9am-7pm Tue-Sun; SLine 1 or 4 to Dongdaemun, Exit 1) FREE With interactive displays and historical artefacts, this modern museum offers an engaging history of the 18.6km-long barrier that has girdled Seoul since the late 14th century. Overlooking Heunginjimun beside a stretch of the City Wall, it also makes a logical embarkation point for a wall hike. Seoul withdrew its Unesco application for the City Wall in 2017 after it was deemed not to possess 'outstanding universal value' (despite being continuously maintained for six centuries). The city intends to resubmit in 2020.

Heunginjimun GATE

(Dongdaemun; Map p74; SLine 1 or 4 to Dongdaemun, Exit 6) The Great East Gate to Seoul's City Wall has been rebuilt several times in its 700-year history and, after recent renovations, it's looking majestic. It's stranded in a traffic island, so it's not possible to enter inside the gate, but there are good photo ops from Dongdaemun Seonggwak Park to the north, which is also where you'll find the City Wall Museum and a trail following the City Wall up to **Naksan Park** (낙산공원; Map p46; http://parks.seoul.go.kr; 54 Naksan-gil; ⊙24hr; SLine 4 to Hyehwa, Exit 2) FREE and Ihwa Mural Village (p54).

Gangnam & Southern Seoul

★Bongeun-sa BUDDHIST TEMPLE

(봉은사; Map p88; ☎02-3218 4895; www.bongeunsa.org; 531 Bongeunsa-ro; ⊙3am-10pm; SLine 2 to Samseong, Exit 6) FREE Located in the heart of ritzy Gangnam, the shrines and halls of the Buddhist temple Bongeun-sa, with its tree-filled hillside location, stand in direct juxtaposition to its corporate high-rise surrounds. Founded in AD 794, the buildings have been rebuilt many times over the centuries. Entry to the temple is through Jinyeomun (Gate of Truth), protected by four king guardians. The main shrine, Daewungjeon, has lattice doors and is decorated inside and out with symbols and art that express Buddhist philosophy and ideals.

★Tangent ARCHITECTURE

(Map p88; Yeongdong-daero; SLine 2 to Samseong, Exit 6) Hyundai Development Company commissioned Daniel Libeskind to work with Seoul-based firm Himma on its headquarters opposite COEX Mall. The result, Tangent, is one of Seoul's boldest architectural statements, an enormous sculpture in glass, concrete and steel, reminiscent of a painting by Kandinsky or an embroidery hoop.

Lotte World AMUSEMENT PARK

(롯데월드; Map p88; ☎02-1661 2000; www.lotteworld.com; 240 Olympic-ro; adult/youth/child ₩36,000/32,000/29,000, passport incl most rides ₩52,000/45,000/41,000; ⊙9.30am-10pm; 👪; SLine 2 or 8 to Jamsil, Exit 3) This huge complex includes an amusement park, an **ice-skating rink** (롯데월드 아이스링크; B3 fl, Lotte World Adventure; per session incl rental adult/child ₩15,000/14,000; ⊙11am-9.30pm Mon-Fri, 10am-10.30pm Sat & Sun; 👪; SLine 2 or 8 to Jamsil, Exit 1), a **folk museum** (3rd fl, Lotte World; museum only adult/youth/child ₩5000/3000/2000; ⊙9.30am-8pm Mon-Fri, to 9pm Sat & Sun), a **hotel** (롯데호텔월드; ☎02-419 7000; www.lottehotelworld.com; r from ₩184,000; ❄@📶🏊; SLine 2 or 8 to Jamsil, Exit 4), a shopping mall (p90), a cinema multiplex, a department store, restaurants and more. Kids and adults alike will love the place, which is basically an indoor Korean version of Disneyland, complete with 'flying' balloons, 3D films, laser and music shows, screen rides, fantasy parades and thrill rides.

The outdoor **Magic Island** (☎02-1661 2000; adult/youth/child ₩36,000/32,000/29,000, passport incl most rides adult/child ₩52,000/45,000/41,000; ⊙9.30am-10pm; SLine 2 or 8 to Jamsil, Exit 3 & 4) is in the middle of Seokchon Lake, and that part may close in bad weather.

Olympic Park PARK

(올림픽 공원; Map p88; ☎02-410 1114; www.olympicpark.co.kr; 424 Olympic-ro; ⊙5am-10pm, car access from 6am; P👪; SLine 8 to Mongchontoseong, Exit 1, or Line 5 to Olympic Park, Exit 3) FREE

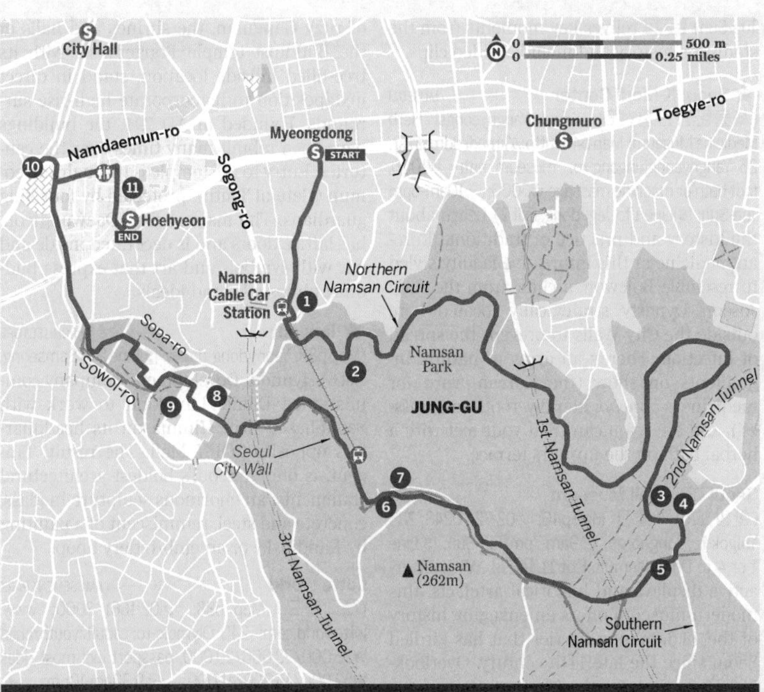

City Walk Namsan Circuit

START SUBWAY LINE 4 TO MYEONGDONG, EXIT 4
END HOEHYEON STATION
LENGTH 6KM; THREE HOURS

Following pedestrian pathways and parts of the Seoul City Wall, this hike takes you around and over Namsan, providing sweeping city views along the way and a chance to enjoy the mountain's greenery and fresh air. It's best done early in the morning, but leafy trees do provide some shade most of the way.

From the subway exit walk up to the **1 cable car station** (p49); just before you reach here you'll see steps leading up the mountainside to the pedestrian-only Northern Namsan Circuit. Walk left for five minutes, and pause to look around the shrine **2 Waryongmyo** (와룡묘; 91-6 Sopa-ro) FREE, before following the road as it undulates gently around the mountain, past routes down to Namsangol Hanok Village and Dongguk University, until you reach the **3 outdoor gym** (uphill from the National Theater of Korea) where you might catch older locals outpacing younger folk on the free-to-use equipment.

You can cut out the next bit by hopping on one of the buses that go to the peak from the **4 bus stop** near here. Otherwise, turn right at the start of the Southern Namsan Circuit road and you'll soon see the **5 Seoul City Wall**, the remains of the original fortress wall of the capital. A steep set of steps shadows the wall for part of the way to the summit; at the fork continue on the steps over the wall and follow the path to **6 N Seoul Tower** (p49) and the **7 Bongsudae** (Mongmyeoksan Beacon ; 5-6 Yejang-dong) FREE signal beacons. Grab some refreshments to enjoy at the geological centre of Seoul, before picking up the Seoul City Wall trail down to pretty **8 Joongang Park**. On the left is **9 Ahn Jung-geun Memorial Hall** (02-3789 1016; 91 Sowol-ro; www.thomasahn.org; 10am-6pm Tue-Sun, to 5pm Nov-Feb). The park continues over a road tunnel down towards the Hilton Hotel with reconstructed sections of the Seoul City Wall. Finish up taking a look at the reconstruction of **10 Sungnyemun** (남대문; Namdaemun; 40 Sejong-daero; 9am-6pm Tue-Sun) FREE, Seoul's picturesque Great South Gate, then browsing **11 Namdaemun Market** (p49) for a snack or a bargain.

This large and pleasant park was the focus of the 1988 Olympics. Strolling its paths takes you past its stadiums surrounded by plenty of greenery, ponds and open-air sculptures. There's a gallery of modern art and two museums on the history of the Baekje dynasty. The park contains the remains of the Mongchon-toseong (Mongchon Fortress), an earth rampart surrounded by a moat, built in the 3rd century AD during the Baekje dynasty.

Activities

★Dragon Hill Spa & Resort SPA

(드래곤힐스파; Map p46; ☎010 4223 0001; www.dragonhillspa.co.kr; 40-713 Hangangno 3-ga; Mon-Fri day/night ₩10,000/12,000, Sat & Sun all day ₩12,000; ⊙24hr; SLine 1 to Yongsan, Exit 1) Think of this foreigner-friendly *jjimjil-bang* as a wellness theme park with a dash of Las Vegas bling and Asian chic thrown in. One of Seoul's largest bathhouses, it has a unisex outdoor pool as well as traditional kiln saunas, ginseng and sauna baths, hot tubs, an ice room, a 'fire-sweating' room and much more. It also has a cinema, arcade games, beauty treatment rooms and multiple dining options. Massages, manicures and mud packs cost extra.

★Bukaksan HIKING

(북악산; Bugaksan; Baegaksan; Map p46; www.bukak.or.kr; ⊙9am-3pm Apr-Oct, from 10am Nov-Mar; SLine 3 to Gyeongbokgung, Exit 3) FREE The tallest of Seoul's four guardian peaks, Bukaksan (342m) was off limits to the public for 38 years following a dramatic assassination attempt by North Korean agents on then-President Park Chung-hee in 1968. Security remains tight along this spectacular 2.5km section of the Seoul City Wall that rises steeply from **Changuimun** (창의문; 118 Changuimun-ro; ⊙9am-4pm; 1020, 7022 or 7212, SLine 3 to Gyeongbokgung, Exit 3) FREE, the old subgate in Buam-dong, hopping over the peak above **Cheongwadae** (청와대, Blue House; Map p52; ☎02-737 5800; www.president.go.kr; 1 Cheongwadae-ro; ⊙tours 10am, 11am, 2pm & 3pm Tue-Sat; SLine 3 to Gyeongbokgung, Exit 5) FREE to the Malbawi Information Center near Sukjeongmun, the main north gate, which can also be accessed from **Samcheong Park** (Map p52; 41 Waryonggongwon-gil; 2 or 11).

This section of the fortress wall is also open only during daylight hours and photography is permitted at designated spots only, such as Baekakmaru, the summit viewpoint. You're also required to show your passport at Changuimun in exchange for a pass, which must be worn at all times. The wall is in excellent condition, and with plenty of soldiers and CCTV cameras, there's a vivid sense of its original purpose as the city's last line of defence. From the subway, take bus 1020, 7022 or 1711 to Changuimun.

Inwangsan HIKING

(인왕산; Map p46; SLine 3 to Gyeongbokgung, Exit 3) Though it lacks the grim-faced soldiers found on Bukaksan, the section of Seoul City Wall snaking up and down Inwangsan (339.9m) offers even more spectacular views, no restrictions on what you can shoot (photographs, that is), and the enigmatic Seonbawi (Zen Rocks) near the summit. From the subway, take bus 1020, 7022 or 1711 to Changuimun.

The views from the top offer a complete panorama of Seoul, with several palaces visible as well as the Seoul City Wall flowing over Bukaksan, Naksan and Namsan. You can clearly see how the old city nestled inside its guardian mountains. The hike, with some sheer stepped sections, is best started just south of Changuimun, the subgate in Buam-dong, finishing at a lower elevation east of Dongnimmun. Along the way you can detour to the shamanistic shrine Inwangsan Guksadang (p55).

Seoul Plaza Ice Skating Rink SKATING

(서울광장 스케이트장; Map p62; www.seoulskate.or.kr; 110 Sejong-daero; per hour incl skate rental ₩1000; ⊙10am-9.30pm Sun-Thu, to 11pm Fri & Sat Dec-Feb; ; SLine 1 or 2 to City Hall, Exit 5) This outdoor ice-skating rink opens in winter with a magical setting in front of the glimmering glass Seoul City Hall (p51) building and art deco Seoul Metropolitan Library (p51). Two rinks are available: a small one for beginners and a larger rink for regular skating. Gloves are required for all skaters and can be rented for ₩1000.

Courses

Seoul Global Cultural Center ART

(Map p62; ☎02-3789 7961; www.seoulculturalcenter.com; 5th fl, M-Plaza Bldg, 27 Myeong-dong 8-gil; ⊙10am-7pm; SLine 4 to Myeongdong, Exit 6) Set up to promote Korean culture to foreigners, this centre offers classes in anything from *hanji* (handmade paper) craft to painting and calligraphy, as well as Korean film screenings, photo ops wearing traditional clothing, or K-Pop dance lessons. Most activities are free; visit the website for schedules and events.

OFF THE BEATEN TRACK

SEONGSU-DONG, SEOUL'S ANSWER TO BROOKLYN

Roughly bookended between Seoul Forest and Konkuk University, the old shoe-making district of Seongsu-dong has experienced a style renaissance in recent years to the extent that it now regularly gets touted as the 'Brooklyn' of Seoul. That might be overstating it a bit, but there are parallels in how disused warehouses and low-rise factories have been repurposed into industrial-chic cafe-bars and boutiques, with stunning interiors that just beg to be Instagrammed.

A haven for street photographers, there's no shortage of edgy street art scattered throughout the 'hood, and the more you wander about, the more you'll discover. Look out for the giant, three-eyed bunny baby known as Mardi, the signature of Thai street artist Alex Face. It can be found, along with most of the best venues, by heading south from Exit 3 of Seong-su subway station.

No newly hip neighbourhood is complete without its own craft-beer brand. Step up Amazing Brewing Co (p83), a Korean-run microbrewery and bar making locally inspired beers like Seoul Forest, which is named after the park next door.

Tours

Seoul Eats Food Tours FOOD
(☎010 6706 7769; www.seouleats.com; per person ₩80,000, for custom group tours ₩375,000) Korean-American Dan Grey is a food blogger and roving gastronome and has regularly worked with visiting US TV chefs such as Anthony Bourdain and Andrew Zimmern. Few foodies are more qualified to introduce Seoul's best eats, either on fixed itineraries or more expensive bespoke tours.

Sool Company FOOD & DRINK
(MMPKorea, Makgeolli Mamas & Papas; Map p62; www.thesoolcompany.com; 343 Samil-Daero) A *makgeolli* (rice wine) appreciation group, the Sool Company (formerly known as the Makgeolli Mamas and Papas) runs regular meet-ups for tastings, *makgeolli*-making classes and brewery tours, among other largely booze-related events. It's exceptionally knowledgeable on the subject.

Festivals & Events

Yeongdeungpo Yeouido Spring Flower Festival CULTURAL
(영등포 여의도 봄꽃축제; www.ydp.go.kr; Yeouido Park; ⏲early Apr) FREE One of the best places to admire the cherry blossoms, this annual event attracts hordes of locals.

Lotus Lantern Festival RELIGIOUS
(Yeon Deung Ho; www.llf.or.kr/eng; ⏲May) FREE On the Saturday before Buddha's birthday, a huge lantern parade takes place from Dongdaemun to Jogyesa, starting at 7.30pm.

Jongmyo Daeje CULTURAL
(www.jongmyo.net/english_index.asp;) FREE On the first Sunday in May, this ceremony honours Korea's royal ancestors, and involves a costumed parade from Gyeongbokgung (p42) through central Seoul to the royal shrine at Jongmyo (p48), where spectators can enjoy traditional music and an elaborate ritual.

Seoul Fringe Festival ART
(www.seoulfringefestival.net; Seoul World Cup Stadium; 1-day pass ₩30,000, festival ticket ₩50,000; ⏲Jul or Aug) This indie arts festival runs for a week and features a line-up of edgy visual and performance arts.

Seoul International Fireworks Festival FIREWORKS
(한화와 함께하는 서울세계불꽃축제; ⏲Sep-Oct) Best viewed from Yeouido Hangang Park, this festival sees dazzling fireworks displays staged by both Korean and international teams.

★ **Seoul Lantern Festival** CULTURAL
(서울빛초롱축제; www.seoullantern.com; Cheong-gye Plaza) FREE For a fortnight in November, both banks of the Cheong-gye-cheon (p42) are illuminated by a fantastical array of lanterns made by master craftspeople.

Sleeping

Seoul offers the lot, from no-frills guesthouses and traditional *hanoks* (traditional wooden homes) to five-star palaces, but reserve well in advance, especially if visiting during busy travel periods such as Chinese New Year and Japan's Golden Week holidays (usually the end of April or early May). Note that many hotels raise their rates at weekends, and some quote without the 10% government tax added.

Gwanghwamun & Jongno-gu

★Doo Guesthouse GUESTHOUSE $$
(Map p52; ☎02-3672 1977; www.dooguesthouse.com; 103-7 Gyedong-gil; s/d without bathroom incl breakfast ₩50,000/80,000; ❄@📶; Ⓢ Line 3 to Anguk, Exit 3) Mixing old and new is this enchanting *hanok* in a garden setting with a traditional-style room where breakfast is served. The shared bathrooms are high quality, with bidets and walk-in showers. The rooms have TVs and DVD players.

Hotel the Designers BOUTIQUE HOTEL $$
(Map p52; ☎02-2267 7474; www.hotelthedesigners.com; 89-8 Supyo-ro; r/ste from ₩132,000/168,000; ❄📶; Ⓢ Line 1 or 3 to Jongno 3-ga, Exit 15) Eighteen designers were given free rein to decorate the suites at this sophisticated love motel, tucked off the main road. Check the website for the different themes: our favourite is Camp Ruka-baik, with a tent, deck chairs, tree-bark-covered poles and guitar for a camping-in-the-city experience. Large discounts when booked online.

Hide & Seek Guesthouse GUESTHOUSE $$
(Map p52; ☎02-6925 5916; www.hidenseek.co.kr; 14 Jahamun-ro 6-gil; s/tw incl breakfast from ₩65,000/75,000; ❄📶; Ⓢ Line 3 to Gyeongbokgung, Exit 5) Stylish design marks out this appealing five-room guesthouse, tucked away in Tongui-dong, beside the remains of an ancient pine tree, and occupying a modern, two-storey house with a broad outdoor terrace. Breakfast is served in the cute Stella's Kitchen cafe.

★Chi-Woon-Jung GUESTHOUSE $$$
(취운정; Map p52; ☎02-765 7400; www.chiwoonjung.com; 31-53 Gahoe-dong; s/d incl breakfast from ₩500,000/1,100,000; ❄📶; Ⓢ Line 3 to Anguk, Exit 2) The *hanok* as an exclusive luxury experience doesn't get much finer than this stunning property that has just four elegant guest rooms, all with beautifully tiled bathrooms and pine-wood tubs. Completely remodelled since Korean president Lee Myung Bak once lived there, it is decorated with beautiful crafts and has a Zen-calm garden wrapped around it with views of Bukchon Hanok Village.

Rak-Ko-Jae GUESTHOUSE $$$
(락고재; Map p52; ☎02-742 3410; www.rkj.co.kr; 98 Gyeo-dong; s/d incl breakfast ₩198,000/275,000; ❄@; Ⓢ Line 3 to Anguk, Exit 2) This beautifully restored *hanok*, with an enchanting garden, is modelled after Japan's ryokan. The guesthouse's mud-walled sauna is included in the price, as is breakfast, but dinner (₩30,000 to ₩50,000) must be booked in advance. The en suite bathrooms are tiny.

Myeong-dong & Jung-gu

There are plenty of guesthouses and hostels just south of Myeongdong station. It makes a convenient base near the station and Namsan, even if shopping is not your focus, but the roads can be steep and inconvenient if you are bringing lots of luggage.

Zaza Backpackers HOSTEL $
(자자 백팩커스; Map p62; ☎02-3672 1976; www.zazabackpackers.com; 18-6 Namsandong-2ga; s/d ₩50,000/60,000; ❄@📶; Ⓢ Line 4 to Myeondong, Exit 3) In the guesthouse enclave that's sprung up along the hill to Namsan, Zaza is one of the best with its contemporary building full of design touches and friendly staff who speak English. Neutrally decorated rooms have their own private washing machine and kitchenette, attracting longer-term guests.

★Small House Big Door BOUTIQUE HOTEL $$
(스몰 하우스 빅 도어; Map p62; ☎02-2038 8191; www.smallhousebigdoor.com; 6 Namdaemun-ro 9-gil; r incl breakfast ₩115,000-250,000; ❄📶; Ⓢ Line 2 to Euljiro 1-ga, Exit 1 or 2) Down a narrow street in central Seoul, this suave little hotel is quite the find. Its white-toned rooms all feature locally designed, handmade furniture and beds, and maximise the use of space with slide-out desks and TVs. Pricier rooms have outdoor sitting areas and sky windows.

★Splaisir BOUTIQUE HOTEL $$
(Map p62; ☎02-772 0900; www.splaisir.com; 15 Namdaemun-ro 5-gil; d & tw incl breakfast ₩131,000-327,000; ❄📶; Ⓢ Line 1 or 2 to City Hall, Exit 8) This hotel has rooms dedicated to Line Friends – cartoon characters from popular Japanese-Korean social-media app Line – so fans of cuteness overload and giant stuffed chickens staring at them while sleeping will be in four-star paradise here near Namdaemun Market. Otherwise, immaculate, minimalist rooms – dressed in bamboo browns and whites holding hinoki-wood soaking tubs and soft beds – are much calmer.

Hotel 28 BOUTIQUE HOTEL $$
(호텔28; Map p62; ☎02-774 2828; www.hotel28.co.kr/; 13 Myeongdong 7-gil; d from ₩110,000; ❄@📶; Ⓢ Line 2 to Euljiro, Exit 6) Opened in 2016, this boutique hotel was founded by veteran actor Shin Young-kyun and takes on a Korean

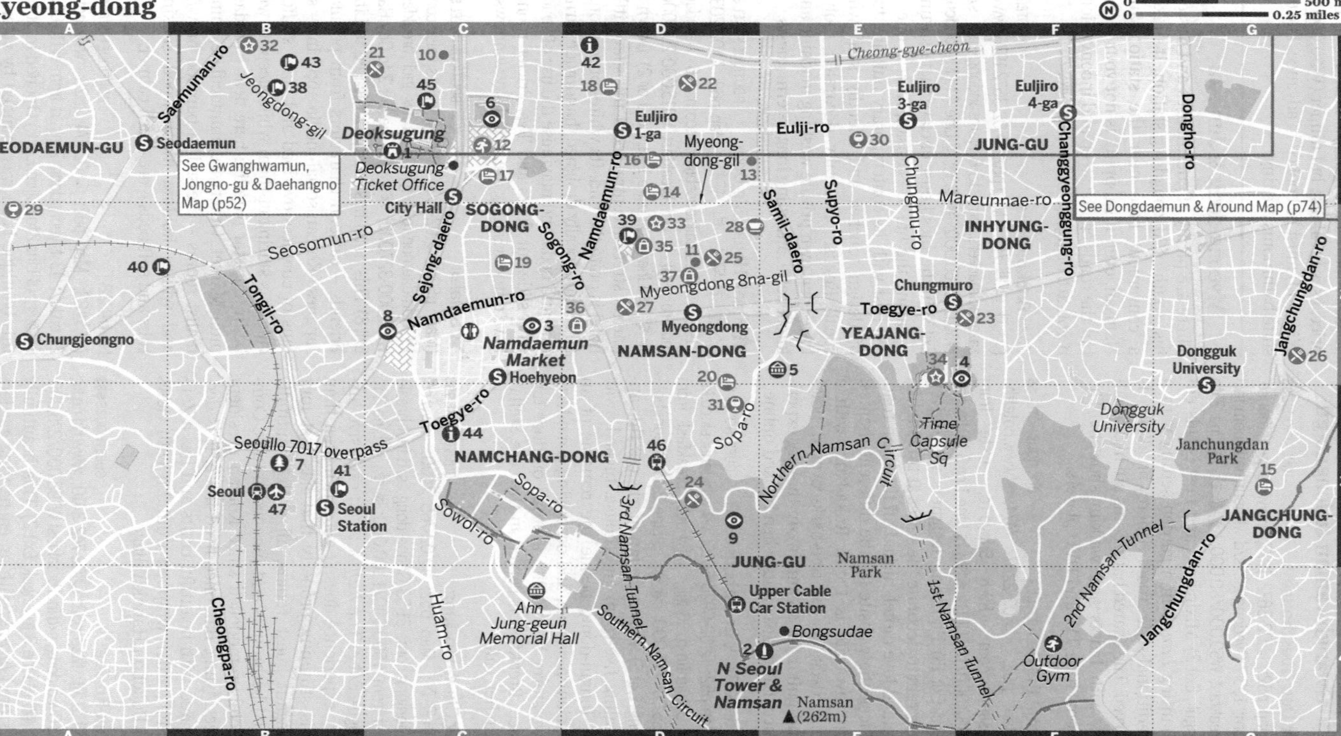

Myeong-dong
500 m
0.25 miles
See Gwanghwamun, Jongno-gu & Daehangno Map (p52)
See Dongdaemun & Around Map (p74)
SEODAEMUN-GU
Seodaemun
Saemunan-ro
Jeongdong-gil
Deoksugung
Deoksugung Ticket Office
City Hall
SOGONG-DONG
Cheong-gye-cheon
Euljiro 1-ga
Euljiro 3-ga
Euljiro 4-ga
Eulji-ro
Myeong-dong-gil
JUNG-GU
Changgyeonggung-ro
Dongho-ro
Chungmu-ro
Supyo-ro
Samil-daero
Mareunnae-ro
INHYUNG-DONG
Seosomun-ro
Sejong-daero
Sogong-ro
Namdaemun-ro
Myeongdong 8na-gil
Tongil-ro
Chungjeongno
Namdaemun Market
Hoehyeon
Myeongdong
NAMSAN-DONG
Chungmuro
Toegye-ro
YEAJANG-DONG
Dongguk University
Jangchungdan-ro
Seoullo 7017 overpass
Seoul
Seoul Station
NAMCHANG-DONG
Sopa-ro
Sowol-ro
Time Capsule Sq
Northern Namsan Circuit
Janchungdan Park
JANGCHUNG-DONG
2nd Namsan Tunnel
3rd Namsan Tunnel
JUNG-GU
Namsan Park
Upper Cable Car Station
Bongsudae
N Seoul Tower & Namsan
Namsan (262m)
Ahn Jung-geun Memorial Hall
Southern Namsan Circuit
1st Namsan Tunnel
Outdoor Gym
Huam-ro
Cheongpa-ro

Myeong-dong

Top Sights
1 Deoksugung C1
2 N Seoul Tower & Namsan E4
3 Namdaemun Market C2

Sights
4 Namsangol Hanok Village F2
5 Seoul Animation Center E2
6 Seoul City Hall C1
Seoul Metropolitan Library .... (see 6)
7 Seoullo 7017 .... B3
8 Sungnyemun C2
9 Waryongmyo D3

Activities, Courses & Tours
10 Panmunjom Travel Centre C1
11 Seoul Global Cultural Center D2
12 Seoul Plaza Ice Skating Rink C1
13 Sool Company D1

Sleeping
14 Hotel 28 .... D1
15 Hotel Shilla G3
16 Metro Hotel D1
17 Plaza C1
18 Small House Big Door D1
19 Splaisir C2
20 Zaza Backpackers D2

Eating
21 Congdu C1
22 Gosang D1
23 Korea House F2
24 Mokmyeoksanbang D3
25 Myeong-dong Gyoja D2
N.Grill .... (see 2)
26 Pyeongando Jokbal Jip G2
27 Yeong-yang Centre D2

Drinking & Nightlife
28 Coffee Libre D2
29 Muldwinda A2
30 The Edge E1
31 Walkabout D3

Entertainment
32 Jump B1
33 Nanta Theatre Jung-gu D2
34 Seoul Namsan Gugakdang E2

Shopping
35 Primera D2
36 Shinsegae D2
37 Stylenanda Pink Hotel D2

Information
38 Canadian Embassy B1
39 Chinese Embassy D2
40 French Embassy A2
41 German Embassy B3
42 KTO Tourist Information Center D1
Netherlands Embassy .... (see 38)
43 New Zealand Embassy B1
44 Seoullo 7017 Information Center C3
45 UK Embassy C1

Transport
46 Namsan Cable Car D3
47 Seoul Station City Airport Terminal B3

cinema theme. Each room has stills of films that Shin starred in, and the lobby and the hallways are decorated with film reels. The hotel also collaborates with entertainment company YG for its hotel restaurant called YG Republique, located on the 1st floor.

Metro Hotel HOTEL $$
(메트로호텔; Map p62; ☎02-2176 3199; www.metrohotel.co.kr; 14 Myeong-dong 9ga-gil; s/d/tw incl breakfast from ₩83,000/143,000/198,000; ❄@📶; Ⓢ Line 2 to Euljiro 1-ga, Exit 6) An excellent midrange choice, this small, professionally run hotel has boutique aspirations. Splashes of style abound, from the flashy, metallic lobby to its laptops. Room size and design vary – ask for one of the larger ones with big windows (room numbers that end in 07).

Plaza HOTEL $$$
(더 플라자; Map p62; ☎02-771 2200; www.hoteltheplaza.com; 23 Taepyeong-ro 2-ga; r from ₩290,000; ❄@📶🏊; Ⓢ Line 1 or 2 to City Hall, Exit 6) You can't get more central than the Plaza, opposite the striking rising glass edifice of City Hall. Rooms sport a smart design with giant angle-poise lamps, circular mirrors and crisp white linens contrasting with dark carpets. It also has some chic restaurants and a good fitness club with a swimming pool.

Western Seoul

★Kpopstay HOSTEL $
(Map p78; ☎010 9955 1969; http://kpopstay.com; 6-153 Changjeon-dong; dm ₩23,000-29,000, q ₩150,000; ❄📶; Ⓢ Line 2 to Hongik University, Exit 8) There is a stream of K-Pop on the TVs at this memorabilia-adorned hostel in the heart of Hongdae's bar area next to Hongik University. But even if you aren't a K-Pop fan, designer-like dorms make Kpopstay an excellent choice – soft beds in pod-style bunks with total-privacy curtains and especially large individual lockers.

Urbanwood Guesthouse HOSTEL $

(Map p78; ☎070-8613 0062; www.urbanwood.co.kr; 3rd fl, 48-20 Wausan-ro 29-gil; s/d incl breakfast from ₩60,000/80,000; ❄📶; Ⓢ Line 2 to Hongik University, Exit 8) Creatively decorated in bright colours and modern furnishings, this cosy guesthouse feels more like a cool arty apartment. Martin, the convivial English-speaking host, knows the area well and will whisk you up a mean coffee on the professional barista machine in the well-appointed kitchen.

Come Inn HOSTEL $

(Map p78; ☎070-8958 7279; www.comeinnkorea.com; 20-10 Wausan-ro 21-gil; dm/s/tw without bathroom incl breakfast ₩15,000/33,000/45,000; ❄@📶; Ⓢ Line 2 to Hongik University, Exit 9) In the centre of Hongdae is this compact, 3rd-floor guesthouse offering private rooms and female-only dorms, all sharing common bathrooms. There's a comfy lounge and a broad outdoor terrace with views across the area.

Wowfactor Stay GUESTHOUSE $$

(Map p78; ☎010 9615 2789; www.wowfactorstay.com; 28 World Cup buk-ro 5ga-gil; d/q incl breakfast from ₩80,000/120,000; ❄@📶; Ⓢ Line 2 to Hongik University, Exit 1) The husband-and-wife team who converted this house have keen design sensibilities. K-Pop-fanatic Jacqueline chooses photogenic, homey decor and cooks delightful Korean breakfasts designed to wow on social media. Colour-themed studios are chic, with premium bedding, and all have their own modern bathroom. It's a few blocks from Hongdae's epicentre of shopping and bars, but within a quiet garden.

Lee Kang Ga GUESTHOUSE $$

(Map p78; ☎02-323 5484; www.leekanghouse.com; 4th fl, 12 World Cup buk-ro 11-gil; d incl breakfast from ₩85,000; ❄@📶; 🚌15, 7711, 7737 or 7016, Ⓢ Line 2 to Hongik University, Exit 1) Near the **War & Women's Human Rights Museum** (전쟁과여성인권박물관; ☎02-392 5252; www.womenandwar.net; 20 World Cup Buk-ro 11-gil; adult/teenager/child ₩3000/2000/1000; ⏲1-6pm Tue-Sat; 🚌6, 8, 15, 7016 or 7737, Ⓢ Line 2 to Hongik University, Exit 1), this appealing guesthouse is worth the trek from Hongdae. Rooms are attractively decorated with *hanji* (traditional paper) wallpaper, silky pillows and pine-wood furniture, and a few have balconies and washing machines. There are great views from the rooftop kitchen and garden.

Northern Seoul

★Kims HOMESTAY $$

(그림가네 게스트하우스; Map p46; ☎010 9073 4457; ghbuamthekims@naver.com; 13, Baekseokdong 1-gil; dm/s ₩55,000, tw/d ₩90,000; ❄📶; 🚌1020, 7017 or 7212 to Changuimun) A more relaxed alternative to downtown digs is this beautifully designed, modern homestay in the hills above the city. The swish family home of a retired Korean couple, it has several room configurations available, including one with a balcony offering glorious views of Bukaksan (p59). Mrs Kim knocks up a gourmet breakfast.

Eugene's House HOMESTAY $$

(Map p52; ☎02-741 3338; www.eugenehouse.co.kr; 36 Hyehwa-ro 12-gil; s without bathroom ₩55,000, d/q ₩110,000/200,000; ❄📶; Ⓢ Line 4 to Hyehwa, Exit 1) This traditional *hanok* homestay has rooms ranging from a tiny single to a four-futon set-up, with the owner and his family (he speaks a bit of English) living in one corner of the quadrangle. Cosy, quiet and with a lived-in feel, it has a good location just below Seongbuk-dong.

Itaewon & Yongsan-gu

★Itaewon G Guest House HOSTEL $

(이태원 G게스트하우스; Map p73; ☎010 2082 8377; www.gguest.com; 14-38 Bogwang-ro 60-gil; dm/s/d incl breakfast ₩17,000/40,000/72,000; ❄📶; Ⓢ Line 6 to Itaewon, Exit 3) Run by the welcoming and convivial Shrek Lee, this hostel is easily the best budget digs in Itaewon. Fourteen dorms and four twins are stacked in a converted block at the end of the lane that houses trendy nightclub **Soap** (소프, Club Soap, Soap Seoul; Map p73; ☎070-4457 6860; www.soapseoul.com; 14-9 Bogwang-ro 60-gil, Yongsan-gu; admission incl 1 free drink ₩20,000; ⏲10pm-5am Thu-Sat). It's a good place to meet other travellers, either in the downstairs kitchen or chilling on the rooftop.

Philstay Hostel B&B GUESTHOUSE $

(Map p73; ☎02-749 8855; www.philstay.co.kr; 120-4 Itaewon-dong; dm ₩20,000/d ₩ 60,000/tr ₩ 75,000/f ₩130,000; 🚭❄📶; Ⓢ Line 6 to Itaewon, Exit 1) Offering clean, modern rooms kitted out with minifridges, TVs and Japanese toilets, this hostel is one of the better choices on the hill overlooking Itaewon's nightlife. It has a communal kitchen and roof terrace, but no bar or restaurant.

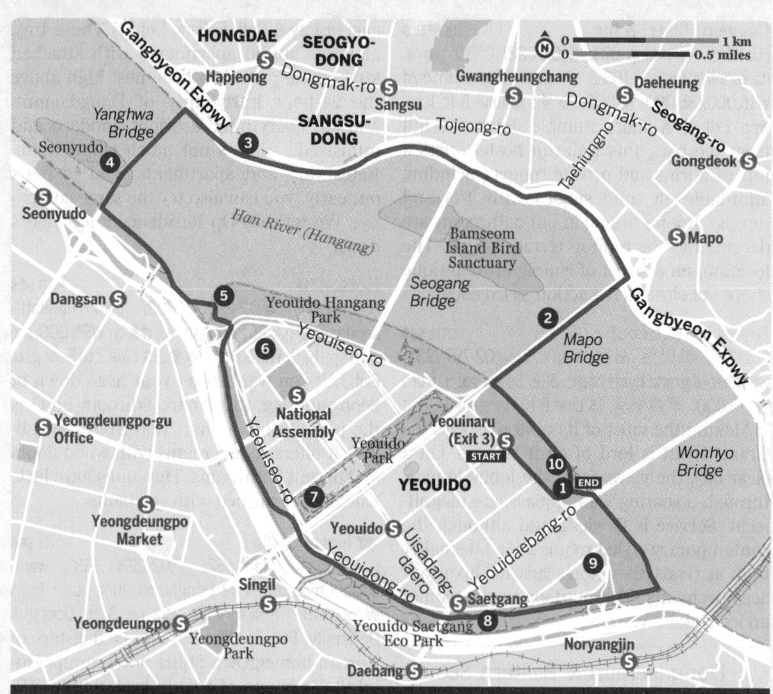

Cycling Tour
Han River Cycle Ride

START SUBWAY LINE 5 TO YEOUINARU STATION, EXIT 3
END YEOUIDO HANGANG PARK
LENGTH 15KM; THREE HOURS

It's possible to walk this 15km route around Yeouido and across the river via the island park of Seonyudo, but it's quicker and more fun to use a bicycle, which you can rent at several outlets in Yeouido Hangang Park, the starting point for the ride.

Walk east from the subway exit in Yeouido Hangang Park, where you'll find a 1 **bicycle rental stall** (first hour ₩3000, every extra 15 minutes ₩500; ⏲9am-5pm); bring some form of photo ID for them to keep as a deposit.

Cycle west and out of the park across the 2 **Mapo Bridge**, taking the blue ramp down to the north bank of the river. Head west for about 4km until you reach a steep cliff, at the top of which is 3 **Jeoldusan Martyrs' Shrine** (절두산 순교성지; ☎02-3142 4434; www.jeoldusan.or.kr; 6 Tojeong-ro; ⏲shrine 24hr, museum 9.30am-5pm Tue-Sun). Continue west to the Yanghwa Bridge and carry your bike up the stairs to the pathway on the west side. On an island about halfway along the bridge is the beautifully landscaped 4 **Seonyudo Park** (선유도공원; http://hangang.seoul.go.kr; 343, Seonyu-ro; ⏲6am-midnight). There are wonderful river views from the park (which used to be a water-filtration plant), as well as a cafe at which you can take a break. Continue from the park back to the south bank of the Han River and pedal back towards Yeouido. At the western tip of the island you can pause to view the ritzy 5 **Seoul Marina** and the 6 **National Assembly** (국회의사당; ☎02-788 3656; http://korea.assembly.go.kr; 1 Uisadang-daero; ⏲9am-5pm Mon-Fri, to 4pm Sat & 1st Sun of month). Also have a look around central 7 **Yeouido Park**, which includes a traditional Korean garden.

Continue along the bike paths on the southern side of the island; 8 **Yeouido Saetgang Eco Park** here is wilder and more natural. As you round the eastern tip of Yeouido look up to see clouds reflected in the gold-tinted glass of the 63 City skyscraper and its 60th-floor 9 **63 Sky Art Gallery** (p54). After returning your bike to the rental stall look out for the quirky 10 **monster sculpture** based on the hit horror movie *The Host*.

Itaewon Hostel & Inn HOSTEL $
(이태원 인; Map p73; ☎02-6221 0880; www.itaewoninn.com; 103-2 Bogwang-ro; dm/s/d ₩16,000/35,000/70,000; ; Line 6 to Itaewon, Exit 4) A short stumble down the hill from the bars, this well-run hostel offers a mix of dorms and private rooms (including affordable en suite singles with TVs and towels). Rooms are plain but bathrooms are decent, and the rooftop terrace is vast. The location, on a street of characterful antique shops yet close to the action, is excellent.

Grand Hyatt Seoul HOTEL $$$
(그랜드 하얏트 서울; Map p73; ☎02-797 1234; www.seoul.grand.hyatt.com; 322 Sowol-ro; r from ₩375,000; ; Line 6 to Hangangjin, Exit 1) Making the most of its hilltop aspect, the Grand Hyatt is lord of all it surveys. On a clear day, the views from the lobby lounge, through a soaring wall of glass, are magnificent. Service is flawless, and although the contemporary-styled rooms are a bit smaller than at rivals, they don't lack for luxurious accoutrements. The outdoor pool becomes an ice rink in winter.

Dongdaemun & Eastern Seoul

★ **K-Grand Hostel Dongdaemun** HOSTEL $
(케이 그랜드 호스텔; Map p46; ☎02-2233 9155; 339-1 Wangsimni-ro; d/tr/f incl breakfast from ₩40,000/60,000/70,000; ; Line 2 to Wangsimni, Exit 4) A spotlessly clean, superbly run western-style hostel, the K-Grand occupies the top half of a 10-storey building, with great views as standard from its spacious en suite rooms. Sealing the deal is a sociable kitchen with free tea and coffee, English-speaking staff, cheap laundry, two subway stations close by and a wonderful rooftop terrace.

Uhbu's Guesthouse GUESTHOUSE $
(Map p46; ☎070-8125 4858; 19-5 Gosanja-ro 33-gil; incl breakfast dm/d ₩22,000/63,000, d without bathroom ₩52,000; ; Line 1 to Jegi-dong, Exit 3) There are mixed and female dorms and three tiny doubles in this brightly painted *hanok*, one of many time-worn nuggets in a shabby city block that has somehow escaped redevelopment. You also get a communal kitchen and covered courtyard, plus free brekkie and Korean-style pyjamas courtesy of the English-speaking owner.

Uljiro Co-Op Residence APARTMENT $$
(Map p74; ☎02-2269 4600; http://rent.co-op.co.kr; 32 Eulji-ro 6-ga, Jung-gu; studios from ₩77,000; ; Line 2, 4 or 5 to Dongdaemun History & Culture Park, Exit 12) These tiny, all-white studio apartments with attached kitchenette provide a little nest high above the 24-hour hurly-burly of Dongdaemun Market. Everything is bright, modern and minisized – there's not much elbow room. Rates vary and apartments tend to book out early; you can also try the same company's Western Co-Op Residence a few doors down.

Hotel Atti HOTEL $$
(Map p46; ☎02-2205 0702; http://hotelatti-seongsu.com/; 96 Seongsui-ro; d & tw ₩98,000, ste with spa bath ₩178,000; ; Line 2 to Seongsu, Exit 3) If you want to get your head down in Seongsu-dong, this smart, 80-room hotel is the place to be. A short hop from the subway, it offers stylish rooms with wood floors and decent bathrooms. The suites have little balconies furnished with spa baths.

★ **Hotel Shilla** HOTEL $$$
(신라호텔; Map p62; ☎02-2233 3131; www.shillahotels.com; 249 Dongho-ro, Jung-gu; r from ₩250,000; ; Line 3 to Dongguk University, Exit 5) The luxurious flagship of Korea's homegrown Shilla hotel group, Hotel Shilla is one of Seoul's best, with a VIP location on 9 acres of private hillside near Namsan (there's a regular shuttle bus up from the subway exit). Highlights include an all-season outdoor pool and La Yeon, the hotel's modern Korean haute cuisine restaurant, with three Michelin stars.

Gangnam & Southern Seoul

Kimchee Gangnam Guesthouse HOSTEL $
(김치 강남 게스트하우스; Map p84; ☎02-518 6696; www.kimcheeguesthouse.com; 23 Seolleung-ro 133-gil; dm/s/tw incl breakfast ₩25,000/30,000/45,000; ; Line 7 to Gangnam-gu Office, Exit 3) A rare budget choice for ritzy Gangnam, this friendly guesthouse is set in a posh-looking old apartment building in a residential street. The mixed dorms are modern and spacious, while private rooms are more on the boxy side. Unwind in the basement with stylish cafe, vintage furniture and full kitchen.

★ **Tria Hotel** HOTEL $$
(호텔 트리아; Map p84; ☎02-553 2471; www.triahotel.co.kr; 16 Teheran-ro 33-gil; r/ste from ₩86,000/113,000; ; Line 2 to Yeoksam, Exit 8) An excellent-value, midrange option that's very affordable for this end of town, the 50-room boutiquey Tria has lots going for it. Opt for any room above standard

and you'll get a whirlpool bath. The hotel is tucked away in the streets behind the Renaissance Hotel, a five-minute walk from the subway exit.

H Avenue Hotel MOTEL $$

(에이치 에비뉴 호텔; Map p84; ☎02-508 6247; 12 Teheran-ro 29-gil; r from ₩85,000; ; Line 2 to Yeoksam, Exit 8) Fantastic value, this love motel is most notable for its roof-terrace rooms that come with their own roof-deck swimming pools and views over Namsan and the nearby cathedral; stay mid-week for the best deals. While essentially a love motel, it comes without all the usual, weird trappings.

La Casa Garosugil HOTEL $$

(라까사 호텔 서울; Map p84; ☎02-546 0088; www.hotellacasa.kr; 83 Dosan-daero 1-gil; s/d incl breakfast from ₩178,000/224,000; ; Line 3 to Sinsa, Exit 6) The first venture into the hospitality business by classy Korean furniture and interior-design store Casamia packs plenty of chic style. The rooms are attractive and spacious with quirky details such as the travel-themed pillowcases, while the lobby also has plenty of design features and art books. It's handy for Garosu-gil.

★**Park Hyatt Seoul** HOTEL $$$

(파크 하얏트 서울; Map p88; ☎02-2016 1234; www.seoul.park.hyatt.com; 606 Teheran-ro; r from ₩355,000; ; Line 2 to Samseong, Exit 1) A discreet entrance – look for the rock sticking out of the wall – sets the Zen-minimalist tone for this gorgeous property. Each floor only has 10 rooms with spot-lit antiquities lining the hallways. Spacious open-plan rooms have floor-to-ceiling windows that boast city views and come with luxurious bathrooms classed among the best in Asia.

Eating

Gwanghwamun & Jongno-gu

★**Koong** DUMPLINGS $

(궁; Map p81; ☎02-733 9240; www.koong.co.kr; 11-3 Insa-dong 10-gil; dumplings ₩11,000-14,000; ⏲11.30am-9.30pm; Line 3 to Anguk, Exit 6) Koong's traditional Kaeseong-style dumplings are legendary and more than a mouthful. Only order one portion, unless you're superhungry, or enjoy them in a flavourful soup along with chewy balls of rice cake. In summer the *pyeonsu* (flower-shaped zucchini and leek stuffed dumplings) are a lighter option.

Gwanghwamun Jip KOREAN $

(광화문집; Map p52; ☎02-739 7737; 12 Saemunan-ro 5-gil; kimchi stew ₩7000; ⏲9am-10pm; ; Line 5 to Gwanghwamun, Exit 8) Following the same recipe since the 1980s, Gwanghwamun Jip is one of the most famous kimchi *jiggae* (stew) restaurants in South Korea. The homey interior is cramped but the food is truly fabulous. Its stew perfectly combines fermented kimchi with fatty pork for a spicy, refreshing taste. For an extra ₩5000, add a large rolled omelette on the side.

Chosun Gimbap KOREAN $

(조선김밥; Map p52; ☎02-723 7496; 78 Yulgok-ro 1-gil; gimbap from ₩4500; ⏲11am-2.30pm & 3.30-8pm; ; Line 3 to Anguk, Exit 1) Right behind the National Museum of Modern and Contemporary Art, Chosun Gimbap is a rare cheap eat in the area. Its signature dish, the *chosun gimbap*, is packed with freshly prepared Korean root vegetables and feels more like a proper meal than most other *gimbap* (seaweed rice rolls). The space is small so prepare to wait to sit.

Rogpa Tea Stall VEGETARIAN $

(사직동 그 가게; Map p52; ☎070-4045 6331; www.rogpa.com; 18-1 Sajik-ro 9-gil; mains ₩7000-11,000; ⏲noon-8pm Tue-Sun; ; Line 3 to Gyeongbokgung, Exit 1) You'll feel whisked to the Himalayas at this charming fair-trade cafe that raises awareness about the Tibetans' situation (Rogpa is Tibetan for 'friend and helper'). Everything is freshly made, beautifully presented and rather delicious. All but the chicken curry are vegetarian. Dig into a tofu curry followed by a sweet *dosa* (crispy lentil pancake) and soy-milk chai.

Seoureseo Duljjaero Jalhaneunjip DESSERTS $

(서울서둘째로잘하는집; Map p52; ☎02-734 5302; 122-1 Samcheong-ro; desserts ₩5000; ⏲11am-9pm Tue-Sun; Line 3 to Anguk, Exit 1) Little has changed at 'Second Best Place in Seoul', a tiny tea and dessert cafe, since it opened in 1976. Apart from the medicinal teas it serves wonderful thick *danpatjuk*, red-bean porridge with ginseng, chestnut and peanuts.

★**Ikseon Dimibang** EUROPEAN $$

(익선디미방; Map p81; ☎02-747 3418; www.instagr.am/ikseon_dimibang; 17-27 Supyo-ro 28-gil; set lunch ₩18,000, mains ₩18,000-26,000; ⏲noon-3pm & 5-10pm; Line 1, 3 or 5 to Jongno 3-ga, Exit 4) The converted *hanok* that houses this chic bistro in the revamped old neighbourhood

1

3

TOPIC IMAGES INC / GETTY IMAGES ©

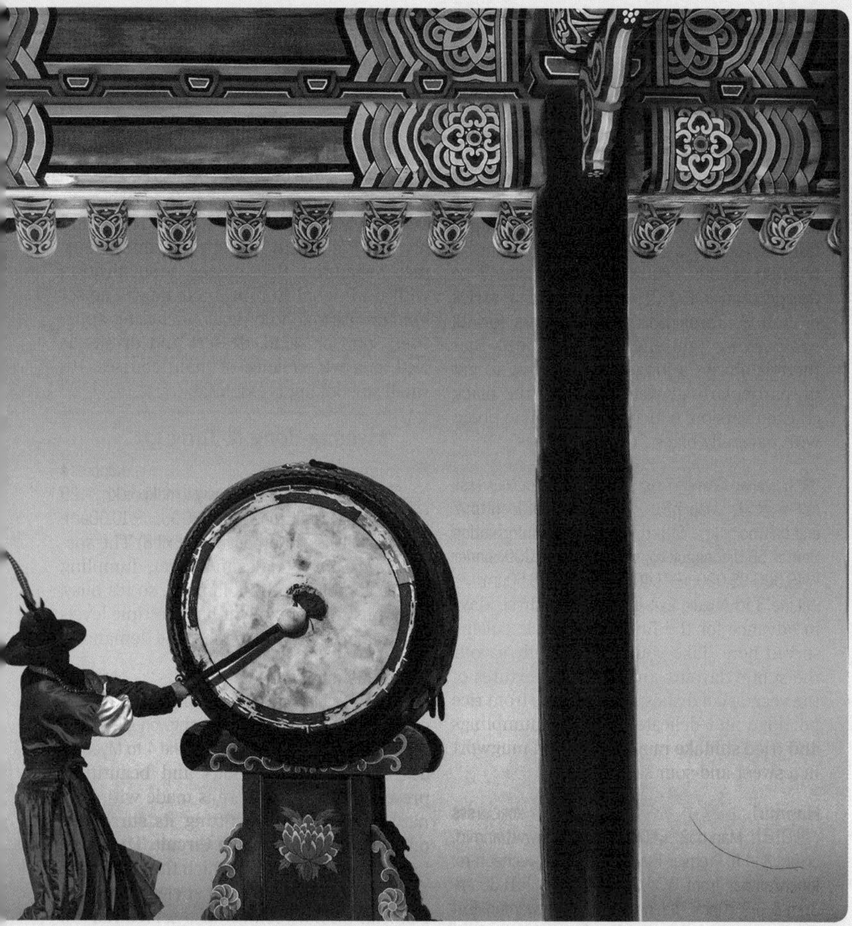

1. Gyeongbokgung (p42), Seoul, South Korea Ringing the temple drum at the Palace of Shining Happiness, which once housed 3000 staff serving the royal family.

2. Dongdaemun Design Plaza & Park (p56), Seoul, South Korea Designed by the late Zaha Hadid, the now iconic cultural complex is made from aluminium and concrete.

3. Cheong-gye-cheon (p42), Seoul, South Korea This once-buried stream under Seoul's streets has been transformed into a riverside park, and is now home to many festivals including the Lotus Lantern Festival (p23).

ESCAN / SHUTTERSTOCK ©

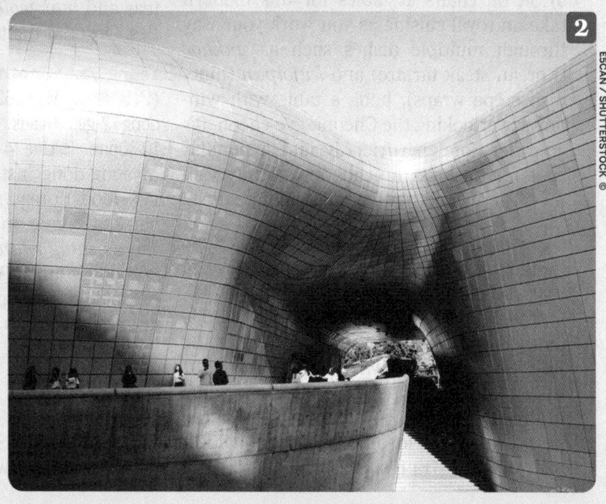

of Ikseon-dong is Korean, but the dishes are contemporary European. Excellent scorched prawn risotto is served on bright metal plates to match the sleek copper furniture. Fusion touches are seen in seafood pasta with chillies from Cheongyang. Good-value weekday set lunches include a main, salad and drink.

Tosokchon KOREAN $$

(토속촌; Map p52; ☎02-737 7444; http://tosokchon.com; 5 Jahamun-ro 5-gil; mains ₩16,000-24,000; ⌚10am-10pm; Ⓢ Line 3 to Gyeongbokgung, Exit 2) Spread over a series of *hanok*, Tosokchon is so famous for its *samgyetang* (ginseng chicken soup) that there is always a long queue waiting to get in, particularly at weekends. Try the black chicken version, which uses the silkie breed with naturally black flesh and bones.

★Balwoo Gongyang VEGETARIAN $$$

(발우공양; Map p81; ☎02-2031 2081; http://eng.balwoo.or.kr; 5th fl, Templestay Information Center, 56 Ujeongguk-ro; set lunch ₩30,000, dinner ₩45,000-95,000; ⌚11.40am-3pm & 6-8.50pm; ✎; Ⓢ Line 3 to Anguk, Exit 6) Reserve three days in advance for the fine temple-style cuisine served here. Take your time to fully savour the subtle flavours and different textures of the vegetarian dishes, which range from rice porridge and delicate salads to dumplings and fried shiitake mushrooms and mugwort in a sweet-and-sour sauce.

Hanmiri KOREAN $$$

(한미리; Map p52; ☎02-757 5707; www.hanmiri.co.kr; 2nd fl, Premier Place, 8 Cheonggyecheon-ro; lunch/dinner from ₩34,000/56,000; ⌚11.30am-3pm & 6-9.30pm; Ⓢ Line 5 to Gwanghwamun, Exit 5) Sit on chairs at tables for this modern take on royal cuisine as you work your way through multiple dishes such as *yukhoe* (Korean steak tartare) and *kujolpan* (nine-dish crêpe wraps); book a table with windows overlooking the Cheong-gye-cheon. It's gourmet, foreigner-friendly and a popular spot for business lunches and family visitors. There's another branch in Gangnam.

Ogawa JAPANESE $$$

(오가와; Map p52; ☎02-735 1001; 19 Saemunan-ro 5-gil; set menu lunch/dinner ₩50,000/70,000; ⌚noon-2.30pm & 6-10.30pm Mon-Fri; Ⓢ Line 5 to Gwanghwamun, Exit 1) In the basement of the Royal Building, Ogawa's expert chefs craft sushi and sashimi, piece by piece, and serve it directly over the kitchen counter – in the best Japanese style, although still with Korean twists. Extra dishes, such as udon and abalone porridge, mean you certainly won't leave hungry. Booking is essential as space is limited.

GastroTong SWISS, EUROPEAN $$$

(가스트로통; Map p52; ☎02-730 4162; www.gastrotong.com; 10 Jahamun-ro 8-gil; set course lunch/dinner from ₩30,000/50,000; ⌚11.30am-3pm & 5.30-10.30pm; 📶; Ⓢ Line 3 to Gyeongbokgung, Exit 3) Swiss-German chef Roland Hinni and his wife Yong-Shin run this charming gourmet restaurant that blends sophistication with traditional European cooking. The set lunches are splendid deals, including appetiser, soup or salad, dessert and drinks as well as a wide choice of main courses. It's small so booking is essential.

Myeong-dong & Jung-gu

Myeong-dong Gyoja NOODLES $

(명동교자; Map p62; www.mdkj.co.kr; 29 Myeongdong 10-gil; noodles ₩8000; ⌚10.30am-9.30pm; Ⓢ Line 4 to Myeongdong, Exit 8) The special *kalguksu* (noodles in a meat, dumpling and vegetable broth) is famous, so it's busy, busy, busy. Fortunately it has multiple levels and a nearby branch to meet the demand.

Mokmyeoksanbang KOREAN $

(목멱산방; Map p62; ☎02-318 4790; http://mmmroom.com; 627 Namsangongwon-gil; mains ₩7000-17,000; ⌚11am-9pm; Ⓢ Line 4 to Myeongdong, Exit 3) The delicious and beautifully presented bibimbap here is made with only natural seasonings, befitting its surrounds on the Northern Namsan Circuit. The traditional wooden house in which the restaurant is based is named after the ancient name for Namsan (Mokmyeok); it also serves Korean teas and *makgeolli* (rice wine) in brass kettles. Order at the till.

Yeong-yang Centre KOREAN $$

(영양센터; Map p62; ☎02-776 2015; 52 Myeongdong 2-gil; mains ₩10,00-22,500; ⌚10.30am-10.30pm; Ⓢ Line 4 to Myeongdong, Exit 6) A Myeong-dong institution since 1960, this is fast food Korean-style: the tasty deep-fried chicken comes in various portion sizes or there's *samgyetang* (ginseng chicken soup). A good set lunch (₩10,000) with salad, soup, bread and pickled radish is available until 4pm on weekdays and 2pm on weekends.

★Congdu KOREAN $$$

(콩두; Map p62; ☎02-722 7002; 116-1 Deoksugung-gil; set course lunch/dinner from ₩29,800/49,800; ⌚11.30am-3pm & 5.30-10pm; Ⓢ Line 5 to Gwanghwamun, Exit 6) Feast on art-

fully plated, contemporary twists on Korean classics, such as pine-nut soup with soy milk *espuma* (foam) or raw blue crab, at this serene restaurant tucked behind the British embassy. Meals come as a set menu only and dessert includes delicious *yuja* (citrus fruit) ice cream with Korean biscuit 'gravel'. The main dining room becomes an open roof terrace in good weather.

★Korea House KOREAN $$$
(한국의집; Map p62; ☎02-2266 9101; www.koreahouse.or.kr; 10 Toegye-ro 36-gil; set menu lunch ₩29,000-47,000, dinner ₩68,200-150,000, performances ₩50,000; ⊙lunch noon-2pm Mon-Fri, dinner 5-6.30pm & 7-8.30pm, performances 6.30pm & 8.30pm except 3rd Mon, shop 10am-8pm; Ⓢ Line 3 or 4 to Chungmuro, Exit 3) Scoring a hat trick for high-quality food, entertainment and shopping is Korea House. A dozen dainty, artistic courses make up the royal banquet. The *hanok*, the *hanbok*-clad waitresses, the *gayageum* (zither) music, and the platters and boxes the food is served in are all part of the experience.

★Gosang KOREAN $$$
(고상; Map p62; ☎02-6030 8955; 67 Suha-dong; lunch/dinner set course ₩39,800/58,000; ⊙11.30am-3pm & 5.30-10pm Mon-Fri, to 9pm Sat & Sun; 🖉; Ⓢ Line 2 to Euljiro 1-ga, Exit 4) One worth dressing up for, this classy restaurant specialises in vegetarian temple dishes that date from the Goryeo dynsasty. It's all set-course, traditional-style banquets here, and there's also a meat option. It's in a posh food court in the basement of the Center 1 Building.

Western Seoul

★Namul Meokneun Gom KOREAN $
(나물 먹는 곰, Bear Eats Greens, Bob Cafe; Map p78; ☎02-323 9930; 367-31 Seogyo-dong; mains ₩8800-18,000; ⊙noon-10pm) You can enjoy the bright lights of Hongdae's student hang-outs but still dine at this converted *hanok* restaurant hidden in a quiet courtyard. The menu of Korean dishes at 'Bear Eats Greens' are easy to understand, with photos and English explanations of the dishes such as *ojingeo duruchigi* (spicy stir-fried squid), or the *jjimdak soban* (braised chicken set meal for two).

Tuk Tuk Noodle Thai THAI $
(Map p46; ☎070-4407 5130; http://blog.naver.com/tuktuknoodle; 161-8 Seongmisan-ro; mains ₩9000-15,000; ⊙noon-3.30pm & 5-10pm; Ⓢ Line 2 to Hongik University, Exit 3) Credited with kicking off a trend for more authentic Thai restaurants in Seoul, Tuk Tuk's Thai chefs whack out a broad menu of spicy dishes that don't compromise on flavour. Their success saw them move to this minimally decorated two-level space deep into a quiet area of Yeonnam-dong, which still requires queueing on weekends.

Raw Vega VEGAN $
(Map p78; ☎010 8562 7133; www.fb.me/rawvega.seoul; 22 Sinchon-ro 12-gil; mains ₩7500-10,500; ⊙11am-7pm Wed-Sun; ❄📶🖉; Ⓢ Line 2 to Sinchon, Exit 8) Can purely raw, vegan, gluten-free and organic dishes be tasty? Yes! Take this tiny cafe's pad thai, which spices up veggie spirals (in place of noodles) with a creamy peanut and coconut dressing. Other inventive surprises include walnut taco 'meat' in cabbage shells, cashew nut 'cheese' burgers, almond-milk matcha smoothies, and coffee coconut-milk ice cream.

Sobok DESSERTS $
(소복; Map p78; ☎02-6014 0861; www.sobokorea.com; 58 Eoulmadang-ro, Seogyo-dong; ice cream ₩5500; ⊙1-11pm; 📶👪; Ⓢ Line 6 to Sangsu, Exit 1) One of the most photogenic dessert spots in Seoul, Sobok creates desserts based on Korean ingredients. Its menu varies season to season, but the year-round bestseller is the *injeolmi* (bean powder) soft serve. Each serving comes with a small piece of ice-cream-covered *tteok* (rice cake), a spoonful of honey and a flower.

Ddobagi Chicken KOREAN $
(또바기치킨; Map p78; ☎02-3142 0991; 27 Wausan-ro, Sangsu-dong; dishes ₩9000; ⊙5pm-2am Mon-Sat, to 1am Sun; ❄👪; Ⓢ Line 6 to Sangsu, Exit 4) One of the most famous and best-value chicken joints in Seoul. Portions are smallish, but the fried exterior is crispy-perfect and the juiciness of the meat will have you dreaming about it for days. Half-and-half combinations are the most popular; choices include original, sweetly marinated, soy marinated and spicy.

Dongmu Bapsang KOREAN $
(동무밥상; Comrade's Table; Map p46; ☎02-322 6632; 10 Yanghwajin-gil; noodles ₩10,000; ⊙11.30am-3pm & 5-9pm Tue-Sat; ❄👪; Ⓢ Line 2 or 6 to Hapjeong, Exit 5) One of the most authentic North Korean restaurants in Seoul, using quality ingredients to produce simple flavours. Owner-chef Yu Jeong-chol worked at one of the most famous restaurants in Pyongyang before defecting. North Korean specialities from the short menu such as

naengmyun (Pyongyang-style iced noodles) and *mandu-guk* (dumpling soup) are not to be missed.

★**Hongik Sutbul Galbi** BARBECUE $$
(홍익숯불갈비; Map p78; ☎02-334 3354; 146-1 Eoulmadang-ro; mains ₩12,000-16,000; ⏲3.30pm-4am; ⓢLine 2 to Hongik University, Exit 7 or 8) Real charcoal (rather than a hotplate) brings out the flavours of the fine cuts of pork and beef at this *galbi* (beef ribs) joint; look for the stove on the street corner. Staff will do most of the cooking, then just wrap the smoky meat and sides in lettuce. It's open late, but expect to queue at dinner-time.

Tamra Sikdang KOREAN $$
(탐라식당, Tamra Restaurant; Map p78; ☎02-337 4877; 19 Wausan-ro 3-gil; mains from ₩9000; ⏲5pm-1am Mon-Sat; ; ⓢLine 6 to Sangsu Station, Exit 4) 'Tamra' is an old name for Jeju and this restaurant specialises in Jeju-style cuisine – even using ingredients brought over from the southern island. The most popular dish on the pork-heavy menu is *ddombae-gogi*: sliced, broiled pork served with lettuce and raw garlic. Pair your meal with one of the Jeju-speciality alcohols in stock.

Northern Seoul

★**Jaha Sonmandoo** KOREAN $
(자하손만두; Map p46; ☎02-379 2648; 12 Baekseokdong-gil; dumplings from ₩6500; ⏲11am-9.30pm; ⓢLine 3 to Gyeongbokgung, Exit 3) Around lunchtime and on weekends Seoulites queue up at this posh mountain-side *mandu* (dumpling) house for elegantly wrapped dough parcels stuffed with veggies, beef and pork, served either boiled or in soup. A couple of orders is enough of these whoppers; the sweet cinnamon tea to finish is free. From the subway, take bus 1020, 7022 or 7212.

Gyeyeolsa Chicken FAST FOOD $
(계열사; Map p46; ☎02-391 3566; 7 Baekseok-dong-gil; chicken ₩20,000; ⏲noon-11.30pm Tue-Sun; ; ⓢLine 3 to Gyeongbokgung, Exit 3) The fried-chicken purists here say 'cluck-off' to chilli and other gimmicks, simply serving delicious, golden-fried chicken pieces heaped together with crisp potato wedges. One basket serves two nicely. It's a popular spot, and it packs you in tight. From the subway, take bus 1020, 7022 or 7212.

Scoff BAKERY $
(Map p46; ☎070-8801 1739; 149 Changuimun-ro; baked goods ₩2000-5000; ⏲11am-6pm Wed-Sun; ⓢLine 3 to Gyeongbokgung, Exit 3) British baker Jonathan exhibits admirable bake-off skills in his selection of sweet treats ranging from scones and ginger cake to coconut macaroons – but the lemon sponge gets our vote. Ideal for a takeaway nibble while wandering Buam-dong. From the subway, take bus 1020, 1711, 7016, 7018, 7022 or 7212.

Hyehwa Kalguksu NOODLES $
(혜화 칼국수; Map p52; ☎02-743 8212; 13 Changgyeonggung-ro 35-gil; noodles ₩9000; ⏲11am-10pm; ⓢLine 4 to Hyehwa, Exit 4) This throwback Korean eatery, painted duck-egg blue, serves simple bowls of *guksi* noodles in a milky-white, beef-bone broth with leeks and zucchini. Homey and simple, it also does delicious cod fritters that look like giant fish fingers.

Deongjang Yesool KOREAN $
(된장예술, Bean Art and Wine; Map p52; ☎02-741 4516; 9-2 Daehak-ro 11-gil; set meal ₩11,000; ⏲11am-10pm; ; ⓢLine 4 to Hyehwa, Exit 3) Serves a tasty fermented-bean-paste-and-tofu stew that comes with a big variety of nearly all vegetarian side dishes at a bargain price – no wonder it's well patronised by the area's student population. Look for the stone carved lions flanking the door.

Itaewon & Yongsan-gu

★**Casablanca Sandwicherie** SANDWICHES $
(Map p46; ☎02-797 8367; 33 Sinheung-ro, Haebangchon; sandwiches ₩7000-8000; ⏲noon-10.45pm Tue-Sun; ; ⓢLine 6 to Noksapyeong, Exit 2) These mouth-watering, deep-filled sandwiches served on wide, half-loaves of pillowy bread are beloved by locals and expats. Try the wickedly seasoned (and messy) Moroccan chicken. Also does North African–style *shakshuka* (spicy, baked eggs in tomatoes; ₩10,000) and a thick lentil soup (₩3000). There's a long fridge of craft beer in the cosy dining room.

Plant Cafe & Kitchen VEGAN $
(플랜트; Map p73; ☎02-749 1981; www.plantcafeseoul.com; 2nd fl, 117 Bogwang-ro, Yongsan-gu; meals from ₩12,000; ⏲11am-9pm Mon-Thu, to 10pm Fri & Sat; ; ⓢLine 6 to Itaewon, Exit 4) Vegan wraps, avocado burgers, chickpea tagines and peanut stews are just some of the virtuously delicious highlights at this popular vegan hang-out started by a local food blogger. The plant-filled space is also a tranquil spot to nurse a cup of homemade *yuja* tea or on-tap kombucha.

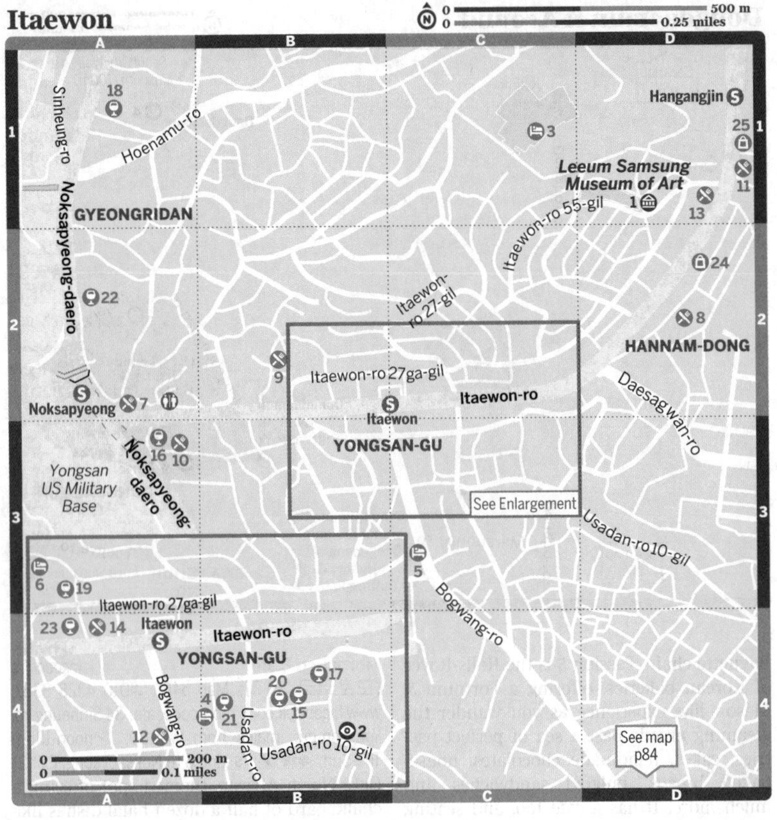

Itaewon

Top Sights
1 Leeum Samsung Museum of Art D1

Sights
2 Stairway Flea Market B4

Sleeping
3 Grand Hyatt Seoul C1
4 Itaewon G Guest House B4
5 Itaewon Hostel & Inn C3
6 Philstay Hostel B&B A3

Eating
7 Coreanos Kitchen A2
8 Downtowner D2
Gino's NY Pizza .... (see 7)
9 HBC Gogitjib B2
10 Linus' BBQ A3
11 Passion 5 .... D1
12 Plant Cafe & Kitchen A4
13 Rose Bakery D1
14 Tartine A4

Drinking & Nightlife
15 Always Homme B4
16 Cakeshop A3
17 Grand Ole Opry B4
18 Magpie Brewing Co A1
19 Mowmow A3
20 Queen B4
21 Soap B4
22 Southside Parlor A2
Sunset Beach .... (see 14)
23 Venue/ A4

Shopping
Comme des Garcons .... (see 13)
24 Vinyl & Plastic D2
25 Yongsan Crafts Museum D1

Passion 5 BAKERY, DESSERTS $
(Map p73; 272 Itaewon-ro, Hannam-dong; sandwiches from ₩5000; ⏰7.30am-10pm; Ⓢ Line 6 to Hangangjin, Exit 2) A luxe spin-off of the Paris

Dongdaemun & Around

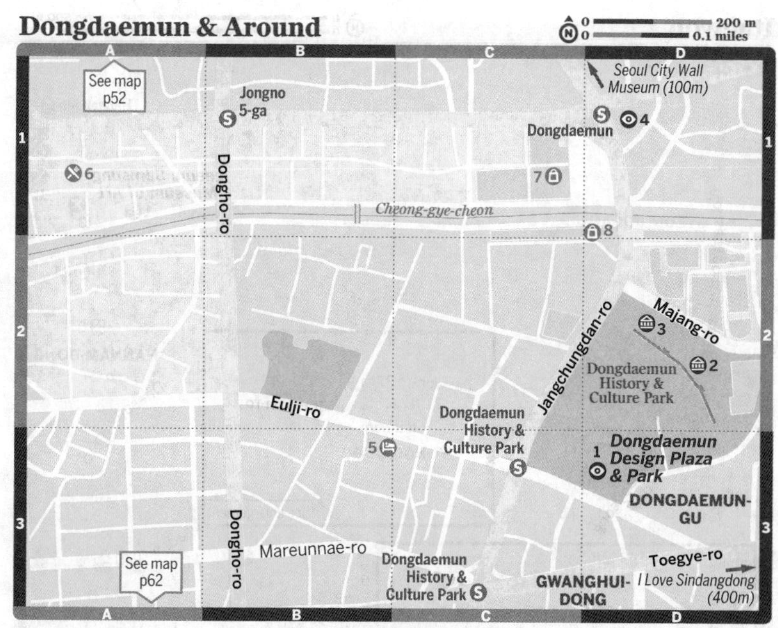

Baguette chain, Passion 5 is the Rolls-Royce of Korean bakeries, offering a Fortnum & Mason–like experience as you wander the gleaming arcade past a sea of perfect pastries, cakes, handmade chocolates, house-baked breads, bulgogi sandwiches and much more. It has a cafe too, and seating throughout the complex.

HBC Gogitjib KOREAN, BARBECUE $

(HBC 고깃집; Map p73; 118-9 Itaewon-dong; barbecue ₩16,900; ⌚5pm-1am Mon-Fri, to 2am Sat & Sun; 📶; Ⓢ Line 6 to Itaewon, Exit 1) Hungry revellers flock here for the nightly all-you-can-eat barbecue deal (₩16,900 per person), which includes beef rib-eye and all the pork cuts on the menu for 90 minutes of protein guzzling. Sides are self-serve, and it has local beers and *soju* (local vodka).

Coreanos Kitchen MEXICAN $

(Map p73; www.coreanoskitchen.com; 46 Noksapyeong-daero 40-gil; tacos for 2 ₩8000; ⌚noon-11pm, last order 10.15pm; Ⓢ Line 6 to Itaewon, Exit 2) Lively KoMex restaurant specialising in 'skizzles' (essentially fusion fajitas) served on tabletop skillets in epic sharing portions. Tacos come in pairs; the corn tortillas are made in-house. Try to snag a terrace table for views over Itaewon.

Morococo Cafe MOROCCAN $

(모로코코 카페; Map p46; ☎010 4228 8367; www.facebook.com/morococococafe; 34 Sinheung-ro, Yongsan-gu; mains from ₩9000; ⌚noon-10pm Tue-Sun; ❄📶✍; Ⓢ Line 6 to Noksapyeong, Exit 2) Cute North African–themed spot offering a chalkboard of half a dozen halal dishes like carrot salad, claypot lamb and the popular 'Morocco Over Rice' (₩9000) – shrimp, chicken, lamb or vegan with rice and veggies. Libations include spiced Moroccan tea and *'nas nas'* coffee (espresso dripped over foamed milk), bottled craft beer and wine.

Tartine CAFE $

(Map p73; ☎02-3785 3400; www.tartine.co.kr; 4 Itaewon-ro 23-gil; small pecan pie ₩7800; ⌚10am-10.30pm; Ⓢ Line 6 to Itaewon, Exit 1) This humble bakery-cafe just off Itaewon's main party strip bakes the best pecan pie this side of the Pacific, along with cranberry cheesecake, butter tart, apple crumble and lots more sweet-pie variations. Max out your sugar high with a cement-thick hot chocolate.

Downtowner BURGERS $

(다운타우너; Map p73; ☎070-8820 3696; www.instagram.com/downtownerseoul; 28-4 Itaewon-ro 42-gil, Yongsan-gu; burgers from ₩6800; ⌚11.30am-9.30pm Tue-Sun; 📶; Ⓢ Line 6 to Hangangjin, Exit 3) Foodies queue daily for the

Dongdaemun & Around

much-lauded burgers here, painstakingly assembled (with Instagram in mind) and wrapped in cute zebra-striped paper. Pimp up your patty with cheese and bacon or the more popular avocado, and don't miss out on the guac fries. Oh, and the chicken strips.

★Linus' BBQ BARBECUE $$
(Map p73; ☎02-790 2930; www.facebook.com/linusbbq; 136-13 Itaewon-ro; sandwich plus sides from ₩12,000; ⏱11.30am-3.30pm & 5.30-10pm; ⓢLine 6 to Noksapyeong, Exit 3) The portions are more modest than your typical Southern smokehouse, but the pulled pork and beef-brisket rolls with 'skinny ass' fries are some of the tastiest (and prettiest) plates of western food in Seoul. Count on a friendly, laid-back vibe in the industrial-styled dining space, with a good choice of craft beers and cocktails.

Gino's NY Pizza PIZZA $$
(지노스 뉴욕 피자; Map p73; ☎02-792 2234; www.facebook.com/ginoskorea; 46 Noksapyeong-daero 40-gil, Yongsan-gu; pizzas for 2 from ₩17,000; ⏱noon-10pm Tue-Sun; ⓢLine 6 to Noksapyeong, Exit 2) This wildly popular upstairs kitchen bakes an authentic range of New York-style pizzas along with appetisers like garlic knots, wings and messy fries. The queues got so big they opened another, more casual, venue opposite that sells pizza by the slice (closed Tuesdays). Craft beers and cocktails available.

Dongdaemun & Eastern Seoul

★Gwangjang Market KOREAN $
(광장시장, Kwangjang; Map p74; www.kwangjangmarket.co.kr; 88 Changgyeonggung-ro, Jongno-gu; dishes ₩4000-15,000; ⏱8.30am-10pm; ⓢLine 1 to Jongno-5ga, Exit 8, or Line 2 or 5 to Eulji-ro 4-ga, Exit 4) This sprawling fabric market is now best known as Seoul's busiest *meokjagolmok* (food alley), thanks to the 200 or so food, kimchi and fresh-seafood vendors that have set up shop amid the silk, satin and linen wholesalers. It's a hive of delicious sights and smells. Foodies flock here for the golden fried *nokdu bindaetteok* (mung-bean pancake; ₩4000 to ₩5000) – paired beautifully with *makgeolli* (rice wine).

Most diners squeeze on to benches at one of the many vendors threading through the centre of the alleyways, where you can munch on *mandu* (Korean dumplings), *jokbal* (braised pig's trotters), bibimbap and *boribap* (mixed rice and barley topped with a selection of veggies). Gwangjang Market is also a popular place to try *sannakji,* raw octopus tentacles that wriggle and writhe on the plate (₩15,000).

Onion BAKERY $
(어니언; Map p46; ☎070-7816 2710; www.instagram.com/cafe.onion; 8 Achasan-ro 9(gu)-gil; coffee from ₩4500; ⏱8am-10pm Mon-Fri, 10am-10pm Sat & Sun; ❄📶; ⓢLine 2 to Seongsu, Exit 2) Seoul's hippest cafe-bakery, Onion is the epitome of industrial-chic cool, set within a semi-derelict concrete building that just begs to be photographed. Scenesters queue out the door to take their turn loading trays with artisanal baked goods, sandwiches and frankly fabulous coffee, before finding a little perch of exposed brick to call their own.

I Love Sindangdong KOREAN $
(아이러브 신당동; Map p46; ☎02-2232 7872; www.ilovesindangdong.com; 302-4 Sindang-dong; tteokbokki for 2 from ₩11,000; ⏱24hr, closed 1st & 3rd Mon of month) The *tteokbokki* at this raucous restaurant comes in bubbling saucepans as part of a witches' brew of rice cakes, fish cake, instant ramen, veggies, egg and tofu in a volcanic sauce. It's pure comfort food and great fun; you can pay extra to pimp it up with seafood and cheese. Also on offer are *gimbap* (Korean sesame-oil flavoured rice wrapped in seaweed), cheap draught beer and occasional live music.

Pyeongando Jokbal Jip NORTH KOREAN $

(평안도 족발집; Map p62; ☎02-2279 9759; 174-6 Jangchungdan-ro; jokbal for 2 from ₩30,000; ⏰11.30am-11pm; Ⓢ Line 3 to Dongguk University, Exit 3) Out of sight in an alleyway, this is one of the best spots in town to try *jokbal* (braised pigs trotters). Staff maintain a continuous cleaving of pig forelegs to keep up with diners gorging on collagen-rich pork slices wrapped in leaves with garlic and other condiments. *Jokbal* is said to pair perfectly with *soju* (local vodka), so don't hold back.

Share D Table INTERNATIONAL $$

(쉐어드테이블; Map p46; ☎02-467 0303; Seongsu-dong 2(i)-ga, Seongdong-gu; mains around ₩15,000; ⏰10am-11pm, last food order 9pm; ❄📶; Ⓢ Line 2 to Seongsu, Exit 4) One of several beautifully converted warehouse hang-outs in the Seongsu 'hood, Share D Table is more food focused, with separate vendors hawking pizza, pasta, Thai and tapas. And, of course, third-wave coffee and cakes, plus craft beer from Amazing Brewing Co (p83) nearby. Note the retro bathhouse-style decor by the entrance – all the rage in Seoul.

Gangnam & Southern Seoul

Bad Farmers CAFE, VEGETARIAN $

(Map p84; ☎02-515 8400; www.badfarmers.com; 31 Apgujeong-ro 4-gil; salads ₩11,500-13,800; ⏰11.30am-3.30pm & 4.30-9pm Mon-Thu, to 9.30pm Fri & Sat, to 8pm Sun; 🖉🐾; Ⓢ Line 3 to Sinsa, Exit 8) One of the first in Seoul to catch on to the healthy-food trend, Bad Farmers is the place for your daily dose of green eats. Recognisable for its bright-red exterior, the spacious, sun-filled restaurant specialises in salads, cold-pressed juices and open sandwiches. There are plenty of options for vegetarians and vegans, and there's even 'pet parking' for furry friends.

Jilhal Bros KEBAB $

(질할브로스; Map p88; ☎02-542 1422; www.fb.me/JilhalBros; 32 Apgujeong-ro 79-gil; bowls from ₩6500; ⏰11am-10pm; Ⓢ Line 7 to Cheongdam, Exit 10) Nestled in K-Pop paradise (between entertainment companies JYP and SMTown), Jilhal Bros has managed to capture the hearts of sunglasses-adorned celebrities ordering takeaway. Imitating the famous Halal Guys cart in midtown Manhattan, Jilhal Bros serves up chicken or lamb over rice with a simple salad as well as wraps and *gyros*.

Haru JAPANESE $

(하루; Map p84; ☎02-514 5557; 56 Eonju-ro 172-gil, Gangnam-gu; mains ₩6000-9000; ⏰11.40am-4pm & 5-9.40pm; Ⓢ Bundang Line to Apgujeongrodeo, Exit 5) Haru's decades-long run alone could be considered a feat in Seoul – not to mention the constant (fast moving) lines out the door and topping local 'best cheap eats' lists. The pan-soba is particularly queue-worthy – two fistfuls of freshly made cold buckwheat noodles with icy broth on the side. Or point to the photo menu's hot and juicy *donkatsu* (fried pork cutlet) cooked to perfection.

Min's Kitchen FUSION $$

(민스키친; Map p84; ☎02-544 1007; www.minskitchen.kr; 10-4 Dosan-daero 45-gil; mains ₩10,000-60,000, set lunch/dinner from ₩28,000/98,000; ⏰11.30am-3pm & 5.30-10pm Mon-Sat; Ⓢ Bundang Line to Apgujeongrodeo, Exit 5) Korean cuisine, while delicious, can overwhelm with punchiness. Min's Kitchen opts for fresh, delicate flavours in dishes such as shrimp bibimbap. The long menu is not radical but is done well, with its best modern touches shining through artful tasting menus including bulgogi 'taco' and acorn jelly.

★ **Jungsik** KOREAN $$$

(정식당; Map p84; ☎02-517 4654; www.jungsik.kr; 11 Seolleung-ro, 158-gil; 5-course lunch/dinner from ₩88,000/130,000; ⏰noon-3pm & 5.30-10.30pm; Ⓢ Bundang Line to Apgujeongrodeo, Exit 4) This place was voted number 25 in *Asia's 50 Best Restaurants* in 2018; neo-Korean cuisine hardly gets better than this. At the Apgujeong outpost of the New York restaurant named after creative chef-owner Yim Jungsik, you can expect inspired and superbly presented contemporary mixes of traditional and seasonal ingredients over multiple courses. Book at least one month in advance.

★ **Normal by Ryunique** FUSION $$$

(노멀바이류니끄; Map p84; ☎02-546 9279; 42 Apgujeong-ro 10-gil; mains from ₩27,000, Quick Ryunique ₩60,000; ⏰noon-3pm & 5pm-10.30pm Mon-Fri, noon-10.30pm Sat & Sun; Ⓟ❄; Ⓢ Line 3 to Sinsa, Exit 8) 'Normal' is the casual counterpart to restaurant **Ryunique** (류니끄; Map p84; ☎02-546 9279; www.ryunique.co.kr; 40 Gangnam-daero 162-gil; set lunch/dinner ₩120,000/230,000; ⏰noon-3pm & 6-10.30pm; Ⓟ❄; Ⓢ Line 3 to Sinsa, Exit 8), one of Asia's Top 50 restaurants. A contemporary bistro that makes fine dining affordable, the menu consists of American- and French-inspired dishes à la carte or one of two set meals. The

excellent seven-course Quick Ryunique can include a shrimp rice-paper wrap, langoustine ramen and berry mousse dessert.

Samwon Garden KOREAN $$$
(삼원가든; Map p84; ☎02-548 3030; www.samwongarden.com; 835 Eonju-ro; mains ₩39,000-81,000, set menu galbi ₩41,000-65,000; ⏲11.40am-10pm; Ⓢ Line 3 to Apgujeong, Exit 2) Serving top-class *galbi* (beef ribs) for over 30 years, Samwon is a Korean idyll, surrounded by beautiful traditional gardens including several waterfalls. It's one of the best places in the city for this kind of barbecued-beef meal. There are also more inexpensive dishes such as *galbitang* (beef short rib soup) for ₩15,000.

Gati ITALIAN $$$
(가티; Map p84; ☎02-517 3366; www.instagr.am/restaurant_gati; 24 Dosan-daero 1-gil; mains ₩25,000-38,000, set menu ₩49,000; ⏲11.30am-3pm & 5.15-9.45pm Mon-Fri, from noon Sat & Sun; Ⓢ Line 3 to Sinsa, Exit 8) This fine Italian restaurant is as casually cool as its all-black-wearing diners, but the food is seriously top-notch. Homemade squid-ink linguine with scallops in roe cream is a standout. Opt for the praise-worthy four-course set menu and you'll notice fusion touches in the *galbi* beef salad or sashimi. Nearby artsy Garosu-gil is good for a postdinner stroll.

Drinking & Nightlife

Gwanghwamun & Jongno-gu

★Cobbler COCKTAIL BAR
(코블러; Map p52; ☎02-733 6421; www.facebook.com/BarCobbler; 16 Sajik-ro 12-gil; drinks from ₩20,000; ⏲7pm-3am Mon-Sat; 📶; Ⓢ Line 3 to Gyeongbukgung, Exit 7) This high-end bar is located inside a *hanok* within a nest of lonesome alleyways. Owned by Robin Yoo (a pioneer in Korea's cocktail scene), it has no menu; instead the bartender recommends some excellent cocktails, such as gin sour with lavender notes, or something from a wide range of whiskeys. Everybody is given a piece of cobbler pie upon entrance.

Dawon TEAHOUSE
(다원; Map p81; ☎02-730 6305; 11-4 Insa-dong 10-gil; teas ₩7000; ⏲11am-9.50pm; Ⓢ Line 3 to Anguk, Exit 6) The perfect place to unwind under shady fruit trees in a courtyard with flickering candles. In colder weather sit indoors in *hanok* rooms decorated with scribbles or in the garden pavilion. The teas are superb, especially *omijacha hwachae* (fruit and five-flavour berry punch), a summer drink.

Sik Mool BAR
(식물; Plant Cafe; Map p81; ☎02-747 4858; www.fb.me/plantcafebar; 46-1 Donhwamun-ro 11da-gil; ⏲11am-midnight Sun-Thu, to 1am Fri & Sat; Ⓢ Line 1, 3 or 5 to Jongno 3-ga, Exit 6) Four *hanok* were creatively combined to create this chic designer cafe-bar that blends old and new Seoul. Clay-tile walls, Soviet-era propaganda posters, mismatched modern furniture and contemporary art surround a young crowd sipping cocktails, coffee and wine and nibbling on house-made pizza. Sik Mool and its creator, fashion photographer Louis Park, are often credited as spearheading Ikseon-dong's popularity.

Daeo Sochom CAFE
(대오서점; Map p52; ☎010 570 1349; 55 Jahamun-ro 7-gil, Jongno-gu; ⏲11am-10pm Tue-Sun; Ⓢ Line 3 to Gyeongbokgung, Exit 2) Opened as a bookshop in 1951 by Mrs Kwong and her husband Mr Cho, this charming, ramshackle cafe is still run by the same family and oozes bygone-days atmosphere with lots of memorabilia and quirky decor. Entry is ₩5000, which gets you a choice of drink.

Dalsaeneun Dalman Saenggak Handa TEAHOUSE
(달새는 달만 생각한다; Map p81; ☎02-720 6229; 14-3 Insa-dong 12-gil; teas ₩7000-9000; ⏲10am-11pm; Ⓢ Line 3 to Anguk, Exit 6) 'Moon Bird Thinks Only of the Moon' is packed with plants and rustic artefacts. Birdsong, soothing music and trickling water add to the atmosphere. Huddle in a cubicle and savour one of its teas, which include *gamnipcha* (persimmon-leaf tea). *Saenggangcha* (ginger tea) is peppery but sweet.

Cha Masineun Tteul TEAHOUSE
(차마시는뜰; Map p52; ☎02-722-7006; 26 Bukchon-ro 11na-gil; ⏲10am-10.30pm; Ⓢ Line 3 to Anguk, Exit 1) In the Bukchon Hanok Village area overlooking Samcheong-dong and Gwanghwamun is this lovely *hanok* with low tables arranged around a courtyard. It serves traditional teas, and a delicious bright-yellow pumpkin rice cake fresh from the steamer.

AleDang CRAFT BEER
(에일당; Map p52; ☎070-7766 3133; www.instagr.am/alepub; 33-9 Supyo-ro 28-gil, Ikseon-dong; beer ₩6800-15,000; ⏲noon-11pm; Ⓢ Line 1,3 or 5 to Jongno 3-ga, Exit 4) The courtyard of this converted *hanok* in Ikseon-dong makes the

Hongdae

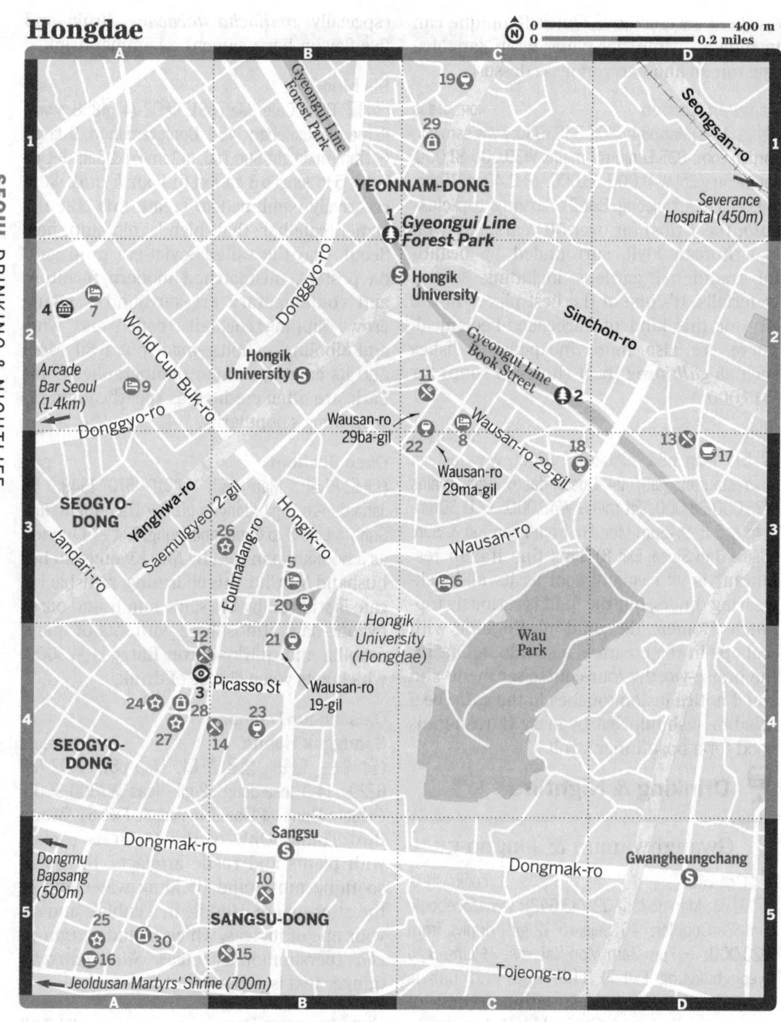

craft beers here extra special. A four-beer sampler includes citrusy light Punk IPA, and brews by Seoul's Magpie Brewing. There's also pizza, coffee, classic rock and even a disco ball.

Myeong-dong & Jung-gu

★Muldwinda BAR

(물뛴다; Map p62; ☎02-392 4200; www.facebook.com/muldwindakr; 43 Kyonggidae-ro; ⊙5pm-midnight Mon-Thu, 11am-2pm & 5-11pm Sat & Sun; S Line 2 or 5 to Chungjeongno, Exit 7) Seoul's most sophisticated *makgeolli* (rice wine) bar is a place for connoisseurs of Korean liquors and those who'd like to learn a bit more about the depth and breadth of local tipples. Set up by graduates from the nearby Susubori Academy (where you can learn how to make *makgeolli*), it serves good food and is decorated with class.

The Edge COCKTAIL BAR

(디엣지; Map p62; ☎010 3596 4049; www.facebook.com/theedgeseoul; 2F, 8 Eulji-ro 12-gil; drinks from ₩5000; ⊙noon-midnight Tue-Thu, to 1am Fri, 2-8pm & 10pm-3am Sat & Sun; ; S Line 2 or 3 to Euljiro 3-ga, Exit 10) The Edge is half record shop and half cafe and bar. The venue focus-

Hongdae

Top Sights
1 Gyeongui Line Forest Park........B1

Sights
2 Gyeongui Line Book Street........C2
3 KT&G SangsangMadang........A4
4 War & Women's Human Rights Museum........A2

Sleeping
5 Come Inn........B3
6 Kpopstay........C3
7 Lee Kang Ga........A2
8 Urbanwood Guesthouse........C2
9 Wowfactor Stay........A2

Eating
10 Ddobagi Chicken........B5
11 Hongik Sutbul Galbi........C2
12 Namul Meokneun Gom........A4
13 Raw Vega........D3
14 Sobok........B4
15 Tamra Sikdang........B5

Drinking & Nightlife
16 Anthracite........A5
17 Bread Blue........D3
18 Café Sukkara........C3
19 Channel 1969........C1
Gopchang Jeongol........(see 8)
20 Hongdae Playground........B3
21 Labris........B4
22 Sorori Wolhyang........C2
Su Noraebang........(see 12)
23 Suzie Q........B4

Entertainment
24 DGBD........A4
25 Mudaeruk........A5
26 Nanta Theatre Hongdae........B3
27 Owl's Rooftop........A4
XIndie Ticket Lounge........(see 14)

Shopping
Free Market........(see 20)
28 Gentle Monster........A4
29 GRDS........C1
30 Veronica Effect........A5

es on selling records by day, but invites DJs and sells drinks after dark. On Saturdays there is a DJ night featuring hip-hop, soul and electronic music. Space is limited but cocktails are decent and affordable.

Walkabout BAR
(Map p62; ☎010 6785 5847; www.fb.me/walkaboutnu; 49 Toegye-ro 20-gil; ⏰4pm-midnight Mon-Sat, to 10pm Sun; 📶; Ⓢ Line 4 to Myeongdong, Exit 3) Among Myeong-dong's guesthouse enclave leading up to Namsan, this travel-themed bar is run by a couple of young travel nuts who serve Korean craft beers on tap. There is also good Thai food.

Coffee Libre CAFE
(Map p62; ☎02-774-0615; www.coffeelibre.kr; Myeong-dong Cathedral, 74 Myeong-dong-gil; ⏰11am-8pm; Ⓢ Line 4 to Myeongdong, Exit 4) A tiny branch of this speciality coffee roaster has a somewhat bizarre location within the Myeong-dong Cathedral complex, but it makes for a good pit stop to refuel on single-origin pour-overs, aeropress or espressos.

Western Seoul

★ **Anthracite** CAFE
(Map p78; ☎02-322 0009; www.anthracitecoffee.com; 10 Tojeong-ro 5-gil; ⏰11am-midnight Mon-Sat, to 11pm Sun; 📶; Ⓢ Line 6 to Sangsu, Exit 4) An old shoe factory is the location for one of Seoul's top independent coffee-roaster and cafe operations. Drinks are made using the hand-drip method at a counter made out of an old conveyor belt. Upstairs is a spacious lounge and there's outdoor seating on the roof.

Café Sukkara BAR
(Map p78; ☎02-334 5919; www.sukkara.co.kr; Sanwoollim Theatre Bldg, 327-9 Seogyo-dong; ⏰11am-3.30pm & 4.30-11pm Tue-Sun, food from noon; 📶; Ⓢ Line 2 to Hongik University, Exit 9) There's a fantastic range of drinks at this shabby-chic, farmhouse-style cafe with a contemporary Japanese flair. They make their own juices and liquors – try the black shandy gaff, a mix of homemade ginger ale and Magpie Brewery dark beer. Some very tasty dishes include butter-chicken-like vegetarian curry, and ploughman's lunches with smoked ham or tofu cheese.

Sorori Wolhyang BAR
(소로리 월향; Map p78; ☎02-336 9765; 11-4 Wausan-ro 29ba-gil; ⏰2pm-midnight Mon-Sat; 📶; Ⓢ Line 2 to Hongik University, Exit 8) Specialising in artisanal *makgeolli* (rice wine) from around Korea, and other local liquors, this cosy basement bar is a great place to sample traditional alcoholic drinks. Various fruity and nutty flavours of *makgeolli* are complemented by decent food, such as *pajeon* (scallion pancakes).

Gopchang Jeongol BAR

(곱창전골; Map p78; ☎02-3143 2284; 8 Wausan-ro 29ra-gil; beer ₩5000; ⏰7pm-4am; Ⓢ Line 2 to Hongik University, Exit 5) Fans of this veteran music bar (opened 1999) in the heart of Hongdae love it for its old-school vibes, '70s interior and for solely playing Korean music. Hear Korean rock legends such as the Kim Sisters and admire the collection of rare Korean rock vinyl. There's standard *soju* (local vodka) and local beer; if it's crowded you might have to order food.

Su Noraebang KARAOKE

(수노래방; Map p78; ☎02-322 3111; www.skysu.com; 67 Eoulmadang-ro; room per hr ₩2000-20,000; ⏰24hr; Ⓢ Line 6 to Sangsu, Exit 1) Sing your heart out and be noticed at this luxe karaoke bar: some rooms resemble lounge bars, while others have floor-to-ceiling windows fronting onto the street so you can show off your K-Pop moves. Rates rise from noon to 6am, with the most expensive period from 8pm to the early hours.

Channel 1969 LOUNGE

(채널1969; Map p78; ☎010 5581 1112; www.facebook.com/channel.1969.seoul; B1, 35 Yeonhui-ro; drinks from ₩6000; ⏰6pm-3am; 📶; Ⓢ Line 2 to Hongik University, Exit 3) One of the last truly alternative spaces in the Hongdae-Yeonnam-dong area, this cultural space and bar turns itself into a club and lounge on weekends and is especially popular with the artsy crowd. Drinks are cheap and a lot of mingling happens outside where partygoers go for a smoke or a breath of fresh air.

Arcade Bar Seoul BAR

(지능계발; Map p46; ☎02-336 1945; www.instagram.com/arcadebarseoul; 82 Mangwon-ro 2-gil; beer from ₩6000; ⏰noon-11.30pm Tue-Thu, to midnight Fri-Sun; 📶; Ⓢ Line 6 to Mangwon, Exit 2) This two-storey bar and cafe is all about its dozen vintage video games on the basement level. Drinks include decent coffee and a few craft beers on tap; video games (from ₩500) range from 'Street Fighter' to 'Pac-Man'. Occasionally, the bar attempts a party vibe in the basement with a fog machine and loud EDM.

Bread Blue CAFE

(Map p78; ☎070-4405 0723; 3 Sinchon-ro 12da-gil; coffee ₩3500; ⏰9.30am-10pm Mon-Fri, to 9pm Sat & Sun; 📶; Ⓢ Line 2 to Hongik University, Exit 6) This vegan bakery-cafe is one of the few places to get an excellent soy latte in Seoul. Dairy-free temptations include dense matcha muffins, macaroons, filled panini, garlic bread, tofu pizza swirls and tiramisu.

Hongdae Playground BEER GARDEN

(홍익문화공원; Map p78; 19-3 Wausan-ro 21-gil; ⏰24hr; Ⓢ Line 2 to Hongik University, Exit 8) An icon of Hongdae and known simply as 'Playground', small Hongik Munhwa park turns into an impromptu outdoor party most nights. Weekends are especially sociable when students and foreigners grab a *soju* or beer from shops nearby and hold rowdy dance-offs to music by 'DJs' and buskers.

Labris LESBIAN

(라브리스; Map p78; ☎02-333 5276; 81 Wausan-ro; cover incl 1 drink ₩10,000; ⏰9pm-6am Fri & Sat; Ⓢ Line 6 to Sangsu, Exit 1) This 8th floor, comfortable, women-only space is lesbian-oriented but not exclusively so. A female DJ plays dance music, and there are cocktails and *anju* (bar snacks). Fridays can be very quiet.

Suzie Q BAR

(수지큐; Map p78; ☎02-338 9929; 10 Wausan-ro 15-gil; ⏰5-11pm Sun-Thu, to 2am Fri & Sat; 📶; Ⓢ Line 2 to Hongik University, Exit 8) A dark and wonderful LP bar in Hongdae lined with over 15,000 records. Jot down your song requests and pass it to the cool older DJ who *might* play one on vinyl, if it pleases him. Tip: rock, Korean classics and even disco rule in this basement. Solo beer drinkers very welcome.

Northern Seoul

★ **Suyeon Sanbang** TEAHOUSE

(수연산방; Map p46; 8 Seongbuk-ru 26-gil; tea from ₩8500; ⏰11.30am-10pm; Ⓢ Line 4 to Hansung University, Exit 6) Seoul's most charming teahouse is housed in a 1930s *hanok* and surrounding garden that once belonged to famous writer Lee Tae-jun, who settled in the North after the Korean War to an unknown fate. Apart from a range of medicinal teas and premium-quality, wild green tea, it also serves traditional sweets; the salty-sweet pumpkin soup with red-bean paste is a taste sensation.

Sanmotoonge CAFE

(산모퉁이; Map p46; ☎02-391 4737; www.sanmotoonge.co.kr; 153 Baekseokdong-gil; ⏰11am-10pm; Ⓢ Line 3 to Gyeongbokgung, Exit 3) Being featured in a Korean TV drama can do wonders for your business, but punters would still flock to this mountainside hot spot regardless for the wonderful views and hi-

Insa-dong

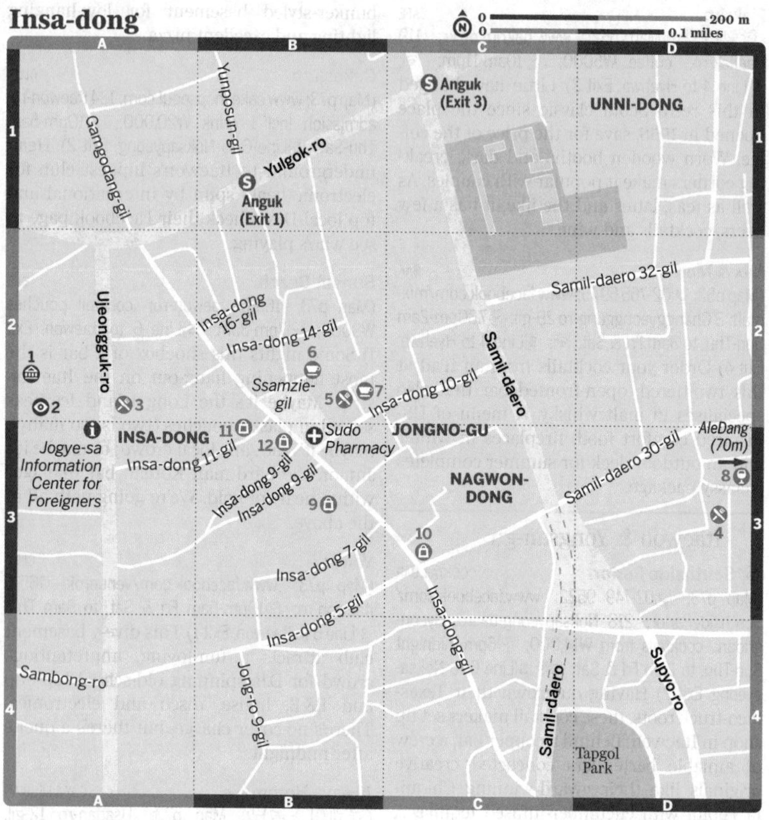

Insa-dong

Sights
- 1 Central Buddhist Museum A2
- 2 Jogye-sa A2

Eating
- 3 Balwoo Gongyang A2
- 4 Ikseon Dimibang D3
- 5 Koong B2

Drinking & Nightlife
- 6 Dalsaeneun Dalman Saenggak Handa B2
- 7 Dawon B2
- 8 Sik Mool D3

Shopping
- 9 Insa-dong Maru B3
- 10 Jilkyungyee C3
- 11 KCDF Gallery B3
- 12 Kukjae Embroidery B3

larious clutter of *objets d'art* and bric-and-brac both inside and on the terraces. Order drinks and snacks at the counter then snag the perfect sunset perch.

Club Espresso COFFEE
(Map p46; www.clubespresso.co.kr; 132 Changuimun-ro; ⏲9am-10pm; Ⓢ Line 3 to Gyeongbokgung, Exit 3) Pouring some of Seoul's best coffee since 1990, this elegant roaster, cafe and shop imports its beans from all corners of the globe; there are usually a couple of free samples on the go. The caffeine kick should give you the energy to climb nearby Bukaksan. From the subway, catch bus 1020, 7022 or 7212.

Hakrim CAFE

(학림다방; Map p52; www.hakrim.pe.kr; 119 Daehak-ro; coffee ₩5000; ⌚10am-11pm; 📶; Ⓢ Line 4 to Hyehwa, Exit 3) Little has changed in this retro Seoul classic since the place opened in 1956, save for the price of the coffee. Worn wooden booths and dark, creaking corners make it popular with couples. As well as teas, lattes and the like, it has a few beers, cocktails and wine.

Mix & Malt BAR

(Map p52; ☎02-765 5945; www.facebook.com/mixmalt; 3 Changgyeonggung-ro 29-gil; ⌚7.30pm-2am Sun-Thu, to 3am Fri & Sat; 📶; Ⓢ Line 4 to Hyehwa, Exit 4) Order your cocktails from an iPad at this two-tiered, open-fronted bar that also specialises in malt whisky. A menu of US-inspired comfort food, fireplaces in winter and an outdoor deck for summer completes a classy package.

Itaewon & Yongsan-gu

★ **Southside Parlor** COCKTAIL BAR

(Map p73; ☎02-749 9522; www.facebook.com/SouthsideParlor; 218 Noksapyeong-daero, Gyeongridan; cocktails from ₩14,000; ⌚6pm-midnight Sun-Thu, to 2am Fri & Sat; 📶; Ⓢ Line 6 to Noksapyeong, Exit 2) Having outgrown their Texas-taco-truck roots, these cocktail makers set up shop in Itaewon. Behind a copper bar, a crew of amiable bartenders concocted creative originals like their award-winning Chiquita Pepita with cucumber-infused tequila. A quality food menu includes Texas staples like fried chicken tacos and smoked *queso*. Weekday food specials help the medicine go down.

Grand Ole Opry BAR

(Map p73; 16 Usadan-ro 14-gil; beer ₩3000; ⌚6pm-1am, to 3am Fri & Sat; Ⓢ Line 6 to Itaewon, Exit 3) Bang in the middle of Itaewon's red-light district, this honky-tonk dive bar is a throwback GI hang-out and something straight out of a movie. The original owner, Mama Kim, still works the bar; she bought the club in 1975. Grab a ₩3000 drink, have a chinwag about Itaewon's colourful history, then do-si-do over to the wooden dance floor.

★ **Magpie Brewing Co** MICROBREWERY

(Map p73; www.magpiebrewing.com; 244-1 Noksapyeong-daero; beer from ₩7000; ⌚3pm-1am; Ⓢ Line 6 to Noksapyeong, Exit 2) Seoul craft-beer pioneers Magpie pour some of the finest brews in Seoul from this rough-and-tumble alleyway venue, opened in 2011. Pull up a stool at the tiny bar or duck into the bunker-styled basement for low-hanging lighting and excellent pizza.

Cakeshop CLUB

(Map p73; www.cakeshopseoul.com; 134 Itaewon-ro; admission incl 1 drink ₩20,000; ⌚10pm-5am Thu-Sat; Ⓢ Line 6 to Noksapyeong, Exit 2) Head underground to Itaewon's hippest club for electronic beats spun by international and top local DJs. Check their Facebook page to see who's playing.

Sunset Beach BAR

(Map p73; 165-6 Itaewon-ro; cocktail pouches ₩9000; ⌚7pm-3am; Ⓢ Line 6 to Itaewon, Exit 1) Some nights this shoebox of a bar is the most happening hang-out on the Itaewon strip. Maybe it's the Long Island Ice Teas served in plastic pouches (two is too many); maybe it's the zany local crowd; or maybe it's Junior, the hard-man Korean bar manager with a heart of gold. We're going with all of the above.

Venue/ CLUB

(Map p73; www.facebook.com/venuerok; 165-6 Itaewon-ro; ⌚10pm-5am Fri & Sat, to 3am Thu; Ⓢ Line 6 to Itaewon, Exit 1) This dive-y basement club attracts a fun-loving, unpretentious crowd for DJs spinning old-school hip-hop and R&B, house, disco and electronica. There's no cover charge, but there's a queue after midnight.

Always Homme GAY & LESBIAN

(올웨이즈옴므; Map p73; Usadan-ro 12-gil; ⌚9pm-4am Sun-Thu, to 5am Fri & Sat; Ⓢ Line 6 to Itaewon, Exit 3) The most welcoming gay bar on the strip, this place has flirty-friendly staff, low-playing music and a cosy open-air lounge set-up.

Mowmow BAR

(모우모우; Map p73; 54-3 Itaewon-ro 27ga-gil; makgeolli from ₩12,000; ⌚5pm-3am Mon-Thu, 3pm-5am Sat, to 1am Sun; Ⓢ Line 6 to Itaewon, Exit 1) Order your *makgeolli* (rice wine) by the half-litre or litre at this homey bar and restaurant up the hill from the main Itaewon dining alley. Or pair a *makgeolli* cocktail with a *jeon* (Korean savoury pancake) crammed with creative and filling combos like pork belly, kimchi and cheese.

Queen GAY & LESBIAN

(Map p73; www.facebook.com/queenbar; 7 Usadan-ro 12-gil; ⌚10pm-3am Thu, to 5am Sat & Sun; Ⓢ Line 6 to Itaewon, Exit 3) The undisputed queen of Homo Hill, this eternally popular gay bar is still the place to party in Itaewon.

CRAFT BEER VALLEY

At the epicentre of the craft-beer revolution in Seoul, the area north of Noksapyeong subway station has come to be known as Craft Beer Valley thanks to the string of brewers who set up shop in the vicinity. In a short time, this localised scene has paved the way for a greater diversity and quality of beer in Seoul, resulting in a shift in tastes that's seen locals gain a thirst for India Pale Ales (IPAs), amber ales, German-style wheat beers and smoky stouts.

Previously, government restrictions meant the industry was dominated by a handful of major brewers churning out industrial lagers like Hite, Cass and OB. It was this lack of diversity that led to an article in the *Economist* claiming that North Korean beer tasted infinitely better than its southern counterpart. Ouch. This proved to be the spark that lit the fuse, leading to a loosening of restrictions enabling small-scale breweries to produce commercially. The rest is history, and now every second bar and restaurant in Itaewon sells craft beer, both local and imported.

Dongdaemun & Eastern Seoul

★Daelim Changgo CAFE

(대림창고; Map p46; ☎02-498 7474; 78 Seongsui-ro, Seongdong-gu; pizzas from ₩25,000; ⏲10am-11pm; 📶; Ⓢ Line 2 to Seongsu Station, Exit 3) Hands down the most stunning converted *changgo* (warehouse) venue in 'Seoul's Brooklyn', Daelim Changgo is the ultimate synthesis of Seoul's obsessions for cafes, design, art and selfies. Choose from single-origin coffee, draught beers and wood-fired pizza and find a spot in either of two cavernous former workshops to sit and marvel at the funky wall art, sculptures, and interior garden complete with buzzing neon flowers.

Baesan Warehouse Cafe CAFE

(바이산 대림창고; Map p46; ☎02-6238 8130; 78 Seongsui-ro; coffee from ₩6000; ⏲11am-11pm; Ⓢ Line 2 to Seongsu, Exit 3) Anywhere else in Seoul (except maybe Hongdae), this vast, industrial-chic hang-out would be the cream of the crop with its street-art styling, quality baked goods and teas made to look like craft beer (they do sell real beer too). It's just that Daelim Changgo next door is possibly the most spectacular cafe in Asia. What you gonna do?

Amazing Brewing Co BREWERY

(Map p46; ☎02-465 5208; www.amazingbrewing.co.kr; 4 Seongsuil-ro 4-gil; 250mL pours from ₩5000; ⏲6pm-1am Mon-Fri, from 4pm Sat & Sun; 📶; Ⓢ Line 2 to Ttukseom, Exit 5) Amazing serves around 20 of its own beers at this hip brewing facility and bar. Seoul Forest, a New England pale ale, is named after the park next door. Another beer named Cosmos Hawking Radiation...well, that's anyone's guess. There are international guest beers too, and you can order hot dogs, wings and pizza.

Hidden Track MICROBREWERY

(히든트랙; Map p46; 6 Yangnyeongsi-ro, Dongdaemun-gu; beers from ₩5500; ⏲6pm-1am Mon-Sat; Ⓢ Line 6 to Anam, Exit 3) This basement microbrewery pub serves its own, mostly German-style beers on tap, as well as pizza and snacks. If you make it out here, the surrounding student neighbourhood is lively and packed with cheap eats.

It's a 10-minute walk south from Anam subway, just off the roundabout.

Gangnam & Southern Seoul

★Club Octagon CLUB

(Map p84; www.octagonseoul.com; 645 Nonhyeon-ro; admission before 11pm & after 4am ₩10,000, 11pm-4am ₩30,000; ⏲Thu-Sat 10pm-6am; Ⓢ Line 7 to Hak-dong, Exit 4) Voted number seven in the world's top clubs by *DJ Mag* in 2018, Octagon is one of Gangnam's best for serious clubbers. High-profile resident and guest DJs spin house, trap, hip-hop and techno in a warehouse-sized space over its powerful Funktion 1 sound system to an appreciative crowd here to party till dawn.

Art C Company BAR, CAFE

(아트씨컴퍼니; Map p84; ☎02-549 0110; www.artc-company.com; 33 Apgujeong-ro; coffee/cocktails from ₩4000/16,000; ⏲9am-3am; Ⓢ Line 3 to Sinsa, Exit 8) A three-storey design and music-themed cafe located in an alley adjacent to Garosu-gil. Each floor brings a slightly different atmosphere, from cafe decorated with vinyl records and turntables, to kitsch basement bar and lounge decorated with towering contemporary artworks and pumping out retro and hip-hop music until 3am. The rose-petal-topped 'Rose Garden' cocktail is delicious and not too strong.

Apgujeong, Gangnam & Yongsan-gu

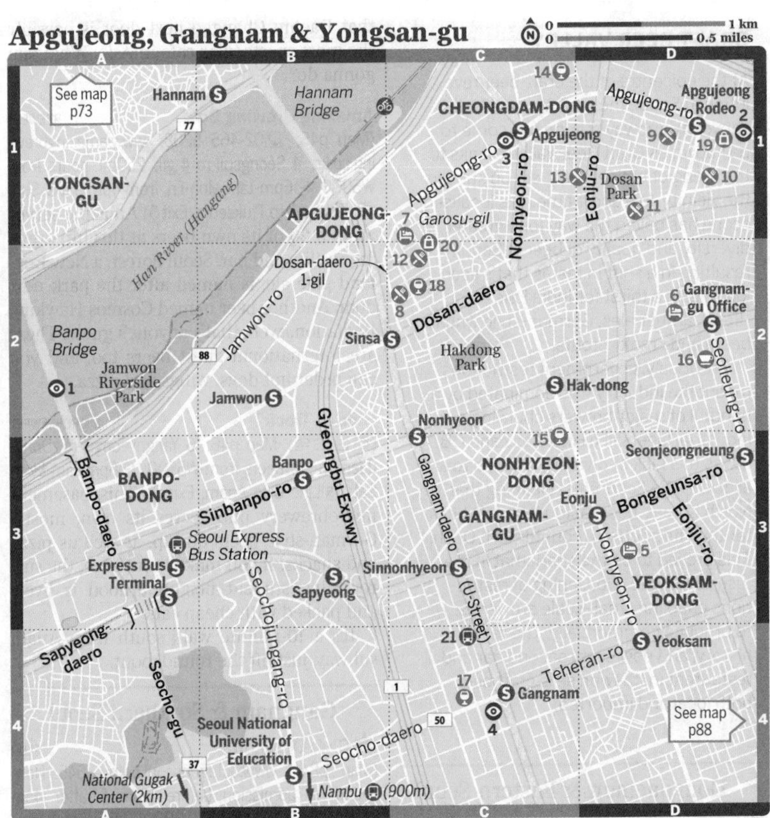

Cafe More CAFE

(카페모아; Map p46; ☎02-880 0888; 1717 Nambusunhwan-ro; coffee from ₩2000; ⏰8am-10.30pm; 📶👪; Ⓢ Line 2 to Bongchon, Exit 4) Part coffee shop and part Braille library, this bright and spacious cafe caters to the sight-impaired community. The library consists of hundreds of Braille books and two computers, and the cafe often donates a part of its profits to charities for the sight-impaired, in addition to making a decent cup of coffee.

Pongdang MICROBREWERY

(Map p84; ☎02-6204 5513; www.pongdangsplash.com; 49 Apgujeong-ro 2-gil; ⏰5pm-1am Mon-Thu, to 2am Fri, 4pm-2am Sat, 4pm-midnight Sun; Ⓢ Line 3 to Sinsa, Exit 6) The original bar for this Korean microbrewery does a good selection of pale ales, and Belgian and wheat beers, enjoyed at Pongdang's bar or tables surrounded by arcade machines.

Neurin Maeul BAR

(느린마을, Slow Brew Pub; Map p84; ☎02-587 7720; http://slowbrewpub.com; 7 Seochodae-ro 73-gil; ⏰11am-11pm; Ⓢ Line 2 to Gangnam, Exit 9) The Gangnam branch of this Baesangmyeon Brewery bar is a bit snazzier than others, but remains a good place to sample quality traditional Korean alcohol. Its signature Neurin Maeul *makgeolli* (rice wine) is the standout – it's divided into the four 'seasons', which refers to the differing production stages; you can sample each before ordering. Look for the rusty shipping container.

Greenmile Coffee CAFE

(Map p84; ☎02-517 2404; www.facebook.com/greenmilecoffee; 11 Seolleung-ro 127-gil; coffee from ₩4000; ⏰8am-7pm Mon-Fri; 📶; Ⓢ Line 7 to Gangnam-gu Office, Exit 2) Fitted out in designer furniture and caffeine-related paraphernalia, this cool little cafe is a great spot for coffee. It roasts all its single-origin beans on-site, sourced from Africa to Latin Ameri-

Apgujeong, Gangnam & Yongsan-gu

Sights
1 Banpo Bridge Rainbow Fountain A2
2 K-Star Road D1
3 K-Wave Experience C1
4 Samsung D'Light C4

Sleeping
5 H Avenue Hotel D3
6 Kimchee Gangnam Guesthouse D2
7 La Casa Garosugil C1
Tria Hotel .... (see 5)

Eating
Bad Farmers .... (see 7)
8 Gati C2
9 Haru D1
10 Jungsik D1
11 Min's Kitchen D1
12 Normal by Ryunique C2
Ryunique .... (see 12)
13 Samwon Garden D1

Drinking & Nightlife
14 Art C Company C1
15 Club Octagon C3
16 Greenmile Coffee D2
17 Neurin Maeul C4
18 Pongdang C2

Shopping
19 10 Corso Como Seoul D1
20 Steve J & Yoni P C2

Transport
21 Bus Stop for Everland Amusement Park C4

ca. As well as the usual espresso, pour-overs and cold drip, it's also the proud owner of laboratory-like, halogen-powered equipment that does sensational siphon brews.

☆ Entertainment

★Seoul Racecourse HORSE RACING
(서울경마장, Let's Run Park; Map p46; 02-509 2309; www.kra.co.kr; Gyeongmagongwon-daero, Gwacheon-si; ₩2000, Champions Suite ₩15,000; Fri-Sun, races from 10.45am; ; Line 4 to Seoul Racecourse Park, Exit 2) Enjoy a day at the races at Seoul's impressive and hugely popular horse-racing track. A 40,000-capacity grandstand faces the sandy track and its backdrop of verdant hills, where giant screens show the odds, the races and close-ups of the horses. You'll need a T-Money card (see p399) to get you through the turnstiles; once inside, make a beeline for the ground floor Foreigner Information Desk to collect the day's form guide in English and a handy leaflet explaining how the betting system works.

★Nanta Theatre Jung-gu PERFORMING ARTS
(명동난타극장, Myeongdong Nanta Theatre; Map p62; 02-739 8288; www.nanta.co.kr; 3rd fl, Unesco Bldg, 26 Myeongdong-gil; tickets ₩40,000-60,000; 5pm & 8pm Mon-Thu, 2pm, 5pm & 8pm Fri-Sun; Line 4 to Myeongdong, Exit 6) Running since 1997, with no end in sight, this is Korea's most successful nonverbal performance. Set in a kitchen, this high-octane, 90-minute show mixes magic tricks, *samulnori* folk music, drumming, kitchen utensils, comedy, dance, martial arts and audience participation. It's top-class entertainment that has been a hit wherever it plays. There's another **venue** (Map p78; 357-4 Seogyo-dong; tickets ₩40,000-60,000; shows 5pm & 8pm; Line 2 to Hongik University, Exit 9) in Hongdae.

Mudaeruk LIVE MUSIC
(무대륙; Map p78; 02-332 8333; www.mudaeruk.com; 12 Tojeong-ro 5-gil; from ₩15,000; ; Line 6 to Sangsu, Exit 4) The 'Lost Continent of Mu' has been hiding out in Sangsu-dong all these years? Join those in the know for live bands, piano, improv jazz or electronic music in the basement on weekends. Upstairs is a stylish cafe-bar with craft beer, sharing boards of food and great fish and chips.

Owl's Rooftop LIVE MUSIC
(옥탑방 부엉이; Map p78; 02-332 6603; http://fb.me/owlsrooftop; 2nd fl, 43 Dongmak-ro 9-gil; 6pm-1am Sun-Thu, to 3am Fri & Sat, live music from 8pm; Line 2 to Hongik University, Exit 8) FREE With live jazz, bands and acoustic music, great Korean food (clam and tofu stew; apple barbecue pork) and beer (or bottles of berry *makgeolli*), this place, with views over a buzzing corner of Hongdae, makes for a good night, or at least a great start.

National Gugak Center TRADITIONAL MUSIC
(국립국악원 예악당; Map p46; 02-580 3300; www.gugak.go.kr; 2364 Nambusunhwan-ro; tickets from ₩10,000; 9am-6pm Tue-Sun; Line 3 to Nambu Bus Terminal, Exit 5) Traditional Korean classical and folk music and dance are performed, preserved and taught at this centre, which is home to the Court Music Orchestra, the Folk Music Group, Dance Theater and

TICKETS

Interpark (http://ticket.interpark.com) Tickets for theatre, concerts and sporting events.

KTO Tourist Information Center (p91) Sells daily discount tickets for shows.

Daehangno Information Center (Map p52; Marronnier Park, 104 Daehak-ro; 11am-8pm Tue-Sat, to 7pm Sun; Line 4 to Hyehwa, Exit 2) Tickets for shows staged at the dozens of venues around Daehangno.

Contemporary Gugak Orchestra. The main theatre, Yeak-dang, puts on an ever-changing program by leading performers every Saturday, usually at 3pm.

Jump PERFORMING ARTS
(Map p62; 02-722 3995; www.hijump.co.kr; 22 Jeong-dong; tickets ₩40,000-60,000; hours vary; Line 5 to Gwanghwamun, Exit 6) A long-running comedy performance that features a wacky Korean family all crazy about martial arts. The nonverbal show mixes Korean taekwondo and *taekkyeon* with slapstick and doesn't require any Korean-language knowledge.

Shopping

Gwanghwamun & Jongno-gu

★ Kyobo Bookshop BOOKS, MUSIC
(Map p52; 02-3973 5100; www.kyobobook.co.kr; B1, Kyobo Bldg, 1 Jong-ro; 9.30am-10pm; Line 5 to Gwanghwamun, Exit 4) Kyobo's flagship branch sells a wide range of English-language books and magazines (you'll find them on the left from the main entrance), as well as stationery, electronics and CDs and DVDs in its excellent Hottracks (www.hottracks.co.kr) giftware section.

Insa-dong Maru ARTS & CRAFTS
(인사동마루; Map p81; 02-2223 2500; www.insadongmaru.co.kr; 35-4 6 Insa-dong-gil; shops 10.30am-8.30pm, cafes & restaurants to 10pm; Line 3 to Anguk, Exit 6) Around 60 different Korean designer shops selling crafts, fashion and homewares are gathered at this slick complex. Spread over several levels, the complex surrounds a central rest area where a piano invites passers-by to give impromptu concerts.

KCDF Gallery ARTS & CRAFTS
(Map p81; 02-736 0088; www.kcdf.kr; 44 Insa-dong gil; 10am-8.30pm; Line 3 to Anguk, Exit 6) The Korean Craft and Design Foundation's gallery showcases some of the finest locally made products including woodwork, pottery and jewellery. It's the ideal place to find a unique, sophisticated gift or souvenir.

Jilkyungyee FASHION & ACCESSORIES
(질경이; Map p81; 02-7325606; www.jilkyungyee.co.kr; 14-1 Insa-dong; 9am-6pm; Line 3 to Anguk, Exit 6) Lee Ki-Yeon trained as an artist in the late 1970s when she became interested in natural dyeing and traditional Korean fashion. She went on to establish this fashion brand selling tastefully designed *hanbok* (traditional), everyday and special-occasion clothing for both sexes. The styles are easy to wear and are often more contemporary in their design than you'll find elsewhere.

Kukjae Embroidery ARTS & CRAFTS
(Map p81; 02-732 0830; www.suyeh.co.kr; 41 Insa-dong-gil; 10am-8.30pm; Line 3 to Anguk, Exit 6) Exquisite traditional embroidery pieces, including handbags, cushions and pillows, from Kukjae have often been presented as official gifts by Korean presidents to visiting dignitaries. You'll also find *bojagi* patchwork cloths here used for gift wrapping or display.

Myeong-dong & Jung-gu

★ Shinsegae DEPARTMENT STORE
(신세계백화점; Map p62; 02-2026 9000; www.shinsegae.com; 63 Sogong-ro; 10.30am-8pm; Line 4 to Hoehyeon, Exit 7) Wrap yourself in luxury inside the Seoul equivalent of Harrods. It's split over two buildings, the older part based in a gorgeous 1930 colonial building that was Seoul's first department store, Mitsukoshi. Check out local designer fashion labels, and also the opulent supermarket in the basement with a food court.

Stylenanda Pink Hotel FASHION & ACCESSORIES
(스타일난다 핑크호텔; Map p62; 02-752 4546; www.stylenanda.com; 37-8, Myeong-dong 8-gil; 11am-11pm; ; Line 4 to Myeongdong, Exit 7) One of the most popular brands for affordable, young women's casual fashion, Stylenanda's flagship store is especially notable for its pink design. The 1st floor showcases its make-up brand, 3CE, with a full make-up bar. The 5th floor has a swimming-pool-themed cafe and, during the summer, there's a rooftop cafe with a great view of the neighbourhood.

K-POP AND K-INDIE

From the glossy, manufactured K-Pop industry to the underground indie scene, Seoul offers an eclectic assortment of live music.

Hongdae is *the* place for Seoul's K-Indie scene, where intimate venues host local indie, punk, metal and hip-hop acts. Call in to the **XIndie Ticket Lounge** (Map p78; ☎02-322 2218; http://xindieticket.kr; 41-1 Eoulmadang-ro; ⏲1-9pm Tue-Sun; Ⓢ Line 6 to Sangsu, Exit 1) for booking and information on the music scene.

Concerts by visiting megastars are held at arena venues such as **YES 24 Live Hall** (Map p46; www.yes24livehall.com; 20 Gucheonmyeon-ro; Ⓢ Line 5 to Gwangnaru, Exit 2), while touring bands and K-Pop acts often perform at the Olympic Stadium or Gymnastic Stadium at Olympic Park (p57).

The chilled-out **Greenplugged festival** (www.gpsfestival.com; Nanji Hangang Park; ₩119,000; ⏲May) features mostly established and up-and-coming Korean indie, folk and pop bands. Or just book a room at Kpopstay (p63) to be surrounded by K-glam 24/7. Other music-related sights and venues include the following:

K-Star Road (Hallyu Star Ave; Map p84; Apgujeong Rodeo St; ⏲24hr; Ⓢ Bundang Line to Apgujeongrodeo, Exit 7) FREE Gangnam's 'Hallyuwood Walk of Fame' pays homage to K-Pop stars.

K-Wave Experience (Map p84; 2nd fl, Gangnam Tourist Information Center, 161 Apgujeong-ro; ⏲10am-7pm; Ⓢ Line 3 to Apgujeong, Exit 6) FREE Live your K-Pop fantasies with a full makeover to transform you into a star.

SMTown coexartium (Map p88; www.smtownland.com; 513 Yeongdong-daero; ⏲11am-10pm) FREE Interactive shrine to K-Pop with a photo hall full of real props, hologram museum and augmented reality concerts.

DGBD (디지비디; Map p78; ☎02-322 3792; http://cafe.daum.net/dgbd; 23 Jandari-ro; ₩10,000; ⏲8-11pm; Ⓢ Line 2 or 6 to Hapjeong, Exit 3) K-Indie bands like Crying Nut came into the spotlight at this legendary live-music venue.

Indie Art-Hall GONG (Map p46; ☎02-2632 8848; www.gongcraft.net; 30 Seonyuseo-ro 30-gil; Ⓢ Line 5 to Yangpyeong, Exit 2) Steel factory turned art space with live gigs by K-Indie rockers.

Primera COSMETICS

(Map p62; www.primera.co.kr; 22 Myeongdong 4-gil; ⏲10am-10pm; Ⓢ Line 4 to Myeongdong, Exit 5) The flagship store of this Korean cosmetics brand specialises in organic skin products and essential oils using germinated sprouts.

Western Seoul

★**Free Market** GIFTS & SOUVENIRS

(Map p78; www.freemarket.or.kr; Hongdae Playground, 19-3 Wausan-ro 21-gil; ⏲1-6pm Sat Mar-Nov; Ⓢ Line 2 to Hongik University, Exit 9) Going strong since 2002, this weekly market helps to propel talented young creatives in to big-time retail. It's a great opportunity to meet the crafters and buy a unique souvenir, be it a hand-painted cap, a colourful piece of jewellery or a leather bag. A good line-up of singers and bands plays all afternoon too.

Gentle Monster FASHION & ACCESSORIES

(Map p78; www.gentlemonster.com; 48 Dongmak-ro 7-gil; ⏲noon-9pm; Ⓢ Line 2 or 6 to Hapjeong, Exit 3) Sunglasses at night is *the* Hongdae look and this hip place is where to pick up the edgiest of shades and frames as worn by K-Popsters and TV stars. Imaginative and fun art installations change roughly every 25 days on the ground floor.

D-Cube City MALL

(Map p46; www.dcubecity.com; Kyungin-ro; ⏲shops 11am-9.30pm Mon-Fri, to 10pm Sat & Sun; Ⓢ Line 1 or 2 to Sindorim, Exit 1) Seoul's shopping malls hardly come any more stylish than this one in the previously industrial hub of Guro. The interior spaces surround a waterfall that cascades down seven floors, and plenty of terraces allow relaxing in fine weather. There are good restaurants and a superbly designed Korean food court in the basement.

Veronica Effect BOOKS

(베로니카 이펙트; Map p78; ☎02-6273 2748; www.veronicaeffect.com; 10 Eoulmadang-ro 2-gil; ⏲11.30am-9pm Mon-Sat; Ⓢ Line 6 to Sangsu, Exit 4)

Jamsil

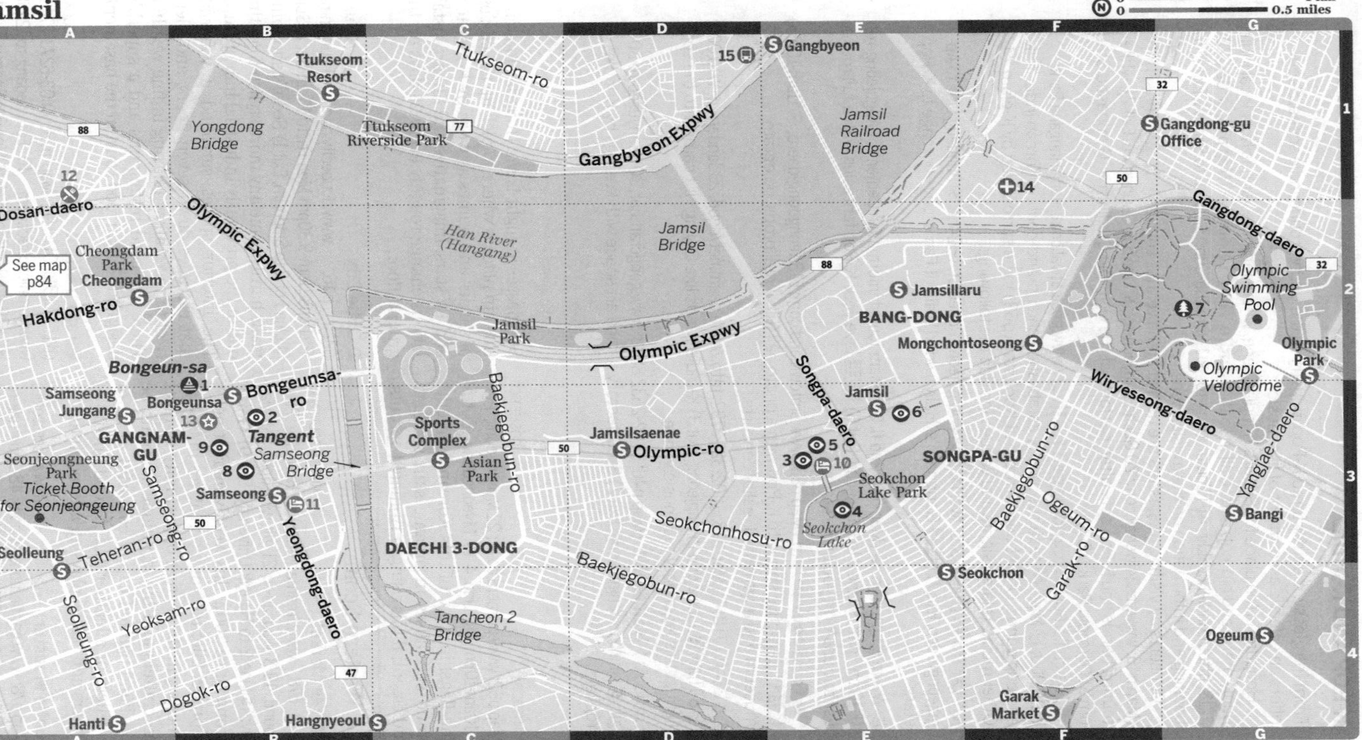
Jamsil
1 km
0.5 miles
Ttukseom Resort
Ttukseom-ro
15
Gangbyeon
Yongdong Bridge
Ttukseom Riverside Park
77
Gangbyeon Expwy
Jamsil Railroad Bridge
Gangdong-gu Office
32
88
12
Dosan-daero
Olympic Expwy
Han River (Hangang)
Jamsil Bridge
50
14
Gangdong-daero
See map p84
Cheongdam Park
Cheongdam
Hakdong-ro
Jamsillaru
Olympic Swimming Pool
BANG-DONG
7
Jamsil Park
Olympic Expwy
Mongchontoseong
Olympic Park
Bongeun-sa
Olympic Velodrome
1
Bongeunsa-ro
Samseong Jungang
Bongeunsa
2
Baekjegobun-ro
Jamsil
6
Wiryeseong-daero
Songpa-daero
13
Sports Complex
GANGNAM-GU
Tangent
Jamsilsaenae
Olympic-ro
9
Samseong Bridge
5
SONGPA-GU
Seonjeongneung Park
8
Asian Park
3
10
Seokchon Lake Park
Baekjegobun-ro
Yangjae-daero
Ticket Booth for Seonjeongeung
Samseong
11
4
Bangi
Samseong-ro
Seokchonhosu-ro
Seokchon Lake
Ogeum-ro
DAECHI 3-DONG
Seolleung
Teheran-ro
Yeongdong-daero
Baekjegobun-ro
Seokchon
Garak-ro
Seolleung-ro
Yeoksam-ro
Tancheon 2 Bridge
Ogeum
47
Dogok-ro
Garak Market
Hanti
Hangnyeoul

Jamsil

Top Sights
1 Bongeun-sa B2
2 Tangent B3

Sights
3 Lotte World E3
4 Lotte World Adventure & Magic Island E3
5 Lotte World Folk Museum E3
6 Lotte World Tower E3
7 Olympic Park G2
8 SMTown coexartium B3
9 Starfield Library B3

Activities, Courses & Tours
Lotte World Ice Skating Rink .... (see 3)

Sleeping
10 Lotte Hotel World E3
11 Park Hyatt Seoul B3

Eating
12 Jilhal Bros A1

Entertainment
13 Megabox COEX B3

Shopping
COEX Mall .... (see 9)
Lab 5 .... (see 9)
Lotte World Mall .... (see 6)

Information
14 Asan Medical Center F1

Transport
CALT .... (see 9)
15 Dong-Seoul Bus Terminal D1

This independent bookshop specialises in art books, graphic novels, vintage foreign books and works by local artists. Yu Seung-bo, who runs the shop with his partner Kim Hye-mi, is an artist who also teaches bookmaking and illustration classes on-site. The vintage books can be pricey, but there are plenty of very affordable books by local artists too.

GRDS SHOES
(그라더스; Map p78; 02-332 0477; www.grds.com; 46 Yeonhui-ro 1-gil; 1-9pm Tue-Sun; Line 2 to Hongik University, Exit 3) A young, local brand, GRDS combines comfortable Italian soles with sleek and modern Korean designs. At this offline location, it even displays cross-sections of its shoes to show how much of an emphasis it puts on comfort. Styles focus on simple lines and muted colours.

Itaewon & Yongsan-gu

Yongsan Crafts Museum ARTS & CRAFTS
(Map p73; 02-2199 6180; 274 Itaewon-ro; 10am-7pm Tue-Sun; Line 6 to Hangangjin, Exit 3) A fantastic place to buy top-quality traditional Korean handicrafts like *hanji* (Korean paper) ornaments and baskets, *najeon* (inlaid lacquerware), porcelain tea sets, *tal* (masks) and *bangjja* (bronzeware). Even if you're not buying, the museum-like shop floor makes it well worth a browse. You can find craft workshops on the 2nd floor.

Vinyl & Plastic MUSIC
(Map p73; 02-2014 7800; 248 Itaewon-ro; noon-9pm, to 6pm Sun; ; Line 6 to Itaewon, Exit 3) Vinyl is alive and kicking at this warehouse-sized music shop that invites you to listen to the latest releases on a dozen or so turntables before buying. Opened by Hyundai Card, a Korean credit-card company, it also sells headphones and Bluetooth speakers. An upstairs cafe has digital jukeboxes on the tables and outdoor balcony seating.

Comme des Garcons FASHION & ACCESSORIES
(Map p73; 261 Itaewon-ro; 11am-8pm; Line 6 to Hangangjin, Exit 1) Uberstylish flagship boutique of the Japanese label. Take the lift to the 4th floor then work your way down through the mazelike corridors. Take a break at **Rose Bakery** (Map p73; 261 Itaewon-ro; dishes from ₩11,000; 10am-8pm;) on the ground floor.

Dongdaemun & Eastern Seoul

★ **su;py** CLOTHING
(Map p46; 02-6406 3388; www.supyrocks.com; 71 Seongsui-ro, Seongdong-gu; 11am-10pm Tue-Sun; Line 2 to Seongsu, Exit 3) See what's coming next in Korean fashion at this fabulously well-designed boutique, which offers streetwear, gifts and bags on the ground floor and more formal styles upstairs. Even if you're not buying, the shop design, especially upstairs, deserves your attention. There's also su;py cafe next door.

Seoul Yangnyeongsi Herb Medicine Market HEALTH & WELLNESS
(Map p46; www.seoulya.com; Jegi-dong; 9am-7pm; Line 1 to Jegi-dong, Exit 2) Also known

as Gyeongdong Market, Korea's biggest Asian medicine market runs back for several blocks from the traditional gate on the main road and includes thousands of clinics, retailers, wholesalers and medicine makers. If you're looking for a leaf, herb, bark, root, flower or mushroom to ease your ailment, it's bound to be here.

Dongdaemun Market MARKET

(동대문시장; Map p74; Dongdaemun; ⌚24hr Mon-Sat; Ⓢ Line 1 or 4 to Dongdaemun, Exit 8) The bargaining never stops at this colossal retail and wholesale cluster, best visited at night when local buyers come clamouring for deals. The labyrinthine market buildings comprise some 30,000 retailers; only serious shopaholics need apply. Head to the multilevel **Pyounghwa Clothing Market** (평화시장; ⌚7-10pm) for fashion and accessories (though don't expect haute couture), and the **Dongdaemun Shopping Complex** (⌚8am-7pm Mon-Sat) for a broader range of goods.

Seoul Folk Flea Market MARKET

(서울풍물시장; Map p46; 19-3 Cheonho-daero 4-gil, Dongdaemun-gu; ⌚10am-7pm, closed 2nd & 4th Tue of month; Ⓢ Line 1 or 2 to Sinseol-dong, Exit 6 or 10) You could kit out half the world's hipster cafes from the teetering stacks of dusty ornaments, table lamps, musical instruments and valve radios crammed inside this two-storey, canvas-tented market. You might also dig up some traditional Korean bric-a-brac like wooden masks and ink drawings. A cheap food court ladles up *sundubu jjigae* (tofu and kimchi stew) for ₩4000.

Gangnam & Southern Seoul

★**10 Corso Como Seoul** FASHION & ACCESSORIES

(Map p84; www.10corsocomo.co.kr; 416 Apgujeong-ro; ⌚11am-8pm, cafe to 11pm; Ⓢ Bundang Line to Apgujeongrodeo, Exit 3) Inspired by its shopping complex in Milan, this outpost of the fashion and lifestyle boutique is about as interesting as Gangnam retail can get. The blend of fashion, art and design includes several local designers and big-ticket global labels. There's also a brilliant selection of international books and CDs to browse, and a chic cafe for an espresso or glass of wine.

Lab 5 FASHION & ACCESSORIES

(Map p88; ☎02-551 5000; http://lfive.co.kr/lab5; COEX Mall, 513 Yeongdong-daero; ⌚10am-10pm; Ⓢ Line 2 to Samseong, COEX Exit) There's no need to root around Dongdaemun Market for the latest hot K-designers with this shop in the COEX Mall showcasing the designs of 100 rising stars, including participants of *Project Runway Korea*.

Steve J & Yoni P FASHION & ACCESSORIES

(Map p84; ☎070-7730 5467; www.stevejandyonip.com; 45 Gangnam-daero; ⌚11am-10pm; Ⓢ Line 3 to Sinsa, Exit 8) Collaborating on the superfashionable women's streetwear in this boutique are local designers Steve J and Yoni P. Their T-shirts, sweatshirts and colourful printed clobber are stocked by high-class boutiques around the world, but their flagship store is down this happening little street in Hannam-dong.

Lotte World Mall MALL

(Map p88; www.lwt.co.kr; 300 Olympic-ro; ⌚10.30am-10pm; Ⓢ Line 2 or 8 to Jamsil, Exit 1) At the base of Korea's **tallest building** (롯데월드타워, Seoul Sky; ☎02-3213 5000; adult/child ₩27,000/24,000; ⌚9.30am-11pm; Ⓟ 🚻) lies its largest shopping mall, comprising six floors of luxury and duty-free department stores, a mega cinema complex and a concert hall. There's also a department store at the nearby amusement park (p57).

COEX Mall MALL

(Map p88; ☎02-6002 5300; www.starfield.co.kr; 513 Yeongdong-daero; ⌚10am-10pm; Ⓢ Line 2 to Samseong, COEX Exit) One of Seoul's premier malls and the world's largest underground mall, the shiny COEX is a vast maze of department stores loaded with shops selling fashion, lifestyle, accessories and electronics, as well as the **Starfield Library** (☎02-6002 3031; ⌚10.30am-10pm), SMTown coexartium (p87) shrine to K-Pop and a **multiplex cinema** (www.megabox.co.kr; 524 Bongeunsa-ro; tickets ₩9000; ⌚7am-2am). It's also a launching point to the airport (p91), and has several hotels.

ℹ Information

DANGERS & ANNOYANCES

- Motorists can be impatient with pedestrians, so take extra care when crossing the road.
- Drunks in Seoul tend to be better behaved than elsewhere, so walking around at 3am shouldn't pose a problem. There's always an exception, of course, so it's best not to antagonise people who have been drinking.
- Police in full riot gear, carrying shields and batons, are a not-uncommon sight in central Seoul. Student, trade-union, anti-American, environmental and other protests can occasionally turn physical. Keep well out of the way of any confrontations.

DISCOUNT CARDS

Korea Pass (www.lottecard.co.kr/app/html/koreapass/IHKPAZZ_V100.jsp) A prepaid card providing discounts on a range of goods and services. It can be bought at Lotte Mart and 7-Eleven branches and the A'REX booth at Incheon Airport.

Discover Seoul Pass (www.discoverseoulpass.com) Available in 24-hour, 48-hour or 72-hour versions (₩39,900/55,000/70,000), it gets you free/discounted entry into dozens of attractions and works as a rechargeable transport card. Buy it from CU convenience stores at Incheon Airport, from Tourist Information Centers or online as a mobile app.

MEDICAL SERVICES

Asan Medical Center (Map p88; ☎02-3010 5100; http://eng.amc.seoul.kr; 88 Olympic-ro 43-gil; ⊙international clinic 8.30am-5.30pm Mon-Fri; Ⓢ Line 2 to Seongnae, Exit 1)

Severance Hospital (Map p46; ☎02-2228 5800; www.yuhs.or.kr; 50-1 Yonsei-ro; ⊙international clinic 9.30-11.30am & 2-4.30pm Mon-Fri, 9.30am-noon Sat; Ⓢ Line 2 to Sinchon, Exit 3)

Sudo Pharmacy (Map p81; ☎02-732 3336; 40 Insadong-gil, cnr Insadong 10-gil; ⊙8.30am-7.45pm Mon-Sat, noon-7pm Sun; Ⓢ Line 3 to Anguk, Exit 6)

SMOKING

It is forbidden to smoke in all bars, restaurants, hotels and public buildings, while walking along the street, or outside subway stations or bus stops. Generally, smokers duck into a side road or alleyway for a quick puff.

TOURIST INFORMATION

There are scores of tourist information booths around the city. In major tourist zones such as Insa-dong and Namdaemun Market, look for red-jacketed city tourist guides, who can also help with information in various languages.

The **KTO Tourist Information Center** (Map p62; ☎02-1330; www.visitkorea.or.kr; 2nd fl, 40 Cheonggyecheon-ro; ⊙9am-8pm; 🚻; Ⓢ Line 1 to Jonggak, Exit 5) is the best of Seoul's many tourist centres, offering knowledgeable staff, free internet, ample brochures and maps, and free experiences include trying on *hanbok*, and cooking and craft classes.

ℹ Getting There & Away

Most likely you'll arrive at Incheon International Airport. If you're travelling from within Korea, your arrival point could also be Gimpo International Airport, or Seoul or Yongsan train stations, or one of the long-distance bus stations. Ferries to Incheon, west of Seoul, connect the country with China. Flights, cars and tours can be booked online at www.lonelyplanet.com/bookings.

AIR

The main international gateway is **Incheon International Airport** (www.airport.kr), 52km west of central Seoul on the island of Yeongjong-do. Regularly ranked as one of the world's best airports, this top-class operation was enhanced even further in 2018 with the opening of Terminal 2 in time for the 2018 Winter Olympics.

Korean Air (www.koreanair.com), the nation's biggest airline, serving 123 countries worldwide, operates out of the new Terminal 2.

The bulk of domestic flights (and a handful of international routes) touch down at the more central Gimpo International Airport (p395), 18km west of the city centre.

Local airline **Air Busan** (☎02-1666 3060; www.airbusan.com) operates from here.

BOAT

Ferries (from ₩115,000, 12 to 24 hours) connect Incheon, west of Seoul, with a dozen port cities in China. To reach Incheon's port (ferries leave from Yeonan Pier or International Terminal 2), take subway Line 1 to Incheon station and then take a taxi (around ₩6000). Ferries to Japan leave from Busan (p182).

BUS

Most long-distances buses depart from **Seoul Express Bus Station** (Map p84; ☎02-536 6460-2; 194 Sinbanpo-ro; Ⓢ Line 3, 7 or 9 to Seoul Express Terminal). Regional services to the east may run from **Dong-Seoul Bus Terminal** (Map p88; ☎02-1688 5979; www.ti21.co.kr; 50 Gangbyeonnyeok-ro; Ⓢ Line 2 to Gangbyeon, Exit 4), while services to some destinations in the south go from **Nambu** (off Map p84; ☎02-521 8550; www.kobus.co.kr; 292 Hyoryeong-ro;

> ### ℹ LUGGAGE CHECK-IN
>
> If you're flying Korean Air, **Asiana** (☎02-2669 8000; www.flyasiana.com) or Jeju Air, you can check in your luggage and go through immigration at the **City Airport Terminal** (Map p62; www.arex.or.kr; Seoul Station; ⊙check-in 5.20am-7pm; Ⓢ Line 1 or 4 to Seoul Station) inside Seoul Station, then hop on the A'REX train to Gimpo or Incheon. If you're south of the river, a similar service operates from **CALT** (City Airport; Map p88; ☎02-551 0077; www.calt.co.kr; COEX Mall, 22 Teheran-ro 87-gil; 1-way ₩15,000; ⊙bus 4.15am-9.30pm; Ⓢ Line 2 to Samseong, Exit 5), which allows check-ins for most major airlines, before transferring by limousine bus to Incheon (₩16,000, 65 minutes) or Gimpo (₩7500, 45 minutes) airports.

S Line 3 to Nambu Bus Terminal, Exit 5), in Gangnam.

TRAIN

Most trains leave from Seoul Station, which has high-speed (KTX) and local services to many parts of the country. Yongsan Station handles connections to the southern provinces, Cheongnyangni Station connections east and, Yeongdeungpo Station south of the river; services heading south.

For current fares and detailed schedules, visit the website of the Korea National Railroad (www.letskorail.com).

Getting Around

TO/FROM INCHEON INTERNATIONAL AIRPORT

City limousine buses run to destinations around Seoul (₩9000 to ₩15,000, 5.30am to 10pm, every 10 to 30 minutes). Deluxe **KAL limousine buses** (www.kallimousine.com; ₩14,000) drop passengers at major hotels.

Regular metered taxis charge around ₩60,000 to ₩80,000 for the 70-minute journey to central Seoul. From midnight to 4am regular taxis charge 20% extra.

A'REX Airport Express (Airport Railroad Express; www.arex.or.kr; express train 1-way adult/child ₩9000/7000, all-stop train basic 1-way adult ₩4150, to terminal 2 ₩4950) trains run from the airport to Seoul Station from 5.20am to 11.45pm. Express trains take 43 to 48 minutes and depart every 30 minutes. All-stop trains take an hour.

TO/FROM GIMPO INTERNATIONAL AIRPORT

City/KAL limousine buses run every 10 minutes to central Seoul (from ₩5000/7000, around 40 minutes, depending on traffic).

Subway lines 5 and 9 connect the airport with the city (₩1450, 35 minutes).

A taxi costs around ₩35,000 to the city centre and takes from 40 minutes to an hour.

A'REX trains run to Seoul station (₩1300, 15 minutes).

BICYCLE

The Seoul Bike bicycle-sharing scheme can be used by visitors. The green-and-white bikes and their similarly coloured docking stations can be found at over 150 locations across the city.

To use, first purchase a voucher at www.bikeseoul.com to obtain an unlock code, which is then keyed in on the bike itself (selecting the 'Foreign Tourist' option).

Bicycles can also be rented at several parks along the Han River, including on Yeouido, Ttukseom Resort, Seoul Forest Park and Olympic Park. Rental is around ₩3000 per hour, and you'll need to leave some form of ID as a deposit.

PUBLIC TRANSPORT

Bus, subway, taxi and train fares can all be paid using the rechargeable touch-and-go T-Money card (also called CITYPASS+), which gives you a ₩100 discount per trip and means that you can connect subway and bus as a single fare, providing less than 30 minutes has elapsed between transfer. The card can be bought for a nonrefundable ₩2500 (and reloaded with credit) from machines at most subway stations, as well as bus kiosks and convenience stores displaying the T-Money logo.

Bus

Seoul has a comprehensive and reasonably priced bus system (http://bus.go.kr) that runs from 5.30am to midnight. Some bus stops have bus route maps in English, and most buses have their major destinations written in English on the outside and a taped announcement of the names of each stop in English, but few bus drivers understand English.

Red buses Long-distance express buses that go to the outer suburbs with few stops.

Green buses These link subways within a district.

Blue buses All-stop buses going to outer suburbs.

Yellow buses Short-haul buses that circle small districts.

Subway

Seoul has an excellent, user-friendly subway system, which connects up with destinations well beyond the city borders, including Suwon and Incheon. The minimum fare of ₩1350 (₩1250 with a T-Money card) takes you up to 12km, and the system runs from 5.30am to midnight.

Most subway stations have lifts or stair lifts for wheelchairs, and escalators are common.

Taxi

Flagfall for regular orange- or grey-coloured taxis for 2km is ₩3000 and rises ₩100 for every 144m or 35 seconds after that if the taxi is travelling below 15km/h. A 20% surcharge is levied between midnight and 4am. Deluxe taxis are black and cost ₩5000 for the first 3km and ₩200 for every 164m or 39 seconds, but they don't have a late-night surcharge.

Few taxi drivers speak English; have your destination written down in Korean. **International Taxi** (☎02-1644 2255; www.intltaxi.co.kr) has English-speaking drivers; reserve in advance for 20% extra.

Around Seoul

Includes ➡

Best Places to Eat

- Sinpo Market (p111)
- Samchi St (p110)
- Yeonpo Galbi (p103)
- Pungmi (p111)

Best Places to Stay

- Hotel Dono (p103)
- Seopori Hotel (p114)
- Jeondeung-sa Temple (p117)
- Hotel Atti (p110)

Why Go?

Seoul's staggeringly efficient mass transit system makes its surrounding areas incredibly accessible, whether for easy day trips or longer excursions. And despite such proximity, cities such as Suwon, the provincial capital of Gyeonggi-do with its World Heritage–listed fortress, or Incheon with its intriguing multicultural background, have a vibe all their own.

It's just as easy to get back to nature around Seoul, too. The well-trodden mountain trails of Bukhansan National Park may be only a subway ride away from the city, but they are a world away in atmosphere. And further north, the most unlikely nature reserve of all, the long-depopulated Demilitarized Zone (DMZ), is the region's grimly voyeuristic tourist drawcard. Throw into the mix the dreamy sweep of West Sea islands easily reached by ferry from Incheon, and one of the world's great megacities just got even bigger.

When to Go

Incheon

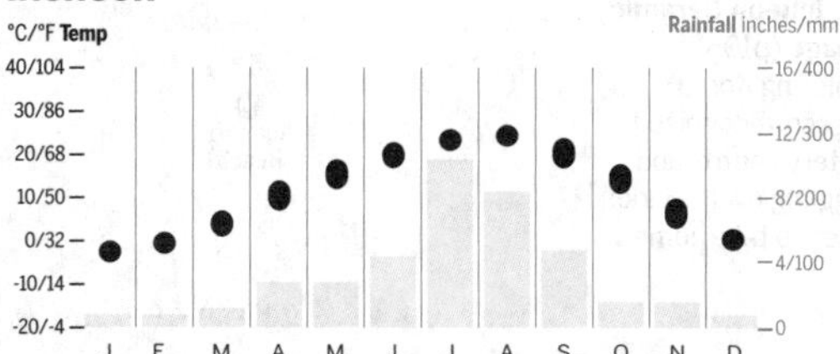

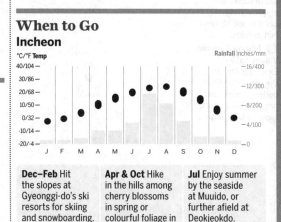

Dec–Feb Hit the slopes at Gyeonggi-do's ski resorts for skiing and snowboarding.

Apr & Oct Hike in the hills among cherry blossoms in spring or colourful foliage in autumn.

Jul Enjoy summer by the seaside at Muuido, or further afield at Deokjeokdo.

Around Seoul Highlights

1. **DMZ** (p96) Peeking into North Korea for a bizarre terror-meets-tourism experience.
2. **Incheon** (p107) Uncovering Korea's concession-era past with a stroll through Chinatown and the Old Port area.
3. **Suwon** (p99) Marching along the World Heritage–listed fortress walls in Gyeonggi-do's capital city.
4. **Bukhansan National Park** (p99) Joining Seoul's army of retiree walkers and hiking up granite peaks to stunning mountainside temples.
5. **Deokjeokdo** (p114) Catching a ferry out to this laid-back West Sea island and its seriously stunning beach.
6. **Goryeogungji Palace** (p115) Starting your explorations of fascinating Ganghwado at these hilltop ruins.
7. **Icheon Ceramic Village** (p105) Exploring Korea's Unesco-recognised pottery centre, and haggling over celadon vases to take home.

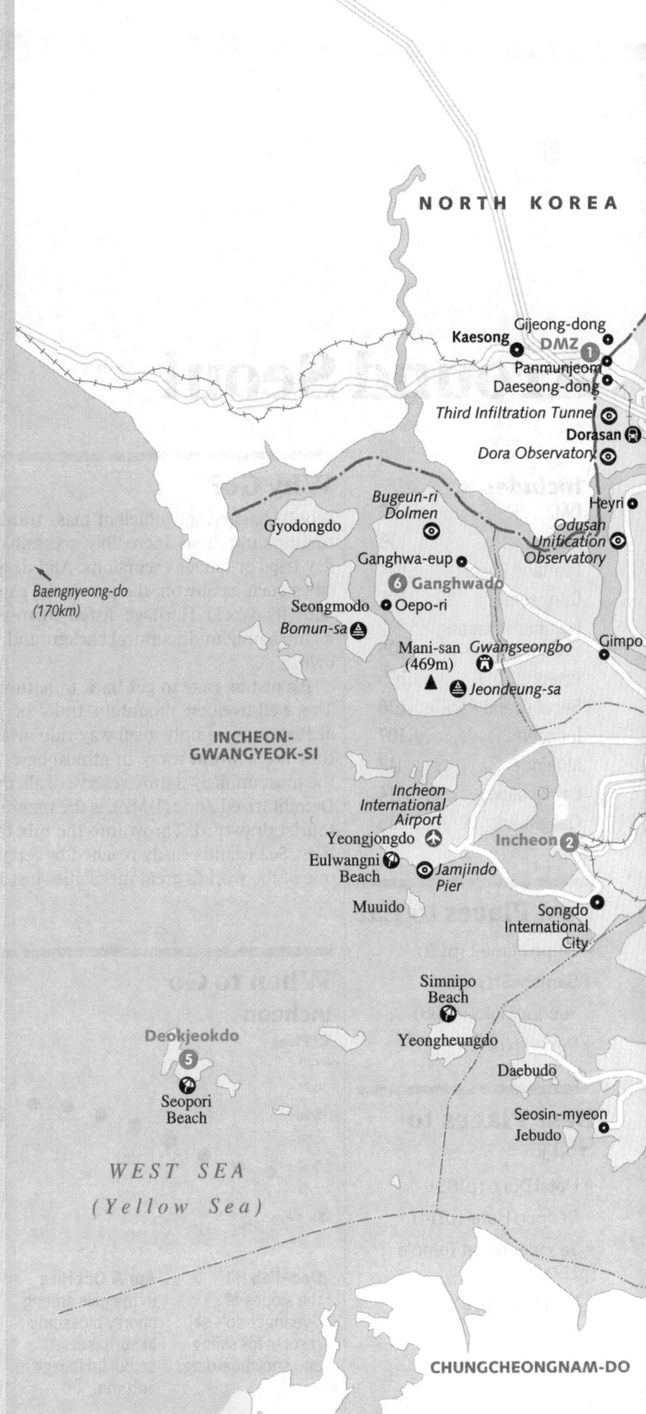

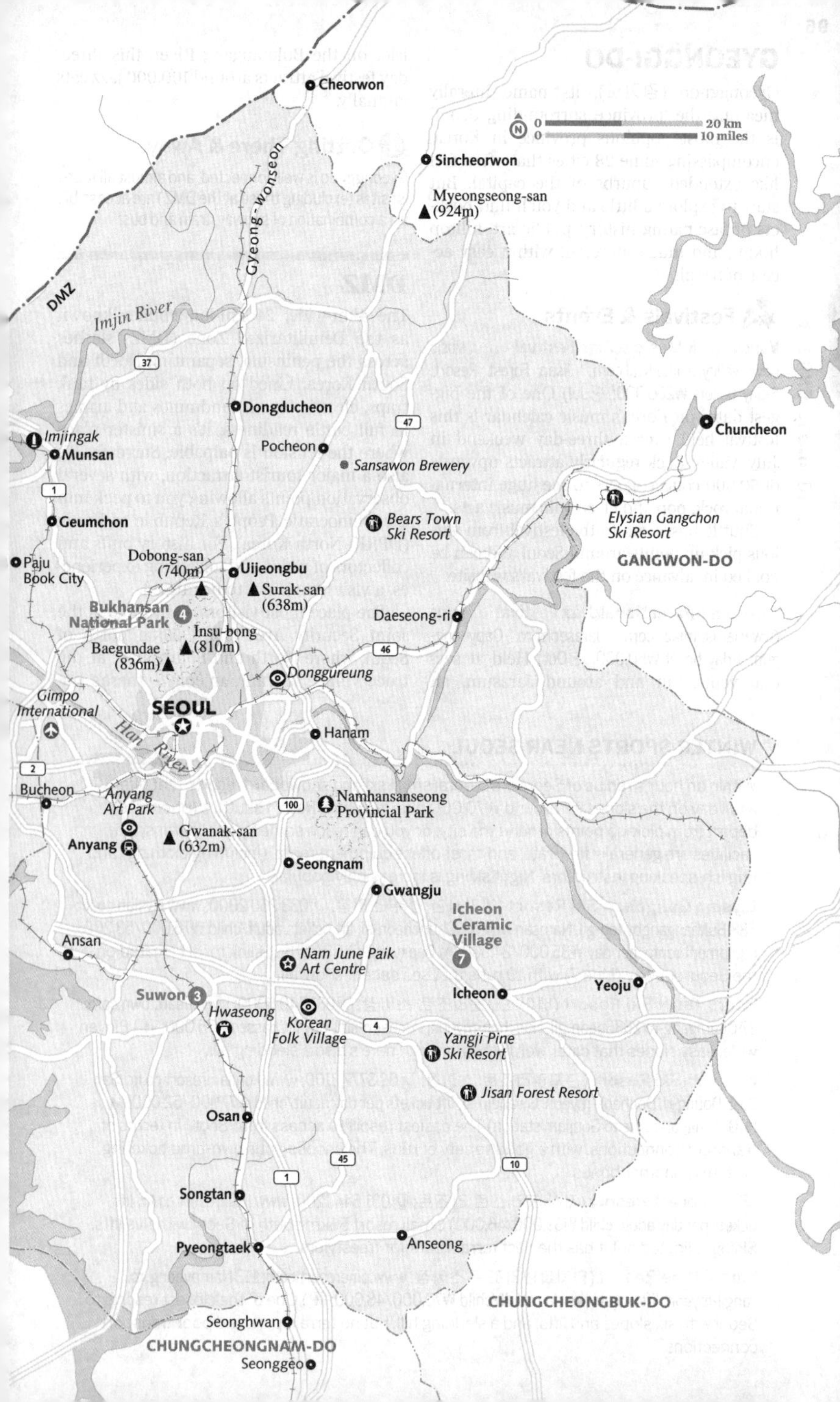

0 20 km
0 10 miles
Cheorwon
Sincheorwon
Myeongseong-san
(924m)
Gyeong-wonseon
DMZ
Imjin River
37
Dongducheon
47
Chuncheon
Imjingak
Munsan
Pocheon
Sansawon Brewery
1
Geumchon
Bears Town
Ski Resort
Elysian Gangchon
Ski Resort
Paju
Book City
Dobong-san
(740m)
Uijeongbu
Surak-san
(638m)
GANGWON-DO
Bukhansan
National Park
4
Insu-bong
(810m)
Daeseong-ri
Baegundae
(836m)
46
Donggureung
Gimpo
International
SEOUL
Han
River
Hanam
2
Bucheon
Anyang
Art Park
100
Namhansanseong
Provincial Park
Anyang
Gwanak-san
(632m)
Seongnam
Gwangju
Icheon
Ceramic
Village
7
Ansan
Nam June Paik
Art Centre
Suwon
3
Icheon
Yeoju
Hwaseong
Korean
Folk Village
4
Yangji Pine
Ski Resort
Jisan Forest Resort
Osan
45
10
1
Songtan
Anseong
Pyeongtaek
CHUNGCHEONGBUK-DO
Seonghwan
CHUNGCHEONGNAM-DO
Seonggeo

GYEONGGI-DO

Gyeonggi-do (경기도), its name literally meaning the 'province surrounding Seoul', is the most populous province in Korea, encompassing some 28 cities that often feel like extended suburbs of the capital. But start to explore a little and you'll find pockets of fascinating history, public art, hilltop hiking and much more, all within easy access of Seoul.

Festivals & Events

Valley Rock Music & Arts Festival MUSIC
(www.valleyrockfestival.com; Jisan Forest Resort; 3-day tickets ₩260,000; ⏲Jul) One of the biggest dates on Korea's music calendar is this festival held over a three-day weekend in July. Valley Rock regularly attracts upwards of 50,000 concert-goers to see huge international rock, pop and electronic music acts.

Shuttle buses run to the festival from various pick-up points around Seoul and can be booked in advance on the festival's website.

Jarasum International Jazz Festival MUSIC
(www.jarasumjazz.com; Jaraseom-ro, Gapyeong-gun; 1-day ticket ₩50,000; ⏲Oct) Held at several venues in and around Jarasum, an islet on the Bukhangang River, this three-day festival attracts around 100,000 jazz cats annually.

Getting There & Away

Gyeonggi-do is well connected, and almost all tourist sites (excluding those at the DMZ) are accessible via a combination of subway, train and bus.

DMZ

The 4km-wide, 240km-long buffer known as the Demilitarized Zone (DMZ) slashes across the peninsula, separating North and South Korea. Lined on both sides by tank traps, electric fences, landmines and armies in full battle readiness, it's a sinister place where the tension is palpable. Surreally, it's also a major tourist attraction, with several observation points allowing you to peek into the Democratic People's Republic of Korea (DPRK; North Korea). For history buffs and collectors of weird and unsettling experiences, a visit here is not to be missed.

The place most visitors want to go is the Joint Security Area (JSA), 55km north of Seoul, where North and South meet at the truce village of Panmunjeom – there's no-

WINTER SPORTS NEAR SEOUL

Within an hour's radius of Seoul are several small ski and snowboard resorts that offer a full day on the slopes for around ₩70,000 plus gear hire. Resort shuttles (often free) depart from pick-up points around the city, or you can reach some by public transport. Facilities are generally first-rate, and most offer equipment rental (including clothing) and English-speaking instructors. Night skiing is increasingly popular.

Elysian Gangchon Ski Resort (엘리시안 강촌 스키장; ☎033 260 2000; www.elysian.co.kr; 688 Bukhangangbyeon-gil, Namsan-myeon, Chuncheon-si; lift tickets adult/child ₩76,000/53,200, equipment rental per day ₩35,000/24,500; MBaekyang-ri) Small-but-slick resort located on the Seoul subway (Line 7) with 10 runs that see decent snowfall.

Bears Town Ski Resort (베어스타운리조트 스키장; ☎031 540 5000; www.bearstown.com; 27 Geumgang-ro 2536beon-gil, Naechon-myeon, Pocheon-si; 1-day lift passes ₩75,000; 👪) Eleven wide, easy slopes that cater well for beginners. There's also a sledding hill.

Konjiam Ski Resort (곤지암리조트 스키장; ☎02 3777 2100; www.konjiamresort.co.kr; San 23-1, Doung-ri, Docheok-myeon, Gwangju-si; lift tickets per day adult/child ₩77,000/52,000; 👪; SGyeonggang Line to Gonjiam station) The easiest resort to access from Seoul in terms of transport connections, with a good variety of runs. The choose-your-own-time ticketing system is another bonus.

Jisan Forest Resort (지산 포레스트 리조트; ☎031 644 1200; www.jisanresort.co.kr; lift tickets per day adult/child ₩69,000/46,000) Small resort 56km south of Seoul with five lifts. Skiing is limited but it has the best terrain park for freestylers.

Yangji Pine Resort (양지파인리조트 스키장; www.pineresort.com; 112 Nampyeong-ro, Yangji-myeon; lift tickets per day adult/child ₩70,000/48,000; 👪) One of the closest resorts to Seoul with six slopes and lifts, and a sledding hill, but no terrain park and poor transport connections.

LOCAL KNOWLEDGE

LIVING INSIDE THE DMZ

The 1953 *Korean Armistice Agreement* created two villages in the DMZ. On the south side, less than 1km from Panmunjeom, is Daeseong-dong (대성동 or 'Freedom Village'), where around 200 people live in modern houses with high-speed internet connections and earn a tax-free annual income of more than US$80,000 from their 7-hectare farms. There's an 11pm curfew and headcount, and soldiers stand guard while the villagers work in the rice fields or tend their ginseng plants.

On the North Korean side of the line is Gijeong-dong (기정동). The North translates this as 'Peace Village', but the South calls it Propaganda Village because virtually all the buildings are believed to be empty or just facades – the lights all come on and go off here at the same time. The village's primary feature is a 160m-high tower flying a flag that weighs nearly 300kg, markedly larger than the one on the South Korean side. It's believed that some workers from the Kaesong Industrial Complex (defunct at time of research) were living in Gijeong-dong.

Both villages occasionally blast the other with propaganda from loudspeakers, but these were silenced in April 2018 days before the two sides held their historic summit at the DMZ.

where else in South Korea where you can get so close to DPRK soldiers without being arrested or fired at.

Sights

Joint Security Area AREA

(JSA, Panmunjeom) Unquestionably the highlight of any trip to the DMZ is the Joint Security Area (JSA) at Panmunjeom. An improbable tourist destination, it's here where the infamous Military Demarcation Line separates South and North Korea. Soldiers from both sides often stand metres apart eyeballing one another from their respective sides of the blue-painted UN buildings. You'll be taken inside the meeting room – where the 1953 truce was signed – the only place where you can safely walk into North Korea.

Tours kick off with a briefing by US or Republic of Korea (ROK, South Korea) soldier guides at Camp Bonifas, the joint US–ROK army camp just outside the DMZ, before being transferred to another bus to the JSA.

Within the blue conference room at the JSA, where official meetings are still sometimes held, microphones on the tables constantly record everything said, while ROK soldiers stand guard inside and out in a modified taekwondo stance – an essential photo op. Their North Korean counterparts keep a steady watch, usually, but not always, from a distance.

Though your tour will be a quiet one, the soldier guide will remind you that this frontier is no stranger to violent incidents. One of the most notorious was in 1976 when two US soldiers were hacked to death with axes by North Korean soldiers after the former tried to chop down a tree obstructing the view from a watchtower. Camp Bonifas, the joint US–ROK army camp just outside the DMZ, is named after one of the slain soldiers.

Back on the bus you'll be taken to one of Panmunjeom's lookout posts from where you can see the two villages within the DMZ: Daeseong-dong in the South and Gijeong-dong in the North. You'll also see the Bridge of No Return where POW exchange took place following the signing of Armistice Agreement in 1953. Ironically, the forested surrounds here, long since abandoned, are some of the most ecologically pristine in Korea, and are even thought to be home to the Siberian tiger.

Third Infiltration Tunnel TUNNEL

(제3땅굴; ⌚9am-5pm Tue-Sun) Since 1974, four tunnels have been found running under the DMZ, dug by the North Koreans so that their army could launch a surprise attack. Walking along 265m of this 73m-deep tunnel is not for the claustrophobic or the tall: creeping hunched over, you'll realise why visitors get issued hard hats. The guide will point out how the North Koreans painted the rocks black so they might claim it was a coal mine.

Dora Observatory OBSERVATORY

(binoculars ₩500; ⌚10am-5pm Tue-Sun) Peer through binoculars for a voyeuristic glimpse into the Democratic People's Republic of Korea (DPRK; North Korea). On a clear day you can make out Kaesong city and Kaesong

Industrial Complex, where for a time cheap North Korean labourers were employed by South Korean conglomerates. You'll also spot the 160m-high North Korean flag in Gijeong-dong, facing South Korea's paltry 98m erection.

Dorasan Train Station LANDMARK
(도라산역; ₩500) Awaiting the next departure to Pyongyang (and onward trans-Eurasian intercontinental travel), Dorasan train station stands as a symbol of hope for the eventual reunification of the two Koreas. The shiny new international customs facilities built in 2002 remain unused.

Added in 2015, the Dorasan Unification Platform has an optimistic exhibition on German reunification that's housed in an old train carriage, and a clock counting the hours since the Korean peninsula has been officially divided.

Imjingak MEMORIAL
FREE This park is dedicated to the 10 million South Koreans separated from their families when the peninsula was divided postwar. Also here is the Freedom Bridge, connecting North and South, where 13,000 POWs were exchanged in 1953, plus a steam train derailed during the war.

Dorasan Peace Park PARK
This mildly diverting park has a couple of modern Korean tanks, some deer, an outdoor photo display and a few saplings called, groovily, the Paul McCartney Beatles Forest.

Tours

The only way to visit the DMZ is on either a coach or train tour. For an organised bus tour with an English-speaking guide, prices vary from ₩70,000 to ₩135,000, depending on the length of the tour, and whether the JSA (p97) and lunch are included.

Koridoor Tours ADVENTURE
(02 795 3028; www.koridoor.co.kr; ₩96,600; office 8am-5pm Mon-Sat; S Line 1 to Namyeong, Exit 2) Run by the USO, the US army's social and entertainment organisation, these tours to the DMZ have long been regarded as one of the best. Try to book at least a month in advance. Lunch isn't included.

Panmunjom Travel Centre ADVENTURE
(Map p62; 02 771 5593; http://panmunjomtour.com; Koreana Hotel, 9th fl, Office B/D; tours ₩77,000-130,000) A reputable company with knowledgeable guides, and notable for having a North Korean defector who sometimes (but not always) comes along to answer your questions. Prices include lunch.

Getting There & Away

The only way into this heavily restricted area is on an organised tour, either by coach or the DMZ train from Seoul station.

To visit the JSA or ride the DMZ train you'll need to bring your passport. Note citizens of certain countries are not permitted to enter the JSA. There are also strict dress and behavioural codes; usually collared shirts for men, and no ripped jeans, revealing clothing or open-toed shoes. Alcohol consumption is also prohibited. Only children over 10 years are permitted.

VISITING THE DMZ BY TRAIN

A fun and cheap way to tour the DMZ (minus the JSA) is to ride the frankly bizarre DMZ train operated by Korail, which trundles out of Seoul Station at 10.15am Wednesday to Sunday on its way to Dorasan, the last station before North Korea. With its carriages emblazoned with pink flowers and love hearts, you could almost be going to Pyongyang Disneyland, not one of the most fiercely guarded frontiers on the planet.

It takes a leisurely 1½ hours to reach the DMZ, during which time you can buy beer and crisps from the train kiosk and look at a display of Korean war photographs. Crossing the heavily fortified Imjin River, you'll pass the remains of a bridge destroyed in the Korean War before arriving at Imjingang station for a passport check. Then it's the final leg to Dorasan, where you transfer to coaches to begin a tour that includes Dora Observatory (p97), Dorasan Peace Park and the Third Infiltration Tunnel (p97).

The DMZ train tour (₩31,000) should be booked at least one day in advance from the Seoul Travel Guide Centre inside Seoul station. It's also possible to book just the train on the Korail website (www.letskorail.com), but you'll still need to pay for the tour and a return ticket on board the train if you want to get further than Imjingang station. Passports are a must.

WORTH A TRIP

BUKHANSAN NATIONAL PARK

Sweeping mountaintop vistas, maple leaves, rushing streams and remote temples draw more than 5 million hikers and rock climbers annually to the granite-peak-studded **Bukhansan National Park** (북한산 국립공원; ☎031 873 2791; http://english.knps.or.kr; Ⓢ Line 1 to Dobongsan or Mangwolsa) FREE. Even though the park covers nearly 80 sq km, it's so close to Seoul (45 minutes by subway) that it does get crowded, especially weekends.

The park is divided into the Bukhan-san area in the south and Dobong-san area in the north, each featuring multiple scenic – but strenuous – hikes to mountain peaks. Bring plenty of water.

In the northern area a popular excursion is the hike up Dobong-san (740m), which climaxes with the spectacular ridgetop peak climb. Along the way be sure to take signed detours to visit atmospheric forested temples Cheonchuk-sa (천축사) on the way up and Mangwol-sa (망월사) on your descent – around a four-hour trek in total.

The southern part has South Korea's highest peak, Baegundae (836m), a 3½-hour return trip via the Bukhansanseong trail. For rock climbers, nearby Insu-bong (810m) has some of the best multipitch climbing in Asia and routes of all grades.

For Dobong-san, take subway Line 1 to Dobongsan station, a 15-minute walk from Dobong Park Information Centre, which has a basic hiking map in English. If you take the route down via Wondol-bong (recommended) you'll finish at Mangwolsa station.

Baegundae is accessed from Bukhansanseong or Jeongneung; both have information centres with maps. For Bukhansanseong take subway Line 3 to Gupabal station and then take bus 704. For Jeongneung take Line 4 to Gireum station and bus 110B or 143.

Suwon

☎031 / POP 1,200,000

A popular day trip out of Seoul, sprawling Suwon (수원) is the largest city in Gyeonggi-do province, with World Heritage–listed fortifications still looping around its heart. Suwon almost became the country's capital in the 18th century, when Joseon dynasty ruler King Jeongjo built the 5.7km-long walls in 1794–96 ahead of moving the royal court south. However, the king died, power remained in Seoul, and Suwon ended up with one hell of a tourist sight. The city is located around 30km south of Seoul.

Sights

★Hwaseong FORTRESS

(화성; www.swcf.or.kr/english; adult/child ₩1000/500; ⊙24hr) The World Heritage–listed fortress wall that encloses the original town of Suwon is what brings most travellers to the city. Snaking up and down Paldal-san (143m), the fortification wall stretches a scenic 5.7km past four majestic gates, command posts, pavilions, observation towers and fire-beacon platforms. Built by King Jeongjo and completed in 1796, it was constructed of earth and faced with large stone blocks and grey bricks, nearly all of which have been restored.

It takes around two hours to complete the circuit. Try to go outside the wall for at least part of the way, as the fortress looks much more impressive the way an enemy would see it.

Start at Paldalmun (팔달문), also known as Nammun (South Gate); the most iconic of Hwaseong's four main gates, it stands at the heart of the city on a busy roundabout. From here follow the steep steps off to the left up to the Seonam Gangu (서남각루, Southwest Pavilion), an observation point near the peak of Paldal-san.

At the top of Paldal-san, near **Seojangdae** (서장대, Western Command Post), is the large Hyowon Bell, which you can can pay to ring (three tolls for ₩1000), and **Seonodae** (서노대, West Crossbow Platform), an octagonal tower on the summit that was used by crossbow archers, and offers spectacular panoramic views of the city.

On the north edge of the fortress wall is Hwahongmun (화홍문), a water gate that bridges the Suwon-cheon gurgling beneath it. Nearby Dongbukgongsimdon (동북공심돈), the northeast observation tower, has a unique oval shape and stands three storeys tall (8m), with a spiral staircase threading the centre of the structure.

Further on, the Bongdon Beacon Towers (봉돈), a row of brick chimneys, were used to send messages and alerts around the

Suwon

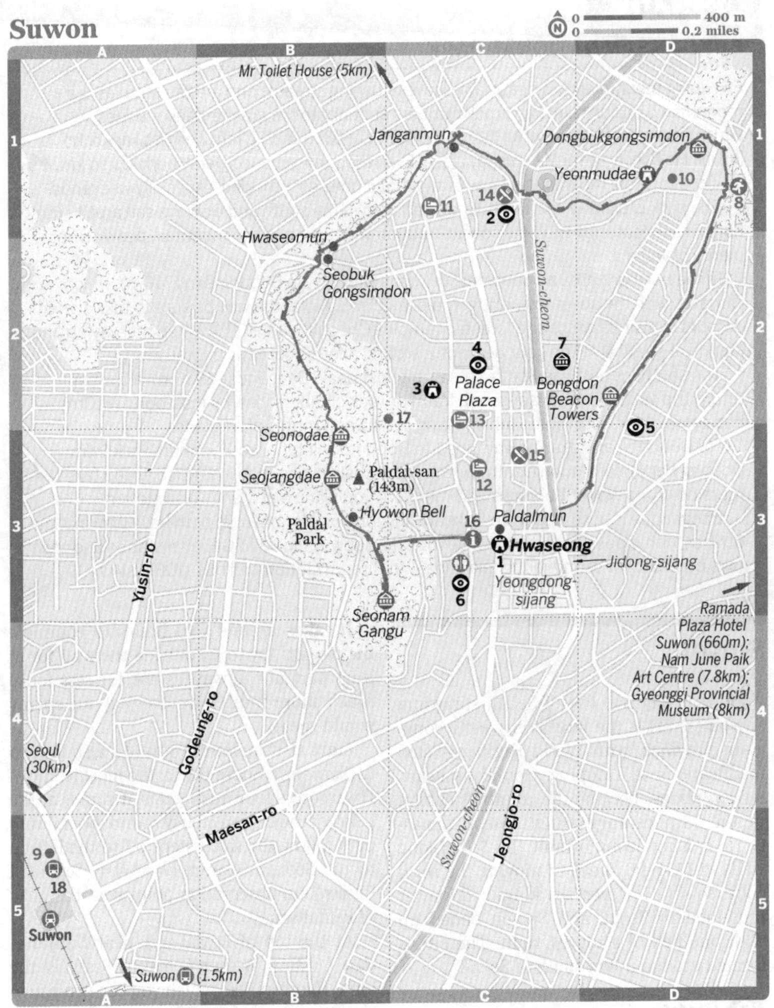

country using a system of fire and smoke signals. They would have had a clear line of sight to Hwaseong Haenggung (p101) in order to alert the king of various threats.

If you don't fancy the walk, head up the hill at the rear of the palace to the find the Hwaseong Trolley (p104) that winds in and out of the fortress wall to the archery field (p102) at **Dongjangdae** (동장대, East Command Post), also nicknamed Yeonmudae, a reference to its second function as a training camp. The grassy area was used as a sword and archery training ground for 200 years after the fortress opened.

Other notable structures in the fortress complex include Janganmun (장안문), the main north gate of Hwaseong and the largest gate of its kind in Korea. Visitors coming from Seoul would have entered the city here. It was reconstructed in the 1970s. The northwest watchtower Seobuk Gongsimdon (서북공심돈) stands guard next to Hwaseomun (화서문), the west gate, surrounded by its own fortress walls in miniature.

If you want to find out more about the fortress, including how detailed court records aided the 1970s reconstruction process, check out the **Suwon Hwaseong**

Suwon

Top Sights
1 Hwaseong..C3

Sights
Alternative Art Space Noon.........(see 2)
2 Haenggung-dong Mural Village...........C1
3 Hwaseong Haenggung........................C2
4 IPark Museum of Art..........................C2
5 Ji-dong Mural Village........................D3
6 Paldal-sa..C3
7 Suwon Hwaseong Museum................C2

Activities, Courses & Tours
8 Flying Suwon.....................................D1
9 Suwon City Tour................................A5
10 Yeonmudae Archery Centre...............D1

Sleeping
11 Hotel Dono.......................................C1
12 Hwaseong Guesthouse.......................C3
13 Suwon Hostel....................................C2

Eating
14 Yeonpo Galbi....................................C1
15 Yongsung Fried Chicken.....................C3

Information
Suwon Tourist Information Centre..........................(see 18)
16 Tourist Information Booth.................C3

Transport
17 Hwaseong Trolley..............................C2
18 Shuttle Bus to Korean Folk Village..........................A5

Museum (수원화성박물관; adult/child ₩2000/free; ⏲9am-6pm, closed 1st Mon of month).

In August the fortress is illuminated with light shows at night.

Korean Folk Village CULTURAL CENTRE
(한국민속촌; ☎031 288 0000; www.koreanfolk.co.kr; 90 Minsokchon-ro, Yongin-si; adult/teenager/child ₩18,000/13,000/11,000; ⏲9.30am-6.30pm May-Sep, to 6pm Oct-Apr; 🚼; 🚌10-5, 37) This 245-acre themed experience is designed to transport you back to the Joseon dynasty as you wander through picturesque grounds filled with thatched and tiled buildings relocated here from around Korea. Performers wearing *hanbok* (traditional clothing) craft pots and handmake paper, while others tend to vegetable plots and livestock. Throughout the day there are shows by traditional musicians, dancers, acrobats and tightrope walkers, and you can watch a staged wedding ceremony.

The Folk Museum offers a fascinating snapshot of 19th-century Korean life, and there are many hands-on activities for kids, as well as a child-oriented amusement park, which costs extra, plus several traditional restaurants.

From Suwon station, take bus 37 or 10-5 to Korean Folk Village, or there's a free shuttle bus that leaves from outside the station at 10.30am, 12.30pm and 2.30pm. The last shuttle bus leaves the folk village at 4.30pm (5pm on weekends). After that time, walk to the far end of the car park and catch city bus 37 (₩1300, one hour, every 20 minutes) back to Suwon station.

Mr Toilet House MUSEUM
(해우재, Haewoojae; ☎031 271 9777; www.haewoojae.com; 458-9 Jangan-ro, Jangan-gu; ⏲10am-6pm Tue-Sun, to 5pm winter; 🚌65, 301) FREE A contender for Korea's wackiest museum, Mr Toilet House is the former residence of Suwon's mayor, the late Sim Jae-duck. Appropriately designed like a toilet, it houses hilarious poo-related exhibits and a sculpture garden, as well as covering more serious sanitation issues – the museum is also an NGO established to improve public sanitation worldwide. Kids will love it, and there's a children's museum across the road with an observatory deck for viewing the toilet house. Jae-duck was famous for his efforts in beautifying Suwon's public toilets in the lead-up to the FIFA World Cup (2002), decorating them with art, flowers and classical music – many of them remain around the city today.

To get here take bus 65 or 301 (25 minutes) from Hwaseong Haenggung and get off at Dongwon High School, from where it's a 10-minute walk. A taxi from Suwon station should cost about ₩10,000.

Nam June Paik Art Centre GALLERY
(백남준아트센터; ☎031 201 8500; http://njpac-en.ggcf.kr; 10 Paiknamjune-ro, Giheung-gu, Yongin-si; ⏲10am-6pm Tue-Sun; 🚌10, 66, Ⓢ Bundang Line to Sanggal, Exit 4) FREE This gallery features the pioneering new-media work of internationally acclaimed avant-garde artist Nam June Paik (1932–2006). It's not far from Korean Folk Village.

From Suwon station take bus 10 or 66 or the Budang Line subway to Sanggal station (from where it's a 10-minute walk). En route you'll pass Gyeonggi Provincial Museum (p102), worth a stop for its fine collection of cultural artefacts.

Hwaseong Haenggung PALACE
(화성행궁; adult/child ₩1500/700; ⏲9am-6pm Tue-Sun) Sitting at the base of Paldal-san

WORTH A TRIP

SANSAWON BREWERY & MUSEUM

If you're partial to a day out at a winery, brewery or distillery, mixed in with a bit of culture amid nature, then a day trip to **Sansawon Brewery & Museum** (산사원; ☎031 531 9300; www.sansawon.co.kr; 25 Hwadong-ro 432beon-gil, Hwahyeonmyeon, Pocheon-si; ⏲8.30am-5.30pm) could be for you. A producer of traditional Korean alcohol, Sansawon is all about high-quality, chemical-free *soju* (local vodka) and *makgeolli* and other rice wines; far removed from the nasty hangovers you can get from convenience-store booze. For ₩2000 you get a sampler and shot glass for unlimited tasting.

Also here is a museum of traditional brewery equipment (but with no information in English). Outside stand rows of ceramic vats containing *soju* left to age. It's a lovely outdoor area; you might consider packing a picnic lunch and buying a bottle to enjoy on the lawn.

It's worth getting in touch with Sool Company (p60) to see if these experts in the field are running tours. Otherwise take the bus from Dong Seoul terminal (across from Gangbyeon subway on Line 2) to Pocheon (₩6000, 70 minutes). From here it's a 10-minute taxi ride for around ₩8000.

(143m), King Jeongjo's palace was built in the late 18th century as a residence for when he visited to worship at his father's tomb. The palace was mostly destroyed during the Japanese colonial period and has been meticulously reconstructed. From March to November, various traditional performances are held at the plaza in front of the palace, including a **changing-of-the-guard ceremony** (⏲2pm Sun) and **martial-arts display** (⏲11am Tue-Sun).

Every October a grand royal procession is re-enacted here as part of Suwon's annual festival.

Gyeonggi Provincial Museum MUSEUM
(6 Sanggal-ro, Giheung-gu, Yongin-si; ⏲10am-8pm Mon-Fri, to 10pm Sat & Sun) FREE This well-curated museum features cultural relics from around the province. A stop here is worth tacking on if you're visiting the Nam June Paik Art Centre (p101).

Alternative Art Space Noon GALLERY
(대안공간눈; ☎031 244 4519; www.spacenoon.co.kr; ⏲noon-7pm Tue-Sun) FREE This vibrant little gallery exhibits local artists in a converted '70s home within Haenggung-dong Mural Village.

IPark Museum of Art ARTS CENTRE
(SIMA, 수원시립아이파크미술관; http://sima.suwon.go.kr; adult/child ₩4000/1000; ⏲10am-6pm Tue-Sun) This contemporary-styled museum on the plaza in front of Hwaseong Haenggung (p101) hosts a variety of art-related exhibitions across its five galleries.

Haenggung-dong Mural Village AREA
This low-rise '70s neighbourhood has been adorned with eye-catching murals, and makes for a relaxing stroll in conjunction with a visit to quirky gallery Alternative Art Space Noon.

Ji-dong Mural Village AREA
(지동 벽화마을) There are more whimsical murals adorning the walls of houses here just outside the eastern wall of Suwon Hwaseong (p99).

Paldal-sa TEMPLE
(팔달사) Consider popping in to this well-frequented, laid-back Buddhist temple lost amid shops a short stroll southeast of Paldalmun, the iconic South Gate of Hwaseong (p99), before starting your ascent on the fortress.

Activities & Tours

Flying Suwon BALLOONING
(adult/youth/child ₩18,000/17,000/15,000) This hot-air-balloon experience rises on ropes up to 150m offering a near-bird's-eye view of the city's World Heritage–listed fortifications. There's space for 20 passengers, and the ride lasts for about 20 minutes.

Yeonmudae Archery Centre OUTDOORS
(10 arrows ₩2000; ⏲9.30am-5.30pm; 👪) In the northeast corner of the fortress (p99), this archery centre allows you to fire arrows at targets, a sport Koreans dominate at the Olympics. Sessions are held every 30 minutes.

Suwon City Tour BUS
(☎031 256 8300; adult/youth/child ₩11,000/8000/4000; ⏲9.50am & 1.50pm Tue-Thu & Sun) These 3½-hour tours take in most of Suwon's main sights and are a good option for those short on time. Tours are purchased at and depart from the tourist information centre (p103) at Suwon station.

Sleeping

Suwon Hostel HOTEL $
(수원호스텔; ☎031 245 5555; 4 Paldallo 2-ga, Paldal-gu; d from ₩30,000, q ₩50,000; ❄📶) More of a government hotel than a hostel, this place offers exceptional value for money with large, western-style or *ondol* (traditional, sleep-on-a-floor-mattress) rooms with retro furnishings. The on-site education centre is part of Suwon Cultural Foundation. Note the 'no alcohol' policy.

Hwaseong Guesthouse GUESTHOUSE $
(☎010 5316 3419; www.hsguesthouse.com; 11 Jeongjo-ro 801beon-gil, Jeongju-ro; dm/s/d ₩18,000/30,000/35,000; ❄@📶) It ain't the Ritz, but these spacious dorms and doubles are the cheapest in town, sharing bathrooms and a communal kitchen with cooking facilities.

Hotel Dono HOTEL $$
(☎031 258 8881; www.hoteldono.com; 68 Sinpung-ro, Paldal-gu; d ₩100,000; ❄📶) High-quality digs offering spacious, modern rooms within easy access of Hwaseong (p99). Rates include pick-up from Suwon station, and iced coffee on arrival. The Suwon Centre for Traditional Culture, a open-air folk-arts complex, is next door.

Ramada Plaza Hotel Suwon HOTEL $$$
(라마다프라자 수원호텔; ☎031 230 0031; www.ramadaplazasuwon.com; 150 Jungbu-daero; r from ₩172,000; ❄@📶) The Ramada is a modern affair with decent rooms and facilities, including a gym, deli and restaurants. It's about five minutes by taxi east of Suwon's fortress (p99). Book online for sizeable discounts.

Eating

Suwon is renowned for its *galbi* (beef ribs), usually eaten at long-standing city-centre restaurants like Yeonpo Galbi.

Yeonpo Galbi KOREAN $$
(연포갈비; 56-1 Jeongjo-ro 906beon-gil; ribs from ₩20,000; ⏲11.30am-10pm) This famous restaurant grills up all manner of mouth-watering *galbi* (beef ribs). At lunch, go for the special Suwon version of *galbitang* (₩12,000) – ribs in a seasoned broth with noodles and leeks. Find it down the steps from Hwahongmun, the water gate on the north edge of the fortress wall.

Yongsung Fried Chicken FAST FOOD $$
(용성통닭, Yongseong Tongdak; ☎031 242 8226; 800-7 Jeongjo-ro; chicken ₩15,000; ⏲11.30am-1am Wed-Mon; 📶) A popular *chimaek* (chicken and beer) spot for golden-fried, juicy chicken pieces and cheap jugs of cold brew.

Information

The **main tourist information centre** (☎031 228 4673; www.swcf.or.kr/english; ⏲9am-6pm; Ⓢ Suwon, Exit 4) is on the left as you come out of the railway station.

There are several **tourist information booths** (☎031 228 4672; ⏲9am-6pm) at points around Suwon's fortress walls.

The Suwon City Tour is a good option for those short on time.

Getting There & Away

BUS

Long-distance buses depart from **Suwon bus terminal** (www.suwonterminal.co.kr), heading to major cities including Incheon (₩4800, 1½ hours, every 15 minutes), Busan (₩24,900, five hours, 10 daily), Daegu (₩19,900, 3½ hours, six daily) and Gwangju (from ₩16,000, three hours, every 30 minutes).

There's also an airport bus (from ₩12,000, 70 minutes) leaving every 30 minutes opposite the Suwon tourist information centre (p103).

TRAIN

From Seoul, the Budang Line and Line 1 run to Suwon (₩1850, one hour). KTX trains from Seoul are speedier (from ₩4600, 30 minutes) but not as frequent.

From Suwon train station, high- and regular-speed trains depart frequently to cities all over Korea, including Busan (from ₩26,900, 5½ hours), Daegu (from ₩18,200, three hours), Daejeon (₩8100, 70 minutes) and Jeonju (from ₩15,100, three hours). High-speed trains take about half the time, but are double the cost.

Getting Around

From Suwon train station, buses 11, 13, 35 and 36 go to Paldalmun (₩1100, 10 minutes), the iconic South Gate of the fortress. A taxi costs around ₩5000.

To get to the city's bus terminal (p103), catch bus 5, 5-1 or 7-1 (₩1100, five minutes) from Suwon train station.

A free **shuttle bus** (⌚10.30am, 12.30pm & 2.30pm) leaves from outside Exit 4 of Suwon train station to Korean Folk Village (p101) at 10.30am, 12.30pm and 2.30pm.

The **Hwaseong Trolley** (adult/teenager/child ₩3000/2000/1000; ⌚10am-5.20pm) links the fortress to the archery field at Yeonmudae.

Everland Resort

Set amid rolling hills 40km south of Seoul, Everland Resort is Korea's largest theme park. While it might lack the polish of Disney (and a certain mouse), the gorgeous setting, kid-friendly attractions, discounted tickets for international visitors and one world-class roller coaster make for a winning family day out. The resort also incorporates a separate water park, Caribbean Bay, which only opens in summer.

Sights

★Everland AMUSEMENT PARK

(에버랜드; ☎031 320 5000; www.everland.com; adult/teenager/child ₩54,000/46,000/43,000; ⌚9.30am-10pm Sep-Jun, to 11pm Jul & Aug; 🚌5002) Opened in 1976, Everland is Korea's largest theme park, with five zones of rides, fantasy buildings and impressive seasonal gardens. The lush hillside setting, 40km south of Seoul, is part of the appeal. Thrill-seekers will want to head straight to T Express, a gargantuan wooden roller coaster added in 2008 that boasts a 45m near-vertical drop. But its the littler kids who'll find the most fun here, with gentle rides, animal attractions, shows and two parades daily.

At night, the illuminated park takes on a magical atmosphere, and if you can last until 9.30pm you'll catch the fireworks. Appealingly retro in places, some of Everland's rides, like the big wheel, are actually decommissioned relics left just for show.

Caribbean Bay AMUSEMENT PARK

(캐리비안 베이; www.everland.com; adult/child ₩50,000/39,000; ⌚9am-7pm Sep & Jun, 8am-10pm Jul & Aug) An impressive indoor and outdoor water park with white-knuckle luges, flumes, tubes, a lazy river and a not-so-lazy wave pool. It's best avoided on summer weekends, when you'll be queuing even for the hot tub. Caribbean Bay is part of Everland theme park but requires a separate ticket.

TOP TIP

Save money on Everland tickets by buying online – the park permits reputable websites to sell discounted QR code tickets (around 40% off) to international visitors. There's also a 'Ticket Office for Foreigners' booth at the main entrance that sometimes gives discounts.

Hoam Art Museum GALLERY

(호암미술관; ☎031 320 1801; http://hoam.samsungfoundation.org; adult/child ₩4000/3000, free with Everland ticket; ⌚10am-6pm Tue-Sun) Good luck trying to persuade the kids to exit Everland to go see an art museum, but if you manage it you'll be richly rewarded with the personal collection of Lee Byung-chull, the founder of Samsung Group, which also runs the theme park. Korean modern art, together with wooden furniture, silk paintings, ceramics and calligraphy from earlier dynasties, are displayed in a traditional-styled building adjacent to the serenely beautiful Hee Won Korean gardens.

A free shuttle bus runs from Everland Resort's main entrance to the Hoam Art Museum; the last bus is at 4.30pm.

Samsung Transportation Museum MUSEUM

(삼성화재교통박물관; ☎031 320 9900; www.stm.or.kr; adult/child ₩6000/5000; ⌚10am-6pm Tue-Fri) An impressive collection of classic automobiles and sports cars are buffed to a sheen at this kid-friendly museum. A free shuttle bus goes here from Everland bus terminal.

Sleeping & Eating

The on-site hostel might suit families wishing to overnight and visit both Everland and Caribbean Bay; otherwise there's little reason to sleep over.

Snack vendors and restaurants are found all over the park, and you can take your own food in with you. Garden Terrace sells draught Cass (Korean beer) for ₩4000.

Home Bridge Cabin Hostel HOSTEL $$

(☎031 320 9740; www.everland.com; Everland Resort; r from ₩140,000; ❄@) This log-cabin-style villa tucked inside Everland Resort attracts large school groups, with *ondol* (traditional, sleep-on-a-floor-mattress) rooms sleeping from four to 20.

Getting There & Away

To get here from Seoul take bus 5002 (₩2000, 50 minutes, every 15 minutes) from the **Everland**

bus stop (Map p84) in Gangnam. From outside Suwon's train station, hop on bus 66 or 66-4 (₩1700, one hour, every 30 minutes).

Donggureung

The largest and most attractive of the World Heritage–listed royal tombs scattered around Seoul and Gyeonggi-do, **Donggureung** (동구릉; Map p46; 197 Donggureung-ro; adult/child ₩1000/500; 6am-6pm Tue-Sun; 88, S Jungang Line 1 to Guri, Exit 1) is the burial place of seven kings and 10 queens from the Joseon dynasty. The tombs are set over 196 hectares of forested paths, and it takes around 1½ hours to explore the site in its entirety. It's located 20km northeast of central Seoul in Guri.

All the tombs are similarly arranged on large grassy mounds according to the rules of Confucianism and feng shui. The entrances are marked by a simple red-painted wooden gate, stone pathway and hall for conducting rites in front of the humped burial mounds decorated with stone statuary – typically a pair of civil officers and generals, plus horses and protective animals such as tigers and rams.

The most notable tomb is that of King Taejo (1335–1408), the founder of the Joseon dynasty. In contrast to the other neatly clipped plots in this leafy park, his mound is covered in bushy pampas grass from his home town of Hamhung (now in North Korea) that – in accordance with the king's predeath instructions – has never been cut. Also don't miss the tombs at Mongneung, the only tombs that you can scramble up to and explore close-up. A walking-tour map is available from the History Centre Museum, which also has a good overview of the area.

To reach the complex take the Jungang Line 1 to Guri station where you can connect with bus 88, or take a 40-minute walk to the site.

Namhansanseong Provincial Park

The World Heritage–listed fortress of **Namhansanseong** (남한산성 도립공원; adult/child ₩2000/1000; 10am-5pm Tue-Sun; S Line 8 to Namhansanseong, Exit 1), 20km southeast of central Seoul, once guarded the city's southern entrance. Today it's famous for hiking trails that hug the 17th-century fortress walls, of which 12.3km still remain, taking you through beautiful pine and oak forests, and wild flowers.

Your first stop should be Namhansanseong Emergency Palace, the beautifully reconstructed complex of the king's quarters, which also has a hiking map of the fortress.

The most popular hiking route is the two-hour loop that leads you past the main gates of Bukmun (North Fortress), Seomun (West), Nammun (South) and South Command Post, with sweeping panoramas. Or you can trek the entire wall's perimeter in around seven hours. Be sure to mix up trails that lead in and out of the wall to change your views.To get here, take subway Line 8 to Sanseong, then get a taxi or take bus 9 from Exit 2 of the station to the park's south gate, a total journey of around one hour from central Seoul.

Icheon

031 / POP 215,206

The famed pottery centre of Icheon (이천; not to be confused with Incheon) has origins in the craft that date back to the early Joseon dynasty. It's a tradition that continues today, centred on the Icheon Ceramic Village, a touristy enclave of workshops and retailers 6km north of town that's worth a visit for those with an interest in learning about, purchasing or even making pottery. Surrounded by mountains some 60km southeast of Seoul, Icheon makes for an easy day trip out of the capital.

Sights

★Icheon Ceramic Village AREA

(이천 도예촌; www.icheon.go.kr; Gwango-dong; 10am-5pm; 114, 24-7, 20-4) This leafy cul-de-sac off a busy main road is the centre of Icheon's porcelain and celadon trade, a thriving tradition that dates back to the Joseon dynasty. Containing some 40 ceramics shops, kilns and a couple of cafes, it gets going daily from mid-morning, and one or two places, including Hankook Dojakwon (p106) beside the arched gate to the village, offer the chance to shape and fire your own cup, vase or pot. Prices here can be considerably cheaper than in Seoul, though you'll still need your bargaining hat on. For as little as ₩5000 you can buy a cup or plate, with larger items like green celadon vases starting at around ₩50,000.

To get there, take local bus 114, 24-7 or 20-4 (₩1500, 15 minutes) from outside Icheon's bus terminal, disembarking at the

stop just past the village gate. A taxi should cost about ₩7000.

Icheon World Ceramics Centre ARTS CENTRE
(Cerapia; www.kocef.org; galleries ₩3000; ⌚9am-6pm Tue-Sun) This art complex within **Seolbong Park** (설봉공원; http://tour.icheon.go.kr; ⌚9am-5pm) has several galleries showcasing contemporary ceramic art from Korea and around the world. There's also an opportunity to buy pieces, and participate in workshops for crafts like pottery and glassblowing. Be sure to wander through the gardens to the traditional Korean kiln at the rear of the complex.

Icheon World Ceramics Centre is also the venue for the Ich eon Ceramic Festival.

Activities

★Hankook Dojakwon ARTS & CRAFTS
(Korean Ceramic Gallery; Icheon Ceramic Village; workshops from ₩20,000; ⌚10am-6pm) If you fancy making your own cup, bowl or million-won vase, visit this cluttered workshop and ceramics retailer beside the Icheon Ceramic Village (p105) entrance. For ₩20,000, you can don a smock and sit down at a slippery mass of spinning clay. The gallery will pack up your creation and post it back to your home country for an extra fee.

Festivals & Events

Icheon Ceramic Festival ART
(www.ceramic.or.kr; ⌚late Apr–mid-May) If you're in town between April and May, you might catch the annual Icheon Ceramic Festival, during which artists and enthusiasts descend on Seolbong Park to buy and sell ceramics, and take part in a program of craft activities.

Gyeonggi International Ceramic Biennale ART
(GICB; www.kocef.org/eng; ⌚Apr-May) Ceramic artists from around the world gather for this ceramics exhibition held at various venues around Icheon.

Sleeping & Eating

The town centre has a handful of beery *hof* (local pubs).

Miranda Hotel HOTEL $$
(미란다호텔; ☎031 639 5000; www.mirandahotel.com; r ₩141,000; ❄@📶; 🚌8, 21) Incheon's snazziest hotel (though don't get your hopes up) overlooks a small lake with a pavilion on an island. There's also a bowling alley and **spa complex** (미란다호텔 스파플러스; ⌚6am-10pm) attached.

Naratnim KOREAN $$
(나랏님 이천쌀밥; ☎031 636 9900; set meals from ₩13,000; ⌚9.30am-10pm; 🚌114, 24-7, 20-4) One of several cavernous restaurants just north of Icheon Ceramic Village (p105) known for an impressive abundance of *banchan* (side dishes) served together with Icheon's famous rice. Dining here is for a minimum of two people.

You'll spot Naratnim easily: it's the huge, faux-traditional wooden building with the curved, tiled roof. No English menu.

Shopping

Icheon Ceramics Store CERAMICS
(Icheon Ceramic Village; ⌚10am-5pm) One of the largest emporiums in Icheon Ceramic Village (p105) with good prices and room to negotiate. Note that the celadon vases are often sold in pairs here.

Information

The **tourist information centre** (⌚10am-5pm) within Seolbong Park has a good local area map, but staff have limited English.

Getting There & Around

Buses run from **Dong-Seoul Bus Terminal** (Map p88; ☎02 1688 5979; www.ti21.co.kr; 50 Gangbyeonnyeok-ro; Ⓢ Line 2 to Gangbyeon, Exit 4) to Icheon (₩4700, one hour, every 15 to 40 minutes). Once in Icheon, it's another 15 minutes by local bus or taxi to Icheon Ceramic Village.

Seoul Grand Park

Indeed grand in scale, this family-friendly entertainment complex includes an excellent contemporary art museum and the interactive Gwacheon National Science Museum. There are also hiking trails, a campground, an amusement park and a river that's a pleasant location for a picnic.

Sights

Gwacheon National Science Museum MUSEUM
(국립과천과학관; Map p46; www.sciencecenter.go.kr; Seoul Grand Park, Gwacheon; adult/child ₩4000/2000; ⌚9.30am-5.30pm Tue-Sun; 👪; Ⓢ Line 4 to Seoul Grand Park, Exit 3) While aimed at kids, this interactive science museum can be enjoyed by all. Set within a

gigantic futuristic building, there are plenty of entertaining, hands-on exhibits that cover everything from dinosaurs to space exploration, though English captions are few. Note that several exhibits have limited capacity, so check upon arrival if you need a ticket, which are free apart from for the **planetarium shows** (adult/child ₩2000/1000). The traditional Korean Science Hall is also worth checking out for cultural insights.

Admission is free for kids under seven years old.

National Museum of Modern and Contemporary Art MUSEUM
(MMCA; 국립현대미술관; Map p46; ☎02 2188 6000; www.moca.go.kr; Seoul Grand Park, Gwacheon; ⏲10am-6pm Tue-Fri & Sun, to 9pm Sat & Wed; Ⓢ Line 4 to Seoul Grand Park, Exit 2) FREE The best reason for making the trip out to Seoul Grand Park is to visit this large and striking museum spread out over three floors and surrounded by a sculpture garden. The standout installation here is Nam June Paik's *The More the Better* (1988), an 18m-tall, pagoda-shaped tower of 1000 TV screens. Commenting on our increasingly electronic universe, it seems both prescient and quaintly nostalgic in today's smartphone era.

Special exhibition entry costs vary.

Seoul Land AMUSEMENT PARK
(서울랜드; Map p46; ☎02 509 6000; www.seoulland.co.kr; Seoul Grand Park, Gwacheon; day pass adult/youth/child ₩42,000/39,000/36,000; ⏲9.30am-9pm summer, to 6pm winter; 👪; Ⓢ Line 4 to Seoul Grand Park, Exit 2) Keep the kids happy all day at this family amusement park with five themed areas, special shows and classic fairground rides, from bumper cars to a looping coaster. The Everland and Lotte World theme parks are better overall, but small children will still be very happy here.

It's accessed via the Elephant Tram Car, which links it with the park entrance.

Sleeping & Eating

The **Seoul Grand Park Campsite** (https://grandpark.seoul.go.kr/eng_grand/camping/reserv/reserv02.jsp) is fully equipped and popular with families. Tents can be reserved online (Korean language only).

You can get a hearty of bowl of noodles at the row of Korean restaurants outside Exit 5 of Seoul Grand Park station.

Getting There & Around

Take subway Line 4 to Seoul Grand Park station, around 45 minutes from City Hall. The Science Museum is close to the park's main entrance, but to reach the other attractions you'll save time by taking the **Elephant Tram Car** (Map p46; adult/youth/child ₩1000/800/700) or the ski-resort-style **Sky Lift** (Map p46; adult/youth/child ₩5500/400/3500).

INCHEON METROPOLITAN CITY

One of Korea's six *gwangyoek-si*, or 'metropolitan cities', Incheon is the country's third largest, second only to Seoul and Busan (though it can seem like an extension of the former). But what sets Incheon apart is that it also administers the dreamy sweep of West Sea islands or *do*, the largest of which, Ganghwado, is only separated from the mainland by a narrow channel. Remarkably, the region continues to grow as giant swaths of coast are reclaimed and developed into new urban centres such as Songdo, an ambitious and futuristic 'smart city', as yet not fully realised.

Incheon

☎032 / POP 2,900,000

South Korea's third-largest city, Incheon (인천) is an expanding metropolis and industrial port. Its colourful Chinatown and Open Port areas are the most tourist-friendly parts of the city to explore, and are easily accessible via subway from Seoul. Come here to eat Chinese food, discover pockets of concession-era architecture, stroll the seafront boardwalk at Wolmido and visit the fish market at Yeonan, where you can catch ferries to the West Sea islands or beyond to China.

Located 36km west of Seoul, Incheon is the place where Korea opened up to the world in 1883, ending centuries of self-imposed isolation. In 1950, during the Korean War, the American General Douglas MacArthur led UN forces in a daring landing behind enemy lines here.

Sights

Wolmido AREA
(월미도; http://wolmi.incheon.go.kr; 🚌2, 23, 45) Historically notable as the site of the Incheon Landing Operations during the

Incheon

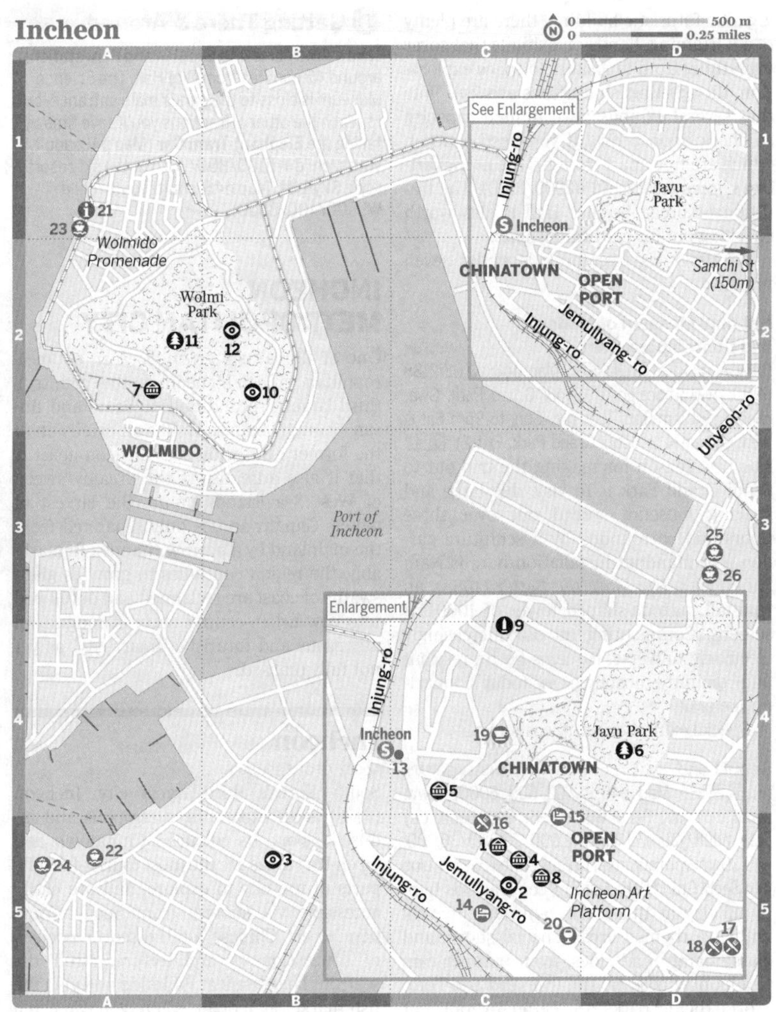

Korean War, today the former island of Wolmi (it was joined to the mainland in 1989), is a leisure area offering a Coney Island–style waterfront boardwalk and small amusement park. It also has the forested Wolmi Park (p110) with tranquil walking trails leading to traditional gardens, the Wolmi Observatory (p110) with its panoramic views, and the Korean Emigration History Museum (p109).

Construction began in 2007 on a monorail encircling Wolmido, but safety concerns have caused endless delays; it is now slated to open in 2019, with plans to eventually connect to Incheon station.

Incheon Fish Market MARKET

(인천종합어시장, Grand Fishery Market; www.asijang.com; Yeonan; 5am-9pm;) This large fish and seafood market has row upon row of vendors hawking every kind of edible sea beast, which can be consumed right here at several small restaurants and cafes.

Bus 12 or 24 will get you here from Dong-incheon subway station.

Incheon

Sights

1 Daebul Hotel ... C5
2 Incheon Art Platform ... C5
3 Incheon Fish Market ... B5
4 Incheon Open Port Museum ... C5
5 Jajangmyeon Museum ... C4
6 Jayu Park ... D4
7 Korean Emigration History Museum ... A2
8 Modern Architecture Museum ... C5
9 Songwol-dong Fairy Tale Village ... C4
10 Wolmi Observatory ... B2
11 Wolmi Park ... A2
12 Wolmido ... B2

Activities, Courses & Tours

13 Incheon City Tour ... C4

Sleeping

14 Harbor Park Hotel ... C5
15 Hotel Atti ... C5

Eating

16 Dadabok ... C5
Pungmi ... (see 5)
17 Sinpo Market ... D5
18 Sinpo Woori Mandoo ... D5

Drinking & Nightlife

19 Cafe Castle ... C4
20 Caligari Brewing ... C5

Information

21 Tourist Information Centre ... A1
Tourist Information Centre ... (see 13)

Transport

22 Coastal Ferry Terminal ... A5
23 Ferry to Yeongjongdo ... A1
24 International Ferry Terminal ... A5
25 International Ferry Terminal 2 ... D3
26 Weidong Ferry Company ... D3

Incheon Art Platform ARTS CENTRE
(www.inartplatform.kr; Open Port; ⏲9am-6pm Tue-Sun) FREE This attractive complex of 1930s and '40s brick warehouses was turned over to the Incheon Foundation for Arts and Culture, which has created gallery spaces and artist residency studios. Performances and events are also held here, and there is a light-filled cafe with plenty of art books.

The platform offers residency programs and studio space for artists; visit the website for more info.

Incheon Landing Operation Memorial Hall MUSEUM
(인천상륙작전기념관; www.landing915.com; Songdo; ⏲9am-6pm Tue-Sun; 🚌8, 16, 521, Ⓢ Suin Line to Songdo, Exit 1) FREE This sombre, strikingly designed museum commemorates the daring attack in which some 70,000 UN and South Korean troops took part in a surprise landing in Incheon in 1950, supported by 260 warships. The displays include newsreel films of the Korean War, plus guided missiles and amphibious landing crafts.

Buses 8, 16 and 521 come here from Dongincheon subway, or you can take the subway from Incheon to Songdo, from where it's a 25-minute walk.

Daebul Hotel MUSEUM
(대불호텔; Hotel Daibutsu; Open Port; ₩1000; ⏲9am-5.30pm) Dubbed the 'first western hotel in Korea', this three-storey brick building is a recreation of an old merchants hotel that stood on this spot from 1888 to 1978 (the original foundations are viewable through glass). Upstairs, mock-ups of historical guest rooms are designed to give Korean visitors a taste of old-world western culture.

Jajangmyeon Museum MUSEUM
(Chinatown; ₩1000; ⏲9am-6pm) Housed in a building dating from 1907, this imaginative museum celebrates the origins of the much-loved noodle dish *jajangmyeon,* thought to be adapted from the snacks of Chinese labourers who came over from Shandong Province to work in Incheon's Open Port area at the turn of the 20th century.

There's not much in English here, so pick up the leaflet.

Korean Emigration History Museum MUSEUM
(http://mkeh.incheon.go.kr; ⏲9am-6pm Tue-Sun) FREE This museum offers interesting insights into the outbound journeys of Korean migrants, with a focus on those settling throughout the Americas. It's located at the base of Wolmi Park (p110).

Incheon Open Port Museum MUSEUM
(인천개항박물관; www.icjgss.or.kr/open_port; Open Port; adult/teenager/child ₩500/300/200; ⏲9am-6pm) Built in 1897, this is one of three former Japanese banks along the same street. Exhibitions within present the history of Incheon's Open Port area since foreign concessions were first established here in 1883.

Incheon Metropolitan City Museum MUSEUM
(인천광역시립박물관; http://museum.incheon.go.kr; Songdo; ⏲9am-6pm Tue-Sun; 🚌8, 16, 521,

Ⓢ Suin Line to Songdo, Exit 1) FREE The city's main museum offers an excellent collection of celadon pottery and some interesting historical displays dating from the Three Kingdoms. It's located next to the Incheon Landing Operation Memorial Hall (p109).

Buses 8, 16 and 521 come here from Dongincheon subway, or you can take the subway from Incheon to Songdo, from where it's a 25-minute walk.

Jayu Park PARK

(자유공원; Open Port) You can explore this picturesque hilltop park, designed by a Russian civil engineer in 1888, while walking between Chinatown and the Open Port area. It contains the monument for the centenary of Korea–USA relations and a statue of General MacArthur, who led the Allied amphibious landings at Incheon, turning the tide of the Korean War.

Modern Architecture Museum MUSEUM

(Open Port; adult/youth/child ₩500/300/200; ⌚9am-6pm) Housed within a former concession-era Japanese bank, this museum examines the historic diversity of the Open Port area's architecture – modernist, Gothic, Japanese imperial and Chinese – much of which has been lost over the years.

Songwol-dong Fairy Tale Village PUBLIC ART

(인천 송월동 동화마을) As if a princess had waved a magic wand over its streets, this once-gritty neighbourhood has been transformed into a children's wonderland of brightly coloured, fairy-tale-themed murals. While it's aimed at kids, it's quirky enough to warrant a visit by all.

Wolmi Park PARK

(월미공원; http://wolmi.incheon.go.kr/index.do; Wolmido; ⌚6am-10pm, garden 9am-8pm) FREE This large, forested park has walking trails, a replica of a traditional Korean garden, and the hilltop **Wolmi Observatory** (월미산 유리전망대; ⌚6am-10pm) FREE, offering views across the port and towards Yeongjongdo. The Korean Emigration History Museum is at the park's southern end.

Tours

The excellent **Incheon City Tour** (www.travelicn.or.kr/open_content/english/citytour; single route ₩5000, all routes ₩10,000; ⌚10am-4pm) bus has three hop-on, hop-off circular routes, but the most useful is the 'Harbour Line' (₩5000 for an all-day pass). Departing from the **tourist information centre** (http://english.incheon.go.kr; ⌚9am-6pm) outside Incheon station every half-hour between 10am and 4pm, it calls at the fish market, Yoenan Pier, Songdo International City, the museums, the Open Port area and Wolmido.

Ganghwa Tour TOURS

(☎032 772 4000; 8hr tours ₩10,000; ⌚Sun Apr-Oct) Sunday tours of Ganghwado (p115) leave only if there are enough people booked. Book by phone at least four days in advance.

Festivals & Events

Pentaport Rock Festival MUSIC

(www.pentaportrock.com; Songdo-dong; 3-day tickets ₩200,000; ⌚Jul-Aug) This multiday rock, indie and metal fest held annually in Incheon attracts major international bands.

Sleeping

Incheon has a dearth of decent hotels and no hostels. For upmarket digs, nearby Songdo International City is a better bet.

Hotel Atti MOTEL $

(호텔 아띠; ☎032 772 5233; ymj5599@naver.com; 88, Sinpo-ro 35beon-gil, Open Port; r from ₩50,000; ❄@📶) A friendly budget option with a perfect location between Chinatown and the Open Port area. Rooms come with thoughtful additions like charging cables and wash-kits, and you can enjoy free popcorn, coffee and noodles by the check-in desk. Prices rise on weekends.

Harbor Park Hotel HOTEL $$

(하버 파크 호텔; ☎032 770 9500; www.harborparkhotel.com; 217 Jemullyang-ro; r from ₩110,000; ❄@📶) Housed in a business-like glass building, Harbor Park Hotel offers plain but well-equipped rooms with views of the working harbour. Facilities include a fitness centre and top-floor buffet restaurant.

Eating

In Chinatown you can sample local takes on Chinese cuisine including *jajangmyeon* (noodles in black bean sauce), *jjampong* (noodles in a spicy seafood soup) and *onggibyeong* (dumplings baked inside clay jars).

Incheon's well-known seafood can be enjoyed at source at the city's fish market (p108), or along **Samchi St** (동인천 삼치거리; Uhyeon-ro 67beon-gil, Dongincheon-dong, Jung-gu; samchi around ₩13,000; Ⓢ Dongincheon, Exit 8).

Dadabok CHINESE $
(다다복; 032 765 9888; 24 Chinatown-ro 55beon-gil, Gaho-dong, Jung-gu; dumplings from ₩5000; 11am-7.30pm) Set back from the bedlam of Chinatown, this unassuming restaurant is the local pick for Incheon's tastiest *mandu* (filled dumplings), with a choice of pork or shrimp, either pan-fried, steamed or boiled. Note the early closing time.

Sinpo Market KOREAN $
(신포시장, Sinpo-sijang; Sinpo-dong; street-food items ₩1000-10,000; 10am-8pm; S Dong-incheon) Several stalls along this pair of covered arcades specialise in *dakgangjeong* (fried chicken in a sweet, spicy sauce). The best vendors usually have a line of locals patiently queuing for their takeaway box. Another popular snack here is *hotteok* (fried, syrup-filled pancakes).

Sinpo Woori Mandoo KOREAN $
(신포우리만두; 032 772 4958; www.sinpomandoo.co.kr; dumplings from ₩4000; 10am-10pm) Feast on steamers of dumplings with fillings like pork and kimchi, along with Korean classics including bibimbap (rice, egg, meat and veggies with chilli sauce), pork cutlet and cold noodles at this cheap and cheerful chain restaurant (this is the original location) just outside the western entrance to Sinpo Market.

Pungmi CHINESE $
(풍미; 032 772 2680; Chinatown; meals ₩5000-10,000; 10am-9pm) Pimp up your *jajangmyeon* (noodles in black bean sauce) with seafood or spice at this oriental-styled restaurant operating here since 1957. Also serves classics like sweet and sour pork and egg rolls, and complimentary tea. Learn more about your lunch by visiting the Jajangmyeon Museum (p109) just around the corner.

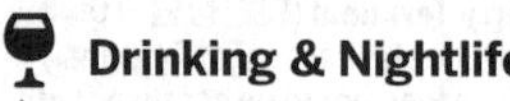

Drinking & Nightlife

★**Caligari Brewing** BREWERY
(칼리가리 브루윙; www.caligaribrewing.com; 2-1 Haeandong 3(sam)-ga; beers from ₩5900; 5pm-1am;) One of the best spots for a beer in the Old Port area, this brewery with attached taproom slots perfectly into its old warehouse setting. A row of towering tanks faces a small bar pouring a range of craft beers, and you can order snacks and pizza if you're feeling peckish.

Cafe Castle CAFE
(Cafe 성; 032 773 2116; Chinatown; coffees ₩5000; noon-10am;) FREE Enjoy coffee, tea, cocktails and snacks at this homey cafe with a fantastic harbour view from its rooftop garden. Tricky to find, it's at the top of the steps that go up from the centre of Chinatown, next to the red arch.

Information

Tourist information booths at **Incheon station** (032 777 1330; http://english.incheon.go.kr; 9am-6pm), **Wolmido promenade** (032 765 4169; http://english.incheon.go.kr; 6am-9pm), the **bus terminal** (032 430 7257; http://english.incheon.go.kr; 10am-6pm) and outside the subway station (p110) have very helpful staff, and lots of excellent maps, brochures (in English) and suggestions for Incheon, Songdo and the islands.

Getting There & Away

Incheon International Airport (p395) isn't in Incheon itself, but rather on Yeongjongdo, over an hour away by bus.

INCHEON–CHINA FERRIES

Ferries link several Chinese ports with Incheon, including Tianjin (for Beijing), Dalian, Qingdao, Yingkou, Qinhuangdao, Yantai, Shidao, Lianyungang, Weihai and Dandong. Best suited for those with a penchant for slow travel, the mostly overnight trips take 12 to 26 hours to cross the West Sea (or Yellow Sea, as China calls it).

The cheapest fares get you a thin mattress in a shared dorm, or you can shell out for a small cabin with twin beds and TV. Child fares are usually half the adult fare, and some companies offer a student discount.

Ferries to China depart from either International Ferry Terminal (p112) or International Ferry Terminal 2 (p112). You'll need to arrange visas in advance.

Weidong Ferry Company (032 7770 4958; www.weidong.com; International Ferry Terminal 2, 147 Hang-dong, Incheon Port; 9, 23, 24, 72, M Line 1 to DongIncheon) operates modern, well-equipped boats from Incheon to Qingdao, Tianjin and Weihai. It's based at International Ferry Terminal 2 and has a good English website (www.weidong.com) and a Facebook-chat ticket reservation facility.

BOAT

Ferries to the various West Sea islands sail from the **Coastal Ferry Terminal** (인천항연안여객터미널; Incheon Coastal Passenger Terminal) building at Yeonan Pier, not to be confused with the **International Ferry Terminal** (인천항 제1국제여객터미널; Incheon Port International Passenger Terminal) next door with boats bound for China. Note that China-bound ferries sailing to Tianjin, Qingdao and Weihai embark from **International Ferry Terminal 2** (인천항 제2국제여객터미널; www.icferry.or.kr; Ⓢ Suin Line to Sinpo station, Exit 1), 4km away.

A passenger and car **ferry** (₩3500; ⏲7am-6pm) makes the short hop between Wolmido and Yeongjongdo.

To/From West Sea Islands

The Coastal Ferry Terminal is the point of embarkation for 14 of the West Sea's inhabited islands, including Deokjeokdo (p114). Note that cancellations sometimes occur in the event of bad weather.

To discover more about the the West Sea islands (excluding Ganghwado and Yoengjongdo), see www.ongjin.go.kr.

BUS

From **Incheon Bus Terminal** (☎032 430 7114; www.ictr.or.kr/eng/index.asp; Ⓢ Incheon Line 1 to Incheon Bus Terminal) you can take direct long-distance buses all over South Korea, from Suwon (₩4500, one hour) to Busan (from ₩24,100, 4½ hours). For Seoul it's faster, cheaper and easier to connect via the subway.

SUBWAY

Subway Line 1 from Seoul station (₩1850) takes around 70 minutes; the line branches at Guro so make sure you're on an Incheon-bound train.

Getting Around

BUS & TAXI

Buses and taxis to various destinations leave from outside Dongincheon and Incheon stations. For Incheon airport and Yeongjongdo, take bus 306 from Dongincheon station (₩2250, 70 minutes, every 15 minutes).

If you're heading to Yeonan Pier to catch a West Sea islands boat from the Coastal Ferry Terminal or a China-bound boat from International Ferry Terminal, take bus 12 or 24 from Dongincheon, or hail a taxi (₩8000). For International Ferry Terminal 2 you can take bus 23 from Incheon station or a taxi (₩3000), but it's better to go by subway.

For Wolmido, hop on bus 2, 23 or 45 from outside Incheon station. A taxi costs ₩3000.

SUBWAY

Incheon station is the western terminus for Line 1 of Seoul subway (70 minutes to Seoul station), and the northern terminus of the Suin Line for connecting trains to Songdo International City.

International Ferry Terminal 2 is conveniently situated just outside Sinpo station, one stop south of Incheon on the Suin Line.

Muuido

If you're looking for a beachside escape within easy reach of Seoul, the tiny island of Muuido (무의도) fits the bill. Broad stretches of golden sand and forested walking trails are just a short ferry hop away from more developed Yeongjongdo (home to Incheon airport). A road bridge was under construction at time of research, however, so you might want to get there before the developers do.

Note also that swimming is only possible during high tide; at low tide the water recedes substantially, turning the area into mudflats.

Sights

Hanagae Beach BEACH

(하나개 해수욕장; www.hanagae.co.kr; adult/child ₩2000/1000) Hanagae Beach is Muuido's best, with plenty of golden sand, a handful of seafood restaurants and basic beach huts under the pine trees or on the beach. Walking trails loop around the headland to the south. Kids will enjoy the giant zip-wire ride over the sand (summer only).

So-Muuido ISLAND

(₩2000) The tiny, car-free island of So-Muuido can be accessed via a footbridge from Muuido's southeastern tip. It's a charming fishing community with a clifftop walk and lovely seaside panoramas.

Silmi Beach BEACH

(실미해수욕장) The northernmost of the two main beaches on Muuido's west coast, Silmi is 2km southwest from the ferry terminal. Quieter than Hanagae Beach, at low tide you can walk across the the sand to the unpopulated islet of Silmido.

Sleeping & Eating

Both Hanagae and Silmi Beaches offer camping (BYO tent) and basic accommodation in beach huts. Rates at hotels and pensions rise on weekends and during July

Yeongjongdo & Muuido

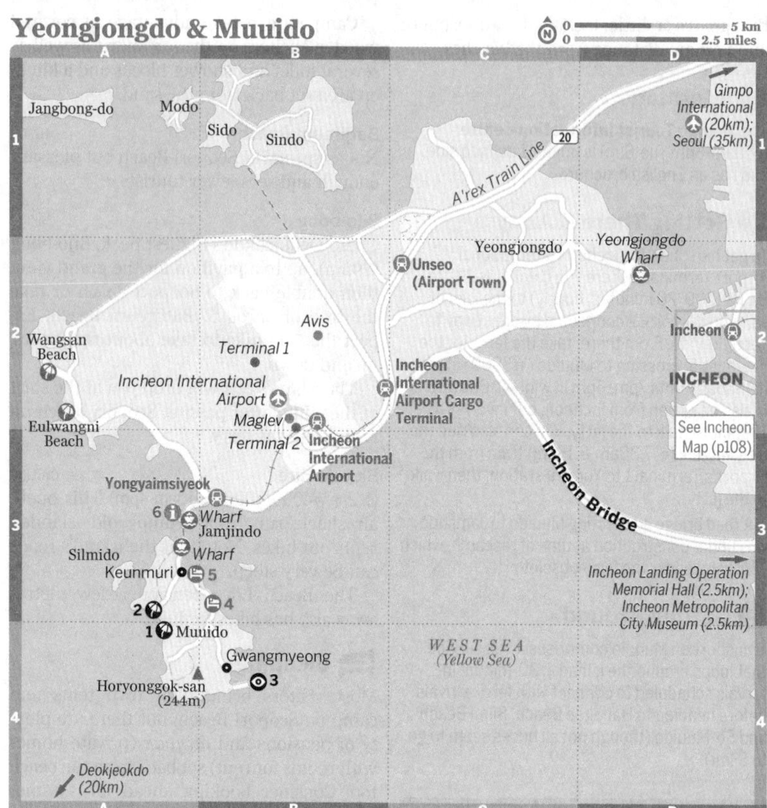

and August. There's a row of seafood restaurants at Keunmuri wharf.

Hanagae Beach Huts HUT$
(Hanagae Beach; huts ₩30,000) The best budget choice on the island is this row of stilted beach boxes plonked directly on Hanagae Beach (p112). Huts are basic heated *ondol* (traditional, sleep-on-a-floor-mattress) rooms, with *very* thin bedding and shared bathrooms. There's a ₩10,000 key deposit, and showers costs ₩1000. There are also private pension rooms for ₩50,000 to ₩100,000, which offer value for groups.

Island Garden PENSION $$
(섬뜰아래; ☎010 3056 2709; www.islandgarden.kr; r ₩70,000-150,000, camping ₩50,000; ❄📶) Offering apartment-style rooms, plenty of sea-facing decking and its own grassy plot for camping, Island Garden also has a tiny private beach. The friendly owners speak some English.

Yeongjongdo & Muuido

Sights

1 Hanagae Beach A4
2 Silmi Beach A3
3 So-Muuido B4

Sleeping

Hanagae Beach Huts .... (see 1)
4 Island Garden B3
5 Seaside Hotel A3

Information

6 Muuido Tourist Information Centre A3

Seaside Hotel HOTEL $$
(☎032 752 7737; www.seasidehotel.co.kr; r from ₩70,000; ❄📶) All the pleasantly decorated accommodation at this hotel – both large western-style and *ondol* (traditional, sleep-on-a-floor-mattress) rooms – have sea views,

though it's a little lacking in atmosphere and is some distance from the beaches.

Information

The **Muuido Tourist Information Centre** (9am-6pm Tue-Sun) is on the Jamjindo side, and has an English brochure.

Getting There & Away

To get here, head to Incheon International Airport Terminal 1 where you catch bus 222 or 2-1 (₩1200, 20 minutes, hourly) to the islet of Jamjindo (잠진도), connected by causeway to Yeongjongdo. From there, take the ferry for the five-minute crossing to Muuido (₩3800 return, half-hourly until 7pm, 6pm in winter). Bus 306 is also an option from Incheon, but involves a 15-minute walk to the jetty. You can also ride the free **Maglev** (7.30am-8.15pm) train from the airport's Terminal 1 to Yongyu station, then walk to the jetty.

A road bridge connecting Muuido to Jamjindo was under construction at time of research, which will likely render the ferry obsolete.

Getting Around

Transport on Muudio comprises a bus service that loops around the island in 30-minute intervals scheduled to connect with ferry arrivals before heading to Hanagae Beach, Silmi Beach and So-Muuido (though not all buses seem to go to Silmi).

Deokjeokdo

Deokjeokdo (덕적도) is one of the most scenic and laid-back of the West Sea islands. Beyond a blissful beach and breathless hilltop hike, there's nothing much else to do here apart from sit back and soak up the tranquillity.

Located 70km southwest of Incheon, Deokjeokdo is just about doable as a day trip, but you'll get more out of the journey (and be more relaxed) if you spend the night. Outside of warm weekends, expect to be one of the island's only visitors.

Sights & Activities

★Seopori Beach BEACH

(서포리해변) The spectacular 2km-long Seopori Beach, located along Deokjeokdo's southern shore and backed by a thick grove of 200-year-old pine trees, is a sleepy sanctuary of pristine nature and the main island attraction for travellers. Nearby Batjireum Beach (p114), 4km north, is another option.

Campers can take advantage of covered wooden shelters on the foreshore, as well as several toilet and shower blocks and a kitchen area set back from the sand.

Batjireum Beach BEACH

Not as special as Seopori Beach but pleasant enough and sees fewer tourists.

Bijo-bong HIKING

Climb Deokjeokdo's highest peak, Bijo-bong (292m), up to a pavilion for the grand view, then double back to Seopori Beach or take the trail onwards to Batjireum Beach. Expect the 7km hike to take about two hours, up and down.

The island's bus will drop you at the start of the climb after passing Seopori Beach on route from the ferry.

Bicycle Hire CYCLING

(1/2hr ₩4000/7000; 10am-4pm) This open-air shack, run by a grumpy old islander, rents out bikes. Note that the island's roads can be very steep.

The Beach Love pension a few metres away also has bikes for hike.

Sleeping

Most visitors bring their own tents and camp on Seopori Beach, but there are plenty of pensions and *minbak* (private homes with rooms for rent) set back from the beach too. Consider booking ahead for summer weekends.

★Seopori Hotel PENSION **$$**

(010 2106 4282; www.seoporia.com; ondol low/high season ₩120,000/200,000, cabins ₩100,000;) This snazzy pension on a hillside set back from the beach offers bright, *ondol* (traditional, sleep-on-a-floor-mattress) rooms that can sleep up to seven and come furnished with bathrooms, kitchenettes and sea-facing balconies. Or you can choose cosy pine cabins that sleep four to five people; each comes with its own barbecue facilities (charcoal costs ₩10,000). There's a well-equipped communal kitchen, a swimming pool (open July and August only) and wi-fi.

Beach Love PENSION **$$**

(비치사랑펜션; 010 5248 0007; www.beachlove.co.kr; Seopori Beach; r from ₩50,000;) This popular pension offers spotless, *ondol* (traditional, sleep-on-a-floor-mattress) rooms furnished with bathrooms and kitchenettes; the upstairs balcony rooms are a bit dearer. Also has bicycle hire (₩4000/15,000

per hour/day) and use of a barbecue. It's around 50m east of the convenience store in Seopori's tiny local town.

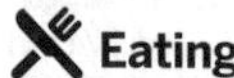

Eating

Choose from a tiny handful of restaurants behind Seopori Beach and at the ferry wharf. The island's only convenience store, also at Seopori Beach, is handy for buying alcohol.

Deokjeokdo Chinese Restaurant CHINESE $
(☎010 7393 9410; noodles ₩5000; ⏲11am-7pm) The *jajangmyeon* (noodles in black bean sauce) and egg rolls at this homey shack a few steps from Beach Love pension are the real deal. There's no name inside or out. The restaurant has plenty of cold beer.

Island Restaurant KOREAN $
(Memoria Restaurant; ☎032 832 3613; fried shrimp ₩10,000; ⏲11am-7pm) English is spoken at this homespun restaurant on the 2nd floor above Memoria Pension. Choose from dishes like pork cutlet, fried shrimp and spaghetti, but don't expect everything to be available. Accepts credit cards.

Shopping

Artisan Market MARKET
Open daily in time for the departing afternoon ferries (but best on weekends), this line of stalls sells fresh shellfish, seaweed products and local jams to take back to the mainland.

CU Convenience Store ALCOHOL
The hub of Deokjeokdo's not-so-thriving social life. Drop in for cold beer, salty snacks and local gossip.

Getting There & Away

Several daily ferries depart from Incheon's Coastal Ferry Terminal (p112) for the one-to-two-hour journey (₩42,000 return). Sailing times vary according to season, but the last ferry back to the mainland departs Deokjeokdo around 4pm.

Getting Around

The island's only bus waits at the ferry wharf for new arrivals and deposits them 12km away at Seopori Beach, or a little further on for the climb up Bijo-bong. It performs the same journey in reverse around 45 minutes before each afternoon ferry departure.

Local taxis cruise around in summer looking for wayward wanderers to take back to the ferry wharf, or to offer sightseeing tours of the island (around ₩20,000).

Ganghwado

☎032 / POP 65,500

South Korea's fifth-largest island, Ganghwado (강화도) is worth a side trip for its hilltop temples and other low-key attractions, as well as its fascinating history. For a brief period in the mid-13th century, when the Mongols were rampaging through the mainland, the island became the location of Korea's capital. Situated at the mouth of the Han River, Ganghwado continued to have strategic importance – it was the scene of bloody skirmishes with French and US forces in the 19th century as colonial powers tried to muscle in on the 'hermit kingdom'.

Sights

Ganghwado's main town, Ganghwa-eup (강화읍), is where all buses crossing the bridge from the mainland end up, and makes a logical base from which to embark on your tour of the island's attractions.

Note that Ganghwado is big, and buses infrequent, so you'll need a day or two to explore it properly. Local bus 7 (runs Thursday to Sunday) offers a handy sightseeing loop, taking in Ganghwa History Museum, Ganghwa Peace Observatory and Gapgot Dondae. If time is tight, consider taking a tour. Several leave from Seoul – check with the KTO Tourist Information Centre (www.visitkorea.or.kr). There's also one that starts from Geonam station on Sundays (₩10,000; book four days in advance by calling ☎032 772 4000).

★Goryeogungji Palace PALACE
(고려궁지; Ganghwa-eup; adult/child ₩900/600; ⏲9am-6pm) The partially restored remains of a small palace, dating back to the Goryeo dynasty (918–1392), sit on a hillside in Ganghwa-eup. The palace was completed around 1234, a few years after King Gojong moved his capital to Ganghwado to better resist Mongol invasion.

Directly down the hill from the palace is the Ganghwa Anglican Church (c 1900), notable in that it is designed like a traditional Korean temple. Follow the alleyways down to the Yongheunggung Royal Residence, where King Cheoljong lived in the 19th century.

The palace and town were once encircled by a 7km fortress wall, snaking over the surrounding hilltops much like the one in Seoul. Destroyed in 1866 by French troops

who invaded Korea in response to the execution of nine French Catholic missionaries, it has since been partially rebuilt, and three major gates have been renovated.

The palace is a 15-minute walk from the bus terminal.

Ganghwa Dolmen Park ARCHAEOLOGICAL SITE

(강화 고인돌 유적; 24hr) FREE Skip across this grassy field beside Ganghwa History Museum to marvel at Bugeun-ri Dolmen (부근리 고인돌), a trio of giant stones hefted into a megalithic tomb – the two 'door' stones are missing. Dating from the Bronze Age, the top stone is estimated to weigh 75 tonnes. It's a scenic spot with expansive valley views; no wonder the site was chosen for its auspicious purpose.

There are close to 150 dolmen scattered throughout Ganghwa, 70 of which are World Heritage–listed.

Bomun-sa TEMPLE

(보문사; 032 933 8271; Seongmodo; adult/youth/child ₩2500/1700/1000; 9am-6pm; 31, 35) Situated high in the pine-forested hills of the west-coast island of Seongmodo, this temple has some superbly ornate painting on the eaves of its buildings. The grotto and 10m-tall Buddha rock carving are standouts. The walk to reach Bomun-sa is steep and has many stairs – catch your breath at the top.

To get here, take bus 31 or 35 from Ganghwa bus terminal, which crosses a road bridge over to Seongmodo (one hour).

Mani-san MOUNTAIN

(마니산; adult/child ₩2000/700; 9am-6pm) It's a steep one-hour climb of more than 900 steps, to reach the top of scenic Mani-san (469m). At its summit you'll find **Chamseongdan** (참성단; 10am-4pm), a large stone altar said to have been originally built and used by Dangun, the mythical first Korean.

Mani-san is 15km from Ganghwa-eup; take bus 3 or 7A (50 minutes). A taxi from Ganghwa-eup (₩20,000) takes half an hour.

Jeondeung-sa BUDDHIST TEMPLE

(전등사; 032 937 0125; www.jeondeungsa.org; adult/youth/child ₩3000/2000/1000; 7am-sunset) This temple in Ganghwado's southeast commands a forested hilltop setting within the walls of Samrangseong Fortress. A free vegetarian lunch is served from around noon; wash your own dishes afterwards. You can also spend the night as part of the Templestay (p117) program (₩80,000).

Ganghwa History Museum MUSEUM

(http://museum.ganghwa.go.kr; adult//child ₩3000/2000; 9am-6pm Tue-Sun; 1, 3, 23, 25) Covering 5000 years of the island's history, the exhibits at this imaginative museum start with Ganghwa's ancient (and Unesco-listed) dolmen sites and continue up to the US Navy attack on the island in 1871.

Your ticket also gets you into the Ganghwa Natural History Museum next door, an ambitious little place containing a sperm-whale skeleton and some competent taxidermy. Both are a 20-minute bus ride from Ganghwa bus terminal.

Ganghwa Peace Observatory OBSERVATORY

(강화평화전망대; adult/child ₩2500/1700; 9am-6pm; 1, 2) This multiplex observatory just 2km from North Korea offers prime views into the 'hermit kingdom'. Through binoculars (₩500 for two minutes) you can spy villages, workers in rice fields, military towers and distant mountain ranges. There's a short, introductory video in English, but you'll need to request it to be played. Bus 26 will get you here, with bus 27 returning to Ganghwa-eup terminal (35 minutes).

Gapgot Dondae FORTRESS

(갑곶돈대; ₩2700; 9am-6pm Tue-Sun; 5) This fortress and observation post was one of several built along the coast to guard the Ganghwa strait here during the 13th century at the time of the Mongol invasions. An attached museum has rusting cannons among other artefacts. Bus 5 comes here from Ganghwa bus terminal (15 minutes).

Activities

Fortress Wall Hike HIKING

Starting at Ganghwa-eup's historic West Gate, follow the section of reconstructed fortress wall south up the hillside, which soon rises sharply. It's then a breathless 2km march along the denuded nub of the wall to a lofty pavilion with fabulous views. From there you can carry on down to Ganghwa-eup, completing the loop, or continue on other marked walking trails.

Festivals & Events

Azalea Festival CULTURAL

(Apr) Every April, walkers hike up Goryosan (436m) to snap photos of a carpet of azalea blossoms on the peak.

Sleeping

Apart from the options here, there are several chilled out *minbak* (private homes with rooms for rent) on Seongmodo, the tiny island just west of Ganghwado that houses Bomun-sa.

Hotel Everrich HOTEL $$
(호텔에버리치; ☎032 934 1688; www.hoteleverrich.com; d ₩110,000;) Perched on the side of a mountain and offering expansive views towards the mainland, this 70-room hotel has a nature-lodge vibe, with minimalist white rooms, a pool and a pleasant Italian restaurant. Trails above the hotel connect up with the fortress wall hike.

Take a taxi here from the bus terminal; otherwise it's a long walk.

Jeondeung-sa Temple TEMPLESTAY $$
(☎032 937 0152; http://eng.templestay.com; dm incl food & activities from ₩80,000) Part of the Templestay program, the hilltop temple of Jeondeung-sa encourages visitors to check in and then tune in to their inner Buddha. Prices include vegetarian meals, cultural activities and dawn wake-up calls.

Namchidang GUESTHOUSE $$
(남취당; ☎032 937 0119; http://kyl3850.com/pension/index.php?uid=3; r from ₩100,000;) This purpose-built *hanok* (traditional wooden home) has wood-fired *ondol* (traditional, sleep-on-a-floor-mattress) rooms and free bicycle hire. It's a couple of kilometres from Jeondeung-sa; buses 3, 7 and 41 run here from Ganghwa bus terminal.

Eating & Drinking

Ganghwado is known for its eel dishes. A couple of good eel-barbecue joints styled like log cabins can be found just beyond Ganghwa-eup's reconstructed West Gate.

Bomun-sa is known for plates of *twigim* (tempura) seafood accompanied by local ginseng-infused *makgeolli* (rice wine).

Wangjajeong KOREAN $$
(왕자정; Ganghwa-eup; meals ₩8000-25,000; ⏲10am-9.30pm;) Enjoy healthy, delicious vegetarian dishes such as *mukbap* (acorn jelly rice) and *kongbiji* (bean soup) while overlooking the walls of Goryeogungji Palace (p115).

Jungnim Dawon TEAHOUSE
(죽림다원; Jeongeungsa-sa; tea ₩5000; ⏲9am-5.30pm) This atmospheric teahouse and garden within Jeondeung-sa is frequented by resident monks sipping on traditional Korean teas, while presumably contemplating the meaning of life, the universe and everything.

Information

The **tourist information centre** (☎032 930 3515; www.ganghwa.incheon.kr; Ganghwa-eup bus terminal; ⏲9am-6pm) can provide you with English-language maps and bus times.

There's another tourist information centre in the car park at Gapgot Dondae just after you cross the bridge from the mainland.

Getting There & Away

Frequent buses run from near Seoul's Sinchon station to Ganghwa-eup's **bus terminal** (강화터미널; Ganghwa-eup; ₩2900, 1 hour 50 minutes) – they go every 10 minutes from 4am to 10pm. From Incheon, you can jump on bus 800 from Jemulpo station (₩2100, 1 hour 40 minutes).

Getting Around

While buses from Ganghwa-eup connect all points of the island, they run infrequently, usually every hour, so it pays to get info on bus schedules.

Cycling can be a good way of exploring Ganghwado, which has quieter roads than the mainland plus decent bike-lane provision.

From the Gapgot Dondae fortifications, a 15km cycle path runs alongside the seaside highway towards the southern Gangwha Choji Bridge, past eel restaurants, rice fields and several more stone fortifications lining the coast including those at Gwangseongbo (광성보) and Chojijin (초지진).

Gangwon-do

Includes ➡

Best Places to Eat

- ➡ Byoldang Makguksu (p122)
- ➡ Todam Sundubu (p137)
- ➡ Geumhak Kalguksu (p137)
- ➡ Bikini Burger (p137)
- ➡ Emoi Vietnam Kitchen (p142)
- ➡ Pino (p137)

Best Places to Stay

- ➡ House Hostel (p128)
- ➡ Kensington Stars Hotel (p127)
- ➡ Lakai Sandpine Resort (p136)
- ➡ Haslla Museum Hotel (p139)
- ➡ James BLuE Hostel (p128)

Why Go?

Mountainous Gangwon-do (강원도) gives you some of South Korea's most spectacular natural parks and scenic landscapes, up-close Demilitarized Zone (DMZ) experiences, and laid-back coastal towns and beaches on the East Sea. This is where many Seoulites escape – to get lost in the hills, chow down on Chuncheon's fiery chicken dish *dakgalbi* or the raw fish of the coastal towns, or leap into a frenzy of sports such as skiing in Pyeongchang, which hosted the 2018 Winter Olympics.

While the province may not have that much by way of cultural antiquities, what it does have – Gangneung's 400-year-old Dano Festival, for instance – it celebrates with zest. And Gangwon-do can be quirky too. Near Samcheok you'll find a park full of unabashed phallic sculptures standing cheek by jowl with a humble fishing village, while Gangneung has a museum dedicated to its founder's lifelong obsession with all things Edison.

When to Go

Chuncheon

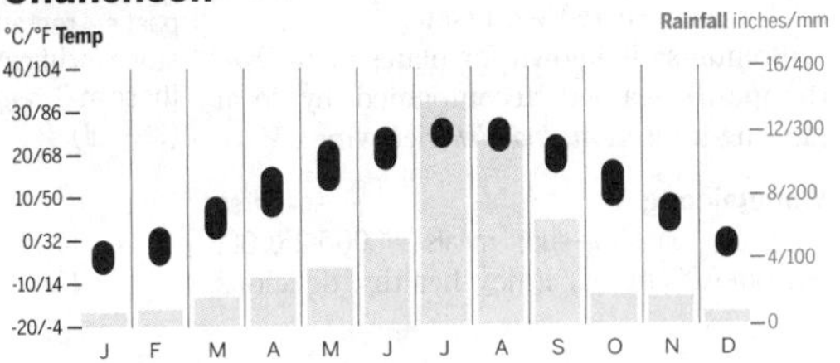

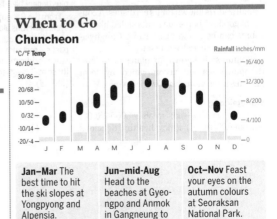

Jan–Mar The best time to hit the ski slopes at Yongpyong and Alpensia.

Jun–mid-Aug Head to the beaches at Gyeongpo and Anmok in Gangneung to enjoy the summer.

Oct–Nov Feast your eyes on the autumn colours at Seoraksan National Park.

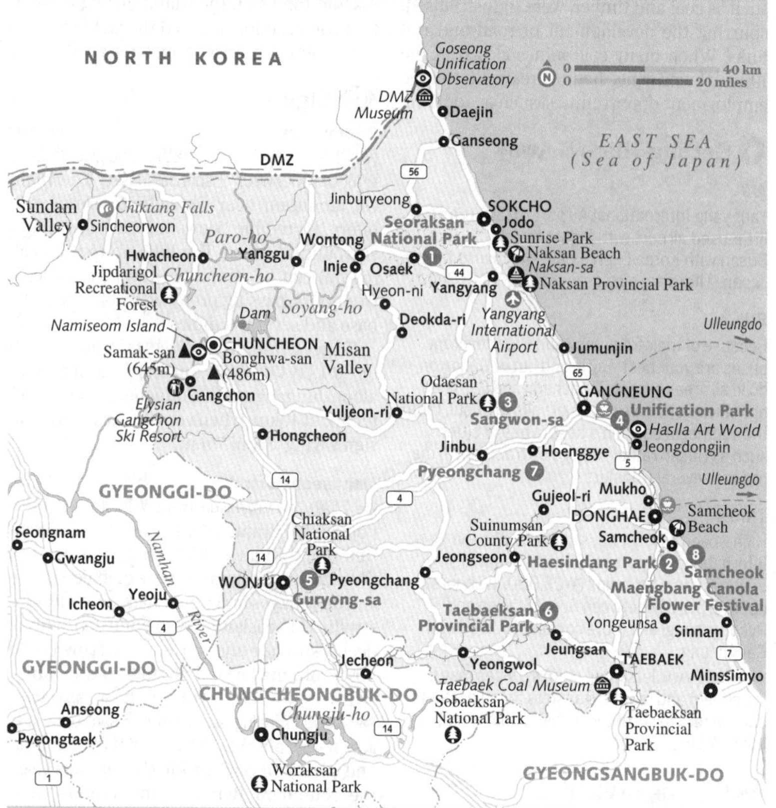

Gangwon-do Highlights

1. **Seoraksan National Park** (p123) Climbing through the stunning, misty mountains, hunting out temples, waterfalls and solitude.
2. **Haesindang Park** (p140) Watching and joining in with the crowds eyeing up the park's extraordinary phallic sculptures.
3. **Sangwon-sa** (p132) Exploring the historic fabric of this Buddhist temple before hiking into the hills.
4. **Unification Park** (p138) Hunching up to stoop about in a real North Korean submarine near Jeongdongjin.
5. **Guryong-sa** (p145) Joining the Templestay program and discovering tranquillity and peace in them mountains.
6. **Taebaeksan Provincial Park** (p139) Making a pilgrimage to the mountaintop altar to Dangun.
7. **Pyeongchang** (p142) Skiing at the Olympic venues in Yongpyong and Alpensia ski resorts.
8. **Samcheok Maengbang Canola Flower Festival** (p141) Wading into a sea of yellow canola flowers in spring for photo-ops.

History

Gangwon-do is the southern half of a province that once straddled the border (the North Korean half is romanised as Kangwon-do). Some areas north of the 38th parallel belonged to North Korea from 1945 till the end of the Korean War, and it's not uncommon to come across families with relatives in North Korea.

During the war this province saw many fierce battles for strategic mountaintops. Subsequently its rich natural resources,

such as coal and timber, were industrialised, spurring the development of road and rail links. When many coal mines closed in the 1990s, the province had to create alternative employment opportunities, such as tourism.

Getting There & Away

AIR

Yangyang International Airport (p130) is a little-used airport with flights to Jeju-do and Busan with Korea Express Air, which also flies to Japan. There are also seasonal flights to China.

BUS

Because of their frequency and wide coverage, buses are your best way in and out of Gangwon-do in all areas except Chuncheon and Gangneung, which both have good rail links to Seoul. From the southeast coast, it's best to bus to cities such as Busan rather than go by train, which may require several transfers.

TRAIN

High-speed KTX services connect Incheon International Airport (p395) and Seoul to Pyeongchang. Six trains (₩22,000, 1½ hours) operate per day between Seoul Station and Pyeongchang, and more connect to Jinbu and Gangneung.

Korail (www.letskorail.com) services may be infrequent and require transfers to the northern and eastern parts of the province that aren't on the KTX Line.

Getting Around

You can rent a car in cities such as Chuncheon, Sokcho and Gangneung; highways are excellent, though tolls and speed cameras are frequent.

Chuncheon

033 / POP 275,000

The charms of Gangwon-do's capital, Chuncheon (춘천, meaning 'Spring River'), dwell in its shimmering lake views, gorgeous surrounding mountains, and doses of the fiery chicken dish *dakgalbi*. It's also a good base for outdoor activities, and its superb transport links with Seoul makes it a popular weekend getaway for denizens of the capital.

With several universities Gangwon-do also has a youngish vibe, with a burgeoning shopping and nightlife scene.

On Jungdo, construction on the city's drawcard-to-be Legoland has ground to a halt, and the theme park may never be built, even though the bridge to the city has been completed. The discovery of prehistoric ruins and tombs on the island during foundation construction silenced the jackhammers and concrete mixers, maybe for good.

Sights

Samak-san MOUNTAIN

(삼악산; 033 262 2215; adult/youth/child ₩1600/1000/600; sunrise-sunset) The highest mountain near Chuncheon, Samak-san offers incredible views of the town and surrounding lakes. The hike up to the peak (645m) can be strenuous and takes at least two hours, passing pretty waterfalls near the base and several temples.

To get to the ticket office, take bus 3, 5, 50 or 50-1 (₩1300, 15 minutes) heading south along Jungang-no in Chuncheon. Get off after about 10km, when you see the green road sign saying 'Seoul 79km'.

Namiseom Island ISLAND

(남이섬; www.namisum.com; ₩10,000) Part of popular TV drama *Winter Sonata* was set on this island in an artificial lake southwest of Chuncheon. It's home to rows of majestic redwoods, ginkgos and pines, making it ideal for strolling. The island is also home to roaming deer, ostriches and various waterfowl, and hosts rotating art and photography exhibits.

It's a touristy park with a **zip wire** (₩38,000 including island entry; 9am-6pm, later in summer), **electric triway** (₩24,000 per hour) and plenty of *Sonata* kitsch – it calls itself the Naminara Republic and visitors need 'visa' tickets (kids under three are free), which include entrance and a return **ferry trip** (7.30am-9.40pm) – but it's a fine spot for a breath of fresh air.

To get there, hop on a train from Chuncheon to Gapyeong (₩3000, 17 minutes, hourly) and then walk 1.6km (25 minutes) or bus it (₩1300, three minutes) to Gapyeong Wharf.

Korean War Memorial MEMORIAL

The evocative statues at this memorial to the Battle of Chuncheon are shown midaction, holding North Koreans at bay at the opening of the Korean War on 25 June 1950. It's a moving memorial, despite the nationalist dynamics to the artwork.

A more sober, mournful and poignant commemorative statue can be found a short walk north: three soldiers helping each other, with the cut-out of a helmeted rifle stuck in the ground carved expertly in the stonework.

Chuncheon

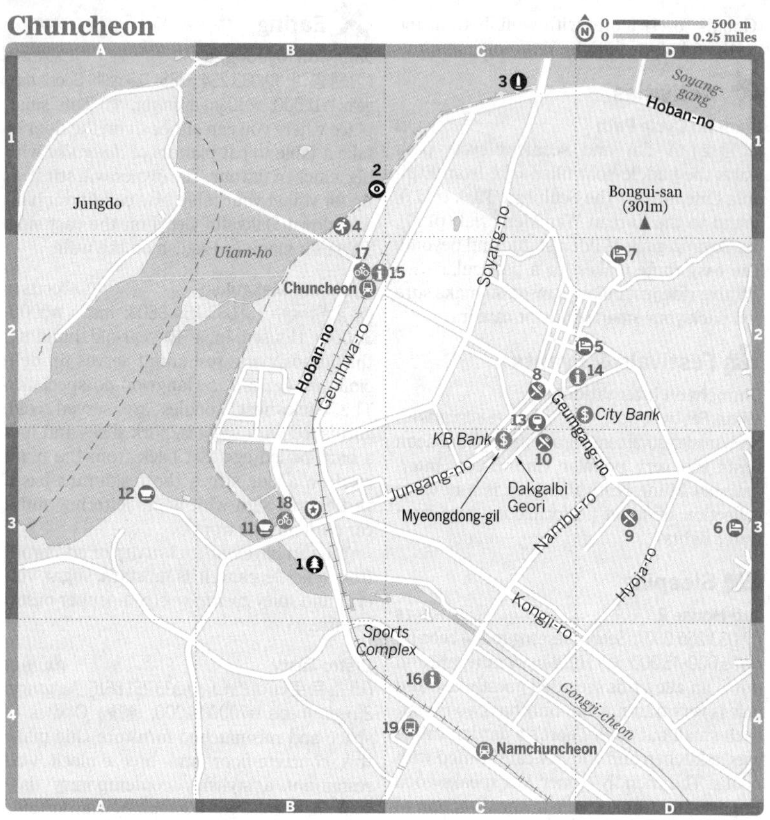

Chuncheon

Sights
1 Gongjicheon Sculpture Park B3
2 Korean War Memorial B1
3 Soyang-gang Maiden C1

Activities, Courses & Tours
4 Uiam-ho Cycle Path B1

Sleeping
5 Grand Motel D2
6 Jati House 2 .... D3
7 Sejong Hotel Chuncheon D2

Eating
8 Bistro Tasty C2
9 Byoldang Makguksu D3
10 Jangwon Myeongga C3

Drinking & Nightlife
11 Ethiopia Café B3
12 Gallery Cafe A3
13 Jackson Bill C2

Information
14 Chuncheon City Hall Department of Tourism D2
15 Tourist Information Booth B2
16 Tourist Information Centre C4
Tourist Information Office .... (see 19)

Transport
17 Bicycle Rental B2
18 Bicycle Rental B3
19 Express & Intercity Bus Terminals C4

Gongjicheon Sculpture Park PARK
(공지천 조각공원) Families and teens picnic and sit in the shade of trees in this park dotted with sculptures, some of them hard to fathom. It's a very pleasant diversion if you are tired from walking Chuncheon's large distances, and there's a small water fountain for a drink and a handy supermarket

(Gongji Forest Store) with wi-fi, both at the north end of the park by Yetgyeongchun-ro.

Activities

Uiam-ho Cycle Path CYCLING

(의암호) A flat and scenic bicycle path skirts the paddle-boat filled lake from Ethiopia Café, next to the Sculpture Park (p121), round to the Korean War Memorial (p120), the Soyang-gang Maiden statue and beyond. The easy route makes for a particularly attractive ride just before sunset, so make sure you pack your smartphone or camera.

Festivals & Events

Chuncheon International Mime Festival PERFORMING ARTS

(www.mimefestival.com; late May) Chuncheon hosts the very popular Chuncheon International Mime Festival, which is a raucous collection of street performances and even water fights.

Sleeping

Jati House 2 GUESTHOUSE $

(033 255 0507; Seobudaeseong-ro 184 beon-gil; r ₩35,000-45,000;) Hidden away uphill and down an alley, this secluded guesthouse and cafe is very tranquil, but only has two rooms, each small but cute. There's a garden full of cats, a kitchen and a lovely cafe stuffed with books. The friendly owner Jati speaks good English and Chinese. It's in the direction of Kangwon National University.

Sejong Hotel Chuncheon HOTEL $$

(춘천 세종 호텔; 033 252 1191; www.chunchonsejong.co.kr; d/ondol from ₩135,000/145,000;) Nestled on the slope of Bonguisan, this rather plush hotel offers unrivalled views of Chuncheon and the surrounding countryside, ensconced within an attractive setting, with a rockery and landscaped waterfall feature that blooms with azaleas in spring. Rooms have a warm glow, with all the mod cons, and some ground-floor rooms have a patio. The cheapest rooms get mountain views. American breakfast is ₩10,000.

Grand Motel MOTEL $$

(그랜드모텔; 033 243 5022; Okcheon-no 39-6; r from ₩40,000;) This motel, run by a kind and helpful family, stands out from the surrounding love motels for comfortable, good-sized rooms sans tackiness. The owners can provide information for sightseeing in Chuncheon and nearby. Rates rise by 25% on Friday and Saturday.

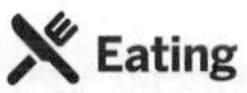

Eating

Jangwon Myeongga KOREAN $

(장원명가; 033 254 6388; Dakgalbi Geori; dakgalbi ₩11,000; 10am-midnight;) This small place where you can either sit on the floor or take a table to eat platters of *dakgalbi* with big, chicken flavour. The owner will stir it all up for you at your table. You can find it halfway down Dakgalbi Geori on the east side. There's a menu in English on the wall.

Byoldang Makguksu NOODLES $$

(별당막국수; 033 254 9603; meals ₩5000-35,000) Housed in a 40-year-old building, this atmospheric restaurant serves up delicious *makguksu*, a Gangwon-do speciality. The buckwheat noodles are served cold, garnished with veggies, pork slices and half a hard-boiled egg. Set back from the main road on a side street, the restaurant has a vertical red sign with white lettering and a car park out the front.

You can have *makguksu* dry or add broth from a kettle, as well as mustard, sugar, vinegar and spicy *gochujang* (red-pepper paste) to taste.

Bistro Tasty ITALIAN $$

(비스트로테이스티; 033 251 8616; Jungangro 2(i)-ga; meals ₩7000-14,000;) Oodles of space and mismatched-furniture chic make this concrete-floor and breeze-block wall restaurant a stylishly contemporary date spot for locals, yet it's equally comfortable for solo diners. If ordering a burger, specify how you would like it cooked or otherwise it will turn up medium-rare. Set dishes, such as seafood linguine (₩12,000) with bread and a glass of wine, are excellent value.

Drinking & Nightlife

Gallery Cafe CAFE

(033 254 1917; www.artncompany.kr; snacks from ₩4000; 10am-11pm) Part of the Art n Company gallery, this stylish hillside cafe has a great tea selection and commands lovely views of Uiam-ho, accompanied by smooth, jazzy sounds. It's in the MBC broadcasting building; from the city centre, take a taxi or walk along the boardwalk around the lake and head up the steps. For eats, there's whipped cream cake, tiramisu and cookies.

Jackson Bill BAR

(010 2993 7754; 50-6 Joyang-dong; 5pm-1am) This old-school watering hole between Myeong-dong and the bend of Dakgalbi Geori is overseen by amiable veteran Mr

Oh, who sits in front of 8000 vinyl records and takes requests, digging out oldies from the '70s and '80s upon request. Mr Oh first set up at the US Army base in town (Camp Page), then moved here when the soldiers moved out.

It's on the 2nd floor, so look for the stairs heading up, on the north side of the alley, with a chicken sign high up on the other side of the lane. Draught beers start at about ₩4000.

Ethiopia Café CAFE
(이디오피아; ⊙10am-9pm) Ethiopia Café is the main establishment at the lakefront, near the Memorial Hall for Ethiopian Veterans of the Korean War with its triple-pointedroof. It's mainly notable for its location rather than for its coffee, drinks or interior ambience.

Information

The best place for tourist information for the region is the Chuncheon City Hall Department of Tourism, but the building was being reconstructed at the time of writing. There is also a basic **tourist information office** (☎033 250 3896; www.chuncheon.go.kr; ⊙9am-6pm) at the bus terminal, a **tourist information booth** (☎033 250 4312) outside Chuncheon station and another **tourist information centre** (☎033 244 0088) around 600m north of the bus terminal; all have maps in English, but staff only speak Korean.

If you stay with Jati at Jati House 2 or have a coffee in her sedate cafe, she can supply you with information.

City Bank (⊙9am-4pm Mon-Fri)
KB Bank (⊙9am-4pm Mon-Fri)
Police (☎112)

Getting There & Away

BUS

The **Express & Intercity Bus Terminals** (Gyeongchun-ro) are beside each other. Departures from the latter include Gwangju (₩24,500, five hours, hourly); buses leave either terminal for Daegu (₩18,000, four hours, hourly). A short taxi ride takes you to the city; the highway is unpleasant to walk along. Buses (₩21,000, 2½ hours, regular) also run from Bay 13A of Incheon International Airport direct to Chuncheon centre, which saves you hauling your bag onto the metro.

TRAIN

ITX trains run on the Gyeongchun Line from Seoul's Cheongnyangni train station (₩6400, one hour, hourly) and Yongsan station (₩7300, 1¼ hours, hourly) to Chuncheon station, also stopping at Namchuncheon in Chuncheon, which is a little further to central Myeongdong-gil. From either station it's a quick taxi ride to Chuncheon, though it is an easy walk from Chuncheon station.

Seoul's Gyeongchun metro line also runs trains from Sangbong to Namchuncheon and Chuncheon stations (₩2850, one hour, every 15 minutes), taking in scenic mountain views.

Getting Around

Most short taxi rides around Chuncheon cost about ₩5000. The local train between Chuncheon and Namchuncheon stations costs ₩1150.

There's **bicycle rental** (per hour/day ₩3000/10,000; ⊙9am-7pm) from a stall opposite the Ethiopia Café, or from a **bike shop** (per 1hr/2hr/day ₩3000/5000/10,000; ⊙9am-7pm) by the stairs to Chuncheon station, where you can also buy clear route maps.

Seoraksan National Park

☎033

One of the most beautiful and iconic parks on the entire Korean Peninsula, and a draw for Koreans and travellers alike, Seoraksan National Park is a Unesco Biosphere Protection site. Seorak-san (Snowy Peaks Mountain) is the third-highest mountain in South Korea, with its highest peak, Daecheong-bong (대청봉), soaring to 1708m. Set within this landscape are two stately Buddhist temples, Sinheung-sa (p126) and Baekdam-sa (p126). Certain natural preservation areas are closed to the public. Ask at the visitor centre (p127) for details on free guided tours and hikes (the minimum number of participants is five).

Sights

Seoraksan National Park NATIONAL PARK
(설악산 국립공원; ☎033 636 7700; http://english.knps.or.kr; adult/child ₩3500/500; ⊙sunrise-sunset) One of South Korea's most beloved and beautiful national parks, Seoraksan is most celebrated for its oddly shaped rock formations and ancient Silla-era temples. It's also a hiker's paradise, a stunning realm of gnarled rock formations, dense forests, abundant wildlife, hot springs and plunging waterfalls. Peak season is July and August, while in mid-October visitors flock to see the changing colours of the autumn leaves – best appreciated over a bottle of *meoruju* (wild fruit wine).

Embedded within this setting are two famous Buddhist temples: Sinheung-sa (p126)

Seoraksan National Park

A
B
C
D
1
2
3
4
5
6
7
46
Ganseong (26km)
Yongdae-ri
Bukcheon
Shuttle Bus to Baekdam-sa
Namgyo-ri
46
Baekdam-sa Bus Stop
1
Sibiseonnyeotang Valley
INNER SEORAK
Dumun Pokpo
Suryeom-dong Valley
An-san (1430m)
Inje (12km); Yanggu (25km)
Daeseungnyeong Pass
Daeseungnyeong (1210m)
Daeseung Pokpo
44
7
Jugeok-bong (1401m)
Gari-bong (1519m)
451

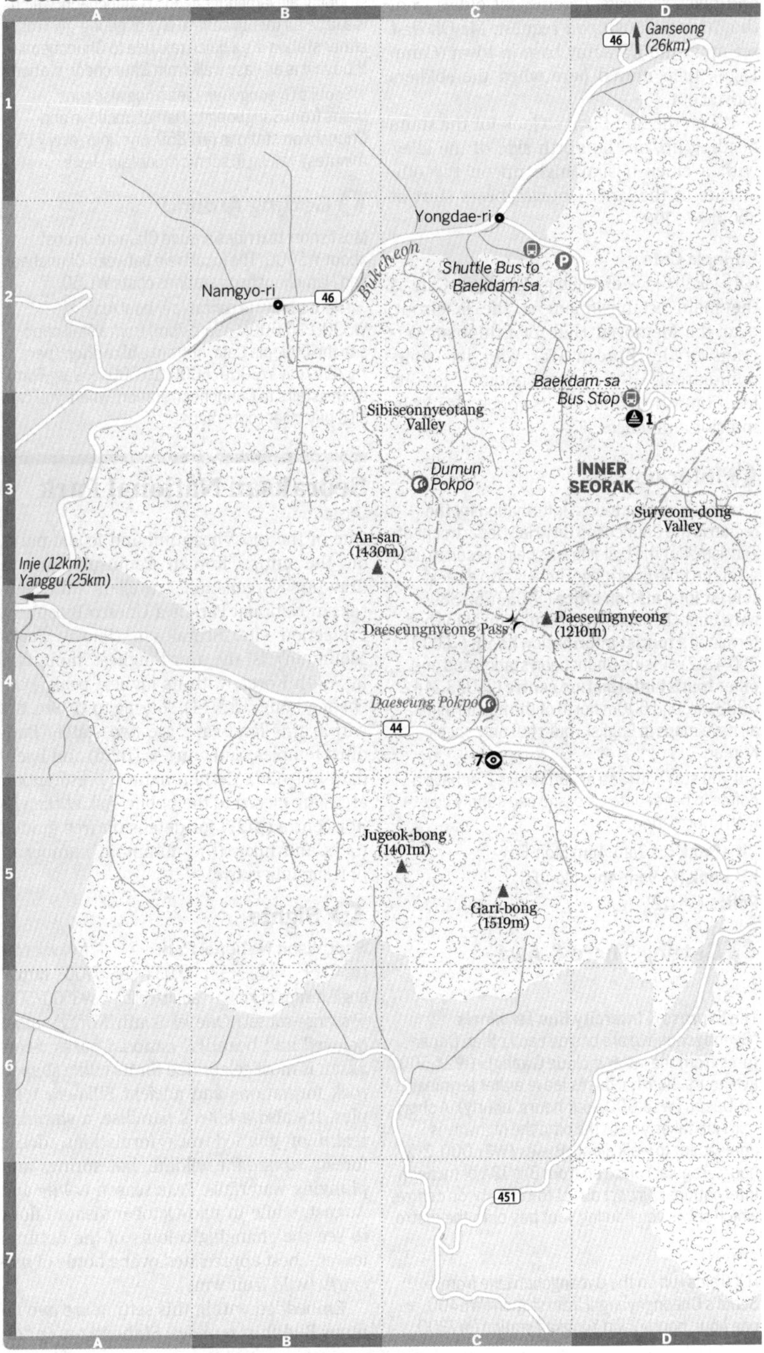

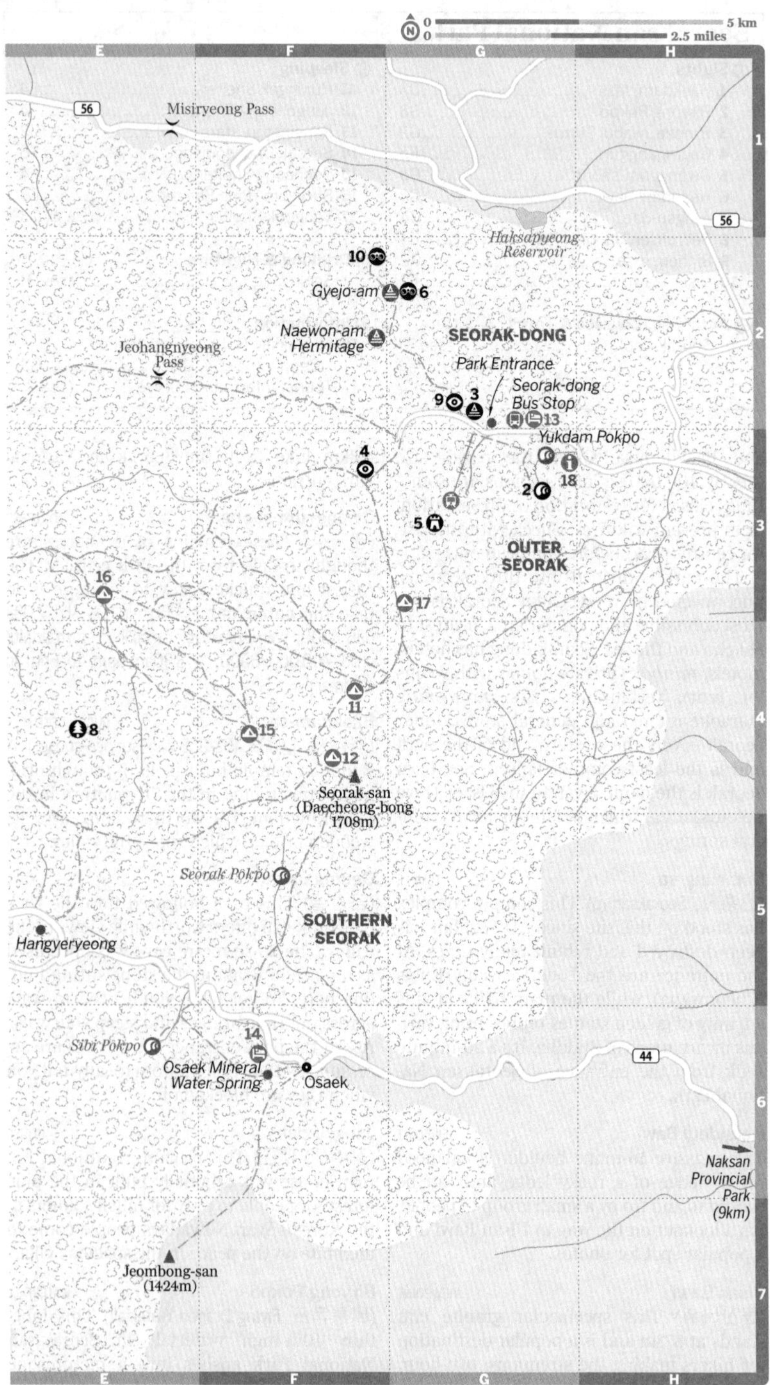

0 5 km
0 2.5 miles
E
F
G
H
1
2
3
4
5
6
7
56
Misiryeong Pass
Haksapyeong Reservoir
10
Gyejo-am
6
Naewon-am Hermitage
SEORAK-DONG
Jeohangnyeong Pass
Park Entrance
9
3
Seorak-dong Bus Stop
13
Yukdam Pokpo
4
18
2
5
OUTER SEORAK
16
17
11
8
15
12
Seorak-san (Daecheong-bong 1708m)
Seorak Pokpo
SOUTHERN SEORAK
Hangyeryeong
14
Sibi Pokpo
Osaek Mineral Water Spring
Osaek
44
Naksan Provincial Park (9km)
Jeombong-san (1424m)

Seoraksan National Park

Sights

Activities, Courses & Tours

Sleeping

Drinking & Nightlife

Information

and Baekdam-sa. Given the park's size (nearly 400,000 sq km), sections are sometimes closed for restoration or preservation, or to prevent wildfires. Check with the visitor centre (p127) before you head out.

The park is divided into three sections, unconnected by road: Outer Seorak is the most accessible and popular area, nearest to Sokcho and the sea. Seorak-dong has hotels, motels, *minbak* (private homes with rooms for rent), restaurants, bars, *noraebang* (karaoke rooms) and general stores. Inner Seorak covers the western end of the park and is the least commercialised; Southern Seorak is the name given to the Osaek (Five Colours) area, which is famous for its mineral springs.

Sinheung-sa TEMPLE

(신흥사; Seoraksan-ro) This temple complex has stood on this site since AD 652, but has been destroyed and rebuilt many times. At the entrance are the Four Heavenly Kings (Cheonwang), while the main hall contains a trinity of golden statues representing various incarnations of Buddha. It's a 20-minute walk from the entrance of Seoraksan National Park.

Heundeul Bawi VIEWPOINT

This massive 16-tonne boulder is balanced on the edge of a rocky ledge and can be rocked to and fro by a small group of people. It's a lookout on the way to Ulsan Bawi and a popular spot for photos.

Ulsan Bawi VIEWPOINT

(울산바위) This spectacular granite cliff stands at 873m and is a popular destination for hikers making the strenuous, two-hour, 4.3km hike from the Seoraksan National Park entrance.

Gwongeum-seong FORTRESS

(권금성) These remains of a fortress are thought to date from the 13th century. The easiest and quickest way to get here is to take the **cable car** (설악 케이블카; ☎033 636 4300; www.sorakcablecar.co.kr; return adult/child ₩10,000/6000; ⌚8.30am-5pm, to 6pm in summer).

Baekdam-sa BUDDHIST TEMPLE

(백담사; ☎033 462 2554; ⌚sunrise-sunset) A Buddhist temple built in 1957, though originally constructed in the 7th century in the Silla Kingdom. It's worth walking over its wooden bridge, which spans the valley.

Geumganggul CAVE

(금강굴) This cave hollowed into the rock of Seorak-san offers worthwhile views of the valley. The 23-sq-metre cave was once used as a place to worship the stone sitting Buddha here. To get here, you'll need to walk across multiple bridges and steep stairways. Ask at the park entrance if the caves are accessible as they don't automatically tell you when they are blocked off.

Jangsu-dae HOUSE

(장수대) FREE This elegant, traditional Korean house was originally built in the pine forest for people to pray for fallen soldiers in the Korean War. Nowadays people come to meditate on the peace in the spacious villa.

Biryong Pokpo WATERFALL

(비룡폭포, Flying Dragon Waterfall) This long, thin 40m-high waterfall in Seorak-san National Park gushes into a picturesque

pool and is a 2km climb up from the Seoraksan National Park Visitor Centre.

Sleeping

The road from Yongdae-ri to the park entrance (1km) is flanked by farmhouses, *minbak* (from around ₩20,000 per room) and restaurants. It's a good place to spend the night if you'd like to wake up to your own slice of rural Korean idyll.

There are four mountain shelters (₩12,000 to ₩13,000, depending on the season) along the Outer Seorak routes to Daecheong-bong – at **Jungcheong** (☎033 672 1708; http://english.knps.or.kr; per person Dec-Apr ₩12,000, May-Nov ₩13,000), **Yangpok** (per person Dec-Apr ₩12,000, May-Nov ₩13,000), **Huiungak** (☎033 672 1708; http://english.knps.or.kr; per person Dec-Apr ₩12,000, May-Nov ₩13,000) and **Socheong** (per person Dec-Apr ₩12,000, May-Nov ₩13,000). Reservations are accepted only for Jungcheong and Huiungak, which is just 100m below the peak. **Suryeom-dong Shelter** (☎033 462 2576; per person Dec-Apr ₩12,000, May-Nov ₩13,000) is on the trail from Baekdam-sa. Check for shelter closures at http://english.knps.or.kr/experience/shelters.

Seorak Oncheonjang MOTEL $$
(설악온천장; ☎033 672 2645; r ₩30,000; ❄@📶) This motel has pleasant rooms spread over two neat white buildings, with the lobby in the rear one. The *oncheon* (hot-spring spa; summer and autumn only) is free for guests, as is wi-fi. Owner Mr Lim can speak some English. Rates rise to ₩40,000 on Friday and Saturday, and go up to ₩70,000 during peak periods.

★ **Kensington Stars Hotel** LUXURY HOTEL $$$
(켄싱턴호텔; ☎033 635 4001; www.kensington.co.kr; d/ondol/tw ₩209,000/209,000/300,000; ❄@📶) Just 300m from the park entrance, in the crook of a mountain, is this English oasis with Edwardian armchairs in the lobby and two red London Routemaster double-decker buses outside (including a No 52 that ran through Notting Hill). The floors have themes such as movies and sports, and autographed memorabilia abounds; check out the Beatles records in the Abbey Road lounge.

There's also a veranda outside the Abbey Road lounge upstairs, with excellent views – anyone can visit.

Eating & Drinking

As in many national parks, the restaurants around Seoraksan serve popular fare such as *sanchae* bibimbap (₩9000) and *sanchae-jeongsik* (mountain-vegetable banquet dishes; ₩11,000), both of which feature local vegetables. You can grab a filling bowl of ramen for ₩6000 at the cable car restaurant.

Seolhyang CAFE
(雪香; drinks ₩8000; ⏲8am-6.30pm) Inside the park and on the outskirts of Seorak-dong, this charming traditional Korean cafe has a terrific range of freshly roasted coffees and sits by a bridge leading to the main pavilion of Sinheung-sa temple. It's the perfect spot to refuel with a coffee and a cookie or two.

Information

The **Seoraksan National Park Visitor Centre** (☎033 636 7700; ⏲10am-5pm Tue-Sun) at the entrance to Outer Seorak has some information in English as well as maps. A **tourist information office** (⏲9.30am-5.30pm) inside the park entrance has a smaller selection, as well as lockers (₩2000 to ₩3500 per hour).

Getting There & Away

The access road to Outer Seorak branches off the main coast road at Sunrise Park, halfway between Sokcho and Nak-san. From outside Sokcho's intercity bus terminal, along Jungang-no, or opposite its express bus terminal, catch bus 7 or 7-1 (₩1200, 30 minutes, every 10 minutes), which terminates at the bus stop at the park entrance at Seorak-dong.

Buses from Sokcho's intercity bus terminal run every hour to Osaek (₩4000) and Jangsu-dae (₩5600). From Dong-Seoul, there are also seven buses daily to Osaek (₩17,800, 2½ hours) from 6.30am. At Osaek, buy your bus ticket (cash only) at the general store about 10m from the bus stop on the highway.

Also from Sokcho's intercity bus terminal, buses bound for Jinburyeong (six daily from 6.30am to 5.50pm) make stops at Yondae-ri (₩6800) and Namgyo-ri (₩7100). From Yongdae-ri, it's a 1km walk to the park entrance. There, you can hike or take a **shuttle bus** (adult/child one way ₩1800/1000, 15 minutes, every 20 minutes) to the **stop** at Baekdam-sa; it runs from 7am to 5.30pm.

Sokcho

☎033 / POP 100,000

Despite its proximity to Seoraksan National Park, Sokcho (속초) is more of a fishing

town than a tourist hub. The main commercial activity – and its attendant aromas – are clustered along the waterfront. For most domestic tourists the main draw is the chance to sup on fresh raw fish with the tang of salt in the air. Vintage seafood restaurant Abai Shikdang has been particularly attractive to visitors since it appeared in K-drama *Autumn in My Heart*. The beaches get crowded on New Year's Eve when people gather to watch the first sunrise of the year.

Sokcho is only about 60km from the border and was part of North Korea from 1945 to the end of the Korean War. Most of the coastline is lined with barbed wire. At night, remember that lights in the water are to attract squid; lights on the beaches are to detect infiltrators.

Sights

DMZ Museum MUSEUM
(DMZ박물관; ☎033 680 8463; www.dmzmuseum.com; adult/child ₩2000/1000; ⊙9am-5.30pm Mar-Oct, to 5pm Nov-Feb) This large museum has a surprising amount of English in its narration of the history of the DMZ, as well as exhibits such as US POW letters and extensive photos.

It's inside the Tongil Security Park, on the left side of the road as you approach the Goseong Unification Observatory.

From central Sokcho or the bus stop right outside the intercity bus terminal, catch bus 1 or 1-1 (₩5020, 1½ hours, 44km, every 15 minutes) headed north, but ask if they go to the DMZ as not all do. Get off at Machajin (마차진; a round-trip taxi from Sokcho might cost in the region of ₩70,000) and walk about 10 minutes up to the Tongil Security Park (통일안보공원). Here you present identification and purchase your admission ticket. If you don't have your own vehicle, the staff might be able to help you hitch a ride, but don't count on it. It's 10km to the observatory; pedestrians, bicycles and motorbikes are not allowed.

Goseong Unification Observatory Building HISTORIC BUILDING
(고성 통일전망대; ☎033 682 0088; adult/child/parking ₩3000/1500/3000; ⊙9am-4pm mid-Aug–mid-Jul, to 5.30pm mid-Jul–mid-Aug) While this area was part of North Korea in 1945–53, today this building is the closest most South Koreans can get to glimpsing that world. There are binoculars (₩500 for two minutes) installed on the viewing deck, and inside the observatory is a large map labelled (in Korean only) with mountain names and the locations of military installations (red text for North Korea, white text for South Korea). Kiosks here sell liquor, cash, postage stamps and other souvenirs from North Korea.

On a clear day, you can get a good view of Kumgang-san, about 20km to the west. The North-bound highway and railroad fell quiet after South Korea suspended Kumgang-san tours in July 2008, when a South Korean tourist was shot by North Korea.

Despite the solemnity of the place, the car park is cluttered with souvenir shops and restaurants. On the other side of the lot is the Korean War Exhibition Hall, which provides something of a primer on the war.

Lighthouse Observatory LIGHTHOUSE
(속초등대전망대; 1-7 Yeongnang-dong; ⊙sunrise-sunset) The views of distant Seorak-san and the East Sea aren't bad, and are best at dusk or dawn. Binoculars are available.

Sleeping

★House Hostel HOSTEL $
(더하우스 호스텔; ☎033 633 3477; www.thehouse-hostel.com; dm/s/d Sep-Jun ₩18,000/23,000/35,000, Jul&Aug ₩30,000/40,000/60,000; ❄📶) A five-minute walk from the intercity bus terminal, this place combines the niceties of Korean motel rooms – minifridge and basic toiletries – with free amenities such as bikes, laundry and breakfast (cereal, bread and coffee) and a very cheap coffee machine (₩200). The quirky common lounge and charming, light-filled breakfast room are great for meeting travellers.

There's also a large lounge area downstairs beyond the breakfast room with darts and table football. The English-speaking young owner Yu sits down with all guests for a thorough and excellent overview of the area with a map. Rooms are comfortable and beds come with electric underblankets. Watch out for the first flight of stairs, which has one step higher than the others, and can send you flying. There's no lift and you need to make up your bed.

James BLuE Hostel HOSTEL $
(☎033 637 2789; www.hostel-jamesblue.com; 466-36 Dongmyeong-dong, off Jungang-no; dm/r ₩20,000/40,000; 🚭❄📶) This is a hostel all grown up. Rooms are clean and common areas close at night for proper rest for all. Bonuses include heated floors, strong showers, reliable wi-fi and a helpful English-

Sokcho

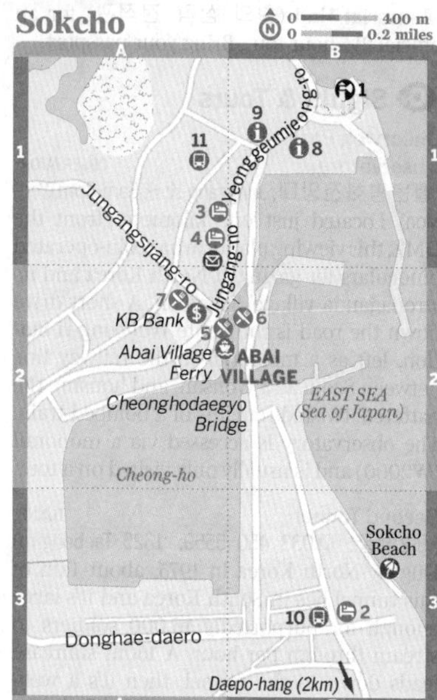

Sokcho

Sights
1 Lighthouse Observatory B1

Sleeping
2 Good Morning Hotel B3
3 House Hostel A1
4 James BLuE Hostel A1

Eating
5 88 .... A2
6 Abai Shikdang B2
7 Jungang-sijang A2

Drinking & Nightlife
Cafe Nadoo .... (see 6)

Information
8 Tourist Information Booth B1
Tourist Information Booth .... (see 10)
9 Tourist Information Office B1

Transport
10 Express Bus Terminal B3
11 Intercity Bus Terminal A1

speaking owner, James. Buses to Seorak-san are nearby, though early risers note: breakfast starts at 8am. Rates increase 25% on Fridays and Saturdays, and 50% July to August and October.

Good Morning Hotel HOTEL $$
(굿모닝 호텔; 033 637 9900; 1432-1 Joyang-dong; r ₩60,000;) This spiffy nine-storey hotel is one of the nicest near the beach; its good-looking rooms have contemporary dark-wood floors, tasteful decor and floor-to-ceiling windows to take advantage of the views. Rates rise by ₩20,000 on Saturday.

Eating & Drinking

Abai Shikdang SEAFOOD $$
(아바이식당; 033 635 5310; meals ₩10,000-30,000) A fine place to try squid *sundae* (sausage) in Abai, a collection of vintage seafood restaurants between the canal and the sea. To get there, take the old-fashioned ferry (a floating platform attached to a hand-pulled cable; ₩200) across the harbour and walk under the elevated bridge road on the far side.

88 SEAFOOD $$
(88생선구이; 033 633 8892; 468-55 Jungang-dong; barbecue per person ₩14,000; 8.30am-9pm) On a corner on the waterfront, 88 does delicious fish barbecue at your table, but doesn't serve solo diners and staff don't speak much English. Plonk down and they handle the grilling, checking and dishing up of tender squid, mackerel, flounder and other fish served with rice and kimchi. Look for the large '88' signs.

Jungang-sijang SEAFOOD $$
(중앙시장; Jungangsijang-ro; mains from ₩10,000; 10am-10pm) The basement of this fish market has plentiful indoor casual restaurants with tanks of (soon to be) seafood. Most places are perched away from the constantly wet floor.

Cafe Nadoo CAFE
(033 635 9773; Abaimeul-gil 24; drinks ₩4000; 10am-9pm;) In the old-timey Abai Village, this small but chic spot is hewn from raw concrete, has a friendly owner and serves coffee, tea and lemonade. It's a great spot to take a seat (there are only a handful) and watch the comings and goings outside.

Information

There are small **tourist information booths** (1330; 9am-6pm Feb-Dec) outside the express and intercity bus terminals, and the ferry pier. English-speaking staff alternate between them on different days.

KB Bank (9am-4pm Mon-Fri)
Post Office (9am-6pm Mon-Fri)

Getting There & Away

AIR

Yangyang International Airport (양양국제공항; www.airport.co.kr/yangyangeng/index.do) has flights to Jeju-do and Busan within South Korea with Korea Express Air, which also flies to Japan. There are also seasonal flights to China. The airport is 17km south of Sokcho and can be reached by bus (₩8200, 25 minutes) from the intercity bus terminal (p130). A taxi will cost around ₩25,000.

BUS

Buses leave Sokcho **Express Bus Terminal** (속초고속버스터미널; ☎033 631 3181; 1418 Joyang-dong) for Seoul (₩17,300, 2½ hours, every 30 minutes). Bus departures for Busan, Chuncheon, Daegu, Dong-Seoul and Gangneung leave from Sokcho **Intercity Bus Terminal** (속초버스터미널; ☎033 633 2328; www.sokchoterminal.com; Jangan-ro). Buses also run direct to Incheon International Airport (₩30,000, 3½ hours, five daily) and Gimpo Airport (₩25,000, 3 hours, five daily).

Getting Around

Many local buses (1, 1-1, 7, 7-1, 9 and 9-1) connect the intercity bus terminal to the express bus terminal and Daepo-hang, via the town's main street Jungang-no. Buses 7 and 7-1 go to the Seoraksan area and national park entrance, while buses 9 and 9-1 link Sokcho with Naksan Provincial Park and Yangyang. To get to Abai Village take the **ferry** (아바이마을 갯배; ☎033 633 3171; 39 Jungangbudu-gil; adult/child ₩500/300).

Cheorwon

Say 'DMZ' (Demilitarized Zone) and most people think of Panmunjeom. But the little-touristed town of Cheorwon (철원), 85km northeast of Seoul, presents a more haunting version. Under North Korea's control from 1945, it saw fierce fighting during the Korean War and was built anew after the war, as part of South Korea. But even today it abounds with army trucks and military checkpoints. It's one way to see the DMZ without paying an exorbitant fee and being hustled onto coaches.

Most of the war sites lie within the Civilian Control Zone that spans 20km from the border, so visitors must present identification and register with the **Hantan-gang Tourism Office** (한탄강관광지 관리사무소; ☎033 450 5558; ⏰9am-6pm) at the **Iron Triangle Memorial Hall** (철의 삼각 전적관) for an official 2½-hour tour. Bring your passport.

Sights & Tours

Cheorwon Peace Observatory OBSERVATORY
(철원평화전망대; Junggang-ri; ⏰6am-8pm Wed-Mon) Located just one kilometre from the DMZ, this viewing platform has coin-operated binoculars for gazing at North Korea and its 'propaganda village' Seonjeon. A short drive down the road is the petite Woljeong-ri Station, left as a memorial to the railway line between Seoul and Wonsan, and housing the battered, twisted remains of a bombed train. The observatory is accessed via a monorail (₩2000) and is usually only visited on a tour.

Second Tunnel TUNNEL
(제2땅굴; ☎033 450 5559; 1825 Taebong-ro) Dug by North Korea in 1975, about 1km of this tunnel lies in South Korea and it's large enough for purportedly 16,000 soldiers to stream through per hour. A 150m staircase leads down to the tunnel, then it's a well-lit, albeit damp, 500m stretch to where the tunnel was discovered, just 300m from the border.

Former Labor Party Headquarters HISTORIC BUILDING
(철원 노동당사; 265 Geumgangsan-ro, Cheorwon-gun) After passing a few battle-scarred buildings, most tours of Cheorwon end here, at the former Labor Party (that is, Communist Party) HQ. The surviving grandiose-communist facade is evocative, but its associations are less than pleasant: when Cheorwon was part of North Korea, many civilians were imprisoned and tortured here.

Cheorwon Tour TOURS
(adult/youth/child without transport ₩4000/3000/2000; ⏰9.30am, 10.30am, 1pm & 2.30pm or 2pm in winter, Wed-Mon) For this official 2½-hour tour of the DMZ (Demilitarized Zone) in Cheorwon, you must have your own vehicle or hitch a ride. There's usually a tour shuttle bus (₩8000) available on weekends. If not, a three-hour taxi ride to cover the sights would be about ₩100,000.

Getting There & Away

Buses from Dong-Seoul run to Cheorwon (₩9300, 2½ hours, every 30 minutes from 6am), from where you can catch a taxi to Iron Triangle Memorial Hall in about 15 minutes.

Getting Around

You will generally need to join a tour to take in the sights, which is convenient (and necessary to visit the Cheorwon Peace Observatory); otherwise you will need to have your own vehicle or hitch a ride between stops.

Naksan Provincial Park

Occupying a 24km-long section of coastline, Naksan Provincial Park (낙산도립공원) south of Sokcho is home to the must-see Buddhist Naksan-sa, with its towering effigy of the Goddess of Mercy and spacious temple grounds, as well as the pleasant sands of Naksan Beach. The area works very well as a stop-off on the road between Sokcho and Gangneung.

Sights

Naksan-sa TEMPLE

(낙산사; ☎033 672 2448; adult/youth/child ₩3000/1500/1000; ⏲5am-7pm) This temple was originally established in AD 671 and enjoys a glorious perspective overlooking the sea. Also facing the sea is a majestic (but modern, dating from 1977) 16m-tall statue of the Goddess of Mercy, Gwaneum (관음), presiding over the East Sea from a promontory. The temple has fallen victim to the forest fires that have periodically swept by, razing the temple buildings (most recently in 2005).

Immediately below the statue is a small shrine, with a window strategically constructed so that a kneeling devotee can look up and gaze upon the statue's face. Further down a side path is a pavilion with a glass-covered hole through which you can see the sea cave below. From 11.30am to 1.30pm, complimentary vegetarian meals are served at the temple cafeteria; leave a donation by the shrine in the kitchen if you wish.

Most of the temple complex has been stoutly rebuilt since the last fire and the surrounding pine forest is recovering as well. A monument of colourful temple hall roof tiles that survived has been preserved in a huge mound, which serves as a moving tribute to the former temple.

The 16m-tall statue is known as the Seawater Gwaneum (해수관음). Gwaneum's full name in Korean is Gwanse'eum Bosal (관세음보살), the sounds of which derive from her Chinese name 觀世音菩薩 (Guanshiyin Pusa), which literally means 'the Bodhisattva who listens to the sounds of the World'. She is therefore a goddess (more strictly a bodhisattva, or Buddha-to-be) who lends a compassionate ear to those who come to her needing sympathy. She is also known as Avalokiteśvara or Guanyin, and is worshipped in China, Vietnam, Japan, Cambodia and other nations. In Tibet she is manifested in earthly form as the Dalai Lama.

There is a very good homestay here, if you would like to spend the night and also, if you are inclined, find out about Buddhist practice (though that is voluntary).

Naksan Beach BEACH

(낙산해수욕장) Below Naksan-sa is this beach, one of the best on the east coast and of course, busy in summer, when accommodation prices can triple. At other times it's a pleasant place to stay if you want to avoid Sokcho's fishing-town feel.

Insect Ecology Museum MUSEUM

(⏲9am-6pm) This interesting museum is dedicated to an intriguing range of beetles, butterflies and other insects from around the world. Captions are in Korean and Latin only, but some of the butterflies – including specimens from Brazil – are really very beautiful. Kids will love it. It's upstairs from the Yangyang Tourist Information Centre (p132).

Sleeping & Eating

It's not worth coming to Naksan Provincial Park to dine, but there are several cafes and restaurants by the beach. The temple of Naksan-sa has a canteen that offers a free vegetarian meal between 11.30am and 1.30pm (but a donation would be appreciated).

Naksan Beach Hotel HOTEL $$

(☎02 742 0337; d ₩150,000, ste ₩200,000-300,000; P⊖❄📶) Just beneath the temple of Naksan-sa and enjoying splendid sea views from high up, this luxury hotel has an elegant arc shape and a neat, minimalist lobby. As well as modish, contemporary rooms, there's a sauna, a fitness room and a kids' room; however, the out-front car park means people can see into your room if the net curtains are open.

The Suites Hotel Naksan HOTEL $$

(☎033 670 1100; http://naksan.suites.co.kr/eng; 440-5 Bunji, Josan-ri; r from ₩95,000; P❄@📶) The beach glistens right outside your balcony here, or ascend to the roof terrace for even more spectacular views from a sun

lounger. Rooms are spacious, plush and bright in modern, muted colours. The karaoke lounge, free laundry and table tennis are family-friendly additions.

Information

Yangyang Tourist Information Centre (양양 관광안내센터; ⊙9.30am-6pm) This very helpful tourist office across the way from the bus drop-off has loads of literature and good advice for travellers, with a little English spoken. The Insect Ecology Museum is upstairs.

Getting There & Away

Bus 9 and 9-1 (₩1500, 15 minutes, every 15 minutes) can be picked up outside either of Sokcho's bus terminals, heading in the direction of Yangyang. Get off at Naksan Beach. You can approach Naksan-sa via the beach, or walk backwards along the highway and follow the signs to approach it from the landward side.

Odaesan National Park

Odaesan National Park (오대산 국립공원) combines splendid hiking, superb views and two prominent Buddhist temples – Woljeong-sa and Sangwon-sa – into a fantastic sensory and spiritual experience.

Odae-san (Five Peaks Mountain) is a high-altitude massif; the best times to visit are late spring and early to mid-autumn, when the foliage colours are richest. There are two main entrances to the park: from the south at Dongsan-ri and from the northwest at Sogeum-gang. The former leads to the temples and the main hiking trail.

Sights

★Sangwon-sa BUDDHIST TEMPLE

(상원사; ☎033 339 6800; www.woljeongsa.org; incl Woljeong-sa adult/youth/child ₩3000/1500/500; ⊙dawn-dusk) Sangwon-sa's intricately decorated bronze bell was cast in AD 725 and is the oldest bell in Korea (and one of the largest as well). Another prized object is the wooden statue of the bodhisattva of wisdom Munsu (in Sanskrit, Manjusri) – it was made in the 15th century, it is said, on the order of King Sejo after the bodhisattva cured his skin disease.

The ceiling of the Munsu Hall – in which the bodhisattva is housed – is hung with a galaxy of votive effigies of the bodhisattva, while the steps up to the temple are decorated with pink lanterns. Several other halls can be examined, including the small Spirit Mountain Hall as well as a row of commemorative steles inscribed in *hanja* and *hangul*. One of the temple halls has been converted to a charming cafe (p134). The temple's name means 'Upper Courtyard Temple'.

The temple is 10km uphill from Woljeong-sa, where a hiking trail begins. From Jinbu bus terminal, 12 local buses run daily to Sangwon-sa (₩3000, 40 minutes).

Woljeong-sa BUDDHIST TEMPLE

(월정사; ☎033 339 6800; www.woljeongsa.org; incl Sangwon-sa adult/youth/child ₩3000/1500/500; ⊙5am-9pm, museum 9.30am-5.30pm Wed-Mon Apr-Oct, to 4.30pm Nov-Mar) This Silla-era temple was founded in AD 645 by the Zen Master Jajang to enshrine relics of the historical Buddha. Although it fell victim to fires and was even flattened during the Korean War, one treasured structure that has survived from the Goryeo dynasty is the octagonal nine-storey pagoda in the main courtyard, with the figure of a kneeling bodhisattva before it. The newer buildings around it are decorated with intricate religious art.

There is a museum of Joseon-era Buddhist and the temple also runs a popular Templestay program, with a 3.50am wake-up and various programs if you wish to learn about Buddhist ritual and belief. From Jinbu bus terminal, 12 local buses per day run to Woljeong-sa (₩1900, 20 minutes).

Gwaneum-am BUDDHIST TEMPLE

(관음암; ⊙dawn-dusk) This temple is named after and dedicated to the Goddess of Mercy (Gwaneum), worshipped by those seeking consolation or by women wanting children.

Activities

Hiking Trails HIKING

The main hiking trail begins at Sangwon-sa and is a fairly steep 6.5km climb to the highest peak Biro-bong (1563m), about three hours return. Gung-ho hikers can continue from Biro-bong along a ridge to Sangwang-bong (1493m), then back down to the road and to the temple (12.5km, five hours).

A separate trail runs 13.3km from Sogeumgang to Jingogae, passing several waterfalls, including Guryong Pokpo, Nagyeong Pokpo and Noin-bong (1338m). The route takes about seven hours one way. Parts of the trail may be shut during the dry months due to fire hazard.

Odaesan National Park

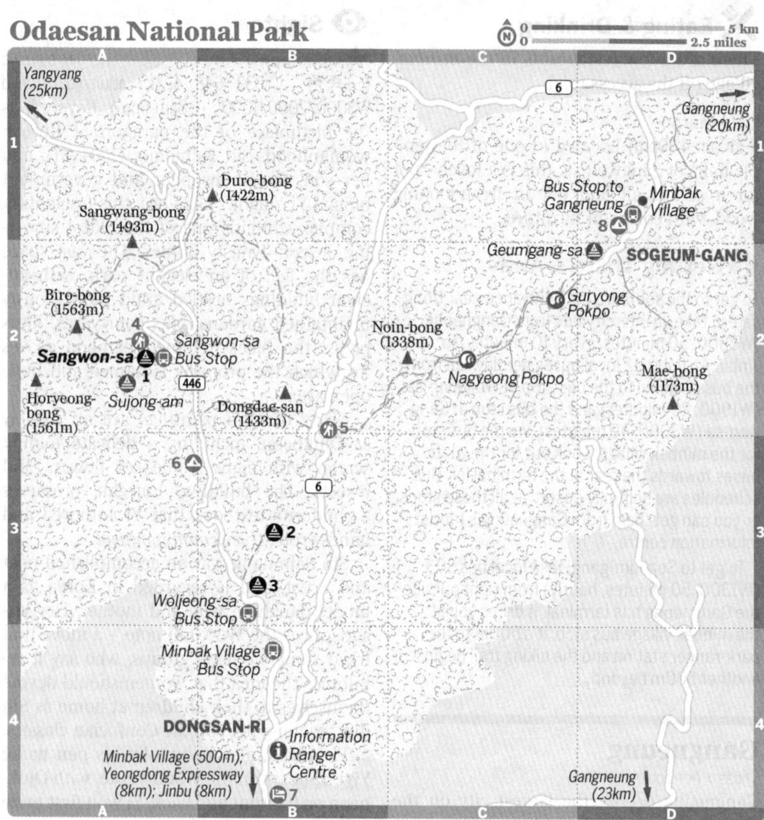

Sleeping

A small village with *minbak* accommodation is on the left side of the access road, about 1km from the turnoff from Hwy 6. It's a 40-minute walk south of Woljeong-sa, or you can take the bus. Halfway between the temples is **Dongpigol Camping Ground** (per tent ₩3000-6000). Sogeum-gang also has a *minbak* village and **campground** (☎033 661 4161; campsites ₩15,000-19,000; 📶). Temple accommodation is offered at Woljeong-sa.

Kensington Hotel Pyeongchang LUXURY HOTEL **$$$**
(켄싱턴호텔 평창; ☎033 330 5000; r/ste ₩180,000/280,000; ❄📶🏊) This tall deluxe hotel is about 2.5km from the southern park entrance, with sweeping views all around. Rooms are suitably plush and during low season you should be able to garner discounts of up to 50%. There are two restaurants.

Odaesan National Park

Top Sights
1 Sangwon-sa A2

Sights
2 Gwaneum-am B3
3 Woljeong-sa B3

Activities, Courses & Tours
4 Hiking Trails A2
5 Jingogae B2

Sleeping
6 Dongpigol Camping Ground A3
7 Kensington Hotel Pyeongchang B4
8 Sogeumgang Camping Ground D1

Drinking & Nightlife
Cafe Maroo .... (see 1)

Eating & Drinking

There are a few restaurants in the *minbak* village off the access road.

Cafe Maroo CAFE

(⌚10am-4.30pm) Located in one of the temple halls of Sangwon-sa, this is a lovely spot for a coffee, all laid out in fresh-looking wood, with colourful furniture.

Getting There & Away

To get to the southern park entrance near Dongsan-ri, take an intercity bus from Gangneung (₩3900, 50 minutes, every 10 minutes) to Jinbu. At Jinbu, 12 local buses per day run from the bus terminal to the bus stop at Woljeong-sa (₩1900, 20 minutes) and the bus stop at Sangwon-sa (₩3000, 40 minutes), via the bus stop for the minbak village. Look out for the white buses towards the rear of the terminal lot. Bus schedules are helpfully posted at all these stops, or you can get them from Gangneung's tourist information centre.

To get to Sogeum-gang, take local bus 303 (₩1300, 50 minutes, hourly) from right outside the Gangneung bus terminal. It drops you at the minbak village bus stop; it's 500m to the park-ranger station and the hiking trail begins another 500m beyond.

Gangneung

☎033 / POP 200,000

Gangneung (강릉), the largest city on the Gangwon-do coast, hosted many events of the 2018 Winter Olympics including figure and speed skating, ice hockey and curling.

Gangneung's appeal lies towards the sea, particularly near Gyeongpo, while its cultural hot spots – well-preserved Joseon-era buildings in the unmissable Ojukheon and the 400-year-old shamanist Dano Festival – are matched by quirky modern attractions, such as a museum lovingly dedicated to Thomas Edison and a North Korean submarine.

With a decent bar scene, the town is a good place to linger for a few days if you're looking for an experience that's off the beaten track without being too small-town. Try to arrive in spring, when azaleas cover the town in gorgeous splashes of colour. The city tree is the pine, found in abundance by Gyeongpo Beach. The main shopping area is in the city centre, in the warren of lanes near Jungang-sijang.

Sights

★Ojukheon HISTORIC BUILDING

(오죽헌; ☎033 648 4271; adult/youth/child ₩3000/2000/1000; ⌚8am-6pm) Revered as the birthplace of the paragon of Korean womanhood, Sin Saimdang (1504–51), and her son, the philosopher and government official Yi Yulgok (1536–84), this fascinating complex contains one of the oldest surviving Joseon-dynasty homes. The vast space has the feel of an elegant park, with ancient buildings nestled amid punctiliously maintained gardens, plus courtyards, lotus pools, the black-stemmed bamboo groves for which the property is named and huge open areas.

Many of Sin's paintings are on display at Ojukheon, including a delicate folding screen with eight studies of flowers and insects. The building, Eojegak, preserves a children's textbook that Yi authored and hand-wrote, *Gyeokmongyogyeol*.

Sin Saimdang was an accomplished poet and artist, and is regarded in Korea as a model daughter, wife and mother. Her visage graces the ₩50,000 note – a move that irked some women's groups, who say it reinforces the idea that women should devote themselves to their children at home as Sin did, teaching her son the Confucian classics.

Yi Yulgok, also known by his pen name Yiyi, appears on the ₩5000 note, with Ojukheon on its front and back. Yi won first prize in the state examination for prospective government officials and went on to serve the king. Unfortunately his advice to prepare against a possible invasion by Japan was ignored – to the kingdom's peril after Yi's death, when the Japanese invaded in 1592.

You can also find the Gangneung City Museum, with its displays of art, calligraphy and ceramics, within the grounds. English captions are limited.

Ojukheon is 4km from central Gangneung. From outside the bus terminal, take bus 202 (₩1200, 10 minutes, every 30 minutes) and make sure it's the one heading to Gyeongpo (경포). The bus stop outside Ojukheon is well signposted.

Gyeongpo Beach BEACH

(경포해수욕장) The largest beach on the east coast, and the third-busiest in South Korea, has 1.8km of flat, white sand bordered by pine trees and pleasant waters. It's besieged by visitors during the official sea-

son (13 July to 20 August). At other times, the noisy strip of beachside restaurants and motels doesn't detract too much from the charm of the famous wind-twisted pine trees, which provide good photo-ops.

Gyeongpo-ho & Gyeongpodae Pavilion HISTORIC BUILDING
(경포호 | 경포대) Immediately behind Gyeongpo Beach is Gyeongpo-ho, which attracts local residents looking for a little peace and quiet. There's a 4km bicycle path along the lakeshore, passing traditional pavilions. The most prominent is Gyeongpodae, from which it is poetically said that you can see five moons: the moon itself and its four reflections in the sea (now obscured by pine trees), in the lake, in your obligatory glass of alcohol and in your own mind.

Look out for the huge stone rock carved with *hanja* characters '人無遠慮難成大業', which mean 'people who don't think far enough find it hard to achieve great things'.

A lovely Cherry Blossom Festival is held here in early April, which is really the time to go. If you just miss the cherry blossom, don't worry: the azaleas then flower and make for a gorgeous spectacle.

Rent a bike from any of the outfits to the north along the shore of the lake. Gyeongpodae is a short walk from the Chamsori Gramophone & Edison Museum.

Gangneung Seongyojang HISTORIC BUILDING
(강릉선교장; ☎033 640 4799; adult/youth/child ₩3000/2000/1000; ⏲9am-6.30pm) Dating from the late Joseon dynasty, this national cultural property for 300 years was the home of a *yangban* (aristocratic) family. It was built for a descendant of the brother of King Sejong (the monarch who invented *hangeul*, the Korean phonetic alphabet), and has been restored in keeping with the original floor plan and architectural style. The complex includes residential quarters, a library and a pavilion overlooking a lotus pond.

It's very pretty but somewhat lifeless, like a movie set; in fact, a number of Korean films and TV shows have been shot here. The servants' quarters have unfortunately been turned into a gift shop, but you can try your hand at some traditional games outside. To get here, take bus 202 and get off about five minutes after Ojukheon.

Chamsori Gramophone & Edison Museum MUSEUM
(참소리 축음기 에디슨 과학 박물관; ☎033 655 1130; www.edison.kr; adult ₩17,000, child ₩8000-13,000; ⏲9am-5pm; 👪) This whimsical museum is a sheer delight. It combines the two loves of private collector Son Sung-Mok: gramophones and Thomas Edison. There are hundreds of antique gramophones (or phonographs, as Edison termed them) and music boxes, as well as a colourful collection of Edison's other inventions and related devices, from cameras and kinetoscopes to toys, TVs and typewriters. Some of these items are the only one of their kind.

Though the tour is in Korean only, the guide demonstrates the use of some antique music boxes and other contraptions – good fun for children and anyone interested in 'retro' technology. Take bus 202 for Gyeongpo and get off at the Gyeongpo Beach stop (five minutes after Seongyojang), from where it's a five- to 10-minute walk back.

Anmok Beach BEACH
(안목해수욕장) This fine beach strewn with golden sand and shells is framed between the blue, blue sea and a long line of cafes; it's a lovely place for a stroll, to feel the sea breeze in your hair and catch some rays.

GETTING INTO THE SPIRIT

The highlight of Gangneung's calendar is the shamanist **Dano Festival** (단오제, Danoje), celebrated for one week on the fifth day of the fifth lunar month (usually in June). It's one of the biggest holidays in Korea and has been recognised by Unesco as a 'Masterpiece of the Oral and Intangible Heritage of Humanity'. For foreigners, it's a great opportunity to revel Korean-style, while learning about some of the country's oldest spiritual beliefs.

Danoje is the climax of a month-long series of shamanist and Confucian ceremonies for peace, prosperity and bountiful harvests. On the first day there's a lantern parade to welcome a mountain spirit, who unites with his 'wife', another spirit dwelling in Gangneung. During the festival people present their wishes to both, while female shamans perform the *dano gut*, a rite of singing, dancing and sacrificial offering to the spirits to implore their blessings. On the final day the people send the male spirit back to the mountain.

Gangneung

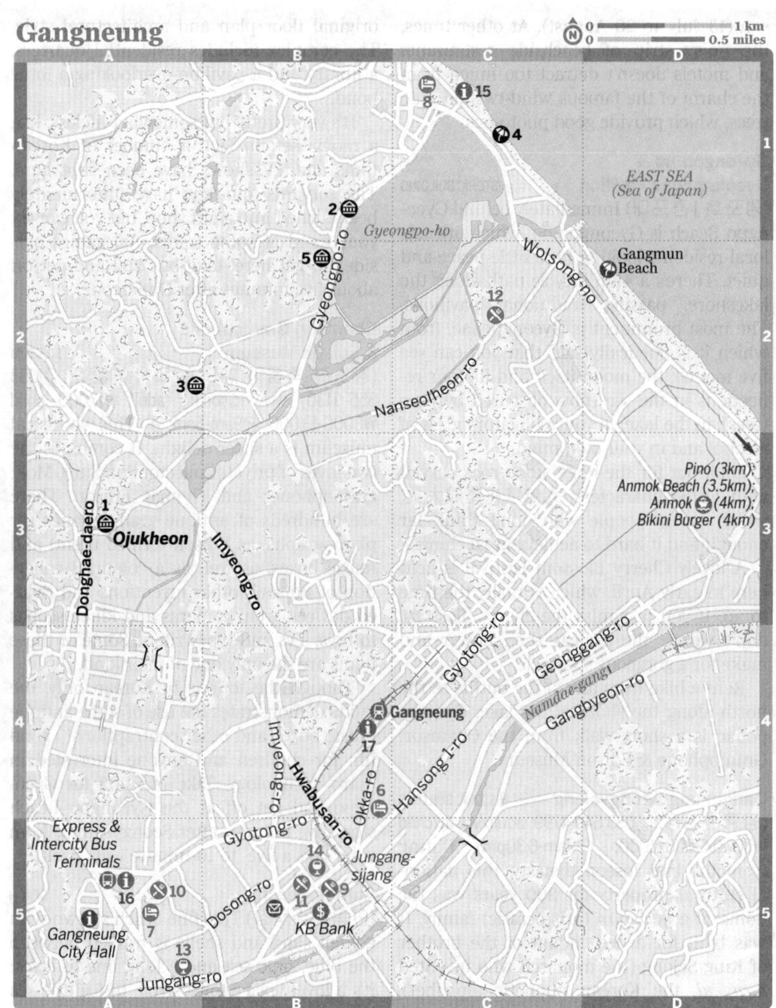

Buses 501, 502, 503, 504, 505, 508, 509 and 510 can take you right there.

Sleeping

Alps Hotel HOTEL $$

(Alps Hotel 알프스 호텔; 14 Dongbusijang-gil; r from ₩40,000;) With huge beds, bright, white linen, underfloor heating and flat screen TVs, this simple but comfortable place is tucked away down a side street; it's very affordable and central, though little English is spoken.

Equus Motel MOTEL $$

(에쿠스모텔; 033 643 0114; r ₩40,000;) This love motel has pretty sleek rooms that offer good value for money in the bus terminal area. Rooms have neat black decor and enormous TVs, and better rooms come with treadmills and whirlpool baths. Rates rise by ₩10,000 on Saturday. English is very limited.

★**Lakai Sandpine Resort** RESORT $$$

(1644 3001; www.lakaisandpine.co.kr; 536 Haean-ro; studio/ondol/ste from ₩75,000/90,000/95,000;) This delightfully

Gangneung

Top Sights

1 Ojukheon A3

Sights

2 Chamsori Gramophone & Edison Museum B1
3 Gangneung Seongyojang A2
4 Gyeongpo Beach C1
5 Gyeongpo-ho & Gyeongpodae Pavilion B2

Sleeping

6 Alps Hotel B4
7 Equus Motel A5
8 Lakai Sandpine Resort C1

Eating

9 Geumhak Kalguksu B5
10 Haengun Sikdang A5
11 Terarosa B5
12 Todam Sundubu C2

Drinking & Nightlife

13 Budnamu Brewery A5
14 Bumpin' Bar B5

Information

15 Tourist Information Booth C1
16 Tourist Information Centre A5
17 Train Station Tourist Information Booth B4

landscaped choice is right by the sea. A large variety of contemporary and stylish rooms are at hand, including a vast penthouse and very spacious *ondol* rooms. Staff are professional and the setting is just lovely.

The resort boasts five restaurants and cafes, so you won't actually need to leave. Rounding it all off are a sauna, spa, outdoor pool and kids' pool.

Eating

Geumhak Kalguksu NOODLES $
(금학 칼국수; mains from ₩6000; ⏲9am-9pm) This small, ramshackle place with a little garden and simple blue plastic furniture serves delicious and generous helpings of *jang kalguksu* – buckwheat noodles in a piquant broth poured into a large metal bowl and sprinkled with seaweed and sesame seeds. It's down the narrow alley next to Starbucks, at the bend in the alley.

Haengun Sikdang KOREAN $
(행운 식당; ☎033 643 3334; meals ₩6000-9000) This popular spot offers good, simple fare such as *kimchi jjigae* (kimchi stew) or *doenjang jjigae* (soybean-paste stew); if you like squid or octopus, try the stir-fried *ojingeo bokkeum* (오징어볶음) or *nakji bokkeum* (낙지볶음). Look for the light-brown sign and blue umbrella outside.

Todam Sundubu VEGETARIAN $
(토담 순두부; ☎033 652 0336; meals ₩7000-10,000; ⏲7am-7pm; ✎) In Chodang, this rustic eatery serves up simmering *sundubu* (uncurdled tofu) inside a quaint wooden house with traditional floor seating. Look for the white vertical sign with red lettering beside Heogyun-Heonanseolheon Park (허균·허난설헌 기념공원). To get to Chodang, take bus 206, 207 or 230 (₩1200, 30 minutes) from outside the bus terminal.

Terarosa CAFE $
(테라로사; ☎033 648 2760; www.terarosa.com; coffee ₩5000, snacks from ₩2000; ⏲9am-10pm; ❄📶✎) With a sofa in the corner, bare brick walls and wooden floor, this polished, good-looking and friendly cafe roasts and brews about 20 varieties of coffee, bakes its own bread and serves cookies and cheesecake. It's along the second lane to the west of McDonald's on Jungang-ro. There are two other branches in town.

★**Bikini Burger** BURGERS $$
(비키니버거; ☎033 651 0208; mains from ₩10,000; ⏲11am-9pm; 📶) Hop off the bus to Anmok Beach and you're at this small place by the sea that serves up some seriously scrumptious burgers. The menu is skimpy, but each burger is so packed with flavour it doesn't matter, so don't miss out. Walk it all off along the lovely beach.

Pino ITALIAN $$
(피노; ☎033 652 3300; 42-1 Palsong-gil; mains from ₩18,000, lunch set ₩23,000; ⏲10am-10pm; 📶) On a quiet road off Songjeong Beach, popular Pino goes for the concrete bunker/distressed industrial vibe with considerable aplomb, but beyond its textured walls, the menu is excellent. Try the crab pasta with cream sauce, or just settle for a pizza. Delicious, matched by outstanding service.

Drinking & Nightlife

★**Budnamu Brewery** BAR
(버드나무 브루어리; ☎033 920 9380; ⏲noon-midnight) This splendid craft beer house is a superb place to immerse yourself in a world of beery flavour: try a Zeumeu Blanc – delightful and slightly zingy, with a touch of banana flavour – or a Baegilhong

Red Ale, with darker tones, or a full-bodied Ojook Stout. The whole menu's a treasure trove for ale fiends.

Bumpin' Bar BAR

(☎033 644 3574; ⏰7pm-2am Mon-Sat; 📶) This gem, down an alley opposite Terarosa, lives in a ramshackle wooden house with a low ceiling. Park yourself at the beautiful, dark bar, constructed of old pine planks from a Buddhist temple that was destroyed in a fire. There's no beer on tap, just a chilled cabinet of local (from ₩6000) and a few international beers, plus spirits.

ℹ Information

The **tourist information centre** (☎033 640 4537; www.gntour.go.kr; ⏰9am-8pm) is beside the bus terminal, with English-, Mandarin- and Japanese-speaking staff who can book accommodation for you and assist with almost anything in customary Korean fashion. There is another very helpful **branch** (⏰9am-6pm) just within the entrance of the new train station building. A small **tourist information booth** (⏰9am-6pm) can be found on Gyeongpo Beach.

Gangneung City Hall (강릉시청; www.gn.go.kr) also provides guides to festivals such as the Dano Festival, but it was under construction at the time of writing.

KB Bank (Geumseong-ro; ⏰9am-4pm)

Post Office (Imnyeong-ro; ⏰9am-6pm)

ℹ Getting There & Away

BOAT

Gangneung has a ferry to the island of Ulleungdo. Services depart from the **Anmok Ferry Terminal** (☎033 653 8670; one way/return ₩54,000/108,000) at 8.40am or 9am daily (2½ hours). To get to the terminal, take bus 202 or 303 (₩1300) from the bus terminal or a taxi (₩6000, 15 minutes).

BUS

Gangneung's **Express & Intercity Bus Terminals** (Haseulla-ro) share the same building, near the entrance to Hwy 7. Express buses from Gangneung head to Dong-Seoul (₩13,700, 2½ hours, every 40 minutes) and Gangnam (₩21,000, every 20 minutes).

TRAIN

Gangneung built a new and impressive train station for the 2018 Winter Olympics. A new KTX line was laid, with trains running from Seoul Cheongnyangni station (₩26,000, every hour, 1½ hours). Alternatively, trains also run from Seoul station (₩27,000, hourly). There's also a special 'seaside train' to Samcheok.

ℹ Getting Around

Buses 202 and 303 connect the bus terminal with the train station twice hourly (₩1800). Bus 202 goes directly to Gyeongpo (경포). Bus 202-1 goes between Gyeongpo and the city centre (시내) terminating at Gangneung station. A useful bus timetable in English is available at tourist information centres.

A booth beside the northeast end of Gyeongpo-ho by the Gyeongpo Beach bus stop rents out bicycles (₩5000/30,000 per hour/day).

Jeongdongjin

The coast south of Gangneung has a couple of unique sights that merit a day trip if you have the time. Where else can you squeeze inside a North Korean submarine and examine its cramped quarters before exploring the bridge of a former US warship almost right alongside?

◉ Sights

Unification Park HISTORIC SITE

(통일 공원; ☎033 640 4469; adult/youth/child ₩3000/2000/1500; ⏰9am-5.30pm Mar-Oct, to 4.30pm Nov-Feb) The main two spectacles at this seaside attraction are a warship and a red and green North Korean submarine. The 35m-long submarine was spying on military facilities near Gangneung in 1996 when it ran aground off Jeongdongjin. The damage to the rear of the vessel is still visible, but what is perhaps most incredible is the astonishingly cramped interior. The much larger warship was built in America in 1945, saw action in WWII and the Vietnam War, and was donated to South Korea in 1972.

The warship's interior has been refurbished as an exhibition on Korean naval history with glimpses of sleeping quarters and mess halls. It's interesting to wander the decks, inspect the 40mm and 5in guns and patrol the bridge, the captain's office and the radio transmission room.

When the submarine ran aground, the commander burned important documents (the fire-blackened compartment is still visible) and the 26 soldiers made a break for shore, hoping to return to North Korea. It took South Korea 49 days to capture or kill them (except one, who went missing); during the manhunt 17 South Korean civilians and soldiers were killed and 22 injured.

WORTH A TRIP

BIG WHITE MOUNTAIN

In the heart of 'Korea's alps', Taebaeksan (태백산) is one of the most sacred mountains in the country. The small town of Taebaek (태백) is a jumping-off point for exploring **Taebaeksan Provincial Park** (태백산도립공원; ☎033 552 1360; http://taebaek.go.kr; San 80, Sodo-dong; adult/youth/child ₩2000/1500/700; ⊙sunrise-sunset), which offers year-round hiking on trails that snake up to Janggun-bong (1568m) and Cheonjedan (천제단), an altar connected with Korea's mythical founder, Dangun. Included in the park ticket is admission to the **Taebaek Coal Museum** (태백 석탄 박물관; ☎033 552 7720; www.coalmuseum.or.kr; 195 Cheonjedan-gil, Taebaek-san Provincial Park; ⊙9am-6pm; 👪), which documents the history of coal mining in the region.

Each winter in the park, the **Taebaeksan Snow Festival** (태백산 눈축제; ☎033 550 2828, 033 550 2085; http://festival.taebaek.go.kr; 168 Cheonjedan-gil; adult/youth/child ₩2000/1500/700; 👪; 🚌6, 7) features giant snow sculptures and other wintery activities, including an igloo restaurant and K-pop performances. It is among the largest and most well-attended ice festival in the country.

Getting There & Around

Buses connect Taebaek to Dong-Seoul (₩23,800, three hours, once or twice hourly), Samcheok (₩7100, 2½ hours, hourly) and Busan (₩32,500, four hours, six daily).

Seven trains run to Seoul's Cheongnyangni station (₩17,600, four hours) daily. The flashy, retro tourist O-train (₩27,800, four hours, 7.45am) from Seoul station is a fun way to get here. It runs a loop and returns to Seoul from Taebaek at 6pm.

Buses 6 and 7 leave from Taebaek's bus terminal (₩1500, 20 minutes, every 30 minutes) for the provincial park. To find the right bus, go inside the bus station and find the glass doors in the right-hand waiting area.

There are also military planes to the north, an exposed 20-minute walk along the highway.

Unification Park is 4km north of the Jeongdongjin train station along the coastal road. As you exit the train station, turn left and look for the bus stop along the row of restaurants. Take bus 111, 111-1, 112 or 113 (₩1300, 20 minutes, hourly) and get out right after the warship, at the third stop once you hit the coastal road.

Haslla Art World ARTS CENTRE

(하슬라아트월드; ☎033 644 9419; www.haslla.kr; 33-1 Gangdong-myeon, Jeongdongjin-ri San; adult/child ₩10,000/9000; ⊙8.30am-6pm; 👪) Sitting atop a hill, this park has contemporary Korean sculptures set amid a pleasant 11-hectare garden with winding paths and boardwalks. On a clear day, there are incredible sea views. It's a nice ramble for an hour or so, but the artworks are generally underwhelming, albeit quirky. Round up your visit with some traditional Korean tea at the Sea Café (a drink is included in the admission price).

The adjacent Haslla Museum Hotel has five art galleries; they're also open to ticket holders.

The park is 1.5km north of Jeongdongjin train station. Take bus 11, 112, 113, or 114 (₩1300, five minutes, hourly), and walk up a steep slope to the park entrance.

Sleeping

★Haslla Museum Hotel HOTEL $$$

(하슬라 뮤지엄 호텔; ☎033 644 9411; www.haslla.kr; d from ₩198,000; ❄📶) This architectural oddity by the Haslla Art World is an oasis of design: beds are shaped like large wooden bowls, rooms are furnished with quirky pieces of art and all have great ocean views. Rates rise 20% on Friday and Saturday and nearly double during peak times in summer.

Getting There & Away

BUS

Bus 109 (₩1700, 45 minutes, hourly) leaves from the bus stop outside Gangneung's bus terminal for Jeongdongjin, which is 20km south. Shuttle buses (₩2000, 45 minutes, 10 daily) also leave from the train station; the ticket office is just inside the main door.

Buses 111, 111-1, 112 and 113 (₩1300, 35 minutes, hourly) also leave from central Gangneung.

TRAIN

Eleven trains daily connect Jeongdongjin to Gangneung (₩2600, 15 minutes). Jeongdongjin is also a stop on the 'seaside train' that runs between Gangneung and Samcheok.

Getting Around

Local buses are infrequent so taxis are a better option. A trip between any of the sights costs ₩5000 to ₩8000.

Samcheok

033 / POP 80,000

With lovely green hills all about, sedate little Samcheok (삼척) is the gateway to an unusual mix of sightseeing spots. Within an hour's bus ride are spectacular limestone caves, an inimitable 'penis park' (phallic sculptures, not body parts) within a lovely wooded setting and pretty beaches tucked away in quiet coves. The town has a rousing Full Moon Festival in February, with tug-of-war competitions.

Sights

★Haesindang Park — PARK

(해신당 공원; 033 570 3568; incl Fishing Village Folk Museum adult/youth/child ₩3000/2000/1500; 9am-6pm Mar-Oct, to 5pm Nov-Feb) Of all the things you'd expect to find in a fishing village like Sinnam (신남), a 'penis park' is probably not one of them. There are more than 50 phallic sculptures, some taking the form of park benches or drums, attracting a large crowd of both young and old, including kids. It's a cheeky, eye-opening 20- to 30-minute walk if you don't stop, but you *will* stop. If you head downhill, you can detour towards the end to some rocky coves.

The phallic obsession originates with a local legend about a drowned virgin whose restless spirit was affecting the village's catch. A fisherman discovered that she could be appeased if he answered the call of nature while facing the ocean, so the village put up phalluses to placate her. A small shrine to this spirit stands at the seaward tip of the park, and binoculars look out to the statue commemorating where she drowned. The name Haesindang (해신당) literally means 'God of Sea Hall'.

There's an elaborate series of penis sculptures representing the 12 animals of the Chinese zodiac, and outside the park stands a red lighthouse with the same, uh, peculiarities. Penises spring forth from sculpted fish mouths, penis stools are there to sit on if you're tired and there's even a phallic waterwheel. The park also contains the Fishing Village Folk Museum (p141) as well as lovely trees, flowers, lotus-filled ponds and gorgeous sea views.

From Samcheok's intercity bus terminal, take bus 24 (₩1800, 40 minutes, hourly) from the platform on the right. You can enter Haesindang Park from the top of the headland (where there's a huge car park lot) or from the entrance in Sinnam. The easier walk is to start at the top, work your way down and exit at the village. The bus journey itself is lovely, past pines, crystal waters and glittering coves.

Maengbang Beach — BEACH

(맹방 해수욕장) Maengbang Beach is about 12km south of town. It's less frantic than Samcheok Beach and has no buildings, although tented stalls spring up during beach season (10 July to 20 August). The beach is on the route of buses 21, 23 and 24 (₩1800, 25 minutes) – get off at the Geundeok Nonghyeop or Agricultural Technology Center stops.

In spring, this is the venue of the alluring Samcheok Maengbang Canola Flower Festival (p141), when the fields glow yellow with flowers.

If you're heading to Haesindang Park on bus 24, you can stop off at Maengbang Beach either on the way out or on your return.

Hwanseongul — CAVE

(환선굴; 033 570 3255; adult/youth/child ₩4000/2800/2000; 8.30am-6.30pm Mar-Oct, 9.30am-5.30pm Nov-Feb) One of the largest caves in Asia, it has almost 2km of steel stairways that take visitors through cathedral-sized caverns, up, down and around its varied formations. Some curious formations to look out for are the heart-shaped hole over the correspondingly named Bridge of Love, the rimstone that resembles a fried egg, and a difficult-to-spot calcite growth that resembles a tiny statue of the Virgin Mary.

As with many caves in Korea, while Hwanseongul's natural beauty is breathtaking, garish lighting and kitschy names have been added to 'enhance' the experience.

Bus 60 (₩2900, 45 minutes, 8.20am, 10.20am and 2.20pm) heads from Samcheok's intercity bus terminal for the cave. The last bus leaves the cave at 7.30pm.

Samcheok Beach BEACH
(삼척 해수욕장) Samcheok Beach is found immediately to the north of town. The beach has shallow waters, making it popular with families, and there's the usual assortment of motels and restaurants. Bus 11 (₩1800, 20 minutes, five daily) runs from Samcheok's intercity bus terminal to Samcheok Beach. You can also jump on the train from Samcheok train station; Samcheok Beach station is the next stop along to the north.

Fishing Village Folk Museum MUSEUM
(어촌 민속 전시관; incl Haesindang Park adult/youth/child ₩3000/2000/1500; 9am-6pm Tue-Sun Mar-Oct, to 5pm Tue-Sun Nov-Feb) The ship-shaped Fishing Village Folk Museum focuses on the history of fishing and shamanist rituals in the region, and sexual iconography in other cultures.

Mystery of Caves Exhibition MUSEUM
(동굴 신비관; 033 574 6828; adult/youth/child ₩3000/2000/1500; 9am-6pm Mar-Oct, to 5pm Nov-Feb;) Located on the south side of the river is a building that resembles a wedding cake dripping with various colours of icing. Exhibits (some in English) contain elaborate detail on cave formation. There's also a 20-minute IMAX film at 10.30am, 2pm and 3pm.

Festivals & Events

Samcheok Maengbang Canola Flower Festival HORTICULTURAL
(삼척 맹방유채꽃축제; Apr) Head out to Maengbang Beach in April when the bright-yellow fields of canola (rapeseed) are in bloom for fantastic photo-ops and various events and exhibitions.

Sleeping

★Moon Motel MOTEL $$
(033 572 4436; 432-63, Jeongsang-dong; d/tw ₩50,000/60,000;) Standing tall conveniently just a block back from the bus terminals is this superb love motel. Rooms are spotlessly clean, with huge beds, coffee sachets, computers, large flat-screen TVs, work desk and sofas; bathrooms are spacious and clean. English is very limited, but that's not a problem as service is polite and helpful.

Check-in includes a free airline-style toothbrush and a razor (for men).

Eating & Drinking

There are numerous bars stuffed away down the side streets of Jungang-ro, which bisects the town, and on Jungang-ro itself, but most are rather brash and charmless.

Bonjuk ASIAN $
(본죽; 033 572 6281; www.bonjuk.co.kr; mains from ₩7500; 9am-9.30pm Mon-Sat & 1st & 3rd Sun of the month) This small but inviting chain restaurant specialises in sweet and savoury porridge (*juk*) that can be eaten day or night. There's a well-presented English menu, though the staff's English is limited. Try bulgogi octopus porridge, shrimp porridge, tuna and vegetable porridge or, if you want something sweet, aim for red bean or sweet pumpkin porridge. Portions are ample.

You can find it on the road just to the west of Dunkin Donuts on Cheokju-ro.

Comma Food ASIAN $
(mains from ₩3500; 11am-6pm) This place in Jungang Market has a takeaway stall (No A06) and a sit-down restaurant opposite. Grab a Vietnamese *bánh mì* baguette, a stuffed and fully loaded beef or chicken burrito, hot dogs, spring rolls and more. It's friendly and the food is ample and tasty.

Eunmi Gamjatang KOREAN $
(은미 감자탕; 033 574 5333; 48-13 Jungangsijang-gil; meals ₩5000-8000; 10am-10pm) This friendly eatery specialises in hearty *gamjatang* (meaty bones and potato soup) served in a *jeongol* (hotpot) or *ttukbaegi* (뚝배기; earthenware dish). You'll need at least two people to order it; otherwise you'll end up with a massive dish for one. Solo diners can aim for the *galbitang* or *yukgaejang* (spicy beef soup with vegetables).

Information

The **tourist information centre** (033 575 1330; www.samcheok.go.kr; 9am-6pm) is beside the express bus terminal. Staff speak English and Japanese; detailed bus schedules are available in English for buses to Hwanseongul and Haesindang Park.

Getting There & Away

BUS

The express and intercity bus terminals sit beside each other. Express buses to Seoul (₩17,500, 3½ hours) run to Gangnam (every 35 minutes) and Dong-Seoul (hourly).

TRAIN

A special 'sea train' (바다열차) runs between Samcheok and Gangneung. Train carriages have been remodelled so that passengers face the extra-large windows looking out to sea (instead of the conventional front–back arrangement). From Samcheok, the train makes stops at Donghae, Jeongdongjin and several beach stations before terminating at Gangneung (₩13,000 to ₩16,000, 1¼ hours). The sea views are lovely, but the route also passes some unattractive stretches of industrial landscape.

Trains depart Samcheok at 12.18pm and 3.48pm, and return from Gangneung at 10.34am and 2.10pm, with a further service in the morning on weekends. There are extra services in May and August.

Trains take a scenic route to Andong (₩11,500, 3½ hours, daily) from Donghae, which you can get to by local bus 11 from outside the intercity bus terminal (₩1550, 25 minutes, every 10 minutes).

Wonju

033 / POP 306,000

The closest major town to Chiaksan National Park (p145), Wonju (원주) is not a particularly interesting place, but it's home to several universities and military bases and has a youthful vibe.

Sleeping & Eating

Cello Motel MOTEL
(첼로모텔; Seowon-daero; r from ₩50,000;) Right across from the bus terminal, this love motel is in a handy location and is comfortable, though some rooms are decorated in a kind of Liberace-slept-here super kitsch style. Minimal English, but a very pleasant owner.

Emoi Vietnam Kitchen VIETNAMESE $
(에머이; www.emoi.biz; Seowon-daero; from ₩6000; 11am-10.30pm;) Steaming *pho* is served up swiftly in colourful ceramic bowls in a spacious environment of green wood and yellow brickwork. Emoi does a brisk trade and it's not surprising – the *pho chin* (rice noodles in a beef broth) is lip-smackingly good and there's an English photo menu. Add the plates of chilli and pickled garlic to taste.

Information

No banks take foreign cards in Wonju, so come armed with enough cash.

Getting There & Away

From the **express bus terminal** (원주 고속버스 터미널; Seowon-daero) buses run to Seoul Gangnam (₩10,400, 1½ hours, every 10 to 15 minutes), Gangneung (₩7900, 1½ hours, hourly) and Dongdaegu (₩20,200, four hours, four per day).

Buses from the **intercity bus terminal** (원주시외버스터미널; Seowon-daero) head to Cheongju (₩8400, 1½ hours, hourly) and Gwangju (₩7,900, two to four hours, every 1½ hours).

ITX trains (₩9300, 1¼ hours, hourly) run between Wonju and Seoul's Cheongnyangni station. There are also trains to Andong (₩9200, 2¼ hours, five daily).

Pyeongchang

033

Pyeongchang county (평창군) hosted the 2018 Winter Olympics. Travellers still come for the snow; two main ski resorts in the area, Alpensia and Yongpyong (p143), hosted most of the 2018 events. Alpensia served as the main Olympic Village, hosting the ski jumping, luge, bobsleigh and cross-country skiing, while Yongpyong, which is one of northeast Asia's better ski resorts, hosted the downhill slalom events. The region is naturally best-visited and most popular during the ski season, when accommodation prices are highest, but off-season the region is highly scenic and more affordable.

The town of Hoenggye (횡계) serves as a transit hub for both ski resorts and provides cheaper eating options, a bit of nightlife, and basic accommodation.

Activities

Alpensia Ski Resort SNOW SPORTS
(알펜시아리조트 스키장; 033 339 0000; www.alpensia.co.kr; 325 Solbong-ro; lift tickets per day adult/child ₩80,000/60,000, equipment rental per day ₩36,000/27,000) With just six runs, Alpensia in Baekdusan is a small but well-serviced resort that hosted the 2018 Winter Olympics. Far less crowded than its neighbour, Yongpyong, Alpensia is a fine place for family skiing and beginners, with one long easy slope, several intermediate runs and an advanced run, as well as an alpine coaster. There's also very scenic night skiing.

The resort village at the bottom of the slope has three hotels (guests get a 30% discount on lift tickets), restaurants and a

OFF THE BEATEN TRACK

SKIING THE KOREAN ALPS

In the mountains west of Taebaek, **High1 Ski Resort** (하이원 스키장; www.high1.co.kr; 500, High1-gil; lift tickets per day adult/child ₩76,000/60,000, ski gear rental ₩28,000/22,000; ; Gohan, Gohan) is a modern ski resort that ranks among the best skiing facilities in South Korea. At 1340m, the resort sees plenty of powder on its 18 slopes, which are served by five lifts and four gondolas. Skis, boards and clothing are available for rent, single day lessons start from ₩280,000 and there's night skiing.

With officially certified slopes capable of staging international competitions, there's a good range of difficulty levels at High1, with long, relaxed low-incline baby runs for novices that commence from the top of the mountain (meaning even beginners can take in the panoramic views), alongside advanced runs where, depending on the time of year, you may find moguls. The resort is also home to Korea's first ski school for the disabled. There are slope webcams on the website if you want to peruse skiing conditions.

Sleeping options include the comfy **High1 Hotel** (하이원호텔; 033 1588 7789; www.high1.com; 399 Gohan 7-gil; d/ste from ₩160,000/300,000;), as well as the high-rise **Kangwonland Hotel** (강원랜드호텔; 033 1588 7789; www.high1.com; 265 High1-gil, Sabuk-eup; d/ste from ₩300,000/600,000;) right at the ski base.

Intercity buses (₩21,200, three hours, 23 daily) run from Dong Seoul Express Bus Terminal and Incheon airport (four hours) to the town of Gohan.

Trains depart go from Seoul's Cheongnyangni station (₩14,400, four hours, seven daily). On weekends, the tourist **O-train** (₩26,400, 7.45am, 3½ hours) is a lot of fun, kitted out in kitschy 1970s decor.

A free shuttle bus connects Gohan with all areas of High1 Ski Resort. Turn right out of the train station, walk down the drive and look for the bus shelter on the right.

water park, and nearby is a ski-jump stadium, cross-country and biathlon courses, a golf course and a casino. Lessons cost from adult/child ₩80,000/60,000 for a full day (four hours). There are also several summertime-only hiking trails surrounding the resort.

Yongpyong Ski Resort SNOW SPORTS
(용평리조트 스키장; 033 335 5757; www.yongpyong.co.kr; 715 Olympic-ro, Daegwanryeong-myeon; lift tickets per day adult/child ₩76,000/61,000, equipment rental per day ₩33,000/27,000) Korea's most beloved ski resort, and one of its largest with 31 slopes and 15 lifts, Yongpyong is a perennial favourite with snow-seekers each winter. The resort gets an average of 250cm of snow (the season runs November to March), and on a clear day it's possible to glimpse the East Sea from the slopes.

The surrounding buildings, including the giant Dragon Plaza ski house, manage to be charming but not kitschy. The resort also has cross-country trails and two half-pipes, and lessons are available in English (and four other languages). Night lift passes are available between 9pm and 12.30am (adult/child ₩38,000/30,000).

Sleeping

Yongpyong Hostel HOSTEL $
(용평호스텔; 02 3270 1231; www.yongpyong.co.kr; dm/r ₩14,000/80,000;) Hidden among the pines like a Swiss chalet, this budget option is only three minutes from the Yongpyong slopes. It doesn't have any lounges to socialise in, but it provides a place to crash if you can ignore the noisy teens that tend to stay here. It's open November to March and mid-July to mid-August. Booking is available by phone or email.

Holiday Inn Resort Alpensia HOTEL $$
(홀리데이인 알펜시아 평창 리조트; 033 339 0000; www.holidayinn.com; 225-3 Yongsan-ri; r ₩162,000;) The spacious and comfy rooms here overlook the ski slopes, some with ski in/out options. The rooms are large and functional, with balconies and big bathrooms. There's a lobby lounge with slope views and a Korean restaurant. Don't get it confused with the other all-suite Holiday Inn (p144) in Alpensia.

Boutique Olive HOTEL $$
(부티크 올리브; 033 336 3444; 314-10 Hoenggye-ri, Daegwanryeong-myeon; condos from ₩100,000;) This budget condo

complex is located in the centre of Hoenggye and is a decent option as a serviceable crash pad for nearby Alpensia (p143) and Yongpyong (p143) ski resorts. Rooms are ok, basic but clean, with kitchenettes and en suite bathrooms. Downstairs are several pubs, cafes and restaurants.

★InterContinental Alpensia Pyeongchang Resort LUXURY HOTEL $$$
(인터컨티넨탈 알펜시아 평창 리조트; ☎033 339 0000; www.ihg.com; 225-3 Yongsan-ri; r /ste ₩180,000/385,000; P⊖❄@📶≋) One of the more luxurious ski accommodation options in Korea is this InterContinental-managed hotel at the foot of Alpensia Ski Resort (p142). The grand lobby lounge with open fireplace has delicious views of the slopes and rooms are spacious, with soft beds, flat-screen TVs and terraces, some overlooking the slopes.

There's an on-site Western restaurant, and a spa with segregated Korean sauna and heated indoor soaking pools.

Staff speak excellent English and service is to a high international standard. Amazingly, good discounts often make this a more affordable option than the other hotels in the Alpensia complex, possibly because it's two minutes' walk further from the slopes.

Dragon Valley Hotel HOTEL $$$
(드래곤밸리호텔; ☎02 3270 1231, 033 330 7111; www.yongpyong.co.kr; r ₩320,000-340,000, ste ₩550,000-880,000; ❄📶≋) This choice is the best hotel in Yongpyong, close to the slopes with attentive staff, excellent rooms and a choice of restaurants. Rooms vary in size from 34-sq-metres to 78-sq-metres, while the largest suite is 87-sq-metres.

Holiday Inn & Suites Alpensia HOTEL $$$
(홀리데이인 알펜시아 평창 스위트; ☎033 339 0000; www.holidayinn.com; 225-3 Yongsan-ri; ondol/ste ₩225,000/300,000; P⊖❄@📶) Right at the foot of Alpensia's slopes, this suite-only Holiday Inn has western, Korean-style and wheelchair-accessible rooms, and is popular with families. Rooms are utilitarian but modern, with good mountain views. Be warned that it books out quickly during ski season.

Eating

The ski resorts have cafeteria-style restaurants in their lodges, and most of the resort hotels also have restaurants serving Korean and Western food; expect high-ish prices. The town of Hoenggye is a good place to find cheaper dining options.

Getting There & Away

BUS

Yongpyong or Alpensia are accessible via private shuttle buses from Incheon International Airport (one way adult/child ₩36,000/20,000, 3½ hours, five daily), Gimpo Airport (adult/child ₩30,000/16,000, three hours, five daily) and from various pick-up points around Seoul, including Seoul Station, Dongdaemun Gate and Sinchon Station (adult/child ₩21,000/16,000, three hours, six daily). Tickets can be booked in advance (see resort websites for details) or bought from the driver, though spots tend to fill up, especially on weekends.

Buses run to Hoenggye from Dong-Seoul (₩14,500, every 45 minutes). From here, free shuttle buses (10 minutes, 15 daily 5.30am to 11.30pm) depart for Yongpyong from the post office next to the bus terminal, but you'll have to take a taxi (₩11,000, 10 minutes) to Alpensia. A taxi from Hoenggye to Yongpyong costs around ₩10,000.

Intercity buses also go from Gangneung's bus terminal to Hoenggye (₩2600, 30 minutes, every 10 to 15 minutes).

TRAIN

High-speed KTX services connect Seoul to Pyeongchang. Six trains (1½ hours, ₩22,000) operate per day between Seoul Station and Pyeongchang, and considerably more connect to nearby Jinbu and Gangneung.

Getting Around

There is no regular transportation between the two resorts; a taxi can cost upwards of ₩20,000 for the 15-minute one-way journey and can be arranged by a hotel concierge on either side.

Chiaksan National Park

This park may be the smallest of the national parks in Gangwon-do, but it is still over 182 sq km in size and offers challenging hikes in some simply spectacular scenery.

It's also a very doable weekend trip from Seoul. The park is splashed with colour in spring as the azaleas flower and gorgeous autumn hues later in the year before winter snow adds further allure.

Chiaksan National Park

Sights

Chiaksan National Park NATIONAL PARK

(치악산 국립공원; ☎033 732 5231; http://english.knps.or.kr; adult/child ₩2000/500; ⏲sunrise-sunset) Scenic and mountainous Chiaksan (the name means 'Pheasant Peak Mountain') National Park is home to the lovely Guryong-sa and a host of other temples, and is top-notch hiking territory. A popular route threads up from Guryong-sa to 1288m-high Biro-bong (three hours, 5km) past the waterfalls of Seryeom Pokbo (세렴폭포), which can be extended by a further two hours down to Hwanggol (황골) where you can get the bus back to Wonju, the main access town. Parking at the park costs ₩2000.

There are also hiking trails from Geumdae-ri and Seongnam-ri – both accessible by bus from Wonju – which run about 6km to the peak Namdae-bong (1181m).

Guryong-sa BUDDHIST TEMPLE

(구룡사, Turtle Dragon Temple; ☎033 731 0503; www.templestay.com) Set among the verdant hills of Chiaksan National Park, this colourful and vibrant temple is a beauty, its main courtyard festooned with vibrantly coloured lotus lanterns and orchids placed outside the main hall. Among other shrines is a small hall to Gwan-eum, the Goddess of Mercy. The temple is home to a Templestay operation, if you want to overnight here and deeply fathom the silence of the mountains (but book ahead; no English spoken).

The temple is colloquially known as 'Nine Dragon Temple' in honour of a myth that the temple was built upon a pond in which dwelt nine dragons that were chased away by a monk; its name, however, literally means 'Turtle Dragon Temple', out of respect to a turtle rock that once existed here and protected the complex, but was destroyed, bringing misfortune upon Guryong-sa. The name of the temple was therefore changed to Turtle Dragon Temple – which has the same pronunciation in Korean as Nine Dragon Temple – to reverse its demise and afford it protection.

Sangwon-sa BUDDHIST TEMPLE

(상원사) This temple was built by the Buddhist monk Ja Jang (590–658) in 643, rebuilt in 705, burnt down in 1946 and restored again in 1947. The oldest remains is a Munsu child figure.

Sleeping

There is a lovely templestay operation at Guryong-sa, but apply ahead. *Minbak* (private homes with rooms for rent) can be found in the village outside the park's Guryong-sa entrance. There are **campgrounds** (대곡야영장; per site ₩7000-9000) in summer available at Daegok near Guryong-sa – pass the temple and walk for 10 minutes. There are no mountain shelters. The alternative is to return to Wonju, where you can find motels near the bus terminal.

Getting There & Away

To get to Guryong-sa, exit Wonju's intercity bus terminal and either take bus 51 (₩1200) to Wonju train station, or grab a taxi (₩2500). Then take either bus 41 or 41-1 (₩2000, 40 minutes, every 25 minutes), which terminate at the car park bus stop near the park entrance. Guryong-sa is a very pleasant 800m walk alongside the river further ahead.

Bus 82 runs a loop service to Hwanggol (₩1200, 30 minutes, hourly) from the stop on Bonghwa-ro (perpendicular to and just west of Seowon Dae-ro), while buses 21, 23 and 24 run to the Geumdae-ri bus stop and 23 runs to the Seongnam-ri bus stop (₩1200).

Gyeongsangbuk-do

Includes ➡

Best Places to Eat

- Gaejeong (p152)
- Kisoya (p166)
- Sukyeong Sikdang (p165)
- Kyusan (p152)
- Hyundai Department Store Food Hall (p152)

Best Places to Stay

- Grand Daegu Hotel (p152)
- Baramgot Guesthouse (p165)
- Rak Ko Jae (p177)
- Empathy Guesthouse (p151)

Why Go?

Korea's cultural warehouse, Gyeongsangbuk-do (경상북도) is resplendent in both natural beauty and heritage sites, including enchanting temples, ancient pagodas, rock-carved Buddhas and sublime tombs. Gyeongju is often called 'the museum without walls' for its historical treasures. The rounded *tumuli* (burial mounds) in the centre of town are beautiful and serene pyramids – reminders of the dead they still honour.

The region's major city, Daegu, has a historic centre peppered with heritage churches and an excellent medicinal-herb market, with superb restaurants and craft beer bars. Haein-sa is a must-see temple-library amid gorgeous mountain scenery that contains the *Tripitaka Koreana*, 1000-year-old wooden tablets inscribed with sacred Buddhist texts. The ancient town of Andong offers multiple options, while off the coast sits the rugged island of Ulleungdo, with endless opportunities to enjoy spectacular coastal landscapes.

When to Go

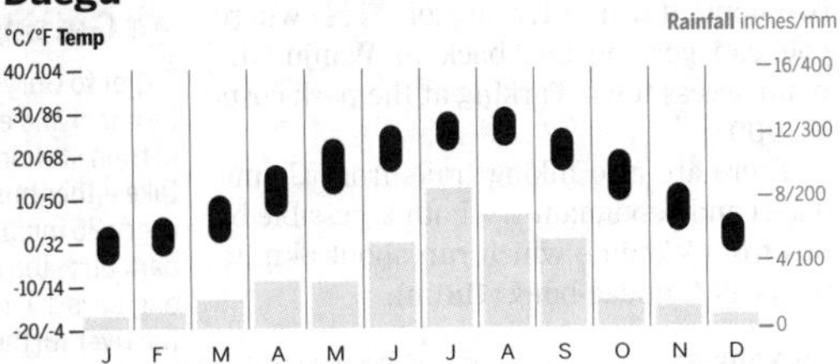

Apr–Jun Lovely temperatures and low humidity; a great time to travel here.

Mid-Aug Catch Ulleungdo's squid festival and enjoy delicious seafood in a unique island setting.

Late Sep–early Oct Andong's Mask Dance Festival, a highlight of the Korean arts calendar.

Gyeongsangbuk-do Highlights

1 Gyeongju (p158) Wandering among the sublime, ages-old *tumuli* and ancient tombs in the centre of town.

2 Daegu (p148) Exploring the city's old quarter and bumping into an impressive cathedral, old churches and missionary homes.

3 Haein-sa (p155) Marvelling at the 80,000-plus wooden tablets of the Buddhist sutras at this serene temple.

4 Hahoe Folk Village (p176) Meandering the lanes and seeking out the mysterious spirit tree at the heart of the hamlet.

5 Ulleungdo (p169) Trekking along the rocky island coastline and admiring the stunning scenery and sea views.

6 Andong (p173) Searching out ancient pagodas and walking along the lengthy and serene riverside walkway.

7 Dosan Seowon (p174) Jumping on a bus from Andong to immerse yourself in the introspective tranquillity of this Confucian academy.

8 Jikji-sa (p156) Voyaging into a dreamy Buddhist realm at this scenic mountain temple.

9 Yangdong Folk Village (p167) Being spoilt for choice photographing the charms of this traditional village.

History

At the centre of South Korea, this area was once the capital of the Silla empire (57 BC–AD 935), and as such was a central part of Korean government and trade. During this almost thousand-year-long empire, the Silla rulers created alliances with China to defeat

Japanese threats, as well as to repel other Korean invaders. During this time Confucian laws were widely adopted and informed all aspects of Korean life, including who, where and when a person could marry.

Getting There & Away

Gyeongsangbuk-do's airports include Daegu International Airport (p154) and Pohang Airport (p169), while airports outside the province at Busan (Gimhae) and Ulsan are useful too.

High-speed KTX train connect Dongdaegu station in Daegu with Seoul, Busan and Daejeon. KTX trains also run to Seoul from Gyeongju. It's most useful to use the bus to get around Gyeongsangbuk-do, but the train is handy between various cities, such as Gyeongju to Dongdaegu station in Daegu and Andong to Seoul, Daegu and Gyeongju. Ferries run from Pohang to Ulleungdo.

Daegu

053 / POP 2.45 MILLION

South Korea's fourth-largest city is a pleasant and progressive place with a fascinating traditional-medicine market; a historic central area packed with heritage, old churches and missionary residences; some excellent eating options; and a humming city centre that's good fun to explore. The city is a popular place for exchange students and English teachers, and the large student population gives Daegu (대구) a young and carefree feel.

A simple, three-line subway system makes getting around easy, and Daegu (sometimes spelled Taegu) is also a great hub for day trips; including to Haein-sa (p155) and Jikji-sa (p156), both of which offer templestays.

The name Daegu means 'Big Hill', deriving from the *hanja* characters you will see on maps and signs: 大邱.

Sights

★Our Lady of Lourdes Cathedral CATHEDRAL

(계산동 성당, Daegu Gyesan Catholic Church; Map p153; 10 Seoseong-ro) An icon and motif of Daegu, this lovely cruciform church is quite a sight, with its twin spires. Originally constructed in wood, the first incarnation went up in flames in 1899. A brick-and-stone replacement was quickly completed by 1902. Check out the interior, with its still extant luminous stained glass, and note the large crucifix out the front that makes for a good photo op with the church behind. The name in Korean is named after the district, Gyesan (Osmanthus Hill).

★Daegu Jeil Church CHURCH

(대구제일교회, The First Presbyterian Church of Daegu; Map p153) This red brick structure is one of the city's historic churches. Within the church is a fascinating history of the building and a collection of Bibles and Christian material in Korean, as well as numerous historic photographs. Look out for the fascinating examples of Korean Christmas cards from the early 1960s.

The name in Korean simply means Daegu Number One Church. The house of worship was founded in 1898 and was the first church in the province; the bell tower was added in 1936. The church is usually open, but if you find it shut, ask at the tourist information kiosk opposite and they may find someone to fling open the doors and flick on the lights.

★Daegu National Museum MUSEUM

(국립대구박물관; Map p150; 053 768 6051; http://daegu.museum.go.kr; 10am-7pm Tue-Sun) FREE This excellent museum has English labelling throughout most of its collection – and what a collection it is. Armour, jewellery, Buddhist relics from various different eras, Confucian manuscripts, clothing and textiles are all beautifully displayed in well-lit glass cases, and there's normally at least a couple of temporary exhibits as well. From Banwoldang metro, take bus 414 or 349; or from Dongdaegu station take bus 414 from across the road on the bridge. The electric boards inside the bus announce 'Nat'l Museum'.

Daegu Hyanggyo Confucian School SCHOOL

(대구향교; Map p150; www.daeguhyanggyo.org; M Line 1 or 3 to Myeongdeok, Exit 5) FREE This tranquil Confucian School at the heart of Daegu is an oasis of introspective calm that dates from 1398 (though it was burned down by the Japanese and rebuilt in the late 16th century). The main hall containing the portrait of Confucius is not generally open to visitors, but you can wander the grounds and soak up the Confucian peacefulness of the place. Look out for Mr Young-chae Cho who is a mine of information and speaks impeccable English.

Daegu's Herbal Medicine Market MARKET
(대구약령시; Map p153; Ⓜ Line 1 or 2 to Banwoldang, Exit 4) This market, west of the central shopping district, has a history as vast as its scope. It dates from 1658, making it Korea's oldest medicine market and still one of its largest. The shops spill onto the street with fragrant curiosities from lizards' tails to magic mushrooms (the latter only with a prescription); you might also catch a glimpse of someone receiving acupuncture. Start at the museum to learn the uses of every spiky herb.

Bullo-dong Tumuli-gongwon TOMB
(불로동 고분 공원; 053 940 1224; 9am-6pm) FREE In the north end of the city, Bullo-dong Tumuli-gongwon is an enormous open space covering some 330,000 sq metres. The grassy hillocks that rise like bumps across the valley are *tumuli* – burial mounds, similar to those in Gyeongju (p158). Dating from the 2nd to the 6th century AD, the *tumuli* are for both nobles and commoners – the higher the location on the hill, the higher the status of the person.

Monument to the Old City Wall MONUMENT
(Map p153) This monument records the existence of the old city wall that once ringed the town. The wall was pulled down in 1905, but its history survives in road names such as Dongseong-no (East City Wall Road) and Bukseongno (North City Wall Road). The monument is affixed with a brass plaque that details the extent of the bastion.

Gyeongsanggamyeong Park PARK
(경상감영공원; Map p153) Once known as Central Park, this is a beautiful spot to flee Daegu's modernity and fumes; a place of birdsong, where old folk and couples gather in the evening and where shade can be found during the day. The park was originally the location of Gyeongsanggamyeong, where the Gyeongsangbuk-do governor resided and worked, hence the array of traditional buildings.

Daegu Modern History Museum MUSEUM
(대구근대역사관; Map p153; 9am-7pm Apr-Oct, to 6pm Nov-Mar Tue-Sun; Ⓜ Line 1 to Jungang-no) FREE Located within the fabulous former Joseon Siksan Bank building (check out the brickwork), which dates from 1918, this very educational museum gives you the lowdown on modern Daegu, concentrating on the city's 20th-century history: its colonial past, architecture, literary heritage and contributions to democracy. The CGI-simulated bus journey around early-20th-century Daegu is only in Korean, but is still fascinating.

Daegu Arboretum GARDENS
(대구수목원; 9am-6pm Tue-Sun; Ⓜ Daegok, Exit 3) These superb botanical gardens in the south of town offer shade from the sun and a huge range of trees and plants, as well as several large greenhouses that contain more exotic specimens. It's a 1.4km walk to the arboretum from the metro station.

Cheongna Hill AREA
(청라언덕; Map p153) Not far from Our Lady of Lourdes Cathedral is this very historic hilly area of Daegu, which contains various early-20th-century missionary houses and residences; it's a charming diversion into the city's European-style history and heritage. Note the colossal modern church right alongside the area.

Daegu Yangnyeongsi Museum of Oriental Medicine MUSEUM
(대구약령시 한의약박물관; Map p153; 053 257 4729; 9am-6pm Tue-Sun; ; Ⓜ Line 1 or 2 to Banwoldang, Exit 14) FREE An interactive museum on the upper two levels has re-creations of traditional clinics and video quizzes, but offers a decreasing number of English captions as you ascend. It's a visually exciting introduction to oriental medicine such as *insam* (ginseng) and reindeer horns, with audio guides available in English, Japanese and Chinese.

On the days ending with 1 or 6 (except the 31st), *yangnyeong-sijang* (a wholesale market) takes place downstairs. You can find it right opposite the historic Jeil Church.

There is a very helpful tourist information booth as you enter the courtyard containing the museum, which can supply you with maps of this historic district of Daegu as well as a walking trail map.

Activities & Tours

Greenvill BATHHOUSE
(그린빌 찜질방 사우나; Map p153; sauna ₩6000, sauna & bed ₩9000; 24hr; Ⓜ Line 1 or 2 to Banwoldang, Exit 1) This bathhouse and *jjim-jil-bang* (sauna) is not huge, but its clean and has a soothing mixture of hot, warm and cold tubs, plus scorching-hot (81°C) and ice-cold rooms. It's a 24-hour facility, so guests can sleep overnight on wooden pillows, making it a budget sleeping option if you're just staying one night. It's down the

Daegu

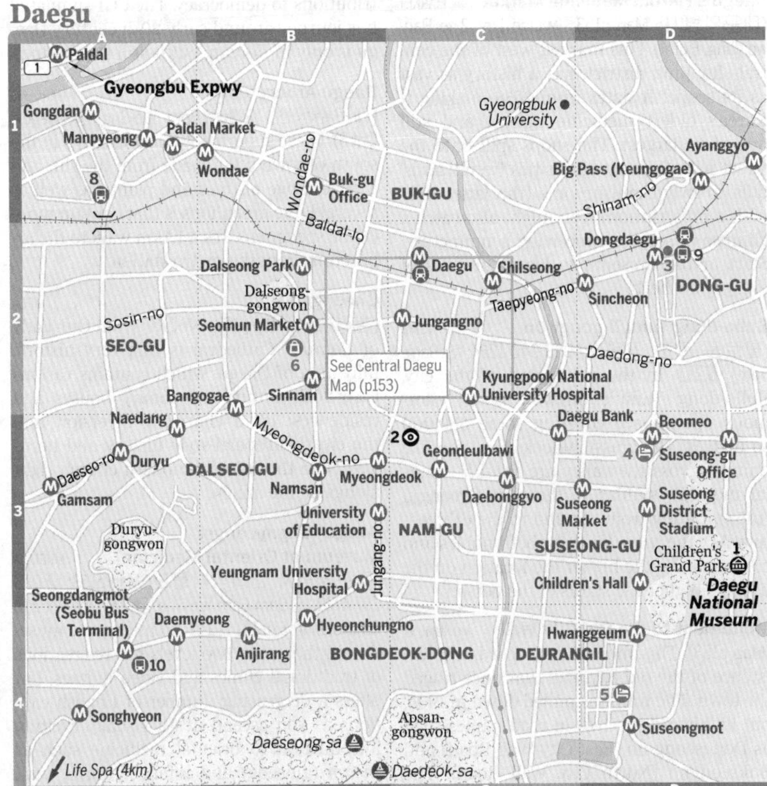

first turn to your right south from the metro station. Take the stairs down to reach the reception desk.

Life Spa BATHHOUSE
(수목원 생활 온천; ☎053 641 0100; www.lifespa.co.kr; ₩10,000; ⏲24hr; Ⓜ Line 1 to Jincheon, Exit 2 or 3) Located in western Daegu, this is a beautiful facility with 1100 sq metres of tubs and sweat rooms, a fitness centre and rooftop pools. After exiting the station, walk to the intersection and turn right. From here, it's a quick taxi ride; ask for '*sumokwon saengwol oncheon*' (수목원 생활 온천).

Daegu City Tour BUS
(Map p150; ☎053 603 1800; http://daegucitytour.com; adult/child ₩5000/3000; ⏲9.30am-4.50pm Tue-Sun) Travellers with limited time might consider Daegu's official double-decker tour. Jump on and off the bus at some of the area's best sites. Buy a ticket and get a full list of hop-on points from tourist information centres, such as at Dongdaegu station, where tours start.

Sleeping

Savoy Hotel MOTEL $
(사보이호텔; Map p153; ☎053 253 8021; www.hotelsavoy.co.kr; r from ₩40,000; Ⓜ Line 1 to Jungangno, Exit 4) This love motel enjoys a fantastic location in central Daegu, alongside a church a stone's throw north of the Daegu Modern History Museum. Rooms are divided into two blocks, one newer than the other, and are comfortable, with PCs, bathrooms, kettles and regularly restocked minifridges (for water and coffee). Breakfast (toast and cornflakes) is simple but sufficient, with a free coffee machine in the lobby.

It's over five floors and there's a lift and staff who speak very good English. Ask for a room with a window that will open. Prices go up by ₩20,000 at weekends.

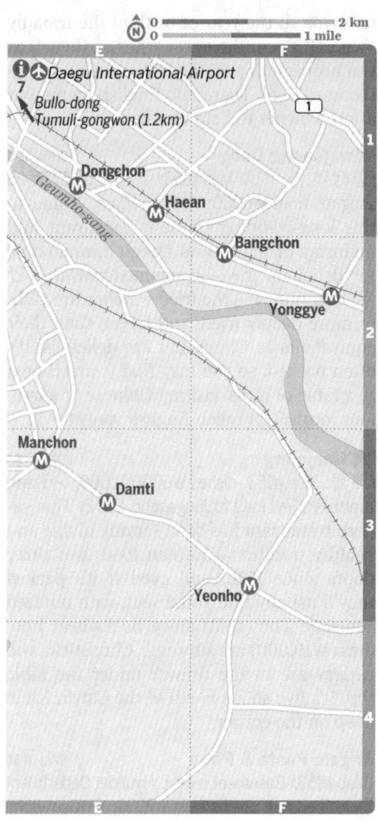

Daegu

Empathy Dongseongro Guesthouse HOSTEL $
(공감 동성로 게스트 하우스; Map p153; ☎070 7708 3145; 4-/6-/8-person dm from ₩23,000/19,000/19,000; ; Ⓜ Jungangno, Exit 3) Aimed more at backpackers just looking for dorm accommodation, this very clean, central and organised upstairs spot is a sister establishment of the Empathy Guesthouse (p151). It has decent dorms and a colourful reception area and kitchen. There's no English sign, so look for the blue-on-white hoarding above the entrance to the stairs.

Empathy Hanok GUESTHOUSE $
(공감 한옥 게스트 하우스; Map p153; ☎070 8915 8991; www.empathyguesthouse.wordpress.com; d/tr/q ₩55,000/90,000/110,000; Ⓜ Line 1 to Jungangno, Exit 1) This charming, traditional-style guesthouse is a sister operation of the Empathy Guesthouse, with private rooms along a historic alley in a traditional courtyard building, overlooked by towering ancient trees. Shower and toilet facilities are shared and there is a common kitchen too. There's only a handful of rooms, so reserve early.

Danim Backpackers HOSTEL $
(다님; ☎010 6713 0053; www.danimbackpackers.com; dm incl breakfast from ₩20,000; ; Ⓜ Line 1 or 2 to Banwoldang, Exit 9) This tiny, simple place has an apartment feel, with just 12 beds in two dorms (one for women only). It has all the necessities, however, including a great location a short stroll from the neon-drenched streets of the city centre, a communal kitchen, free use of laundry facilities, a rooftop and a nearby bar. Staff speak English and are keen to help.

★ **Empathy Guesthouse** GUESTHOUSE $$
(공감 게스트 하우스; Map p153; ☎070 8915 8991; www.empathyguesthouse.wordpress.com; 32 Jungangdaero 79-gil, Jung-gu; incl breakfast dm ₩22,000, tw ₩55,000-70,000; ; Ⓜ Line 1 to Jungangno, Exit 1) This guesthouse is part of the Center for North Korean Defectors (www.nkpeople.or.kr), and 20% of proceeds go to resettlement services. It's a great place to stay with heated floors, a rooftop terrace, curfew-free independent entry, free laundry

and staff who speak excellent English. The sociable lounge is good for hearing insights from volunteers about life for defectors.

Dorm beds are made of wood and there are a couple of twin rooms too. Dorms vary in size from six to 10 beds. The guesthouse has traditional-style *hanok* accommodation just round the corner.

Hotel Ariana HOTEL **$$**
(호텔 아리아나; Map p150; ☎053 763 9000; www.ariana.co.kr; r from ₩120,000; ❄📶; Ⓜ Line 3 to Suseongmot) This smart, well-run property has comfortable and spacious rooms, each with a double and single bed. It's in a good location near the Deurangil restaurant district, and the metro station is just round the corner. The friendly staff speak limited English. No breakfast, but the good cafe on the ground floor serves pastries and pizzas.

Grand Daegu Hotel LUXURY HOTEL **$$$**
(대구 그랜드 호텔; Map p150; ☎053 742 0001; www.daegugrand.co.kr; 563-1 Beomeo 1-dong, Susung-gu; d/f from ₩249,000/260,000; ❄@📶; Ⓜ Line 2 to Beomeo, Exit 3) This immaculate property blends minimalism with style. The location is great and the rooms are extremely comfortable, with king-sized beds and widescreen TVs. Plus there are more liveried bellboys and pruned bonsai trees than you'll know what to do with. The hotel comes equipped with a gym and a sauna. Expect reasonable discounts.

Eating

Hyundai Department Store Food Hall FOOD HALL **$**
(현대백화점 푸드홀; Map p153; Basement level 1, Hyundai Department Store; mains from ₩6000; ⊙10.30am-8pm Mon-Thu, to 8.30pm Fri-Sun; 📶; Ⓜ Banwoldang, Exit 18) This superb place – often packed to its smart-looking rafters – is all you need for a one-stop, under-one-roof dining bonanza. Wander around the stalls and take your pick from Italian, Thai, noodles, burger bars, ramen, bakeries, sushi and Korean, then dig out a table to sit at. You find yourself coming back again and again, your waistline expanding slightly on each visit.

★ **Kyusan** RAMEN **$**
(큐산; Map p153; ☎053 716 7599; mains from ₩7000; ⊙11.30am-10pm; Ⓜ Jungangno, Exit 2) This terrific, welcoming, very popular ramen restaurant is a modern all-wood affair with busy, efficient staff and a short menu of excellent noodle dishes. The name means '93', referring to the year of birth of the friendly owner. It's near the next corner on the left as you head south past the Nike store on Dongseong-ro 6-gil. There's no English menu, but ask the owner to help translate.

Yeongsaeng Deog CHINESE **$**
(영생덕; 永生德; Map p153; ☎053 255 5777; 20 Jong-ro; from ₩6000; ⊙11am-10pm) Come to this long-standing Chinese restaurant and mainstay of the central Daegu dining scene for delicious fried or steamed *mandu* (만두; dumplings) – the fried versions are rather more deeply fried, and larger, than their equivalents in China, but are delicious. It's often packed, so you may find yourself next to a table of nuns, visiting Chinese or garrulous locals. Not much English spoken.

★ **Gaejeong** KOREAN **$$**
(개정; Map p153; dishes ₩6000-11,000; ⊙11am-10pm; 📶; Ⓜ Line 1 to Jungangno, Exit 2) This superb restaurant has been serving divine and healthy traditional Korean food over three floors since 1978; and even if it's packed they'll usually find you a seat, with unfazed courtesy. The (cold) spicy buckwheat noodles (₩10,000) are supreme. Chopsticks and cutlery are in the drawer under the table top. It's five shops north of the Calvin Klein shop on the corner.

Angelo Pasta & Pizza ITALIAN **$$**
(Map p153; Basement level 1, Hyundai Department Store Food Hall; mains from ₩7900; ⊙10am-8pm; 📶) Spaghetti-shaped lines form at busy Angelo's, so find your spot and size up the photo menu. Always wanted to eat excellent pizza with chopsticks? Now's your chance. Get your pointy elbows out, take a seat at the long table or one of the nearby round tables… and enjoy.

Bongsan Jjim-Galbi KOREAN **$$**
(봉산 찜갈비; Map p153; www.bongsanzzim.com; dishes from ₩8000; ⊙10am-10pm; Ⓜ Line 1 to Jungangno, Exit 2) Located on Daegu's famous *jjim-galbi* (slow-cooked beef ribs) street, this quaint restaurant has been serving spicy steamed beef for 40 years. The friendly owner, Mr Choi, speaks English and is happy to accommodate customers who prefer less spice in their food.

Drinking & Nightlife

★ **Brewers Brothers** BAR
(Map p153; 29 Jong-ro; ⊙6pm-1am Mon-Thu, to 2am Fri & Sat; Ⓜ Jungangno, Exit 1) This amiable, homey and easy-going bar – with a touch of

Central Daegu

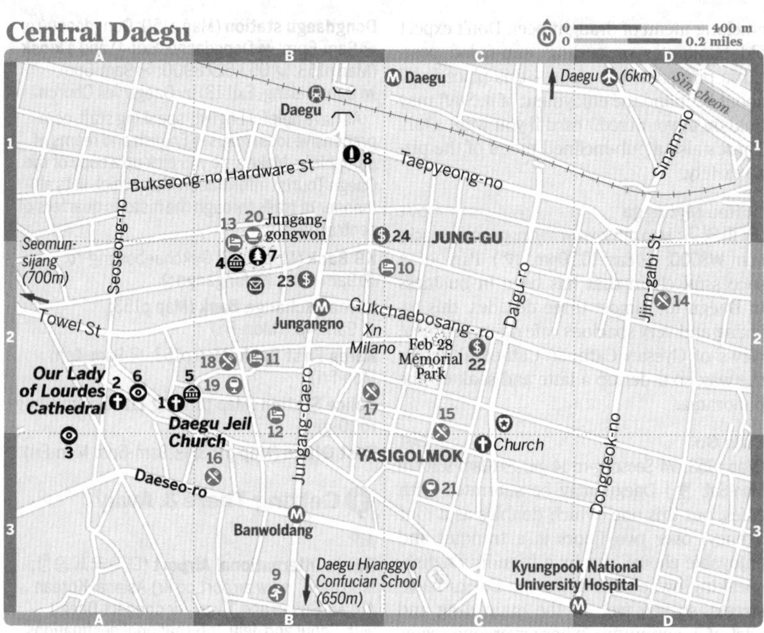

Central Daegu

Top Sights
1 Daegu Jeil Church A2
2 Our Lady of Lourdes Cathedral A2

Sights
3 Cheongna Hill A3
4 Daegu Modern History Museum B2
5 Daegu Yangnyeongsi Museum of Oriental Medicine A2
6 Daegu's Herbal Medicine Market A2
7 Gyeongsanggamyeong Park B2
8 Monument to the Old City Wall B1

Activities, Courses & Tours
9 Greenvill B3

Sleeping
10 Empathy Dongseongro Guesthouse C2
11 Empathy Guesthouse B2
12 Empathy Hanok B2
13 Savoy Hotel B2

Eating
Angelo Pasta & Pizza .... (see 16)
14 Bongsan Jjim-Galbi D2
15 Gaejeong C2
16 Hyundai Department Store Food Hall B3
17 Kyusan B2
18 Yeongsaeng Deog B2

Drinking & Nightlife
19 Brewers Brothers B2
20 Cafe Go B1
Coffee Myungga .... (see 2)
21 Etoh's Drafthouse C3

Shopping
Hyundai Department Store .... (see 16)

Information
Jeil Church Tourist Information Kiosk .... (see 5)
22 KB Bank C2
23 Korea Exchange Bank B2
24 Korea First Bank B1

a London pub feel – delivers a terrific menu of craft beer on tap (served with a small pot of pretzels) and bottled beers, perfect for a boozy evening with backdrop of smooth music. There's also a pub-food menu of fish and chips, sausage and chips, and pizza.

Etoh's Drafthouse BAR
(이토스; Map p153; ☎053 211 9385; 12-3 Dongseong-ro 3-gil; ⏰4pm-1am Mon & Thu, to 2am Fri, 3pm-2am Sat, 3pm-1am Sun; 📶) With a popular, slender terrace over the street, spacious Etoh's sports a homey atmosphere and a

cracking menu of draught beer. Don't expect old banknotes or curling, sun-faded postcards pinned to the walls – this place is all about beer and the enjoyment of it. Staff may hold on to your credit card if you want a tab. There's also a pub-inclined menu of the pizza variety.

Coffee Myungga CAFE
(커피명가; Map p153; www.myungga.com; snacks from ₩3000; ⊙8am-10.30pm; 📶) Part of a successful chain that has been in business in Daegu for almost three decades, this relaxing and very spacious cafe offers supreme views of Gyesan Catholic Cathedral across the way, so order up a latte and soak up the panorama.

Cafe Go CAFE
(Map p153; 74 Seosong-ro 14-gil; ⊙10am-9.30pm Mon-Sat; 📶) Daegu may be saturated with cafes, but this one (which doubles as a tour agency) over two floors is a tranquil and enjoyable choice, run by a friendly English-speaking owner. It's down the Daegu backstreets, so you feel off the main drag and part of a community where everyone seems to know each other. Views upstairs range over the park.

Shopping

Hyundai Department Store DEPARTMENT STORE
(현대백화점; Map p153; ⊙10.30am-8pm Mon-Thu, to 8.30pm Fri-Sun; 📶; Ⓜ Banwoldang, Exit 18) It's worth coming here at night to see the light display, but any time will do for this terrific department store – a modern, geometric architectural marvel in its own right. On the shopping front, you'll find everything here and if you're feeling peckish, just head for the terrific food hall (p152).

Seomun-sijang MARKET
(서문시장; Map p150; ⊙9am-6pm Mar-Oct, to 5pm Nov-Feb, closed 2nd & 4th Sun; Ⓜ Line 2 to Seomun Market, Exit 1) This hulking, multistorey complex has more than 4000 stalls in six sections including clothing, silk and street food. Bustling yet orderly, it's been one of Korea's big three markets since 1669, even if the current buildings have little of that historic character. Outside the subway exit, turn 180 degrees and walk round the corner.

Information

Daegu has a tourist information centre at all major transit points, including at the **airport** (Map p150; 221 Gonghang-ro, ⊙9am-6pm), **Dongdaegu station** (Map p150; Dongdaegu-ro; ⊙9am-6pm; Ⓜ Dongdaegu, Exit 4) and a **kiosk** (Map p153; ☎053 627 8900; ⊙9am-6pm; Ⓜ Banwoldang, Exit 18) by Daegu Jeil Church.

All have helpful English-speaking staff, comprehensive local maps in English and reams of pamphlets. Make sure you pick up a copy of the Daegu Tourist Information Map, which lists all manner of trails through the historic quarters of central Daegu.

KB Bank (Map p153; Gukchaebosang-ro; ⊙9am-4pm; Ⓜ Jungangno)

Korea Exchange Bank (Map p153; ⊙9am-4pm Mon-Fri)

Korea First Bank (Map p153; ⊙9am-4pm Mon-Fri)

Police Station (Map p153; ☎112; Gongpyeong-ro 10-gil)

Post Office (Map p153; ⊙9am-6pm Mon-Fri)

Getting There & Away

AIR

Daegu International Airport (대구국제공항; Map p150; www.airport.co.kr) Asiana, Korean Air, Air Busan and T'way Air connect Daegu with Seoul and Jeju. International destinations include Shanghai, Bangkok, Taipei, Shenyang, Beijing and destinations in Japan.

Daegu's airport is northeast of the city, about 2km from the express bus terminal. From central Daegu, take Line 1 to Ayanggyo station, Exit 3, and catch bus 401, 101 or Express 1. A taxi from the airport to the centre will cost around ₩10,000 and take about 20 minutes.

BUS

There are three bus terminals in Daegu: an **Express (Gosok) Bus Terminal** (Map p150; ☎053 743 3701; Ⓜ Line 1 to Dongdaegu, Exit 4), which incorporates the **Dongbu Intercity Bus Terminal** (East Intercity Bus Terminal; Map p150; ☎053 756 0017; Ⓜ Line 1 to Dongdaegu, Exit 4), by Dongdaegu train station; and the **Seobu** (West Intercity Bus Terminal; Map p150; ☎053 656 1583; Ⓜ Line 1, Seongdangmot, Exit 3) and **Bukbu** (North Intercity Bus Terminal; Map p150; ☎053 357 1851; Ⓜ Line 2, Duryu, Exit 1) intercity terminals. Buses to some destinations leave from multiple terminals, so it may be worth checking departure times of several terminals if you're looking for a bus at a specific time. Visit www.kobus.co.kr for more information.

TRAIN

Dongdaegu station on the east side of the city is the main station for long-distance trains. It's near the express bus terminal. Daegu station, closer to the centre, is mostly for *Tonggeun* (commuter-class) and *Mugunghwa* (semi-express) trains.

You'll find good connections from Dongdaegu station to Seoul including frequent KTX (₩43,400, two hours) and *Mugugahwa* (₩21,000, four hours) trains. A frequent KTX service to Busan is available (₩17,100, one hour), though consider *Saemaul* (₩11,400, 1¼ hours) or *Mugunghwa* (₩7700, 1½ hours) services to increase your departure options without adding a significant amount of travel time. A new KTX train connecting Daejeon and Daegu takes 45 minutes. Check www.korail.go.kr for schedules and fares. Trains also run from Dongdaegu to Gyeongju (₩5000, 1¼ hours, hourly).

Getting Around

Local bus fares are ₩1250, but can vary with longer routes. Two efficient subway lines crisscross the city centre as well as a third monorail line; subway and monorail train tokens cost ₩1350.

Haein-sa

055 / POP 500

Haein-sa TEMPLE

(해인사; 055 934 3105; www.haeinsa.or.kr; ₩3000; 8.30am-6pm) Holding 81,258 woodblock scriptures, making it one of the largest Buddhist libraries of its kind, this Unesco World Heritage–listed temple should be on every visitor's not-to-be-missed list. As well as being one of Korea's most significant temples, Haein-sa is also one of the most beautiful: part of its magic lies in the natural setting of mixed deciduous and coniferous forest surrounded by high mountain peaks and rushing streams. At prayer times (3.30am, 10am and 6.30pm) the place can feel otherworldly.

Known as the *Tripitaka Koreana*, the blocks are housed in four buildings at the temple's upper reaches, complete with simple but effective ventilation to prevent deterioration. Although the buildings are normally locked and you can only approach to a certain distance, the blocks are visible through slatted windows, though you may have to do a fair amount of peering to allow your eyes to adjust to the light.

The main hall, Daejeokkwangjeon (대적광전; 大寂光殿), the Great Hall of Tranquil Light, was burnt down in the Japanese invasion of 1592 and again (accidentally) in 1817, though miraculously the *Tripitaka* survived. It escaped a third time, during the Korean War, when a South Korean pilot working for the Allied forces refused to allow them to bomb it. The hall is an astonishing sight, with its fabulously carved and decorated ceiling and extraordinary trinity of Buddhas.

The Daebirojeon (대비로전; 大毘盧殿) or Vairocana Hall is notable for containing the two oldest wooden images in Korea, both of the Vairocana Buddha. Don't overlook having a ladle of pure crystal-clear spring water from the Eosujeong (King's Spring) – a well that was mainly used in the past by kings but can now be supped from by all and sundry. The name Haein-sa literally means the 'Stamp of the Sea Temple'.

Haein-sa Museum MUSEUM

(adult/child ₩2000/free; 10am-6pm Mar-Oct, to 5pm Nov-Feb) On the approach to the temple, this excellent museum showcases temple treasures like replicas of the scriptures, Buddhist art and other artefacts, including a collection of ritual *vajra* (dorje); there's even a temple downstairs. It is a short walk from the main road, while the temple itself is a further kilometre up the hillside.

Activities

Gaya-san HIKING

(가야산) Hikers will want to challenge Gayasan (1430m), the main peak in the Gayasan National Park, and a pretty one, though the climb up from Haein-sa is known to be tough. There are many other temples hidden away amid the trees and foliage of the hills, so you can explore largely to your heart's content, though pack water and snacks.

Sleeping

Haein-sa Templestay TEMPLESTAY $

(해인사 템플스테이; 055 934 3110; https://eng.templestay.com; weekday/weekend ₩40,000/60,000) The best and most enjoyable sleeping option is to stay at the temple itself. Don't expect luxury – men and women sleep in separate *ondol* (floor-heated) dorms, but it's a worthwhile option to experience the otherworldly 3.30am prayer service and, of course, the serene and magical temple setting.

Gobau GUESTHOUSE $

(고바우; 055 932 5599; s/d ₩30,000/40,000; meals ₩8000-15,000) This decent place has kind owners and twee, simple, comfy, clean and floor-heated rooms. Try the **restaurant** (7am-midnight) where *sanchae jeongsik* (산채정식; rice with vegetables) is the main dish. It's in the centre of Haein-sa, up the hill beyond the bus terminal.

WORTH A TRIP

PALGONGSAN PROVINCIAL PARK

Palgongsan Provincial Park (팔공산 도립공원) is scenic, mountainous and well visited. Its highest peak, Palgong-san (Mountain of the Eight Meritorious Officers; 1192m) received its name around the end of the Silla period after eight generals saved Wang-Geon, the founding king of the Goryeo kingdom. There are some excellent hiking routes here, but the quickest way to ascend Palgong-san is by **cable car** (팔공산 케이블카; adult/child one-way ₩6000/3000, return ₩10,000/5500; 9.30am-sunset Tue-Sun). The seven-minute ride drops you at the top (820m), where several restaurants offer panoramic views. For the cable car station, take the bus to the last stop (Donghwa Area).

Palgongsan Provincial Park is 20km north of Daegu. Bus 401 (₩1800) runs between Dongdaegu station and the tourist village below Gatbawi. Bus 1 (급행, Geuphaeng; ₩1800, 50 minutes, frequent) connects Donghwa-sa and the bus stop near Dongdaegu station. For Donghwa-sa, get off at the Donghwa-sa stop; for the cable car, wait until the final stop.

Gatbawi (갓바위; www.seonbonsa.org) A medicinal Buddha shrine and national treasure, some 850m above sea level and said to date back to AD 638. This Buddha is famed for the flat stone 'hat' hovering over its head, 15cm thick. Incense wafts and mountain mist make it quite a spiritual experience. Plan on a challenging, though enjoyable, two-hour (return) hike. About 20 minutes into the hike, the trail leads to a small temple. For a longer and not-as-steep hike, pick up the dirt trail behind the temple. For a shorter but steeper walk up stone steps, turn left at the small pagoda in the temple compound. Note: the trails are often packed on weekends.

Donghwa-sa (동화사; ₩2500; 9am-6pm) Palgongsan Provincial Park's most popular destination is the province's leading temple, with a history stretching back to AD 493. For the temple, get off the bus at the Donghwa-sa stop; it's a 800m walk from there.

Haeinsa Tourist Hotel HOTEL $$
(해인사 관광 호텔; 055 933 2000; d & tw /ste from ₩65,000/130,000;) The most comfortable option in Haein-sa is at the top of the hill along the road up from the bus terminal, with a polished lobby, coffee shop, restaurant and sauna – even if it is often eerily deserted. Rooms come with balconies and rates rise roughly 40% on Friday and Saturday. Basic English spoken.

Drinking & Nightlife

Book Tea CAFE
(9am-5.30pm, to 6pm summer, to 5pm winter;) This fabulous cafe in a temple hall at the heart of Haein-sa is arrayed with Buddhist books on shelves. A state of zen calm presides over the neat, minimalist space, with wooden furniture and black-and-white temple photographs adorning the walls. It's a joyous spot for a coffee or a restorative smoothie.

Getting There & Away

Although it's in Gyeongsangnam-do, Haein-sa is most easily accessed by bus (₩7100, 1½ hours, every 40 minutes 6.40am to 8pm) from Daegu's Seobu Intercity Bus Terminal (p154).

While the bus terminates at Haein-sa's small bus station at the top of the hill, where there's a community of motels and shops, get off at the Haein-sa stop (listen for the announcement or tell the bus driver you want to get off at the stop for the temple) and follow the crowds 1.2km up the hillside to the temple complex.

Gimcheon & Jikji-sa

054 / POP 150,000

Gimcheon (김천) is a simple and not particularly interesting town, despite its alluring name, which means 'Gold Spring'. Its main draw is as a base for exploring the nearby temple of Jikji-sa (p156).

Sights

Jikji-sa TEMPLE
(직지사; 054 436 6174; www.jikjisa.or.kr; ₩1200; 7am-6.30pm Mar-Oct, to 5.30pm Nov-Feb) Jikji-sa is a postcard-pretty temple in a wonderfully quiet mountain forest setting. The delicate paintings on the temple buildings have an appealing grace, as do the giant timbers and several historic stone pagodas.

Of the 40 original buildings, about 20 still exist, the oldest dating from a 1602 reconstruction. Highlights include the Daeung-

Palgongsan Provincial Park

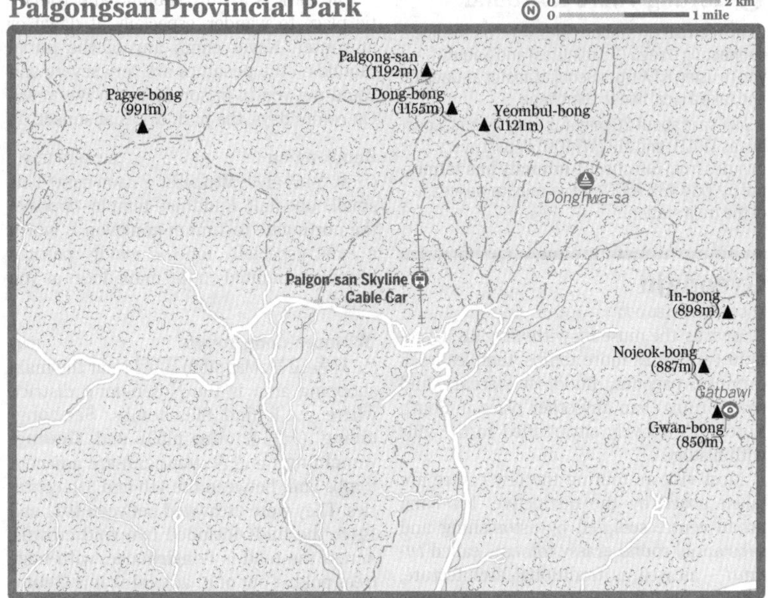

jeon, with stunning Buddhist triad paintings on silk (1774) that are national treasures, and the rotating collection in the temple's Jikji Museum of Buddhist Arts.

The Vairocana Hall contains thousands of small Buddha statues, while 330 lotus flowers decorate the ceiling of the main hall. Many visitors day-trip to Jikji-sa, while some join the **Templestay program** (₩50,000-70,000 per night), a lovely experience and an opportunity to learn *seon* (zen) meditation techniques. There's a well-established tourist village by the bus stop with *minbak* (private homes with rooms for rent), *yeogwan* (small, family-run hotels), a larger hotel, restaurants and cafes.

Jikji-sa is about 20 minutes from Gimcheon by bus. Local buses 11, 111, and 22 (₩1200) depart every 10 minutes from Gimcheon's intercity bus terminal. The temple complex is a pleasant 15-minute walk from the bus stop.

Jikji Museum of Buddhist Arts MUSEUM
(☎054 436 6009; www.jikjimuseum.org; ₩2000; ⏲9am-5.30pm Tue-Sun Mar-Oct, to 4.30pm Nov-Feb) A collection of 2000 Buddhist treasures and relics from temples in Gyeongsang-buk-do. Highlights include a bronze bell cast by a monk, and a large unearthed bronze gong.

Sleeping & Eating

There's an excellent templestay program at Jikji-sa (p156), if you want some serenity and something different.

Rex Motel MOTEL
(렉스모텔; ☎054 437 7995; 145-5 Pyeonghwa-dong; r ₩40,000) This solid choice is run by an old man with limited English. Rooms are spacious, with flat-screen TVs and comfy beds; nothing special, but serviceable. After exiting the train station and turning right, it's around a 10-minute walk down a road off the main drag.

Misoya JAPANESE $
(미소야; ☎054 433 8090; ⏲11am-9pm) This excellent chain Japanese restaurant – described as a 'Japanese Urban Bistro' – is just the place for delicious rice dishes, hot pot, katsu breaded chicken cutlets, bento or steaming bowls of curry udon or soba noodles. There's a clear picture menu and staff are helpful.

Information

KB Bank (Kookmin Bank; 국민은행; ⏲ATM 7am-11.30pm) The only place in town with a global ATM; it's a short walk from the train station.

Getting There & Around

Gimcheon's train station (김천역) is on the line connecting Daegu (50 minutes) and Seoul. If you're using KTX from Seoul, transfer at Daejeon and take a local line to Gimcheon.

Jikji-sa is about 20 minutes away by bus. Local buses 11, 111, and 112 (₩1400) depart every 10 minutes from Gimcheon's **intercity bus terminal** (054 432 7600), a five-minute walk east of the train station.

Gyeongju

054 / POP 280,000

Known as 'the museum without walls', Gyeongju (경주) has more tombs, temples, rock carvings, pagodas, Buddhist statuary and palace ruins than any other place in South Korea. It's a lovely city, stuffed to the gills with history.

Most visitors touring the city centre are taken aback by the distinctive, low-lying urban centre sculpted by astonishing and substantial round grassy tombs – called *tumuli* – as well as traditional architecture, with colourful hip roofs set against a canvas of green rolling mountains.

Two of Gyeongju's not-to-be-missed sites – Bulguk-sa and Seokguram – are in the outlying districts, within reach of public transport. Gyeongju and its surrounding districts covers a vast area – some 1323 sq km – so you should plan on several days' stay if you want to visit some of the lesser-known places.

Sights

Central Gyeongju

★Tumuli-gongwon TOMB

(대릉원; Map p159; ₩1500; 9am-10pm) The huge, walled park has 23 tombs of Silla monarchs and family members. From the outside, they resemble substantial grassy hillocks that echo the mountains outside town. Many of the *tumuli* have yielded fabulous treasures, on display at the Gyeongju National Museum. One tomb, **Cheonmachong** (천마총, Heavenly Horse Tomb; Map p159), is open to visitors, but was shut for restoration at the time of writing. Thirteen metres high and 47m in diameter, the tomb was built around the end of the 5th century.

Facsimiles of the golden crown, bracelets, jade ornaments, weapons and pottery found here are displayed in glass cases around the inside of the tomb.

The park is a truly sublime and romantic place to wander, especially at dawn or at sunset. Never climb any of the burial mounds – the penalties are very severe and could put you in prison for up to two years. On colder days, the park closes at sunset.

Beopjang-sa BUDDHIST TEMPLE

(法藏寺; 법장사; Map p159; dawn-dusk) This small, one-hall Buddhist temple opposite the north gate to Tumuli-gongwon is worth a look, especially for the vividly painted guardians painted on the main doors as you enter.

★Noseo-dong Tombs TOMB

(노서동 고분; Map p159) FREE Near the main shopping area is the Noseo-dong district, where you'll find Silla tombs. **Seobongchong** (서봉총; Map p159) and **Geumgwanchong** (금관총; Map p159) are adjacent tombs built between the 4th and 5th centuries. They were excavated between 1921 and 1946; the finds included two gold crowns. Across the road is Bonghwadae, with huge trees poking out of it; adjoining it is **Geumnyeongchong** (Map p159). Houses covered much of this area until 1984, when they were removed.

★Bonghwangdae TOMB

(봉황대; Phoenix Terrace; Map p159) Sprouting huge trees of vast girth, this is the largest extant Silla tomb – 22m high, with a 250m circumference. It's quite a picture at any time, but particularly at sunset, if you get the right light and the sun is going down behind the hillock. Make sure you don't climb the tomb (it's tempting) – or any of the other mounds – as penalties are severe (up to two years in prison).

Gyeongju National Museum MUSEUM

(국립경주박물관; Map p164; 054 740 7537; http://gyeongju.museum.go.kr; 9am-6pm Tue-Fri & Sun, to 9pm Sat & holidays Mar-Dec) FREE Arguably the best history museum in Korea, the Gyeongju National Museum is where you can appreciate the significance of this ancient city in one fell swoop. The main archaeological hall has dazzling displays of jewellery, weaponry and other ceremonial items from the Silla dynasty, including a 5th-century gold crown that looks like something from *Game of Thrones*. The museum is an easy 150m walk from the east side of Wolseong-gongwon and is well signed.

You'll find an entire building devoted to the findings at **Anapji Pond** (안압지, Dong-

Central Gyeongju

Central Gyeongju

Top Sights
1 Bonghwangdae......B2
2 Noseo-dong Tombs......B2
3 Tumuli-gongwon......C3

Sights
4 Beopjang-sa......B2
5 Cheomseongdae......D4
6 Cheonmachong......C3
7 Geumgwanchong......B2
8 Geumnyeongchong......C3
9 Seobongchong......B2

Sleeping
10 Baramgot Guesthouse......C2
11 Gyeongju Guest House......D2
12 Hanjin Hostel......A2
13 Taeyang-Jang Motel......A2

Eating
14 Daebak Jip......A1
15 Dosolmaeul......B3
16 Jungang Night Market......A1
17 Kisoya......B2
18 Kuro Ssambap......D4
19 Sukyeong Sikdang......C3

Information
20 Express Bus Terminal Tourist Information Kiosk......A3
21 Train Station Tourist Information Kiosk......D1

Transport
22 Express Bus Terminal......A3
23 Gyeongju Train Station......D1
24 Intercity Bus Terminal......A3

gung Palace and Wolji Pond; Map p160; ₩2000; 8am-sunset Sep-May, 7.30am-7pm Jun-Aug), an art hall focusing on Buddhist works and a temporary exhibition hall.

Gyeongju

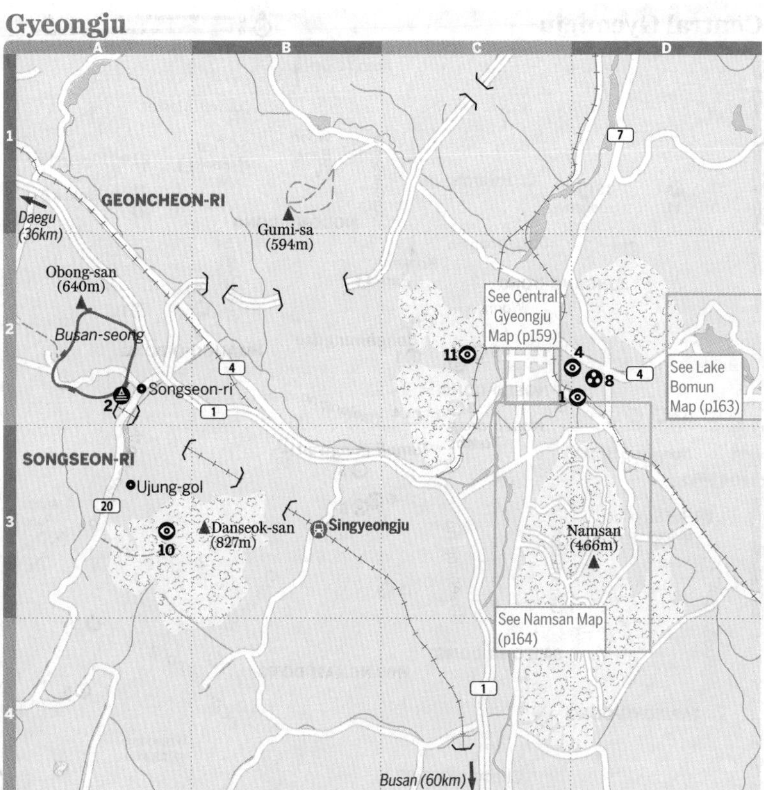

Outside the main hall, the Emille Bell (King Seongdeok's Bell) is one of the largest and most beautifully resonant bells ever made in Asia. It's said that its ringing can be heard over a 3km radius when struck only lightly with the fist. Unfortunately you aren't allowed to test this claim. A couple of ancient stupas can also be found within the grounds.

There are English signs throughout and an interesting multilingual audio guide is available (₩3000). English-speaking tours run on Saturdays at 1.30pm (March to November).

Bunhwang-sa PAGODA

(분황사; Map p160; www.bunhwangsa.org; ₩1500; ⏲sunrise-sunset) This large pagoda was built in the mid-7th century during Queen Seondeok's reign, making it the oldest datable pagoda in Korea. It's a rare example of one made from brick. The magnificently carved Buddhist guardians and stone lions are a feature; the pagoda is unique in that each entrance is protected by two guardians.

Cheomseongdae OBSERVATORY

(첨성대; Map p159; ☎054 772 5134; ⏲8am-6pm Apr-Oct, from 9am Nov-Mar) FREE Southeast of Tumuli-gongwon in the attractive sprawl of Wolseong-gongwon is the Far East's oldest astrological observatory, constructed between AD 632 and 646. Its design conceals amazing sophistication: the 12 stones of its base symbolise the months of the year. From top to bottom there are 30 layers – one for each day of the month – and a total of 366 stones were used in its construction, corresponding (approximately) to the days of the year. The name literally means 'Observe the Stars Platform'.

Banwol-seong RUINS

(반월성; Map p164; Castle of the Crescent Moon) A few minutes' walk south through the trees from Cheomseongdae, Banwol-seong is the

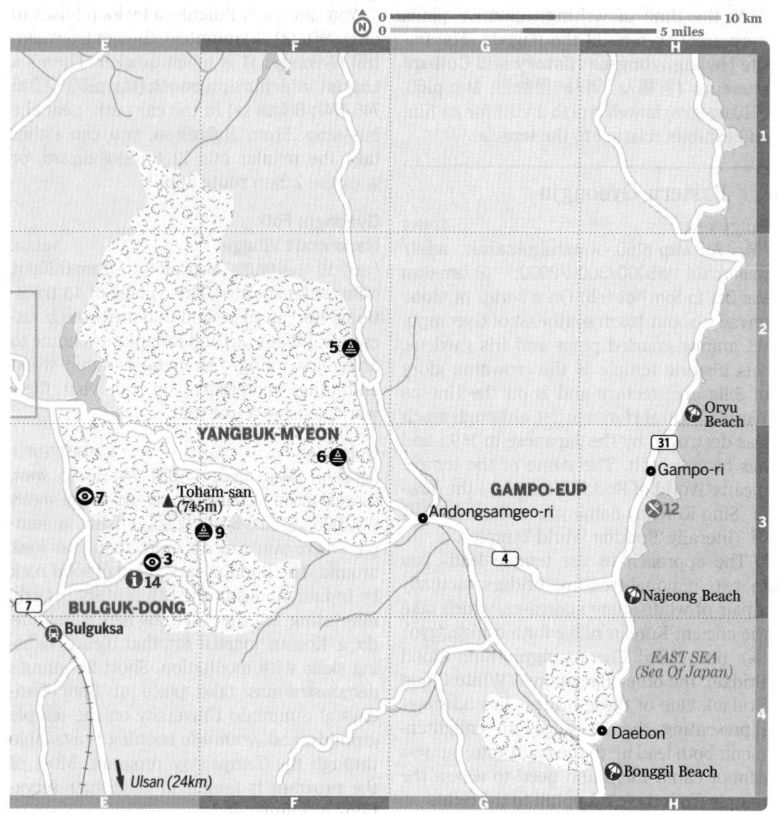

site of a once-fabled fortress. Now it's attractive parkland, where you can see some walls and ruins, as well as a huge and active excavation site. The only intact building is the early-18th-century Seokbinggo (Stone Ice House), which was once used as a food store and was restored in 1973. The *hanja* 石氷庫 (meaning 'Stone Ice House') is carved on the lintel over the entrance.

Hwangnyong-sa Site RUINS
(황룡사지, Yellow Dragon Temple; Map p160) The ruins of this simply vast 6th-century temple are a sad and desolate spectacle: once the nation's largest Buddhist temple, its standout feature was a huge nine-storey, 80m-tall pagoda (the world's tallest wooden building at the time), whose foundation stones can still be seen. The entire temple and pagoda was sent up in flames by the Mongols in 1238. The surviving foundation stones give an idea of the scale of the compound, which was astonishing in size.

Gyeongju

Sights

1 Anapji Pond D2
2 Bokdu-am Hermitage A2
3 Bulguk-sa E3
4 Bunhwang-sa D2
5 Girim-sa F2
6 Golgul-sa F3
7 Gyeongju Folk Handicraft Village E3
Hwangnyong-sa History and Culture Museum .... (see 8)
8 Hwangnyong-sa Site D2
9 Seokguram F3
10 Sinseon-sa A3
11 Tomb of General Kim Yusin C2

Eating

12 Gampo Hogung Raw Fish Center H3
13 Nahbi C2

Information

14 Bulguk-Sa Tourist Information Booth E3

At the time of writing, tentative plans were afoot to rebuild the pagoda. The on-site **Hwangnyong-sa History and Culture Museum** (황룡사 역사 문화관; Map p160; ⏲10am-9pm) is well worth a visit for its film and exhibits relating to the temple.

Eastern Gyeongju

Bulguk-sa TEMPLE
(불국사; Map p160; www.bulguksa.or.kr; adult/youth/child ₩5000/3000/2000; ⏲7am-6pm Mar-Oct, to 5pm Nov-Feb) On a series of stone terraces about 16km southeast of Gyeongju, set among gnarled pines and iris gardens, this historic temple is the crowning glory of Silla architecture and is on the Unesco World Cultural Heritage list, although much was destroyed by the Japanese in 1593 and has been rebuilt. The name of the temple means 'World of Buddha Temple' – the *hanja* (Sino-Korean) name you will see is 佛國寺 (literally 'Buddha World Temple').

The approach to the temple leads you to two national-treasure bridges (actually a pair of white stone staircases, which take the ancient Korean name for a bridge, 'gyo': 橋); one called Cheongungyo (Blue Cloud Bridge), the other Baegungyo (White Cloud Bridge). One of these bridges has 33 steps, representing the 33 stages to enlightenment; both lead up to the main gate, but you cannot climb them and need to access the temple from the road uphill to the right.

The main hall is the Daeungjeon Hall (大雄殿, Main Buddha Hall) which dates from 1765, as the original was burned in the late 16th century. In front of the main hall are two more national treasures: two pagodas that somehow survived Japanese destruction. The first, Dabotap (Many Treasures Pagoda), is of plain design and typical of Silla artistry, while the other, Seokgatap (Sakyamuni Pagoda), is much more ornate and typical of the neighbouring Baekje kingdom. When the latter was restored in 1966, it was found to contain a copy of a sutra that is one of the world's oldest woodblock print books. The pagodas are so revered that replicas appear in the grounds of the Gyeongju National Museum (p158).

Other halls you will find are the much more recently constructed Nahanjeon Hall (where Buddha is flanked by 16 *nahan*, or arhats) and a shrine to the Goddess of Mercy (Avalokitesvara), the Gwon-eum-Jon (the original dated from the 8th century, but this is a 20th-century reconstruction).

You can reach Bulguk-sa by loop buses 10 or 11 (₩1500, 30 minutes), though from central Gyeongju 11 is much quicker. There's a **tourist information booth** (Map p160; ☎046 746 4747; Bulguk-sa) in the car park, near the bus stop. From Bulguk-sa, you can either take the regular bus 12 to Seokguram, or walk the 2.2km route uphill.

Gyeongju Folk Handicraft Village VILLAGE
(경주민속공예촌; Map p160; ⏲9am-6.30pm, closes earlier in winter) This village of 45 traditional Korean tiled- and thatched-roof houses near Toham-san and Bulguk-sa is home to artisans working with metal, ceramic, wood and other materials; you can visit their workshops on a free tour.

Golgul-sa BUDDHIST TEMPLE
(골굴사; Map p160; ☎054 744 1689; www.sunmudo.com; templestay per night incl meals ₩50,000; ⏲8am-6pm) FREE Finally, a temple where you can do more than just look around. The Buddha carved out of solid rock by Indian monks in the 6th century is fairly interesting, but the real draw here is *sunmudo,* a Korean martial art that blends fighting skills with meditation. Short 20-minute demonstrations take place at 3pm Sundays at Sunmudo University on the temple grounds, and *sunmudo* training is available through the Templestay program. Most of the program is taught in English; reservations recommended.

From Gyeongju intercity bus terminal, take a bus towards Gampo-ri or Yangbuk-myeon (bus 100 or 150) and ask the driver to drop you at Andongsamgeo-ri, where the turnoff to the temple is off to the left. Golgul-sa is a 20-minute walk down the road.

Seokguram BUDDHIST SITE
(석굴암, Stone Grotto Temple; Map p160; adult/child/youth ₩5000/3500/3000; ⏲6.30am-6pm Apr-Oct, 7am-5.30pm Nov-Mar) In the mountains above Bulguk-sa is this world-famous Unesco-listed Buddhist grotto, a magical place when rain and mists envelop the mountaintops and chipmunks dance in the thick woods. Sitting within its rotunda is a statue of Buddha surrounded by over three dozen guardians and lesser deities, including an 11-faced Gwan-eum (관음). The set up is a little underwhelming, though: Buddha sits behind glass that reflects light and you can actually see very little as you must stand at a distance.

The carving of Gwan-eum (the Goddess of Mercy) is not visible, hidden behind the main statue, so you have to make do with a poor-quality photograph. Photography is not allowed.

Buddha's position gazing over the East Sea (visible in clear weather) has long made him regarded as a protector of his country. Seokguram was quite a feat of engineering when it was constructed in the mid-8th century. Huge blocks of granite were quarried far to the north at a time when the only access to the Seokguram site (740m above sea level) was a narrow mountain path.

But it is the setting that is most rewarding, after you are quickly filed past the image of Buddha, so revel in the mountain scenery. The 2.2km walk down the steps to Bulguk-sa is enjoyable and not strenuous, or you can continue uphill to the peak of Toham-san, 1.4km distant. Bus 12 runs hourly between the car parks for Bulguk-sa and Seokguram (₩1500, 20 minutes). From the Seokguram car park, it is a 400m walk along a shaded gravel track to the grotto.

Lake Bomun Resort LAKE

(보문 단지; Map p163) Bomun is a tourist district around an artificial lake 5km east of central Gyeongju. Tradition-seekers will find the tandem bikes, paddle boats, conference centres and such less appealing, but it is home to Gyeongju's most luxurious lodgings. The lake and extensive parklands are lovely for strolling or cycling, though the area doesn't have the character of the town centre.

Traditional dancing and musical performances are held on a regular basis from April to October at Bomun Outdoor Performance Theatre, below the information centre by the lake.

Girim-sa BUDDHIST TEMPLE

(기림사; Map p160; ₩4000; ⏲8am-8pm) Girim-sa is one of the largest complexes in the vicinity of the Silla capital, about 3.5km down the road from Golgul-sa. Its size compares with that of Bulguk-sa, but the complex lacks a 'wow' factor, which might explain why it receives comparably fewer visitors.

From Golgul-sa, there is no public transport to Girim-sa. If you're without personal transport, the choices are walking 3.5km down the road alongside rice paddies, or asking for a lift.

Lake Bomun

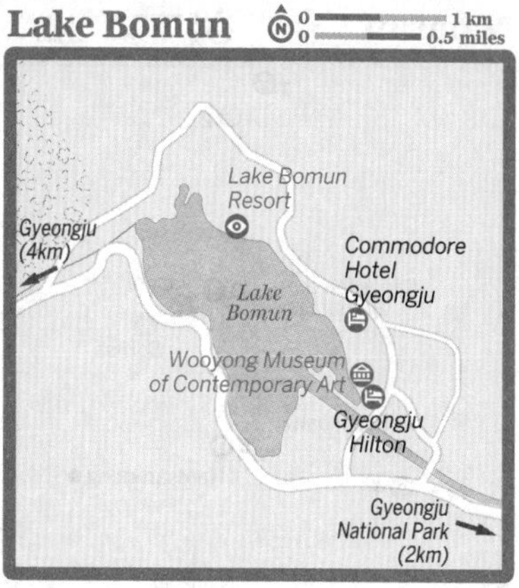

Wooyong Museum of Contemporary Art MUSEUM

(우양미술관; Map p163; ☎054 745 7075; www.wooyangmuseum.org; adult/child ₩5000/3000; ⏲10am-6pm; P) This modern art museum has three exhibition spaces with seasonal exhibitions plus a permanent collection containing paintings, sculpture and mixed media. It's a sister to Artsonje Center Seoul, and a worthwhile stop if you're in the area. Find it behind the **Hilton** (경주 힐튼호텔; Map p163; ☎054 745 7788; www.hilton.com; 484-7, Bomun-ro; r from ₩121,500; ❄📶🏊).

Southern Gyeongju (Nam-san)

Samneung TOMB

(삼릉; Map p164) The reason to come to this pine grove is to start a hike up Nam-san. On your way up, you may pass the *tumuli* of three Silla kings. Another tomb, located away from the others, is said to contain King Gyeongae, who was killed when robbers raided Poseokjeongji during an elaborate banquet, setting the stage for the dynasty's collapse.

Sangsabawi LANDMARK

(상사바위; Map p164) Sangsabawi resembles a mere rock but is permeated with a morbid legend telling of an older man who, suffering from unrequited love for a village girl, hanged himself and transformed into the rock. This gave Sangsabawi its name, loosely translating as Lovesick Rock.

Ongnyong-am BUDDHIST SITE

(옥룡암; Map p164) In the upper corner of this hermitage are boulders covered with Korea's greatest collection of relief carvings.

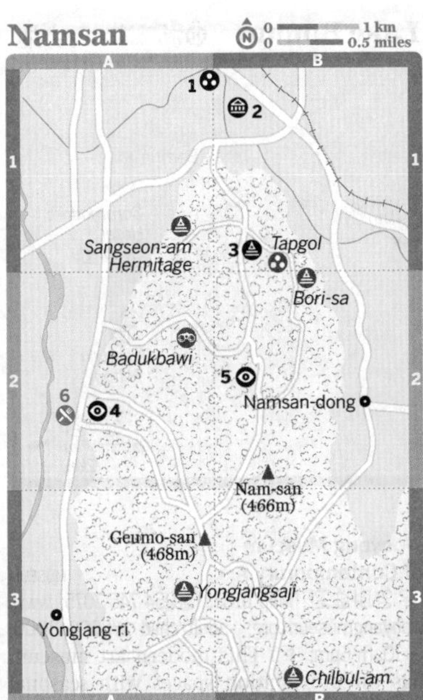

Namsan

Sights

1 Banwol-seong A1
2 Gyeongju National Museum B1
3 Ongnyong-am B1
4 Samneung A2
5 Sangsabawi B2

Eating

6 Sigol Yeohaeng A2

The 24 different representations of Buddha were carved into rock with the belief that stone would preserve them for eternity.

Western Gyeongju

Bokdu-am Hermitage BUDDHIST SITE

(Map p160) Close to the summit of the thickly forested Obong-san (640m), Bokdu-am features a huge rock face out of which 19 niches have been carved. The three central niches hold a figure of the historical Buddha flanked by two bodhisattva (Munsu and Bohyeon); the remainder house the 16 *nahan* (arhat) monks who have attained Nirvana. Just below the hermitage is a stunning viewpoint from the top of a couple of massive boulders. It's a great place for a picnic lunch.

The carvings are recent and although there's an unoccupied house up here, the actual hermitage was burned down in 1988 after an electrical fault started a blaze. There is also a statue of Gwanseeum, the Goddess of Mercy (whose name means the one who 'listens to the cries of the world'), just beyond the rock face.

The trail is easy to follow, but bring water as there are no springs along the way. The walk up will take around an hour. From the bus stop in Songseon-ri (송선리), follow the creek up along the narrow road about 500m to a small temple, Seongam-sa. The trail starts just to the left of this temple and is well marked in Korean.

A further 3.8km up the road from the bus stop for Bokduam and Jusaam, remote **Sinseon-sa** (신선사; Map p160) near the top of Danseok-san (827m), is believed to be one of the oldest cave temples in Korea. About 50m to the right as you face the temple are some ancient rock carvings in a small grotto. The temple was used as a base by General Kim Yu-shin in the 7th century and has seen renovation work since then. It's about a two-hour circuit walk from the bus stop. There's a little village along the way, about 2.5km from the bus stop.

Bus 300 (₩1800, every 25 minutes) travels to Obong-san and stops near Jusaam. If you're looking for a more direct route to Sinseon-sa, take bus 350 (₩1800, every one to two hours) and get off at Ujung-gol (우중골). From the intercity bus terminal, catch either bus at the stop near Paris Baguette on Daejung-no.

Tomb of General Kim Yusin TOMB

(Map p160) This royal tomb has 12 statues carved with the likeness of the signs of the Chinese zodiac watching over the resting place.

Sleeping

Hanjin Hostel HOSTEL $

(한진장여관; Map p159; ☎054 771 4097; www.gyeongjuhostel.com; dm/s/tw ₩15,000/25,000/40,000; 📶) Going since 1977, this hostel is all about its friendly English-speaking and easy-going owner Clint Kwon, a mine of local info who shares excellent local advice and history (his father accommodated probably the first Lonely Planet writer in Korea). Rooms are simple and dated, but prices are low and pervasive sensations of dependable, old-school travelling culture permeate the place.

The courtyard and roof deck are gathering spots for travellers. Laundry is ₩6000 per load. It's on the road with McDonald's at its southern end.

Taeyang-Jang Motel MOTEL $
(태양장 여관; Map p159; ☎054 773 6889; r/ste ₩30,000/40,000; ❄@) This decent love motel has a friendly enough owner. Rooms are spacious, with good bathrooms and all modern conveniences including huge widescreen TVs and in-room PCs.

Gyeongju Guest House HOSTEL $$
(경주 게스트 하우스; Map p159; ☎054 745 7100; www.gjguesthouse.com; dm/tw/tr incl breakfast ₩18,000/50,000/65,000; ⊖❄@☜) Just a short distance from the train station, this solid budget option has a spacious and modern communal area, a sparkling kitchen and very clean sleeping areas. Guests also get a free laundry and discounted bicycle rental (₩5000 per day). Staff speak basic English.

Baramgot Guesthouse GUESTHOUSE $$
(바람곳게스트하우스; Map p159; ☎054 771 2589; www.baramgot.kr; 137 Wonhyo-ro; dm/d incl breakfast ₩18,000/50,000; ⊖❄@☜) You'll love returning to serene Baramgot at the end of a day of walking. Drop a cushion onto the wooden floor of the charming sitting area and meet other travellers or watch a projected movie. Then finally get true rest on comfortable beds. Bathrooms are reassuringly clean, and shared ones sport ample showers. Basic English spoken.

Commodore Hotel Gyeongju HOTEL $$$
(코모도호텔 경주; Map p163; ☎054 745 7701; www.commodorehotel.co.kr/eng; r from ₩144,000, sauna ₩5400; ❄☜) Perhaps the best located of the lakeside hotels, with some of the most attractive grounds, the Commodore is less impressive on the inside, with rather dated decor. That said, there is nice woodwork in the rooms, Gyeongju green and terracotta-coloured motifs downstairs, and one of the city's favourite saunas. Rates increase 25% Friday and Saturday.

Eating

Jungang Night Market MARKET $
(중앙 야시장; Map p159; mains from ₩5000; ⏲6-11pm Sep-Oct & Feb-Apr, 7pm-midnight Jun-Aug, 6-11pm Fri & Sat Nov-Jan) This terrific night market is on the northeast corner of the Jungang Market, with a whole line of stalls selling all manner of food, from vegetarian pasta cooked up at a Filipino stall, to dishes from Pakistan and, of course, Korea. Take your own beers along from a supermarket and grab a seat at a table.

Sigol Yeohaeng KOREAN $
(시골 여행; Map p164; meals ₩5000-12,000; ⏲9am-9pm) Opposite the entrance to Samneung (p163), this 20-year-old restaurant specialises in *mukun kimchi* (묵은 김치), a spicy noodle-and-broth dish made with kimchi aged at least three years.

Daebak Jip KOREAN $
(대박집; Map p159; mains ₩2500-10,000; ⏲11am-2pm) A good place to eat late, this delicious local hang-out does excellent barbecue pork and beef dishes at low prices. The service is very friendly, even if there's no English menu or English spoken – the pictorial menu saves the day.

★ **Sukyeong Sikdang** KOREAN $$
(숙영 식당; Map p159; mains from ₩9000; ⏲11am-8.30pm) Since 1979, this cosy restaurant with a delightfully cluttered and rustic interior has been serving tasty *pajeon* (파전, scallion pancake; ₩10,000) made from organic ingredients and homemade, ice-cold and slushy *dongdongju* (동동주, rice wine), which goes for ₩6000 for almost a litre or ₩10,000 for almost two. It's near the east wall of Tumuli-gongwon and has English-, Korean- and Chinese-speaking staff. The rice wine is not strong, so there's no need to go easy on it.

★ **Dosolmaeul** KOREAN $$
(도솔마을; Map p159; mains ₩15,000; ⏲11.30am-9pm Tue-Sun) This very atmospheric place is a traditional family-run courtyard restaurant beside Tumuli-gongwon, with a delicious and broad menu featuring dishes such as steamed octopus with hot sauce, or seafood, meatball and vegetable stew. The best deal, however, is the ₩18,000 traditional Korean set dinner for two, a delicious feast of around 20 small dishes.

★ **Nahbi** CAFE $$
(나비; Map p160; 69 Dongmun-ro; ⏲9am-7pm Tue-Sat, to 3pm Sun) Run by the ever-so-friendly Hae Yong – who can put together a decent BLT sandwich for you to munch on as you peruse the book-stuffed walls. Looking for that elusive first edition? It could be here. Hae Yong speaks excellent English and organises meals out on Tuesday evenings for foreigners and Koreans to mix. The name Nahbi means Butterfly. It's not too far north

of the East Gate (Dongmun), which was being restored at the time of writing and that lends its name to the road.

Kisoya JAPANESE $$
(기소야; Map p159; ☎054 746 6020; meals ₩10,000-30,000; ⏰10am-3pm & 5-10pm) Friendly and inviting Kisoya serves up a mouth-watering array of Japanese dishes with a Korean slant. Mains are generous set meals of the classics from bento boxes to sashimi and noodle soups. Don't miss the superb chicken-fillet bento box.

Kuro Ssambap KOREAN $$
(구로쌈밥; Map p159; per person ₩12,000; ⏰11am-9pm) An eclectic collection of birds, rocks, figurines, pottery and other folk arts make this a unique place to dine on this strip of otherwise rather similar *ssambap* (lettuce wrap) restaurants just to the north of Wolseong-gongwon. Orders include 28 refillable side dishes.

Gampo Hogung Raw Fish Center SEAFOOD $$$
(감포 호궁 회센타; Map p160; crab meals from ₩30,000; ⏰7am-midnight) King crab and raw fish are the specialities of this bustling restaurant near Gampo harbour. Crab dinners start with a small selection of sides and finish with a pot of spicy fish soup. It's customary to negotiate the price of a crab meal before entering, although English isn't spoken, so bring a Korean friend or prepare for some interesting bargaining.

Information

There are several handy tourist information kiosks and offices, including at the **Express Bus Terminal** (Map p159; ☎054 772 9289), **Train Station** (Map p159; ☎054 772 3843; ⏰9am-6pm) and Bulguk-Sa (p162). All have English-speaking staff and comprehensive English-language maps.

Kookmin Bank (Map p159; ⏰9am-4pm Mon-Fri)

Nongyyup Bank (Map p159; ⏰9am-4pm Mon-Fri)

Post Office (Map p159; ⏰9am-4pm Mon-Fri)

SC First Bank (Map p159; ⏰9am-4pm Mon-Fri)

Woori Bank (Map p159; ⏰9am-4pm Mon-Fri)

Getting There & Away

BUS

Buses link Gyeongju's express bus terminal with Busan's Gimhae airport (₩9000, 3½ hours, 18 daily).

Gyeongju's **express bus terminal** (Map p159; ☎054 741 4000) and **intercity bus terminal** (시외버스터미널; Map p159; ☎054 743 5599) are adjacent to one other.

Express Bus Terminal

DESTINATION	PRICE (₩)	DURATION (HR)	FREQUENCY
Busan	4800	1	hourly
Daegu	4900	1	every 40min
Gimhae Airport	9000	3½	18 daily
Seoul	19,100	4½	hourly

Intercity Bus Terminal

DESTINATION	PRICE (₩)	DURATION (HR)	FREQUENCY
Busan	4800	1	every 15min
Daegu	4900	1	every 40min
Pohang	3400	1	every 15min
Ulsan	4900	1	4 daily

TRAIN

Gyeongju has a direct KTX service with regular services from to Seoul (₩49,300, two hours) and Busan (₩11,000, 30 minutes), but it serves the rather out-of-town Singyeongju station (to the southwest of Gyeongju), rather than the central old Gyeongju station. Arriving at Singyeongju station, take bus 50, 60, 61, 70, 201 or 700 to the city centre (15 minutes).

From the old **Gyeongju train station** (Map p159; ☎054 743 4114) there are services to Pohang (₩2600, 30 minutes, regular) and Dongdaegu (₩5000, 1¼ hours, hourly), but you'll need to change trains in Dongdaegu or Pohang to reach Seoul. Also change at Dongdaegu to reach Busan.

Getting Around

BICYCLE

Hiring a bicycle is a great way to reach the sights. There are some bike trails around Namsan (but it's rather hilly) and Lake Bomun. There are bicycle-rental shops everywhere, including several scattered around the town centre and one opposite the Gyeongju National Museum (p158). Rates are approximately ₩3000 to ₩4000 per hour or ₩12,000 to ₩15,000 per day. Check with your accomodation for bike deals.

BUS

Many local buses (₩1500) terminate just outside the intercity bus terminal. For shorter routes (eg to Bulguk-sa), buses can be picked up along Sosong-no and Daejeong-no.

Buses 10 (clockwise) and 11 (anticlockwise) run a circuit of most of the major sights including Bulguk-sa, Nam-san and Lake Bomun, as well as the bus terminals and Gyeongju train station (every 15 minutes). You can grab the bus for Bulguk-sa from the **bus stop** (Map p159) south of the express bus terminal. Bus 150 departs from the train station to the eastern sights, via the Lake Bomun Expo arena (every 30 minutes). Bus 100 makes a similar initial route.

Buses make announcements in English for major attractions, but can be standing-room only on busy weekends.

TAXI

Taxis are often available for day hire outside train and bus stations (₩150,000/200,000, five/seven hours). One-way between Lake Bomun and the city centre is ₩10,000.

Around Gyeongju

Yangdong Folk Village

054

Reaching Joseon-era Yangdong Folk Village (경주 양동마을) is not particularly straightforward, but you will be rewarded with an intimate look at traditional architecture in an authentic setting.

Designated as a cultural preservation area, the entire photogenic village (replete with stone walls, straw-thatched roofs and green gardens) is a photographer's dream. Set aside a half-day to admire the 180 or so houses typical of the *yangban* class – a largely hereditary class based on scholarship and official position. Most of the homes here are still lived in, so you need to observe the usual courtesies when looking around; some of the larger mansions stand empty and are open to the public. There are no entry fees to any of the buildings. Descriptive plaques with English explanations can be found outside some of the more important structures.

The tea shop **Uhyangdaok** (우향다옥; 054 762 8096; 143 Yangdong-ri; dishes ₩5000-17,000; noon-10pm), in a rustic building, offers simple treats like green tea, wine and light meals. No English is spoken, but the owner goes to much effort to ease communication. If you want to stay the night, there are two small *ondol* rooms (₩35,000) for rent where early breakfast is possible, but you need to book it in, or there are a few *hanok*-style places to stay the night within the village.

Getting There & Away

From Gyeongju, buses 200, 201, 202, 203 and 206 (₩1600, 50 minutes, regular) will get you to within 1.5km of Yangdong; alight at the Yangdong Folk Village Bus stop. From the bus stop, follow the train line and then go under it. There's only one road into the village; it's about a 30-minute walk.

Oksan

054 / POP 200

The small and very plain village of Oksan-ri (옥산리) is home to the historic walled cluster of traditional houses called Dongnakdang and the famous Confucian academy of Oksan Seowon, both attractively situated next to a stream. There's also a further Confucian academy here and a notable and unusual pagoda, as well as hiking opportunities, making the place an absorbing day trip from Gyeongju. The name Oksan means 'Jade Mountain'.

Sights

Dongnakdang HISTORIC SITE

(독락당; 24hr) FREE A 10-minute walk beyond Oksan Seowon up the valley road will bring you to Dongnakdang, a beautiful collection of well-preserved buildings, constructed in 1515 and expanded in 1532 as the residence of Yi Eon-jeok after he left government service. The walled compound is partly occupied by descendants of Master Yi himself and sits scenically next to a stream, though it was empty when we last visited. You can walk down the steps to the river, cross the stepping stones, and hike into the hills.

If you want to reach Dongnakdang first, take the 203 bus from Gyeongju to its final stop; then you can walk down the road to Oksan Seowon.

Oksan Seowon CONFUCIAN SITE

(옥산 서원) Established in 1572 in honour of Yi Eon-jeok (1491–1553), Oksan Seowon was one of the most important *seowon*, or Confucian academies. Enlarged in 1772, it was one of few to escape destruction in the 1860s. An early-20th-century fire destroyed some of the buildings, however; today only 14 structures remain, so it's not large and can be quickly explored. With its location at the base of the hills and next to a gushing river, the academy has perfect *pungsu* (feng shui).

To the left of the main entrance (as you face it) is Sesimdae (세심대), a series of flat rocks next to the waterfalls that surge past

the academy. The name literally means 'Terrace for cleansing the mind/heart' (signs in *hanja* saying 洗心臺 point to it); it is indeed a most entrancing and relaxing spot.

Thirteen-Storey Stone Pagoda PAGODA
(십삼층석탑) Built upon a square base and tapering in stages to its top, this very attractive and unique pagoda dates from the 9th century and is on the left side of the road between Dongnakdang and Jangsan Seowon. The pagoda is part of the now vanished temple of Jeonghye-sa (정혜사).

Jangsan Seowon CONFUCIAN SITE
(장산 서원) Closed when visited last, this rebuilt Confucian academy originally dates from the late 18th century. Look for the signs to the academy, indicated in *hanja*: 章山書院. If it's not open, you can at least peer over the surrounding wall.

Sleeping

Oksan Motel MOTEL $
(옥산 모텔; ☎054 762 9500; www.oksanmotel.com; r from ₩35,000; ❄📶) Not far from the Oksan Seowon, this place has modern *ondol* or bedrooms with a shower, and a patio in front of the property.

Drinking & Nightlife

Oksan Coffee Store CAFE
(옥산상회; ⌚8.30am-9pm) A small, family-run cafe right by the Oksan Seowon bus stop. It also doubles as a convenience store, so you can stock up on drinks and munchable goodies if you want to go hiking.

Getting There & Away

Bus 203 (₩1800, 70 minutes, 10 daily) to Angang-ri runs from Gangbyeon-no just east of Gyeongju's Intercity Bus Terminal (p166), reaching Oksan Seowon and Dongnakdang. For Dongnakdang, continue to the last stop; for Oksan Seowon, get off at the penultimate stop, which is also the main stop for the village.

Pohang

☎054 / POP 508,000

Pohang (포항) is mainly known for being home to the world's second-largest steel plant, Posco (Pohang Iron and Steel Company), which mires views from its beach. Most people pass through here on the way to the island of Ulleungdo or as a base to visit Bogyeong-sa, but don't linger.

Sights

Bogyeong-sa BUDDHIST TEMPLE
(보경사; ₩3500; ⌚7am-7pm) You'll need a full day to explore the offerings in and around this temple about 30km north of Pohang. Bogyeong-sa is a gateway to a beautiful valley boasting 12 waterfalls, gorges spanned by bridges, hermitages, stupas and the temple itself. There are splendid hikes including up Naeyeon-san (930m), from where the waterfalls gush down. The 20km return trip to the summit – Hyangno-bong – from Bogyeong-sa takes about six hours (take lots of water).

The well-maintained trail to the gorge and waterfalls branches off from the tourist village. It's about 1.5km to the first waterfall, 5m-high Ssangsaeng Pokpo. The sixth waterfall, Gwaneum Pokpo, is an impressive 72m and has two columns of water with a cave behind it. The seventh waterfall, about 30m high, is called Yeonsan Pokpo. Further up the trail, the going gets difficult; the ascent of Hyangno-bong should only be attempted if the day is young.

The temple is 15 minutes' walk from where the buses from Pohang terminate, and there's a tourist village with souvenir shops, restaurants, *minbak* and *yeogwan*.

Bus 500 (₩1600, 45 minutes, every 30 to 90 minutes) runs between Pohang's intercity bus terminal and the temple, though some buses require a transfer at Cheongha. The easiest route is to catch one of three or four buses that travel directly to the temple; check with the tourist office to find out the latest timings. Otherwise, take bus 500 to Cheongha, get off at the tiny terminal and wait for a connecting bus (₩1300, 15 minutes, every 10 to 90 minutes). A taxi from Cheongha to the temple costs ₩15,000.

Sleeping & Eating

Ibeujang Motel MOTEL $
(이브장 모텔; ☎054 283 2253; d from ₩35,000; ❄) Small but clean rooms with bright furnishings and huge old-school TVs, the red lamps being the only hint that this is a love motel. It's very conveniently located for the intercity bus terminal.

Design Motel A2 MOTEL $$
(디자인 모텔 A2; ☎054 249 5533; weekday r from ₩45,000, weekend r ₩50,000-60,000; ❄📶) Right on the beachfront, this hotel with a design sensibility and boutique pretensions

offers slightly more imaginative accommodation than its neighbours, with free coffee and popcorn, bathtubs in the middle of the rooms and 3D TVs. Each room is decorated differently (choose carefully from the room menu) and those with sea frontage really make the most of their views.

Yuk Hae Gong SEAFOOD **$$$**
(육해공; dishes from ₩25,000; ⏰noon-5am) Take a seat in the outdoor patio overlooking the beach and enjoy *jogae gu-e* (조개 구이, barbecued shellfish). Shells filled with seafood, cheese and onion look, smell and taste wonderful. It's often brimming with a boisterous late-night crowd – look for the restaurant with a gravel patio floor. If full, many nearby shops have a similar menu.

ℹ Information

There's little English spoken at the **tourist information booth** (☎054 245 6761; ⏰9am-6pm Mon-Sat Jul & Aug, to 5pm Sep-Jun) outside the intercity bus terminal, nor at Pohang station, but there are plenty of English-language brochures and maps. A booth outside the ferry terminal is not regularly staffed.

Korea Exchange Bank (⏰9am-4pm Mon-Fri)
SC First Bank (⏰9am-4pm Mon-Fri)

ℹ Getting There & Away

AIR

From Pohang Airport (포항공항) Korean Air has daily flights to Gimpo International Airport in Seoul; Air Pohang flies to Jeju.

BOAT

Ferry services (standard/1st class ₩64,500/70,700, 3¼ hours, one to two per day) run to Ulleungdo from the ferry terminal.

BUS

Buses depart from Pohang's **intercity bus terminal** (☎054 272 3194) and the express bus terminal (a five-minute taxi ride from the intercity bus terminal).

Intercity Bus Terminal Departures

DESTINATION	PRICE (₩)	DURATION (HR)	FREQUENCY
Andong	15,500	2	every 1-2hr
Busan	8100	1½	every 10min
Daegu	6700	2	every 10min
Gyeongju	3400	1	every 15min
Seoul	23,300	4½	every 30min

Express Bus Terminal Departures

DESTINATION	PRICE (₩)	DURATION (HR)	FREQUENCY
Daejeon	20,900	3¼	hourly
Gwangju	26,000	4	5 daily
Masan	11,400	2¼	5 daily
Seoul	19,500	4½	every 40min

TRAIN

There are regular speedy KTX trains from **Pohang station** (☎054 275 2394; 137-1 Lin-ri, Heunghae-eup) to Seoul (₩53,600, 2½ hours, 12 daily). Trains also run to Gyeongju (₩2600, 30 minutes, every one to two hours).

ℹ Getting Around

Local buses cost regular/deluxe ₩1000/1500. Bus 200 runs between the airport and the intercity bus terminal. Bus 105 and 200 run between the intercity bus terminal and the Ulleungdo ferry terminal south of Bukbu Beach. A taxi between Pohang station and Bukbu Beach takes 20 minutes and costs ₩6000.

Ulleungdo

☎054 / POP 10,235

The island of Ulleungdo (울릉도), the top of an extinct volcano that rises majestically from the sea floor into incredibly steep cliffs, offers some of the most spectacular scenery in Korea; think mist-shrouded volcanic cliffs, traditional harbour towns and a breathtaking jagged coastline.

In the rainy season the green hues are even more vivid, saturating the hills like an overtoned colour photograph. In autumn the hills are a patchwork of reds, greens and yellows from the turning leaves.

Located 135km east of the Korean Peninsula, Ulleungdo today is mainly a fishing community that sees enough tourism to warrant a sprinkling of hotels and restaurants.

Sights

Dodong-ri PORT
(도동리; Map p172) Dodong-ri is the island's main tourist hub, meaning the greatest selection of lodging and dining options. Behind the ferry terminal, a spiral staircase leads to a seaside walking trail offering spectacular views of the sea crashing into jagged rocks. About 1.5km down the path is a lighthouse and a trail leading to Jeodong-ri (it's a two-hour return trip). The one-hour return

Ulleungdo

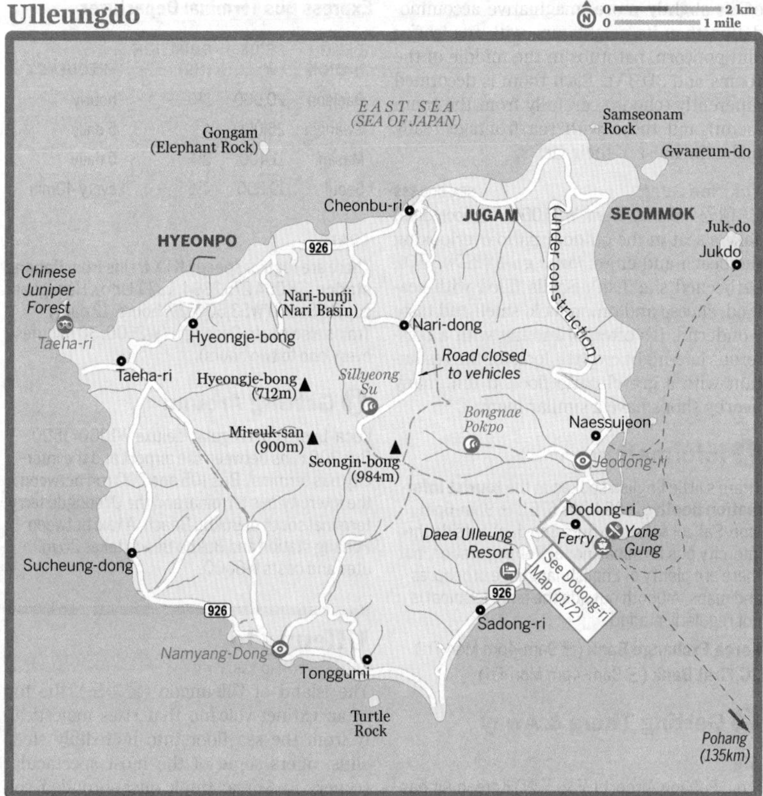

walk to the lighthouse is an incredible highlight, but you'll need a flexible schedule as the path closes with strong ocean tides.

Dodong-ri is the island's administrative centre and largest town. Like a pirate outpost, its harbour is almost hidden away in a narrow valley between two forested mountains, making it visible only when approached directly.

Mineral Spring Park PARK

(약수 공원; Map p172) The highlight of this park, a 350m climb above Dodong-ri, is the **cable car** (독도전망대 케이블카; Map p172; return ₩8500; ⏰5.30am-8pm) across a steep valley to Manghyang-bong (316m). The ride up affords stunning views of the sea and a bird's-eye view of Dodong-ri. Visit early or late in the day to avoid crowds, and avoid the weekends entirely, if possible. The park's namesake *yaksu gwangjang* (mineral-water spring) is near the top. The water has a distinctive flavour (think diet-citrus-soft drink-meets-quartz) and some claim drinking it has all sorts of medicinal benefits.

Sunset Point Pavilion VIEWPOINT

(Ilmoljeon Mang-dae; Map p172) Sunset Point Pavilion is a steep 15-minute walk above Dodong-ri, commanding great views of the ocean and the sunset. To get there, follow the western creek out of town and cross the bridge after the school. A small overgrown trail continues up to the pavilion.

Daewon-sa TEMPLE

(Map p172) This small temple might be simple, but being walking distance from Dodong-ri makes it a good resting spot for a return stroll.

Taeha-ri VIEWPOINT

(태하리; Map p170; ₩5000; ⏰8am-5pm) There is a terrific view of the northern coastline from Hyangmok Lighthouse (향목 등대) in the northwest corner of the island, about

20km from Dodong-ri. To get there you take a monorail on a five-minute, 304m ride up a sharp cliff (39° angle). You will be dropped off at the base of a 500m trail leading up to the lighthouse. Buses to Taeha-ri leave the Dodong-ri terminal (₩1700, 40 minutes, every 40 minutes).

Jeodong-ri PORT

(저동리; Map p170) Jeodong-ri is a fishing village with picturesque sea walls, fishing nets and seagulls. The boats with the lamps strung around like oversize holiday lights are for catching squid.

Bongnae Pokpo WATERFALL

(봉래폭포; Map p170; ₩1400; ⊙6am-7pm Apr-Oct, 8am-5pm Nov-Mar) A steep 1.5km walk from Jeodong-ri is Bongnae Pokpo. The source of the island's drinking water, the waterfall is quite spectacular during summer.

On the return trip, cool down in Cheonyeon Natural Air Conditioner (천연에어콘 풍혈), a cave that maintains a year-round temperature of 4°C.

Buses serve the car park from Dodong-ri via Jeodong-ri (₩1700, 15 minutes, every 40 minutes).

Namyang-Dong VILLAGE

(남양동; Map p170) The coastal road from Dodong-ri to Taeha-ri leads through Namyang, a tiny seaside community with spectacular cliffs covered with Chinese juniper and odd rock formations.

Activities

Boat Trips

Jukdo Sightseeing Boats BOATING

(Map p172; ₩18,000; ⊙10am & 3pm) Sightseeing boats run to Jukdo, a nature reserve 4km from Ulleungdo. Visitors are welcome to take a picnic to eat on the island. The trip takes about 1½ hours including walk or picnic time. Most hotels and hostels can help you book these trips, which depart from the **ferry terminal** (Map p172) at Dodong-ri.

Round-Island Tour BOATING

(Map p172; ₩25,000) A round-island tour is a great way to admire Ulleungdo's dramatic landscape. Tours depart from Dodong-ri ferry terminal at 9am and 3pm (six daily in July and August), and last around two hours.

Hiking

Seongin-bong HIKING

(Map p170) Various pathways lead to the summit of Seongin-bong (984m), but the two main routes run from Dodong-ri (about five hours return) or Nari-bunji (four to five hours return).

From Dodong-ri, take the main road towards Daewon-sa (p170). Just before you reach the temple, there is a fork in the trail and a sign (in Korean) pointing the way to Seongin-bong (a steep 4.1km).

From Nari-bunji, enter the thick forest, adhering to the right-hand path, and you'll arrive at fields of chrysanthemum. Further on you'll pass a traditional home. Finally, at the entrance to the virgin forest area and picnic ground, the steep ascent of Seongin-bong (one hour) takes you through a forest of Korean beech, hemlock and lime.

Just below the peak, as you descend to Dodong-ri, is a trail off to the right, down to Namyang-dong (1½ hours).

Sillyeong Su HIKING

(신령수; Map p170) If you're not up for a major hike, try the 5km-return trip from the Nari basin bus stop to Sillyeong Su (신령수), a mountain spring. The walk cuts through a thick forest and is an easy one-hour stroll.

Sleeping

Ulleungdo has lots of choices for those on a budget, but is very poorly prepared for those wanting more comfort or luxury. Room rates rise steeply in peak season (from ₩50,000 to ₩100,000 in July, August and holidays) – coinciding with a flood of boisterous Korean travellers on package tours – so book ahead. Most hotels are in or around Dodong-ri.

Khan Motel HOTEL $$

(칸모텔; Map p172; ☎054 791 8500; d from ₩80,000; ❄📶) One of the best options on the island is this classy if rather minimalist place with *ondol* and western-style rooms. The rooms are on the small side, though the large TVs and computers are pluses. The owner is a great resource for guests looking for hard-to-find ferry tickets during the busy travel season.

Pension Skyhill PENSION $$

(스카이힐 펜션; Map p172; ☎054 791 1040; www.skyhill.or.kr; d/ondol from ₩70,000/60,000; ❄📶) Near the top of town, this is a popular destination for groups of university students, so rooms and communal areas – such as a shared kitchen and rooftop barbecue facilities – look a little used. However, it's a convenient stroll from several restaurants and is one of the cheapest deals in town.

Dodong-ri

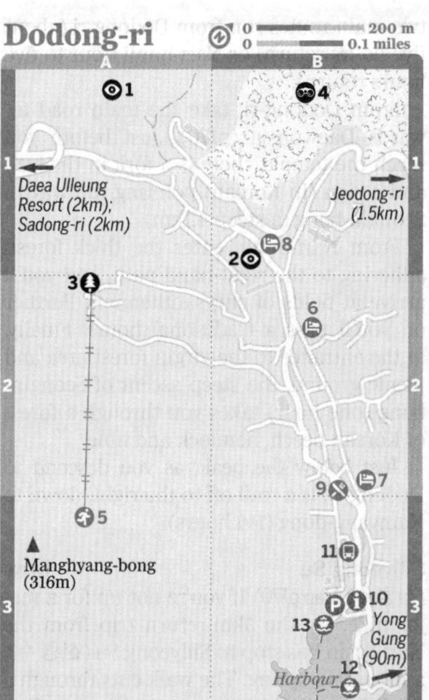

Dodong-ri

Sights
1 Daewon-sa A1
2 Dodong-ri B1
3 Mineral Spring Park A2
4 Sunset Point Pavilion B1

Activities, Courses & Tours
5 Dokdo Island Observatory Cable Car A3
Jukdo Sightseeing Boats .... (see 12)
Round-Island Tour .... (see 12)

Sleeping
6 Hotel Ulleungdo B2
7 Khan Motel B2
8 Pension Skyhill B1

Eating
9 99 Sikdang B2

Information
10 Information Booth B3

Transport
11 Bus Terminal B3
12 Ferry Terminal B3
13 Ferry to Jukdo B3

Hotel Ulleungdo HOTEL $$
(울릉도 호텔; Map p172; ☎054 791 6611; ondol/r ₩50,000/80,000; ❄☜) While it's the only hotel in Dodong-ri officially accredited for tourism, the Ulleungdo remains a large *yeogwan* with lots of simple but clean *ondol* rooms and a restaurant. It's a popular choice for groups who want to economise by sharing a room and don't mind the minimal furnishings.

Daea Ulleung Resort HOTEL $$$
(대아 리조트; Map p170; ☎054 791 8800; www.daearesort.com; r/ste from ₩170,000/240,000; ❄@☒) The island's most expensive property, this impressive resort has amazing mountaintop views of the sea, but the rooms are overpriced for what they are: unexciting and smallish, albeit perfectly comfortable and clean. From mid-July to August there's an outdoor swimming pool, and room prices spike. The hotel is in Sadong-ri, a ₩5000 taxi ride from Dodong-ri.

Eating

Outdoor seafood stalls are ubiquitous in Ulleungdo. There are a few scattered *mandu* (dumplings), *naengmyeon* (cold buckwheat noodles) and *gimbap* (seaweed rice rolls) shops, where you can eat for as little as ₩3000, and some casual restaurants by the harbour with outdoor seating. Most restaurants can be found in Dodong-ri.

99 Sikdang SEAFOOD $$
(99 식당; Map p172; ☎054 791 2287; dishes ₩7000-23,000; ⏲6.30am-10pm) One of the island's most famous restaurants – its owner will tell you proudly about its many appearances on Korea's food-obsessed TV channels – this is a place to delight in seafood barbecue and dishes such as *ojing-eo bulgogi* (오징어 불고기, squid grilled at the table with vegetables and hot-pepper sauce) and *ttaggaebibap* (따개비밥, shellfish with rice).

Yong Gung SEAFOOD $$
(용궁; Map p170; dishes from ₩16,000; ⏲8am-10pm) Sit near the seafront with a bottle of *soju* (local vodka) and a platter of raw fish, and watch the ocean crash onto the rocky shoreline at this ramshackle but quietly charming place. Mr Jeong (who speaks passable English) and his brother personally catch the seafood by diving for sea creatures each morning. It's about 500m from the ferry terminal on the seaside walking trail.

Information

The helpful **information booth** (Map p172; ☎054 790 6454; www.ulleung.go.kr/english; ⏰9am-6pm) by the Dodong-ri ferry terminal occasionally has English speakers on duty, but this can't be relied upon.

You can change money or withdraw cash from the 24-hour bank machine at Nonghyup Bank in Dodong-ri.

Getting There & Away

You can get to Ulleungdo by **ferry** (Map p170; ☎054 242 5111; www.daea.com) from Pohang (standard/1st class ₩64,500/70,700, 3¼ hours) to the island ferry terminal (Map p172). There is one morning departure daily year-round (weather permitting; strong winds or even morning rain can mean cancellations), and there are two daily departures during summer. If assigned seats are unavailable you can buy a floor-seating ticket in a common room for a slight discount. It's possible to take vehicles on the standard daily ferry, the *Sunflower* (₩5000 per vehicle), but not on the supplementary summer ferry, the *Ocean Flower*.

It is best to reserve (no deposit required) your tickets to and from the island, especially during summer – ask at the tourist office for someone to do this for you. Otherwise you can buy your ticket at the terminal first thing in the morning, but go early and expect to wait. Jukdo Sightseeing Boats (p171) leave from the harbour wharf (p171).

Getting Around

Buses run between the bus terminal (Map p172) at Dodong-ri and Jeodong-ri every 30 minutes (₩1200, 10 minutes). There are 18 buses daily from Dodong-ri via Namyang-dong (₩1700, 25 minutes) to Cheonbu-ri (₩1700, one hour), where you can transfer to Nari-bunji via a van (₩1200, 10 minutes, eight daily). Timetables are posted at the Dodong-ri bus terminal.

Andong

☎054 / POP 184,000

Famous for its mackerel, particularly strong *soju* (local vodka), wooden masks and myriad ancient sites, Andong (안동) is the capital of Gyeongsangbuk-do and makes a terrific base for exploring the numerous historical and cultural diversions in the surrounding area. The city itself has a very laid-back vibe and is strikingly friendly, with a good selection of places to eat and stay. The old *hanja* name for the city that you will see outside the train station and in other places is 安東 (Peaceful East), pronounced exactly the same in modern-day Mandarin Chinese (Āndōng).

Sights

Andong Folk Village VILLAGE

(안동민속촌) On a hillside east of town and on the far side of Weolyeonggyo Bridge (월영교), Andong Folk Village is a repository for traditional homes moved to prevent them from being submerged by the construction of Andong Dam in 1976. Relocated and partially reconstructed traditional-style buildings range from the thatched farmhouses of peasant to elaborate mansions of government officials with multiple courtyards. The village looks so authentic that the TV network KBS has used it as a set for historical dramas on multiple occasions.

The village is about 4km east of Andong, close to the dam wall on the opposite side of the river from the main road. Take buses 3, 3-1 or 3-2 (₩1200) from next to the tourist office and hop off at *minsokchon* (folk village). A taxi costs about ₩6000. Otherwise it is around a 40-minute walk, during which you can stop by the Seven-Storey Brick Pagoda, cross the Weolyeonggyo Bridge and return by the wooden walkway on the far side of the Nakdong River.

Andong Folklore Museum MUSEUM

(안동 민속박물관; ☎054 821 0649; ₩1200; ⏰9am-6pm Mar-Oct, to 5pm Nov-Feb) Near the Andong Folk Village, this museum offers clear displays of Korea's folk traditions from birth through to death.

Seven-Storey Brick Pagoda BUDDHIST PAGODA

(칠층전탑) Just east of town along the railway line, you will come to this beauty – the oldest and largest brick pagoda in Korea. At almost 17m in height, the pagoda stands at the former site of the Beopheung-Sa (법흥사), and is indeed the only surviving part of the temple. Note the carvings on the pagoda base and that part of the finial at the top is missing. The pagoda dates originally from the 8th century. Today the pagoda stands between the railway line and a large traditional Korean house, dating from 1704.

Jebiwon Seokbul BUDDHIST SHRINE

(제비원석불) The body and robes of this Buddha are carved on a boulder over 12m high – on top of which are the head and hair, carved out of two separate pieces of rock. It's an impressive stark sight to behold emerging from the tall greenery. Above the Buddha is an ancient stupa, while on the approach to the Buddha – an object of great veneration to worshippers – is a temple hall. Note the

Andong

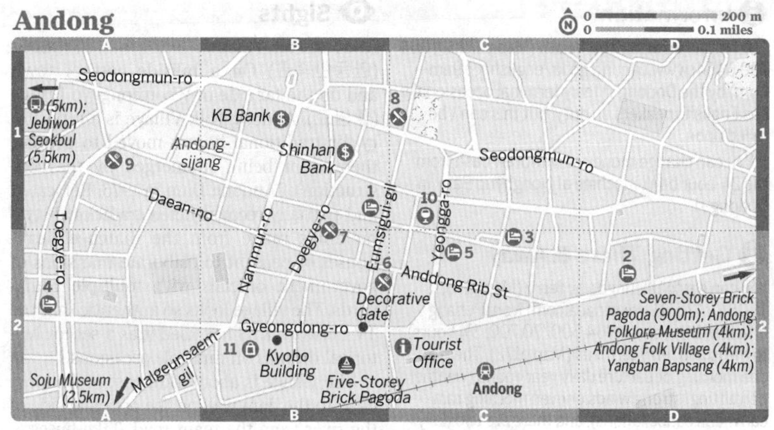

galaxy of small gold Buddhas on the walls in front of the Buddha.

Catch bus 54 (₩1200, every 30 minutes) from opposite the Kyobo building and ask the driver to drop you off at Jebiwon, otherwise known as Ichon-dong. The bus-stop back to Andong is on the far side of the road.

Dosan Seowon CONFUCIAN SHRINE
(도산서원; 154 Dosanseowon-gil, Dosan; ₩1500) This sublime and hoary Confucian academy has a tranquil setting enveloped by mountains and perched over the river. The quiet, introspective halls are fronted by a huge willow tree; the museum within contains explanations of woodblock printing and all manner of Confucian texts and intricate philosophical schemata. Walk along the river to the terrace at the end for lovely views over the water. Reach it via bus 67 from Andong (₩1300), which continues to Cheongnyangsan Provincial Park (p177).

Soju Museum MUSEUM
(소주 박물관; www.andongsoju.net; 9am-5pm Mon-Sat) FREE The heady 45% *soju* (local vodka) of Andong may not be to your taste, but its significance has been preserved with its designation as an intangible cultural property. Located on the grounds of the Andong Soju Brewery, the museum houses a couple of displays that detail the distilling process, the drinking ceremony and a history of *soju* labels. A (thimble-sized) taste of the liquor is given at the end of your visit.

The museum is in the south of Andong, across the Nakdong-gang, and is best reached by taxi (₩5000). Catch bus 80 (₩1200, 10 minutes) from opposite the Kyobo building.

Activities

Wooden Walkway HIKING
This long walkway reaches back to the city of Andong on the far side of the river from the Andong Folk Village (p173), from where you can cross the bridge back to town. It's a beautiful walk, pinched between the wooded hillsides and the river.

Festivals & Events

Andong Mask Dance Festival DANCE
(054 841 6397; www.maskdance.com; late Sep-early Oct) This festival, which brings together a colourful array of national and international mask dance troupes, is a great

reason to visit Andong. It is usually held in tandem with the folk festival, showcasing performances of traditional music and dance. Check with the tourist office (p176) for details.

Andong Folk Festival DANCE

(⏲late Sep-early Oct) Andong's folk festival showcases performances of traditional music and dance. Check with the tourist office (p176) for details.

Sleeping

Happy Guesthouse HOSTEL $

(해피 게스트하우스; ☎010 8903 1638; s/d incl breakfast ₩25,000/40,000; ❄@) Things are happy a short walk from the action, though this place looks grim from the outside. Incense infuses the traditional downstairs dining room, while upstairs there are spotless new rooms with private bathrooms and mats for sleeping rolled directly onto the floor. There are PCs, Korean breakfast options (pumpkin rice porridge) and a helpful English-speaking owner.

Gotaya Guesthouse GUESTHOUSE $

(고타야 게스트하우스; 古陀耶旅館; ☎010 4367 0226; 205-17 Dongbu-dong; dm incl breakfast ₩17-30,000, s/tw ₩50,000/60,000; ⊖❄@) Named after the old name for Andong, this pleasant enough place is a decent choice. There's free laundry on the ramshackle but sunny roof terrace, English-speaking staff, warm, clean dorms and small spaces that lend themselves to meeting travellers, as well as a generally inviting demeanour.

Andong Hotel HOTEL $

(안동 호텔; ☎054 858 1166; www.andonghotel.net; s/d/ste from ₩50,000/60,000/80,000; ❄@) One of the better options among in town, the Andong Hotel is right in the centre of things. Despite horribly kitschy decor, the hotel has spacious rooms, good bathrooms, desktop PCs in each room and helpful staff. Rates rise ₩10,000 Friday and Saturday.

Andong Park Hotel HOTEL $$

(안동파크호텔; ☎054 853 1501; www.andongparkhotel.com; d/tw/VIP ₩50,000/60,000/70,000; ❄@) Andong's establishment choice boasts staff with negligible English, but reasonable prices; expect rather gurgly pipes and old sealant around the baths. Suites are spacious, with old-fashioned bathtubs and flat-screen TVs. Standard rooms are smaller, but comfortable enough. Wi-fi is good. Few guests opt for the breakfast (₩12,000).

Sharp Motel MOTEL $$

(샵 모텔; ☎054 854 0081; www.sharphotel.com; s/d ₩40,000/50,000; ❄@) Centrally located and offering good-standard, relatively tasteful rooms, all with huge flat-screen TVs, in-room PCs and fridges. The Sharp is a love motel, but not obviously so.

Eating

You could eat each meal in Andong on Eumsigui-gil (aka Food St), the restaurant row in the town centre, marked by the decorative gate and lit-up archways, or the next door Andong Rib St, where there's a proliferation of tasty rib joints.

Andong-Gwan KOREAN $

(안동관; Eumsigui-gil; mains from ₩8000; ⏲11am-9pm) This lovely, traditional corner restaurant is decorated with *hanja* calligraphy, with private dining rooms or an open section where you can sit on the floor and feast on boiled dumplings (만두), hot pot bulgogi, bibimbap and other tasty dishes, washed down with glasses of *soju* (소주, local vodka) or *makgeolli* (막걸리, rice wine). Look out for the restaurant with the *hanja* outside that says 安東館.

Momo KOREAN $

(모모; ☎054 853 3346; 183 Seodongmun-ro; mains from ₩8000; ⏲10am-10pm;) The spruce, efficient and neat-looking light-mustard-coloured restaurant does a great line in hamburger steaks, grilled beef bulgogi steaks and garlic pepper steaks, served quickly and offering good value.

Mammoth Bakery BAKERY $

(맘모스 베이커리; coffee ₩3000, breads ₩1000-4000; ⏲8am-10pm) Friendly staff serve good espresso and fresh tasty treats, making Mammoth a good choice for brekkie. If the weather is nice, enjoy your drink on the outdoor patio. If you get an Americano, enjoy a single refill for just ₩500. It's a bit old-fashioned – Mammoth even has a fax number, so you could fax through your order.

Jaerim Galbi KOREAN $$

(재림 갈비; Eumsigui-gil; servings ₩9000-22,000; ⏲10am-11pm) A good-value barbecue place serving pork ribs, bulgogi, prime beef rib and grilled beef steaks. The menu is very simple but the smell from the street is mouth-watering.

Yangban Bapsang KOREAN $$
(양반 밥상; meals ₩8500-18,000; ⏲10am-9pm) Mackerel served golden – skin crispy, flesh tender – melts on the tongue the way mackerel was meant to. Not far from Andong Folk Village (p173), it's across the street from the entrance to the wooden bridge.

Sinseon Jjimdak KOREAN $$
(신선찜닭; ☎054 842 9989; 178-2 Nam-mun-dong; mains from ₩18,000) Many of the restaurants in the market where this restaurant is located will charge you ₩25,000 for two (even if it's just you) for a plate of *andong jjimdak* (simmered chicken), but this restaurant will cook it up for you for a reasonable, solo price.

Drinking & Nightlife

★**Yam Bar** BAR
(☎054 843 0994; 116-4 Dongbu-dong; 📶) This is your Andong nightlife choice with a superb range of craft menu of beer and attentive service. There's also a decent supply of food to soak up the hoppy flavours, including – if you are so inclined – fried spam, served in a tin (fiddly, but not impossible, with chopsticks). It's just north of Hotel Yam.

Shopping

Homeplus MALL
(홈플러스; ⏲10am-midnight) The colossal Homeplus Mall is not just *the* most hulking landmark in town, but an all-under-one-roof shopping bonanza, with long hours. There's a small cafe on the ground floor.

Information

KB Bank (⏲9am-4pm Mon-Fri)
Shinhan Bank (⏲9am-4pm Mon-Fri)

Getting There & Away

BUS

Andong mainly uses the newer **bus terminal** (안동 터미널; ☎054 857 8296) around 5km northwest from the town centre. To get into town take bus 0, 1, 2,11, 46, 51 or 76 (₩1200) and get out at Andong station, or it's a quick cab ride (₩5000).

Departures from Andong

DESTINATION	PRICE (₩)	DURATION (HR)	FREQUENCY
Busan	17,800	2½	every 30-60min
Daegu	9700	1½	every 30min
Daejeon	15,000	3	every 30min
Dong-seoul	19,900	3	every 30min
Gyeongju	10,100	1¾	7 daily
Juwang-san	8600	½	6 daily
Pohang	15,500	2	every 2hr
Ulsan	14,700	2¾	8 daily

TRAIN

Departures from Andong

DESTINATION	PRICE (₩)	DURATION (HR)	FREQUENCY
Daegu	8000	2	1 daily
Dongdaegu (transfer to Busan)	8200	2	3 daily
Gyeongju	8300	2	3 daily
Seoul	24,100	4	8 daily
Seoul	16,500	5½	2 daily

Getting Around

The **tourist office** (☎054 840 6974; www.andong.go.kr; ⏲9am-6pm) hands out a helpful local bus timetable with English explanations. The town is small enough to get around on foot, and local buses serve all the outlying sights. Note that Cash Bee cards are not accepted on buses in Andong.

Hahoe Folk Village

A delightful traditional riverside village and a Unesco World Heritage site, **Hahoe Folk Village** (Hahoe Minsok Maeul; 안동 하회마을; www.hahoe.or.kr/english/sub1.asp; adult/child ₩5000/2500; ⏲9am-6pm Mar-Oct, to sunset Nov-Feb) is a great place to commune with the traditional fabric of old Korea and, in the busy months, with large crowds of visitors. Avoid the weekends, go off-season and be rewarded with a glimpse of bucolic enchantment and the gentle rhythms of countryside village life. Cross the river or drive to Buyongdae Cliff (부용대) for the bird's-eye perspective and search out the sacred Goddess Samsin Tree at the heart of Hahoe.

The name Hahoe (하회 – pronounced 'ha hway') means 'River Returning', which reflects the village's position at a looping bend in the Nakdong River. Some Korean folk villages can seem a bit artificial but Ha-

hoe has 230 residents who give the place life and the sensation of a working community; this also means it is important to respect people's privacy if you step beyond a house threshold (residents are of course used to visitors, but keep this in mind).

Before you hop aboard the shuttle bus to the village from the Andong bus drop-off point, take time to explore the **Hahoe Mask Museum** (하회동 탈 박물관; ☎054 853 2288; ₩3000; ⊙9.30am-6pm), with its intriguing collection of Korean and international masks. There are also Byeolsingut Talnori masked dance performances near the car park; enquire at the **tourist office** (⊙9am-6pm Apr-Sept, to 5pm Oct-Mar) for details on times and also to pick up a map of the village.

The shuttle bus will deposit you in the village, where you are free to explore at will. The village is full of traditional residences, pretty thatched houses (63 in total), old pavilions and rural panoramas. Hunt down the Presbyterian Church (하회 교회) with its brick spire and wander down by the river to the Mansongjeong Pine Forest (만송정숲). Not far from the pine forest, a small ferry (₩4000) crosses the river to Buyongdae Cliff on the far bank.

The Confucian academy of **Byeongsan Seowon** (병산서원; ⊙9am-6pm Apr-Oct, to 5pm Nov-Mar) FREE is a 30- to 40-minute walk east of the village, or you can take one of the three daily buses from Andong that pass through the village and continue to the academy.

Sleeping

Many homes in Hahoe have *minbak* (private homes with rooms to rent) for rent from around ₩50,000, some with *jjimjil-bang* (saunas) as well. Look out for the signs, or ask at the tourist information office.

Rak Ko Jae GUESTHOUSE
(락고재; ☎054 857 3410; www.rkj.co.kr; d incl breakfast Nov-Mar from ₩160,000, Apr-Oct from ₩180,000; ❄📶) A four-room, upmarket guesthouse facing the river and blending seamlessly with the surrounding thatched-roof *hanok* (traditional wooden homes). The name in Korean literally means 'Happiness old House'. Each traditional room comes with modern comforts like cable TV and a fridge, plus an odd *hinoki* (pine) bathtub. There's a mud-walled *jjimjil-bang* (sauna, cash only) also, for that true traditional bathing experience.

Dinner (₩30,000 per person) is available from December to March and needs to be reserved three days in advance.

Drinking & Nightlife

Susimheon CAFE
(수심헌; 修心軒; coffee from ₩3000) This cafe at the heart of the village serves coffee and bottles of the local Andong *soju* firewater (from ₩6000 to ₩30,000).

Entertainment

Byeolsingut Talnori DANCE
(⊙2pm Sat & Sun Jan & Feb, 2pm Wed-Sun Mar-Dec) Byeolsingut Talnori masked dance performances take place in a small stadium near Hahoe's car park. These shows are a must-see – plus they're free, although donations are demanded by hard-working *halmeoni* (grandmas).

Times of performances do tend to change from year to year, so check at the tourist information office for details.

Getting There & Around

Bus 246 (₩1800, 50 minutes, 12 daily) runs to Hahoe from Andong. The last bus back to Andong is at 7.10pm. A shuttle bus runs every 10 to 15 minutes for the 1km run from the Andong bus drop-off to the village itself.

Cheongnyangsan Provincial Park

Cheongnyangsan Provincial Park (청량산 도립공원) boasts spectacular views and tracks wandering along cliff precipices. In addition to the mountain Cheongnyang-san, the summit of which is Changin-bong (870m), there are 11 scenic peaks, eight caves and a waterfall, Gwanchang Pokpo. A spiderweb of tracks radiates out from the main temple, Cheongnyang-sa (p178) and most are well marked.

It takes about five hours to complete a round-trip of the peaks, returning to the bus stop, or about 90 minutes to the temple and back again.

Sights

Cheongnyang-sa BUDDHIST TEMPLE
(청량사) The largest temple in the park is Cheongnyang-sa. Built in AD 663, the tem-

ple is quite scenic, sitting in a steep valley below the cliffs. The are a number of other hermitages in the park too.

Cheongnyangsan Museum MUSEUM
(청량산박물관; 1725-2 Gwanchang-ri, Cheongnyang-ro; 9am-6pm) FREE A modest effort with artefacts related to the area's agricultural history.

Sleeping & Eating

If you want to stay the night, there are a dozen *minbak* options, as well as shops and restaurants, across the street from the park entrance.

Drinking & Nightlife

Ansimdang TEAHOUSE
(안심당; 054 673 6389; Cheongnyangsan-gil; snacks from ₩5,000; 10am-5pm) Located at the base of Cheongnyang-sa (p178) is this pleasant teahouse, a perfect place to relax.

Getting There & Away

From Andong, bus 67 (₩2200, one hour, six daily) continues past the Confucian Academy of Dosan Seowon to the park.

Juwangsan National Park

Beautifully situated among the Baekdu mountains, **Juwangsan National Park** (주왕산 국립공원; ₩2000; sunrise-1hr before sunset), a 106-sq-km national park, is notable for its sublime limestone pinnacles, verdant valleys, splendid gorges, caves, ancient temples and waterfalls. Lying just within the entrance to the park is temple of Daejeon-sa (대전사), which dates from the 7th century. Most visitors reach the park by bus from Andong (₩8600 to ₩11,200, 1½ hours, six per day) via the town of Cheongsong (₩6800, 20 minutes, every 30 minutes).

The popular hike from Daejeon-sa to the 720m peak of Juwang-san (주왕산) takes around 1¼ hours and can be followed by a 15-minute trek along the ridge to Kaldeunggogae (732m), from where you can make your way back down to Daejeon-sa (about 1¾ hours) via Hurimaegi (50 minutes), a picturesque valley of trees and a creek straddled by a wooden bridge. You can detour on the way down to Juwanggul Cave, accessed via a path that passes the hermitage of Juwang-am.

Other temples and hermitages in the park include Gwangam-sa and Juwang-am.

Juwangsan National Park

Sights

1	Daejeon-sa	A3
2	Gwangam-sa	A2
3	Hurimaegi	C2
4	Juwang-am	B3
5	Juwanggul Cave	B3
6	Juwangsan National Park	A3
7	Mujanggul Cave	B3
8	Naewonmaeul	C2
9	Yeonhwagul Cave	B2

Sleeping

10	Bangalo Minbak	A3
11	Hyangchon Sikdang-Minbak	A3

Information

Information Centre ....(see 12)

Transport

12	Bus Terminal	A3

Cave enthusiasts can eke out Mujanggul Cave and Yeonhwagul Cave.

Naewonmaeul, in the park, is a tiny village where craftspeople perform woodworking.

Hiking within the park is prohibited at night.

Sleeping & Eating

If you want to overnight at Juwangsan, the *minbak* village (*minbakchon*) opposite the Juwangsan bus terminal has a large number of accommodation options, but quality varies, so hunt about first. Room rates can double on weekends and in July, August and October. There's also a wide choice of restaurants in the *minbak* village and the main road leading to the park entrance.

Hyangchon Sikdang-Minbak B&B $
(향촌 식당 민박; 054 873 0202; r from ₩35,000) With the largest sign near the park entrance, this *minbak* and restaurant is hard to miss and it also has some of the area's nicest rooms. Downstairs in the restaurant, the *jeongsik* meal (₩10,000) comes with soup and a colourful array of leafy side dishes, some of which are picked by the owner in the local mountains.

Bangalo Minbak CHALET $$
(방갈로 민박; 054 874 5200; Gongwon-gil; r weekdays/weekends ₩30,000/60,000) About 500m from the park entrance, this place has a log-cabin exterior with central court-

Juwangsan National Park

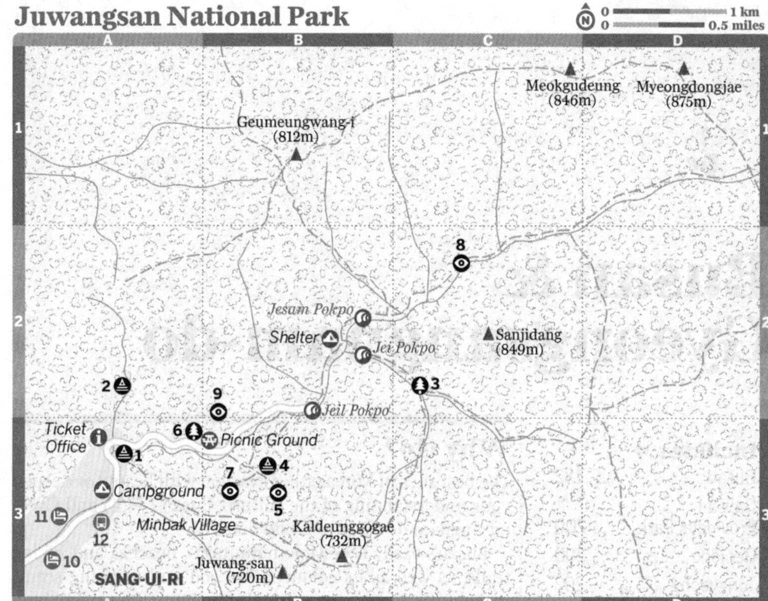

yard. Rooms have *ondol* (traditional, sleep-on-the-floor mattresses) or beds and there's also a simple on-site restaurant.

Information

The main gateway to the park is the town of Cheongsong, about 15km away. At the park entrance, the **information centre** (☎054 873 0014; 2nd fl, bus terminal; ⏲9am-5.30pm) has English and Korean maps detailing hiking routes, distances and estimated calories burned. Be sure to check here for local trail conditions.

Getting There & Away

BUS

Buses (₩8600 to ₩11,200, 1½ hours, six per day) to Juwangsan from Andong go via the town of Cheongsong (₩6800, 20 minutes, every 30 minutes). Check the timetable inside the Juwangsan **bus terminal** for detailed schedules.

Departures from Juwangsan

DESTINATION	PRICE (₩)	DURATION (HR)
Andong	8600-11,200	1½
Busan	19,300	3¾
Cheongsong	1600	½
Dongdaegu	16,400	3
Dongseoul	24,100	5
Yeongcheon (transfer to Gyeongju)	13,000	2

Busan & Gyeongsangnam-do

Includes ➡

Best Places to Eat

- ➡ Jacky's Seafood (p191)
- ➡ Noran Mahura (p193)
- ➡ Sol Taphouse (p193)
- ➡ Ddungbo Halmae Gimbap (p203)
- ➡ Dajeong Sikdang (p207)

Best Places to Stay

- ➡ Hotel1 (p189)
- ➡ Ibis Ambassador Busan City Centre Hotel (p188)
- ➡ Paradise Hotel (p189)
- ➡ Westin Chosun Beach Hotel (p189)
- ➡ Dong Bang Hotel (p205)
- ➡ Nexon (p203)

Why Go?

The best sites in Korea either awe you with beauty or deepen your understanding of the culture. Busan (부산) and Gyeongsangnam-do (경상남도) do both.

Busan's easily accessible mountains, beaches and hiking trails, as well as its colourful seafood and drinking scene, make it very easy to love. It's also home to the world's largest shopping and entertainment complex and a bedazzling world-class cinema centre.

Gyeongsangnam-do's natural beauty – the verdure of rolling mountains and the vibe of yesteryear coastal towns untouched by tourist development – is closer than you think, thanks to an efficient transport system. Hop on a bus and you'll be rewarded with outstanding trails in Jirisan National Park, glorious temples in hideaway locations, and lush rice paddies in just about every rural community. For marine treasures, board a ferry and go island-hopping around Tongyeong. On land or by sea, Gyeongsangnam-do is accessible, affordable and waiting to be explored.

When to Go

Busan

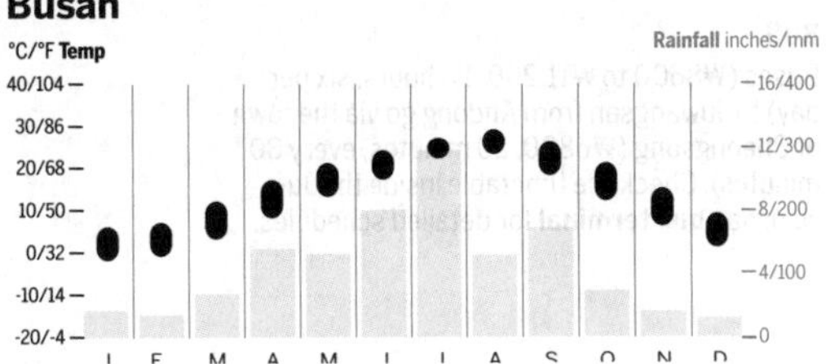

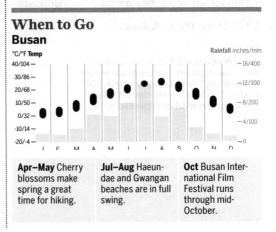

Apr–May Cherry blossoms make spring a great time for hiking.

Jul–Aug Haeundae and Gwangan beaches are in full swing.

Oct Busan International Film Festival runs through mid-October.

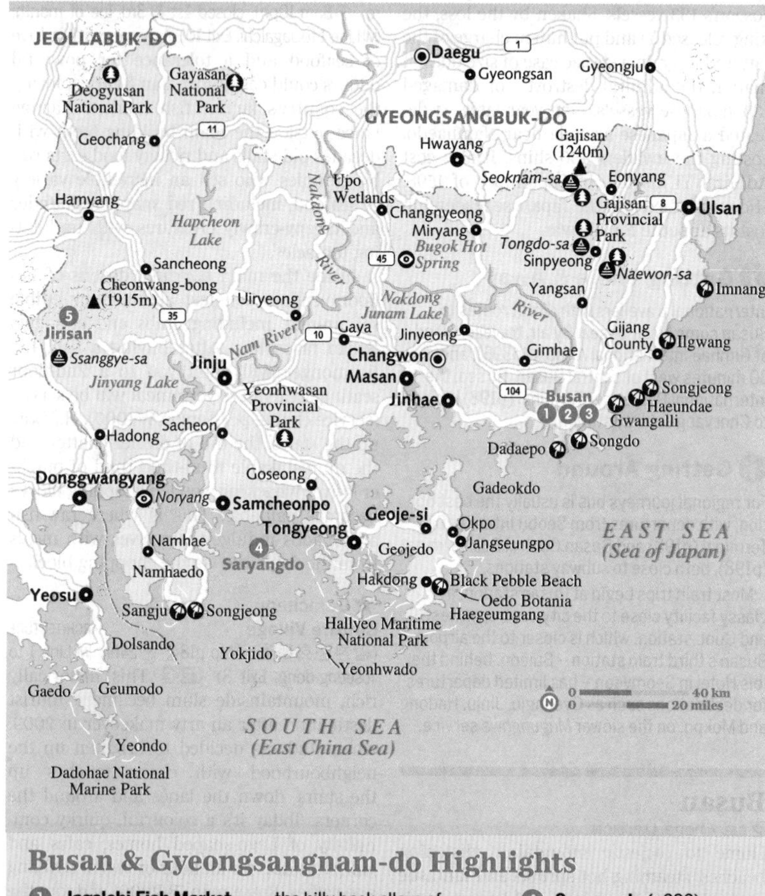

Busan & Gyeongsangnam-do Highlights

1. **Jagalchi Fish Market** (p182) Shocking your taste buds with raw fish at Korea's largest seafood market in Busan.
2. **Gamcheon Culture Village** (p182) Exploring the hilly back alleys of this colourful Busan neighbourhood.
3. **BIFF** (p188) Attending a world-class film festival in Busan.
4. **Saryangdo** (p202) Challenging yourself by hiking a beautiful island off the coast of Tongyeong.
5. **Jirisan** (p209) Exploring one of the best places to hike in Korea.

History

Gyeongsangnam-do has a long history of warfare, though it's difficult to beat the Imjin War for destruction, treachery and the birth of an icon. In 1592 the Japanese were eager to secure a land route to China, but the Joseon government refused assistance, so the Japanese attacked. Led by Toyotomi Hideyoshi, the Japanese landed 160,000 troops at several places, including Busan and Jinju, where the Koreans made an unsuccessful stand against a superior enemy.

The war's local star was Admiral Yi Sun-sin, a brilliant tactician credited with the development of the turtle ship, an ironclad vessel instrumental in harassing Japanese supply lines. Despite his significant wartime contributions, Yi was arrested for disobeying orders thanks to a clever ruse concocted by the Japanese, who were eager to see the good admiral removed from the war. With Yi behind bars, the Japanese launched a massive assault that destroyed all but 13 of

Joseon's 133 vessels. Shaken by the loss, the king released Yi and put him in charge of the tattered navy. In a classic case of size doesn't matter, the admiral destroyed or damaged 133 Japanese vessels. One year later, Yi defeated a Japanese armada near Namhaedo, costing the invaders 450 ships. It also cost Admiral Yi his life. In September of 1598, Hideyoshi died and the Japanese leadership lost its appetite for the war.

Getting There & Away

International travellers with direct routes to Busan come by air or sea. By air, travellers land at Gimhae International Airport (p395), about 30 minutes west of central Busan. By sea, the International Passenger Terminal (p198) is close to Choryang subway station.

Getting Around

For regional journeys bus is usually the best option, with departures from Seobu Intercity Bus Terminal (p198) and Busan Central Bus Terminal (p198), both close to subway stations.

Most train trips begin at Busan station, a glassy facility close to the city centre, or west-end Gupo station, which is closer to the airport. Busan's third train station – Bujeon, behind the Ibis Hotel in Seomyeon – has limited departures for destinations such as Gyeongju, Jinju, Hadong and Mokpo, on the slower *Mugunghwa* service.

Busan

051 / POP 3.4 MILLION

Home to majestic mountains, glistening beaches, steaming hot springs and fantastic seafood, South Korea's second-largest city is a rollicking port town with tonnes to offer. From casual tent bars and chic designer cafes to fish markets teeming with every species imaginable, Busan (부산) has something for all tastes. Rugged mountain ranges slice through the urban landscape, and events such as the Busan International Film Festival underscore the city's desire to be a global meeting place.

While Busan is within the boundaries of Gyeongsangnam-do, it is a separate administrative unit with its own telephone area code.

Sights

Nampo-dong

★Jagalchi Fish Market MARKET
(자갈치 시장; Map p190; 051 245 2594; http://jagalchimarket.bisco.or.kr; 52 Jagalchihaean-ro; 8am-10pm, closed 1st & 3rd Tue of month; Line 1 to Jagalchi, Exit 10) Anyone with a love of seafood and a tolerance for powerful odours could easily spend an hour exploring the country's largest fish market. Narrow lanes outside the main building teem with decades-old stalls and rickety food carts run by grannies who sell an incredible variety of seafood, including red snapper, flounder and creepy-crawly creatures with undulating tentacles.

Inside the main building, dozens of 1st-floor vendors sell just about every edible sea animal, including crabs and eels, two Busan favourites. After buying a fish, the fishmonger will point you to a 2nd-floor seating area where your meal will be served (service charge per person ₩4000). Halfway up the stairs, the din of dinner chatter and the unmistakable thud-thud-thud of butcher knives whacking wooden chopping blocks becomes palpable. This is where raw-fish aficionados indulge themselves with meals from the fish tank, via the chopping block.

★Gamcheon Culture Village ARCHITECTURE
(감천문화마을; Map p184; 24hr; Line 1 to Toseong-dong, Exit 8) FREE This historically rich, mountainside slum became a tourist destination after an arty makeover in 2009, when students decided to brighten up the neighbourhood with clever touches up the stairs, down the lanes and around the corners. Today it's a colourful, quirky community of Lego-shaped homes, cafes and galleries, ideal for an hour or two of strolling and selfies. Buy a map (₩2000) and join the scavenger hunt. Comfortable walking shoes recommended.

From the metro station, cross the street and walk to the bus stop in front of the hospital. Catch minibus 2 or 2-2 (₩900, 10 minutes) up the steep hill to the village. A taxi from the hospital (₩3000) is faster.

Busan Tower TOWER
(부산타워; Map p190; 051 661 9393; 37-55 Yongdusan-gil; adult/child ₩5000/3000; 10am-11pm) If the haze is not too thick, daytime views of container-ship traffic in the harbour from this 188m-high tower provide a sense of the port's scale of operations.

Busan Museum of Movies MUSEUM
(부산영화체험 박물관; Map p190; 051 715 4200; www.busanbom.kr; 12 Daechong-ro 126beon-gil, Jung-gu; adult/child ₩10,000/7000; 10am-

LOCAL KNOWLEDGE

BUSAN ON THE BIG SCREEN

As the host of the Busan International Film Festival (p188), one of the most important film festivals in Asia, Busan has welcomed lovers of the cinematic arts for over two decades. But the city itself drew the international spotlight in 2018 when it served as a backdrop in Marvel's record-breaking blockbuster Black Panther. When selecting locations, director Ryan Coogler said he looked for unique settings that featured a traditional side of Asia, choosing famous Busan locations like Jagalchi Fish Market (p182), Gwangandaegyo Bridge and Gwangan Beach (p185) for some of the film's most prominent scenes.

In 2016 the city played a role in the Korean zombie-apocalypse thriller *Train to Busan* (부산행), where a workaholic Seoul banker and his young daughter board a KTX train bound for Busan that becomes overrun with infected passengers during the rail journey. Animator Yeon Sang-Ho made his directorial debut with the critically acclaimed flick, which premiered during the Midnight Screenings at Cannes. During the screening, French studio Gaumont set its sights on a remake, outbidding big-time Hollywood studios like Fox and Sony; it will be their first English-language film set in the US.

6pm Tue-Sun;) The museum opened in July 2017 as the first film exhibition and experience in South Korea. Inside, visitors can pose with statues of their favourite superheroes as well as experience different aspects of moviemaking, including an interactive green-screen room and a 'movie-karaoke' studio where you can add your own voiceover to popular film clips. The virtual reality room, where visitors watch films through special VR glasses, is also a hit. It's the perfect indoor activity for adults and children alike. Last entrance at 5pm.

Busan Modern History Museum MUSEUM
(부산 근대역사관; Map p190; 051 253 3845; http://museum.busan.go.kr/modern/index; 104 Daecheong-ro; 9am-6pm Tue-Sun; M Line 1 to Jungang, Exit 5) FREE The hour it takes to walk through this small museum will be time well spent. There's a surprising amount of English material documenting the history of the Busan port, Japanese influence and the Korean War. It's in a building north of Yongdu-san Park, 300m west of the central post office.

Yongdu-san Park PARK
(용두산 공원; Map p190; 051 860 7820; http://yongdusanpark.bisco.or.kr; 37-55 Yongdusan-gil; 10am-11pm; M Line 1 to Nampo, Exit 1) Close to the shopping in Nampo-dong, this humble park is home to the 118m-high Busan Tower.

Seomyeon

Busan Citizens Park PARK
(부산 시민공원; Map p184; 051 850 6000; http://english.busan.go.kr/bscitypark; 73 Simingong-won-ro; 5am-11pm; M Line 1 to Bujeon Station, Exit 7) Built on a former US army base, this pleasant city park features nearly one million trees and shrubs of 97 different species. Its paths stretch past peaceful streams, fountains and squares, and there's a history museum, artificial sand beach, maze and cafes.

Haeundae

★Haeundae BEACH
(해운대해수욕장; Map p189; 051 749 4000; U-dong Haeundae-gu; M Line 2 to Haeundae, Exit 3 or 5) Haeundae is the country's most famous beach. During the peak August travel season, umbrellas mushroom across the 2km-long beach while frolickers fill the water with inner tubes rented from booths behind the beach. It's a fun family outing with 100,000 friends, though the marketing material portraying Haeundae as a world-class resort is bunkum.

Busan Museum of Art MUSEUM
(부산 시립 미술관; Map p184; 051 744 2602; http://art.busan.go.kr; 58 APEC-ro; 10am-8pm Tue-Sun; M Line 2 to Busan Museum of Art, Exit 5) FREE This is a modest gallery, hardly a must-see, but is an interesting diversion on a rainy day. It houses works by local Busan artists, plus a handful of international exhibitions and an outdoor sculpture park.

Nurimaru APEC House ARCHITECTURE
(Map p189; 051 744 3140; 116 Dongbaek-ro) Located on Dongbaekseom Island, the grounds of this contemporary memorial and conference hall offers great sea views and are a nice place for a stroll.

Busan

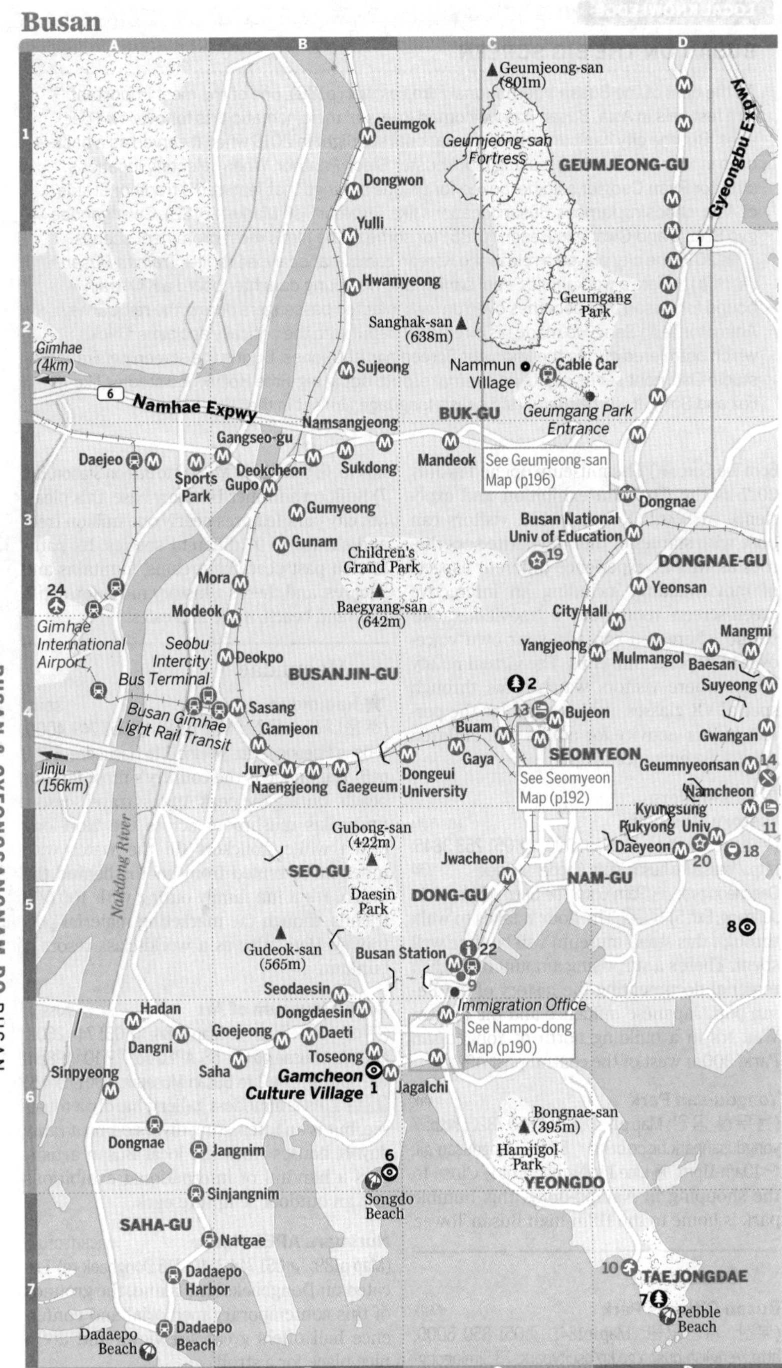
Geumjeong-san (801m)
Geumjeong-san Fortress
GEUMJEONG-GU
Gyeongbu Expwy
Geumgok
Dongwon
Yulli
Hwamyeong
Sanghak-san (638m)
Geumgang Park
Sujeong
Nammun Village
Cable Car
Geumgang Park Entrance
Gimhae (4km)
Namhae Expwy
BUK-GU
Namsangjeong
Gangseo-gu
Daejeo
Sports Park
Deokcheon
Gupo
Sukdong
Mandeok
See Geumjeong-san Map (p196)
Dongnae
Gumyeong
Busan National Univ of Education
Gunam
Children's Grand Park
19
DONGNAE-GU
Mora
24
Baegyang-san (642m)
Yeonsan
Modeok
City Hall
Gimhae International Airport
Seobu Intercity Bus Terminal
Deokpo
Mangmi
Yangjeong
Mulmangol
Baesan
BUSANJIN-GU
2
Suyeong
13
Sasang
Bujeon
Busan Gimhae Light Rail Transit
Gamjeon
Buam
Gwangan
Gaya
SEOMYEON
Jinju (156km)
Jurye
Naengjeong
Gaegeum
Dongeui University
See Seomyeon Map (p192)
Geumnyeonsan
14
Namcheon
Kyungsung Pukyong Univ
11
Gubong-san (422m)
Daeyeon
20
18
Nakdong River
SEO-GU
Jwacheon
NAM-GU
Daesin Park
DONG-GU
8
Gudeok-san (565m)
Busan Station
22
9
Seodaesin
Immigration Office
Hadan
Dongdaesin
Goejeong
Daeti
Dangni
See Nampo-dong Map (p190)
Toseong
Saha
Gamcheon Culture Village
1
Sinpyeong
Jagalchi
Bongnae-san (395m)
Hamjigol Park
Dongnae
Jangnim
6
YEONGDO
Songdo Beach
Sinjangnim
SAHA-GU
Natgae
Dadaepo Harbor
10
TAEJONGDAE
7
Pebble Beach
Dadaepo Beach
Dadaepo Beach

Gwangan & Yongho

Gwangan BEACH

(광안리해수욕장, Gwangalli; Map p184; ☎051 622 4251; 219 Gwanganhaebyeon-ro; Ⓜ Line 2 to Geumnyeonsan, Exit 3) Among the city's seven beaches, Gwangan is the best option for access and quality (the other beaches are Haeundae (p183), Dadaepo, Songdo, Songjeong, Ilgwang and Imnang). Although the wall of commercial development behind the beach diminishes the daytime experience, Gwangan shines at night. The multicoloured light show illuminating the Diamond Bridge is grand.

Outside the metro station, rotate 180 degrees and turn right at the corner. Or take Line 2 to Gwangan station, Exit 3 or 5.

Igidae PARK

(이기대; Map p184; ☎051 607 6398; 25 Yongho 3sam-dong; Ⓜ Line 2 to Namcheon, Exit 3) If the trails of Geumjeong Fortress seem more like work than pleasure, there are opportunities to explore Busan's natural beauty at a more leisurely pace. Igidae is a nature park that's ideal for a two-hour stroll. Most visitors take the coastal route for the sweeping views of Haeundae across the bay.

From the metro station, walk to the first major intersection and turn left. The park is a 20-minute walk down the road.

UN Cemetery CEMETERY

(재한 유엔 기념공원; Map p184; ☎051 625 0625; www.unmck.or.kr; 93 UN Pyeonghwa-ro, Nam-gu; ⏲9am-5pm; Ⓜ Line 2 to Daeyeon, Exit 3) This is the only United Nations cemetery in the world and is the final resting place of 2300 men from 11 nations, including the UK, Turkey, Canada and Australia, that supported the South in the 1950–53 Korean War. There's a moving photo exhibit, along with knowledgeable volunteers who share stories about the people in the images.

The cemetery is a 15-minute walk from the station.

Dongnae & Geumjeong-san

★Beomeo-sa BUDDHIST TEMPLE

(범어사; Map p196; ☎051 508 3122; www.beomeosa.co.kr; 250 Beomeosa-ro; ⏲8.30am-5.30pm; Ⓜ Line 1 to Beomeosa, Exit 5) This magnificent temple is Busan's best sight. Despite its city location, Beomeo-sa is a world away from the urban jungle, with beautiful architecture set against an extraordinary mountain

Busan

Top Sights
1 Gamcheon Culture Village B6

Sights
2 Busan Citizens Park C4
3 Busan Museum of Art E4
4 Gwangan E4
5 Igidae E5
6 Songdo Marine Cable Car B6
7 Taejongdae Park D7
8 UN Cemetery D5

Activities, Courses & Tours
9 City Tour Busan C5
Spa Land ......(see 21)
10 Taejongdae Gonpo Cruise D7

Sleeping
11 Gwangan Hound Hotel D5
12 Hotel1 ......E4
13 Ibis Ambassador Busan City Centre Hotel C4

Eating
14 Brunch Cafe Ean D4
Ecotopia ......(see 11)
15 Millak Town Raw Fish Centre E4
16 Noran Mahura F4
Sol Taphouse ......(see 11)

Drinking & Nightlife
Beached ......(see 11)
Eva's Gwangan ......(see 11)
Galmegi Pub ......(see 11)
17 HQ Gwangan E4
18 The Commonplace D5
Thursday Party ......(see 12)

Entertainment
Busan Cinema Center ......(see 21)
19 Busan IPark C3
20 Daeyeon Cinema Theatre D5
Lotte Giants ......(see 19)
Monk ......(see 18)

Shopping
Bujeon Market ......(see 13)
21 Lotte Department Store – Centum City E4
Shinsegae Centum City ......(see 21)

Information
22 Busan Station Tourism Office C5
Gimhae Airport – Domestic Terminal Info ......(see 24)
Gimhae Airport – International Terminal Info ......(see 24)
Gimhae International Airport Domestic Terminal Currency Exchange ......(see 24)
Gimhae International Airport International Terminal Currency Exchange ......(see 24)
23 Kangsan Travel F4

Transport
24 Gimhae International Airport A3

backdrop. Beomeo-sa can be a busy place on weekends and holidays, as the path leading to the temple is the northern starting point for trails across Geumjeong-san. Before heading back to the city, visit the *pajeon* (파전, green onion pancake) restaurants near the bus stop.

At street level from Beomeo-sa station, spin 180 degrees, turn left at the corner and walk 200m to the terminus. Catch bus 90 (₩1200, 20 minutes, every 15 minutes) or take a taxi (₩5000) to the temple entrance.

To fully appreciate the beauty of this temple, sign up for the templestay program. The predawn chanting is hauntingly beautiful. Signing up for a templestay is usually completed online. Reservations are required, often two weeks in advance. Payment is by bank transfer.

Seokbul-sa BUDDHIST TEMPLE
(석불사; Map p196; 051 332 1690; 1 Mandeok-dong; 7am-7pm) Hard to find, difficult to reach and a wonder to behold, this hermitage has Buddhist images meticulously etched into stone. Visually powerful in scale and impact, it's the kind of work that moves visitors to exclaim 'wow' as they step back and arch their necks to get the full picture. The quickest route here begins with a ride on the **Geumgang Park cable car** (금강공원 케이블카; Map p196; http://geumgangpark.bisco.or.kr; one way/return adult ₩5000/8000, child ₩4000/6000; 9am-5pm; Line 1 to Oncheonjang, Exit 1); up top, follow the trail signs.

The most interesting – and strenuous – route to Seokbul-sa is to add it to your Geumjeong Fortress hike (carry plenty of water). From Nammun, the path indicated by the Mandeokchon (만덕촌) sign leads to a collection of restaurants and a foot volleyball court. Keep going straight until you can't go any further, then turn right onto a narrow path. Eventually this leads to a larger path heading down the mountain-

side. Look for a sign that reads '석불사 입구' (Seokbul-sa entrance), which points you down a steep, rocky trail. Way down at the bottom, turn right at the concrete road and walk uphill to the temple.

On the way back, you can either return to Nammun and then follow the signs to the cable car, or keep walking down the concrete road from the temple – you'll end up near Mandeok station on Line 3.

Geumgang Park PARK

(Map p196; ☎051 860 7880; 155 Ujangchun-ro; ⊙9am-5pm) This park features a cable car, located about 150m from the park entrance; follow the *Ropeway* signs.

Geumjeong Fortress HISTORIC SITE

(금정산성; Map p196) FREE Travellers climbing Geumjeong-san (금정산, Geumjeong Mountain) expecting to see a fort will be disappointed because there isn't one. Geumjeong Fortress consists of four gates and 17km of stone walls encircling 8 sq km of mountaintop. Not all is lost, though, because this is where you'll find some of the city's best hiking, and the opportunity to see Korean hikers sporting the very latest in alpine fashion. Most hikers start at Beomeo-sa or the Geumgang Park Cable Car.

Hikers looking for a sturdy workout begin at the northern leg of the trail, which is on the left side of Beomeo-sa. The steep walk to the main ridge takes about an hour. Follow the trail left and head to Bukmun (북문, North Gate). The 8.8km hike from Beomeo-sa to Nammun (남문, South Gate) is a comfortable walk with a couple of steep stretches.

The least arduous route is by cable car from Geumgang Park at the southern base of the mountain. From the mountaintop cable-car platform, it's a 20-minute walk to the South Gate.

Yeongdo & Southern Busan

Taejongdae Park PARK

(태종대유원지; Map p184; ☎051 405 8745; www.taejongdae.or.kr; 24 Jeonmang-ro; ⊙4am-10pm; Ⓜ Line 1 to Nampo, Exit 6) On the southern tip of Yeongdo (영도, Yeong Island), experience the city's rugged coastline along a well-groomed walking path. For those less inclined to hoof it, there's a train (adult/child ₩2000/100) that stops at the park's various sights. Yeongdo Lighthouse is the best spot for photograph-worthy views of the cliffs and ocean.

Exit the metro station and walk along the Jagalchi side of the street towards Lotte department store; turn right at the main road. The bus stop (₩1200, bus 8, 30, 88) is down the street, or take a taxi from the metro station (₩8000).

Songdo Marine Cable Car CABLE CAR

(Busan Air Cruise; Map p184; ☎051 247 9900; www.busanaircruise.co.kr; 171 Songdohae-byeon-ro; adult/child standard cabin ₩15,000/11,000, glass floor cabin ₩20,000/15,000; ⊙9am-10pm; 🚌7, 26 or 96 to Songdo Beach bus stop, Ⓜ Line 1 to Jagalchi, Exit 2) Originally launched in 1964 as Korea's first cable car, the Songdo Beach attraction reopened in 2017, measuring a distance of 1.62km – four times what it was before its 1988 closure. There are 39 cars – 13 of them with glass floors – that traverse emerald waters, offering for surreal views of the hillsides and cliffs. The journey starts from a station next to Songnim Park on Songdo's east side, ending at an observatory station at Amnam Park in the west.

Take metro Line 1 to Jagalchi Station, Exit 2. Turn left at the corner, walk 50m and cross the street to Chungmudonggyocharo bus stop. Take bus 7, 26, 71 or 96 and get off at the Songdo Beach bus stop.

Haedong Yonggungsa TEMPLE

(해동 용궁사; ☎051 722 7744; www.yongkungsa.or.kr/en; 86 Yonggung-gil, Gijang-eup; 🚌181 to Yonggungsa Temple stop, Ⓜ Line 2 to Haeundae, Exit 7) FREE One of the country's few temples situated on the coast, Haedong Yonggung offers spectacular views of the temple grounds and surrounding ocean. Located quite north of the city, it gets congested on the weekends – but the vistas, elaborate altars, statues of towering zodiac animals and a giant gold Buddha make the venture well worth it.

Activities

★Spa Land SPA

(Map p184; ☎051 745 2900; www.shinsegae.com; 1st fl, Shinsegae Centum City; adult/youth weekdays ₩13,000/10,000, weekends ₩15,000/12,000; ⊙6am-midnight, last entry 10.30pm; Ⓜ Line 2 to Centum City, Exit 3) You can't really experience Busan unless you've been naked in a room full of strangers inside Asia's largest bathhouse. The bathing area in Spa Land isn't particularly impressive, but the *jjimjil-bang* (the area where people wear loose-fitting

clothes) is immense – there's a panoply of relaxation rooms of various temperatures and scents. Kids under 13 are not permitted.

Taejongdae Gonpo Cruise CRUISE
(Map p184; ☎051 405 2900; www.taejongdae.or.kr; 24 Jeonmang-ro; adult/child ₩10,000/7000; ⏲9am-5pm) This noisy 45-minute cruise runs along the coast with views of Igidae.

Tours

Mipo Wharf BOATING
(미포 선착장; Map p189; 33-1 Dalmaji-gil 62beon-gil; adult/child ₩22,000/13,000; ⏲hourly 10am-10pm; Ⓜ Line 2 to Haeundae, Exit 3 or 5) The small pier at the eastern end of Haeundae beach runs 50-minute return trips to the nearby Oryuk-do Islets and Gwangan bridge.

City Tour Busan BUS
(부산 시티 투어버스; Map p184; ☎051 464 9898; www.citytourbusan.com; 206 Jungang-daero, Busan Station; adult/child ₩15,000/8000; ⏲tour times vary; Ⓜ Line 1 to Busan station, Exit 1) City Tour runs six daytime routes with different themes. Buy a Loop Tour ticket and you can jump on and off that bus all day. Three different evening tours drive towards Haeundae, Gwangan bridge and the major hotels. All buses start at Busan station.

Festivals & Events

★Busan International Film Festival FILM
(부산국제영화제; ☎1688 3010; www.biff.kr; ⏲Oct) It's all glitter, glamour and gossip in October when the Busan International Film Festival (BIFF) takes centre stage. Not just about movies – there were 300 films from 76 countries in 2017 – the real buzz centres on which Korean female starlet will wear the most revealing dress on the red carpet. Screenings are at six theatres, including the Busan Cinema Center (p195).

Busan International Fireworks Festival FIREWORKS
(부산국제불꽃축제; ☎051 501 6051; www.bfo.or.kr/festival_eng; ⏲Oct) The Busan International Fireworks Festival lights the sky with bedazzling night-time choreography of light, colour, lasers and music along Gwangan beach, all set against the glimmering Diamond Bridge.

Sleeping

Seomyeon, at the intersection of two subway lines, is a practical choice for travellers who plan on seeing the sights. Between Haeundae station and the beach, there's a swath of choices, from guesthouses to luxury rooms. Prices here are higher in July and August.

Seomyeon

Blue Backpackers HOSTEL $
(Map p192; ☎051 634 3962; www.bluebackpackers.com; 454-1, Bujeon 2-dong, Busan Jin-gu; dm/r ₩20,000/40,000; ❄@📶; Ⓜ Line 1 or 2 to Seomyeon, Exit 7) Rooms with individual baths, a central location and free toast on the roof make this a great budget choice. It's a 10-minute walk behind Lotte Hotel in Seomyeon.

Ibis Ambassador Busan City Centre Hotel BUSINESS HOTEL $$
(이비스 앰배서더 부산; Map p184; ☎051 930 1110; https://ibis.ambatel.com/busan; d from ₩100,000; ❄@📶; Ⓜ Line 1 to Bujeon, Exit 1) Towering over Bujeon Market (p197), Ibis wins for location (a five-minute walk from Seomyeon), cheery staff and understated, chic rooms, which have LCD TVs. Starbucks and a convenience store are on street level.

Toyoko Inn Busan Seomyeon BUSINESS HOTEL $$
(토요코인 부산서면; Map p192; ☎051 638 1045; www.toyoko-inn.com; d/tw ₩58,300/80,300; ❄@📶🍽; Ⓜ Line 1 or 2 to Seomyeon, Exit 8) One of several branches of the Toyoko Inn in Busan, this property caters to Japanese businessmen and offers rather cramped, no-frills rooms and a modest-but-free breakfast. It's a few minutes' walk from Seomyeon.

Lotte Hotel BUSINESS HOTEL $$$
(롯데 호텔; Map p192; ☎051 810 1000; www.lottehotelbusan.com; d & tw from ₩470,000; ❄@📶🍽; Ⓜ Line 1 or 2 to Seomyeon, Exit 5 or 7) This business-class hotel in Seomyeon has many contemporary rooms, but the older ones are uninspiring and the staff service at times seems gauche. There's a casino here but it's small, though the Japanese tourists don't seem to mind.

Haeundae

Pobi Guesthouse HOSTEL $
(포비 게스트 하우스; Map p189; ☎051 746 7990; www.pobihouse.com; 1394-328, 2nd fl, Jung-dong, Haeundae-gu; dm from ₩15,000; ❄@📶; Ⓜ Line 2 to Haeundae, Exit 3 or 5) Everything a guesthouse needs is here: Haeundae beach locale, knowledgeable staff and a friendly cat. Prices rise on weekends.

Haeundae

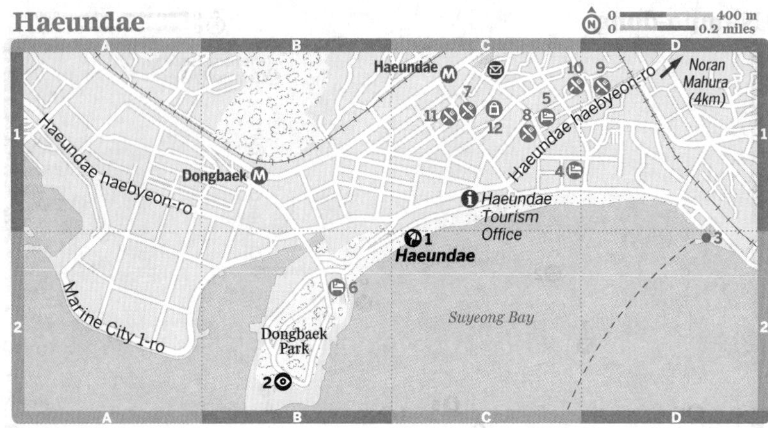

From the metro exit, walk straight and turn left at the Haeundae Market entrance. Walk to the end of the street and turn right. The guesthouse is down the road on the left.

★Westin Chosun Beach Hotel LUXURY HOTEL $$$
(웨스틴 조선 비치 호텔; Map p189; ☎051 749 7000; www.starwoodhotels.com; d from ₩390,000; ❄@🛜🏊; Ⓜ Line 2 to Haeundae, Exit 3 or 5) Busan's oldest international hotel gets better with age. A hint of retro (shaken, not stirred), with modern touches creates a James Bond – à la Sean Connery – sort of dashing cool. It's a little removed from the main action on Haeundae beach, which gives the place a secluded feel.

★Paradise Hotel LUXURY HOTEL $$$
(파라다이스 호텔; Map p189; ☎051 742 2121; www.busanparadisehotel.co.kr; tw from ₩480,000; ❄@🛜🏊; Ⓜ Line 2 to Haeundae, Exit 3 or 5) Fantastic views of Haeundae beach, grovelling service and decent on-site dining make the Paradise stand out. The rooms are somewhat worn and the casino is modest, but amenities like the outdoor rooftop hot spring make up for that.

Gwangan & Yongho

★Hotel1 HOTEL $
(Map p184; ☎051 759 1011; www.hotel1.me; 203 Gwanganhaebyeon-ro; from ₩48,000; ❄🛜) The tiny, minimalist rooms in this slick and serene capsule hotel feature high-key, all-white-marble finishings and stunning views of the beach and Gwangan Bridge. Some sleep up to four people, many have flat-screen TVs, and all include a set of buffalo plaid pyjamas. Hip common spaces include a rooftop terrace and open-air lounge chair cafe on the 1st floor.

Gwangan Hound Hotel BOUTIQUE HOTEL $$
(하운드호텔 광안; Map p184; ☎051 755 0072; www.gwanganhound.wnh.co.kr; 12, Namcheonbada-ro 33beon-gil, Suyeong-gu; d ₩60,000; P❄@🛜; Ⓜ Line 2 to Geumnyeonsan, Exit 3) The Hound Hotel is a boutique hotel that combines design with beautiful views. The Hound's prices are reasonable considering its prime waterfront location, and everything is

Haeundae

Top Sights
1 Haeundae C2

Sights
2 Nurimaru APEC House B2

Activities, Courses & Tours
3 Mipo Wharf D2

Sleeping
4 Paradise Hotel C1
5 Pobi Guesthouse C1
6 Westin Chosun Beach Hotel B2

Eating
7 Boribap & Cheonggukjang C1
8 Gijang Fresh Eel C1
9 Haeundae Somunnan Amso Galbijip D1
10 Milmyeon Jeonmunjeom C1
11 Sulbing C1

Shopping
12 Save Zone Building C1

Nampo-dong

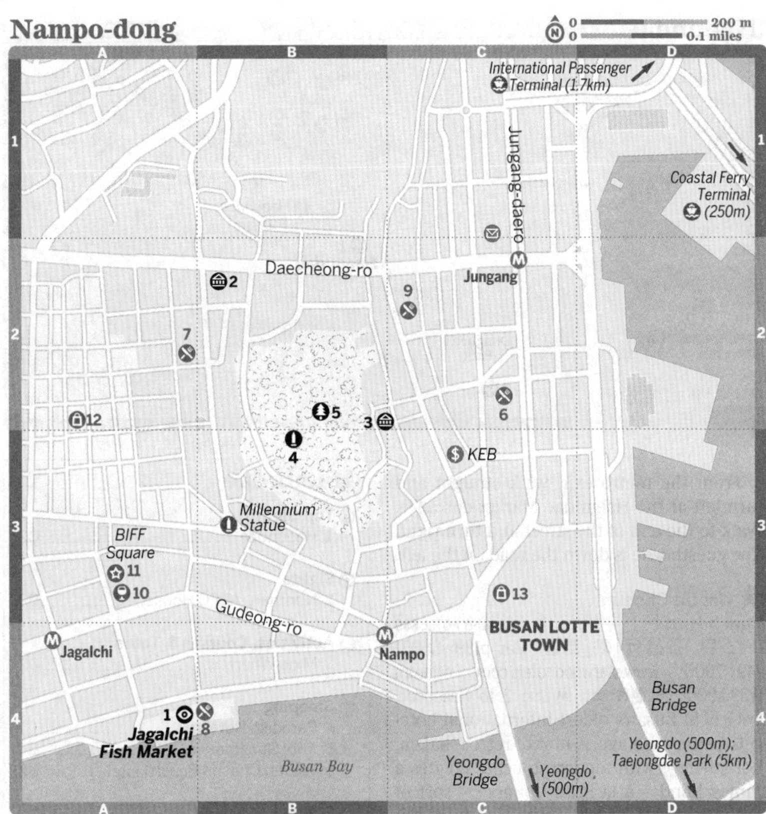

impeccably clean. There's also a rooftop terrace perfect for summer nights.

Dongnae & Geumjeong-san

Nongshim Hotel HOTEL **$$$**
(호텔농심; Map p196; ☎051 550 2100; www.hotelnongshim.com; 23 Geumganggongwon-ro 20beon-gil; tw from ₩360,000; ; Line 1 to Oncheonjang, Exit 1) Perhaps the only full-service hotel in the north end of Busan, business travellers stay here if they require relatively quick access to the airport and the industrial area around Yangsan.

Eating

Unsurprisingly, given its proximity to the ocean, Busan's culinary scene is illuminated by fresh seafood. Traditional Korean restaurants, most of which specialise in only a handful of dishes, are easy to find throughout the city's various districts. In the tourist-frequented areas of Gwangan and Haeundae, you'll find restaurants serving an array of international fare.

Nampo-dong

Ddoongbo Jip KOREAN **$**
(뚱보집, Fatty's House; Map p190; ☎051 246 7466; 3 Jungang-daero 41beon-gil, Jung-gu; jjukumi ₩12,000; ⏲10.30am-11pm; ; Line 1 to Jungang, Exit 1) Open since '82, the name of this hole-in-the-wall literally means 'Fatty's House'. It's famous for its *jjukumi* (web-foot octopus): the spicy, chewy delicacy is grilled over charcoal and often paired with the house *bossam* (grilled pork). The atmosphere is lively and the portions are generous so be ready to eat and drink to your heart's content. Closed every fourth Sunday.

Though there's little English spoken, there are only two or three menu items and big pictures of each, so ordering is easy.

Dolgorae KOREAN $
(돌고래; Map p190; ☎051 246 1825; 17 Junggu-ro 40beon-gil; meals from ₩5000; ⏲7am-10pm; Ⓜ Line 1 to Nampo, Exit 1) The interior looks like a penitentiary, but this humble restaurant near the Gukje Market (p196) serves up tasty standards such as *doenjang jjigae* (된장찌개, soybean stew) and *soondubu jjigae* (순두부찌개, spicy tofu stew). Each dish comes with a kimchi that's sweeter than most. It's down a narrow lane; look for the yellow sign.

★ **Jacky's Seafood** SEAFOOD $$
(돼지초밥 횟집; Map p190; ☎051 246 2594; 52 Jagalchihaean-ro, 2F; ⏲10am-10pm, closed 1st & 3rd Tue of month; Ⓜ Line 1 to Jagalchi, Exit 10) Buying a raw-fish dinner couldn't be easier thanks to Jacky, the affable owner of this seafood restaurant. He speaks fluent English and uses signboards to help customers make smart seasonal food choices. It's on the 2nd floor of the main Jagalchi building.

Myeongseong Chobap SUSHI $$$
(명성 초밥; Map p190; ☎051 807 2950; 520-37 Bujeon-dong; sushi sets from ₩12,000, raw fish ₩30,000-60,000; ⏲10am-10.30pm; Ⓜ Line 1 to Jungang, Exit 3 or 5) No-frills Japanese restaurant specialising in quality sushi and sashimi. Enjoy at a table or saddle up to the bar.

Seomyeon

★ **Yetnal Jjajang** KOREAN $
(옛날짜장; Map p192; ☎051 809 8823; 15 Gaya-daero 784beon-gil; meals from ₩4000; ⏲11am-10pm; Ⓜ Line 1 or 2 to Seomyeon, Exit 7) A sterling example of a successful restaurant owner who won't update the interior. According to superstition, the good fortune a successful shop enjoys could be lost if the interior were changed. Consequently, some shoddy-looking restaurants, like this one, serve great food. See noodles get hand-pulled as you enjoy the excellent *jjajangmyeon* (짜장면, black bean-paste noodles) and *jjambbong* (짬뽕, spicy seafood soup).

Gyeongju Gukbap KOREAN $
(경주국밥; Map p192; ☎051 806 2706; 29 Seomyeon-ro 68beon-gil; soup ₩7000; ⏲24hr; Ⓜ Line 1 or 2 to Seomyeon, Exit 3) It may look like all the other *dwaeji gukbap* (돼지국밥, pork and rice soup) restaurants off Seomyeon's Youth St but, judging by the number of celebrity autographs on the wall, this one is special. Hard to find outside the province, this must-try authentic Busan dish is simple, hearty and straightforward, just like the people of this fair city.

Podo Cheong BARBECUE $
(포도청; Map p192; ☎051 806 9797; 11-7 Jungang-daero; per serving ₩7000; ⏲11am-12.30am; Ⓜ Line 1 or 2 to Seomyeon, Judies Taewha Exit) It's not the best *sutbul galbi* (숯불갈비, charcoal-fired barbecue) restaurant, but it is good. The main draw at this busy place is the backyard barbecue feel in the patio. Lean *moksal* (목살, pork chop) tastes great, though most Koreans will choose *samgyeopsal* (삼겹살, fatty pork).

Haeundae

Milmyeon Jeonmunjeom KOREAN $
(밀면전문점; Map p189; ☎051 743 0392; 21 Jungdong 2-ro 10beon-gil; dishes from ₩6000; ⏲11am-9.30pm) A 10-minute walk stands between Haeundae (p183) beach and a chilly bowl of Busan's signature *milmyeon* (밀면), a spicy noodle soup in an icy, meat-based broth. Order a side of steamy dumplings and enjoy this refreshing meal (much needed after basking on the sand) downstairs where

Seomyeon

Seomyeon

Sleeping
1 Blue Backpackers A4
2 Lotte Hotel A2
3 Toyoko Inn Busan Seomyeon D1

Eating
4 Gyeongju Gukbap B2
5 Podo Cheong C4
6 Yetnal Jjajang B2

Drinking & Nightlife
7 Emo B2
8 Maru B1
9 Output C2
10 Yaman Joint C3

Shopping
11 Judies Taewha C3
12 Lotte Department Store – Seomyeon B2
13 Yeonggwang Bookstore B1

there's floor seating, or on the 2nd floor where there are plenty of tables and chairs.

Sulbing DESSERTS $
(설빙; Map p189; ☎051 746 6411; www.sulbing.com; 20 Gunam-ro; desserts from ₩6000; ⏲11am-10.30pm; Ⓜ Line 2 to Haeundae, Exit 5) No serious foodie should visit Busan without trying *sulbing*, a wonderfully subtle dessert invented in this city. It's a bowl of shaved frozen milk topped with soybean powder and sliced almonds. A splash of condensed milk adds a hint of sweetness. New variations experiment with yoghurt, fruit and chocolate.

From the metro station, walk 100m; it's on the 2nd floor of a building near a small car park. *Sulbing* shops can be found in most busy areas, such as Seomyeon, Kyungsung-Pukyung and Nampo-dong.

Boribap & Cheonggukjang KOREAN $
(보리밥 앤 청국장; Map p189; 9-4 Gunam-ro; meals from ₩6000; ⏲11am-9.30pm Wed-Mon;

Ⓜ Line 2 to Haeundae, Exit 3 or 5) This small shop in Haeundae serves excellent traditional Korean meals featuring stews made from pungent *cheonggukjang* (청국장, fermented soybean paste). The mackerel set (고등어 정식) comes with a fish baked to perfection.

It's on a lane on the north side of the Save Zone building.

★Noran Mahura SEAFOOD $$
(청사포 노란 마후라; Map p184; ☎051 703 3586; 60 Cheongsapo-ro 128beon-gil; set meals from ₩30,000; ⏲2pm-sunrise; Ⓟ) This cosy restaurant, not far from a lighthouse, is where people come for a drink to watch the sunset and unexpectedly stay for the sunrise. Meals include *jogae gui* (조개구이, barbecued shellfish) with an amazing salsa-like sauce. It tastes even better with *soju* (local vodka) at sunrise.

Gijang Fresh Eel KOREAN $$
(기장산곰장어; Map p189; ☎051 742 8201; 42 Gunam-ro; 2-person sets from ₩24,000; ⏲3pm-2am) For adventurous foodies, this restaurant serves eel from the tank in front of the shop. The meat is so fresh it continues to writhe as it sits on the tabletop gas grill. Customers choose one of two sauces: salty or spicy. It's on the lane called Haeunde Market Street; look for the shop with customers waiting in line.

Haeundae Somunnan Amso Galbijip KOREAN $$$
(해운대 소문난 암소 갈비집; Map p189; ☎051 746 0033; 32-10 Jungdong 2-ro 10beon-gil; ribs from ₩36,000; ⏲11.30am-9.30pm; Ⓜ Line 2 to Jungdong, Exit 7) This local favourite has been serving up exquisite *galbi* (beef short ribs) since 1964. Also try the popular *gamja-guksu* (감자국수, potato noodles), which sizzle on the edge of the grill and soak up flavour from the beef drippings. A meat coma awaits.

Gwangan & Yongho

Brunch Cafe Ean CAFE $
(브런치카페 이안; Map p184; ☎051 628 5791; 28 Namcheonbada-ro 22beon-gil; mains from ₩8000; ⏲10am-5pm Mon-Fri, to 9pm Sat & Sun; Ⓜ Line 2 to Geumnyeonsan, Exit 5) If you've grown weary of soup and rice for breakfast, start your day with a sugar fix at this sweet little brunch cafe inside a renovated house. Flip through indie magazine ephemera – English-language selections include the likes of *Kinfolk* – while enjoying crêpes, French toast, pancakes or waffles. For something a bit healthier, there's also a selection of sandwiches, salads and homemade yoghurt.

Sol Taphouse PIZZA $
(솔탭하우스, Slice of Life, Pizzeria Sol; Map p184; ☎051 757 4278; 4F, 153 Gwanganhaebyeon-ro, Gwangan 2(i)-dong, Suyeong-gu; slices from ₩4000; ⏲5pm-1am Mon-Thu, 3pm-2am Fri, noon-2am Sat, noon-midnight Sun; ❄📶🖉👪; Ⓜ Line 2 to Geumnyeonsan, Exit 5) Touted as Busan's best pizza, Sol Taphouse delivers craft beer plus authentic New York–style pizzas from the kitchen of Slice of Life. The classics such as pepperoni and cheese are done well, but Spicy Garlic and The Bronx (pepperoni, bacon, mushroom and veggies) are easily the most popular pizzas. There are at least a dozen local craft beers on tap and views over Gwangalli Beach.

Ecotopia VEGETARIAN $$
(에코토피아; Map p184; ☎051 628 2802; 28 Suyeong-ro; mains from ₩6000; ⏲10am-8pm; Ⓜ Line 2 to Namcheon, Exit 1) A bright, eco-chic

BUSAN'S SPECIALITY FOOD

Busan is a coastal city, so it's not surprising that seafood flavours much of the local cuisine. Raw fish, called *hoe* (회; sounds like 'when' without the 'n'), is a popular dish enjoyed with a group of friends and is widely available and affordably priced (compared to most cities).

A typical *hoe* dinner starts with appetisers such as raw baby octopus still wriggling on the plate. A platter of sliced raw fish is the main course. Fish is dipped into a saucer of *chogochujang* (초고추장), a watery red-pepper sauce, or soy sauce (간장) mixed with wasabi (와사비). The meal is customarily finished with rice and a boiling pot of *maeuntang* (매운탕, spicy fish soup).

Most Koreans say *hoe* has a delicate taste and smooth texture. Western travellers may find the taste bland and chewy. A small platter starting at ₩40,000 is rarely sufficient for a pair of raw-fish fans. Raw fish is often accompanied with *soju* (local vodka).

cafe where everything except the kimchi is vegetarian (blame the fish sauce); most dishes can be prepared vegan as well. Hits include fresh cress tofu bibimbap and a tasty vegetable gratin.

Millak Town Raw Fish Centre SEAFOOD $$
(민락회센터; Map p184; ☎051 752 4545; 1 Millaksubyeon-ro; ⏰10am-1am; Ⓜ Line 2 to Gwangan, Exit 5) Buy a fish for ₩30,000 (or more) and walk upstairs to eat; the woman selling you the fish will indicate which floor. Inside the seating area, your fish will be prepared and served for ₩5000 per person. It's the tall building at the northeast end of Gwangan beach. Little English is spoken here, so you'll need to rely on sign language.

Dongnae & Geumjeong-san

Dongnae Halmae Pajeon KOREAN $$$
(동래 할매 파전; Map p196; ☎051 552 0792; 43-10 Myeongnyun-ro 94beon-gil; meals ₩18,000-35,000; ⏰noon-10pm; Ⓜ Line 1 to Dongnae, Exit 2) With large wooden tables and rich earthy colours, this is one of the most attractive places to experience *pajeon* (파전, green onion pancakes), a classic Busan dish. From the station, walk to the first light. Cross the street, walk right and turn left at the first road beside KT Plaza. Turn right past the motels and you'll see it on the left.

Drinking & Nightlife

Nampo-dong

Fermentation Kitchen COCKTAIL BAR
(발효주방, Barhyo Kitchen; Map p190; ☎010 3041 1320; www.facebook.com/barhyokitchen; 2F, 83 Gwangbok-ro jung-gu; makgeolli from ₩16,000; ⏰noon-12.30am Sun-Thu, to 1.30am Fri & Sat; 📶; Ⓜ Line 1 to Nampo, Exit 3) Fermentation Kitchen is a great place to sample *makgeolli* (traditional Korean rice wine). The restaurant-bar serves special carbonated *makgeolli* in wine glasses alongside modern takes on Korean dishes. While *makgeolli* purists might not prefer the venue's high-end feel, the prices are reasonable.

Seomyeon

★Output CLUB
(Map p192; outputbusan@gmail.com; 36 Seojeon-ro 10beon-gil; ⏰10pm-5am Mon-Sat; Ⓜ Line 2 to Seomyeon, Exit 7) Busan's best underground DJs spin electronic and hip-hop beats for a slick, counter-culture crowd, all aglow in red light.

Yaman Joint LOUNGE
(Map p192; ☎051 803 0420; 18 Jungang-daero 680beinga-gil; ⏰7pm-3am Sun-Thu, to 4am Fri & Sat) Vibes are cheerful and carefree at this Jamaican-themed lounge in Seomyeon, which draws an international crowd with DJs spinning reggae and hip-hop. There's a small stage for live acts (beatboxing, anyone?), plus shisha, colourful frozen cocktails and jerk chicken.

Maru TEAHOUSE
(마루; Map p192; ☎051 803 6797; Saesak-ro 17-1, Jin-gu; ⏰10am-10pm; Ⓜ Line 1 or 2 to Seomyeon, Exit 9) Splendid herbal teas and a warm interior make this an excellent alternative to the sterile sameness of chain coffee shops. The dark and earthy twin flower tea (쌍화차) is a speciality.

Exit the Yeonggwang Bookstore (p197), turn left and walk left around the corner. Look for a green signboard with 마루 150m down the street.

Emo BAR
(이모; Map p192; Bujeon-ro; ⏰8pm-7am; Ⓜ Line 1 or 2 to Seomyeon, Lotte department store Exit) One of many orange *pojangmacha* (tented street stall) tents behind Lotte department store in Seomyeon serving drinks and unusual side dishes, such as grilled chicken anus.

Gwangan & Yongho

★The Commonplace WINE BAR
(문화골목 다반; Map p184; ☎051 625 0730; ⏰5pm-1am; Ⓜ Line 2 to Kyungsung-Pukyong, Exit 3) There's nothing common about this exceptional coffee and wine bar. Stylishly decorated, with an ubercool vibe, comfy sofas and friends dissecting existentialism over a glass of red wine, it's on the 1st floor of the architecturally intriguing Golmok (골목) complex. For something less Sartre and more Chomsky, try Nogada, the downstairs beer bar.

From the metro station, turn right at the first street then left at the second street. It's tucked away on a lane halfway down the road on the right side.

HQ Gwangan BAR
(Map p184; ☎010 7544 8830; ⏰7pm-late Mon-Sat, 4-10pm Sun; Ⓜ Line 2 to Gwangan, Exit 3 or 5) This busy expat bar has cheap shots, pub

BUSAN'S NIGHTLIFE DISTRICTS

The neon burns brightly in the popular nightlife district near Kyungsung and Pukyong National Universities (or 'KPU') and is frequented by hungry, thirsty, frugal students. Seomyeon is the spot for bumpin' dance clubs, while the busy commercial district around Pusan National University is a good bet for low-cost bars. For a taste of expat nightlife, head to Gwangan.

grub, trivia nights, TV sport and a splendid view of Gwangan bridge.

From the metro station, walk to the beach road and turn left at the Lotteria fast-food restaurant.

Galmegi Pub MICROBREWERY
(Map p184; ☎051 611 9658; www.galmegibrewing.com; 3-4 Namcheon 2-dong, Suyeong-gu; beers from ₩5000; ⏰6pm-midnight Sun-Thu, to 1am Fri & Sat; Ⓜ Line 2 to Geumyeonsan, Exit 3) Craving craft beer? Busan's first craft brewery has an evolving menu, including black, blonde and pale ales. There are five other locations in Busan, but this one has the advantage of being close to Gwangan beach.

From the metro exit, spin 180 degrees, turn right at the first street and walk towards the beach road. It's near Starbucks.

Eva's Gwangan BAR
(Map p184; ☎051 728 5653; 35 Namcheonbada-ro; ⏰6pm-4am; Ⓜ Line 2 to Geumnyeonsan, Exit 3) Weary English instructors flock to this breezy, beach-vibe bar to unwind over cheap draught beer after a hard day of teaching phonics.

Thursday Party BAR
(Map p184; 193 Gwanganhaebyeon-ro; ⏰6pm-5am; Ⓜ Line 2 to Gwangan, Exit 3 or 5) This bar is a regular date spot for the university crowd because of the cheap draught, free curry-flavoured popcorn and pounding K-Pop. There are two locations on the Gwangan beach road, plus branches in Seomyeon, Haeundae and Kyungsung-Pukyoung.

Beached SPORTS BAR
(Map p184; 177 Gwanganhaebyeon-ro; ⏰4pm-late; Ⓜ Line 2 to Geumnyeonsan, Exit 1) Craig, the owner, calls it a dive bar with the best view of the Gwangan bridge. And he's right. A busy expat tavern, it's one of the few places in town to watch rugby, drink Kiwi beer and listen to Led Zeppelin.

From the metro station, turn right at the first corner, walk down to the beach road and look left.

★ Entertainment

☆ Nampo-dong

Megabox Busan Theatre CINEMA
(메가박스부산극장; Map p190; ☎1544 0070; www.megabox.co.kr; 36 BIFF Gwangjang-ro; tickets ₩6500) Screening Korean and a handful of international films, this cinema is opposite the famous *hotteok* (fried, syrup-filled pancakes) carts in Nampo-dong.

☆ Haeundae

Busan Cinema Center CINEMA
(영화의전당; Map p184; ☎051 780 6000; www.dureraum.org; tickets adult/youth ₩6000/4000; ⏰9am-9pm; Ⓜ Line 2 to Centum City, Exit 12) An important venue for the Busan International Film Festival (p188), this complex plays a mix of Korean and foreign films in its smaller venues. The magnificent complex has the world's longest cantilevered structure. The 127,000 LED lights streaming across its concave surface create an urban architectural spectacle at night.

☆ Gwangan & Yongho

Monk JAZZ
(Map p184; http://cafe.daum.net/clubmonk; 25 Yongso-ro; ⏰7pm-2am Mon-Sat; Ⓜ Line 2 to Kyungsung-Pukyong, Exit 3) The sweet sound of live jazz fills the room most nights from 9pm to 11pm with professional Korean performers – expats jam Wednesday nights.

From the station, turn right at the first street. Walk to the third intersection; it's on the right.

Daeyeon Cinema Theatre CINEMA
(대영시네마, CGV Daeyeon; Map p184; www.cgv.co.kr; 305 Suyeong-ro; Ⓜ Line 2 to Kyungsung Univ-Pukyong Natl Univ, Exit 6) Catch a film or escape the summer heat for a couple of hours. Shows Hollywood films in English with Korean subtitles, as well as Korean films.

Geumjeong-san

Top Sights

1 Beomeo-sa.....A1

Sights

2 Geumgang Park.....A3
3 Geumgang Park Cable Car.....A4
4 Geumjeong Fortress.....A2
5 Seokbul-sa.....A4

Sleeping

6 Nongshim Hotel.....B4

Eating

7 Dongnae Halmae Pajeon.....B4

Shopping

8 Lotte Department Store – Dongnae.....B4

Transport

9 Busan Central Bus Terminal.....B1
10 Busan Express Bus Terminal.....B1
11 Busan Intercity Bus Terminal.....B1

☆ Dongnae & Geumjeong-san

Lotte Giants BASEBALL

(롯데 자이언츠; Map p184; ☎051 590 9000; www.giantsclub.com/eng; 45 Sajik-ro; tickets from ₩7000; Ⓜ Line 3 to Sports Complex, Exit 9) The Lotte Giants baseball experience inside Sajik stadium neatly captures the essence of Busan: boisterous, fun-loving and occasionally naughty (especially when the visiting pitcher holds the man on first base). Expect cheap tickets, no limit on how much food and drink fans can bring in, and good fun with the orange bags. From the metro station, walk towards HomePlus.

Busan IPark FOOTBALL

(부산 아이파크; Map p184; ☎051 941 1100; www.busanipark.com; best seat ₩10,000; Ⓜ Line 1 to Dongdaesin Station, Exit 1) Busan IPark, the city's pro football team, plays 19 home matches between March and November at Gudeok Stadium. Games are thinly attended, so getting a good seat won't be a problem.

Shopping

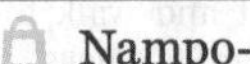

Nampo-dong

Lotte Department Store – Gwangbok DEPARTMENT STORE

(Map p190; ☎051 678 2500; www.lotteshopping.com; 20-1, 7-ga, Jungang-dong; ⏰10.30am-8pm; Ⓜ Line 1 to Nampo, Exit 10) Branch of Korea's biggest department store in Nampo-dong.

Gukje Market MARKET

(국제시장; Map p190; ☎051 245 7389; Sinchang-dong 4(sa)-ga; ⏰8.30am-8.30pm; Ⓜ Line 1 to Jagalchi, Exit 7) West of Nampo-dong, this traditional market has hundreds of small booths with a staggering selection of items, from leather goods to Korean drums.

Seomyeon

Yeonggwang Bookstore BOOKS

(영광도서; Map p192; ☎051 816 9500; www.ykbook.com; 10 Seomyeonmunhwa-ro; Ⓜ Line 1 or 2 to Seomyeon, Exit 9) One the city's oldest bookshops, with a decent selection of English books.

Bujeon Market MARKET
(부전시장; Map p184; ☎051 818 1091; 23 Jungang-daero 783beon-gil; ⏰4am-8pm; Ⓜ Line 1 to Bujeon, Exit 5) You could easily spend an hour getting lost in this enormous traditional market specialising in produce, seafood and knick-knacks.

Lotte Department Store – Seomyeon DEPARTMENT STORE
(Map p192; ☎051 810 2500; www.lotteshopping.com; 772 Gaya-daero; ⏰10.30am-8pm; Ⓜ Line 2 to Seomyeon, Lotte Exit) The Lotte department store branch located in Seomyeon.

Judies Taewha MALL
(쥬디스태화; Map p192; ☎051 804 9700; 694 Jungang-daero; Ⓜ Line 1 to Seomyeon, Exit 2) An old department store converted into a vertical shopping mall.

Haeundae

Shinsegae Centum City DEPARTMENT STORE
(신세계 센텀시티; Map p184; ☎1588 1234; www.shinsegae.com; 35 Centumnam-daero; ⏰10.30am-8pm; Ⓜ Line 2 to Centum City, Shinsegae Exit) The world's largest shopping complex – bigger than Macy's in New York – has everything you'd expect in a temple of commerce. There's a skating rink, indoor golf driving range, shops with seemingly every brand name in the universe and a place to recuperate – Spa Land (p188) – before you do it again.

Lotte Department Store – Centum City DEPARTMENT STORE
(롯데백화점 센텀시티점; Map p184; ☎051 730 2500; www.lotteshopping.com; 1496 U-dong, Haeundae-gu; ⏰10.30am-8.30pm; Ⓜ Line 2 to Centum City, Lotte Exit) Need to buy a $5000 handbag? You can probably find one at this Lotte outlet in Haeundae beside Shinsegae.

Save Zone Building DEPARTMENT STORE
(Map p189; ☎051 740 9000; www.savezone.co.kr; 21 Gunam-ro 29beon-gil; ⏰10am-10pm) A local discount department store.

Dongnae & Geumjeong-san

Lotte Department Store – Dongnae DEPARTMENT STORE
(Map p196; ☎051 605 2500; www.lotteshopping.com; 502-3 Oncheon-dong; ⏰10.30am-8pm; Ⓜ Line 1 to Myeongnyun, Exit 1) Department store in Dongnae. From the metro station, take the overhead crosswalk.

ℹ Information

MONEY

Most banks exchange currency, though the level of service varies. For international withdrawals, your best bet is a **KB Kookmin Bank** (Map p192; ☎051 817 8131; 2 Saessak-ro) ATM. Look for the yellow asterisk and 'b' logo, and the 'global' ATM inside. **Busan Bank** (Map p192; ☎051 803 0851; www.busanbank.co.kr; 1 Saessak-ro; ⏰9am-4pm) and **KEB** (외환은행; Map p190; www.keb.co.kr/main/en; 18 Gwangbok-ro) are local banks with branches all over the city. If you need to get US dollars outside banking hours, go to Nampo-dong and look for the old women sitting on chairs whispering 'changee'.

There are currency exchange desks in both the **domestic** (Map p184; ⏰6am-4pm) and **international** (Map p184; ⏰6am-9pm) terminals at Gimhae International Airport (www.airport.co.kr/gimhaeeng/index.do).

POST

The **main post office branch** (부산 중앙 우체국; Map p190; ☎051 600 3000; www.koreapost.go.kr; 63 Jungang-daero; ⏰9am-6pm Mon-Fri; Ⓜ Line 1 to Jungang, Exit 9) is near the ferry terminal; there's also one in **Haeundae** (우체국; Map p189; ☎051 746 0100; www.koreapost.go.kr; 11 Jungdong 1-ro; ⏰9am-6pm).

TOURIST INFORMATION

Busan Station Tourism Office (부산역 관광 안내소; Map p184; ☎051 441 6565; 206 Jungang-daero; ⏰9am-8pm; Ⓜ Line 1 to Busan station, Exit 8 or 10) Maps and helpful staff on the 2nd floor.

Gimhae Airport – Domestic Terminal Info (Map p184; ☎051 974 3774; ⏰6am-11pm or last arrival) Round kiosk with maps and tourist pamphlets.

Gimhae Airport – International Terminal Info (Map p184; ☎051 974 3772; ⏰6am-11pm or last arrival) Near exit gate two – look for the red and blue signs.

Haeundae Tourism Office (해운대 관광안내소; Map p189; ☎051 749 4335; http://eng.haeundae.go.kr; 11 Jung-dong2ro; ⏰9am-6pm; Ⓜ Line 2 to Haeundae, Exit 3 or 5) Offers lots of tourist informational material.

Immigration Office (부산출입국관리사무소; Map p184; ☎Immigration Contact Centre 1345, 051 461 3091; 17-26 Jungangdong 4-ga, Jung-gu; ⏰9am-6pm; Ⓜ Line 1 to Busan Station, Exit 2) Visa and immigration services.

Kangsan Travel (Map p184; ☎051 747 0031; www.kangsantravel.com; 20 Centum 3-ro; ⏰9am-noon & 1-6pm Mon-Fri; Ⓜ Line 2 to Jangsan, Exit 9) Agency offering services in English.

Getting There & Away

Domestic travellers usually come to Busan via KTX train service, though there are good bus connections from most major destinations. International travellers can fly directly to Gimhae International Airport (p395), 27km west of Busan's city centre.

AIR

From Gimhae International Airport (p395) there are frequent international flights to Japan and regional cities such as Beijing, Hong Kong, Bangkok, Chiang Mai and Cebu.

On domestic routes, the Busan–Seoul flight on Korean Air, Asiana or AirBusan (one hour, every 30 minutes from 7am to 9pm) usually requires reservations on weekends and holidays. Most flights from Busan to Seoul land at Gimpo airport, which has few international connections. If you're flying out of the country, catch the A'REX (p92), which runs between Seoul station and Incheon International with a stop at Gimpo airport. Flights also connect Busan and Jeju-do (one hour, every 30 to 90 minutes from 7am to 8pm).

BOAT

The **International Passenger Terminal** (부산항 국제여객터미널; ☎051 400 1200; www.busanpa.com; 45-39 Choryang-dong; ⊙8am-11.30pm; Ⓜ Line 1 to Choryang, Exit 6) is about a 15-minute walk from Choryang subway station. From Exit 6, turn left at the first intersection and follow the signs for the terminal. Alternatively, use Exit 4 and pick up a shuttle (adult/child ₩1200/300). Purchase tickets on the 3rd floor. Several companies operate services to various Japanese ports.

Ferries to Jeju-do (one way from ₩51,500) depart Busan's **Coastal Ferry Terminal** (부산항 연안여객터미널; ☎051 400 3399; www.busanpa.com; 24 Chungjang-daero; Ⓜ Line 1 to Jungang, Exit 10) on Monday, Wednesday and Friday at 7pm and arrive 12 hours later.

BUS

Buses run every 30 to 60 minutes from the airport's domestic terminal to regional cities, including Gyeongju (₩11,000, 1½ hours), Changwon (₩8300, two hours) and Ulsan (₩7900, two hours).

Dongbu Terminal Departures

DESTINATION	PRICE (₩)	DURATION (HR)	FREQUENCY
Gyeongju	4800	¾	twice hourly
Pohang	8100	1½	4 per hour
Samcheok	28,200	4	4 daily
Seoul	37,700	4½	twice hourly
Tongdo-sa	2200	½	3 per hour

Intercity (부산 시외 버스터미널; Map p196; ☎051 508 9966; www.dbterminal.co.kr; Ⓜ Line 1 to Nopo, Exit 3) and **express** (부산 고속 버스터미널; Map p196; ☎051 508 9201; www.kobus.co.kr; Ⓜ Line 1 to Nopo, Exit 3) buses depart from the **Central Bus Terminal** (부산종합버스터미널; Map p196; www.bxt.co.kr; Ⓜ Line 1 to Nopo, Exit 3) at Nopo-dong station.

Seobu Terminal Departures

DESTINATION	PRICE (₩)	DURATION (HR)	FREQUENCY
Gohyeon	7900	1½	twice hourly
Hadong	11,000	2½	hourly
Jinju	7700	1½	3 per hour
Namhae	11,900	2½	at least hourly
Ssanggyae-sa	14,000	3½	10am & 4pm
Tongyeong	11,500	1¾	2 per hour

Seobu intercity bus terminal (부산 서부 시외버스터미널; Map p184; ☎051 559 1000; www.busantr.com; Ⓜ Line 2 to Sasang, Exit 3 or 5) is outside Sasang station, with street-level access through a department store.

TRAIN

Most trains depart from and arrive at Busan's central station. There are also departures from Gupo, a western station with easy access to metro Line 3 that saves the hassle of going to the city centre. Between Busan and Seoul (adult/child ₩59,800/29,900, every 30 to 60 minutes), KTX is the quickest service, with most trips taking three hours or less.

Saemaul services take five hours to reach Seoul (adult/child ₩42,600/21,300, eight daily). The *Mugunghwa* service is only about 30 minutes slower and quite a bit cheaper (adult/child ₩28,600/14,300, 14 daily).

Busan's smallest station, Bujeon, services regional cities and towns such as Gyeongju (adult/child ₩6600/3300, 20 daily), Hadong (adult/child ₩11,000/5500, four daily) and Mokpo (adult/child ₩25,100/12,500, 6.25am daily). Check **Korea Rail** (www.letskorail.com) online to confirm fares and schedules.

If you're heading to Japan, a Korea-Japan Co-Ticket (aka Korea-Japan Joint Ticket) provides discounted travel between the two countries. It covers Korea Rail services, the ferry crossing between Busan and Fukuoka or Shimonoseki and Japan Rail services. The application procedure is slightly complicated and tickets must be reserved seven days in advance; see www.korailtours.com for details.

Getting Around

TO/FROM THE AIRPORT

Bus A limousine bus from Gimhae airport runs to Seomyeon and the major hotels in Haeundae (₩7000, one hour, every 30 minutes). A second route goes to Seomyeon, Busan station and Nampo-dong (₩6000, one hour, every 40 minutes). The most economical link between the airport and city (₩1200) is bus 307 from Gupo station.

Taxi A taxi from the airport to Seomyeon takes 30 minutes and costs between ₩20,000 and ₩35,000 depending on traffic. A 10-minute taxi from Deokcheon station costs ₩8000.

Train The Busan–Gimhae Light Rail Line connects Sasang and Daejeo stations with the airport (₩1400, 15 minutes). Buy a chip from the vending machine. Put the chip on the magnetic reader when entering the turnstile. When leaving the station, put the chip in the turnstile.

BUS

Busan's bus system is extensive and offers access to parts of the city and surrounding areas that aren't serviced by the handful of metro lines, such as Songdo Beach and Taejongdae Park. It's typical for travellers to use them; adult cash fares are ₩1300/1800 for regular/express buses. ₩100 discounts are available when paying with a Hanaro or other transport card.

SUBWAY

Busan's four-line subway uses a two-zone fare system that costs ₩1400 per ride for one zone and ₩1600 for longer trips if using single-journey paper tickets; a one-day pass costs ₩4500. Using a rechargeable transport card like Hanaro (₩6000 plus travel credits, available at subway vending machines) is handy for long stays – you get a small discount on fares and avoid the hassle of buying a ticket for each trip, and can also use the card on local buses, the Busan–Gimhae Light Rail and taxis. Subway trains generally run between 5.10am and 12.30am.

TAXI

Taxis are plentiful and easy to hail on the street. Basic fares start at ₩3300 (with a 20% night premium). Avoid black-and-red deluxe taxis if possible, because the fares can be high.

TRAIN

The Busan–Gimhae Light Rail and the Donghae Line commuter train are convenient ways to get to the outer stretches of Busan. The Busan–Gimhae Light Rail (₩1400 to ₩1600) connects with subway Line 2 at Sasang station and Line 3 at Daejeo station. The Donghae Line (₩1400 to ₩1600) runs from Bujeon Station in Seomyeon along the coast to Ilgwang (with plans to expand to Ulsan sometime in 2019), and connects with subway Line 2 at BEXCO.

FERRY DEPARTURES FOR JAPAN

COMPANY	DESTINATION	DEPARTURES	FREQUENCY	DURATION (HR)	PRICE (₩), ADULT, ONE WAY
Dae-Ma (www.daea.com)	Izuhara; Hitakatsu	9.30am; 9.10am	Tue, Thu, Sat, Sun; Mon, Wed, Fri, Sat	1¼; 2¼	from 85,000
Future (www.kobee.co.kr)	Fukuoka; Izuhara; Hitakatsu	8.30am	daily	3; 2; 1¼	115,000; 85,000; 75,000
JR Kyushu (www.jrbeetle.co.kr)	Fukoka; Hitakatsu	8am & 3.30pm; 12.15pm	daily	3; 1¼	140,000; 80,000
Kampu (www.kampuferry.co.jp)	Shimonoseki	9pm	3 per week	11	from 88,000
Korea Ferry (www.koreaferry.kr)	Fukoka	10.30pm	6 per week	11½	from 90,000
PanStar (www.panstar.co.kr)	Osaka	3pm	Tue, Thu, Sun	19	from 140,000
Pukwan (www.pukwan.co.kr)	Shimonoseki	9pm	3 per week	11	from 95,000

Gajisan Provincial Park

Vast in both sprawl and beauty, Gaijisan Provincial Park (가지산 도립공원) stuns with lush forest against craggy terrain. Known as the 'Yeongnam Alps', the park is part of the Baekdudaegan range and divided into sections anchored by four Buddhist temples, which serve as the entrances to the network of trails. In autumn, the turning foliage paints the park with bold, warm colours and summiting its highest peak, Gajisan (가지산, Mt Gaji; 1240m), rewards climbers with sweeping mountain views.

Sights

Seoknam-sa BUDDHIST TEMPLE
(석남사; www.seoknamsa.or.kr; 557 Seongam-ro; park entrance adult/youth ₩1700/1300; ⏲3am-8pm; 🚇Eonyang terminal) This temple is a visual masterpiece filled with enchanting contours, colours and contrasts. It begins at the park entrance with an 800m walk through a heavily wooded forest, where patches of sunlight struggle to break through the thick canopy of foliage. Home to female monks, the temple is just beyond a fork in the path that is the starting point for a 6.4km hike up Gajisan.

From Busan's Central Bus Terminal, catch a bus to the small but confusing Eonyang terminal (₩3300, 35 minutes, every 20 minutes) and buy a ticket for Seoknam-sa (bus 1713, ₩2000, 20 minutes, every 15 to 30 minutes). On the way back, bus 807 is another option to Eonyang (₩1200, every 15 to 30 minutes). It stops outside the bus terminal.

Tongdo-sa BUDDHIST TEMPLE
(통도사; ☎055 382 7182; www.tongdosa.or.kr; 108 Tongdosa-ro; adult/youth/child ₩3000/1500/1000; ⏲8.30am-5.30pm; 🚇Line 1 to Nopo, Exit 3) Tongdo-sa is noted for a *sari,* a crystalline substance thought to develop inside the body of a pure monk. The *sari* is enshrined in a fenced area and cannot be seen. It is a focal point of devotion, which is why Tongdo-sa does not have a Buddha statue in the main hall, a rarity in Korea. Tongdo-sa operates an English-language templestay program. Inside the temple compound, stop by the Tongdo-sa Museum.

Buses to Tongdo-sa depart Busan's Central Bus Terminal (₩2200, 25 minutes, every 20 minutes) and stop at Sinpyeong bus terminal. Exit the terminal through the back lot, turn right and walk 10 minutes to the gate.

Tongdo-sa Museum MUSEUM
(통도사 성보 박물관; www.tongdomuseum.or.kr; adult/youth ₩2000/1000; ⏲9am-5pm Wed-Mon; 🚇Line 1 to Nopo, Exit 3) This museum inside the Tongdo-sa (p200) compound houses a collection of Buddhist paintings with limited viewing hours (9am to 11.30am and 1pm to 5pm) to minimise light exposure. There are 30,000 artefacts with full-day access, including gongs, roof tiles and wooden printing blocks. Before entering, place your shoes at the front door.

Sleeping & Eating

Camping, motels and pensions can be found near Seoknam-sa temple. There are Korean restaurants in the rural areas outside of Seoknam-sa and Tongdo-sa.

Getting There & Away

To get to the eastern (Yangsan) side of the park from Busan, take the intercity bus (₩6980, one hour) to Ulsan's Eonyang terminal. From there, it's a 35-minute ride on bus 1713 (₩3300) to Seoknam-Sa, where there is a trail to enter the park.

Geojedo

☎055 / POP 261,371

Connected to the mainland by the 8km Busan–Geoje Fixed Link bridge and tunnel, Korea's second-largest island, Geoje-do (거제도), is famous for its massive shipbuilding industry and natural beauty. The coastal scenery varies between pastoral and industrial, with the best views in and around Haegeumgang (해금강). Geoje-do has one of the highest income levels in Korea, which accounts for the high cost of travelling in some parts of the island and the surprisingly intense traffic congestion in central Geoje-si. Geoje-si is sometimes called Gohyeon, a name that refers to the city's central area.

Sights

Haegeumgang NATIONAL PARK
(해금강) Haegeumgang, a collection of breathtaking rocky islets and a jagged coastline, forms part of the Hallyeo Maritime National Park – famous for life-affirming sunrises, stirring sunsets and exhilarating drives. About an hour by car from Geoje-si, the road to Haegeumgang is filled with twists and turns requiring caution as drivers occasionally stop in unusual places to admire ocean views or buy snacks from roadside vendors.

Oedo Botania ISLAND

(외도; ☎070 7715 3330; www.oedobotania.com; adult/youth/child ₩11,000/8000/5000; ; 11) Geojedo's busiest tourist attraction is a tiny island-sized botanical garden 4km off the coast. It's popular with Korean travellers, but unless you absolutely adore manicured gardens, long waits (if ferries are cancelled or delayed) and pushy lines, consider avoiding the place.

By car from Geoje-si, follow the road signs to Jangsangpo and look for the sign pointing to Oedo terminal.

Historic Park of Geoje POW Camp MUSEUM

(거제도 포로수용소 유적공원; ☎055 639 8125; www.pow.or.kr; adult/youth/child ₩7000/5000/3000; ⊙9am-6pm Apr-Oct, to 5pm Nov-Mar) In Geoje-si, this modest but worthwhile museum provides hard-to-find information about the POW camp experience during the Korean War. Just by the gate is a tourist info centre that has maps but no English-speaking staff. The new Geoje Tour Monorail is accessed here.

From the Gohyeon intercity bus terminal, it's a 30-minute walk; a ₩5000 taxi ride will get you here in a few minutes.

Hakdong Mongdol Beach BEACH

(학동 몽돌해변; Geojejungang-ro, Hakdong Jct) The black-pebble beach in Hakdong is a cosy destination for family outings and romantic getaways, about 30 minutes by car from Geoje-si. Summer crowds flock to the 1.2km-long beach to laze on the bumpy rocks (bring a thick blanket), throw stones and fish off the pier. The rest of the year is rather quiet.

Activities

Geoje Tour Monorail RAIL

(☎055 639 0650; 16 Gyeryong-ro, Historic Park of Geoje POW Camp; incl park entry adult/youth/child ₩14,000/12,000/9000; ⊙9am-5pm Apr-Oct, to 4pm Nov-Mar) Opened in March 2018, this monorail – accessed from inside the Historic Park of Geoje POW Camp – travels up the Gyeryong Mountain ridge and offers views of the Hallyeo Sea and the remains of the camp from an upper observation deck. It's a 25-minute ride each way.

Sleeping

Hotel B HOTEL $$

(☎055 635 9797; www.hotelb.net; 56-2 Seomun-ro; r from ₩55,000; P@) If you need to stay overnight in Geoje-si, try this property with stylish rooms with different wallpaper themes. The larger, more expensive rooms have spacious bathrooms. It's one of the taller buildings behind the bus terminal.

Geoje Tiffany Pension MOTEL $$

(거제 티파니 리조텔; ☎055 636 8866; http://geojetiffany.co.kr; r from ₩50,000;) Hakdong has an impressive selection of motels of varying quality, some closer to the beach than others. Geoje Tiffany Pension is beside the beach. It's nothing fancy; just nice, clean rooms with bathroom and a friendly owner who speaks English. It's a short walk to nearby restaurants.

Samsung Hotel HOTEL $$$

(☎055 631 2114; www.sghotel.co.kr; 80 Jangpyeong 3-ro; r from ₩245,000; P@) Here's the business-class hotel that engineers, technicians and ship-industry professionals choose when visiting Geojedo. Not far from the Samsung shipyard, this upmarket property is one of the few hotels in Gyeongsangnam-do with an indoor swimming pool.

Palm Tree Pension PENSION $$$

(☎055 636 2241, 010 3566 6645; www.palmtree.kr; 1063 Geoje-daero; r standard/deluxe ₩120,000/300,000;) Beautiful and private, the Palm Tree is a gorgeous pension with balconies overlooking the sea. The snazzy deluxe rooms have kitchenettes and spas. It's in a secluded area a couple of kilometres from Hakdong's black pebble beach. About 30 minutes by car along the coastal road from Geoje-si, look for the property with a windmill.

Eating

Green Restaurant KOREAN $$

(그린 식육 식당; ☎055 636 7535; 933 Geoje-daero; servings from ₩9500) If the dozen-or-so raw-fish restaurants near the black pebble beach (p201) in Hakdong don't look appealing, try the barbecued pork at this small shop. Both *samgyupsal* (삼겹살, fatty pork belly) and *moksal* (목살, pork chop) are available.

Getting There & Away

From the Gohyeon intercity bus terminal, there are frequent connections to Busan's Seobu terminal (₩7900, 1½ hours, every 10 to 30 minutes), Tongyeong (₩3400, 25 minutes, every 20 minutes) and Jinju (₩6900, one hour, hourly).

Getting Around

Outside Geoje-si, the island's biggest town, public transport is not well developed. Although there are local buses, connections are inconvenient, so personal transport on the island is recommended. It's relatively easy to drive to and from Busan thanks to the Busan–Geoje Fixed Link bridge, but you'll have to pay the ₩10,000 toll for cars.

Tongyeong

055 / POP 137,208

On the southern tip of Goseong Peninsula, Tongyeong (통영) is a coastal city wedged between Namhaedo and Geojedo. Most of the picturesque sights are in and around Gangguan (강구안), a pretty harbour made for sunset strolls. Visiting Tongyeong's truly spectacular sights – any one of the 151 islands dotting the coastline – usually requires an overnight stay and an early-morning ferry departure to some of the most pristine territory in the province.

Sights

★Saryangdo ISLAND

(사량도; 055 647 0147) Jagged ridges, 400m-high peaks, ropes, ladders and awe-inspiring views await travellers looking for a challenging hike. Most travellers disembark the ferry (return ₩10,000, 40 minutes, departs 7.30am, 9.30am, noon, 2pm and 4.10pm) on Saryandgo and catch a bus to the other side of the island to begin the five-hour trek.

From Tongyeong's bus terminal, catch bus 10-5 (₩1200, 40 minutes) or a taxi (₩14,000, 20 minutes) to the Gaochi ferry terminal (가오치 사량도행 여객터미널).

Bijindo ISLAND

(비진도) Bijindo is actually two islands joined together by a sand bridge, which makes for some outstanding photography. It's a popular getaway destination for couples and families looking for a place to picnic amid sandy beaches and a quiet sense of bliss. Weekends and summer months can be busy and less blissful. Local accommodation is available but expensive. The ferry crossing (return ₩17,250, departs 7am, 11am and 2.30pm) takes one hour.

Hallyeosudo Cable Car CABLE CAR

(한려수도 케이블카; 055 649 3804; http://cablecar.ttdc.kr; 205 Balgae-ro; one way/return adult ₩7500/11,000, child ₩5000/7000; 9.30am-5.30pm Sep-Mar, to 6pm Apr-Aug, closed 2nd & 4th Mon of month; 141) Stretching out 1975m, this is Korea's longest cable-car ride. Near the top of Mireuk-san (461m), the view of Hallyeo Maritime National Park is dramatic. If you're up for a two-hour hike, buy a one-way ticket, walk down the back end of the mountain and head towards the Undersea Tunnel (p203). Pick up a map from the booth near the ticket window. If you're coming here on the weekend, arrive early because wait times can be long.

The cable-car ticket office is a ₩7000 taxi ride from the passenger ferry terminal and ₩10,000 from the intercity bus terminal.

Yeonhwado ISLAND

(연화도; 055 641 6184) Peaceful and remote, Yeonhwado is a small island ideal for three-hour hikes. From the ferry (return ₩18,400, one hour, departs 6.30am, 9.30am, 11am, 1pm and 3pm), follow the path left past the brown cow up to the mountain ridge where you'll find Yongmeori, a spectacular arrangement of rocks that look like a dragon's head. There are a couple of *minbak* (private homes with rooms for rent) here, but Yeonhwado is usually a day trip.

Somaemuldo ISLAND

(소매물도; 055 645 3717) Sharp cliffs and crashing waves on dramatic rock formations make this a worthwhile journey. At low tide, walk across the land bridge and climb to the lighthouse. Some accomodation is available on the island. The ferry (return ₩16,050, 1½ hours) departs Gangguan at 7am, 11am and 2.30pm.

Nammang-san MOUNTAIN

(남망산; 055 648 8417; 139 Nammang-gil) Set aside an hour or more to enjoy the views atop this mountain beside Gangguan harbour. On the way up, you'll pass a modest sculpture park with 15 pieces of art. Up top there's a statue of Yi Sun-shin and a pavilion providing panoramic harbour views.

Turtle Ship Replicas HISTORIC SITE

(거북선; Gangguan Harbour; adult/youth ₩2000/1500; 9am-6pm, to 5pm in winter) Towards the north end of the Gangguan promenade, there are four turtle ships. Definitely worth a look. While ducking your head inside the ship, try to imagine how 50 sailors and 70 oarsmen might have functioned in these cramped quarters.

Gangguan HARBOUR
(강구안; ☎055 650 4681; Jungang-dong Tonyeong-si) Gangguan is not the only harbour in the city, but it's the prettiest. It's also a busy pier anchored by a promenade that serves multiple civic functions, including dock, basketball court and picnic ground for package-tour travellers who aren't squeamish about a mid-morning *soju* (local vodka) pick-me-up.

Jungang Live Fish Market MARKET
(중앙활어시장; ☎055 649 5225; 14-16 Jungangsijang 1-gil; ⊙8am-8pm) Sure there's lots of fish, but this open-air market, filled with grannies selling food out of plastic tubs, is a good place to buy fruit and veggies before heading out on a ferry trip. The front entrance is near Gangguan harbour.

Undersea Tunnel TUNNEL
(해저 터널; ☎055 650 0582; ⊙24hr) FREE The journey to the Undersea Tunnel is more interesting than the sight itself. Constructed in the early 1930s, the 483m-long tunnel connects both sides of Seoho Bay (서호만). Not much more than a concrete corridor, it does make for a pleasant evening stroll towards the Tongyeong Grand Bridge.

Activities

Tongyeong Seawater Land BATHHOUSE
(통영 해수랜드; ☎055 645 7700; www.tysealand.co.kr; 297 Tongyeonghaean-ro; public bath/jjimjilbang adult ₩6000/10,000, youth ₩5000/9000; ⊙24hr) This is a 24-hour spa and *jjimjilbang* (sauna), so guests can sleep here overnight. It's incredible value for budget travellers, but don't expect a good rest: you're on a hard floor surrounded by cranky babies, drunken snorers and people tiptoeing to the toilet all night. On the bright side, take a bath any time you want.

Sleeping

Nexon MOTEL $$
(넥슨모텔; ☎055 643 6568; 6 Dongchung 3-gil; r from ₩50,000; P ❄ @) The modern design and central location make this motel one of the nicer properties around Gangguan. Decent restaurants and waterfront strolls are minutes from your room. The passenger ferry terminal is across the street, which is ideal for travellers catching an early ferry to a nearby island.

WORTH A TRIP

FERRY EXCURSIONS

It's impossible to describe the full range of ferry trips to the magical islands around Tongyeong. Excursions to Yeonhwado, Bijindo and Somaemuldo depart the passenger ferry terminal (p204) near Gangguan harbour. The ferry to Saryangdo departs the Gaochi terminal in the northwest part of the city. Be sure to pack enough food; groceries on the islands are scant or expensive.

Napoli Motel MOTEL $$
(나폴리모텔; ☎055 646 0202; www.tynapoli.co.kr; 355 Tonyeonghaen-ro; r from ₩50,000; ❄ @) This motel by the northern end of the Gangguan promenade has fairly modern rooms with harbour views. Expect to pay ₩70,000 and up in July and August.

Eating

★Ddungbo Halmae Gimbap KOREAN $
(뚱보 할매 김밥; ☎055 645 2619; 325 Tonyeonghaen-ro; per serving ₩5000; ⊙7am-midnight) Hungry travellers with limited Korean skills come here because there's no need to speak or read a menu: this place only serves *chungmu gimbap* (충무 김밥), a spicy squid-and-radish dish. The waitress will ask how many servings you want and, if necessary, she'll use her fingers to count. It's opposite the turtle ships in Gangguan.

One serving of this spicy dish, which will test the red-pepper tolerance of the hardiest Korean food lover, should be enough for a single person.

Ae Gul Bang BAKERY $
(통영애꿀빵; ☎055 648 8583; 331-2 Tongyeonghaen-ro; 6 balls for ₩6000; ⊙7am-9pm) Stroll the Gangguan harbour road and it's impossible to miss the incredible number of shops selling a honey-covered sticky ball of bread with a paste filling called *gul bang*. Ae Gul Bang is a little different because it's made with rice flour, which gives the bread a soft, chewy texture.

Dong Hae Sikdang KOREAN $$
(동해 식당; ☎055 646 1117; 54 Dongchung 4-gil; meals from ₩8000; ⊙8am-8pm) A few scruffy tables with boisterous fishermen polishing

off their third bottle of *soju* (local vodka) may not look inviting, but this small eatery serves excellent food. The *maeuntang* (매운탕, spicy seafood soup) is brimming with flavour and comes with a wonderful array of side dishes. It's behind the Palace Motel (팔레스 모텔) near the Gangguan harbour.

Information

There are three tourist information booths. Outside the intercity bus terminal and on Gangguan harbour (both open 9am to 6pm), there's a decent selection of material, though you'll need to rely on body language because no one speaks English.

Getting There & Away

The bus terminal is on the city's northern fringe. Local buses 10, 20, 30 and 40 run to Gangguan (₩1200, 25 minutes) from the terminal. A taxi to Gangguan costs ₩7500.

Express buses connect Tongyeong with Jinju (₩7600, 1½ hours, every 30 to 60 minutes), Busan (₩11,500, two hours, every 20 minutes), Gohyeon (₩3600, 25 minutes, every 15 minutes), Gimhae airport (₩13,400, 1½ hours, five daily departures) and Seoul (₩24,600, 4½ hours, every 30 to 50 minutes).

Ferry schedules are available from the desk inside the coastal passenger **ferry terminal** (☎055 642 8392; 234 Tongyeonghaen-ro; ⏲9am-4pm).

Jinju

☎055 / POP 349,788

Famous for bibimbap (rice, egg, meat and veggies with chilli sauce) and its role in the Japanese invasions of the 16th century, Jinju (진주) is a laid-back city with a park-like fortress by the Nam-gang (Nam River). It's the largest city in the area and a convenient transport hub from which to explore the province's western region. With excellent bus connections, it's an easy day trip from Busan.

Sights

Jinju Fortress HISTORIC SITE
(진주성; ☎055 749 5171; Bonseong-dong; adult/youth/child ₩2000/1000/600; ⏲9am-6pm Sun-Fri, to 7pm Sat) Local street signs call it a castle, but it's actually a well-preserved fortress that was partially destroyed during the Japanese invasion of 1592. One of the major battles of that campaign, in which 70,000 Koreans lost their lives, was fought here. Inside the fortress traditional gates and shrines dot the grassy knolls of the heavily wooded park.

The small but interesting Jinju National Museum, inside the fortress, has a worthwhile Imjin War exhibition.

Jinju National Museum MUSEUM
(국립진주박물관; ☎055 742 5951; www.jinju.museum.go.kr; 626-35 Namgang-ro; ⏲9am-6pm Tue-Fri, to 7pm Sat, Sun & holidays) FREE This small but worthwhile national museum inside Jinju Fortress houses a collection of artefacts dating back to the Imjin War (임진왜란, Imjin Wae-ran) – a seven-year bloody tussle between Joseon and Japan's Toyotomi Hideyoshi that began with the latter invading the former in 1592. There's a nifty 3D animated video portraying the invasions; ask for the English-language earphone narration.

Jinju Jungang Market MARKET
(진주 중앙시장; ☎055 741 2151; 8-1 Jinyangho-ro; ⏲4am-10pm) A traditional market with a fantastic variety of street vendors and indoor shops.

Jinyangho Lake Park PARK
(진양호 공원; ☎055 749 5933; www.jinju.go.kr/park; 171-1 Panmun-dong) A lakeside city park with a handful of hotels and cafes, plus an amusement park.

Activities

Jageum Seong BATHHOUSE
(자금성; ☎055 743 8841; 15 Jinyangho-ro 564beon-gil; jjimjil-bang ₩8000; ⏲24hr) In Jinju's red-light district, take a bath and relax in the *jjimjil-bang* (spa) before heading out for dinner and drinks. Then come back and sleep on the floor.

Exit the bus terminal, cross the street, walk left and then turn right at the first corner. Turn left at the small children's playground. It's in the tall building.

Festivals & Events

Nam-gang Lantern Festival LIGHT SHOW
(☎055 761 9111; www.yudeung.com) Around 50,000 glowing tigers, dragons and folktale characters light up the river in early October.

Sleeping

S+ Motel MOTEL $$
(S+모텔; ☎055 742 8580; 8 Namgang-ro 736beon-gil; r regular/special/VIP ₩40,000/50,000/70,000; P ❄ @) Wondering what the 'S' stands for? It might be 'snazzy' because the room decor uses funky tiles and vibrant colours such as cherry red, tangerine orange and lime green.

Jinju

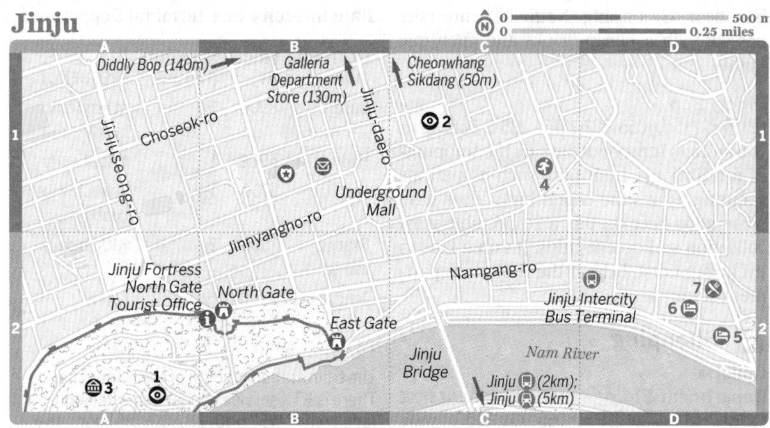

The rooms aren't especially spacious, though the VIP option comes with a king bed.

Dong Bang Hotel BUSINESS HOTEL $$
(동방호텔; ☎055 743 0131; www.hoteldongbang.com; r from ₩115,000; P❄📶) Jinju's only business-class hotel has perfectly cosy rooms with superb river views, although the decor feels somewhat 1980s. The cordial, English-speaking staff make this a very handy property to use as a base for touring the region. Prices jump in July and August. It's a 20-minute walk to Jinju Fortress and the city centre.

Eating

For something different, try one of the eel restaurants (₩15,000 to ₩20,000 per person) along the waterfront near the fortress. Pyeongan-dong, the area behind the Galleria department store, has a good number of bars and restaurants.

Pungnyeon KOREAN $$
(풍년; ☎055 746 0606; 740 Namgang-ro; pork per serving ₩8000, jeongol ₩10,000; ⊙11.40am-2.30pm & 5.30-10pm) A cosy meat restaurant to enjoy barbecued *samgyeopsal* (삼겹살, fatty pork) and hard-to-find *beoseot jeongol* (소고기버섯전골), a beef-and-mushroom casserole.

Cheonwhang Sikdang KOREAN $$
(천황식당; ☎055 741 2646; 3 Chokseok-ro 207beon-gil; meals ₩9000-30,000; ⊙9.30am-9pm, closed 1st & 3rd Mon of month) Housed in a rustic postwar building, Cheonwhang is the place for bibimbap, a bowl of veggies, rice and a splotch of red-pepper paste served with *seonji guk* (선지국, beef-blood soup). Traditionalists might opt for the regional speciality, *yukhoe bibimbap* (육회비빔밥), which adds raw beef seasoned with soy sauce and sesame oil to the mix.

Walk up Jinju-daero towards Galleria and turn right at the first lane past Choseok-ro. Look for the old tile roof, wooden doors and grey-white exterior.

Jinju

Sights
1 Jinju Fortress A2
2 Jinju Jungang Market C1
3 Jinju National Museum A2

Activities, Courses & Tours
4 Jageum Seong C1

Sleeping
5 Dong Bang Hotel D2
6 S+ Motel D2

Eating
7 Pungnyeon D2

Drinking & Nightlife

Serendipity CAFE
(☎055 755 2733; 50 Junji-daero; ⊙noon-10pm) Even with industrial digs featuring exposed pipework, the atmosphere is warm and friendly at this cafe near Gyeonsang National University. It's a great spot for a western-style breakfast.

Soundgarden BAR
(☎010 6478 2248; 18-1 Gajwa-gil; ⊙6pm-2am) A favourite with indie locals and expats, this

bar near Gyeongsang National University has chill vibes, cheap drinks and open mic nights.

Diddly Bop BAR
(디들리밥; ☎055 762 1375; 235-5 Dodong-ro; ⏱6pm-2am) It may not have all the trappings of a traditional Irish pub, such as patrons shouting 'How's the craic?', but it does have some good beer on tap, a respectable vinyl collection and decent chips. It's on a lane in Pyeongan-dong, behind the Galleria department store.

Shopping

Galleria Department Store DEPARTMENT STORE
(갤러리아 백화점; ☎055 791 1000; www.galleria.co.kr; 1095 Jinju-daero; ⏱10.30am-8pm) This multilevel luxury goods department store is a 20-minute walk from the intercity bus terminal. Stop in if you're in the market for a designer handbag or the latest in upmarket Korean skincare.

Information

Jinju Fortress North Gate Tourist Office (진주성 관광안내소; Bonseong-dong) Near the North Gate of Jinju Fortress

Police Station (진주경찰서; www.gnpolice.go.kr/jj; 3 Bibong-ro 24beon-gil; ⏱9am-6pm) A couple of blocks from the post office.

Post Office (진주우체국; ☎055 790 0570; www.koreapost.go.kr; 15 Bibong-ro 24beon-gil; ⏱9am-6pm)

Getting There & Away

AIR

The closest airport is in Sacheon, 20km from Jinju. Four daily flights connect with Gimpo airport in Seoul via Korean Air, which also runs one flight a day to Jeju-do (Asiana offers them daily). Local buses connect Jinju's north-end bus terminal to Sacheon airport (₩3000, 30 minutes).

BUS

There's an express bus terminal south of the river with services to Seoul (₩23,000, every 20 minutes), Daegu (₩11,600, hourly) and Gwangju (₩14,900, every 1½ hours). Most regional travellers use the **Jinju Intercity Bus Terminal** (시외버스터미널; www.jinjuterminal.kr; 712 Namgang-ro) north of the river, which is close to the city centre.

Jinju Intercity Bus Terminal Departures

DESTINATION	PRICE (₩)	DURATION (HR)	FREQUENCY
Busan	8900	1½	at least twice hourly
Hadong	5000	1	twice hourly
Namhae	5700	1½	at least twice hourly
Ssanggyae-sa	7300	2	7.10pm daily
Tongyeong	4900	1½	hourly

TRAIN

The train station is south of the Nam-gang. There is KTX service connecting with Seoul (adult/child ₩57,600/28,800, 3½ hours, five daily), Dongdaegu (adult/child ₩16,300/8100, 1½ hours, twice daily) and Daejeon (adult/child ₩33,300/16,000, 2½ hours, twice daily). Slower *saemaeul* (adult/child ₩12,700/6300, 1½ hours) services run to Gupo station in Busan.

Namhaedo

☎055 / POP 45,476

Namhaedo (남해도), the country's fifth-largest island, is famous for garlic and a slower pace of life clearly evident in the countryside, where some farmers continue to use oxen to plough fields. The drive around the island is arguably one of the most scenic routes in Korea. Rugged ocean views, dense forests and tiny fishing ports untouched by tourist development are best appreciated by travellers with their own transport and an unhurried sense of exploration.

Sights

Bori-am BUDDHIST TEMPLE
(보리암; ☎055 862 6115; www.boriam.or.kr; 665 Boriam-ro; parking ₩4000-7000; ⏱8am-8pm) Between Namhae-gun and Sangju beach, Bori-am is a busy Buddhist hermitage on Geum-san (금산, Geum Mountain, 681m) famous for brilliant sunrises and mesmerising vistas – the kind that move people to reconsider the meaning of life. The hermitage is a 30-minute drive from Namhae-gun, or catch the Bori-am shuttle bus (hourly 8am to 8pm) near the front door of the Namhae-gun bus terminal.

Getting to the mountaintop requires Buddha-like patience. The easiest way up is to take a shuttle bus from the entrance-level car park lot to the upper-level parking

LOCAL KNOWLEDGE

INSIDE THE COVERED WAGON

Spend time walking at night on a busy street in a large Korean city and you're likely to come across a *pojangmacha* (also *pojenmacha*), an orange piece of Korean street culture. Literally meaning 'covered wagon', these food and drink carts draped in a tarpaulin are more than a convenient late-night street pub. They're an institution that delivers a unique social and sensory experience.

It's said that people who love drinking come to the covered wagon because they feel comfortable there. But comfort, in this case, does not mean physical amenities, as most *pojangmacha* are equipped with bench seating, dim lighting and off-site washrooms that require a short stumble to a nearby car park. Comfort instead means a respite from the outside world.

Inside the *pojangmacha*, traditional barriers that prevent Koreans from socialising easily give way to conviviality. Customer talk rambles on between shots of *soju* and drags of cigarettes, and plumes of smoke rise to the top of the tent as grilled chicken anus (닭똥집), sea eel (꼼장어) and mackerel (고등어) sizzle over a charcoal grill. The aromas commingle with the plasticky smell of decades-old tarpaulin, inducing childhood memories of overnight camping trips. It all seems like another world.

area (₩1000 per person). From there it's a 30-minute walk to the hermitage. Some travellers with cars forgo the shuttle bus, preferring to drive to the upper parking area. Space up top is limited, so expect to wait an hour or more if you arrive in the afternoon.

Sangju BEACH
(상주 해수욕장; ☎055 863 3573; www.interkorea.pe.kr/j/eunmorae; 10-3 Sangju-ro) For most of the year this pretty beach with 2km of soft white sand and shallow water is a quiet destination. During summer it's packed with fun-seeking frolickers, triggering 400% price spikes at the nearby motels. The beach is about a 30-minute drive south from Namhae-gun.

Mijo VILLAGE
(미조리; Mijo-ri) This rustic fishing village is an ideal roadside diversion. Walk along the port, zigzag through narrow alleys and sample superb rural food. It's a short drive down the road from Sangju beach.

German Village ARCHITECTURE
(독일 마을; 1074-2 Mulgeon-ri; ⏲24hr) FREE Here's a destination people visit because it's popular, not because it's interesting. Local marketing bumf calls it one of the island's best sites, but the German Village is yawningly underwhelming. There's nothing to do except walk on the street and remark how different the architecture looks compared to the Soviet-inspired apartment blocks spanning Seoul's Han River. If you do come, be prepared for crowds and traffic.

Sleeping

A handful of motels can be found along Hwajeon-ro in Namhae-gun. Behind Sangju beach, where camping is allowed, there are several modest pensions and guesthouses.

Oasis Pension PENSION $$
(오아시스펜션; ☎055 862 6232; 64 Sangju-ro; r standard/ocean view ₩50,000/70,000; ❄📶) If you're spending the night in Sangju beach, try this pension where most rooms come with a double bed and a basic kitchen. Prices jump to ₩200,000 during summer, when the beach is packed. It's on the road running parallel to the beach.

Byzantine Motel MOTEL $$
(비잔틴 모텔; ☎055 864 1515; 31 Hwajeon-ro; r standard/special ₩40,000/50,000; ❄@) If you need to sleep in Namhae-gun, the Byzantine Motel is down a side road outside the bus terminal. It's a standard love motel, but rooms are slightly above average. The town centre is a 10-minute walk away.

Eating

Namhae-gun has a host of restaurants, mostly Korean, off Hwajeon-ro. You'll find a handful of seafood and Korean spots behind Sangju beach, and Mijo has many seafood options.

Dajeong Sikdang KOREAN $
(다정식당; ☎055 867 7334; 5 Mijo-ro 236beon-gil; meals from ₩10,000; ⏲7am-7pm) In Mijo this modest restaurant serves outstanding *dwenjang jjigae* (된장찌개, soybean stew).

The soft tofu with vegetables and seafood is a welcome treat for travellers who need a break from spicy food. Facing the police station, walk left and turn right at the corner. Walk straight, turn left at the shop and take the first right. It's down the road.

Getting There & Away

There are frequent bus connections to Namhae-si from Seobu terminal in Busan, and Jinju. Leaving the island, buses run to Hadong (₩4700, one hour, departing at 7.20am, 8.30am, 11.20am and 5.20pm), Jinju (₩5700, 1½ hours, every 15 to 30 minutes) and Busan (₩11,900, 2¼ hours, every 30 to 45 minutes).

Getting Around

Local buses from Namhae-si to Sangju beach (₩2500, 40 minutes, every 20 to 40 minutes) and Mijo (₩3400, one hour, every 20 to 40 minutes) are available, but the return trip can involve long roadside waits.

Jirisan National Park

☎055

Jirisan National Park (지리산 국립공원) offers some of Korea's best hiking opportunities, with 12 peaks over 1000m forming a 40km-long ridge. Many peaks are over 1500m, including Cheonwang-bong (1915m), the country's second-highest mountain. There are three principal entrances to the park, each with a temple. Two of the three temples, Ssanggye-sa and Daewon-sa (p209), are in Gyeongsangnam-do. From the west, Hwaeom-sa is accessible via Gurye in Jeollanam-do.

The Jirisan Bear Project was established in 2004 to build up a self-sustaining group of 50 wild Asiatic black bears in the national park. In late 2017 a young cub was discovered and is believed to be the third member of the third generation since the creatures were reintroduced to the land.

You'll find a string of Korean food options on the road leading to Ssanggye-sa. Save for the occasional small selection of basic items at some shelters, you're on your own for food inside the park, so bring what you'll need.

Sights

★Ssanggye-sa — BUDDHIST TEMPLE

(쌍계사; ☎055 883 1901; www.ssanggyesa.net; adult/youth/child ₩2500/1000/500; ⊙8am-6pm) The visual imagery of this temple is a feast for the eyes and, like any exquisite dinner, should be savoured with deliberation. Stone walls supporting multiple levels of buildings notched into the mountainside, combined with mature trees and a trickling creek, create a pleasant sensory experience. Three gates mark the path to the main hall – take time to read the signs to appreciate the symbolism of your visit.

One of the most attractive temples in the province, it's a long day trip from Busan. For a relaxed pace, consider an overnight stopover in Jinju or Hadong and an early-morning departure to the temple. There are budget rooms and a few restaurants outside the temple entrance.

Hwaeom-sa — TEMPLE

(화엄사; ☎061 782 7600; www.hwaeomsa.org; 539 Hwaeomsa-ro, Masan-myeon; adult/child/youth ₩3500/1300/1800; ⊙7am-7.30pm) Founded by priest Yeongi in AD 544 after his return from India, this ancient temple dedicated to the Birojana Buddha is enveloped by the beautiful natural surroundings of Jirisan National Park. Last rebuilt in 1636, it has endured five major devastations in its history, including the Japanese invasion of 1592.

On the main plaza is Gakgwang-jeon, a huge two-storey hall. Inside are paintings that are national treasures, nearly 12m long and 7.75m wide, featuring Buddhas, disciples and assorted holies. Korea's oldest and largest stone lantern fronts Gakgwang-jeon, which was once surrounded by stone tablets of the Tripitaka Sutra (made during the Silla era). These were ruined during the Japanese invasion.

Up many further flights of stairs is Hwaeom-sa's most famous structure, Sasaja Samcheung (사사자 삼층석탑), a unique three-storey pagoda supported by four stone lions. The female figure beneath the pagoda is said to be Yongi's mother; her dutiful son offers her tea from another lantern facing her. At the time of research, it was closed for restoration.

The temple is about 25 minutes' walk from the bus stop. Templestays (₩40,000) are possible at Hwaeom-sa. A large tourist village is at the park entrance with a number of restaurants and affordable accommodation; prices rise on weekends.

It is possible to continue from the temple along a trail through Hwaeom-sa Valley. After about 2½ to three hours the trail begins to ascend to a shelter, Nogodan Sanjang (a strenuous four-hour hike). From the shelter,

the trail continues to rise until you are finally on the long spine of the Jirisan ridge.

Daewon-sa TEMPLE
(☎055 974 1112; www.daewonsa.net) Tucked near the eastern border of Jirisan, this temple is an active nunnery where a famed female *sanshin* (mountain spirit) is thought to reside. A templestay program is offered here.

Naewon-sa TEMPLE
(내원사) This temple is about 3km from Samjang-myeon, off route 59. Highlights include a three-tier Silla pagoda and a rare Cheonwang-bosalnim statue.

Chilbul-sa TEMPLE
(칠불사) Founded in 560, this small temple, 7km from Ssanggye-sa, was burned during the Korean War and reconstructed to its original form in 1984.

Buril Pokpo WATERFALL
(불일폭포) It's an easy day trip from Jinju to this small waterfall in Jirisan. The hike to get there is an easy three-hour return trip from Ssanggye-sa.

Activities

Jirisan Hiking Trails HIKING
(지리산 하이킹 트레일; http://eng.jirisan tour.com; park entrance adult/youth/child ₩2500/1000/500) It's impossible to describe the myriad trails within this great park. The traditional course runs east to west (Daewon-sa to Hwaeom-sa), which experienced hikers can complete in three days. Travellers from Busan and Gyeongsangnam-do often begin their journey via Ssanggye-sa, which is close to a bus stop, budget motels and restaurants. Infrequent direct buses depart from Busan; otherwise travel to Hadong and catch a bus to the temple.

A three-night route puts hikers in position for a sunrise view on top of Cheonwangbong. The route starts with a night at the Nogodan shelter. The next two nights are spent at the Baemsagol campground and Jangteomok shelter. On the final day, follow the trail to Jungsan-ri and then catch a bus to Jinju or Busan. Most shelters require reservations, which usually need to be made 15 days in advance.

Travellers with less ambitious plans, but who still want to experience Jirisan's beauty, can hike to Buril Pokpo. Starting from Ssanggye-sa, the mildly challenging trail (2.4km each way, three hours return) winds through a forest along a rippling creek. About two-thirds along the way, just when you've noticed the sound of the creek has disappeared, the trail bursts onto an open field. At the foot of the falls, there's a rocky pool where hikers can meditate to regain their chi.

Sleeping

After a long day of hiking, rest your bones under the stars at one of Jirisan's camping sites. There are also shelters if you're looking for a bit more than a ripstop wall between you and nature.

There are nine camp grounds and facilities are basic. Travellers with a camper might try a car camping space at **Dalgung** (달궁자동차야영장; ☎063 625 8911; http://english.knps.or.kr; 593 Jirisanno; car ₩19,000; P 📶), **Naewon** (내원사자동차야영장; San 106-2; car ₩19,000) and **Deokdong** (덕동자동차야영장; ☎063 630 8900; 395 Jirisanno; car ₩19,000).

Somakgol (소막골야영장; ☎055 972 7775; San 118-1; campsite ₩9000)

Jungsan-ri (중산리야영장; ☎055 972 7775; http://english.knps.or.kr; San 105; car ₩7000; P)

Baengmu-dong (백무동야영장; ☎055 963 1260; http://english.knps.or.kr; 148 Gangcheonni; campsite ₩9000; P 📶)

Buril Pokpo (불일폭포야영장; camping free)

Daeseong Bridge (대성교야영장; ☎055 972 7771; Daesong-ri; camping free)

Baemsagol 1 (뱀사골 제1야영장; ☎063 630 8900; http://english.knps.or.kr; 252 Buun-ri; car/campsite ₩19,000/7000; P 📶)

Baemsagol 2 (뱀사골 제2야영장; ☎063 630 8900; http://english.knps.or.kr/; 29 Wawun-gil; car/campsite ₩19,000/7000)

There are seven shelters across Jirisan. From west to east:

Nogodan (노고단대피소; ☎061 780 7700; http://english.knps.or.kr; San 110-2; per person ₩13,000)

Yeonhacheon (연하천대피소; ☎063 630 8929; http://english.knps.or.kr; 324 Waun-gil; per person ₩13,000)

Byeoksoryeong (벽소령대피소; ☎011 1767 1426; http://english.knps.or.kr; 249-1049 Byeoksoryeong-gil; per person ₩13,000)

Seseok (세석대피소; ☎055 970 1000; http://english.knps.or.kr; Jirisan-daero; per person ₩13,000)

Jirisan National Park

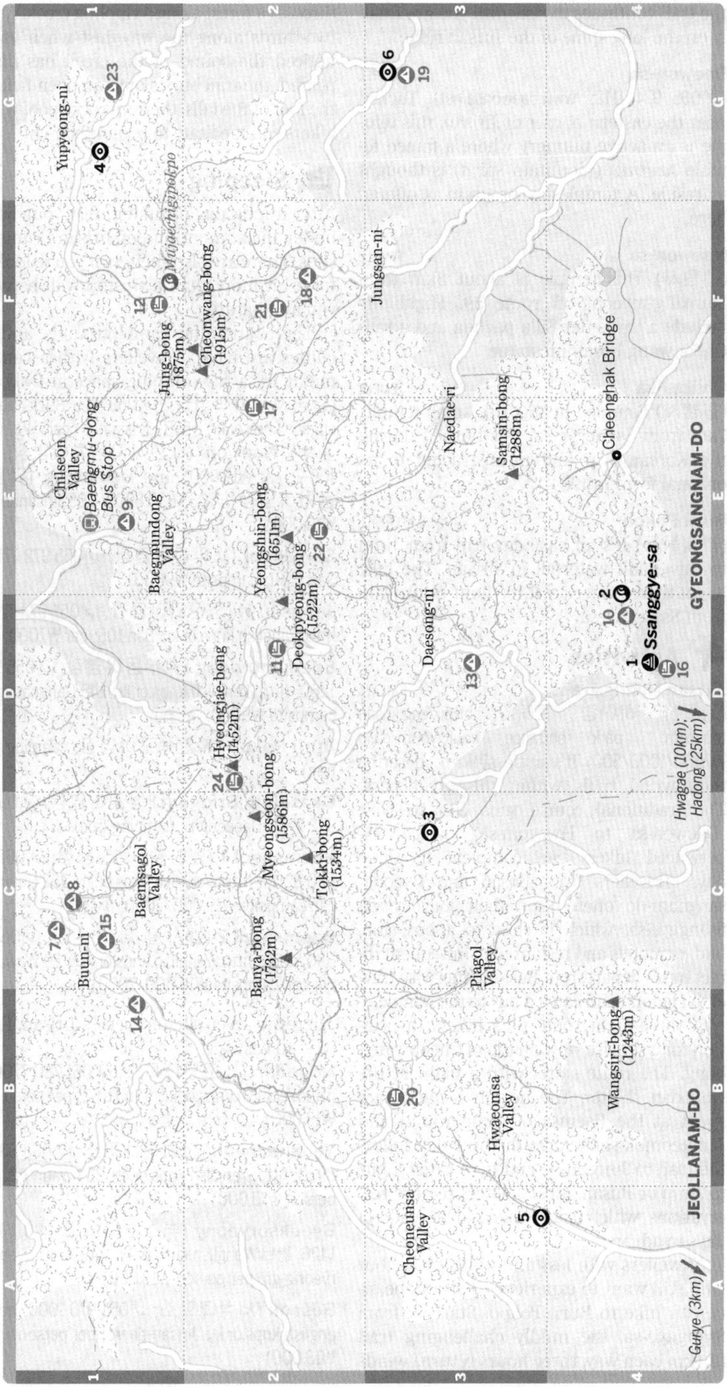

Jirisan National Park

Top Sights
1 Ssanggye-sa ...D4

Sights
2 Buril Pokpo ...E4
3 Chilbul-sa ...C3
4 Daewon-sa ...G1
5 Hwaeom-sa ...A3
6 Naewon-sa ...G3

Sleeping
7 Baemsagol Camping Ground 1 ...C1
8 Baemsagol Camping Ground 2 ...C1
9 Baengmu-dong Camping Ground ...E1
10 Buril Pokpo Camping Ground ...D4
11 Byeoksoryeong Shelter ...D2
12 Chibanmok Shelter ...F1
13 Daeseong Bridge Camping Ground ...D3
14 Dalgung Car Camping Ground ...B1
15 Deokdong Car Camping Ground ...C1
16 Gilson Minbak ...D4
17 Jangteomok Shelter ...E2
18 Jungsan-ri Camping Ground ...F2
19 Naewon Car Camping Ground ...G3
20 Nogodan Shelter ...B3
21 Rotari Shelter ...F2
22 Seseok Shelter ...E2
23 Somakgol Camping Ground ...G1
24 Yeonhacheon Shelter ...D2

Jangteomok (장터목대피소; 055 972 7772; http://english.knps.or.kr; per person ₩13,000)

Rotari (로타리대피소; 055 973 1400; http://english.knps.or.kr; Jirisan-daero; per person ₩13,000)

Chibanmok (치밭목대피소; 055 972 7772; http://english.knps.or.kr; 1404 Pyeongchon-yupyeong-ro; per person ₩13,000)

Jangteomok has enough space for 155 people, and sells torches, noodles and drinks. Seseok is the largest shelter, with space for 240 people. For overnight hikes bring bedding, food, tea and coffee, as most shelters have limited supplies.

Multiday treks require a hiking plan and bookings made 15 days in advance – available spots are often booked up within minutes after the reservation period opens during summer, autumn and weekends. Planning, perseverance and a flexible schedule are required if you want to stay at a shelter. Online reservations can be made at the website of Korea National Park Service (http://english.knps.or.kr), in Korean.

Gilson Minbak INN **$$**
(길손민박; 055 884 1336; 557 Ssanggye-ro; ondol ₩40,000-70,000) Not far from the road leading to Ssanggye-sa, this place has clean rooms with private bathrooms. It's a brown-beige building on a small road off to the right as you walk up to the temple gate. No English is spoken. If full, there are a dozen more *minbak* in the area.

Getting There & Away

Buses to Ssanggye-sa often pass through Hadong, a small village and useful transfer point in the region. If you can't get a direct bus to Ssanggye-sa, travel to Hadong and catch one of the frequent buses to the temple (₩2800, 30 minutes, every 30 to 90 minutes).

En route to Ssanggye-sa from Hadong, buses pass a large bridge and shortly thereafter make a quick stop in Hwagae; don't get off there. Further down the road (usually the next stop), the bus stops in front of a seafood restaurant beside a concrete bridge. Get out here, cross the bridge and follow the winding road to the park entrance. Buy your return bus ticket inside the seafood restaurant beside the bridge.

The signboard lists times for several destinations, though most travellers are best served by heading to Hadong, where buses connect to Busan (₩11,600, 2½ hours, hourly) and Jinju (₩5000, one hour, every 30 to 45 minutes).

If you plan to stay at the Baengmu-dong campground, there's an intercity express bus stop close by.

Jeollanam-do

Includes ➜

Why Go?

This beautiful southwest province is one of Korea's greenest and least developed. The heartland of Jeollanam-do (전라남도) has rolling hills, the towering Sobaek Mountains to the east and 6100km of coastline to the south and west, with more than 2000 islands offshore – fewer than 300 of which are inhabited. The province was largely isolated for centuries and it retains an off-the-beaten-track feel. It also has a rebel edge, and is proud of its ceramic and artistic traditions, its exiled poets and its pro-democracy martyrs.

With a comparatively balmy climate, Jeollanam-do is famous for its bountiful harvests, fresh seafood and green tea, celebrated in several festivals. For all its rural atmosphere, Jeollanam-do has urban elements too: Gwangju, the province's largest city, has a hip vibe and an active arts scene centred on a much-hyped cultural centre.

Best Places to Eat

- ➜ Dokcheon (p233)
- ➜ Wonjo Jangsu Tongdak (p227)
- ➜ Jeonsama (p230)
- ➜ Yeongran Hoet-jip (p234)
- ➜ Sujata (p217)

Best Places to Stay

- ➜ Pedro's House (p215)
- ➜ Gurye Okjam (p220)
- ➜ Yuseongwan (p227)
- ➜ Sinsiwa (p217)

When to Go

Gwangju

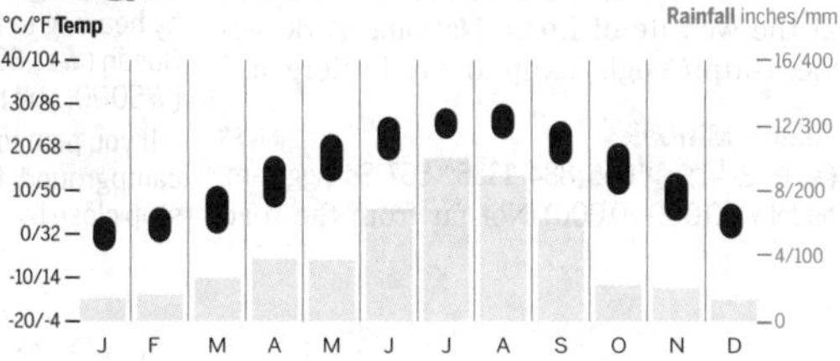

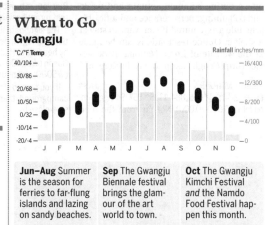

Jun–Aug Summer is the season for ferries to far-flung islands and lazing on sandy beaches.

Sep The Gwangju Biennale festival brings the glamour of the art world to town.

Oct The Gwangju Kimchi Festival *and* the Namdo Food Festival happen this month.

Jeollanam-do Highlights

1. **Gwangju** (p213) Checking out the vibrant arts and nightlife scene, as well as urban hiking and solemn memorials.
2. **Hongdo** (p235) Voyaging to an unspoilt, fabled island.
3. **Daehan Dawon Tea Plantation** (p226) Savouring scenic terrace views and tasting tea in Boseong.
4. **Naganeup-seong Folk Village** (p220) Marvelling at the thatched-roofed houses of an immaculately preserved fortress town.
5. **Suncheon-man** (p221) Spotting migratory birds feasting in rich wetlands.
6. **Mokpo** (p231) Eating still-wriggling octopus and scoping out sunken ships.
7. **Hyangir-am** (p222) Watching the sunrise from a seaside hermitage.

History

Far from Seoul during the Joseon era, Jeollanam-do was a place of exile, often used as a dumping ground for political and religious dissidents. The tradition of political dissent has continued; the province was a hotbed of opposition to the military governments that ruled South Korea in the 1960s and '70s. Students and trade unionists led countless pro-democracy protests and demonstrations, culminating in the 1980 uprising in Gwangju. As a result, development funds were withheld from the region for decades, something that is being rectified today with a flurry of new projects.

Getting There & Away

Gwangju is the major transport hub of the region, with an airport, express buses and KTX train services. The airport only offers flight services between Seoul and Jeju-do. Trains from Seoul's Yongsan Station take two hours.

Bus services between Gwangju and many towns and major cities in the country operate from the U-Square bus terminal.

Gwangju

062 / POP 1.5 MILLION

Gwangju (광주), Korea's sixth-largest city, is defined by its powerful political history and reverence for creativity. Often considered the birthplace of Korean democracy, the effects of the May 18 Democratic Uprising – a 1980 mass protest against South Korea's then-authoritarian military government – remain a strong part of the city's identity. Art abounds at every turn thanks to a wealth of museums, exhibitions and festivals that are bolstered by civic investment.

Sights

Mudeungsan National Park NATIONAL PARK

(무등산국립공원; ☎062 265 0761; http://english.mudeungsan.or.kr; 🚌1187) FREE Overlooking Gwangju, Mudeungsan National Park is a gorgeous green mountain range with a spiderweb of well-signed trails leading to the peak, Cheonwang-bong (1187m), and up to the towering rocky outcrops Seoseok-dae and Ipseok-dae. Just 30 minutes by bus from central Gwangju, it's naturally packed on weekends.

The most popular route starts at the temple Wonhyo-sa, which has an ornate pavilion overlooking the park and a bronze bell dating from 1710. The temple is just uphill from the bus stop. Double back and take the main path 4km up to Seoseok-dae and Ipseok-dae; it's steep going as you get towards the top. Then continue down through Jangbuljae pass to the temple Jeungsim-sa (another 6km), Gwangju's oldest temple. It has a Silla-era iron Buddha backed by red-and-gold artwork, housed in an insignificant-looking shrine behind the main hall. The tiny shrine perched on a rock next to it is dedicated to the Shamanist Mountain God.

Around 250m past Jeungsim-sa, on the way to the bus stop, is the Uijae Museum of Korean Art. This art gallery displays the gorgeous landscape, flower and bird paintings by the famed Heo Baek-ryeon (1891–1977), who lived in a hermitage here in the shadow of the mountains.

The hike takes about five hours; if you're pressed for time, just visit Jeungsim-sa and the Uijae Museum.

The cleverly named bus 1187 (the height in metres of Cheonwang-bong) terminates near Wonhyo-sa; you can catch the bus (every 20 minutes) from the bus terminal or in front of the train station. Bus 9 (every 10 minutes) runs to the Jeungsim-sa area from Geumnam-no 4-ga and the bus terminal.

Unju-sa TEMPLE

(운주사; ☎061 374 0660; www.unjusa.okr; 91-44 Cheontae-ro, Doam-myeon; adult/youth/child ₩3000/2000/1000; ⌚8am-7pm Mar-Oct, to 6pm Nov-Feb; 🚌218, 318-1) Legend has it that Unju-sa originally housed 1000 Buddhas and 1000 pagodas, built because, according to traditional geomancy, the southwest of the country lacked hills and needed the pagodas to 'balance' the peninsula. The remaining 23 pagodas and some 100 Buddhas still make up the greatest numbers of any Korean temple. Some are set on the hillsides, which you can scale.

According to another legend the monuments were all built in one night by stonemasons sent down from heaven, but another theory is that Unju-sa was the site of a school for stonemasons. Whatever their origins, many works are unique and some are national treasures. Back-to-back twin Buddhas face their own pagodas, while another pair of Buddhas lying on their backs are said to have been the last works sculpted one evening; the masons returned back to heaven before the Buddhas could be stood upright.

Buses run from Gwangju bus terminal (₩3650, 1½ hours, every 30 minutes). Check with the driver as only some of the buses go all the way to Unju-sa. The last bus back to Gwangju leaves around 8pm.

Daein-sijang MARKET

(대인시장; 10 Jebong-ro 184beon-gil, Dong-gu; ⌚8am-8pm; Ⓜ Geumnamno 4-ga) By the early 2000s, this traditional market in the city centre was nearly shuttered. As part of the 2008 Gwangju Biennale (p215), artists added colourful murals, giving people a new reason to visit. Today, more than 50 artists also have their studios here, and there are cafes and galleries along with the traditional stalls.

Uijae Museum of Korean Art MUSEUM

(의재미술관; ☎062 222 3040; www.ujam.org; 55 Jeungsimsa-gil, Dong-gu; adult/child ₩2000/1000; ⌚9.30am-5pm Tue-Sun; 🚌9) This gallery displays landscape, flower and bird paintings by the famed Heo Baek-ryeon (1891–1977), whose pen name was Uijae. His rebuilt house is a short walk away. About halfway between Uijae and Jeungsim-sa is the Chunseolheon tea plantation that Uijae established, now cultivated by Jeungsim-sa monks. The gallery is inside Mudeungsan National Park (p214), a 15-minute walk from the bus stop.

Gwangju Folk Museum MUSEUM

(광주민속박물관; ☎062 613 5337; http://gjfm.gwangju.go.kr; 48-25 Seoha-ro, Buk-gu; adult/youth/child ₩500/300/200; ⌚9am-6pm Tue-Sun; 🚌64) Learn about traditional life in Jeollanam-do through the somewhat retro-looking dioramas and models here, which cover everything from kimchi and clothing to courtship rituals and shamanism.

Take the bus (every 20 minutes) from in front of the bus terminal to the Biennale Exhibition Hall stop. Bus 95 (every 15 minutes) also runs here from in front of the Asian Culture Complex.

May 18th National Cemetery MEMORIAL
(국립 5.18 민주묘지; ☎062 266 5187; http://518.mpva.go.kr; 200 Minju-ro, Buk-gu; ⏲8am-6pm Mar-Oct, to 5pm Nov-Feb; 🚌518) FREE Opened in 1997, this is the final burial place for victims of the May 18 Democratic Uprising of 1980, one of the most tragic incidents in modern Korean history. Officially, the casualties include 228 dead or missing and 4141 wounded, but the real numbers are believed to be much higher. A small but emotionally charged museum shows photographs, blood-stained flags, and a hard-hitting film that gives a dramatic account of the traumatic events that still scar the country's political landscape.

On the right, a memorial hall displays photographs of the ordinary folk – from students to grandmothers – who paid the ultimate price during the military government's crackdown. A five-minute walk through the memorial park leads to the reinstated original cemetery, where the victims were hurriedly buried without proper ceremony. The bodies were later reinterred in the new cemetery. Get the bus (one hour, every 30 minutes) in front of the the bus terminal, train station or along Geumnam-ro.

Gwangju Museum of Art MUSEUM
(광주시립미술관; ☎062 613 7100; 52 Haseo-ro, Buk-gu; adult/youth/child ₩500/300/200; ⏲10am-6pm Tue-Sun; 🚌64) Managed by the same folks who put on the Gwangju Biennale, this art museum shows up-and-coming Korean artists along with more established local names, such as Heo Baek-ryeon and Oh Ji Ho.

Take the bus (every 20 minutes) from in front of the bus terminal to the Biennale Exhibition Hall stop. Bus 95 (every 15 minutes) also runs here from in front of the Asian Culture Complex.

Gwangju Biennale Exhibition Hall ARTS CENTRE
(111 Biennale-ro, Buk-gu; 🚌64) Located in the Jung-oe Park Culture Center, this 8100-sq-metre exhibition hall is the setting for the Gwangju Biennale (and in odd-numbered years, the Design Biennale).

Gwangju National Museum MUSEUM
(국립광주박물관; ☎062 570 7000; http://gwangju.museum.go.kr; 110 Haseo-ro, Buk-gu; ⏲10am-6pm Tue-Sun; 🚌48) FREE The Gwangju National Museum's collection traces the region's cultural history, from its prehistorical beginnings through the Joseon period (1392–1897), via artefacts, paintings and calligraphy. Look out for the Chinese ceramics salvaged from a 14th-century shipwreck.

Get the bus (20 minutes, every 30 minutes) from in front of the bus terminal or the train station.

Asian Culture Complex ARTS CENTRE
(국립아시아문화전당; ☎1899 5566; www.acc.go.kr/en; 38 Munhwajeondang-ro; Ⓜ Culture Complex) This arts complex houses galleries, performance spaces, a library and plazas – all designed to boost Gwangju's capital in the art world. It's located on the main site of the May 18 Uprising; the old Provincial Hall building, the target of the protests, has been retained.

Festivals & Events

Gwangju Biennale ART
(www.gwangjubiennale.org) This three-month contemporary art festival takes place every two years (on even-numbered years). Based at the Biennale Exhibition Hall, it features more than 500 artists and foreign curators from 60 countries. On odd-numbered years, the city holds the Design Biennale.

Gwangju Kimchi Festival FOOD & DRINK
(www.kimchi.gwangju.go.kr) Every October Gwangju hosts a five-day kimchi (pickled vegetables) extravaganza with a fairground, market stalls, pottery making, folk music and a *hanbok* (traditional clothing) fashion show. Shuttle buses run to the often-changing venue.

Sleeping

★ **Pedro's House** GUESTHOUSE $
(☎010 9592 9993; www.pedroshouse.com; 18-3 Sangmu-daero 935beon-gil, Seo-gu; dm/d from ₩28,000/55,000; Ⓜ Ssangchon-dong) Gwangju local and veteran traveller Pedro Kim runs this homey guesthouse filled with books and travel souvenirs. The rooms (some with private baths) are spotless, and Kim, who speaks fluent English, knows pretty much everyone and everything in the city. Pedro's is west of the city centre, on the metro.

Gwangju

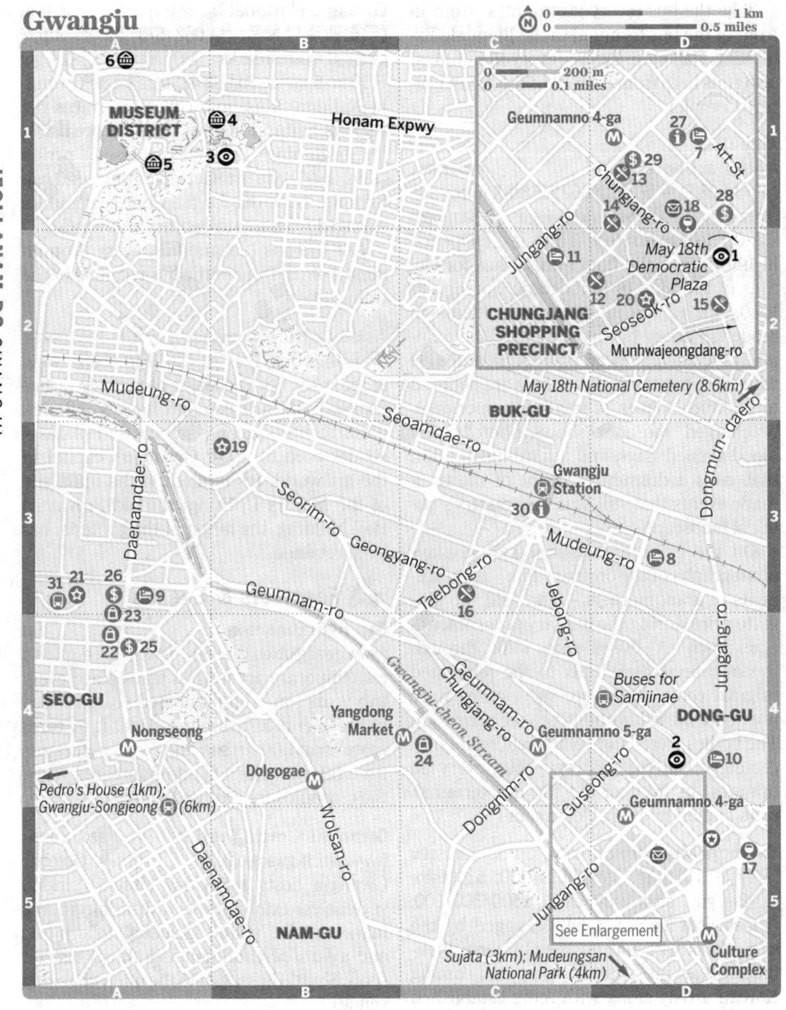

S Plus Motel MOTEL $
(에스플러스 모텔; ☎062 366 3307; 11 Jukbong-daero 78beon-gil, Seo-gu; r ₩35,000-45,000; P❄@📶) The pick of the bunch near the bus terminal, S Plus has rooms kitted out with a sofa, large TV and PCs. Prices jump by ₩10,000 on the weekend. It's 500m east of the Shinsegae Department Store.

Windmill Motel MOTEL $
(윈드밀 모텔; ☎062 223 5333; 150-8 Jungang-ro, Dong-gu; r ₩35,000-60,000; P❄@📶) This love motel on the west end of the Chungjang nightlife district is a local landmark (there's a windmill on top). The staff are friendly and the rooms are clean, if not kitschy, and include flat-screen TVs, fridges and water coolers.

Bando Motel MOTEL $
(반도모텔; ☎062 227 0238; 2-6 Geumnamno 3-ga, Dong-gu; r ₩35,000-45,000; ❄@📶) This basic but clean motel is hidden in an alley between Art St and Geumnamno, behind the NH Bank building and just steps from the action of Chungjang (minus all the noise).

Gwangju

Sights
1 Asian Culture Complex ... D2
2 Daein-sijang ... D4
3 Gwangju Biennale Exhibition Hall ... B1
4 Gwangju Folk Museum ... B1
5 Gwangju Museum of Art ... A1
6 Gwangju National Museum ... A1

Sleeping
7 Bando Motel ... D1
8 Geumsoojang Tourist Hotel ... D3
9 S Plus Motel ... A3
10 Sinsiwa ... D4
11 Windmill Motel ... C2

Eating
12 Bari E ... D2
13 Cheongwon Momil ... D1
14 First Alleyway ... D1
15 Minsokchon ... D2
16 Yeongmi ... C3

Drinking & Nightlife
17 Kunst Lounge ... D5
18 Speakeasy ... D1

Entertainment
19 Gwangju Kia Champions Field ... B3
20 In the Groove ... D2
21 U-Square Culture Centre ... A3

Shopping
22 E-Mart ... A4
23 Shinsegae ... A3
24 Yangdong-sijang ... C4

Information
25 Citibank ... A4
Global ATM ... (see 31)
26 Gwangju Bank ... A3
27 Gwangju International Centre ... D1
28 KEB ... D1
29 Standard Chartered First Bank ... D1
Tourist Information Centre – Bus Terminal ... (see 31)
30 Tourist Information Centre – Train Station ... C3

Transport
31 Gwangju Bus Terminal ... A3

Sinsiwa GUESTHOUSE $$
(신시와; ☎062 233 2755; http://cafe.naver.com/sinsiwaguesthouse; 81-3 Donggyecheon-ro, Dong-gu; d/q from ₩50,000/130,000;) Park Sung-hyun, one-time curator of the Gwangju Biennale, restored this 60-year-old *hanok* himself and opened it as a guesthouse. The three rooms (two with private baths) are simple yet beautiful, decorated with an ever-changing display of works by local artists.

Geumsoojang Tourist Hotel HOTEL $$
(금수장 관광 호텔; ☎062 525 2111; www.geumsoojang.co.kr; 2 Mudeung-ro, 321beon-gil, Dong-gu; r ₩110,000-300,000;) Classy in a retro sort of way, this hotel near the train station has English-speaking staff and comfortable rooms. Book online for a 50% discount. The in-house restaurant serves up a delicious rendition of the Korean *hanjeongsik* (banquet; ₩50,000).

Eating

Sujata VEGETARIAN $
(수자타; ☎062 222 1145; 3 Dongsan-gil 7beon-gil, Dong-gu; meals ₩8000; ⏲11.30am-8.30pm; ; 15, Ⓜ Hakdong/Jeungsimsa) Run by Buddhist monks, Sujata puts on what is possibly the world's best salad bar. It includes soups, stews, noodles, a dozen different greens, countless pickled things, a make-your-own bibimbap (rice, egg and veggies with chilli sauce) section and even cake. It's all vegetarian, but even nonveggies will get their fill here: it's all you can eat.

Look for the red building halfway between the Uijae Museum of Korean Art and the Hakdong/Jeungsimsa subway station.

Cheongwon Momil NOODLES $
(청원모밀; ☎062 222 2210; 174-1 Jungang-ro, Dong-gu; noodles from ₩6000; ⏲10.30am-8.30pm; Ⓜ Geumnamno 4-ga) This humble noodle shop, which specialises in *momil* (모밀; buckwheat noodles) is a Gwangju institution, in business since 1960 (as the sign out the front proudly boasts). Dishes to try include *bibim-momil* (비빔모밀, buckwheat noodles in spicy sauce) and *momil-jjajang* (모밀짜장, buckwheat noodles in black soybean sauce).

First Alleyway INTERNATIONAL $$
(☎070 4127 8066; 5-4 Chungjang-ro an-gil, Dong-gu; meals ₩11,000-15,000; ⏲noon-9.30pm Tue-Thu, to 11pm Fri, to midnight Sat, 11am-8pm Sun; Ⓜ Geumnamno 4-ga) Longtime expat Tim Whitman leads the kitchen here, turning out burgers, pizzas and – as befitting a Canadian – poutine. There's Sunday brunch too. First Alleyway naturally draws an international crowd. It's a few doors down from H&M.

LOCAL KNOWLEDGE

GWANGJU SPECIALITIES

Sample the city's claim to fame dishes, such as *tteokgalbi* (광주떡갈비), hand-formed oblong patties of minced beef and pork with pear, plum, onion and herbs; *oritang* (오리탕), a duck stew; and *boribap* (보리밥), a dish of steamed barley topped with seasonal vegetables. Be sure to try a Namdo *hanjeongsik* (한정식), a table d'hôte offering a cornucopia of some 30 dishes that feature local ingredients and seafood preparations that are unique to the region.

Minsokchon KOREAN $$

(민속촌; ☎062 224 4577; 16-10 Jungang-ro 160beon-gil, Dong-gu; meals ₩8000-18,000; ⏲11.30am-midnight; Ⓜ Culture Complex) Deservedly popular, Minsokchon serves up lean cuts of *so galbi* (소갈비, beef) and *dwaeji galbi* (돼지갈비, pork), set to sizzle over charcoal braziers set into the tables. It has a stylish, rustic interior; look for the traditional facade.

Bari E ITALIAN $$

(바리에; ☎062 224 8241; www.cafebarie.com; 21-9 Bullo-dong, Dong-gu; dishes from ₩12,000; ⏲11am-10pm; 📶; Ⓜ Geumnamno 4-ga) Local fashionistas flock to this earthy corner cafe-restaurant to dig into thin-crust pizzas, pastas and healthy salads while flicking through fashion magazines. There's a wide range of drinks including coffee, juice and German draught beer.

Yeongmi KOREAN $$$

(영미; ☎062 527 0248; 126 Gyeongyang-ro, Buk-gu; meals ₩28,000-48,000; ⏲11am-10pm, closed first Mon of month) There's a whole string of restaurants specialising in *oritang* (오리탕, duck stew) along the aptly named Duck St, but this 80-year-old joint, which seasons its stew with ginseng and jujube, is the most famous. It's pricey, but dishes are meant for sharing.

Drinking & Nightlife

Kunst Lounge LOUNGE

(☎062 223 0009; www.kunst-lounge.com; 4 Dongmyeong-ro, Dong-gu; drinks from ₩8000; ⏲10am-midnight Mon-Sat; Ⓢ Culture Complex) Gwangju's most sophisticated spot does wine by the glass, German beers and a fantastic cheese platter. Located across from the new Asian Culture Complex, Kunst has a suitably artsy vibe.

Speakeasy BAR

(☎010 4713 3825; 160 Jungang-ro, 31-31beon-gil, Dong-gu; drinks ₩6000-8000; ⏲7pm-3am Thu-Sun; Ⓜ Geumamno 4-ga) This 2nd-floor bar hidden down an alley is a favourite with foreigners and has a good selection of imported beers. Bands sometimes play on Fridays or Saturdays. From the front of Burger King, go left for 40m and down the alleyway.

Entertainment

In the Groove JAZZ

(☎062 227 7959; 160 Jungang-ro, 34-2beon-gil, Dong-gu; ⏲8pm-4am Mon-Sat; Ⓜ Geumnamno 4-ga) This mellow basement hideaway features live jazz from 10pm every Friday and Saturday night. There's no cover charge.

Gwangju Kia Champions Field BASEBALL

(광주기아챔피언스필드; ☎062 525 5350; www.tigers.co.kr; 10 Seorim-ro, Buk-gu; tickets from ₩4000; 🚌38) Catch the Kia Tigers professional baseball team in action from April through November. Stock up on snacks from the street vendors outside the stadium, where prices are cheaper. You're permitted to bring in food, beer, coolers and cameras. Games usually start at 5pm or 6.30pm.

Get the bus from in front of the bus terminal; or you can walk from there in 20 minutes (or in 30 minutes from Nongseong metro station).

U-Square Culture Centre ARTS CENTRE

(유·스퀘어문화관; ☎062 360 8432; www.usquareculture.co.kr; 904 Mujin-daero, Seo-gu) The U-Square Culture Centre, adjoining Gwangju's bus terminal, houses cinemas and performance halls.

Shopping

Yangdong-sijang MARKET

(양동시장; 238 Cheonbyeonjwa-ro, Seo-gu; ⏲9am-9pm; Ⓜ Yangdong Market) Voted Korea's best traditional market, sprawling Yangdong sells just about everything, from traditional medicines to clothing.

Shinsegae DEPARTMENT STORE

(신세계; 49-1 Gwangcheon-dong, Seo-gu; ⏲10.30am-8pm) Brand names such as Vuitton and Dior rub shoulders with an art gallery and basement food court-supermarket here. There's also a Starbucks, the favourite haunt of local *doenjangnyeo*, as some Ko-

reans might say (*doenjangnyeo* is a derogatory term for young women who only care about style and fashion). It's behind the bus terminal.

E-Mart FOOD & DRINKS
(20-11 Gwangju-daero 71beon-gil, Seo-gu; ⏲10am-midnight) Stock up on cheap food, drinks and supplies.

Information

Central Post Office (☎062 231 8130; 94 Chungjang-ro)

Police Station (☎062 609 4322; 33 Yesul-gil)

MONEY

Citibank (☎062 224 0709; 181 Geumnam-ro, Dong-gu; ⏲9am-4pm Mon-Fri) Global ATM with high daily withdrawal limit.

Global ATM (Gwangju Bus Terminal) Near the ticket booths.

Gwangju Bank (Shinsegae Department Store) Foreign exchange.

KEB (☎062 232 1111; Geumnam-ro) Global ATM.

Standard Chartered First Bank (☎062 222-4332; 224 Geumnam-ro; ⏲9.30am-4.30pm Mon-Fri) Global ATM.

TOURIST INFORMATION

The expat **Gwangju International Centre** (☎062 226 2733; www.eng.gic.or.kr; Samho Center 1-2F, 196 Jungang-ro, 5beon-gil, Dong-gu; ⏲10am-6pm Mon-Fri, to 5pm Sat; Ⓜ Geunamno 4-ga) offers guidebooks, tourist information, Korean-language classes, tours and social events.

There are also tourist information offices inside the **bus terminal** (☎062 233 9370; 235 Mudeung-ro; ⏲9am-6pm), **Gwangju airport** (☎062 942 6160; 420 25 Sangmu-daero; ⏲9am-6pm) and the **train station** (☎062 233 9370; 235 Mudeung-ro; ⏲9am-6pm).

Getting There & Away

AIR

Two Gwangju–Seoul and 16 Gwangju–Jeju flights run daily; for the latter, look for budget flights on T'Way Airlines (www.twayair.com).

Bus 1000 (₩1400, 30 minutes, every 15 minutes) runs from the airport to the bus terminal and Geumnam-ro. You can also take the metro. A taxi costs around ₩12,000.

BUS

Express and intercity buses to more than 100 destinations depart from the **U-Square complex** (☎062 360 8114; 932 Mujin-daero), 1km north of the Nongseong subway station.

To get to Changpyeong Slow City in Samjinae, pick up bus 303 in Jungheung-dong.

TRAIN

KTX trains (₩47,100, two hours, eight daily) run between Yongsan station in Seoul and the new Gwangju-Songjeong station on the west side of the city. *Saemaeul* (₩34,300, four hours, four daily) and *Mugunghwa* (₩23,000, 4½ hours, four daily) trains run to the older, more central Gwangju station. Trains also continue to Mokpo and Yeosu from both stations.

Getting Around

BUS

Gwangju has more than 80 city bus routes, and most run past the bus terminal with bus stops on all sides. Bus 30 (20 minutes, every 15 minutes) runs between the bus terminal and Gwangju train station. City buses cost ₩1250; pay the driver in cash as you board.

SUBWAY

Currently there is one line that stretches west to the airport and Gwangju-Songjeong station. A single ride is ₩1250; trains run from 5.30am until midnight.

TAXI

Flagfall is ₩2800. The YMCA is an easy drop-off spot for points city centre.

Damyang

☎061 / POP 15,025

Damyang (담양) is famous for its bamboo and has a long tradition of bamboo craftwork. Sadly few artisans remain today, though the spirit of former times returns in May for the annual bamboo festival (www.bamboofestival.co.kr).

Sights

Changpyeong Slow City VILLAGE
(Samjinae; ☎061 383 3807; www.slowcp.com; 57389 Yeonpyeong-gil) South Korea may have developed at a breakneck speed, but it was also the first Asian country to sign on to the international *cittaslow*, or 'slow city' movement. One such city – or rather, village – is Samjinae (삼지내마을), with a population of 4105. Wander the dusty lanes, lined with centuries-old stone walls, past homesteads and heritage houses. 'Slow' food and art experience programs, such as cooking classes, tea ceremonies and paper crafts, can be booked in advance.

Samjinae is in the direction of Damyang. Take bus 303 (₩1750, 40 minutes, hourly)

from Daein Gwangjang and get off at Changpyeong Police Station, where you'll see a sign noting the entrance to the village. Alternatively you can take a taxi from Damyang bus terminal (around ₩20,000).

There are a handful of *minbak* (private homes with rooms for rent; from ₩50,000) here. The tourist information centre in Gwangju can arrange your stay.

Juknokwon GARDENS
(죽녹원, Bamboo Culture Experience; ☎061 380 2680; 119 Juknok-ro; adult/youth/child ₩3000/1500/1000; ⌚9am-6pm; 🚌311) Sandy walking trails wend through this bamboo grove, past pavilions and film locations for Korean dramas. It's one of the area's most popular attractions and can get crowded on weekends. But if you get a quiet moment – enough to hear the wind rustle the leaves – it can be enchanting.

Damyang Bamboo Crafts Museum MUSEUM
(한국대나무박물관; ☎061 380 2909; www.damyang.go.kr/museum; 35 Jukhyangmunhwa-ro; adult/youth/child ₩2000/1500/1000; ⌚9am-6pm; 🚌311) Lightweight and durable, bamboo can be made into pretty much anything – as you'll see at this museum, which is basically a showroom for bamboo products, both traditional and modern.

Sleeping & Eating

There's not much reason to overnight in Damyang – it's an easy day trip from Gwangju. If you feel compelled, however, there are a few motels and pensions in Damyang-gun.

For those looking for something to eat, **Bakmulgwan Apjip** (박물관앞집; ☎061 381 1990; 22 Jukhyangmunhwa-ro; meals ₩12,000-25,000; ⌚11am-9pm; 🚌311) serves Damyang's signature dish: *daetongbap* (대통밥) – rice and nuts cooked inside a bamboo stem – plus bamboo-shoot *doenjang* (fermented soybean paste) and a dozen side dishes, alongside free bamboo-leaf tea. The side rooms have glorious views over rice fields.

Getting There & Around

Intercity buses (₩2300, 40 minutes, every 15 minutes) depart from U Square bus terminal in Gwangju and arrive at Damyang terminal; the museum is a 15-minute walk from there. Bus 311 (₩2100, 40 minutes, every 15 minutes) runs between Gwangju bus terminal and Damyang, stopping off at the museum and Juknokwon. The museum is one stop before Damyang bus terminal and it's about a 30-minute walk between the two sights.

Gurye

☎061 / POP 27,115

The town of Gurye (구례) is the gateway to the southwest entrance of Jirisan National Park (p208). While the bulk of the park lies in the neighbouring province of Gyeongsangnam-do, it is best approached from this direction if you plan to visit Hwaeom-sa (p208), one of Korea's top temples.

Sleeping & Eating

Gurye Okjam GUESTHOUSE $$
(구례 옥잠; ☎010 7435 5353; www.guryeokjam.com; 17 Sangseolsijang-gil; per person from ₩30,000) This guesthouse in a renovated traditional home has thoughtful modern design touches and cosy beds. There are bikes available to borrow, a rooftop lounge area, and the homemade jams with the included breakfast are as sweet as the English-speaking couple who run the place.

Pyeonghwa Sikdang KOREAN $
(평화 식당; ☎061 782 2034; 12 Bukgyo-gil; bibimbap ₩9000; ⌚11am-7.30pm) This small bibimbap joint does a sashimi variety particularly well, with simple but tasty *banchan* (side dishes). Floor seating only.

Getting There & Away

Buses (₩1300, 15 minutes, every 30 minutes) run between Hwaeom-sa and Gurye. From Gurye buses run to Suncheon (₩4200, 50 minutes, every 40 minutes) or Gwangju (₩7800, 1¼ hours, every 30 minutes). Reserved-seat express buses (₩8500, 1½ hours, five daily) also run to Hwaeom-sa from Gwangju.

Suncheon

☎061 / POP 279,435

The southern city of Suncheon (순천) is a convenient base for exploring several of the region's highlights, including the wetlands at Suncheon-man, Naganeup-seong Folk Village and the temples inside Jogyesan Provincial Park (p221).

Sights

Naganeup-seong Folk Village HISTORIC SITE
(낙안읍성민속마을; ☎061 749 8831; 30 Chungmn-gil, Nagan-myeon; adult/youth/child

Suncheon

₩4000/2500/1500; 9am-5pm Dec-Jan, to 6pm Feb-Apr & Nov, 8.30am-6.30pm May-Oct; 63) Among Korea's many folk villages, Nagan is unique for its setting, surrounded by 1410m of Joseon-period fortress walls, built to protect the inhabitants from marauding Japanese pirates. It's Korea's best-preserved fortress town, crammed with narrow, dry-stone alleyways leading to vegetable allotments, and adobe and stone homes thatched with reeds. What's perhaps most interesting, however, is that people still live here.

The Namdo Food Festival (www.namdofood.or.kr), which receives 200,000-plus attendees, is usually held here early in October – it features 300 Korean dishes, eating contests and traditional cultural events.

Some homes double as *minbak* (private homes with rooms for rent from ₩40,000), restaurants and souvenir shops. Buses (₩1200, 40 minutes) leave every 90 minutes from Suncheon bus terminal.

Suncheon-man NATURE RESERVE
(순천만; 061 749 3006; www.suncheonbay.go.kr; 513-25 Suncheonman-gil; adult/youth/child ₩8000/6000/4000; 8am-6pm; 67) At this coastal estuary, inscribed on the Ramsar list of protected wetlands, you can follow walkways through rustling reeds up to an observation hut on a neighbouring hill – a popular sunset viewing spot. Birdwatchers should be on the lookout for hooded cranes, black-faced spoonbills and swans, all of which stop by during their migrations.

If you'd like to get closer to the wildlife, take a birdwatching boat (adult/child ₩8000/4000, 35 minutes, six daily Sunday to Tuesday). There's also a museum with exhibitions on the local ecology.

Buses (₩1200, 20 minutes) leave every 25 minutes from Suncheon bus terminal. This is also a popular place to visit from or on the way to Songgwang-sa (p222).

Sleeping & Eating

Suncheon Guesthouse Namdo HOSTEL $
(순천게스트하우스 남도; 010 4356 3255; 30-17 Jangcheon 2-gil; dm ₩20,000;) In a rambling old house a few minutes' walk north of the bus terminal (turn right at Samoa Motel), Namdo makes for an excellent base. Amenities include cooking and laundry facilities. A colourful mural marks the entrance.

Yeongbunsik KOREAN $
(영분식; 061 742 0933; 16 Isu-ro; meals ₩5000-6500; 11am-10pm) A favourite with local taxi drivers, Yeongbunsik does big portions of hearty staples such as *doenjang-jjigae* (된장찌개, tofu soup), *dolsot bibimbap* (돌솥비빔밥, bibimbap in a stone hotpot) and *donkkaseu* (돈까스; breaded pork cutlet). The restaurant is one block behind the bus terminal, on the left, with a red sign.

Information

There is a tourist information centre inside the **bus terminal** (061 749 3839; 9am-6pm) and in front of the **train station** (061 749 3107; 135 Palma-ro; 9am-6pm). The city runs reasonably priced **tours**, with different schedules daily taking in some of the major sights, meaning you won't have to keep doubling back to the bus terminal. Enquire at the tourist offices.

Getting There & Around

KTX trains run from Yongsan in Seoul to Suncheon (₩44,300, two hours, nine daily); there is also a daily *Saemaul* (₩38,100, 4¼ hours) service.

The intercity bus terminal is in the centre of town. Local buses depart from Palma-ro, in front of the bus terminal.

Jogyesan Provincial Park

Jogyesan Provincial Park (조계산도립공원) is home to two noteworthy temples, Songgwang-sa to the west and Seonam-sa to the east. Two hikes connect the two temples: a spectacular 8km hike and a longer 16km hike over the peak of Janggun-bong (884m).

Jogyesan Provincial Park

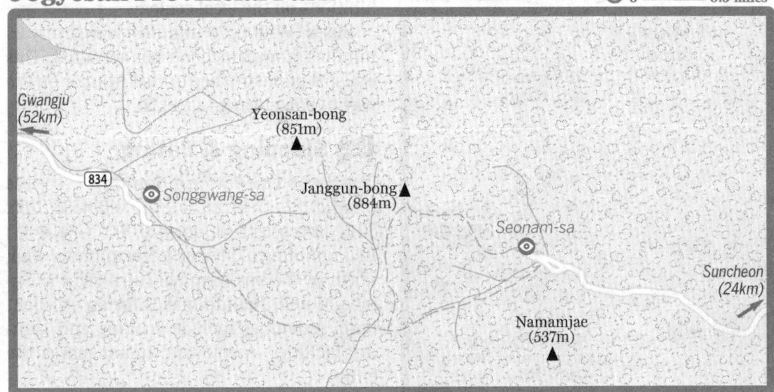

The walk takes six hours if you go over the peak, or four hours if you go around it. Either route is fantastic.

Sights

Songgwang-sa TEMPLE
(송광사; ☎061 755 0107; www.songgwangsa.org; 12 Sinpyeong-ri, Songgwang-myeon; adult/child ₩3000/2000; ⏱6am-7pm Mar-Oct, 7am-6pm Nov-Feb; 🚌111) Songgwang-sa is considered one of the three jewels of Korean Buddhism, along with Tongdo-sa (p200) and Haein-sa (p155), in Gyeongsangnam-do. Featured in the *Little Monk* movie, it is a regional head temple of the Jogye sect, which is by far the largest in Korean Buddhism. It is also one of the oldest Zen temples in Korea, founded in the 10th century, although most of the buildings date from the 17th century. A weekend templestay (₩50,000) is available here.

Songgwang-sa is known for having produced many prominent Zen masters over the years, and today the temple is home to a community of monks.

Seonam-sa TEMPLE
(선암사; ☎061 754 9117; www.seonamsa.net; 802 Jukak-ri, Seungju-eup; adult/youth/child ₩2000/1500/1000; ⏱6am-7.30pm Jun-Sep, 7am-7pm Oct-May; 🚌1) Seonam-sa is a quiet hermitage dating back to AD 529, where the monks study and try to preserve the old ways. Below Seonam-sa is Seungseongyo, one of Korea's most exquisite ancient granite bridges, with a dragon's head hanging from the top of an arch. A templestay is available. To get here, take bus 1 from Suncheon bus terminal (₩1200, one hour, every 45 minutes).

Sleeping

Weekend templestays are available at Songgwang-sa and Seonam-Sa. Lodgings near the car park at Songgwang-sa range from ₩30,000. There's also a tourist village near Seonam-sa.

Getting There & Away

From Gwangju, buses (₩7500, 1½ hours) run to Songgwang-sa at 8.50am, 9.55am, 10.45am, 2.55pm and 3.45pm. From Suncheon, bus 1 runs to Seonam-sa (₩1100, 1½ hours, every 50 minutes) and bus 111 to Songgwang-sa (₩1100, 1½ hours, hourly).

Yeosu

☎061 / POP 295,538

The molar-shaped port city of Yeosu (여수) is halfway along Korea's steep, island-pocked and deeply indented southern coast. Its bustling city centre is nothing special, but its shoreline, peppered with cliffs, islands and peninsulas, is spectacular. The local hero is Admiral Yi Sun-shin (1545–98), who repelled Japanese invaders with his 'turtle ships'. You'll see statues of him, and replicas of the ships, around town; he's also on the ₩100 coin. In 2012 Yeosu hosted the World's Fair International Exposition (called Expo 2012), which resulted in a redevelopment of the waterfront.

Sights

Hyangir-am TEMPLE
(향일암; ☎061 644 4742; 60 Hyangiram-ro, Dolsan-eup; adult/youth/child ₩2000/1500/1000; ⏱dawn-dusk; 🚌111, 113) A Buddhist hermitage

with a 1350-year heritage, Hyangir-am has an enviable location perched halfway up a mountain at the tip of Dolsando, an island connected to Yeosu by a bridge. It's stunning any time of day, but is most enchanting at sunrise, when you can watch daybreak over the ocean while listening to the monks chant. Buses (₩1200; one hour) to Hyangiram start around 4.30am to arrive in time for first light; pick up a schedule at the TIC.

It's a steep 10-minute walk from the bus stop through the tourist village up to the temple. Every restaurant along the way sells *gatkimchi* (갓김치; pickled mustard leaves), a local speciality. There are also some pensions and *minbak* (private homes with rooms to rent) if you're inclined to stay overnight.

Buses (₩1200, one hour) run from outside Jinnamgwan to Hyangiram.

Odongdo ISLAND
(오동도; ☎061 690 7301; 🚌2, 52, 61, 555) This small, craggy island, a favourite destination for locals, is covered in bamboo groves and camellia trees. Walking paths wend round the island taking about half an hour. Take the lift up to the **lighthouse observatory** (⏲9.30am-5.30pm) for the best harbour views. The island is joined to the mainland by a 750m causeway that can be traversed by a **road train** (adult/child ₩800/500, every 20 minutes, ⏲9am-5.30pm).

Buses stop at the causeway entrance; otherwise it's a pleasant 30-minute walk along the coast from Jungang-dong Rotary.

Jinnamgwan HISTORIC BUILDING
(진남관; 11 Dongmun-ro; ⏲9am-6pm) FREE In the centre of town stands this national treasure, Korea's largest single-storey wooden structure (75m long and 14m high). The beautiful pavilion, first constructed in 1599 with 68 pillars supporting its massive roof, was originally used for receiving officials and for holding ceremonies.

On the right, a small but modern museum focuses on Admiral Yi Sun-sin (1545–98) and has maps explaining his naval tactics and victories over Japan in the 1590s.

Fish Market MARKET
Like any port town worth its salt, Yeosu has a bustling fish market.

Expo 2012 Yeosu Korea Memorial Hall MUSEUM
(1 Bangnamhoe-gil; adult/child ₩3000/2000; ⏲9am-7pm Tue-Sun; 🚌2, 6, 7, 333) Originally the Korea Pavilion for Yeosu's 2012 World's Fair International Exposition, this museum showcases the latest in Korean maritime technology, such as tidal-wave power generators.

Activities

Ocean Resort Water Park WATER PARK
(☎061 689 0870; www.theoceanresort.co.kr; 295 Soho-ro; adult/child from ₩65,000/53,000, sauna ₩12,000; ⏲9am-8pm Jun-Aug) The Ocean Resort Water Park has multiple pools and slides, plus a hot-spring sauna (the latter open year-round).

Sleeping

Backpackers in Yeosu HOSTEL $
(백패커스 인 여수; ☎010 2561 2552; www.backpackersinyeosu.com; 1046 Gonghwa-dong; ₩20,000; 🚭❄@📶) This modern hostel has en suite bathrooms in the four-person dorms and ample cooking and lounging facilities. The young staff speak some English. It's a little removed from the action, but very near a stop on bus route 2.

Yeosu Guesthouse Flying Pig HOSTEL $
(여수게스트하우스; ☎061 666 1122; www.yeosuhouse.com; 7 Gonghwabuk 3-gil; dm ₩20,000; 🚭❄@📶) The location here is fantastic, right in the centre of town. There are a few quirks, such as the steep stairs and cramped shared bathrooms. On the other hand, there's free breakfast and the English-speaking owner is friendly and helpful.

Narsha Tourist Hotel HOTEL $$
(나르샤 관광호텔; ☎061 686 2000; www.narshahotel.com; 200-24 Hak-dong; r from ₩110,000; P❄@📶) Though not the cheapest spot on the Hak-dong waterfront strip, this solid midrange option is the most inviting, with helpful English-speaking staff and comfortable, well-appointed rooms, some with sea views.

Motel T MOTEL $$
(모텔티; ☎061 665 5757; 6-12 Gyodongnam 1-gil; r ₩45,000-65,000; ❄@) The owner claims to have the cleanest rooms in the strip and he's probably right. Features include big TVs and large rooms, some with sea views.

Motel Sky MOTEL $$
(모텔스카이; ☎061 662 7780; 5-5 Gyodongnam 1-gil; r ₩70,000-80,000; ❄@📶) A friendly welcome awaits you at this dated but well-maintained motel. The 6th floor has

Yeosu

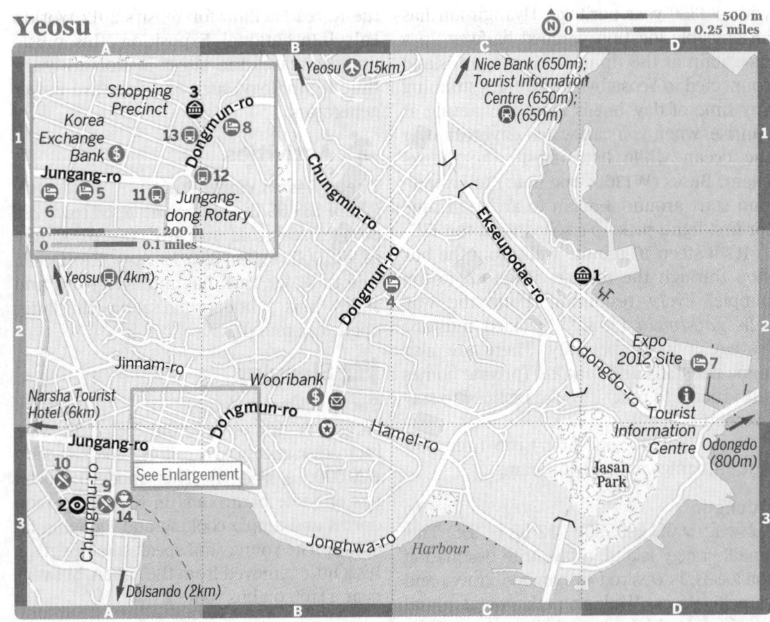

Yeosu

Sights

1 Expo 2012 Yeosu Korea Memorial Hall D2
2 Fish Market A3
3 Jinnamgwan A1

Sleeping

4 Backpackers in Yeosu C2
5 Motel Sky A1
6 Motel T A1
7 MVL Hotel D2
8 Yeosu Guesthouse Flying Pig B1

Eating

9 Gubaek Sikdang A3
10 Gyodong-sijang A3

Information

Tourist Information Centre .... (see 14)

Transport

11 Airport Shuttle Stop A1
12 Buses to Bus Terminal & Train Station B1
13 Buses to Hyangiram A1
14 Ferry Terminal A3

the best views and more expensive rooms have computers.

Ocean Resort RESORT $$$
(☎061 689 0800; www.theoceanresort.co.kr; 295 Soho-ro; r from ₩350,000;) The top draw at this luxury hotel, opened in 2008, is the Ocean Resort Water Park (p223), with its pools, slidesand hot-spring sauna (open year-round). The whole complex sits right on the coast, about 9km west of the city centre. The resort also has a hotel-style tower across the road, with rooms from ₩220,000.

MVL Hotel HOTEL $$$
(☎061 660 5800; www.mvlhotel.com; 111 Odong-do-ro; r from ₩204,000;) The glossy 'Most Valuable Life' hotel has ultramodern rooms with plush beds and bay views.

Eating

Tongbbyeoyechan KOREAN $
(통뼈예찬; ☎061 686 9199; 200-1 Hak-dong; meals from ₩7000; 24hr) Locals love the fiery bowls of *gamjatang* (감자탕, pork bone soup) – a Jeollanam-do speciality and reputed hangover cure – served at this all-night Hak-dong joint. There's a picture menu. It's

around the corner from the Narsha Tourist Hotel (p223).

Gubaek Sikdang KOREAN $$
(구백식당; ☎061 662 0900; 18 Yeogaekseon-teomineol-gil; meals ₩12,000-25,000; ⏰7am-8pm) *Seodae-hoe* (서대회, thin slices of raw fish marinated in *makgeolli* vinegar and chilli paste) is a local speciality and this restaurant is famous for it. To eat it, mix the fish with the rice and stir. *Saengseongui* (생선구이, grilled fish) is another good bet. The *ajumma* (married or older women) staff are friendly and used to dealing with foreigners.

Gyodong-sijang STREET FOOD $$
(교동시장; ☎061 666 3778; 15-10 Gyodongsijang 1-gil; meals ₩15,000-30,000) In the evening, this market fills with 'covered wagons' – makeshift eating and drinking joints, see p207. Several serve *haemul bokkeum* (해물볶음; ₩30,000), a huge two-person (or more) assorted seafood and vegetable sauté, set to bubble at your table.

Mae Hwa Gang San KOREAN $$$
(매화강산; ☎061 692 1616; 200-21 Hak-dong; plates ₩12,000-29,000; ⏰11.30am-10pm) Lovers of red meat will have reason to rejoice at this friendly, family-run, Korean barbecue restaurant serving such favourites as bulgogi and *galbi* (beef ribs). It's along the waterfront in Hak-dong.

ℹ Information

Police station (☎061 660 8239; 2 Hamel-ro; ⏰9am-6pm)

Yeosu Post Office (52 Dongmun-ro; ⏰9am-6pm Mon-Fri)

MONEY

Korea Exchange Bank (☎061 663-8000; 3 Tongjeyeong 4-gil; ⏰9am-4pm Mon-Fri) Exchanges foreign currency.

Nice Bank (2 Mangyang-ro) Global ATM inside the train station.

Wooribank (☎061 662 8111; 51 Dongmun-ro; ⏰9am-4pm Mon-Fri) Exchanges foreign currency; has an ATM.

TOURIST INFORMATION

Tourist Information Centre (☎061 664 8978; www.yeosu.go.kr; Odongdo-ro) At the entrance to Odong-do pedestrian causeway.

Tourist Information Centre (☎061 690 2588; 2 Mangyang-ro; ⏰9am-9pm) The biggest of the tourist information centres is in front of the train station and usually has an English speaker.

Tourist Information Centre (☎061 659 5707; 17 Yeogaekseon terminal-gil) Inside the Yeosu ferry terminal.

ℹ Getting There & Away

AIR

Yeosu airport, 17km north of the city, has flights to Seoul and Jeju-do. An **airport shuttle** (Jungang-ro; ₩3000, 40 minutes) runs from Jungang-dong Rotary; buses are timed to meet departures.

BOAT

The pier for island **ferries** (17 Yeogaekseon terminal-gil) is at the western end of the harbour.

BUS

The express bus terminal and intercity bus terminal are together, 4km north of the port area. Cross the pedestrian overpass to Pizza Hut and from the bus stop, almost any bus (₩1200, 15 minutes) goes to Jungang-dong Rotary.

TRAIN

Yeosu Expo station is the terminus for KTX trains running on the Jeolla line from Yongsan (₩46,500, 3½ hours, nine daily). There are also *Saemaul* (₩39,300, 4½ hours, one daily) and *Mugunghwa* (₩26,400, five hours, nine daily) services.

ℹ Getting Around

BUS

The most useful bus for getting around is No 2, which stops at Yeosu Expo station, Jinnamgwan and Odongdo. Near Jungang-dong rotary are stops for buses that go to the bus terminal and train station (Dongmun-ro), and to Hyangiram (Jinnamsangga-gil).

TAXI

Fares start at ₩2800. It's roughly a 15-minute, ₩10,000 taxi ride from central Yeosu to Hak-dong.

Boseong

☎061 / POP 44,245

The county of Boseong (보성) is famous as Korea's largest producer of green tea, and its namesake town is the gateway to the Daehan Dawon Tea Plantation. A Green Tea Festival takes place here in May; and in Yulpo, a sleepy seaside hamlet in the south of Boseong county, you can even luxuriate in a green tea spa bath.

Sights & Activities

Daehan Dawon Tea Plantation GARDENS

(대한다원; ☎061 853 2595; 763-65 Nokcha-ro; adult/child ₩4000/2000; ⊙9am-6pm) One of Korea's most iconic sights, the Boseong Daehan Dawon Tea Plantation is spectacularly set on a hillside covered with curvy row after row of manicured green tea bushes. It's a popular setting for TV dramas and films. Spring, when the leaves are at their greenest, is the most congenial time to visit.

At the plantation's restaurant you can sample green-tea infused dishes (₩5000 to ₩8000) and drinks.

Korea Tea Museum MUSEUM

(한국차박물관; ☎061 852 0918; www.koreateamuseum.kr; 775 Nokcha-ro; adult/child ₩1000/500; ⊙10am-5pm Tue-Sun) Here you can learn more than you ever thought you needed to know about tea, both in Korea and around the world, and also take part in a traditional tea service (₩2000). The museum is a 1km walk up the hill from the car park behind the bus stop.

Yulpo Haesu Nokchatang BATHHOUSE

(율포 해수 녹차탕; ☎061 853 4566; 678 Dongyul-ri, Hoecheon-myeon; adult/child ₩6000/4000; ⊙6am-8pm, last entry 7pm) Don't just settle for drinking tea – bathe in it at this local spa that includes a green-tea bath among its many tubs.

Sleeping & Eating

Yulpo has a few pensions and car camping close to the water, and there are several seafood restaurants on the waterfront.

Getting There & Away

From Suncheon, buses (₩6300, 50 minutes, every 30 minutes) and trains (₩3800, one hour, six daily) travel to Boseong and continue to Gangjin (₩4500, 45 minutes). There's an express bus from Gwangju (₩8400, 1½ hours). One *Mugunghwa* train at 6.31pm goes from Boseong to Gwangju (₩5200, two hours).

Getting Around

Buses run from Boseong bus terminal to Yulpo Haesu Nokchatang (₩1300, 30 minutes, once or twice an hour), stopping at Boseong train station and Daehan Dawon Tea Plantation (15 minutes).

Haenam

☎061 / POP 23,928

Located at the very southwest corner of the Korean Peninsula, the county of Haenam (해남) is known for agriculture. Just southeast of the small, regional hub of Haenam-eup is Duryunsan Provincial Park, where a cluster of climbable peaks cradle the temple, Daeheung-sa.

Sights

Duryunsan Provincial Park PARK

(두륜산도립공원; ☎061 530 5543; 400 Daeheungsa-gil; adult/youth/child ₩3000/1500/1000) Picturesque views of Korea's southern coastline reward hikers who scale the rocky path up to the peak, Duryun-bong (630m). The hike, which begins just behind the temple museum at Daeheung-sa, takes 1½ hours. It's a hard scramble near the top; it's an easier descent if you follow the stairs down and pick up the trail at the junction Jinburam.

There's also a **cable car** (☎061 534 8992; www.haenamcablecar.com; 88-54 Daeheungsa-gil; adult/child return ₩10,000/7000; ⊙8am-5pm Dec-Mar, to 6pm Apr-Nov) that heads up to a different peak, Gogye-bong (638m), but does not operate on windy days.

Daeheung-sa TEMPLE

(대흥사; ☎061 535 5502; www.daeheungsa.co.kr; 400 Daeheungsa-gil; adult/youth/child ₩3000/1500/1000; ⊙sunrise-sunset) This major Zen temple is thought to date back a millenia, but it remained relatively unknown until it became associated with Seosan, a warrior monk who led a group against Japanese invaders between 1592 and 1598. The backdrop of mountains against the temple is said to be a silhouette of Buddha lying down on his back. Trails behind the temple lead to some mountain hermitages, such as Bukmireuk-am, with its Silla-era (850–932) Buddhist stone carvings.

The temple is inside Duryunsan Provincial Park, a 30-minute walk from the bus stop. Templestays are available (from ₩40,000).

Sleeping

Haenam Youth Hostel HOSTEL $

(해남유스호스텔; ☎061 533 0170; 88-88 Gurim-riu; dm/r ₩10,000/30,000; P ⊖ ❄ @) A three-minute walk beyond the cable car inside Duryunsan Provincial Park is this

WORTH A TRIP

GANGJIN: CERAMICS COUNTY

One of the most important ceramic centres in Korea, the county of Gangjin (강진) has been associated with celadon (glazed green ceramic) for more than 1000 years. It is specifically known for etched celadon, in which shallow patterns are carved while it's still wet and filled in with special glazes through an inlay process.

The exquisite 800-year-old examples of Goryeo-dynasty celadon on display at the **Goryeo Celadon Museum** (고려청자박물관; ☎061 430 3755; www.celadon.go.kr; 33 Cheongjachon-gil, Daegu-myeon; adult/youth/child ₩2000/1500/1000; ⊙9am-6pm) look startlingly contemporary. At the back are pottery workshops (Monday to Friday), where visitors can watch artisans at work on various processes. On the right is an excavated kiln site, discovered in 1968, that dates back to the 12th century. The museum and shops outside sell modern-made Goryeo celadon (the Seoul airport sells similar pieces for 10 times the price). The Gangjin Ceramic Festival is held here during midsummer.

To get to Gangjin, hop on one of the buses running every 30 to 60 minutes along the southern coast from Suncheon (₩10,800, two hours) or Mokpo (₩5500, one hour). Buses also run from Gwangju (₩12,900, 1½ hours, hourly).

The Goryeo Celadon Museum is 18km south of Gangjin. Take a local bus from Gangjin bus terminal for Maryang and get off at the museum (₩1800, 25 minutes, every 40 minutes).

excellent budget option, with clean modern rooms. Dorms have bunk beds while private rooms have *yo* (padded quilt mattresses on the floor); all rooms have bathrooms.

★ **Yuseongwan** GUESTHOUSE $$
(유선관; ☎061 534 2959; 376 Daeheungsa-gil; d ₩50,000; P ⊜) This idyllic traditional *hanok* inn, built around a courtyard, is inside Duryunsan Provincial Park, about two-thirds of the way between the car park and Daeheung-sa. Rooms are small but cosy, and decorated with ink-brush paintings; note that bathrooms are shared – and in a separate building. Don't miss the traditional breakfast (₩8000), brought to your room on a low table.

Next door is a rest stop with floor seating above the gurgling stream – it's a perfect place to stop for an ice cream or *makgeolli* (milky rice wine).

Eating

★ **Wonjo Jangsu Tongdak** KOREAN $$
(원조장수통닭; ☎061 535 1003; 295 Gosan-ro; four people from ₩60,000; ⊙11.30am-9pm) Hungry? Come here to feast on *tongdak* (통닭), chicken served in two courses. First comes a tabletop stir-fry of chicken marinated in a tangy, spicy sauce, followed by the rest of the bird and mung-bean rice porridge. The whole thing, which costs ₩60,000, is meant to serve four. The restaurant is in a brick building with a red sign.

It's halfway between Haenam bus terminal and Daeheung-sa, along the bus route; get off at the Dolgogae bus stop.

Jeonju Restaurant KOREAN $$
(고려청자박물관; ☎061 532 7696; 170 Daeheungsa-gil; dishes from ₩8000; ⊙9am-10pm) This place is famous for mushrooms – choose *pyogojeongol* (mushroom casserole) or *sanchaehan jeongsik* (minced beef, seafood, mushrooms and vegetables). Look for the English sign halfway along the line of restaurants just before the ticket booth for Duryunsan Provincial Park.

ℹ Getting There & Away

Access Duryunsan Provincial Park by bus (₩1200, 15 minutes, every 40 minutes) from Haenam bus terminal.

DESTINATION	PRICE (₩)	DURATION (HR)	FREQUENCY
Busan	31,400	6	7 daily
Gwangju	11,100	1¾	every 30min
Jindo	5900	1	hourly
Mokpo	6300	1	hourly
Seoul	34,300	5	6 daily
Wando	5400	1	hourly

1

2

ART DIRECTORS & TRIP / ALAMY STOCK PHOTO ©

4

TOPIC IMAGES INC / GETTY IMAGES ©

INSUNG JEON / GETTY IMAGES ©

DAENGPANYA ATAKORN / SHUTTERSTOCK ©

1. Hongdo (p235), South Korea Also known as Red Island, Hongdo is a protected nature reserve that can only be visited by boat.

2. Daehan Dawon Tea Plantation (p226), South Korea The county of Boseong is Korea's largest producer of green tea.

3. Mudeungsan National Park (p214), South Korea Overlooking the city of Gwangju, Mudeungsan is a popular hiking spot, including to the city's oldest temple, Jeungsim-sa.

4. Wolchulsan National Park (p234), South Korea Korea's smallest national park, Wolchulsan is packed with natural and engineered features.

Wando

☎061 / POP 53,878

Most travellers view Wando (완도), an island connected to the mainland by a bridge, as a transit point for ferries to Jeju-do. However, it's also home to a fantastic beach and ever-changing views of scattered offshore islands.

Sights

Myeongsasim-ni BEACH

(명사십리; ☎061 550 6929) The southern coast's best beach is a nearly 4km stretch of golden sand backed by a boardwalk and pine trees. There's a popular **campground** (⏲20 Jun-31 Aug; ₩10,000 per person) here, with raised platforms for tents and plenty of showers.

Myeongsasim-ni is on the smaller, neighbouring island of Shinjido; buses (₩1900, 25 minutes, hourly) run here from the Wando bus terminal.

Gugyedeung PARK

(구계등; ☎061 554 1769; 131 Jeongdo-ri; ⏲9am-5pm) On Wando's south coast is a tiny park that offers views of distant cliffs and offshore islands, a pebbly beach, and a 1km nature trail that runs through a thin sliver of coastal woodland. Swimming is dangerous.

The Seobu bus (₩1200, 10 minutes, hourly) runs from Wando bus terminal. Get off at Sajeong and walk 600m down to the park entrance.

Wando Tower OBSERVATORY

(완도타워; ☎061 550 5411; 330 Jangbogodae-ro; adult/student/child ₩2000/1500/1000; ⏲9am-9pm Oct-May, to 10pm Jun-Sep) This 76m-tall tower offers views of Wando harbour and to the islands beyond.

Sleeping

Dubai Motel MOTEL $$

(두바이 모텔; ☎061 553 0688; 37 Haebyeon-gongwon-ro; r ₩40,000-50,000; P❄@📶) There's no desert in sight, but this green waterfront hotel has smart rooms, both western-style and *ondol* (traditional sleep-on-the-floor matresses), and harbour views. Pricier rooms have PCs.

Grand Motel MOTEL $$

(그랜드 모텔; ☎061 535 0100; www.wandogrand.co.kr; 41 Gaepo-ro 56beon-gil; r ₩40,000-50,000; P❄@📶) This is a comfortable, clean place with large rooms overlooking the harbour, fast PCs and free use of the in-house sauna.

Wando

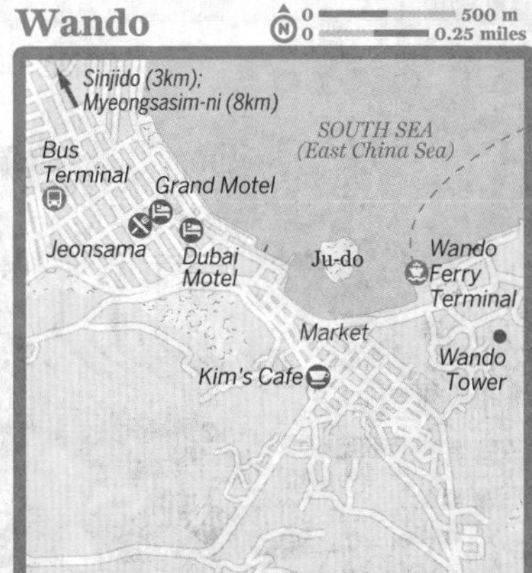

Eating

Wando is Korea's largest producer of *jeonbok* (전복, abalone), and you'll see tanks of them in most restaurants lining the harbour.

Jeonsama KOREAN $$$

(전사마; ☎061 555 0838; 197 Jangboyo-daero; dishes ₩9000-50,000; ⏲9am-9pm) This popular restaurant serves abalone a bunch of different ways, but try what we dub a Korean version of surf-and-turf: *wanggalbi jeonbokjjim* (왕갈비전복찜; for two people ₩50,000) – braised abalone and grilled spare ribs. Yum.

Drinking & Nightlife

Kim's Coffee CAFE

(☎061 555 1158; 40 Cheonghaejinnam-ro; coffee ₩3000-5000; ⏲8.30am-10pm; 📶) This cute-as-pie white cottage looks totally out of place on a street filled with grey, weathered shops. There are fresh juices, cakes and muffins on the menu along with the usual coffees and teas.

Getting There & Away

Ferries depart from **Wando Ferry Terminal** (☎061 554 8000; 335 Jangbogo-daero) for Jeju-do at 9.30am and 4pm on weekdays and at 9am, 3am and 4pm on weekends. The last ferry of the day takes three hours and costs ₩26,700; the others take 1½ hours and cost ₩37,000. Other ferries run to a dozen nearby islands including Cheongsando.

Getting Around

From Wando **bus terminal** (☎061 552 1500; 20 Gaepo-ro 130beon-gil), one local bus heads west (서부, *seobu*) while another heads east (동부, *dongbu*). Both go to the bridge to the mainland before heading back to Wando. The ferry terminal is a 25-minute walk from the bus terminal or a short taxi ride.

Mokpo

☎061 / POP 247,442

The sprawling port city of Mokpo (목포), set on a small peninsula jutting out into the West Sea, is the end of the line for trains and expressway traffic, and a starting point for sea voyages to Jeju-do and the western islands of Dadohae Haesang National Park. Korea's National Maritime Museum is located here, and the craggy peaks of Yudalsan Park rear up in the city centre, offering splendid sea, city and sunset views.

Mokpo is the hometown of late South Korean president and Nobel Peace Prize recipient Kim Dae-jung. It's also the base of the Formula 1 race, held at a racetrack 15km south of town – one of the many recent development projects awarded to long-neglected Jeollanam-do.

Sights

★National Maritime Museum MUSEUM

(국립해양유물전시관; ☎061 270 2000; 136 Namnong-ro; ⏲9am-6pm Tue-Sun; 🚸; 🚌15) FREE This is the only museum in Korea dedicated to the country's maritime history. The highlights are two shipwrecks, one dating from the 11th century and the other from the early 14th century. Thousands of priceless items of Korean and Chinese celadon, coins and other trade items were salvaged from them. Fascinating film footage shows the treasures being salvaged, and part of the actual boats has been preserved. It has excellent English signage.

Yudalsan Park PARK

(유달산; 180 Yudal-ro) Right on the coast, this park is filled with rocky cliffs and pavilions, with views across the island-scattered sea. Follow the main path for about 45 minutes to the peak Ildeung-bawi (일등바위). To head down to Yudal Beach, double back to Soyojeong (소요정) pavilion for the path to Arirang Gogae (아리랑고개), then follow the sign to **Nakjo-dae** (낙조대; Jukgyo-dong) pavilion. From there it's a 10-minute walk down the steps to the beach.

The beach is just a tiny patch of sand, rocks and seaweed, so the main attractions are the island views (partially spoiled by a bridge) and a smattering of bars and restaurants. Bus 1 and most of the other buses that pass by can take you back to the city centre.

Mokpo Culture & Arts Center ARTS CENTRE

(목포문화예술회관; ☎061 270 8484; www.mokpo.go.kr/art; 122 Namnong-ro; ⏲9am-6pm; 🚌15) FREE This grand four-floor atrium building displays the work of local artists who work in all media – from traditional ink to colourful modern splodges, photographs, and the art of bonsai. The centre also houses a 700-seat performance hall.

Gatbawi Culture District AREA

(갓바위공원; Namnong-ro; 🚌15) This area, 4km east of the city centre, has a swath of museums, including the Maritime Museum and the Culture & Arts Center. Just past the museums are the riverside Gatbawi Rocks, which have been heavily eroded into shapes that are supposed to look like two monks wearing reed hats. A pier extends into the river so you can get a good look at this city icon.

Catch the bus (₩1200, 20 minutes, every 30 minutes) from outside the train station (across the street). A taxi costs ₩5000 from the train station.

Namnong Memorial Hall MUSEUM

(남농기념관; ☎061 276 0313; 119 Namnong-ro; adult/child ₩1000/500; ⏲10am-6pm Tue-Sun; 🚌15) This hall contains a collection of paintings by five generations of the Huh family, including work by Huh Gun, a master of Namjonghwa, a Korean art style associated with the Southern School of China.

Mokpo Natural History Museum MUSEUM

(목포자연사박물관; ☎061 274 3655; 135 Namnong-ro; adult/youth/child ₩3000/2000/1000; ⏲9am-6pm Tue-Fri, to 7pm Sat & Sun; 🚸; 🚌15) This museum is aimed at children, with large dinosaur skeletons, live lizards and fish, and thousands of colourful-but-dead butterflies.

Show your ticket stub for free admission to Mokpo Ceramic Livingware Museum (p232).

Mokpo

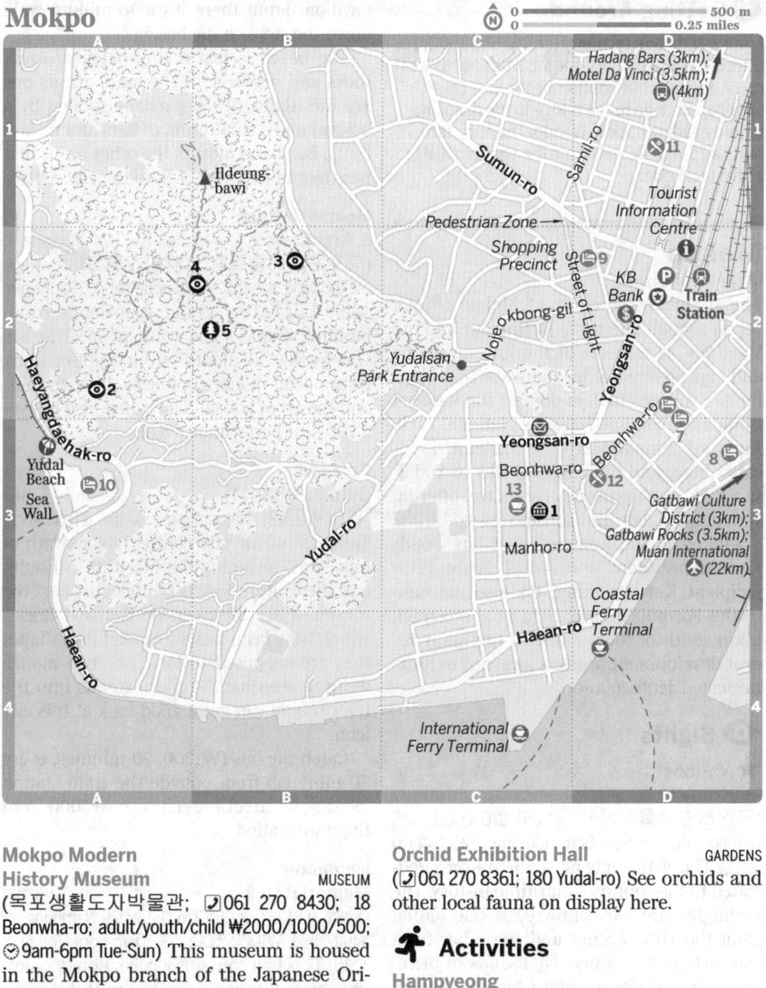

Mokpo Modern History Museum MUSEUM
(목포생활도자박물관; ☎061 270 8430; 18 Beonwha-ro; adult/youth/child ₩2000/1000/500; ⌚9am-6pm Tue-Sun) This museum is housed in the Mokpo branch of the Japanese Oriental Colonization Company, a building from the 1920s. It takes a hard look at the Japanese colonisation of Korea in the early 20th century, telling its story almost entirely through photographs, which also document Mokpo's rapid growth over the last century.

Mokpo Ceramic Livingware Museum MUSEUM
(목포생활도저박물관; ☎061 270 8480; http://doja.mokpo.go.kr; 135 Namnong-ro; adult/youth/child ₩3000/2000/1000; ⌚9am-6pm Tue-Fri, to 7pm Sat & Sun; 🚌15) Traces the history and uses of Korean ceramics, from ancient pottery to biotechnology. Show your ticket stub for free admission to Mokpo Natural History Museum.

Orchid Exhibition Hall GARDENS
(☎061 270 8361; 180 Yudal-ro) See orchids and other local fauna on display here.

Activities

Hampyeong Seawater Sauna SPA
(함평해수찜; ☎061 322 9466; 1007-1 Gungsan-ri, Sonbul-myeon; r ₩30,000; ⌚8am-5pm) Too cold for a swim? Take a detour to the Hampyeong Seawater Sauna, where saltwater is mixed with medicinal herbs and heated with fire-baked stones. Private rooms are available for parties of up to four. You'll be given pyjamas to wear and towels to soak in the water and wrap around your body (don't get in the water – it's too hot).

Buses run roughly hourly from Mokpo to Hampyeong (₩4100, one hour), from where a taxi to the sauna will cost around ₩10,000. Last entry is 3pm.

Mokpo

Sights

1	Mokpo Modern History Museum	C3
2	Nakjo-dae	A2
3	Orchid Exhibition Hall	B2
4	Soyojeong	B2
5	Yudalsan Park	B2

Sleeping

6	Baek Je Hotel	D2
7	F1 Motel	D3
8	Marina Bay Hotel	D3
9	Mokpo 1935	D2
10	Shinan Beach Hotel	A3

Eating

11	Dokcheon	D1
	Namupo	(see 9)
12	Yeongran Hoet-jip	D3

Drinking & Nightlife

13	House Filled with Happiness	C3

Sleeping

Mokpo 1935 GUESTHOUSE $

(목포1935; ☎061 243 1935; http://cafe.daum.net/mokpo1935; 59 Yeongsan-ro; dm/d ₩25,000/100,000;) This beautifully restored, 100-year-old *hanok* is in the heart of the old city, a short walk from the train station. There are dorm rooms in one building and family rooms in another, around a courtyard; bathrooms are shared. It's tricky to find: look up for the sign that says 'Cafe & Bar, Guesthouse' over the entrance to an alleyway.

Fontana Beach Hotel HOTEL $$

(폰타나비치호텔; ☎061 288 7000; www.fontanahotel.co.kr; 69 Pyeonghwa-ro; d from ₩136,000; P) Located along the waterfront Peace Park promenade in Hadang, this hotel is refreshingly understated. Rooms aren't big, but they have picture windows and crisp white linens. The deluxe twin room (with a double and a single bed) is great for families. Staff speak English.

F1 Motel MOTEL $$

(에프원호텔; ☎061 244 7744; 29 Sugang-ro 12beon-gil; r ₩50,000-60,000; P@) The best of the cluster of motels between the train station and the ferry terminal is this dark high-rise. Modern, clean rooms have sofas, heated toilet seats and ultrafast PCs. Note that wi-fi is weak in some rooms.

Shinan Beach Hotel HOTEL $$

(신안비치호텔; ☎061 243 3399; www.shinanbeachhotel.com; 440-4 Jukgyo-dong; r from ₩120,000; P) Traditionally seen as Mokpo's top hotel, it towers over Yudal Beach and is old-fashioned classy. Rooms (mainly *ondol* or twin) have large windows, though the sky lounge is disappointing. Discounts during low season, though prices double during peak.

Marina Bay Hotel HOTEL $$

(마리나베이호텔; ☎061 247 9900; www.marinabayhotel.co.kr; 1 Haean-ro 249beon-gil; d from ₩60,000;) Outside peak season, this hotel – along the waterfront and just a few minutes' walk from the ferry terminal – is an excellent deal. (Prices rise by 20% on weekends and double during summer.) Rooms are bright, airy and modern.

Bobos Motel MOTEL $$

(보보스모텔; ☎061 283 2210; 1034-6 Sang-dong; r ₩50,000; P@) This sleek black and silver tower is clean, sharp and within stumbling distance from Mokpo's popular Hadang nightlife area. Rooms are surprisingly cheerful, given the nightclub lighting in the corridors. Look for the rooftop red English sign.

Baek Je Hotel HOTEL $$

(백제관광호텔; ☎061 242 4411; 10-13 Sang-nak-dong, 1-ga; r from ₩40,000; P@) Location, location, location. The Baek Je is a 10-minute walk from Mokpo's train station and ferries and has compact rooms with dark-wood decor.

Motel Da Vinci MOTEL $$

(모텔다빈치; ☎061 287 0457; 16 Beonyeong-ro; r ₩45,000-70,000; P@) This flashy love motel in Hadang has rooms that are head and shoulders above the local competition (and are thankfully less flashy inside). Twin rooms, for example, come with two PCs and spa tubs.

Eating

★ **Dokcheon** KOREAN $$

(독천식당; ☎061 242 6528; 3-1 Honam-ro 64beon-gil; dishes ₩12,000-19,000; 10am-9.30pm) Mokpo is known for its octopus, particularly for its *nakji tangtangi* (chopped live octopus). This is the best place in town to try it, and if you're not quite up for the challenge of eating it still wriggling, the *nakji bibimbap* (octopus, rice, egg and veggies

OFF THE BEATEN TRACK

WOLCHULSAN NATIONAL PARK

Though it's just 42 sq km in size, making it Korea's smallest national park, **Wolchulsan National Park** (월출산국립공원; ☎061 473 5210; http://english.knps.or.kr; adult/youth/child ₩2000/1000/500; ⏰5am-7pm Mar-Oct, 8am-6pm Nov-Feb) has crags, spires and unusually shaped rocks around every corner, as well as an 8m Buddha rock carving, steel stairways and a 52m steel bridge spanning two ridges. The popular route is the 8km, six-hour hike from Dogap-sa in the west to Cheonhwang-sa in the east (or vice versa) over the park's highest peak, Cheonhwang-bong (809m). Tracks are well signposted, but steep and strenuous in places due to the rocky terrain. Bring lots of water.

If you're not up for a huge hike, head to the more popular Cheonhwang-sa end and hike an hour up a rocky path to the suspension bridge from where sprawling views of the surrounding country unfold.

From the small city of Yeongam (east of Mokpo), buses run the 11km to Dogap-sa (₩1400, 20 minutes, 9.30am and 4.30pm) in the west and the 4km to Cheonhwang-sa (₩1200, 10 minutes, 7.10am, 9am, 10.10am and 4.50pm). Consider taking a taxi from Yeongam.

with chilli sauce) and *nakji yeonpotang* (octopus soup) are excellent too.

It's an ordinary white-tiled building, with signs lit up at night. Seating is on the floor.

Namupo KOREAN $$
(나무포; ☎061 243 8592; 19-1 Sumun-ro; dishes ₩9000-35,000; ⏰9am-10pm) Not in a seafood mood? Try the *galbi* (갈비) grills at this local favourite located in the city centre. There's also a range of fan faves such as bibimbap and *naengmyeon* (cold buckwheat noodles).

Miyabi JAPANESE $$$
(미야비; ☎061 285 7579; www.miyabi.co.kr; 8 Hadangnambu-ro; meals ₩10,000-200,000; ⏰11.30am-9am) Located in Hadang near the Motel Da Vinci (p233), this popular Japanese restaurant has great-value lunch deals (₩10,000 to ₩25,000). Sets such as sushi, tempura and sashimi come with a large selection of Japanese-style *banchan* (side dishes). Prices double at dinner.

Yeongran Hoet-jip KOREAN $$$
(영란횟집; ☎061 243 7311; 42 Beonhwa-ro; dishes ₩45,000; ⏰10am-10pm) Though it may not look like much, this is one of Mokpo's finest *hoe* (raw fish) restaurants, where you can sample the local *mineo* (민어, croaker). Eat it as is or wrapped in *ssam* (leaves) dipped in a sweet and spicy sauce. Dishes are meant for sharing. There's a blue sign out the front.

Drinking & Nightlife

★**House Filled with Happiness** CAFE
(행복이가득한집; ☎061 247 5887; 48 Yudul-ro; drinks from ₩6600; ⏰10.30am-9pm) Mokpo's most attractive cafe, with dark polished wood, dim lights and a wrap-around veranda, is inside a restored Japanese colonial residence. Given the history, the name may seem ironic, but there's no denying that the building itself is beautiful, with a quiet calm.

Moe's Bar & Grille BAR
(1102 Sang-dong; drinks from ₩5000; ⏰9pm-2am) You'll find this scruffy expat hang-out on Rose St, a meandering pedestrian lane about 1km behind Peace Park. Don't read too much into the name: it's more of a beer and darts sort of place than a restaurant. It's above 11am Cafe.

Information

KB Bank (☎061 244 4113; 101 Yeongsan-ro) Foreign exchange and global ATM.
Police Station (☎061 244 1475; 98 Yeongsan-ro)
Post Office (☎061 270 6351; 288 Yeongsan-ro)
Tourist Information Centre (☎061 270 8599; Honam-dong; ⏰9am-6pm) Little English spoken but there is a helpful English map. At the train station.

Getting There & Away

AIR

Muan International Airport (☎1661 2626; www.airport.co.kr/muaneng/main.do; 970-260 Gonghang-ro, Mangun-myeon) is 25km north of the city and has flights to Jeju, Shanghai and Shenyang. There is no direct bus to the airport (a transfer is required at Muan). A taxi (around ₩30,000) is the best option.

BOAT

Mokpo's **Coastal Ferry Terminal** (연안여객선 터미널; 182 Haean-ro) handles boats to smaller islands west and southwest of Mokpo. Sightseeing trips depart from here and cruise around the nearby islands.

The **International Ferry Terminal** (국제 여객선 터미널; 14 Haean-ro) has two sailings a day to Jeju-do. Slower car ferries leave at 9am and take 4½ hours. Fares start at ₩30,000 and vary based on class; fares for under 12s are half price. The faster, pricier *Pink Dolphin* (₩49,650) leaves at 2pm, taking three hours. Contrary to its name, there are no international routes from this terminal.

BUS

Mokpo's bus terminal is several kilometres from the centre of town. Turn left outside the bus terminal, then left at the end of the road and walk down to the main road where bus 1 (₩1200, every 20 minutes) stops on the left. It runs to the train station, the ferry terminals and then on to Yudal Beach.

TRAIN

KTX provides a fast service to Seoul's Yongsan station (₩53,100, 2½ hours, 16 daily).

Getting Around

It's a 15-minute walk from the train station to the ferry terminals or to the entrance to Yudalsan Park.

Local bus 1 (₩1200, every 20 minutes) serves the bus terminal, ferry terminals, train station and Yudal Beach. Bus 15 (₩1200, 20 minutes, every 30 minutes) runs to the Gatbawi Park museums and Hadang from the bus and train stations. Taxis are cheap and plentiful.

Jindo Island

Jindo (진도), Korea's third-largest island, boasts some of the world's largest tides. The island is famous for an unusual natural phenomenon: for a few days each year (usually in spring), the tide drops extremely low, exposing a 2.8km-long, 40m-wide causeway that connects Jindo to the tiny island of Modo-ri.

The experience has long been celebrated among Koreans in legend. As one story goes, a family of tigers was causing so many problems on Jindo that all the islanders moved to nearby Modo, but somehow Grandma Ppong was left behind. She was broken-hearted and prayed to the Sea God to be reunited with her family. In answer to her fervent prayers, the Sea God parted the sea, enabling her to cross over to Modo and meet her family again. Sadly, she died of exhaustion shortly afterwards. Statues, shrines and paintings of her can be seen throughout Jindo.

With the spread of Christianity in Korea, the similarity to the Israelites' crossing of the Red Sea has only brought more enthusiasts. Some 300,000 people make the crossing each year – in tall rubber boots (available for rent, naturally).

The Jindo Miracle Sea Road Festival (http://miracleseaeng.jindo.go.kr), which includes a torchlit procession, musical performances and a memorial ceremony for Grandmap Ppong, is held annually to coincide with the crossing.

Jindo is best accessed from Gwangju (₩12,200, 2¾ hours, every 40 minutes) or Mokpo (₩6500, one hour, every 30 minutes). From Jindo bus terminal, catch a local bus bound for Hoedong (₩1300, one hour, hourly) to the festival site; a taxi should cost about ₩13,000 and take 30 minutes.

Dadohae Haesang (Marine Archipelago) National Park

Consisting of more than 1700 islands and islets and divided into eight sections, Dadohae Haesang (Marine Archipelago) National Park (다도해해상국립공원) occupies much of the coast and coastal waters of Jeollanam-do. Some of the isles support small communities with fishing and tourism income; others are little more than tree-covered rocks.

The town of Mokpo is the gateway to the western sector, including Hongdo and Heuksando, the most visited and scenic of the islands. In July and August the boats fill up, so book ahead.

Sights

Hongdo ISLAND

(홍도; Red Island) This is the most popular and beautiful of the islands west of Mokpo. Some 6km long and 2.5km wide, it rises precipitously from the sea and is bounded by sheer cliffs, bizarre rock formations and wooded hillsides cut by ravines. The island is ringed by islets and its sunsets can be spectacular, but the only way you can see most of it is by boat – with the exception of the villages, Hongdo is a protected nature reserve and entry is prohibited.

It is possible to climb the hill Gitdae-bong for views. There's a small pebbled beach on the south of the island.

Ferries to Hongdo arrive at a sparkling new ferry terminal in Ilgu village, which is protected by a tiny cove. **Boat tours** (₩22,000; ⏲7.30am-12.30pm; two hours) are the best way to appreciate the island and its rocky islets and arches, though the Korean commentary gets a little grating. Towards the end of the tour, a small boat pulls up and fishermen slice up live fish into plates of sashimi (₩35,000).

Heuksando ISLAND
(흑산도) Views of scattered specks of land from the peaks of Heuksando show why Dadohae Haesang means 'marine archipelago'. This island, on the way to Hongdo, is the larger, more populated and more accessible of the two. Fishing villages are linked by trails; walking the full circuit around the island takes about nine hours. Fortunately, local buses (₩1200, hourly) circle most of the island – a recommended trip is up the Bonghwa-dae peak, on the north coast hill, Sangnasan.

Cycling is also a fun way to get around; look for shops offering mountain bikes for hire (₩20,000 per day) near the ferry terminal.

Sleeping & Eating

On Heuksando, the largest village of Yeri has basic *minbak* (private homes with rooms for rent) and *yeogwan* (small, family-run hotels). On Hongdo there are several *minbak* and motels in Ilgu.

There are lots of seafood options on Heuksando and Hongdo, though prices run higher than the mainland.

1004 Hotel MOTEL $$
(1004호텔; ☎061 246 3758; r ₩50,000; ❄) You can't miss the colourful facade of 1004 Hotel, a short walk from the ferry terminal. It has sea-facing rooms and balconies.

Getting There & Away

The same ferries serve Heuksando, 90km west of Mokpo, and Hongdo, another 20km further away. Leaving from Mokpo's Coastal Ferry Terminal, ferries run to Heuksando (adult/child one way ₩34,300/17,150, two hours) and continue on to Hongdo (adult/child one way ₩42,000/21,000, 2½ hours). Ferries depart Mokpo at 7.50am, 8.10am, 1pm and 3.30pm. Return ferries depart from Hongdo at 10.20am and 3.30pm, stopping at Heuksando (₩11,200, 30 minutes) along the way.

Note that you will be asked to show your passport when buying a ferry ticket (and likely again when you board).

Jeju-do

064 / POP 524,790

Includes ➔

Best Places to Eat

- Dasi Boesi (p252)
- Saesom Galbi (p261)
- Yetnal Patjuk (p256)
- Haejin Seafood Restaurant (p244)
- Mint (p255)
- Dasoni (p244)

Best Places to Stay

- Seaes Hotel & Resort (p262)
- Ssari's Flower Hill (p252)
- Baume Couture Boutique Hotel (p243)
- Code 46610 (p266)

Why Go?

Jeju-do (제주도), Korea's largest island, has long been the country's favourite domestic holiday destination thanks to its beautiful beaches, lush countryside and seaside hotels designed for rest and relaxation.

There's plenty on Jeju-do to appeal to those who prefer to be active. Hike up South Korea's highest mountain, Halla-san, or climb the incredible tuff cone Seongsan Ilchulbong, rising straight from the sea, to watch the sun rise from the ridge of a crater. For a less-demanding nature experience, meander along one of the Jeju Olle Trails and explore tangerine-trimmed country roads, jagged coasts and narrow lanes dotted with cottage-style homes made from black lava rock. The ocean is never far away, so plunge into blue seas to view coral as colourful as the sunsets and dig into Jeju-do's unique cuisine, including seafood caught by *haeneyo* (female free divers).

When to Go

Jeju-si

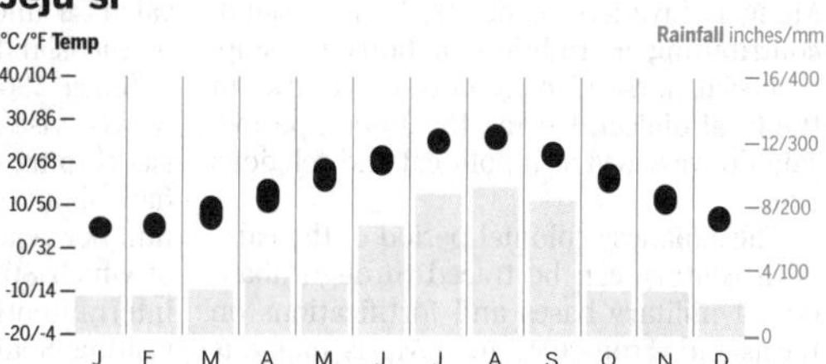

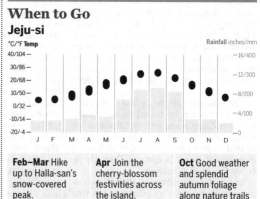

Feb–Mar Hike up to Halla-san's snow-covered peak.

Apr Join the cherry-blossom festivities across the island.

Oct Good weather and splendid autumn foliage along nature trails such as Saryeoni Park.

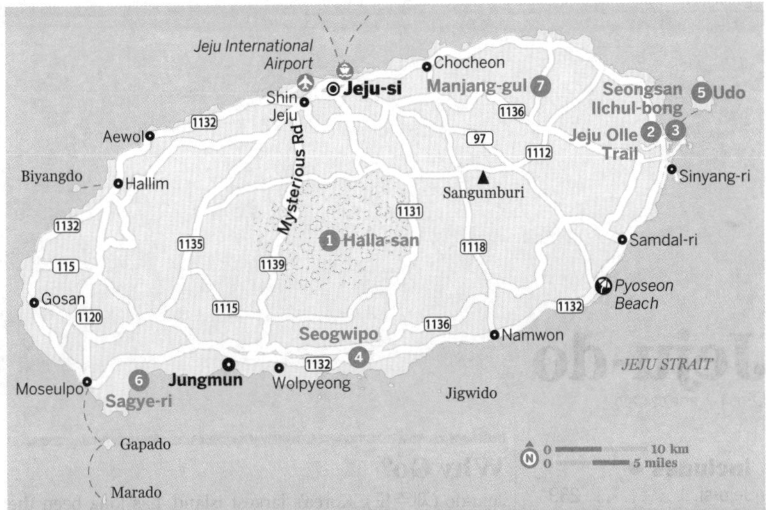

Jeju-do Highlights

1. **Halla-san** (p257) Hiking Korea's highest mountain from long rewarding climbs to easy jaunts.
2. **Jeju Olle Trail** (p250) Exploring the island step by step along a magnificent network of walking trails across the whole of Jeju-do.
3. **Seongsan Ilchul-bong** (p252) Admiring the sunrise and sea from atop the volcanic tuff cone.
4. **Lee Jung-Seop Art Gallery & Park** (p259) Eating, drinking and strolling around Seogwipo's youthful art district.
5. **Udo** (p253) Uncovering serendipitous natural delights on a tiny island off Jeju-do's east coast.
6. **Sanbanggul-sa** (p263) Finding Buddha in a cave at the top of a mountain in Sagye-ri.
7. **Manjang-gul** (p250) Going underground in part of the world's largest lava-tube cave system.

History

According to legend, Jeju-do was founded by three brothers who came out of holes in the ground and established the independent Tamna kingdom. Early in the 12th century the Goryeo dynasty took over, but in 1273 Mongol invaders conquered the island, contributing a tradition of horsemanship, a special horse *(jorangmal)* and quirks in the local dialect. During the Joseon period, Jeju-do was used as a political and religious exile.

The Japanese colonial period of the early 20th century can be traced through abandoned military bases and fortifications on the island. From 1947 to 1954, as many as 30,000 locals were massacred by right-wing government forces in events collectively labelled the 'April 3 Incident'.

Recent decades have seen Jeju-do's economy shift from mainly agriculture to tourism. In 2006 the island was made into a special autonomous province, giving it a level of self-government that is encouraging further economic development. The World Conservation Congress was held here in September 2012 and ambitious carbon-free electricity generation ventures are being tested. Jeju-do has come under fire from conservationists and other protesters for the Korean naval base under construction at Gangjeong on the island's south coast.

Since 2008 the Korean government has waived visa requirements for Chinese tourists coming to Jeju-do. That year the island had about 400,000 visitors. In 2018 that number reached 15 million annual visitors, of which 80% were Chinese, despite China intermittently banning its citizens from visiting South Korea in tour groups from March 2017 because of tensions over the THAAD missile-defense system. Some Jeju-do locals don't want the groups to return, complaining that financial pressures and high land costs are changing the once-sleepy nature of this island, with little trickle-down benefits from the big-name hotels and foreign-owned businesses.

Information

MEDIA

Jeju Weekly (www.jejuweekly.com) News, travel and what's on around Jeju-do.

Getting There & Away

Plenty of budget flights arrive at Jeju-si throughout the day from the mainland. In Seoul this includes both Incheon International Airport and Gimpo International Airport. International destinations include China, Japan, Malaysia, Taiwan and Thailand. Except for holidays and the summer season, it's rarely necessary to prebook. Comfortable ferries sail between Jeju-si and three ports on the peninsula.

Getting Around

CAR

Driving on Jeju-do is easy going. Road signs are in English, most rental cars come with an English-language GPS system and the hire cost is reasonable (around ₩60,000 a day for a compact car, including insurance). You must be at least 21 and have an international driving permit. SK Hertz, Avis and **Jeju Rent-a-Car** (Map p240; ☎064 747 3301; www.jejurentcar.co.kr; Jeju International Airport) have desks in the airport arrivals terminal.

BICYCLE

It's possible to pedal or scooter your way around the island (250km) in three to five days. The designated cycleway is relatively flat, with much of it parallel to the beautiful coast. Pack rain gear. Bicycles (₩10,000 per day) and scooters (₩15,000 to ₩25,000 per day) can be hired in Jeju-si and Seogwipo.

BUS

Services radiate from Jeju-si and Seogwipo and cover most of the island, running around the coast and across the centre roughly every 20 minutes. Pick up an English intercity bus map and timetable from the airport tourist office. The whole island's bus system was overhauled in August 2017, with new route numbers, so beware of outdated information. The new system now provides free wi-fi on board all buses and at most stops, which have useful screens with live next bus information and maps (touch the screen to select English). All regular buses (not red express buses or the Limousine Bus) cost ₩1200 per ride, regardless of distance. It's highly recommended to use the countrywide T-money card, which (in addition to slightly cheaper fares at ₩1150) offers the benefit of two free transfers within 40 minutes of tapping off one ride and making another.

With **Yeha Bus Tours** (☎064 713 5505; www.yehatour.com; adult/youth ₩109,000/89,000; ⏲8.30am-5.30pm) you get bus travel, sight entrance fees, lunch and a guide to explain everything on this one-day excursion. The company operates three routes that run to some of the most popular destinations on the island: east, including Seongsan Ilchul-bong (p252) and Manjang-gul (p250); west, including Hallim Park (p266) and O'Sulloc Tea Museum (p264); and south, including Eoseungsaengak Trail (p258) and **Yakcheon-sa** (약천사; Map p240; ☎064 738 5000; www.yakchunsa.org; 293-28 Ieodo-ro, Daepo-dong; ⏲sunrise-sunset; 🚌600, Yakcheon-sa stop). Tours run from pick-up points at Jeju Airport and Jeju-si, but the company can arrange transfers to many hotels around the island. Contact them for details.

TAXI

Charge is ₩2800 for the first 2km; a 15km journey costs about ₩10,000. You can hire a taxi for around ₩150,000 a day.

> LOCAL KNOWLEDGE
>
> **JEJU-DO FOOD & DRINK**
>
> Jeju-do speciality meats include *heukdwaeji* (pork from the local black-skinned pig), *kkwong* (pheasant) and *basme* (horse), served in a variety of ways, including raw.
>
> All kinds of fish and seafood are available from restaurants and direct from *haenyeo*, the island's famous female divers. Try *galchi* (hairtail), *godeungeo* (mackerel) or *jeon-bok* (abalone), often served in *jeonbok-juk* (a rice porridge). *Okdomgui* is a tasty local fish that is semidried before being grilled.
>
> *Halla-bong* tangerines are common. Also look out for prickly-pear jam, black *omija* tea and honey. Halla-san *soju* (local vodka) is smoother than some.

JEJU-SI

☎064 / POP 515,000

Jeju-do's capital, Jeju-si (제주시) makes a convenient base to explore the island, with a few historic structures, plenty of shopping, the island's hippest bars and a large range of places to eat. Within sniffing distance of the sea, Tapdong-ro has an incredible number of seafood and pork restaurants, which continue along the coastal road at Yongduam Rock with nice seaside views and ample bars and pensions. Boutique sleeping and eating can be found in Shin Jeju. The most interesting sights, such as Jeju Stone Park and Jeju Loveland, are out of town, but easily accessed either by bus or taxi.

Jeju-do

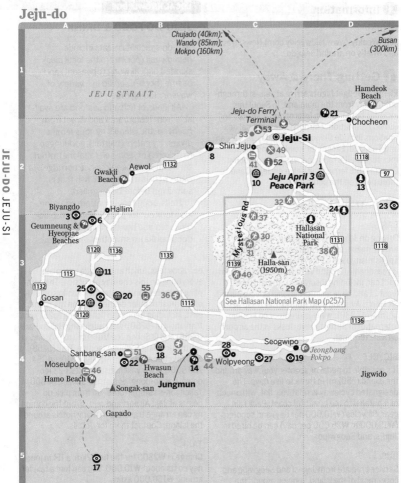

Although Seogwipo in the south is more atmospheric, Jeju-si is the main entry point by air or sea to to the island, with the city centre only 4km east of Jeju International Airport and even closer to its ferry ports, making for an easy stopover before or after any trip.

Sights

★**Arario Museum** MUSEUM
(아라리오뮤지엄; Map p244; ☎064 720 8201; www.arariomuseum.org; 14 Tapdong-ro, Samdoi-dong, Cheju; adult/youth/child ₩10,000/6000/4000; ⏰10am-7pm Tue-Sun) One of the island's most interesting art projects, Arario has four galleries in renovated buildings in and around the Tapdong area hosting permanent and temporary exhibitions by Korean and international artists. The design of these galleries continues and expands a Jeju tradition of thoughtful and artful use of space.

The entry fee into the **Tapdong Cinema gallery** (₩16,000) also gets you into the next-door Tapdong Bike Shop gallery. Arario Museum extends into two galleries housed in old motels – Arario Museum **Dongmun Motel I** (동문모텔 I; Map p244; ☎064 720 8202; www.arariomuseum.org; 37-5 Sanji-ro, Ildoil-dong; adult/youth/child ₩10,000/6000/4000; ⏰10am-7pm

Tue-Sun) and **Dongmun Motel II** (동문모텔 II; Map p244; ☎064 720 8203; 23 Sanji-ro, Geonip-dong) – which are a 20-minute walk from Tapdong, near Sanji-ro.

★ **Jeju April 3 Peace Park** MUSEUM
(제주 4·3 평화공원; Map p240; ☎064 723 4344; www.jejupark43.1941.co.kr; 430 Myeongnim-ro, Bonggae-dong; ⏲9am-6pm Tue-Sun; P) FREE Thoughtful and evocative, this museum chronicles the events that led up to and followed the 'April 3 Incident' – a series of island massacres between 1947 and 1954 that resulted in 30,000 deaths and the destruction of many homes. The reasons behind the deaths are complex and the museum takes a factual and artistic approach that heightens the emotional impact.

Jeju Stone Park PARK
(제주돌문화공원; Map p240; ☎064 710 7731; http://jejustonepark.com; 2023 Jamno-ro, Jocheon-eup; adult/youth ₩5000/3000; ⏲9am-6pm, closed 1st Mon of month; 🚌131, 231) Creating a park dedicated to rocks on a rock-littered island might sound a snooze, but you'll quickly reassess that opinion after touring this beguiling sculpture park. Three walking trails (between 560m and 970m in length) snake past outdoor exhibits, ranging from replicas of the original 47 *dolharubang* (grandfather rocks) to an enchanting forest with hundreds of *dongjasok* (pairs of stone tomb guardians).

Jeju Museum of Art GALLERY
(제주도립미술관; Map p240; ☎064 710 4300; http://jmoa.jeju.go.kr; 2894-78, 1100-ro; adult/youth/child ₩1000/500/300; ⏲9am-6pm Tue-Sun, to 8pm Jul-Sep; 🚌240, 465-1, 465-2) View interesting permanent and temporary exhibits of contemporary visual art at this excellent gallery next to Jeju Loveland (p265). The beautifully designed building appears to float on a pool of water.

Jeju Mokgwana HISTORIC SITE
(제주 목관아; Map p244; ☎064 710 6714; http://mokkwana.jejusi.go.kr; Gwandeok-ro; adult/youth/child ₩1500/800/400; ⏲9am-6pm, archery 10am-noon Sat Apr-Jun, Sep & Oct) Jeju's administrative centre under the Joseon dynasty, destroyed during Japanese rule, has been reconstructed. The cluster of historical buildings have an austere style that is designed to promote virtue. You can have a go at traditional archery, as well as watch displays of centuries-old martial arts. Outside the main gate is the 15th-century pavilion **Gwandeok-jeong** (관덕정; Map p244) FREE, Jeju's oldest building, once used as a training place for soldiers.

Saryeoni Forest FOREST
(사려니숲길; Map p240; ☎064 900 8800; P; 🚌212, 222, 232) FREE On the eastern border of Hallasan National Park, this is a popular weekend walking destination with 15km of forest paths shaded by maples, oaks and cedars, with the occasional roaming deer. Plan on four hours to walk the entire path between the two roadside entrances.

It's on Rtes 1112 and 1118; or take a 30-minute bus from Jeju Intercity Bus Terminal.

Jeju-do

Top Sights
1 Jeju April 3 Peace Park........D2
2 Jeju Folk Village........E3

Sights
3 Biyangdo........A3
4 Gimnyeong Maze Park........E1
5 Haenyeo Museum........F2
6 Hallim Park........A3
Hamel Memorial........(see 22)
7 Hongjodangoe Haebin Beach........F2
8 Iho Tewoo Beach........C2
9 Jeju Glass Castle........A3
Jeju Loveland........(see 10)
10 Jeju Museum of Art........C2
11 Jeju Museum of Contemporary Art........A3
12 Jeju Peace Museum........A3
13 Jeju Stone Park........D2
14 Jungmun Beach........B4
15 Kim Young Gap Gallery Dumoak........E3
16 Manjang-gul........E2
17 Marado........A5
18 Museum of Sex & Health........B4
19 Oedolgae........C4
20 O'Sulloc Tea Museum........B3
21 Samyang Beach........D1
22 Sanbanggul-sa........B4
23 Sangumburi........D2
24 Saryeoni Forest........D2
25 Spirited Garden........A3
26 Udo Lighthouse Park........F2
27 World Cup Stadium........C4
World Eros Museum........(see 27)
28 Yakcheon-sa........C4

Activities, Courses & Tours
29 Donnaeko Trail........C3
30 Eorimok Trail........C3
31 Eoseungsaengak Trail........C3
32 Gwaneum-sa Trail........C2
33 Jeju City Tour Bus........C2
34 Jungmun Beach Golf Club........B4
35 Olle Trail 1........F2
36 Pinx Golf Club........B3
37 Seokgul-am Trail........C3
38 Seongpanak Trail........D3
39 Yellow Tourist Bus 810........E2
40 Yeongsil Trail........C3
Yongmeori Coast........(see 22)

Sleeping
41 Baume Couture Boutique Hotel........C2
Code 46610........(see 6)
Gaga Pension........(see 42)
42 Gentleehouse Jeju........E1
43 Haevichi Hotel & Resort Jeju........E3
One Fine Day Guesthouse........(see 22)
44 Seaes Hotel & Resort........C4
45 Seongeup Folk Village Traditional Houses........E3
46 Springflower Guesthouse........A4
47 Ssari's Flower Hill........F2
Zen Hide Away........(see 22)

Eating
48 Dasi Boesi........F2
49 Dasoni........C2
Dol Hareubang Pizza........(see 12)
Donatos........(see 6)
50 Gwandangnae Sikdang........E3
Hamo Restaurant........(see 46)
Kangsikdang........(see 6)
Mayflower........(see 12)
Su Udon........(see 6)
Woljeong-ri Galbibap........(see 42)
Yetnal Patjuk........(see 50)
Yongrim Sikdang........(see 22)

Drinking & Nightlife
51 Lazybox Café........B4
Woljeong-ri Lowa........(see 42)

Information
Bus Terminal Tourist Information Office........(see 27)
52 Jeju Welcome Center........C2
Tourist Information Centre Jeju Airport........(see 33)

Transport
53 Jeju International Airport........C2
Jeju Rent-a-Car........(see 33)
54 Seongsan Ferry Terminal........F2
55 Yellow Tourist Bus 820........B3

Samyang Beach BEACH
(삼양 검은모래해변; Map p240; Seoheul-gil; 🚌331 or 332 to Samyang 1 Dong stop) The first beach east along Hwy 1132 from Jeju-si is Samyang, which is jet black when wet. In summer join the locals and bury yourself in the iron-rich sand for a therapeutic sand bath, said to relieve dermatitis, arthritis and athlete's foot. Buses 331 and 332 run here from Jeju City Hall (₩1200, 30 minutes, every 20 minutes) via Dongmun Market.

Tapdong Promenade & Waterbreak WATERFRONT
(탑동해안산책로; Map p244; Jungang-ro, Tapdong) Jeju-si doesn't have a beach, but along the seafront runs this pleasant promenade. At the eastern end is a mosaic-decorated sea wall; there's also an old-fashioned **amusement park** (제주월드21; Map p244; ☎064 723 1021; rides ₩4000; ⏰3.30-10.30pm; 👪) and an outdoor band shell that hosts summer music and dance performances.

Iho Tewoo Beach BEACH

(이호테우해변; Map p240; 445 or 447 to Iho Teu Beach stop) The nearest beach to Jeju-si is blessed with an unusual mixture of yellow and grey sand, which means you can build two-tone sandcastles. It's also bookended by two tones of horse-shaped lighthouses, one red, one white. There's shallow water that makes for safe swimming. Buses from Jeju-si (₩1200, every 20 minutes) run from the Intercity Bus Terminal (445, 30 minutes) or City Hall (447, 30 minutes); it's also the westernmost stop on the Jeju City Tour Bus.

Jeju Folklore & Natural History Museum MUSEUM

(민속자연사박물관; Map p244; 064 710 7708; http://museum.jeju.go.kr; Samseong-ro, Ildo 2-dong; adult/youth ₩2000/1000; 8.30am-6.30pm) This wide-ranging eco-museum has exhibits on Jeju-do's varied geological features, including volcanic bombs, lava tubes and trace fossils. Other highlights are excellent wildlife films, the bizarre oar fish and panoramas of the island's six ecological zones.

Yongduam Rock VIEWPOINT

(용두암; Map p244; 15 Yongduam-gil) 'Dragon Head Rock' (so called because the volcanic rocks are said to resemble a dragon) attracts coachloads of tourists. Besides rock-watching, plane-spotting is a popular activity – aeroplanes fly just a few hundred metres overhead on their final approach to the island.

Activities

Tapdong Seawater Sauna SPA

(탑동해수사우나; Map p244; 064 758 4800; http://jejuzzim.com; 6-6 Tapdong-ro 4-gil; bathhouse/jjimjil-bang & overnight sleeping ₩6000/8000; 24hr) Wind down at this public bath and *jjimjil-bang* (upmarket sauna) in Tapdong. It's a 24-hour facility, which also makes it the cheapest sleeping option in Jeju-si.

Tours

Jeju City Tour Bus BUS

(Map p240; 064 748 3211; www.jejugoldenbus.com; day pass adult/child ₩12,000/8000; 9 departures 9am-7pm, closed 3rd Mon of month) A day pass on the blue, white and orange Jeju City Tour Bus is a convenient way to explore multiple sights on a 22-stop hop-on, hop-off circuit in and around Jeju-si. Revamped to incorporate the previous Golden Tour Bus, the new route's key stops include Jeju Folklore & Natural History Museum, Dongmun Market (p245), Jeju Mokgwana (p241), Yongduam Rock and Iho Tewoo Beach. Buses start at Jeju International Airport, then run to Jeju-si Intercity Bus Terminal and City Hall and stop in at the ferry terminals.

Sleeping

Story In Jeju HOSTEL $

(Map p244; 5 Jungang-ro 12-gil; dm incl breakfast from ₩22,000;) The industrial-chic, modern social spaces at this guesthouse carry through to the black metal bunk beds and large lockers and machine-like cleanliness. Staff, though, are warm and can direct you to the market, shopping and places to eat near this quiet location. There is a laundry and in summer barbecues get going on the rooftop.

Yellow Guesthouse HOSTEL $

(Map p244; 010 5301 0907; 4 Gwandeok-ro 15-gil; dm/tw ₩18,000/45,000;) Don't worry, there are only touches of yellow, and the staff are helpful but not overbearing. Dorm bunks are clean and comfortable with privacy curtains and heated bed pads, and there's free laundry use. It's handy for exploring Dongmun Market and Tapdong.

Backpackers in Jeju HOSTEL $

(제주여행자숙소; Map p244; 064 773 2077; http://cafe.naver.com/chejukorea; 1-1 Gwangyang 8-gil, Jeju-si; dm/d/q incl breakfast ₩22,000/48,000/78,000; @) Handy if you want to be in the City Hall party district but in a quiet, large room; this quirky, foreigner-friendly place has a large area map on a blackboard, an extensive LP vinyl collection in the basement cafe-bar and iPads instead of TVs in the private rooms. It's down a lane next to Baskin Robbins.

Ora Stay MOTEL $$

(Map p244; 010 3119 4753; 44 Mugeunseong-gil; r from ₩40,000) Ora is a hybrid, bringing plenty of privacy for hostel prices. In the midst of love motels, this one mixes guesthouse styling with business-like rooms – modern aircon and smart TVs, double-glazed windows for peace, plus spacious bathrooms. It's a short walk to the waterfront and shopping strips.

★**Baume Couture Boutique Hotel** HOTEL $$$

(Map p240; 064 798 8000; www.baume.co.kr; 276-1 Yeon-dong, Shin Jeju; r from ₩210,000; @) Oh so chic, this boutique hotel is Jeju-si's most stylish place to sleep. Up at the rooftop pool (open July and August) there are

Jeju-si

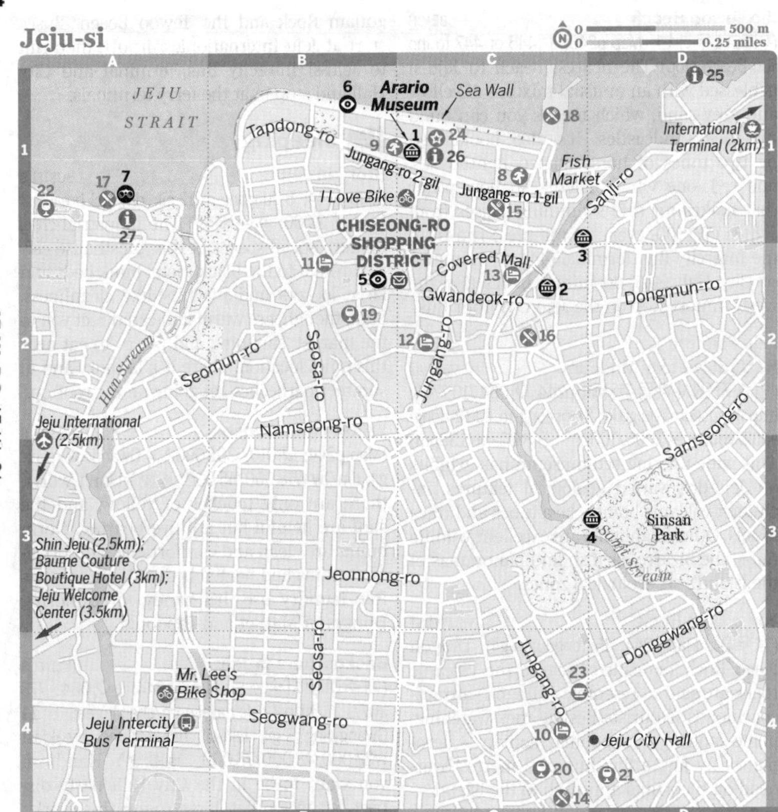

great views of Halla-san, weather permitting. Look for the cool building near the intersection of Singwang-ro and Sin-daero 20-gil.

Eating

★Dasoni VEGAN $

(다소니; Map p240; ☎064 753 5533; 24 Onam-ro 6-gil; mains/set lunch from ₩6000/11,000; ⊙11am-10pm; ❄📶🌿; 🚌312, Ora 1 Dong stop) Sit cross-legged at rustic wooden tables, peering out into the wild garden of this meat-free restaurant. Dishes use local Jeju produce for dishes such as sticky rice wrapped in lotus leaves, or acorn jelly, delighting even non-vegetarians. The lunch photo menu has ample interesting *banchan*, such as green chive *pajeon*. Mention if you don't eat fish as it's used in a couple dishes.

A Factory Bakery BAKERY $

(Map p244; ☎064 720 8223; 3 Tapdong-ro 2-gil, Samdoi-dong; items from ₩3000; ⊙8am-8pm; 📶) The air inside this open-kitchen bakery is filled with the aroma of freshly baked breads, cakes and sweets…and it's not the phoney smell found in some popular brand-name bakeries, though it still favours sweeter flavours, as is the Korean way. Decent sandwiches and coffee are also available.

★Haejin Seafood Restaurant SEAFOOD $$

(해진횟집; Map p244; ☎064 757 4584; 1435-2 Geonip-dong; mains ₩12,000-50,000; ⊙10.30am-midnight) Of the many restaurants overlooking the harbour, Haejin is the largest and one of the most popular places to try Jeju-do's seafood specialities such as cuttlefish, eel, squid, octopus, sea cucumber and abalone. The set meal (₩30,000) feeds two people.

★Bagdad Cafe INDIAN $$

(Map p244; ☎064 757 8182; www.fb.me/bagdad cafejeju; 38 Seogwang-ro 32-gil, Idoi-dong; mains

Jeju-si

from ₩9000; noon-11pm;) This top date spot in the City Hall student district has English-speaking staff and fine fare such as tandoori chicken and peanut butter masala, which tastes great with a large serving of handmade garlic naan. Look for the pink building two blocks west of Jungang-ro.

D-Stone Pub INTERNATIONAL $$
(Modrock; Map p244; 503-5 Yongdamsam-dong; mains ₩13,000-28,000; 5pm-2am;) There's an eclectic range of dishes on the menu, from sweet-potato pork cutlets to quesadillas and burgers, plus a decent selection of imported beers on tap. But really, you'll come here to admire the stunning ocean views while sitting on a patio near Yongduam Rock.

Dongmun Market MARKET $$
(동문재래시장; Map p244; 20 Gwandeong-ro 14-gil; mains ₩10,000-25,000, snacks from ₩500; 8am-9pm) A traditional Korean food market that's fun for a wander and peek at local seafood for sale, which you can have cooked up on the spot at small restaurants. It's also a good place to stock up on *gamgyul*, Jeju's traditional citrus fruit, or to snack on *mandu* (dumplings), *hotteok* (doughnuts), *odeng* (seafood cakes) and black pork cabbage rolls.

Dombaedon BARBECUE $$$
(돔베돈; Map p244; 064 753 0008; Gwandeong-ro 15-gil, Tapdong; 180g serving ₩18,000; 11am-midnight) One of the better options on *heukdwaeji geori* (Black Pork Street), a street dedicated to barbecue restaurants serving the island's tastiest speciality, black pig. It's the corner restaurant with a grandfather statue outside. Minimum two people.

Drinking & Nightlife

★Magpie Jeju CRAFT BEER
(Map p244; 064 720 8227; www.magpiebrewing.com; 3 Tapdong-ro 2-gil, Samdoi-dong; 5pm-1am, closed 1st Mon of month;) Bringing Seoul hipness to Jeju-si's nights, the craft beers here are brewed on the island and served at this broad space with good pizzas and fried chicken. The retro-designed posters for its brews line the walls in an industrial space that is dark enough to come alone or in groups.

Bistro The Barn BAR
(비스트로더반; Map p244; 064 722 0429; 6 Gwandeong-ro 4-gil, Samdoi-dong; 5pm-midnight Tue-Sun;) Dark and relaxed bar run by a well-travelled, English-speaking Jeju native. Craft beer, *soju* (local vodka) and wine match the mismatched antique furniture, soft soulful vinyl music and small

batches of green curry, frittata or whatever has been prepared that day. It's in one of the few hip pockets of the city.

Nilmori Dong Dong BAR

(닐모리동동; Map p244; ☎064 745 5008; www.nilmori.com; 2396 Yongdamsam-dong; ⏰10am-11pm, to 10pm Nov-Mar; 📶) On the coastal road behind the airport is this eclectic cafe-bar-restaurant that often stages craft exhibitions and other arty events. A ₩6000 taxi ride from Shin Jeju, it's a worthwhile stop if you're looking for a place to eat (pizza and pasta from ₩15,000), drink and sample the local arts scene before or after strolling the oceanfront promenade.

Craft Han's BAR

(크래프트 한스; Map p244; ☎064 721 3336; ⏰5pm-2am) Craft beer is on tap along with a decent selection of imported bottled brew at this cosy bar in the youthful City Hall area. Side orders include cheesy, deep-dish, Chicago-style pizza plus salmon and chips. Look for the small building with a woody exterior and dark-green trim.

Panda Coffee Shop COFFEE

(판다 커피숍; Map p244; ☎070-4417 6688; Donggwang-ro; coffee from ₩4000; ⏰10am-midnight; 📶) A cosy coffee shop with a panda theme in the City Hall area. Inside there are a few bears, but don't expect panda insanity. It's quaint and cool with a decent selection of homemade chocolate cookies baked on the premises.

Factory BAR

(Map p244; ☎010 9184 3431; 6, Gwangyang 13-gil; ⏰7pm-3am Tue-Sun) Named after Andy Warhol's studio, the Factory is a dark and moody bar that attracts artists, musicians and other hipsters. It's a favourite haunt for Jeju-si's expat community. There's occasional live music.

ℹ Information

POST

Central Post Office (제주우체국; Map p244; ☎064 722 0084; Gwandeok-ro; ⏰9am-6pm Mon-Fri) Jeju-si's largest post office.

TOURIST INFORMATION

Jeju Welcome Center (Map p240; ☎064 740 6000; www.ijto.or.kr; 23 Seondeok-ro, Yeon-dong; ⏰9am-6pm; 📶) Tourist information and internet access.

Tourist Information Centre Ferry Terminal (Map p244; ☎064 758 7181; ⏰6.30am-8pm) At Jeju's ferry terminal.

Tourist Information Centre Jeju Airport (Map p240; ☎064 797 2525; 1st fl, Jeju International Airport; ⏰6.30am-8pm; 📶) Internet access and helpful English-speaking staff; be sure to get a bus map and schedule.

Tourist Information Centre Tapdong (Map p244; ☎064 728 3919; Tapdong-ro; ⏰9am-6pm) This small office is near the band shell on Tapdong Plaza.

Tourist Information Centre Yongduam (Map p244; ☎064 711 1022; Yongduam-gil; ⏰9am-6pm) Near Yongduam Rock.

FERRIES FROM JEJU-SI

DESTINATION	SHIP	TELEPHONE; WEBSITE	PRICE FROM (₩)	DURATION (HR)	FREQUENCY
Busan	ENA Carferry	☎1661 9559; http://enacarferry.haewoon.co.kr	97,000	12	Tue, Thu, Sat
Chujado & Wando	Red Pearl	☎064 751 5050; www.hanilexpress.co.kr	11,050	1½/4	daily, closed 1st & 3rd Wed
Mokpo	Seastar Cruise	☎064 758 4234; http://seaferry.co.kr	32,300	4½	daily, closed 1st & 3rd Mon
Mokpo	Santalucino	☎064 758 4234; http://seaferry.co.kr	30,000	5½	Sun & Tue-Fri
Usuyeong via Chujado	QueenStar 2	☎064 758 4234; http://seaferry.co.kr	38,000	3	daily, closed 2nd & 4th Wed
Wando	Blue Narae	☎064 751 5050; www.hanilexpress.co.kr	37,000	1¾	daily, closed 4th Wed
Wando	Hanil Car Ferry I	☎064 751 5050; www.hanilexpress.co.kr	26,250	2¾	daily, closed 3rd Sun

Getting There & Away

AIR

Flights connect Jeju-si with several mainland cities, plus a handful of international destinations in China, Japan, Malaysia, Taiwan and Thailand. From Gimpo in Seoul, flights depart every 10 to 30 minutes, dawn to dusk. Except for holidays and the summer season, it's rarely necessary to prebook. Advance one-way fares can start as low as ₩34,000 from Seoul and Busan.

BOAT

Comfortable ferries sail between Jeju-si and three ports on the peninsula. Most ships have three classes: 3rd-class passengers sit on the floor in big rooms; 2nd class gets you a seat; and 1st class gets you a private cabin with bed and bathroom.

Ferries berth at either **Jeju-do Ferry Terminal** (제주항 연안여객터미널; Map p240; ☎1666 0930; http://jeju.ferry.or.kr) or the International Ferry Pier (제주항 국제여객터미널), 1.3km further east. Buses 411, 412 and 415 (₩1200) run regularly between both ferry terminals, and you can walk in about 20 minutes, but a taxi is more convenient. Contrary to the latter terminal's name, there are no international routes.

Getting Around

TO/FROM THE AIRPORT

Jeju International Airport (p395) is 1km from Shin Jeju and 4km from central Jeju-si. The Airport Limousine bus 600 (every 20 minutes, 6.10am to 10.50pm; pay on board or use T-money card), from outside Gate 5, drops off and picks up passengers at major hotels and resorts all around the island, including Jungmun Resort (₩4500, one hour), then to World Cup Stadium (₩5000, 1½ hours) and finishing in Seogwipo (₩5500, 1¾ hours). Buses 102, 110, 120, 130, 150 and 315 shuttle between the airport and the city's Intercity Bus Terminal (₩1200, 10 minutes, frequent); buses 332 and 3001 go to the nearby modern Shin Jeju area (₩1200, 15 minutes, every 20 minutes).

BICYCLE

I Love Bike (아이러브바이크; Map p244; ☎064 723 7775; http://cafe.naver.com/yaya24; Samdo2-dong 14-4, Beon-ji; bicycle per day ₩7000-30,000; ⏰7am-8pm) English speaking, with a large choice of bikes. Look for the shop close to a post-office building near the intersection of Bukseong-ro and Gwandeong-ro 7-gil.

Mr. Lee's Bike Shop (Map p244; ☎064 758 5296; https://mrlees-bike-shop.business.site; 7 Seogwang-ro 5-gil; 125cc scooter for 24hr ₩40,000; ⏰9am-6pm Mon-Fri, 9.30am-3pm Sat) Recommended for bikes, scooters and motorcycles with 125cc engines. You must be an experienced rider with an international driving licence to rent a scooter or motorcycle.

BUS

It is completely possible and convenient to base yourself in Jeju-si and travel by bus across the whole island, with the furthest destinations between one and two hours away.

Streams of city and round-island buses originate from the **Intercity Bus Terminal** (제주시외버스터미널; Map p244; ☎064 753 1153; 174 Seogwang-ro, Orail-dong) on Seogwang-ro and pass the airport or City Hall; tourist information offices can provide a timetable. All regular fares are ₩1200, or slightly cheaper with a T-money card at ₩1150, with the added benefit of two free transfers to other routes within 40 minutes of leaving one route. All buses and most stops have free wi-fi. Most stops also have convenient screens with live departure information and maps in English.

EASTERN JEJU-DO

The coast is what eastern Jeju-do does best. Stretches of pretty beaches lead you to the island's most impressive sight, the extinct tuff volcano Seongsan Ilchul-bong. Nearby is smaller Udo island with sparkling white sand and even bluer water in between ragged coastline and wild hills. There are inland diversions in the east, too, at a museum dedicated to the *haenyeo* women divers; along laneways of a re-enacted folk village showcasing traditional life; among the hedges of Gimnyeong Maze Park; or within the solidified lava tubes of Manjang-gul.

Sights

Gimnyeong Maze Park PARK

(김녕미로공원; Map p240; ☎064 782 9266; www.jejumaze.com; 122 Manjanggul-gil, Gujwa-eup; adult/youth/child ₩4400/3300/2200; ⏰8.30am-6pm; 👪; 🚌711 to Gimnyeong Maze Park stop) This popular maze is fun for adults and children. Created by American expat Fred Dunstin from 2232 Leyland cypress trees, it's fiendishly clever. There is also a cat playground with roaming felines at the entrance.

Getting here by bus is inconvenient, as it's a 30-minute walk from the 201 bus stop on highway Rte 1132, Iljudong-ro, at the intersection with Woldeong-ro (the road to Gimnyeong Maze Park and Manjang-gul). You can take bus 711 (₩1200, hourly) from the intersection as it shuttles between Gimnyeong Beach and Haenyeo Museum, but it is infrequent and does not appear on the

1. Baengokdam Crater, Hallasan National Park (p257), South Korea Formed from a dormant volcano, this national park is the world's only habitat for Korean firs.

2. *Haenyeo* (traditional female free divers; p251), South Korea For centuries Jeju-do women have fished for shellfish, sea cucumbers, spiky black sea urchins and anything else edible.

3. Hallasan National Park (p257), South Korea While flowering azaleas in April and May are notable, autumn is a particularly beautiful time to hike in this national park.

ZKRUGER / SHUTTERSTOCK ©

ANDREW BAIN / GETTY IMAGES ©

'next bus' screen. A taxi from Gimnyeong/Iljudong-ro is ₩6500/2000. You can walk to Manjang-gul from the maze in 15 minutes, which is a cost-effective way to combine both sights in one trip. This is also a stop on the Yellow Tourist Bus 810 (p264).

Manjang-gul CAVE

(만장굴; Map p240; ☎064 710 7905; http://jejuwnh.jeju.go.kr; 182 Manjanggul-gil, Gujwa-eup; adult/youth & child ₩2000/1000; ⏲9am-6pm; 🚌711, Manjang-gul stop) Manjang-gul is the main access point to the world's longest system of lava-tube caves. In total the caves are 7.4km long, with heights between 2m and 23m. In this section you can walk around 1km underground to a 7m-high lava pillar, the cave's outstanding feature. The immense black tunnel with swirling walls looks like the lair of a giant serpent and it's hard to imagine the geological forces that created it aeons ago, moulding rock as if it were Play-Doh.

Take a jacket and good shoes, as the cave ceiling drips, the ground is wet and uneven, and the temperature inside is a chilly 10°C, regardless of the weather outside. The lighting is dim so a torch (flashlight) is a good idea. The ticket office is about 2.5km from the Entrance to Manjang-gul bus stop on Rte 1132 Iljudong-ro, at the intersection with Woldeong-ro; a transfer to local bus 711 (₩1200, hourly) is possible, but arrival times are inconvenient. A taxi from Gimnyeong costs ₩7000.

Sangumburi VOLCANO

(산굼부리; Map p240; ☎064 783 9900; www.sangumburi.net; 768 Bijarim-ro, Jocheon-eup; adult/youth/child ₩6000/4000/3000; ⏲9am-5pm, to 6pm Mar-Oct; 🚌720-1 to Sangumburi Crater stop) Sangumburi is an impressive volcanic crater in the central east of Jeju-do. About 350m in diameter and 100m deep, it only takes a few minutes to walk up to the crater rim, so it's a short visit but you'll want to spend time admiring the expansive plains, distant craters and lush fields.

From Jeju-si (₩1800, 50 minutes, every 25 minutes) buses stop near the ticket office.

Festivals & Events

Jeju Olle Walking Festival SPORTS

(www.jejuolle.org; registration ₩25,000) This three-day festival generally occurs each October or November and includes many food and cultural events, with a focus on a trail a day.

JEJU OLLE TRAIL

Launched by former Korean journalist and Jeju native Suh Myeong-sook in 2007, the Jeju Olle Trail network is one of the great success stories of local tourism. The first route starts in Siheung near Seongsan-ri, and a further 25 routes of between 5km and 22.9km meander mainly along Jeju-do's coast (with some inland diversions) and three outer islands (Udo, Gapado and Chujado).

Olle is the local word for a pathway that connects a house to the main street, signifying one of the project's aims – to open up Jeju's unique culture and scenery to visitors. Although you could hike the entire 430km network of trails in around a month, the Olle's near-spiritual philosophy is one of slow, meandering travel.

If you hike any of the trails, it's worth investing in a passport (₩20,000) that comes with an excellent English-language guidebook providing detailed information on many sights and places to stay and eat along the routes. The passport also gets you discounts at many places and it is fun to collect the stamps, each with a unique image, as a record of your achievements. Passports are available at the foundation's head office in Seogwipo on Trail 6 and at shops or offices at the start/finish point of each trail. If you collect all 78 stamps, you can claim a medal. Visit www.jejuolle.org or www.ollestore.com for details.

The three-day Jeju Olle Walking Festival generally occurs each October or November and includes many special events.

Olle Trail 1 (Map p240; 🚌201, Siheung-ri stop) is a good place to start your Olle Trail experience because of the up-close connection it provides with rural Jeju-do. The 15km trail (four to five hours) runs through farm plots worked by grandmothers, over grassy oreum (craters) where horses and cows graze freely, and along a seaside path leading to one of Jeju-do's most impressive natural treasures, Seongsan Ilchul-bong (p252).

Buses from Jeju-si (₩3300, 1½ hours, every 20 minutes) stop near the trailhead. It's near a wooden sign about 50m from the primary school.

Getting There & Around

Eastern Jeju-do includes the coastal area along Rte 1132 from Gimnyeong to Pyoseon, some inland sites and the ferry to Udo. Most of the coastal destinations can be accessed by bus 201 (₩1200, every 15 minutes from 5.35am to 7.20pm) as it hugs the coast between Jeju-si and Seogwipo via Seongsan Ilchul-bong.

The infrequent bus 711 (₩1200) shuttles between Gimnyeong Beach and Haenyeo Museum in Hado-ri, stopping in at Sehwa, Gimnyeong Maze Park and Manjang-gul. Buses 711-1/711-2 run to/from Gimnyeong hourly but neither appears on 'next bus' screens.

Woljeong Beach

Hideaway Woljeong Beach (월정리 해변) is fast becoming a hot-spot for young couples looking for good times near the ocean. Year-round, it's a fun place to stroll the beach and spend time in the funky oceanside cafes and restaurants. Commercial development, so far, has been small scale, with some of the most interesting guesthouses and hip restaurants springing up on the island.

Sleeping

★Gentleehouse Jeju GUESTHOUSE **$$**
(Map p240; ☎010 8744 9029; http://gentleehouse.com; 24 Woljeong 7-gil; r ₩70,000, Jul & Aug ₩90,000; P❄@📶) People will pinpoint this guesthouse as the moment Woljeong Beach became a hot spot. Gentleehouse is matched with chic new restaurants nearby, yet is enveloped in tranquil farmland. Rooms are comfortable, clean and stylish with neutral tones and splashes of palm green in the communal kitchen and living room.

Gaga Pension PENSION **$$**
(가가펜션; Map p240; ☎064 782 5009; http://gagaps.com; r from ₩59,000, Jul & Aug from ₩89,000; P❄📶; 🚌201, Woljeongni stop) Just steps from Woljeong Beach, this decent property has clean, almost-glamorous rooms with kitchens and balconies with views.

Eating & Drinking

★Woljeong-ri Galbibap RIBS **$$**
(Map p240; ☎064 782 0430; 46 Woljeong 7-gil, Gujwa-eup; mains from ₩15,900; ⏲11am-3pm & 5-8pm; P📶) Is it the delicious *galbi* (barbecued beef ribs) and noodles or the large, chic neon space that guarantees a long queue here? Either way, come early, browse the photo menu, jot your name on the waiting list and explore the nearby beach to work up an appetite – you'll need it to also try the *galbi* sushi, a Woljeong speciality. Solo diners welcome.

Woljeong-ri Lowa CAFE
(월정리 LOWA; Map p240; ☎064 783 2240; 472 Haemajihaean-ro, Gujwa-eup; ⏲9am-10pm; 📶; 🚌201, Woljeongni stop) 🌿 Here's a cafe with a slick interior design, decent drinks, San Miguel to go with a side of fries on the rooftop sunloungers overlooking Woljeong Beach, and friendly, English-speaking staff. Jeju *yujacha* (citron tea) and Jeju green-tea cake are house specialities.

Getting There & Away

From Jeju-si bus 201 (₩1200, 55 minutes, every 20 minutes) runs on Rte 1132; the beach is 500m from the bus stop.

Hado-ri

Tucked into the northeast corner of Jeju, this slice of fishing-town life and its *haenyeo* women divers are often overlooked by tourists in a hurry to get down the road to Seongsan Ilchul-bong. Travellers with a car, and extra time, might consider getting off the main highway here and driving the Sehwa and Hado seashore road for splendid ocean views, stopping off wherever the cobalt-blue waters catch your eye.

Sights

Haenyeo Museum MUSEUM
(해녀 박물관; Map p240; ☎064 710 7771; www.haenyeo.go.kr; adult/youth ₩1100/500; ⏲9am-6pm, closed 1st & 3rd Mon; 🚌201 to Haenyeo Museum stop) The highlight of Hado-ri, this museum does an excellent job explaining the history and culture of the amazing *haenyeo* (women divers) through models of their traditional homes, boats, tools and dress.

Sleeping & Eating

There are lots of small inexpensive restaurants near the beaches, mostly specialising in grilled mackerel, seafood *ramyeon* and *jeonbog* (abalone) everything – with hot stone-pot rice, as sashimi, in rice porridge or simply grilled in their shell.

★Ssari's Flower Hill PENSION **$$**
(Map p240; ☎010 9134 7741; www.jejussari.com; 243 Hado-ri, Gujwa-eup; r incl breakfast ₩60,000, higher weekends & May-Sep;

❄📶) This beautiful countryside guesthouse, surrounded by farms and woods, is an ideal location to get away from it all. Go for lazy walks on Hado beach (a few kilometres down the road), or grab a wine in the 1st-floor coffee shop. Rooms are spacious and white with elegant wood touches. It's run by a Japanese woman and her shaggy dog.

★Dasi Boesi KOREAN $
(다시버시; Map p240; ☎064 783 5575; Haemajihaean-ro, Gujwa-eup; meal for 2 people ₩12,000-20,000 each; ⏰11am-8pm; 🚌701 to museum stop) If you've spent time exploring the Haenyeo Museum (p251), do yourself a favour and eat here. This shop serves delicious feasts of grilled mackerel and tofu stew. On the beach road on the west side of Sehwa Beach, it's a 10-minute walk from the museum. Note: it doesn't serve lone diners.

Getting There & Away

Buses 201 and 260 from Jeju-si Intercity Bus Terminal and City Hall (₩1200, 80 minutes, every 20 minutes) come here. Bus 201 continues on along the east coast to Seongsan Ilchul-bong then south to Seogwipo. Bus 711 (₩1200, hourly) comes here from Gimnyeong Beach via Manjang-gul.

Seongsan-ri & Sinyang-ri

A must-see destination, Seongsan-ri (성산리, Fortress Mountain Village) and the neighbouring village of Sinyang-ri (신양리) are at the foot of a spectacular extinct volcano that rises straight out of the ocean. Black-sand beaches are nearby, as is the lovely island of Udo and the Seopji-koji Peninsula, with breathtaking architecture by the Japanese master Ando Tadao.

Sights

★Seongsan Ilchul-bong VOLCANO
(성산일출봉; Map p254; ☎064 783 0959; http://jejuwnh.jeju.go.kr; 284-12 Ilchul-ro, Seongsan-eup; adult/youth ₩2000/1000; ⏰1hr before sunrise-8pm; 🚌201 or 210 to Seongsan Ilchulbong Tuff Cone Entrance stop) This majestic 182m-high, extinct tuff volcano, shaped like a giant punchbowl, is one of Jeju-do's most impressive sights and a Unesco World Heritage site. The forested crater is ringed by jagged rocks, though there's no lake because the rock is porous. From the entrance, climbing the steep stairs to the crater rim only takes 20 minutes. Doing it in time to catch the sunrise is a life-affirming journey for many Koreans – expect plenty of company.

To do the sunrise expedition, you need to spend the night in Seongsan-ri, a sleepy village filled with motels and restaurants catering to the hiking crowd. The steps up the volcano are easy and clear, but if you're concerned, bring a torch (flashlight). Not an early riser? It's also a popular daytime hike. The Seongsan Sunrise Festival, an all-night New Year's Eve party, is held here on 31 December.

Phoenix Island ARCHITECTURE
(Map p254; ☎064 731 7000; https://phoenixhnr.co.kr; 127-2 Seopjikoji-ro, Seongsan-eup; adult/child ₩2000/1000; ⏰9am-6pm) Coachloads of tourists disgorge at this resort daily to view the scenic location that has been featured in several Korean TV dramas and movies. But the real stars of the Seopji-koji Peninsula are two pieces of architecture by Ando Tadao: **Glass House** (Map p254; 93-66 Seopjikoji-ro, Seongsan-eup), housing the restaurant Mint (p255), and the amazing **Yumin Art Museum** (유민미술관; Map p254; ☎064 731 7791; www.yuminart.org; 107 Seopjikoji-ro, Seongsan-eup; ₩12,000; ⏰9am-6pm Wed-Mon), a gallery with site-specific works that aid meditation. Both

JEJU'S LANDSCAPE GALLERY

Kim Young Gap Gallery Dumoak (김영갑갤러리두모악; Map p240; ☎064 784 9907; www.dumoak.com; 137 Samdal-ro, Seongsan-eup; adult/teenager/child ₩4500/3000/1500; ⏰9.30am-6pm Thu-Tue, to 7pm Jul & Aug; 🅿; 🚌201, Samdal Gyocharo stop) is a countryside gallery dedicated to Kim Young Gap (1957–2005), a talented, self-taught photographer who documented the landscapes of Jeju. In the last years of his life he moved into an abandoned school, which he transformed into a studio (now gallery) and sculpture-filled garden. Explanations in Korean only.

Bus 201 from Jungang Rotary (₩1200, one hour, every 15 minutes) in Seogwipo stops at Samdal Gyocharo bus stop from where it's a 1.4km walk west to the gallery; it's also on Olle Trail Rte 3.

WORTH A TRIP

UDO

The largest of 62 islets surrounding Jeju-do, and supposedly shaped like a sprawled-out cow, Udo (Cow Island), 3.5km off the coast from Seongsan-ri, is a beautiful, occasionally barren place that attracts throngs of tourists, particularly on weekends and holidays. Though light on interesting sights, Udo's main attractions for independent travellers are its rugged natural beauty and the allure of splendid isolation.

On the west coast gorgeous **Hongjodangoe Haebin Beach** (홍조단괴해빈 해수욕장; Map p240; 264 Udohaean-gil, Udo-myeon), now more commonely called Sanho Beach (산호 해수욕장), has brilliant white coral sand stretching out in a crescent-moon-shaped beach. Selfie-seekers usually climb the steep steps up to **Udo Lighthouse Park** (우도 등대 공원; Map p240; 064 783 0180; 337-5 Yeonpyeong-ri, Udo-myeon; sunrise-sunset) FREE for spectacular views of rural Udo from Udo-bong (Udo Peak).

Fifteen-minute **ferries** (Map p254; 064 782 5671; return adult/youth/child/car ₩8500/8100/3200/21,000; 7am to 6.30pm) cross to Udo's western port in Haumokdong (하우목동항), or sometimes southern port in Cheonjin (천진항), from Seongsan in eastern Jeju. Bring your passport. The domed ticket office is at the far end of Seongsan port, a 15-minute walk from Seongsan-ri.

On Udo, you can rent bicycles (daily ₩10,000), scooters (two hours ₩30,000) and quad bikes (two hours ₩30,000). An international driving licence is required to rent motorised vehicles.

It's easiest to ride one of the electric 'circular bus' **shuttle buses** (daily adult/child ₩5000/3000, every five to 10 minutes), which make eight stops at the main sights. Buy tickets at either ferry port before boarding.

buildings are angled to frame Seongsan Ilchul-bong (p252), providing yet more perspectives on the volcano. A taxi here from Seongsan-ri is around ₩5000.

Ilchul-bong Beach BEACH

(Map p254; Seongsan Ilchul-bong; incl with admission to Seongsan Ilchul-bong; 701, Seongsan stop) At the eastern base of Seongsan Ilchul-bong a long staircase leads down to this lovely crescent-shaped cove backed by weather-beaten lava cliff walls and boulders. On the left side of the beach, *haenyeo* divers run a small restaurant and put on a performance of their skills every day at 1.30pm and 3pm. Next to the restaurant, small **speedboats** (Map p254; per trip ₩10,000) can whisk you out to sea for another perspective on Ilchul-bong.

Seongsan Beach BEACH

(Map p254; Ilchul-ro; 201) The long stretch of beach between Seongsan-ri and Phoenix Island is a pleasing contrast of colours – mossy green rocks, black sand and blue waters, all framed by Seongsan Ilchulbong. There are dramatic aerial views of the beach as you scale the extinct volcano.

Sleeping

Seongsanpo Village HOTEL $$

(성산포빌리지; Map p254; 064 782 2373; Ilchul-ro; r ₩60,000;) Sit out on a balcony with a wonderful view of the sea and anything going on along the harbour road. Rooms are old but large and clean. It also has a good restaurant on the ground floor. Look for the light-blue corner building.

Bomulseom PENSION $$

(보물섬; Map p254; 064 784 0039; www.jejubms.com; 252-4 Seongsan-ri, Seongsan-eup; r from ₩60,000;) This hilltop pension has well-kept and -equipped self-catering rooms with enclosed balconies. In July and August a swimming pool is available. It's on a hill, a block off the main road, surrounded by a few other motels.

Phoenix Island APARTMENT $$$

(Map p254; 064 731 7000; https://phoenixhnr.co.kr; 127-2 Seopjikoji-ro, Seongsan-eup; apt from ₩363,000;) The enormous and comfortable self-catering apartments at this resort are great for families or groups of friends to share. You have access to plenty of on-site facilities, nearby beaches and beautiful views of Seongsan Ilchul-bong.

Eating

Umutgae Ilbeonji SEAFOOD $

(우뭇개일번지; Map p254; 064 784 3456; 288 Ilchul-ro, Seongsan-eup; mains ₩7000-9000; 10am-7pm;) This one-woman bistro has fuss-free single dishes – perfect after

Seongsan Ilchul-bong

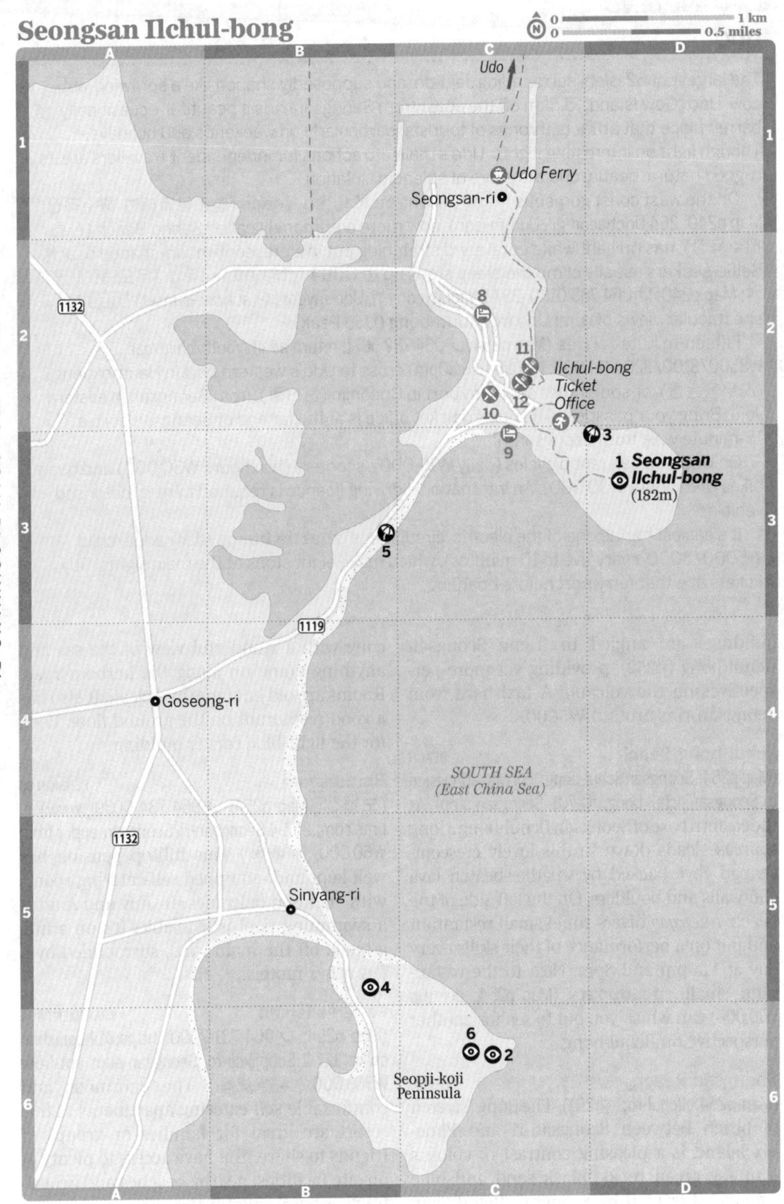

climbing nearby Seongsan Ilchulbong. Each bowl of *jjamppong* (spicy seafood *ramyeon*) holds a bounty of seafood, with even more abalone in the *haejangguk* (hangover soup). Or choose beef bulgogi from the photo menu. Solo diners sit at the bar, where there are complimentary phone chargers. Look for the green awning.

★ **Seongsan Noodles** NOODLES $$
(성산국수; Map p254; ☎064 784 8689; www.instagr.am/seongsan_noodles; Ilchul-ro 288beon-

Seongsan Ilchul-bong

gil; noodles ₩8000; 8am-4pm Fri-Wed;) The glasshouse-like garden restaurant has classy museum looks but is one of the best budget places around. There is only one dish, *guksu* (noodle soup) with generous servings of Jeju black pork and lavished with green onions. Luckily it's great. From Seonsan Ilchul-bong, turn right on the restaurant street until it becomes a path following the coast; Seongsan Noodles is down a driveway on your right.

Haeddeuneun SEAFOOD $$
(해뜨는식당; Map p254; 064 782 3380; 298-22 Seongsan-ri, Seongsan-eup; mains ₩9000-15,000; 8am-9pm) At the top of a hill and close to a cliff with great ocean views, this place is a little apart from the cluster of restaurants at the foot of Seongsan Ilchul-bong. The menu covers many common local options, including abalone rice porridge, sea-urchin soup and seafood hotpot. Look for the red awning at the entrance.

★**Mint** INTERNATIONAL $$$
(Map p254; 064 731 7773; 93-66 Seopjikoji-ro, Seongsan-eup; set lunch/dinner from ₩45,000/60,000; 11am-8pm;) Dining inside Ando Tadao's Glass House is a delightful experience, one best enjoyed during the day when you can take in the coastal views through the floor-to-ceiling windows. The menu offers high-grade local produce such as black pork and fish steak as well as excellent pasta. Coffee and cake is also an enjoyable excuse to linger here.

Shopping

Jeju Seongsan GIFTS & SOUVENIRS
(Map p254; 064 784 8689; Ilchul-ro 288beon-gil; 8am-4pm Fri-Wed) Find unique designer jewellery, candles, stationery and Seongsan Ichulbong-themed souvenirs at this small shop in the same space as Seongsan Noodles.

Getting There & Away

Buses (₩1200) run to Seongsan-ri from Jeju-si Intercity Bus Terminal (buses 201 and 210; 70 to 90 minutes; every 20 minutes) and Jungang Rotary (bus 201; 80 minutes; every 20 minutes) in Seogwipo.

From the **Seongsan ferry terminal** (성산포항 종합여객터미널; Map p240; 064 782 5671; 130-21 Seongsandeungyong-ro, Seongsan-eup; return ticket to Udo adult/youth/child/car ₩8500/8100/3200/21,000) boats sail to Udo (return ₩8500, 15 minutes, at least hourly from 8am to 5pm). Bring your passport.

Pyoseon

064 / POP 5144

This small, quiet town contains a re-enacted 1890s Korean village, and a huge expanse of white sandy beach that, at low tide, stretches as far as the eye can see; in the middle a lagoon forms. Even at high tide the water only reaches 1m deep, making it popular with families who picnic and exercise on the grass. If you like plenty of space, this is the beach to visit.

Sights

★**Jeju Folk Village** VILLAGE
(제주민속촌; Map p240; 064 787 4501; http://jejufolk.com; 631-34 Minsokhaean-ro, Pyoseon-myeon; adult/youth/child ₩11,000/8000/7000; 8.30am-6pm, to 5pm Oct-Feb; 201, Pyeosolli Office stop) The educational Jeju Folk Village gathers together traditional buildings from across the island (some reconstructions, others hundreds of years old) in an attractively designed park. Various sections cover Jeju's culture from shamans to *yangban* (aristocrats), and the differences between mountain, hill-country and fishing villages.

The modern construction has been done in authentic style, and at various places you

can watch craftsmen at work and buy their products. Also here are country-style restaurants serving inexpensive noodle and rice dishes, traditional song and dance performances and, oddly, an ostrich farm.

Sleeping & Eating

Black pork restaurants are around town, with the odd cafe truck and small snack shop nearer the beach, good for a picnic on the grassy area. Within Jeju Folk Village are inexpensive noodle and rice-dish restaurants.

Haevichi Hotel & Resort Jeju RESORT $$$
(Map p240; ☎064 780 8000; www.haevichi.com; 537 Minsokhaean-ro, Pyoseon-ri; r/ste from ₩340,000/443,000;) This luxury resort is owned by Hyundai Motors, which accounts for the display cars in the lobby. The rooms, all of which have balconies and many with sea views, are very chic and spacious; the self-catering suites in the 'resort' side of the complex sleep up to four. Facilities include several restaurants, outdoor swimming pools and a *jjimjil-bang* (luxury sauna; guests/nonguests ₩10,000/20,000).

Getting There & Away

Bus 201 stops here from Jungang Rotary (50 minutes, every 15 minutes) in Seogwipo. For Pyoseon beach, get off at the Pyoseolli Office stop, and walk 15 minutes east.

Seongeup Folk Village

☎064 / POP 1353

A former provincial capital, the village of Seongeup (성읍민속마을) has benefitted from government assistance that has encouraged the preservation and renovation of its traditional rock-walled, thatched-roofed houses. Though modern intrusions include souvenir shops, restaurants and car parks, most of it still looks fantastically feudal. And unlike Jeju Folk Village, Seongeup is the real deal, with people living and working here still.

The core of the village is surrounded by a fortress wall punctuated by ornate entrance gates; Nammoon (the south gate) is the main gate. Give yourself an hour to explore the narrow lanes zigzagging alongside lava rock walls, traditional homes with thatched roofs, more than a few *hareubang* (old grandfather) statues and the occasional baby black pig. If the gate poles are down, you're welcome to enter. Look out for the Confucian school and the 1000-year-old zelkova tree.

Sleeping

★ Seongeup Folk Village Traditional Houses COTTAGE $$
(Map p240; ☎760 3578; cottage from ₩60,000;) The village offers comfortable accommodation in six volcanic-stone and thatched-roof cottages. Inside they have two bedrooms with *ondol* (heated) floors and *yo* (padded quilts) on raised platforms; the bathrooms and kitchens are modern and tastefully decorated.

Eating

Black pork and red bean desserts are some of the traditional dishes to be had here.

★ Yetnal Patjuk KOREAN $$
(옛날 팥죽; Map p240; ☎064 787 3357; 130 Seongeup Minseok-ro, Pyoseon-myeon; mains from ₩6000; ⏰10am-5pm Tue-Sun; ; 🚌720, Seongeup Folk Village stop) Everything about this restaurant, housed in a traditional building, is inviting. Inside the door you're greeted by warm smiles and the sweet earthy aroma of red beans. Excellent soups and porridge are served here, including some made from lotus flowers, pumpkin and seaweed. Wooden tables, exposed beams and heavy earthenware add to the rustic charm. Coming from the south gate, go to the first intersection and turn left. Go about 50m and turn left at the first street. The restaurant is down the road – Seongeup Minseok-ro – on the left. Look for the shop with a gravel car park.

Gwandangnae Sikdang KOREAN $$
(관당네식당; Map p240; ☎064 787 1055; mains from ₩12,000; ⏰8am-7pm) The ebullient owner of this restaurant is known for his succulent black-pig pork dishes – a massive banquet for two is ₩35,000. From the small retail plaza outside the south gate, walk about 50m into the hamlet of traditional buildings. Look for the shop with a weather-worn Korean flag.

Shopping

Seongeup is a good place to buy *galot* (traditional Jeju workclothes) and naturally dyed fabrics. Shops include Garotmandenjip on the village central road, and Sokgungyehtusanpum (속궁예토 산품) next to Nammoon car park.

Getting There & Away

From Jeju-si, take bus 220 (₩1200, 50 minutes, every 20 minutes, Seongeup 1 Ri Office stop).

From Seogwipo, take the 201 east to Pyoseon (₩1200, 50 minutes, every 20 minutes, Pyoseolli Office stop) and transfer to bus 220 to Seongeup (₩1200, 10 minutes, every 20 minutes, Seongeup 1 Ri Office stop). A taxi from Pyoseon is about ₩7000.

HALLASAN NATIONAL PARK

This Unesco World Heritage–listed national park (한라산국립공원) surrounds Halla-san, South Korea's highest peak. At 1950m, hiking up it is strenuous, but worth the effort, and there are some short easy climbs. The densely wooded park surrounding the volcano is the world's only habitat for Korean firs and remains beautiful throughout the seasons, with hillsides of flowering azaleas in April and May being a particularly notable sight. You might spot deer.

Activities

There are seven daytime-only trails up and around Halla-san, but only Seongpanak and Gwaneum-sa go to the peak. The Eoseungsaengak and Seongpanak Trails are the shortest and least strenuous – some people don't even consider them hikes! – but still finish with rewarding sights.

Free maps are available from the information centres at the main trail entrances, but the paths are clearly marked so it's difficult to get lost. Besides, you'll seldom be climbing alone, especially on Sundays. Noted climbing times are generous. However, set out early – if you don't reach the uppermost shelters by certain times (usually 1pm, or noon in the winter), rangers will stop you from climbing higher. Trails open at 6am (5am in summer), and hikers should be off the trails by sunset. Be prepared for wind, sudden weather changes and winter snow.

Gwaneum-sa Trail HIKING
(관음사탐방로; Map p240; 064 756 9950; dawn-dusk; 475, Gwaneumsa Temple Trail Entrance stop) FREE This challenging route (8.7km, five hours) is one of the most scenic trails on Halla-san. It's also the steepest, which can make it murder on your knees coming down. Some travellers recommend hiking up the Seongpanak trail and coming down via Gwaneum-sa.

This is the most difficult trail to get to by bus; some hikers recommend catching a taxi (about ₩18,000) from the Seongpanak Trail car park to Gwaneum-sa campground, where the trail begins. Buses are possible; from Jeju City Hall, take the 281 bus to Jeju National University (₩1200, 18 minutes, frequent) from where you change to Bus

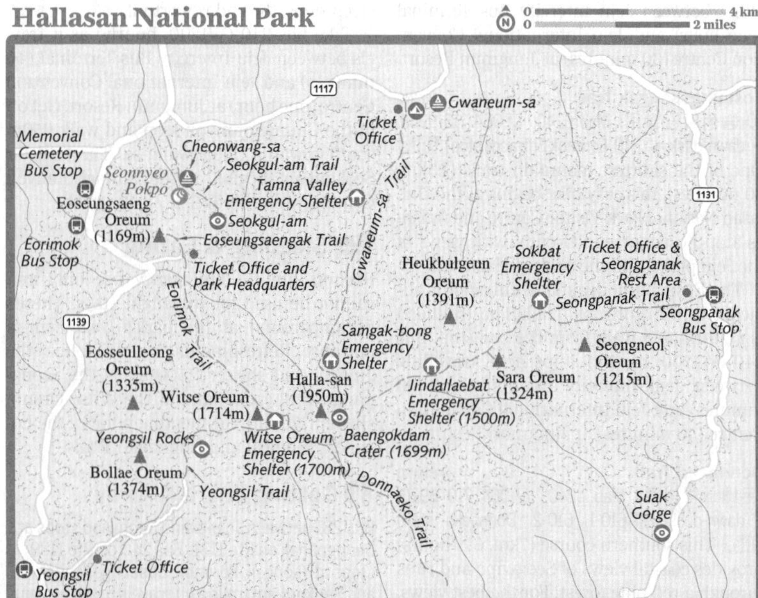

475 (₩1200 or free transfer with T-money, 11 minutes, hourly) to Gwaneumsa Temple Trail Entrance.

Seongpanak Trail HIKING
(성판악탐방로; Map p240; ☎064 725 9950; ⊙dawn-dusk; 🚌780, Seongpanak stop) FREE This popular route (9.6km, 4½ hours) has the most gradual ascent and a side trail to Sara Oreum Observatory. With quick access to Rte 1131 and public transport – the bus stop is beside the car park – it's a busy place. Shops near the car park sell basic food and hiking supplies.

Bus 281 stops here on its frequent travels between Jeju City Hall (32 minutes) and Jungang Rotary Bus Terminal (31 minutes) in Seogwipo.

Yeongsil Trail HIKING
(영실탐방로; Map p240; ☎064 747 9950; ⊙dawn-dusk; 🚌240, Yeongsil Entrance stop) FREE Yeongsil trail (5.1km, 2½ hours) is a short, easy, paved course with grand scenery – panoramas of green *oreum* and pinnacle rocks atop sheer cliffs as you hike through a dwarf fir forest before reaching the mixed deciduous and evergreen forest lower down.

It begins with a 2.1km walk from a park office (first car park) to a resting area (second car park) and finishes with 3.7km of trails to the Witse Oreum shelter.

Bus 240 (₩1200, hourly) stops here, travelling between Jeju Intercity Bus Terminal (one hour) and Jeju International Convention Centre (30 minutes) at Jungmun Resort.

Eoseungsaengak Trail HIKING
(어승생악탐방로; Map p240; ☎064 713 9953; ⊙dawn-dusk; 🚌240, Eorimok Entrance stop) FREE One of the shortest mountain trails (1.3km, 30 minutes), this easy hike begins at the Hallasan National Park Visitor Centre and finishes atop Eoseungtaeng Oreum, with views of the Jeju plains and the peak of Halla-san.

The Eoseungsaengak Trail entrance is adjacent to the Eorimok Trail. The trailhead is a 20-minute walk from the bus stop. Bus 240 (₩1200, hourly) stops here, travelling between Jeju Intercity Bus Terminal (50 minutes) and Jeju International Convention Centre (50 minutes) at Jungmun Resort.

Donnaeko Trail HIKING
(돈내코탐방로; Map p240; ☎064 710 6920; ⊙dawn-dusk; 🚌610-1, 610-2, Donnaeko stop) FREE This southern course (7km, 3½ hours) provides coastal views of Seogwipo and runs through a red pine forest. For the best views, some travellers recommend climbing up Yeongsil or Eorimok and then down Donnaeko.

The 610 bus runs from Cheonjiyeon Pokpo (40 minutes) in Seogwipo and stops conveniently at the Donnaeko Recreation Area; from Jeju City Hall (50 minutes) bus 281 stops at Seogwipo Industry Science High School, 1.2km southeast, from where you can walk.

Eorimok Trail HIKING
(어리목탐방로; Map p240; ☎064 713 9950; ⊙dawn-dusk; 🚌240, Eorimok Entrance stop) FREE After a 20-minute walk from the Eorimok bus stop and visitor's centre, this trail (6.8km, three hours) begins in earnest with a steep climb through a deciduous forest. Halfway up, the dense trees give way to an open, subalpine moorland of bamboo, grass and dwarf firs.

Bus 240 (₩1200, hourly) stops here, travelling between Jeju Intercity Bus Terminal (50 minutes) and Jeju International Convention Centre (50 minutes) at Jungmun Resort.

Seokgul-am Trail HIKING
(석굴암탐방로; Map p240; ⊙dawn-dusk; 🚌240, Chunghonmyoji Cemetery stop) FREE This short course (1.5km, 50 minutes) starts at Cheonwang-sa, runs through Ahheunahhopgol (99 Valley) and terminates at Seokgul-am, a female hermitage. Though novice hikers may wince at the occasional stretch of steep steps, the end is worth it.

Take bus 240 (₩1200, hourly) as it travels between Jeju Intercity Bus Terminal (40 minutes) and Jeju International Convention Centre (one hour) at Jungmun Resort. Get off at the Chunghonmyoji stop and walk 950m south towards Cheonwang-sa. The trail for Seokgul-am begins at the Chunghonmyoji Cemetery (제주시충혼묘지) car park.

Sleeping & Eating

Shelters are for emergency use only and cannot be used for overnight stays. There's a campground at the park's Gwaneum-sa entrance. Refreshments are available at the Jindallaebat shelter (1500m) on the Seongpanak Trail (p257) and at the Witse Oreum shelter (1700m), the meeting point of the Eorimok, Yeongsil and Donnaeko Trails.

Getting There & Away

Bus 281 between Jeju-si and Seogwipo stops at Seongpanak on Rte 1131. Bus 240 on Rte 1139 stops at Yeongsil, Eorimok, Eoseungsaengak and Seokgul-am trails as it travels between Jeju

Intercity Bus Terminal and Jeju International Convention Centre at Jungmun Resort; be sure to check the bus direction before boarding. Bus 610 stops at the Donnaeko trail from Cheonjiyeon Pokpo in Seogwipo. Gwaneum-sa involves taking two buses, so some hikers recommend catching a taxi from Seongpanak to the Gwaneum-sa campground, where the trail begins. Parking is available at most trails for ₩1800.

SOUTHERN JEJU-DO

If you only have a short time on Jeju-do, make Seogwipo your base. It has the best climate and coastal scenery, plus easy access to Halla-san and Seongsan Ilchul-bong. It is a little far from the airport but there are direct buses to and from there. it is also well connected to the atmospheric Buddha in a cave at Sagye-ri and group-package favourite Jungmun Resort.

Getting There & Away

If you base yourself in Jeju-si or elsewhere it's possible to make day trips to the south on long bus rides, either on the Jeju Airport Limousine Bus 600 (₩4500 to ₩5500) as it makes its way through Jungmun Resort and onto World Cup Stadium and Seogwipo, or on local buses, such as the useful bus 202 (₩1200), which travels from Jungang Rotary in Seogwipo on to World Cup Stadium and Jungmun Resort, hugging the coast westwards through Sagye-ri and on to Hallim Park in the northwest.

Seogwipo

064 / POP 186,370

Jeju-do's second-largest city is beautifully situated on a rocky volcanic coastline dotted with lush parks, a deep gorge and two waterfalls. The clear blue waters and mild ocean temperatures make Seogwipo (서귀포; pronounced so-ghee-poh) Korea's best scuba-diving destination and it's also an ideal base for hiking, or day trips across Jeju-do if you don't mind long rides. Its small size makes it easy to walk between most of the sights in town, and at the end of each day you'll find yourself back at Lee Jung Seop-ro, one of the hippest streets on the island. Jungmun Resort is also within easy day-trip distance.

Sights

★Cheonjiyeon Pokpo WATERFALL
(천지연폭포; Map p260; adult/child ₩2000/1000; 7am-10pm) This popular 22m-high waterfall is reached after a 10-minute walk through a beautifully forested, steep gorge. The waterfall can be impressive following heavy rain; at other times it's more noisy than wide. It's well worth visiting in the evening, too, when the illuminated gorge takes on a romantic atmosphere. The falls are on Olle Trail 6; you can easily walk here from town or take the Seogwipo City Tour Bus (p262).

Jeongbang Pokpo WATERFALL
(정방폭포; Map p260; Chilsimni-ro 214beon-gil; adult/youth ₩2000/1000; 8am-6pm) A favourite with photographers, this 23m-high waterfall is a 15-minute walk east of the town centre. At times less dramatic than the island's other waterfalls, its claim to fame is that it's the only waterfall in Asia that falls into the ocean. Enter from the pathway next to Seobok Exhibition Hall.

Saeseom ISLAND
(Bird Island; 새섬; Map p260; dawn-11pm) FREE Densely wooded Saeseom (Sod Island) is ringed by a shady 1.1km trail that is a favourite spot to stroll at sunset. There is also a central public square within the temperate forest conservation zone. Enter from the Saeyeon-gyo bridge.

Oedolgae HILL
(외돌개; Lonely Rock; Map p240; 064 760 3031; Namseongjung-ro; 2, 615-1, 615-2, 627) FREE This unusual volcanic basalt pillar juts out 20m from the sea and has served as a filming location for a number of Korean dramas and TV shows. The walk to this 'lonely rock', by pine trees in Sammae-bong Park to a stunning cliffside, is half the pleasure. It's at the junction of Olle Trail Rtes 6 and 7. Seogwipo City Tour Bus (p262) stops here.

Lee Jung-Seop Art Gallery & Park MUSEUM
(Map p260; 064 760 3567; http://jslee.seogwipo.go.kr; 27-3 Lee Jung Seop-ro; adult/youth ₩1000/500; 9am-6pm Tue-Sun) On the street that is named after him and decorated with images from his distinctive paintings and drawings (in Fauvism style with exaggerated brush strokes and colours), is this small museum devoted to Lee Jung-Seop (1916–56). Outside nearby, in a rocky garden with fragrant trees, is the traditional Jeju house (free admission) in which the artist lived for a short time in 1951. A four-day festival is held in September to celebrate Lee.

Seogwipo

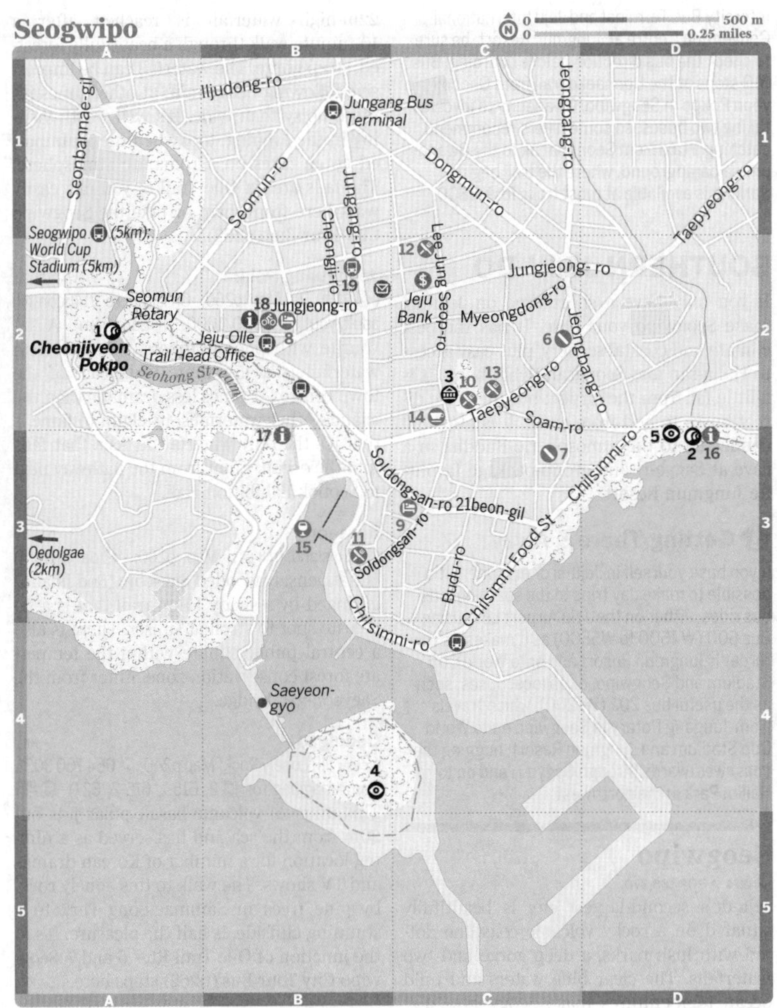

Seobok Exhibition Hall MEMORIAL

(Map p260; ☎064 760 6304; 156-8 Chilsimni-ro; ⏲9am-6pm) FREE This exhibition hall is dedicated to Seobok, who was an envoy of the first Chinese emperor, Qin Shi Huang, and chronicles his visits to Halla-san (p257) in search of a rare elixir. Pull up a bench for good sea views.

Activities

All Blu DIVING

(Map p260; ☎010 4464 3216; www.allblu.co.kr; 172-4 Seogwi-dong, Seogwipo; ⏲9am-6pm) A one-woman diving outfit with MJ, who speaks great English and warmly leads newbie divers to their first splash around Seogwipo, or further afield.

Big Blue 33 DIVING

(Map p260; ☎010 6314 4328; www.bigblue33.co.kr; 9 Soam-ro 12beon-gil, Songsan-dong; ⏲9am-7pm) Formerly run by a German expat and sold in 2018 to a Korean diving enthusiast who speaks English and Korean. A two-tank dive trip costs ₩120,000, with all equipment and guide. An eight-day Master Scuba Diver course costs ₩650,000.

Seogwipo

Sleeping

Backpacker's Home HOSTEL $
(Map p260; ☎064 763 4000; http://backpackershome.com; 24 Jungjeong-ro, Seogwi-dong; dm ₩17,500-21,000; P ❄ @ ☜) One of Seogwipo's better backpacker hostels, this one has spacious dorms – each with its own bathroom, sleeping in sturdy pine bunks with privacy curtains – English-speaking staff, a great outdoor terrace with the occasional social barbecue, a good continental breakfast for ₩1000, and a midnight curfew.

Shinsung Hotel MOTEL $$
(신성호텔; Map p260; ☎064 732 1415; 637-2 Songsan-dong, Seogwipo; r ₩50,000; ❄ @) A good motel with a hard-to-miss metal-and-chequerboard exterior. Rooms include a computer and a spa. Some rooms have balconies, and those with a sea view cost ₩10,000 extra, even if it's too misty to see the sea. It's next to some good casual bars.

Eating

Seogwipo Olle Market MARKET $
(서귀포 올레시장; Map p260; 18 Sinhyojungang-ro 62beon-gil; ⏰7am-9pm) Browse stalls of wonderful fruit, live seafood and street food. It's a good place to pick up snacks for a picnic.

★**Saesom Galbi** BARBECUE $$
(새섬 갈비; Map p260; ☎064 732 4001; 32 Soldongsan-ro 10beon-gil, Seogwi-dong; mains ₩12,000-30,000; ⏰11.30am-10.30pm; P ☜) Perched on a cliff overlooking the harbour, this is the place for barbecued beef or pork. The atmosphere is informal and boisterous thanks to the weathered floors, open dining concept and giddy staff. Side dishes are modest, but the meat is top-notch. Look for a black and white building.

★**b.pork bistro** FUSION $$
(Map p260; www.instagr.am/b.pork_bistro; 417-1 Taepyeong-ro; mains ₩7000-12,000) The lowercase name hints at the minimalist black-and-white bistro so tiny you might miss it posing on the corner – a sign of the Lee Jung Seop-ro area's hip blossoming. Jeju's black pork is showcased in delectable soft-tortilla tacos, pasta and a 'lunchbox' (stir fry and rice) – paired with a glass of Chilean wine here, of course.

Sol Fish FISH & CHIPS $$
(Map p260; ☎064 733 5567; Taepyeong-ro; fish & chips ₩10,000-13,000; ☜) London-good succulent fish and chips come with a choice of cod or a local Seogwipo white fish, plus wedges or salad, and excellent tartare. Grilled mackerel sandwiches are popular too. Look for the small pink building declaring 'Fish & Chips' near the corner with Soam-ro.

Drinking & Nightlife

★**Cafe Mayb** CAFE
(메이비; Map p260; ☎070-4143 0639; www.fb.me/cafemaybe; 34 Lee Jung Seop-ro; ⏰10am-1am; ☜) Creatively decorated inside, with tables spilling onto the street, Seogwipo's most laid-back cafe is the place to meet friends or enjoy downtime with a book.

Rose Marin BAR
(로즈마린 노천카페; Map p260; ☎064 762 2808; 13 Namseongjung-ro, Cheonji-dong; ⌚noon-3am) Rose Marin is a tumbledown waterfront shack with giant trees growing through the floorboards. It's quirky, gritty and delightful. Be sure to try the dried squid, Korea's classic beer-bar side dish.

Information

Jeju Bank (Map p260; Jungjeong-ro; ⌚9am-4pm Mon-Fri) Global ATM with a ₩1,000,000 withdrawal limit.

Post Office (서귀포중앙동우체국; Map p260; Jungjeong-ro; ⌚9am-6pm Mon-Fri) City-centre post office.

TOURIST INFORMATION

Bus Terminal Tourist Information Office (서귀포 시외버스터미널 관광안내소; Map p240; ☎064 739 1391; 33 Woldeukeom-ro; ⌚9am-6pm) Next to the bus terminal in the **World Cup stadium** (제주 월드컵 경기장; Map p240; Shin Seogwipo; ⌚Dak Paper Doll Museum 9am-7pm; Ⓟ; 🚌600).

Jeju Olle Trail Head Office (Map p260; ☎064 762 2190; www.jejuolle.org; 22 Jungjeong-ro; ⌚8am-11pm) Drop by the head office and buy some Olle Trail souvenirs.

Jeongbang Pokpo Tourist Information (정방폭포 관광안내소; Map p260; ☎064 733 1530; Jeongbang Pokpo; ⌚9am-noon & 1-6pm) Office located at Jeongbang Pokpo waterfall (p259). Some English spoken.

Seogwipo Tourist Information Centre (서귀포 종합관광안내소; Map p260; ☎1330; Seohong-dong; ⌚9am-6pm)

Getting There & Away

From the airport in Jeju-si, Airport Limousine Bus 600 (₩5500, 1¾ hours, every 20 minutes) makes its way here via major hotels in Jungmun Resort. Useful cross-island buses (₩1200) include the 181 from the airport to Jungang Rotary (80 minutes, every 30 minutes), and 231 or 281 from Jeju Intercity Bus Terminal to Seogwipo Dongmun Rotary (70 minutes, every 20 minutes), not to be confused with Jeju-si's Dongmun Rotary.

Seogwipo has two intercity bus terminals: a newer one 6km west of town near the World Cup Stadium; and the central Jungang Rotary Bus Terminal (also known as Gu Terminal) at Jungang Rotary. Seogwipo is small enough to walk around, but taxis are plentiful and cheap.

From Jungang Rotary, buses (₩1200, usually departing every 15 to 20 minutes) head east to Seongsan (bus 201; 90 minutes), northwest to Hallim (bus 202; two hours), and north to Seongpanak, the eastern stop for Halla-san (bus 281; 35 minutes).

LOCAL KNOWLEDGE

JUNGMUN RESORT

Jungmun Resort (중문 휴양지; Jungmun Tourist Complex) is South Korea's primary tourist-resort town. Because it's popular, sprawling development – luxury hotels, buffet restaurants and kitschy museums – surrounds the area's pockets of natural beauty. Jungmun does have a couple of nice spots, though they are less impressive than the marketing bumf might suggest. If time is short and you're on a budget, pass on Jungmun and head to some of the island's truly interesting beach areas. If you do decide to stay overnight, aim for **Seaes Hotel & Resort's** (씨에스호텔 앤 리조트; Map p240; ☎064 735 3000; www.seaes.co.kr; r/ste incl breakfast from ₩306,000/428,000; Ⓟ❄@📶) rustically luxurious cottages.

Getting Around

The **Seogwipo City Tour Bus** (Map p260; www.seogwipo.go.kr/group/culture/tourism/electricity.htm; rides with/without T-money card ₩1150/1200; ⌚9am-9.35pm, every 35-40min; 📶) makes it easy to see all of Seogwipo's main sights in and around the city centre in one day.

Notable destinations on its one-way loop, in order, include: Jungang Rotary, Seogwipo Olle Market, Oedolgae, Lee Jung-Seop Art Gallery & Park, Cheonjiyeon Pokpo, Chilsimni Food Street near Seobok Exhibition Hall and Jeongbang Pokpo, then up to Dongmun Rotary.

Explore Seogwipo and Jeju-do the easy way: with your own wheels from **Scooter & Free Zone** (스쿠터 앤 프리존; Map p260; ☎064 762 5296; www.jusfz.co.kr; Seomun-ro, 29 Beon-gil, 38-6 Seogwi-dong; per 24hr 50/125cc scooter ₩30,000/40,000, bicycle/electric bicycle ₩15,000/20,000; ⌚9am-7.30pm). Travellers need an international driving licence to rent scooters and must be aged 21 or over. Lower prices outside of July and August.

Sagye-ri

☎064 / POP 2316

Hugging the southwest corner of the island, this sleepy village boasts a number of terrific sights, including dramatic coastlines and incredible rock formations, but most attractive is the imposing Sanbang-san (395m). Its temples peer out to sea, and at the top of a short hike, a cave holds the dramatic spectacle of a stone Buddha in a cave dripping with water.

Sights

Sanbanggul-sa TEMPLE

(산방굴사; Map p240; 218-10 Sanbang-ro, Andeok-myeon; adult/youth/child/parking ₩1000/700/500/1000; sunrise-sunset; P) A steep, 20-minute walk up the south face of the craggy Sanbang-san is a small stone Buddha in a 5m-high cave called Sanbanggul-sa. From Sagye-ri, the walk up looks more daunting than it really is, but after reaching the cave you'll be delighted because of the powerful 'wow' factor. Lower down, by the defunct ticket office and cafe, are more-modern shrines and statues with free admission. There is a separate ticket office just before the cave.

Buses (₩1200, every 20 minutes) travel between Sanbanggul-sa and Jeju-si Intercity Bus Terminal (bus 250 or 251; 75 minutes), Jungang Rotary (bus 202; one hour) in Seogwipo, or along the west coast from Hallim Park (bus 202; 70 minutes) in the northwest. A taxi from Seogwipo costs about ₩25,000. You can also walk here along Olle Trail Rte 10 from Hwasun beach.

Hamel Memorial MUSEUM

(하멜상선전시관; Map p240; combo ticket with Sanbanggul-sa adult/youth/child ₩2500/2000/1500) The Hamel Memorial is housed in a replica of a Dutch ship. Hendrick Hamel (1630–92), one of the survivors of a shipwreck near Jeju in 1653, was forced to stay in Korea for 13 years before escaping in a boat to Japan. Later he was the first westerner to write a book on the 'hermit kingdom'.

Activities

★**Yongmeori Coast** WALKING

(용머리해안; Map p240; combo ticket with Sanbanggul-sa adult/youth/child ₩2500/2000/1500; 8am-5.30pm) A short walk from Sanbang-gul-sa towards the ocean brings you to the Yongmeori coast, a spectacular seaside trail with soaring cliffs pockmarked by erosion into catacombs, narrow clefts and natural archways. Some say the rock formation looks like a dragon's head, hence the name (dragon, 용, *yong*, and head, 머리, *meori*). From the temple entrance, cross the street and walk towards the shipwreck. Note: the walk along the cliffs closes during very high seas.

Sleeping

One Fine Day Guesthouse GUESTHOUSE $$

(어느멋진날 게스트하우스; Map p240; 010 8991 2983; http://mbbolam.blog.me; 134-1 Sage-ri, Andeok-myeon; dm/r from ₩20,000/60,000;) Kitsch meets comfort in these private and dorm rooms done up in pastel colours and teddy bears to give the place a warm, fuzzy feel. The friendly owner, Mr Park, a Seoul escapee who spent 15 years cooking at the Hilton Hotel, also operates a small on-site French restaurant.

It's on the village's main road, about halfway between Sanbang-san and downhill to the port. Look for the building with the words 'Restaurant and Private Guesthouse'.

Zen Hide Away BOUTIQUE HOTEL $$$

(Map p240; 064 794 0133; http://zenhideaway jeju.com; 186-8 Sagyenam-ro, Andeok-myeon; r from ₩250,000, higher rates Fri & Sat; P) This property oozes a Zen-like appreciation for harmony with nature and balance in decor. Spas are standard in rooms, which also come with seaside views and earthy woodstone finishings. Look for the brick building set back from the road running between Sanbang-san and the port; it contains a large restaurant of the same name.

Eating & Drinking

Yongrim Sikdang SEAFOOD $$

(용림식당; Map p240; 064 794 3652; http://younglim.fordining.kr; Sagyenam-ro; mains from ₩10,000; 11am-10pm) A simple restaurant offering splendid seafood dishes such as *maeuntang* (매운탕, spicy seafood soup). A pair of travellers might choose the set meal (회정식; ₩30,000), which includes raw fish and loads of side dishes. If the weather is nice, ask for a seat on the outdoor patio overlooking the ocean.

It's near the port, on the narrow road running between the village and Sanbang-san. Turn right on leaving Sanbang-gul-sa and head 1km downhill.

Lazybox Café CAFE

(Map p240; 064 792 1254; www.lazybox.co.kr; 177-5 Sage-ri, Andeok-myeon; 10am-7pm;) Located in the small retail strip at the foot of Sanbang-san, this cute cafe serves fair-trade coffee, freshly squeezed juices and homemade cakes. The owners, escapees from Seoul, also run a **guesthouse** (d ₩20,000) km away.

Getting There & Away

Buses (₩1200; every 20 minutes) travel between Sanbanggul-sa and Jeju-si Intercity Bus Terminal (bus 250 or 251; 75 minutes), Jungang Rotary (bus 202; one hour) in Seogwipo, or along the west coast from Hallim Park (bus 202; 70 minutes) in the northwest. A taxi from Seogwipo costs about ₩25,000. You can also walk here along Olle Trail Rte 10 from Hwasun beach.

WESTERN JEJU-DO

The west side of Jeju-do is an inland treasure hunt of quirky museums, and artist hideaways, which are easier than ever to reach without your own wheels. Along the coast, Hallim is finding its hipness with restaurants that lure you in with blue-water views, and small islands promise absolute serenity along Olle Trails. This side of the island takes exploration but rewards you with smaller crowds.

Inland Region

Sights

O'Sulloc Tea Museum MUSEUM
(오설록 녹차박물관; Map p240; ☎064 794 5312; www.osulloc.com; 15 Sinhwayeoksa-ro, Andeok-myeon; 9am-7pm; 255, 771 or 784 to Osulloc stop) FREE Overlooking the verdant plantation of one of Korea's largest growers of *nokcha* (green tea), this museum displays a collection of ancient tea implements, some of which date back to the 3rd century. You can also stroll the fields and shop for its products, such as green-tea shampoo, green-tea cake and green-tea ice cream.

Jeju Glass Castle AMUSEMENT PARK
(유리의성; Map p240; ☎064 772 7777; www.jejuglasscastle.com; 462 Nokchabunjae-ro, Hangyeong-myeon; adult/youth/child ₩11,000/9000/8000; 9am-7pm; 771 or 784 to Yuriuiseong stop) This fascinating theme park features more than 350 glass sculptures created by global artists, including the world's largest glass ball and glass diamond. Glass-blowing and glass-making classes are also run here.

Spirited Garden GARDENS
(생각하는 정원; Map p240; ☎064 772 3701; www.spiritedgarden.com; 675 Nokchabunjae-ro, Hangyeong-myeon; adult/youth/child ₩12,000/10,000/7000; 8.30am-6pm, to 7pm Apr-Sep; 967 to Jeo-jiri stop) *Bunjae* (bonsai) trees may seem esoteric, but this bonsai park has excellent examples, some up to 500 years old. It's the life's work of Mr Sung Bum-young and has hosted presidents and prime ministers from across Asia.

Jeju Museum of Contemporary Art MUSEUM
(제주현대미술관; Map p240; ☎064 710 7801; www.jejumuseum.co.kr; 2114-63 Jeoji-ri, Hangyeong-myeon; adult/youth/child ₩2000/1000/500; 9am-6pm Tue-Sun, to 7pm Jul-Sep; 784 or 820 to Jeju Museum of Contemporary Art Jeoji Munhwayesurin Village stop) At the heart of the Artists Village in Jeoji is this excellent gallery. Permanent exhibitions by Kim Heng-sou and Park Kwang-jin are supplemented by regularly changing shows of other artists. The village is dotted with engaging pieces of modern and traditional architecture. It's on Rte 1115, a short drive from Green Tee-Bonsai Rd.

Eating

Dol Hareubang Pizza ITALIAN $$
(피자굽는돌하르방; Map p240; ☎064 773 7273; www.pizzajeju.modoo.at; 218 Cheongsu-ro, Hangyeong-myeon; mains ₩13,000-59,000; 11am-6.30pm Tue-Sun; 771 or 820 to Jeju Pyeonghwa Museum stop) Tasty 1m-long pizzas topped with sweet potato, bulgogi (marinated beef) and kimchi are served in an old building in the middle of nowhere.

From the southern part of the island, head north on Rte 1120 towards Jeju Glass Castle. Before the northern intersection of 1120 and Rte 1136, turn right on Cheongsu-ro (청수로) – look for the pizza sign. It's the yellow building on a corner lot.

It's about 600m from the **Jeju Peace Museum** (제주 전쟁역사평화박물관; Map p240; ☎064 772 2500; www.peacemuseum.co.kr; 63 Cheongsuseo 5-gil, Hangyeong-myeon; adult/ youth & child ₩6000/4000; 8.30am-5pm).

Mayflower CAFE $$
(카페 오월의 꽃; Map p240; ☎064 772 5995; Nokchabunjae-ro; mains from ₩15,000; 10am-10pm) Enjoy coffee or tea in this self-service cafe that, on the outside, looks like a giant white cloud. Pizza, pasta, pork cutlets and salad are also available. It's on Green Tee-Bonsai Rd, between the Spirited Garden and Jeju Glass Castle.

Getting There & Away

Two useful bus services run a circuit covering isolated sights on the island and include an English-speaking tourist guide aboard. **Yellow Tourist Bus 820** (Map p240; per ride ₩1150; every 30-60min 8.30am-5.30pm;) takes in the west inland, stopping at Jeju Museum of Contemporary Art, Jeju Peace Museum, Spirited Garden, Glass Castle, Jeoji Artists' Village, O'Sulloc Tea Museum and Jeoji Oreum.

The other route is the **810** (Map p240; per ride ₩1150; every 30-60min 8.30am-5.30pm), which makes a loop around the northeast, stopping at many *oreum* (craters) and Jeju Maze Land. Both charge regular local bus fares and you must have a T-money card (no cash). Catch either from any of the sights. Bus 820 originates

JEJU'S SEX MUSEUMS

Although attitudes are changing, Koreans tend to be conservative in public about sex. Pornography, for example, is illegal. So how come Jeju-do has three graphic sex museums? Chatting to locals, a couple of answers come up. The island gives tax breaks to anyone who runs a museum (which explains why Jeju-do has so many 'museums') and many honeymooning and holidaying visitors are already in the mood for frisky fun – these museums provide inspiration and education.

Jeju Loveland (제주러브랜드; Map p240; ☎064 712 6988; www.jejuloveland.com; 2894-72, 1100-ro, Yeon-dong; ₩12,000; ⏲9am-midnight; 🚌240, 465-1 or 465-2) This erotic outdoor theme park created by art students and graduates of Seoul's Hongik University features hundreds of sexy and frequently comic sculptures spread across a quiet green space, plus soft-core art galleries, an adult-toy shop and a cafe selling genital-shaped bread. Open daily and lit up at night, this is one for when other museums are closed. The park is a short drive from Jeju-si on Rte 1139.

Museum of Sex & Health (건강과 성 박물관; Map p240; ☎064 792 5700; www.sexmuseum.or.kr; 1736 Gamsan-ri, Andeok-myeon; ₩12,000; ⏲10am-8pm; 🚌202) In Gamsan-ri in southern Jeju-do, this huge complex has extensive sections devoted to sex education and sex culture from around the world. Laudable for its inclusivity, covering usually taboo subjects in Korea such as homosexuality, it also has some very imaginative installations. Buses running on Rte 1132 between Seogwipo (₩1200, one hour, every 20 minutes) and Hwasun-ri stop near the museum in Andeok-myeon.

World Eros Museum (제주 세계성문화박물관; Map p240; ☎064 739 0059; 33 Woldeukeom-ro; ₩7000; ⏲9am-7pm, last entry 6pm) The smallest of Jeju-do's sex-themed museums and perhaps the most artful and serious. There's a collection of world erotic art, though the lack of English signage makes it a bit inaccessible. The adult-only museum is on the 2nd floor of Seogwipo's World Cup Stadium (p262).

In Seogwipo, frequent local buses run from Jungang Rotary Bus Terminal to World Cup Stadium (₩1200). Airport Limousine Bus 600 (₩4500) also stops here.

at Dongwang Transfer Terminal, with 820-1 running clockwise and 820-2 running anticlockwise.

Bus 202 (every 20 minutes) hugs the coast along Rte 1132 from Jeju-si to Seogwipo via Hallim, Moseulpo and Sagye-ri in the south.

Hallim

☎064 / POP 21,464

On the northwest coast, the pretty town of Hallim (한림) is fringed by two beaches – lovely Hyeopjae (협재해수욕장) and its growing collection of excellent restaurants, and quiet Geumneung (금능해수욕장) – both with white sand and crystal-clear waters, perfect for snorkelling.

Sights

Biyangdo ISLAND

(비양도; Map p240; ☎064 796 7552) Just beyond Hyeopjae's sandy shores sits a tiny island that beckons. It's a curious place; just a hamlet, a couple of restaurants and *minbak* (private homes with rooms for rent) for overnight stays. A hike around the island takes about two hours, including time to reach the lighthouse for excellent panoramic views.

Take a ferry (return ₩6000, 15 minutes, departures 9am, noon and 3pm; passport required) from Hallim Port, which is a long walk or short taxi ride from Hyeopjae beach. The ticket office is next to a police station and the start of Olle Trail 15.

Hallim Park GARDENS

(한림공원; Map p240; ☎064 796 0001; www.hallimpark.co.kr; 300 Hallim-ro, Hallim-eup; adult/youth/child ₩11,000/8000/7000; ⏲8.30am-7pm Mar-Sep, to 6pm Oct-Feb; P 👪; 🚌202 to Hallim Park stop) Hallim Park offers a botanical and bonsai garden, a mini folk village and walks through a lava-tube cave. The caves are part of a 17km-long lava-tube system and are said to be the only lava caves in the world to contain stalagmites and stalactites.

Sleeping & Eating

★**Code 46610** APARTMENT $$$

(코드 46610; Map p240; ☎064 721 0612; 1751-6, Hyeopjae-ri, Hallim-eup; r from ₩150,000;

OFF THE BEATEN TRACK

WESTERN ISLANDS

Near Jeju's southwest tip, the town of Moseulpo (모슬포) is a sizeable fishing port at the junction of Olle Trails 10 and 11 and a jumping-off point for the lonesome islands Gapado and Marado.

There is little to hold people's attention in Moseulpo, but if you want an early start for the islands, there is a handful of hotels and guesthouses, such as homey **Springflower Guesthouse** (Map p240; ☎064 792 6008; www.gojejuguesthouse.com; 1046-1 Hamo-ri, Daejeong-eup; dm/s/d incl breakfast ₩22,000/35,000/50,000; ❄@📶; 🚌202, 250), that are in walking distance of the ferry port. Hit up **Hamo Restaurant** (하모식당; Map p240; ☎064 794 0137; Choenamdanhaean-ro; mains from ₩8000; ⏲8.30am-9pm; 🚌202, 250) for preferry breakfast or a bowl of *miyeokguk* (미역국, seaweed soup).

Gapado (가파도; ☎064 794 3500) The Olle Trail 10-1 (5km, two hours) encircles Gapado (population 300), the nearer and larger of the two pizza-flat volcanic islands, just 5.5km off the coast of Moseulpo. The mostly flat trail meanders along windy coasts and through green fields of flowing barley. There are a few places to grab a bite and rent a bike. **Ferries** (return adult/child ₩13,100/6600 incl park entrance fee; 20min) depart four times daily (9am, 11am, 2pm and 4pm). Note: last return ferry leaves at 4.20pm; see www.wonderfulis.co.kr. Schedules can change in bad weather or rough seas.

Marado (마라도; Map p240; ☎064 794 3500) This barren, windswept island with a rocky coastline has few sights, though you do get bragging rights for reaching Korea's most southerly point, 11km off the coast of Molseupo. Just 4.2km in circumference, it takes about two hours to walk the islet (population 100), which has a Buddhist temple and a Catholic church. **Ferries** (return adult/youth ₩18,000/9000 incl park entrance fee; 30min) have hourly departures from 9.50am to 4.30pm. Note: last return ferry leaves at 3.55pm; see www.wonderfulis.co.kr. Tickets for Marado must be bought at least 40 minutes in advance.

P❄📶; 🚌202) If Hallim's sleepy port and rugged Hyeopjae beach left you feeling nautical, then try sleeping in these converted shipping containers. It's much more comfortable than it sounds, with light-filled spaces and boutique good looks from the equipped kitchens to smart TVs. It's within sniffing distance of the seaside restaurants, or the pizza cafe downstairs.

Kangsikdang KOREAN $$
(강식당; Map p240; ☎064 796 0778; www.instagr.am/kangsikdang; Hyeopjae 1-gil; mains ₩12,000-16,000; ⏲11am-3pm & 5-8pm Wed-Mon) Kangsikdang uses small twists to create great dishes. Three types of organic mushrooms are paired with a secret sauce for an oh-so-creamy pasta; and it elevates the traditional Jeju pork noodle soup, adding spice and bean sprouts. It's on the atmospheric port looking out to Biyangdo.

Su Udon JAPANESE $$
(Map p240; ☎064 796 5830; 11 Hyeopjae 1-gil, Hallim-eub; mains from ₩10,000; ⏲11.30am-3.30pm & 5-6.30pm Wed-Sun, 11am-3.30pm Mon) Who would imagine such perfectly crispy, juicy pork *tonkatsu* or shrimp tempura in a quiet house in Hallim? People are attracted by the blue-water views of Biyago, and surprised by the excellent Japanese udon. Look for a chalkboard (or a queue!) on the path outside; photo menu.

Donatos ITALIAN $$$
(도나토스; Map p240; ☎064 796 1981; www.fb.me/donatos; Hyeopjae 2-gil; pizzas from ₩19,000; ⏲noon-3pm & 5-9pm Mon, Thu & Fri, 5-9pm Wed, noon-9pm Sat & Sun, closed mid-Jan–Mar; 📶; 🚌202) Delicious, authentic pizza from a wood-burning stove is served in a spacious, laid-back atmosphere with rock music in the background. A good selection of international beers, and a ban on children under eight years old, makes it one for adults. It's in a wide building opposite Hyeopjae beach.

ℹ Getting There & Away

Bus 202 (₩1200, every 20 minutes) stops here as it follows the coast between Jeju-si Intercity Bus Terminal (1¼ hours) and Jungang Rotary Seogwipo (1¾ hours).

Jeollabuk-do

Includes ➡

Best Places to Eat

- Hanguk-jip (p272)
- Yetchon Makgeolli (p272)
- Hyundai-ok (p271)

Best Places to Stay

- Seunggwangje (p271)
- Cho Ga Jib (p271)
- Jeonju Tourist Hotel (p271)

Why Go?

The small southwestern province of Jeollabuk-do (전라북도) punches above its weight. At the centre is the capital Jeonju, famous for its *hanok maeul*, a village of hundreds of traditional tile-roofed buildings that house restaurants, cafes and teahouses. Koreans also call Jeonju, a Unesco-listed 'City of Gastronomy', the country's number-one foodie destination: eat once in Jeonju, they say, and you're spoiled for life. It makes sense: this fertile green province is an agricultural heartland whose fresh produce stars in local dishes.

Much of rural Jeollabuk-do is parkland, which means that if you tire of Jeonju's old-world charms, you can stretch your legs on any number of fantastic hiking trails, from the steep peaks of Naejangsan National Park to the gentle hills of Seonunsan Provincial Park. There's also skiing on the slopes of Muju to the east and sandy beaches on the West Sea, from where you can catch ferries to sleepy islands.

When to Go

Jeonju

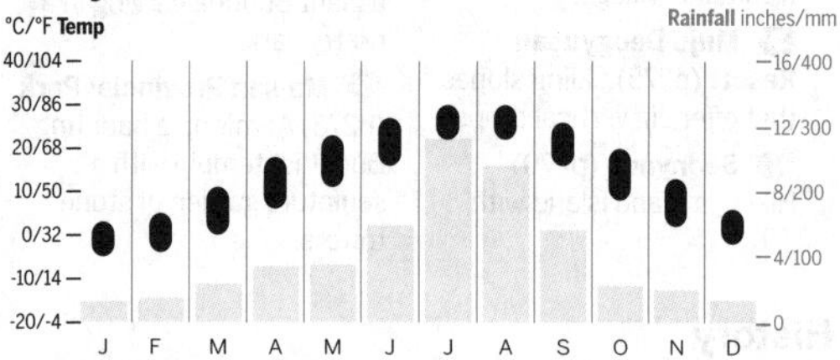

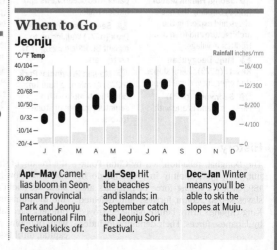

Apr–May Camellias bloom in Seonunsan Provincial Park and Jeonju International Film Festival kicks off.

Jul–Sep Hit the beaches and islands; in September catch the Jeonju Sori Festival.

Dec–Jan Winter means you'll be able to ski the slopes at Muju.

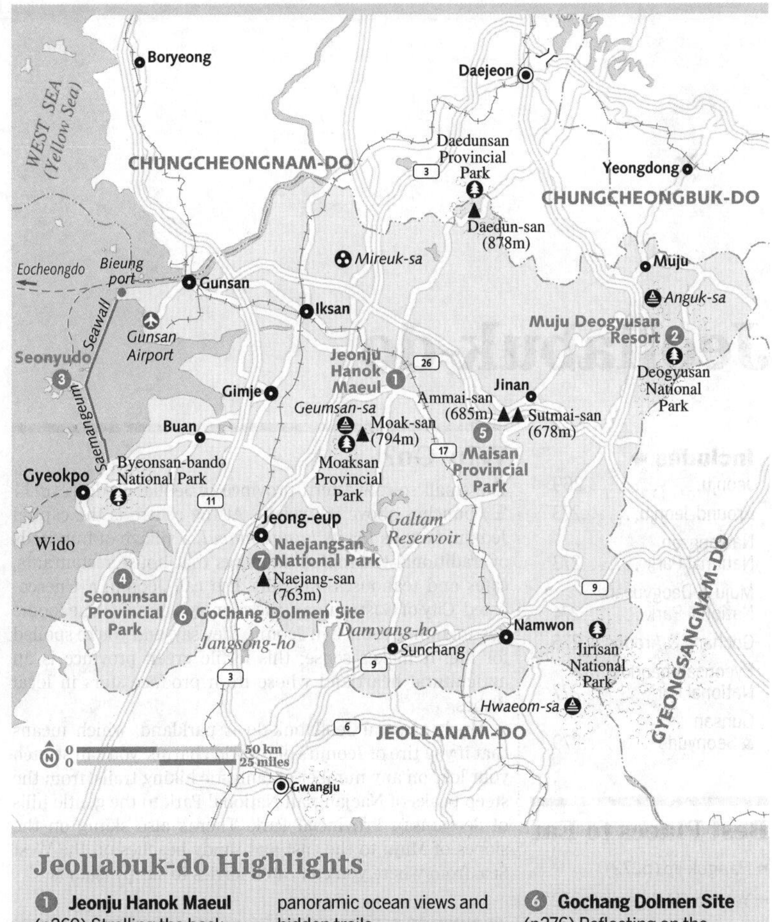

Jeollabuk-do Highlights

1. **Jeonju Hanok Maeul** (p269) Strolling the back alleys and exploring the architecture and food of a traditional village.
2. **Muju Deogyusan Resort** (p275) Skiing slopes that offer big vertical drops.
3. **Seonyudo** (p279) Hiking a grand island with panoramic ocean views and hidden trails.
4. **Seonun-sa Provincial Park** (p277) Walking up to a giant Buddha carving in a pretty park.
5. **Maisan Provincial Park** (p273) Admiring a haunting Buddhist temple with a sculpture garden of stone towers.
6. **Gochang Dolmen Site** (p276) Reflecting on the tides of history while walking amid these prehistoric tombs, some of which weigh more than 30 tonnes.
7. **Naejangsan National Park** (p273) Sipping soothing green tea inside a Buddhist temple building.

History

The Donghak rebellion, led by Chon Pong-jun, took place mainly in Jeollabuk-do in 1893 when a ragtag force of peasants and slaves seized Jeonju fortress and defeated King Gojong's army, before being destroyed by Japanese forces. Their demands included the freeing of slaves, better treatment of the *chonmin* (low-born), the redistribution of land, the abolition of taxes on fish and salt, and the punishment of corrupt government officials. Jeollabuk-do and Jeollanam-do were one joint province, with Jeonju as the capital, until 1896.

Jeonju

☎063 / POP 652,400

Jeonju (전주), the provincial capital of Jeollabuk-do, is famous for being the birthplace of both the Joseon dynasty and Korea's most well-known culinary delight, bibimbap (rice, egg and vegetables with a hot sauce). Centrally located, the city is the perfect base to explore Jeollabuk-do, as it's the regional hub for buses and trains. With almost 10 million visitors annually, Jeonju Hanok Maeul is a popular tourist spot. A half day is hardly enough time to take in the village's outstanding *hanok* (traditional wooden homes) and experiment with new food while exploring a delightful mishmash of streets and alleys.

Sights

★Jeonju Hanok Maeul AREA

(전주한옥마을) This *maeul* (village) has more than 800 *hanok* (traditional wooden homes), making it one of the largest concentrations in the country. Virtually all of them contain guesthouses, restaurants, cafes, and *hanbok* (traditional clothing) rental shops. Though superduper touristy, the cobblestone lanes and unusual architectural lines coupled with wisps of smoke from octopus grills all come together to create an enchanting experience, especially at dusk when an orange hue paints the village with a soft light.

If the thought of afternoon crowds makes the journey here seem less fun, escape to less-explored areas in and around the village. Head to Girin-daero and admire the street art in Jaman Village (자만마을). Walk down the hill and turn right on to the path that runs along the north side of the river. Take time to explore the back alleys and discover hidden gems like Cho Ga Jib (p271). Continuing down the main path beyond Cheongyeonru's gazebo (청연루), head to the 2nd floor of the **Nambu-sijang** (남부시장, Nambu Market; 63 Pungnammun 2-gil) for a drink or meal.

Some places in the village host workshops (eg on making traditional paper or alcohol). These usually require advance reservations and a minimum of two people; ask at a tourist information centre (p272).

Jeondong Catholic Church CHURCH

(전동성당; ☎063 284 3222; www.jeondong.or.kr; 51 Taejo-ro) FREE The easiest landmark to find around the *hanok* village is a tall, red-brick church built by French missionary Xavier Baudounet where Korean Catholics were executed in 1781 and 1801. It's closed to the public except during Mass, when you can respectfully peek at the stained-glass windows.

Those executed here were later interred on the hill southeast of *hanok maeul* known today as **Martyrs' Mountain** (치명자산성지; ☎063 285 5755; www.joanlugalda.com; 89 Baramssoeneun-gil). There are 13 crosses on the hillside marking the burial spot and a small church, accessible via a trail.

Omok-dae HISTORIC BUILDING

(오목대) On a hill overlooking the entire village is a pavilion where General Yi Seong-gye celebrated a victory over Japanese pirates in 1380, prior to his overthrow of the Goryeo dynasty. Cross the bridge to Imok-dae (이목대), a monument to one of Yi Seong-gye's ancestors.

Gyeonggijeon HISTORIC BUILDING

(경기전; ☎063 281 2891; 102 3-ga, Pungnam-dong; adult/youth/child ₩3000/2500/1000; ⏰9am-6pm) This palace is home to shrines, storehouses and guardrooms relating to the Confucian rituals once held here. There is also a replica portrait of Yi Seong-gye, the founder of the Joseon dynasty (1392–1910), whose family came from Jeonju. Teeming with antiquity, the palace – originally constructed in 1410 and reconstructed in 1614 – is a popular spot for selfies. You can **hire costumes** (색동저고리; ☎070-4241 8282; https://koreancolor.modoo.at; 73 Jeon-dong; from ₩10,000; ⏰9am-9pm), such as traditional *hanbok* garments, for period photos. English-language tours are held at 11am and 2pm daily.

Yeomyeong Camera Museum MUSEUM

(여명 카메라 박물관; ☎063 232 5250; 92 Hanji-gil; ₩3000; ⏰10am-6pm, closed Mon) About 400 vintage cameras are on display in this small but worthwhile museum, along with projectors and black-and-white images.

Traditional Wine Museum MUSEUM

(전통술박물관; ☎063 287 6305; http://urisul.net; 74 Hanji-gil; ⏰9am-6pm Tue-Sun) FREE Housed in a beautiful *hanok,* this museum has a *gosori* (traditional still), displays (in Korean) explaining the process of making traditional liquors, and a small gift shop.

Jeonju Hyanggyo HISTORIC BUILDING

(전주향교; ☎063 288 4548; 139 Hyanggyo-gil; ⏰10am-6pm Mar-Sep, to 5pm Oct-Feb) FREE *Hyanggyo* were neighbourhood schools established by *yangban* (aristocrats) in the 1500s to prepare their sons for the *seowon* (Confucian academies), where the students took the all-important government-service

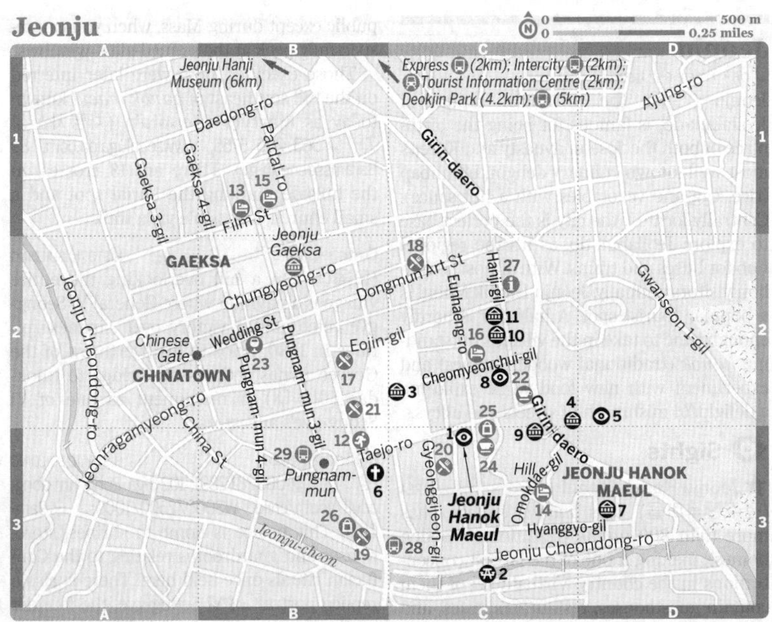

Jeonju

Top Sights

1 Jeonju Hanok Maeul C3

Sights

2 Cheongyeonru Gazebo C3
3 Gyeonggijeon C2
4 Imok-dae C2
5 Jaman Village D2
6 Jeondong Catholic Church B3
7 Jeonju Hyanggyo D3
8 Jeonju Korean Paper Institute C2
9 Omok-dae C3
10 Traditional Wine Museum C2
11 Yeomyeong Camera Museum C2

Activities, Courses & Tours

12 Saeg-dong Jeogori B3

Sleeping

13 Benikea Jeonju Hansung Tourist Motel B1
14 Cho Ga Jib C3
15 Jeonju Tourist Hotel B1
16 Seunggwangje C2

Eating

17 Hanguk-jip B2
18 Hanok Tteokgalbi C2
19 Hyundai-ok B3
20 Veteran C3
21 Yetchon Makgeolli B2

Drinking & Nightlife

22 Cafe Tomorrow C2
23 Deepin B2
24 Gyodong Dawan C3

Shopping

Demiseam .... (see 22)
25 Handicraft Exhibition Hall C3
26 Nambu-sijang B3

Information

27 Hanok Village Tourist Information Centre C2

Transport

Jeondong Catholic Church Bus Stop .... (see 12)
28 Nambu Market Bus Stop C3
29 Pungnam-mun Bus Stop B3

exams. This well-preserved and atmospheric example dates from 1603.

Jeonju Hanji Museum MUSEUM
(전주한지박물관; ☎063 210 8103; www.hanjimuseum.co.kr; 59 Palbok-ro; ⏲9am-5pm, closed

Mon; 101, 380, 381, 383 or 385) FREE Adjacent to a modern-day paper factory, this museum covers the history and processes involved in making *hanji* (traditional Korean paper) and also shows some of the impressive things that can be created with it. At the end, you get to try making your own. A 20-minute northbound bus ride from Jeondong Catholic Church will leave you with long walk to the museum. Consider a short taxi ride (₩5000) instead.

Jeonju Korean Paper Institute ARTS CENTRE
(전주전통한지원; 063 232 6591; 100-10 Hanji-gil; 9am-5pm) FREE See sheets of *hanji* (handmade paper) being manufactured in this institute, housed in a gloriously atmospheric *hanok* (traditional wooden home) down an alley. A slop of fibres in a big tank magically solidifies into paper. Handmade paper products are on sale at the gift shop.

Festivals & Events

Jeonju International Film Festival FILM
(전주 국제영화제; www.jiff.or.kr) This nine-day event every April/May focuses mainly on indie, digital and experimental movies. Around 200 films from 40 countries are shown in local cinema multiplexes.

Jeonju Sori Festival MUSIC
(전주 세계소리축제; www.sorifestival.com) A week-long music festival, with an emphasis on traditional Korean music, held in autumn in the Jeonju Hanok Maeul (p269) and Sori Arts Centre.

Sleeping

★ **Jeonju Tourist Hotel** HOTEL $
(전주 관광호텔; 063 280 7700; 44-5 Jeonju-gaeksa 5-gil; d from ₩30,000) It's not the spiffiest hotel in the Gaeksa market and the room interiors might be a little weathered, but it gets top marks for price and location. A solid choice for budget travellers who want to be a 10- to 15-minute walk to the heart of the *hanok maeul*, it's sometimes booked up on weekends, which is when prices jump.

★ **Cho Ga Jib** HANOK GUESTHOUSE $$
(초가집; 010 5295 2403, 063 288 2403; http://kunsu.co.kr; 25 Omokdae-gil; s/d ₩40,000/50,000) Hard to find, but worth the effort, this utterly charming *hanok* (traditional wooden home) guesthouse is surrounded by a delightful garden. Cosy rooms have modern – though tiny – bathrooms. The friendly woman who runs it (and grew up in the house) speaks some English. During the day, it also serves as a teahouse (until 5pm). It's the only remaining *hanok* building in Jeonju's old city with a thatched-roof signifying a commoner residence. Tile-roofed *hanok* were for the upper class.

Seunggwangje GUESTHOUSE $$
(승광제; 063 284 2323; 12-6 Choemyeonghui-gil; r from ₩60,000;) This humble, 75-year-old *hanok* (traditional wooden home) has the distinction of being owned by Lee Seok, a grandson of King Gojong, and photos of royalty adorn its courtyard. The tiny rooms have TV, fridge, *yo* (padded quilt or mattress on the floor) and small, modern bathrooms. The entrance is down an alleyway. Some English spoken.

Benikea Jeonju Hansung Tourist Motel HOTEL $$
(전주한성관광호텔; 063 288 0014; www.benikea.com; 43-3 Jeonju-gaeksa 5-gil; d incl breakfast from ₩70,000;) A reasonable choice if budget motels and *ondol* rooms (sleeping on the floor) are out of the question, this motel offers western-style rooms with TV and fridge. Staff speak some English. It's in the heart of the Gaeksa district, and rooms facing the main drag can be noisy on weekends.

Eating

Hyundai-ok KOREAN $
(현대옥; 063 282 7214; 2-242 Jeonong 3(sam)-ga; meals ₩5000; 6am-2pm) Jeonju's most beloved restaurant is this 10-seater *kongnamul gukbap* (bean sprout and rice soup) shop inside labyrinthine Nambu market (p269). Ordering is easy: with squid (*ojingeo;* plus ₩3000 for two people) or without. You might also want to ask for it mild – the soup is pretty spicy otherwise.

To find it, enter the Nambu market through the south entrance and turn down the alley on your left, across from the shop selling baskets. But really, all you have to do is ask – everyone knows this place.

Veteran KOREAN $
(베테랑; 063 285 9898; 135 Gyeonggijeon-gil; dishes ₩5000-7000; 9am-9pm) This 'veteran' of the Jeonju dining scene has been dishing out delicious *mandu* (만두, dumplings) and noodle dishes such as *kalguksu* (칼국수) since 1977. The setting is decidedly no-frills, but who cares with food this cheap and good?

Hanok Tteokgalbi KOREAN $
(한옥떡갈비; 063 286 6869; 56 Dongmun-gil; meals from ₩6000; 11am-9pm;) A boon for solo travellers, this modern eatery serves

WORTH A TRIP

DAEDUNSAN PROVINCIAL PARK

Daedunsan Provincial Park (대둔산도립공원) has craggy peaks with spectacular views over the surrounding countryside. It also offers vertigo-inducing thrills: the climb to the summit of Daedun-san (878m) is a steep, stony track that includes a 50m-long cable bridge (금강구름 다리), which stretches precariously between two rock pinnacles, and a long, 127-step steel-cable stairway (삼선구름다리). A short **cable-car ride** (http://daedunsancablecar.com; one way/return ₩6500/9500; ⏲9am-5pm, to 6pm in summer) saves an hour of hiking and puts you close to the bridge and stairway. From the top of the stairway, the mountain peak is a 350m climb up a steep, rocky path. If you're overnighting, **Daedunsan Tourist Hotel** (대둔산온천관광호텔; ☎063 263 1260; 611-70 Sanbuk-ri, Unju-myeon, Wanju-gun; r ₩75,000-90,000; P ⊝ ❄ @) is near the cable-car base station, as well as **San San San** (산산산; ☎063 263 3829; dishes from ₩10,000; ⏲8am-9pm), a folksy restaurant serving *makgeolli* (milky rice wine) and regional favourites.

Daedunsan Provincial Park can be reached by bus from Jeonju's intercity express bus terminal (₩5900, 1¼ hours, 6.40am, 9.40am, 2.20pm and 3.50pm) or Daejeon (₩1400, 55 minutes, every 45 minutes from 6am).

tteokgalbi (떡갈비, short rib patties) – usually a group meal – in single servings. There's a picture menu and big windows out the front.

★**Hanguk-jip** KOREAN $$

(한국집; ☎063 284 2224; 119 Eojin-gil; meals from ₩11,000; ⏲9.30am-9pm) Some folks say this is the best bibimbap restaurant in the city's historic district. The classic Jeonju dish comes with bright yellow mung-bean jelly, a hearty dollop of chilli paste and wild greens; get it in a hot stone pot (돌솥, *dolsot*) or topped with raw beef (육회, *yukhoe*). The building has a temple-like facade.

★**Yetchon Makgeolli** KOREAN $$$

(옛촌막걸리; ☎063 232 9991; 144-4 Paldal-ro; ₩35,000-70,000 for 2-4 people; ⏲3.30pm-midnight) Jeonju's best night out, if you can get a seat. Unlike other *makgeolli* (milky rice wine) bars, where the food is secondary, the dishes here are distractingly good. With the first kettle of wine comes butter-soft pork belly and kimchi; with the second, grilled prawns (and more). It's exceedingly popular and you'll have to queue on weekends. There are many Yetchon Makgeolli bars across the city. The one in the *hanok* village is easy to reach.

Drinking & Nightlife

Gyodong Dawan TEAHOUSE

(교동다완; ☎063 282 7133; 65-5 Eunhaeng-ro; teas ₩6000; ⏲11am-10pm) The *hanok* village's best teahouse is this richly atmospheric spot, where the speciality is *hwangcha* (황차), a golden-hued tea once served exclusively to kings (and grown here in the courtyard). It's served in a ritualistic manner (no photos during this, please). Shoes off at the door; children under 14 not allowed.

Cafe Tomorrow COFFEE

(카페 투모로; ☎063 288 6455; 71 Girin-daero; drinks from ₩5000; ⏲10am-10pm) The coffee is OK, but the view is great. Walk up the steps and take your espresso on the tiny outdoor balcony, or mount the spiral staircase and take in the panoramic view from the roof.

Deepin BAR

(디핀; ☎070-4063 1997; www.facebook.com/deepin1997; 16-16 Jeollagamyeong 4-gil; drinks from ₩3000; ⏲7pm-3am Mon-Thu, to 4am Fri & Sat; 📶) Jeonju's original expat hang-out – going strong since the 1990s – is in the Gaeksa neighbourhood. Look for it down an alleyway on the left as you walk up Wedding St.

Shopping

Demiseam CLOTHING

(데미샘; ☎010 4018 0770; 100-7 Hanji-gil; ⏲10am-6pm) Offers silk scarves coloured with natural dyes and handmade traditional-meets-contemporary clothing from local artisan Han Seowoon.

Handicraft Exhibition Hall ARTS & CRAFTS

(공예품전시관; ☎063 285 0002; 15 Taejo-ro; ⏲10am-7pm) This large complex carries paper, lanterns, lacquerware and more.

Information

As well as the **Hanok Village Tourist Information Centre** (☎063 282 1330; 99 Girin-daero; ⏲9am-6pm) there are several TICs around Jeonju Hanok Maeul, as well as at the bus terminal and train station.

Getting There & Away

The **express bus terminal** (전주고속버스터미널; 063 277 1572; 470 Jeonjucheondong-ro) is a three-minute walk from the **intercity bus terminal** (전주시외버스공용터미널; 30 Garinae-ro). Bus 79 connects the express bus terminal and Jeonju's KTX train station (twice per hour). A taxi from the train station to the bus terminals is about ₩5000.

KTX trains (전주역; Ua 1-dong) connect Jeonju with Seoul's Yongsan station (₩34,400, 1½ hours, 19 daily). *Saemaul* (₩26,200, three hours, two daily) and *Mugunghwa* (₩17,600, 3½ hours, nine daily) also run from Yongsan.

Getting Around

From the bus terminals, walk 500m away from the river to Geuman Sq bus stop, where any number of buses (₩1400) go to Pungnam-mun gateway – useful for destinations around the *hanok maeul*. From the KTX train station catch bus 79, 119 or 535. Other useful stops include Jeondong Catholic Church (p269) and Nambu Market (p269). Taxi fares start at ₩2800. Bus 79 runs from the KTX train station past the bus terminals, to the *hanok maeul* and all the way out to Moaksan Provincial Park (p273).

Around Jeonju

Moaksan Provincial Park

This park (모악산도립공원; 063 290 2752; adult/youth/child ₩3000/2000/1000; 8am-7pm), which contains Moaksan (794m), is a popular destination for hikers on weekends. The main attraction is the temple, **Geumsan-sa** (금산사; 063 548 4441; www.geumsansa.org; 9 Geumsan-ri, Geumsan-myeon; adult/child ₩3000/1000; sunrise-sunset; 79), which dates from AD 599. While there are no buildings here nearly that old, the three-storey Mireukjeon dates from 1635 and has an impressive air of antiquity. Inside is a looming, golden statue of the Maitreya Buddha – the Buddha of the future. Beyond the temple, a trail goes up Janggun-dae (장군대) and along the ridge to the peak in a relatively easy two hours. Minor trails wend past temple hermitages.

Geumsan-sa runs a traveller-friendly templestay program (₩50,000); see the website for details. If quality isn't a concern, try one of the scruffy *minbak* (private homes with rooms for rent) in the commercial area near the bus stop or the tidy motel on the main road opposite the car park.

Catch local bus 79 (₩1700, 45 minutes, every 20 to 40 minutes) at the bus stop between Jeonju's intercity and express bus terminals. Get off at the last stop, 1.2km from the temple.

Maisan Provincial Park

The name of Maisan Provincial Park (마이산도립공원, Horse Ears Mountain) refers to two extraordinary rocky peaks as they appear from the town of Jinan. The east peak is Sutmai-san (Male Mai-san; 678m) while the west peak is Ammai-san (Female Mai-san; 685m). Both 'ears' are made of conglomerate rock, which is rare in Korea. The temple, **Tap-sa** (탑사; 063 433 0012; 367 Maisannam-ro, Maryeong-myeon, Jinan-gun; adult/youth/child ₩2000/1500/1000), at the base of the female ear, has a sculptural garden of 80 stone towers or pinnacles that were piled up by Buddhist mystic, Yi Kapmyong (1860–1957). **Choga Jeongdam** (초가정담; 063 432 2469; meals from ₩8000; 9am-9pm) is a nice spot for a bite to eat nearby here.

An easy 1½-hour, 1.7km hike with a splendid view at the top starts by Tap-sa and takes you back to the car park at the entrance. In April, the cherry trees on the road leading to the park's southern entrance and the nearby lake burst into blossom.

One *minbak* (private home with rooms for rent) is in the southern section of the park; more options are near the park's north gate. There's a **campground** (063 432 1800; www.maisancamp.org; per night ₩12,000, plus per person ₩2000; P) near the southern entrance.

From Jeonju, take a bus to Jinan (₩4600, 50 minutes, every 20 minutes). From there catch a local bus (₩1200, 20 minutes, 9.30am, 1.30pm and 5.20pm) to the southern (남부) entrance. Buses return to Jinan (₩1200, 20 minutes, 9.55am, 12.50pm, 2.05pm, 5.15pm and 7pm) from here. Taxis cost about ₩12,000.

Naejangsan National Park

063

One of the region's best hiking spots, Naejangsan (내장산국립공원) is particularly famous for its brilliant display of autumn leaves in October. Expect the park to be absolutely packed then.

The park's mountainous ridge is shaped like an amphitheatre. A spider's web of trails leads up to the ridge, but the fastest way up is by **cable car** (내장산 케이블카; adult/child one way ₩5500/3500, return ₩8000/5000; 9am-5pm). There's an **observation deck**

Naejangsan National Park

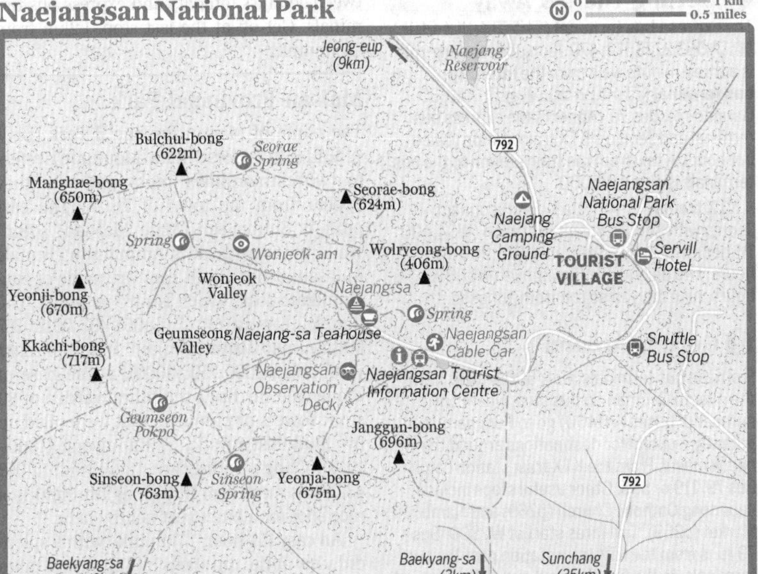

(전망대, Jeonmang-dae) 300m from the top. The hike around the rim is strenuous, going up and down six main peaks and numerous small ones before reaching Seorae-bong (622m), but has splendid views on a fine day.

Sights

Naejang-sa BUDDHIST SITE
(내장사; ☎063 538 8741; www.naejangsa.org; adult/youth/child ₩3000/2000/1000) Naejang-sa has an enviable location, in the centre of Naejangsan National Park and encircled by towering peaks. Though the temple dates from AD 636, the buildings seen today are mostly recent reconstructions. There is a hermitage, **Wonjeok-am** (원적암; ⏱sunrise-sunset), halfway up the ridge.

A **teahouse** (내장사 찻집; ⏱10am-4pm) FREE on the 2nd floor offers respite and green tea. An easy and picturesque 1.2km walk from Naejang-sa goes through Geumsong valley.

Sleeping & Eating

There is a cluster of motels near the main road leading to the park entrance, a five-minute walk from the area bus stop. **Camping** (내장야영장; ☎063 538 7875; high/low season from ₩9000/7000) is available before the park's tourist village.

Servill Hotel MOTEL $$
(세르빌 호텔; ☎063 538 9487; 937 Naejangsan-ro; d ₩40,000-60,000; P ⊖ ❄ @ 📶) Clean, comfortable rooms and an owner who speaks some English make this an excellent place to stay. The attached restaurant does a tasty *sanchae hanjeongsik* (a set meal of local wild vegetables) for ₩20,000 a person.

From the bus stop, follow the main road left for five minutes. Look for the orange building.

Getting There & Away

Jeong-eup is the nearest city. Buses (₩4400, one hour, every 10 to 30 minutes) connect Jeong-eup and Jeonju. Jeong-eup is also a stop on the KTX line from Yongsan (₩39,500, 1¾ hours, 25 daily).

Local bus 171 (₩1500, 30 minutes, every 20 to 30 minutes) runs from the bus terminal to the park **stop**, the last one on the route. From there, it's a 15-minute walk to Naejangsan National Park. Less frequent intercity buses (₩1400, 20 minutes, eight times daily) leave from the bus terminal and terminate at the same bus stop.

Muju & Deogyusan National Park

☎063 / POP 25,100

The small town of Muju (무주) is mainly a jumping-off point for Deogyusan National

Park. The town itself holds little of interest, but it is a handy transport hub for skiers and hikers. Muju is also home to the **Muju Firefly Festival** (무주 반딧불축제; http://english.firefly.or.kr; Muju-eup; ₩10,000; Sep).

Sights & Activities

Deogyusan National Park NATIONAL PARK
(덕유산국립공원; http://english.knps.or.kr; adult/youth/child camping per person per day ₩2000/1500/1000; sunrise-sunset; P) This national park is a hiker's playground and home of Deogyusan Muju ski resort. Gucheon-dong, a small tourist village, marks the start of the park's best hike (two hours, 6km). The trail follows the river and valley past 20 beauty spots to a small temple, **Baengnyeon-sa** (백련사; 580 Baengneonsa-gil, Seolcheon-myeon) FREE, and finishes with a steep, 1½-hour ascent of Hyangjeok-bong (향적봉; 1614m).

A basic **hikers' shelter** (향적봉대피소; 063 322 1614; http://english.knps.or.kr/Experience/Shelters/Default.aspx; Samgong-ri, Seolcheon-myeon; high/low season ₩8000/7000) accommodates trekkers overnight. Yew trees, azaleas and alpine flowers adorn the summit. In the northwest of the park is Jeoksangsan-seong (무주 적상산성), a fortress rebuilt in the 17th century. Walk around the fortress and you'll come across the north, west and south gates. Encircled by an 8km wall is **Anguk-sa** (안국사; 1050, Sanseong-ro, Jeoksang-myeon), a temple housing a Joseon-dynasty archive. While hiking the northwest part of Deogyusan National Park that takes in Jeoksangsan-seong fortress and Anguk-sa, keep your eyes open for the lookout.

Muju Deogyusan Resort SNOW SPORTS
(무주덕유산리조트; 063 322 9000; www.mdysresort.com; 185, Manseon-ro, Seolcheon-myeon; lift tickets adult/child per day ₩88,000/70,000, equipment rental ₩33,000/28,000; ski lifts 8.30am-4.30pm & 6.30pm-midnight, from 6.30am weekends & holidays;) The only Korean ski resort located in a national park, it comprises 30 runs including the highest altitude and longest slope (6.1km) in the country. Snowboarding, sledding, night skiing and lessons are on offer. Equipment can be rented (largest boot size 300 mm). A **gondola** (adult/child single return journey ₩19,000/15,000; 9am-4pm) carries passengers up to the top of Seolcheon-bong, the highest peak inside Deogyusan at 1520m.

Taekwondo Park MARTIAL ARTS
(무주태권도원; English 063 320 0114; www.tkdwon.kr; 1482, Museol-ro, Seolcheon-myeon; adult/youth/child ₩4000/3500/3000; 10am-6pm Tue-Fri, to 7pm Sat & Sun Mar-Oct, to 5pm Tue-Fri, to 6pm Sat & Sun Nov-Feb;) This park devoted to Korea's national sport houses the largest taekwondo stadium in the world. There is also a museum dedicated to the sport, as well as an experience centre where people can try taekwondo for themselves. To reach the park, take a Seolcheon-bound bus from Muju Intercity Bus Terminal.

Sleeping

The best, and most expensive, place to stay in the park is **Hotel Tirol** (티롤호텔; 063 320 7200; www.mdysresort.com; 185, Manseon-ro, Seolcheon-myeon; r/ste from ₩380,000/510,000; P@), an Austrian-style chalet with condominium apartments. Camping is available at several campgrounds, including **Deogyudae Camping Ground** (덕유대야영장; 063 322 3174; 2 Baengnyeonsa-gil, Seolcheon-myeon; tent/car camping ₩12,000/19,000; P), which has showers and tent pitches.

Muju Deogyusan Leisure Biketel MOTEL $
(무주 덕유산 레저바이크텔; 063 324 2575; 9968 Gucheondong-ro, Seolcheon-myeon; d/ondol from ₩11,000/50,000; P@) This bike motel offers a haven for cyclists. The motel features Korean-style *ondol* (traditional, sleep-on-a-floor-mattress) rooms, doubles and cheap dorms, and offers bicycle hire as well as servicing for bicycles, maps and other useful information on cycling in the park.

Getting There & Away

Resort buses (₩20,000 one way, three hours) depart Seoul's Jamsil station during ski season. Intercity buses go to Muju from Seoul Nambu Bus Terminal (₩12,800, 2½ hours, five daily). Buses connect with Jeonju (₩8400, 1½ hours, every one to two hours).

KTX trains (₩33,200, one hour, every 10 to 30 minutes) and SRT (Super Rapid Train; ₩28,800, 55 minutes, every 10 to 30 minutes) services go from Seoul to Daejeon. You'll then need to get to the Daejeon Terminal Complex (₩4000 taxi ride) for an intercity bus (₩4400, 50 minutes, hourly) to Muju.

Getting Around

There's a free shuttle service to the ski resort (5am, 8am, 10.30am, 2.15pm, 4.40pm and 7.30pm) from **Muju bus terminal** (무주 시외 버스공용정류장; 063 322 2245; 351 Hanpung-ru-ro, Muju-eup). For the national park entrance, take the Gucheon-dong bus (₩4200, 40 minutes, 11 daily) from Muju bus terminal.

Deogyusan National Park

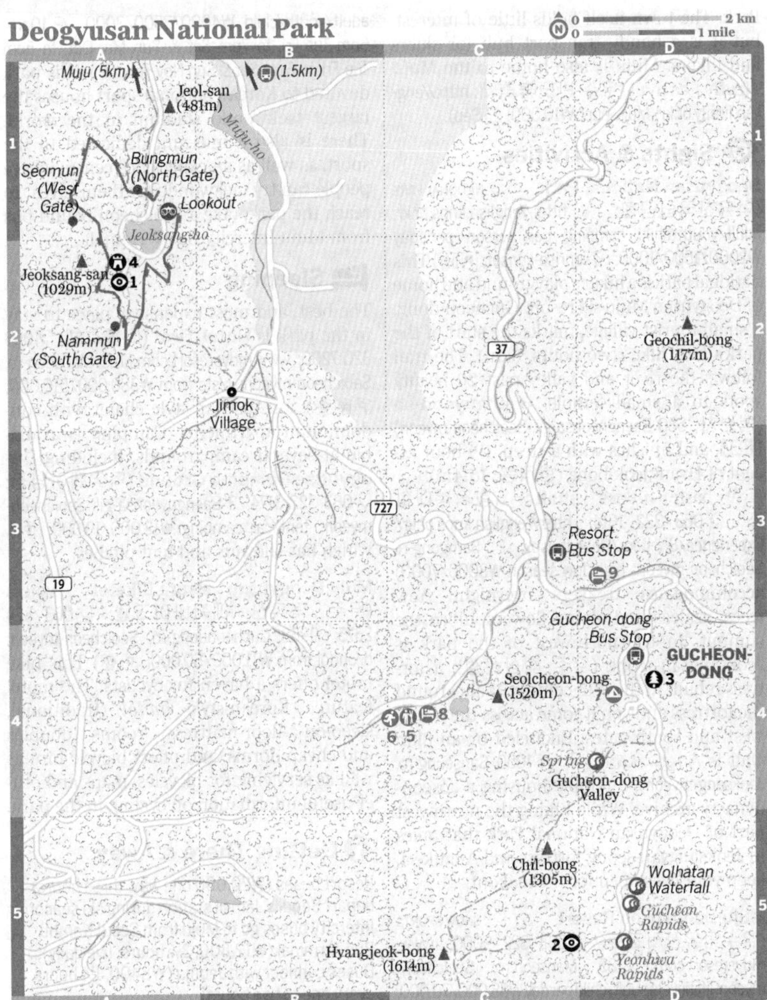

Gochang & Around

063 / POP 60,500

With a handful of worthwhile sights, Gochang (고창) is also the gateway to Seonunsan Provincial Park, with its temple, Seonun-sa.

Sights

Moyang Fortress FORTRESS

(모양성; 063 560 8067; 1 Moyangseong-ro; adult/youth/child ₩2000/1200/800; 9am-7pm Mar-Oct, to 5pm Nov-Feb) An impressive structure built in 1453, Moyang Fortress has a 1.6km-long wall surrounding a complex of reconstructed buildings, and is worth touring if you have a couple of hours to spare. Local legend says if a woman walks three times around the wall with a stone on her head during a leap year, she will never become ill and will enter paradise. To get here, go behind the intercity bus terminal and head left along the stream; the fortress is a 20-minute walk down the road.

Gochang Dolmen Site ARCHAEOLOGICAL SITE

(고창 고인돌군; 063 560 8662; www.gochang.go.kr/dolmen/index.gochang; 74 Goindolgongwon-gil, Gochang-eup; adult/youth/child ₩3000/2000/1000; 9am-6pm Tue-Sun; A-

Deogyusan National Park

Sights

1 Anguk-sa A2
2 Baengnyeon-sa C5
3 Deogyusan National Park D4
4 Jeoksangsan-seong A2

Activities, Courses & Tours

5 Muju Deogyusan Resort C4
6 Seolcheon-bong Gondola C4

Sleeping

7 Deogyudae Camping Ground D4
8 Hotel Tirol C4
9 Muju Deogyusan Leisure Biketel D3

san) History buffs will want to stroll the hills surrounding Gochang and ponder the mystery of 440 dolmens, prehistoric tombs from the Bronze and Iron Ages now registered with Unesco. The site includes a small museum, behind which six trails lead in and around huge boulders dotting the countryside.

Gochang Pansori Museum MUSEUM
(고창판소리박물관; ☎063 560 8061; 100 Dongni-ro; adult/youth/child ₩800/500/free; ⏲9am-6pm Tue-Sun) This small museum has memorabilia on the unique solo opera musical form known as *pansori*. It's not far from the Moyang Fortress entrance.

Seonun-sa TEMPLE
(선운사; ☎063 561 1375; www.seonunsa.org/eng; 250 Seonunsa-ro, Asan-myeon; adult/child/youth ₩3000/1000/2000; ⏲sunrise-sunset) Located in Seonunsan Provincial Park, this Zen temple, founded in 577 and last rebuilt in 1720, is nestled among verdant hills. Just behind the temple is a 500-year-old camellia forest (동백 나무 숲) that flowers around the end of April. Beyond, hiking trails go up to outlying hermitage, such as Seoksang-am (석상암). Seonun-sa has a great templestay (₩50,000), which includes a 'walking meditation' trip up to the hermitages. There's a **youth hostel** (선운산유스호스텔; ☎063 561 3333; www.gochang.go.kr/seonunsan/index.gochang; 334 Samin-ri, Asan-myeon; r ₩50,000-60,000;) in the Seonunsan tourist village.

It's a 30-minute hike to **Dosol-am** (도솔암; ⏲sunrise-sunset) hermitage and just beyond is a giant Buddha rock carving dating from the Goryeo dynasty.

From Dosol-am, you can you can climb up to Nakjodae, and then loop back down to the temple, passing the hermitage **Chamdang-am** (참당암; ⏲sunrise-sunset). The total hike should take about three hours.

Frequent buses to Gochang (local bus ₩1000, 30 minutes, hourly; intercity bus ₩2500, 20 minutes, six times per day) leave the bus stop near the park entrance.

Sleeping & Eating

Top Motel MOTEL $$
(탑모텔; ☎063 563 0600; 125 Boritgol-ro; r from ₩40,000; P) A nice, clean motel a couple of short blocks from the Gochang intercity bus terminal (p277). The 1st-floor cafe serves a respectable espresso.

Sangdam Tofu KOREAN $$
(상담두부; ☎063 562 7807; 270 Gochang-eup; dishes from ₩7000; ⏲noon-10pm) Among a cluster of old-style buildings with thatched roofs, this restaurant serves pungent tofu stew (순두부찌개). In keeping with the traditional motif, remove your shoes before stepping on the stairs. To get here, go behind the bus terminal and walk left for 10 minutes along the stream; it's not far from the Moyang Fortress main gate.

Getting There & Around

Buses connect Gochang with Jeonju (₩6400, 1½ hours, 21 times daily), Gwangju (₩5100, one hour, every 30 to 60 minutes) and Buan (₩4600, one hour, every one to two hours). Local buses (₩1000, 30 minutes, hourly) as well as express buses (₩2500, 20 minutes, six times per day) run to Seonun-sa temple from Gochang's intercity bus terminal (고창 공용버스터미널).

To get to the dolmen site, board a local bus inside the bus terminal to Asan (₩1000, 30 minutes, every 15 to 30 minutes) and tell the driver you want to go to *gochang goindol gun*.

Byeonsan-bando National Park

☎063

Byeonsan-bando (변산반도국립공원) is Korea's only national park that can boast of both mountains and sea. During the summer months, sandy Byeonsan Beach, backed by pines, and Gyeokpo Beach, with its dramatic cliffs and caves, are the top draws. From Gyeokpo, ferries depart for the island Wido, which has a sandy beach. Year-round

Byeonsan-bando National Park

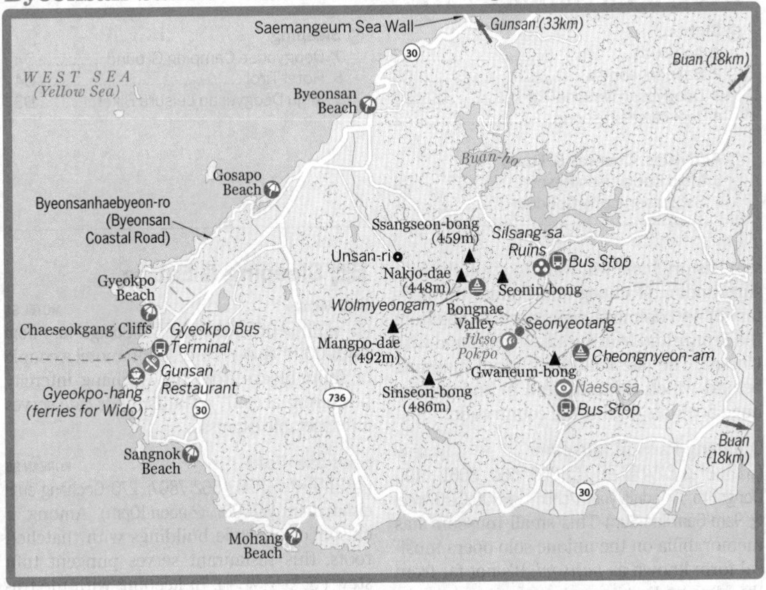

there is hiking in the peaks that frame the temple Naeso-sa. There's a tourist village at Gyeokpo Beach that serves as the transport hub, with eating options and lodgings.

Sights

Naeso-sa TEMPLE

(내소사; ☎063 583 7281; www.naesosa.org; 268 Seokpo-ri, Jinseo-myeon; adult/youth/child ₩3000/1500/500; ⏲sunrise-sunset; Ⓟ) Compared to many temples in Jeollabuk-do, Naeso-sa is a bit underwhelming. Originally built in AD 633 and last renovated in the 19th century, its weathered structures lack the colour typically found in Korean temples. If you do come, it will be for the pleasant park walk and challenging mountain hikes.

Beyond the temple, hike up the unpaved road to the hermitage Cheongnyeon-am (청련암; 20 minutes) for inspiring sea views; another 15 minutes brings you to the ridge where you turn left for Gwaneum-bong. From the peak follow the path, which goes up and down and over rocks for an hour until you reach Jikso Pokpo (직소폭포), a 30m-high waterfall with a large pool. For a more challenging hike head up Nakjo-dae, which is famous for its sunset views. This is a good place to do a templestay (₩40,000); on weekends there is a hiking templestay (₩60,000) in addition to the usual program.

Byeonsan Beach BEACH

(변산해수욕장; Ⓟ) One of the most popular beaches on the west coast, the big draws here are the 2km stretch of white sand backed by a fir-tree forest, shellfish hunting during low tide and superb summer sunsets. From the Buan intercity bus terminal, take bus 100 to Byeonsan Beach (70 minutes).

Gyeokpo Beach BEACH

(격포해수욕장) This small beach easily fills up with inflatable tubes and tents on warm weekends. Aside from swimming, the main attraction is the nearby Chaeseokgang Cliffs, a magnificent formation of layered rock that is accessible during low tide. The beach is a short walk from the Gyeokpo intercity bus terminal.

Eating

Gunsan Restaurant KOREAN $$$

(군산식당; ☎063 583 3234; 16 Gyeokpo port gil; meals from ₩25,000; ⏲8am-10pm; Ⓟ) Like many seafood restaurants in Gyeokpo, this one is geared towards a pair of diners or groups looking forward to an incredible banquet of tastes and textures presented on a table covered with a white sheet of plastic.

Getting There & Away

Take a bus (₩8900, two hours, nine daily) from Jeonju to Gyeokpo. Buan (₩5100, one hour, every 30 minutes) is a useful transfer point, with buses to Naeso-sa (₩2000, one hour, every hour), Gyeokpo (₩3800, 40 minutes, every 30 to 60 minutes) and Gyeokpo Beach (₩2000, 50 minutes, six daily). Bus 301 connects Gyeokpo to Naeso-sa (₩1000, 30 minutes, every two hours from 9am).

Ferries go from Gyeokpo to Wido (₩9100, 50 minutes, every two hours starting at 7.55am) regularly during the week. On weekends, eight ferries depart daily (every one to two hours starting at 7.55am).

Gunsan & Seonyudo

063 / POP 278,500

Seonyudo (선유도) is a giant green park in the middle of the ocean with beaches for lazing, peaks for climbing and hamlets for exploring. It's one of four islands connected by a network of roads and bridges tethered to the Saemangeum Sea Wall. Quiet spaces for picnics or camping are available if you get off the well-worn paths, but that may change. The last time we visited, construction projects were paving the way for more vehicular access, which could change the island's vibe.

If lounging on the 1.6km sandy beach seems too sedate, discover what's up, over and around Mangju-bong (망주봉), a low-rise twin peak (152m) that requires a rope to reach the top. For something less strenuous, rent a bike (₩10,000 per day) or scooter (₩30,000 for two hours) from near the information booth on Jangjado and ride to Sinsido.

The port city of Gunsan (군산), with its huge industrial park and US air force base, has a smattering of architecturally interesting structures, some of which date back to the Japanese colonial period, but they are hard to explore when the daytime air quality becomes nasty. Most travellers visit Gunsan only to catch a bus to Seonyudo.

Sights

Gunsan Modern History Museum MUSEUM

(군산근대역사박물관; 063 454 7870; http://museum.gunsan.go.kr/content/sub01/01_01.jsp; 240 Haemang-ro; adult/youth/child ₩3000/2000/1000; 9am-9pm, closed 1st & 3rd Mon; 1, 2, 8, 17, 18 and 19) The highlight here is a reconstruction of a typical Gunsan block during the 1930s, under Japanese rule. Be sure to pick up a pamphlet, which includes a map of colonial-era buildings in the neighbourhood.

The museum is a ₩5000 taxi ride from Gunsan's intercity bus terminal. By bus, walk to a bus stop on the terminal side of Haemang-ro and take the bus to the Modern History Museum stop.

Eating

Gunsan's gotta-try food is a chewy bun filled with red bean paste from **Lee Sung Dang** (이성당; 063 445 2772; 12-2 Jungang-ro 1-ga; buns from ₩1500; 7.30am-10.30pm, closed 1st & 3rd Sun; 3, 7, 12, 13 and 71), Korea's oldest bakery. If the red bean is too sweet, try the bun filled with a vegetable mix.

Binhaewon CHINESE $

(빈해원; 063 445 2429; 21-5 Jangmi-dong; dishes from ₩5500; 10.30am-9pm; 3 or 71) Don't be put off by the drab exterior of Korea's oldest Chinese restaurant because inside you are in for a treat. The high ceiling, ornate decor and main-room dining table create a vibe that's both kitsch and cool. Standard Korean-Chinese dishes like sweet and sour pork (탕수육) are available. Occasionally requires a wait to get seated. To get here, exit the intercity bus terminal and walk to a bus stop on the terminal side of the road. Get off at Naehan sageo-ri (intersection).

Getting There & Away

Buses (₩5300, one hour, every 15 minutes) connect Jeonju and the **Gunsan Intercity Bus Terminal** (군산시외버스터미널; 18 Haemang-ro), while **Gunsan Express Bus Terminal** (군산고속버스터미널; 30 Haemang-ro) – a short walk from the intercity terminal – has buses to Seoul (₩18,700, 2½ hours, every 15 minutes).

From here, you can get to Seonyudo by bus from **Bieung port** (비응항; 95 Bieung-dong) – take local bus 7, 8, 9 or 85 (₩1400, 60 to 90 minutes, every 15 minutes) or a 20-minute taxi (₩21,000).

With luck, the Gunsan bus will stop opposite the Seonyudo bus stop. If not, get off at the last stop and walk to the other side of the harbour. Look for a bus shelter in front of a building with two tall radio antennae. There's no signage except for a wooden board with a '2' on it. Buses (₩1400, 35 minutes) cross the sea wall and terminate at a roundabout on Jangjado.

Buses heading back to Bieung port depart Jangjado 10 minutes past the hour. From Bieung port, buses heading to Gunsan's intercity bus terminal every 10 to 30 minutes.

One daily ferry departs **Gunsan coastal ferry terminal** (연안여객터미널; 063 472 2711) for Jangjado at 9am (₩12,750 one way, two hours) and returns in the afternoon (3.25pm weekdays, 3.40pm weekends).

Chungcheongnam-do

Includes ➡

Best Places to Eat

- Mushroom (p286)
- Gomanaru (p289)
- Gudurae Dolssambap (p292)
- Korea's Best Seafood Hotpot (p293)

Best Places to Stay

- Pinocchio Pension (p296)
- Lotte Buyeo Resort (p292)
- Mudrin Hotel (p293)

Why Go?

Chungcheongnam-do (충청남도) tends to fly under the radar of most travellers, and that's unfortunate. Some of the best nature within striking distance of Seoul is here. Gorgeous Daecheon Beach is popular, especially during the Boryeong Mud Festival, while those preferring solitude can hop on a ferry to one of the nearby islands. To the north is Taeanhaean National Marine Park, dotted with more islands, beaches and 150km of trails that flit in and out of coastline.

In terms of big-city experiences, Daejeon, the capital manqué, offers the province's best urban diversions, while Sejong, the country's administrative centre, doesn't yet have much to draw tourists. More interesting are the small towns: Gongju and Buyeo were once capitals of the ancient Baekje dynasty, and have retained a surprising number of old fortresses, tombs and relics.

When to Go

Daejeon

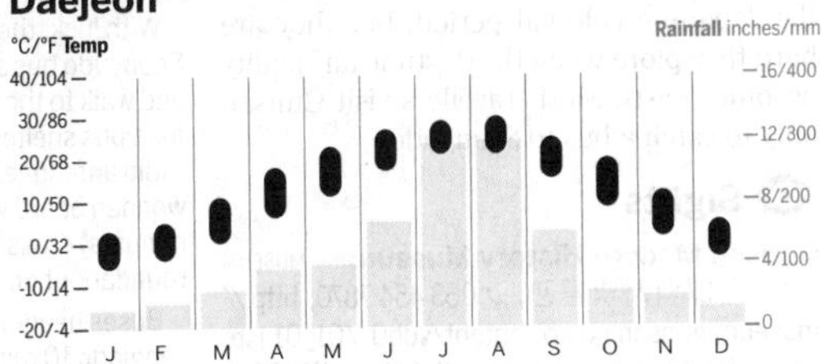

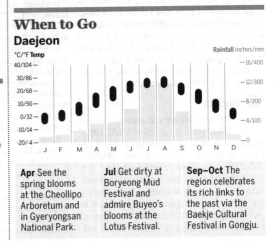

Apr See the spring blooms at the Cheollipo Arboretum and in Gyeryongsan National Park.

Jul Get dirty at Boryeong Mud Festival and admire Buyeo's blooms at the Lotus Festival.

Sep–Oct The region celebrates its rich links to the past via the Baekje Cultural Festival in Gongju.

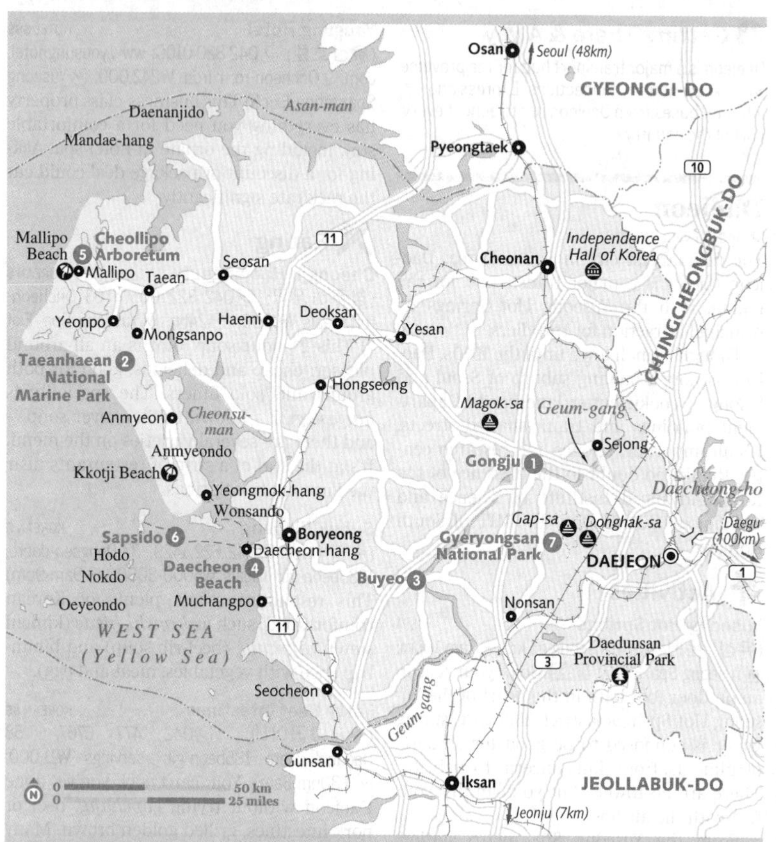

Chungcheongnam-do Highlights

1 **Gongju National Museum** (p288) Exploring Korea's ancient history while marvelling at 1500-year-old treasures from King Muryeong's tomb.

2 **Taeanhaean National Marine Park** (p295) Strolling rugged coastal trails that wind past pristine beaches, mature forests and verdant rice paddies.

3 **Buyeo** (p290) Climbing up the fortress where the valiant Baekje army made its last stand.

4 **Daecheon Beach** (p293) Indulging in playful therapy with thousands of fellow mud worshipers.

5 **Cheollipo Arboretum** (p296) Rejoicing at the variety of flora inside this 64-hectare botanical wonderland.

6 **Sapsido** (p294) Enjoying an evening of seaside solitude on a quiet, sleepy island.

7 **Gyeryongsan National Park** (p285) Taking in panoramic views of sprawling parkland from mountain-ridge hiking trails.

History

When the Baekje dynasty (57 BC to AD 668) was pushed south by an aggressive Goguryeo dynasty in AD 475, this is where the Baekje ended up, establishing their capital first in Ungjin (modern-day Gongju), then moving further south to Sabi (modern-day Buyeo). Its culture was fairly sophisticated, and coincided with the early flourishing of Buddhism in Korea, but after Sabi fell to the joint army of Silla and China in AD 660, the region passed into obscurity.

Getting There & Away

Daejeon is a major transport hub for the province with excellent train connections. Express and intercity buses from Daejeon run to almost every part of the country.

Daejeon

042 / POP 1,512,200

The fifth-largest city in South Korea, Daejeon (대전) is a major transit hub for the region, with the Yuseong Hot Springs its principal attraction for travellers.

Though a small town until the 1970s, Daejeon is now a bulging suburb of Seoul and Sejong, a cookie-cutter landscape of apartment buildings and traffic-snarled streets. It's an important science and research centre, thanks no doubt to the presence of the Korea Advanced Institute of Science and Technology (KAIST, aka the 'MIT of South Korea').

Activities

Yuseong Hot Springs SPA
(유성 온천; www.yuseong.go.kr; 7am-10pm; M Yuseong Spa, Exit 7) FREE Soak your feet in an outdoor foot bath in the heart of the Yuseong Hot Springs district. The 39°C spring water is supposed to be good for all sorts of ailments, from skin concerns to arthritis. There are no towels, but you can dry your feet with the air hose.

From the Yuseong Spa metro station, walk straight and turn right at Oncheon-ro.

Yousung Spa SPA
(042 820 0100; 9 Oncheon-ro; ₩9000; 5am-9pm; ; M Yuseong Spa, Exit 6) The hot spring inside the Yousung Hotel is a real treat. It has indoor and outdoor pools, small waterfalls and a sauna. It's popular and can get crowded on weekends.

Sleeping

Java Hotel MOTEL $$
(자바 호텔; 042 256 6191; 36 Jungang-ro 109beon-gil; d weekday/weekend ₩40,000/50,000; ; M Jungang-ro, Exit 6) Pop accents liven up the spacious, clean rooms at this quiet motel. It's a short walk, or stumble, from Eunhaeng-dong's boozy dining and drinking district.

From the Jungang-ro metro stop, walk up the street for about five minutes and turn right at the Nonghyup bank on the corner. The hotel is down the street.

Yousung Hotel HOTEL $$$
(유성호텔; 042 820 0100; www.yousunghotel.com; 9 Oncheon-ro; r from ₩242,000; M Yuseong Spa station, Exit 6) This business-class property has everything you need for a comfortable stay, including the ornate in-hotel spa. Asking for a discount or package deal could cut the rack rate significantly.

Eating

Cheongju Haejangguk KOREAN $
(청주해장국; 042 822 0050; 63 Oncheon-ro; meals ₩6000; 24hr; M Yuseong Spa, Exit 7) This 24-hour soup joint is an all-around pleaser: cheap and delicious, good for both groups and solo diners. The speciality is *haejangguk* – known as 'hangover soup' – and there are several varieties on the menu. It's at the end of a strip of restaurants near the Yuseong Hot Springs.

Subuk Sikdang KOREAN $
(수북식당; 042 622 1429; 37 Dongseo-daero, 1683beon-gil; meals ₩5000-8000; 9am-9pm) This restaurant serves plenty of Korean comfort food, such as *kimchi jjigae* (kimchi stew), *galbitang* (beef-rib soup) and bibimbap (rice with vegetables, meat and egg).

Tasty Beef Intestines KOREAN $$
(진서방곱이네; 042 477 6767; 58 Daedeok-daero 185beon-gil; servings ₩11,000; 4.30pm-3am) You can't say you've done Daejeon without trying *gopchang*, beef or pork intestines, grilled golden brown. Many people love the chewy texture of ring-shaped innards. Others say they taste like a pencil eraser. This shop in Dunsan-dong is a favourite with the university crowd, so expect flowing beer and a bon vivant atmosphere.

Yeongsuni KOREAN $$
(영순이 샤브칼국수 식당; 042 633 4520; 1717 Dongseo-daero; meals ₩6000-25,000; 10.30am-10.30pm) Choose from a range of hearty set menus with *shabu kalguksu* (샤브칼국수), where you cook your own meat and noodles in a spicy mushroom and vegetable soup. More elaborate sets come with *sangchussam* (상추쌈), grilled meats wrapped in vegetable leaves. Look for a mushroom-headed caricature giving the thumbs up, and the picture menu out front.

Indy INDIAN $$$
(인디; 042 471 7052; www.indyfood.co.kr; 246 Daedeok-daero; set lunch from ₩13,000, dinner mains from ₩19,000; 11.30am-3pm & 5.30-10pm; ; M Government Complex, Exit 2)

Daejeon's favourite Indian joint is located in Dunsan-dong and does authentic classics, from mild *palak paneer* to spicy chicken *vindaloo*.

From the Government Complex metro station, head left down Daedeok-daero and look for the restaurant on your left, past Emart, which is across the street on your right.

Drinking & Nightlife

Lionheart CAFE

(라이언하트 커피; ☎070-8870 6622; 97 Seonhwa-dong; drinks from ₩4500; ⏰7.30am-9pm Mon-Fri, from noon Sun; 📶; Ⓜ Jungang-ro, Exit 6) The espresso is deep and complex, the interior warm and inviting, and there's an original *Abbey Road* LP cover just inside the door. Eun-yeong, the affable English-speaking owner, is a wealth of information about beans and roasting. The cafe is a five-minute walk up the street from the Jungang-ro metro stop. Closed Saturday.

Ranch Pub BAR

(더 랜치펍; ☎042 825 4157; www.facebook.com/ranchpubdaejeon; 88 Gungdong-ro 18beon-gil; drinks from ₩6000; ⏰5pm-2am Mon-Sat; 🚌105, Ⓜ Yuseong Spa station, Exit 7) With 10 beers on draught, this is a favourite haunt of expats and beer lovers. The food is better than the usual pub grub. Closed Sunday.

The bar is near Chungnam University. From Yuseong Spa station, take bus 5 and get off at Hanbit bus stop. Turn left down the side street and the bar will be on your left. A taxi from Yuseong Spa station costs less than ₩5000. If the taxi driver doesn't know the address, say *Hanbit Apt*.

Mustang Pub BAR

(☎010 6567 0803; 220 Daeheung-dong 2f; drinks from ₩5500; ⏰5pm-2am Mon-Sat; Ⓜ Jungang-ro, Exit 3) This small 2nd-floor bar with a neighbourhood-bistro vibe serves draught beers and shots. It's a popular hang-out for students who seem to prefer pizza over beer. A decent place to start your adventure in Eunhaeng-dong. From the Jungang-ro metro stop, walk straight and turn right at the church.

Information

MEDICAL SERVICES

Chungnam National University Hospital (충남대학교병원; ☎042 280 7100; www.cnuh.co.kr; 282 Munhwa-ro; Ⓜ Seodaejeon Negeori, Exit 1) Medical services in English.

Hankook Hospital (한국병원; ☎042 606 1000; 1672 Dongseo-daero)

MONEY

KB Bank (국민은행; ☎042 253 8051; 154 Eunhaeng-dong; ⏰9am-4pm; Ⓜ Jungang-ro, Exit 2) Exchanges foreign currency and has a global ATM.

SC (스탠다드차타드은행 대전지점; ☎042 253 5161; 27-9 Jung-dong) Exchanges foreign currency and has a global ATM.

Shinhan Bank (신한은행; ☎042 636 9581; 145-5 Yongjeon-dong; ⏰9am-4pm) Exchanges foreign currency. There's another branch in the Daejeon Terminal Complex.

TOURIST INFORMATION

There's a grand selection of area maps and local information available at the **information desk** (관광 안내소; ☎042 221 1905; ⏰9am-6pm) inside Daejeon's Korea Train Express (KTX; the fastest trains) station. The tourist information offices inside **Seodaejeon train station** (관광 안내소; ☎042 523 1338; ⏰9am-6pm) and on the **arrivals platform** (관광 안내소; ☎042 633 1355; ⏰9am-6pm) in the Daejeon Terminal Complex, are usually staffed with people who speak English. Staff inside the **Yuseong tourist office** (대전 종합 관광안내센터; ☎042 861 1330; 552-3 Bongmyeong-dong; ⏰9am-6pm; Ⓜ Yuseong Spa, Exit 6) might not speak much English, but they know the area and are eager to help.

Getting There & Away

AIR

The nearest airport is at Cheongju (p300), 40km north. Trains (₩3700, one hour) run 11 times a day from Daejeon station to Cheongju Airport station. Intercity buses (₩3700, 45 minutes, five daily) run from Daejeon Terminal Complex to Cheongju airport.

Intercity buses (₩22,100, 3¼ hours, every 10 to 20 minutes) run from Daejeon Terminal Complex to Incheon International Airport (p395). Frequent express buses depart for the airport from Government Complex station (₩15,900, two hours, every 30 minutes).

BUS

Daejeon has four bus terminals: **Daejeon Terminal Complex** (대전복합터미널, Bokhap; www.djbusterminal.co.kr; 63-3 Yongjeon-dong), the largest facility with express and intercity buses; Seobu (west) intercity bus terminal, also known as Seo Nambu bus terminal (대전서남부터미널); the chaotic Yuseong intercity bus terminal (유성시외버스터미널); and the Dunsan intercity bus terminal (시외버스 둔산정류소) at Government Complex station (mostly connections to Incheon, Seoul, Gwangju and Jeonju).

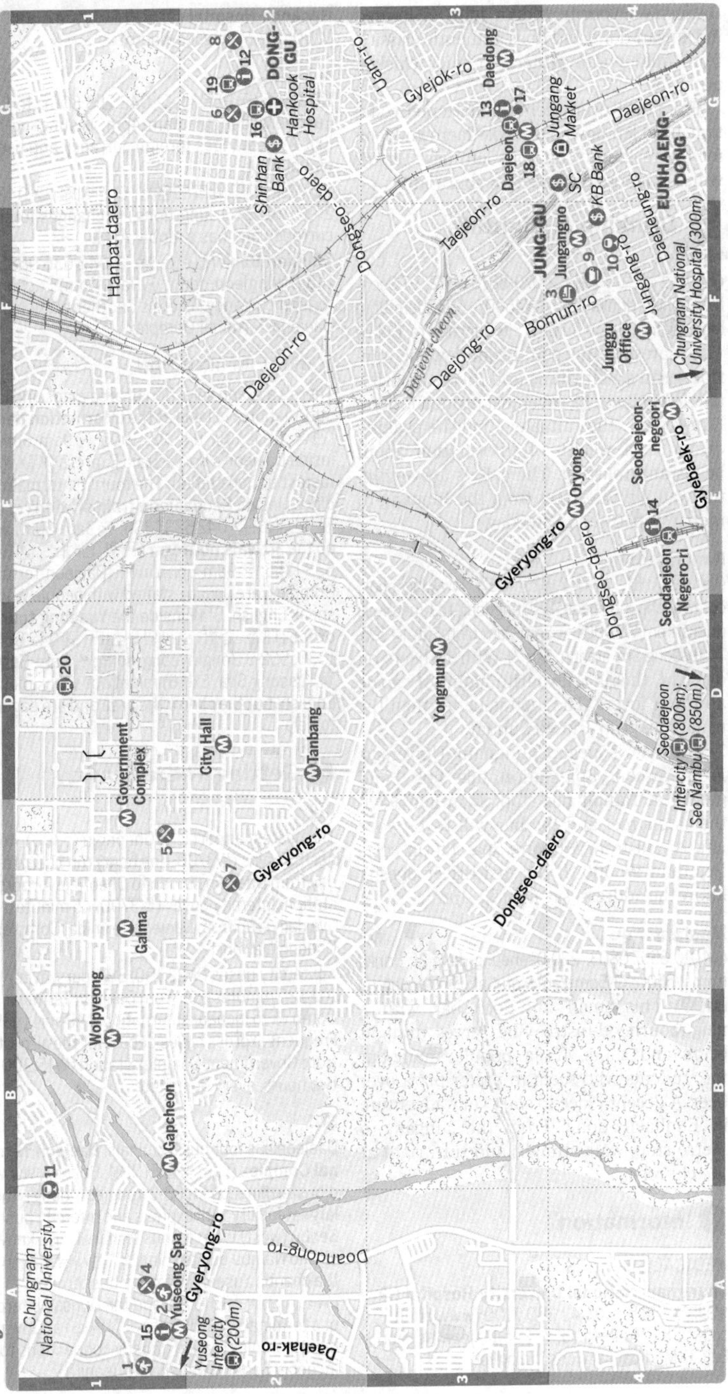

Daejeon

0 1 km
0 0.5 miles

Chungnam National University
11
20
Wolpyeong
Galma
Government Complex
Hanbat-daero
1
15
4
2
Yuseong Spa
Gapcheon
5
Yuseong Intercity (200m)
Gyeryong-ro
City Hall
7
6
19
8
16
12
Shinhan Bank
DONG-GU
Hankook Hospital
Daehak-ro
Doandong-ro
Gyeryong-ro
Tanbang
Daejeon-ro
Dongseo-daero
Uam-ro
Gyejok-ro
Daejeon-cheon
Yongmun
Daejong-ro
Taejeon-ro
13
Daedong
Daejeon
17
18
Dongseo-daero
Gyeryong-ro
Bomun-ro
JUNG-GU
3
Jungangno
SC
Jungang Market
Oryong
9
KB Bank
Dongseo-daero
Junggu Office
10
Jungang-ro
14
Seodaejeon-negeori
Daeheung-ro
Daejeon-ro
Seodaejeon Intercity (800m); Seo Nambu (850m)
Seodaejeon Negero-ri
Gyebaek-ro
Chungnam National University Hospital (300m)
EUNHAENG-DONG

Daejeon

Activities, Courses & Tours
1 Yousung Spa ... A1
2 Yuseong Hot Springs ... A1

Sleeping
3 Java Hotel ... F4
Yousung Hotel ... (see 1)

Eating
4 Cheongju Haejangguk ... A1
5 Indy ... C1
6 Subuk Sikdang ... G2
7 Tasty Beef Intestines ... C2
8 Yeongsuni ... G2

Drinking & Nightlife
9 Lionheart ... F4
10 Mustang Pub ... F4
11 Ranch Pub ... B1

Information
12 Daejeon Bus Terminal Tourist Information Centre ... G2
13 Daejeon Station Tourist Information Centre ... G3
14 Seodaejeon Station Tourist Information Centre ... E4
15 Yuseong Tourist Information Office ... A1

Transport
16 Daejeon Express Bus Terminal Bus Stop ... G2
17 Daejeon Station ... G3
18 Daejeon Station Bus Stop ... G3
19 Daejeon Terminal Complex ... G2
20 Dunsan Intercity Bus Terminal ... D1

TRAIN

KTX trains run every 30 minutes (more frequently in the morning and evening) from Seoul (₩23,700, one hour) and from Busan (₩36,200, 1¾ hours) to Daejeon station (대전역).

From Seoul, there are also hourly *Saemaul* (₩16,000, 1¾ hours) and *Mugunghwa* (₩10,800, two hours) services to Daejeon. From Busan, *Mugunghwa* trains (₩17,800, 2¼ hours) run hourly; *Saemaul* trains (₩26,500, three hours) run seven times a day.

KTX trains (₩23,400, one hour, every 30 to 60 minutes) also run from Yongsan to Seodaejeon train station (서대전역), in the west of the city; some trains continue on to Mokpo and Yeosu in Jeollanam-do.

Getting Around

T-money cards, usable on the metro and bus systems all across the province, can be purchased (₩2500) and charged in metro stations and convenience stores.

BUS

City buses are regular and bus stops have GPS-enabled signs with arrival information. From outside the express bus terminal, useful buses (₩1250 with a T-money card, ₩1400 cash, every 10 to 15 minutes) include the following:

Bus 2, 201, 501 or 701 (15 minutes) To Daejeon train station and Eunhaeng-dong. The bus stop for the latter is along Jungang-ro after Daejeon train station.

Bus 102 or 106 (25 minutes) To Yuseong.

Bus 106 (20 minutes) To City Hall and Dunsan-dong. The bus stop for the latter is just after TimeWorld Galleria.

Bus 701 (35 minutes) To Seobu intercity bus terminal (also called Seo Nambu bus terminal).

METRO

Daejeon's metro line (per trip ₩1250 with T-money card, ₩1400 for a single-ride token, add ₩100 for a two-zone trip) has 22 stations.

TAXI

Taxis are plentiful; fares start at ₩2800. A taxi from the KTX train station to Seobu (Seo Nambu) bus terminal costs about ₩7000.

Gyeryongsan National Park

One of Korea's smallest parks, **Gyeryongsan** (계룡산국립공원; ☎042 825 3003; http://gyeryong.knps.or.kr; adult/youth/child ₩2000/700/400; ⏲6am-7pm) means 'Rooster Dragon Mountain' because locals thought the mountain resembled a dragon with a rooster's head. At the eastern entrance is the temple **Donghak-sa** (동학사; 462 Donghaksa 1-ro; adult/youth/child ₩3000/1500/1000; ⏲8am-6pm); at the western entrance, **Gap-sa** (갑사; 567-3 Gapsa-ro; adult/youth/child ₩2000/1000/500; ⏲8am-6pm). A trail between the two temples runs along streams and small waterfalls (and a few peaks if you wish). The total hike takes between four and six hours, depending on the route. There is excellent English-language signage throughout.

With its easy access from Daejeon, most people start at the eastern entrance, from where it's a 15-minute walk to Donghak-sa,

Gyeryongsan National Park

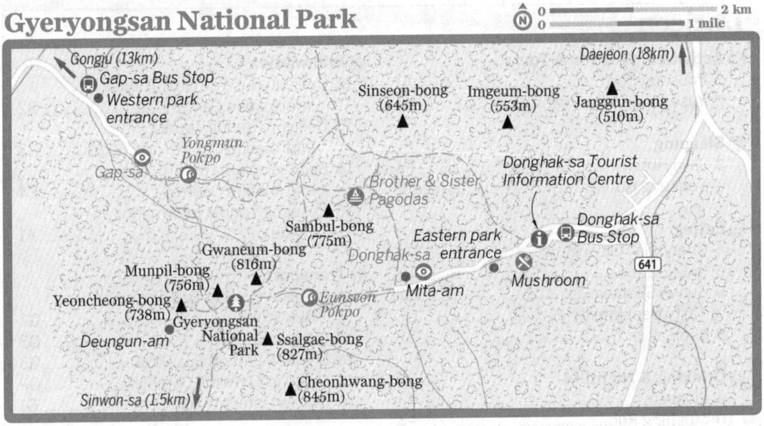

one of Korea's few nunneries. Just before the temple, look for the trail that leads you on an easy one-hour trek up to the Brother & Sister Pagodas (남매탑; Nammaetap) – twin Silla-era pagodas that are said to represent the brother and sister who founded the original hermitage here.

Continue up to Sambul-bong Gogae (Sambul-bong Ridge), where the trail splits. From here you can continue on to the peaks Sambul-bong (775m), Gwaneum-bong (816m) and Yeoncheong-bong (738m), before wending down to Gap-sa (5.5km, four hours), or head directly to Gap-sa (2.8km, 1½ hours). The latter route passes the small waterfall Yongmun Pokpo and the hermitage Sinheung-am.

Depending on your route and schedule, you might come across other hermitages, like Daeja-am, Deungun-am or Mita-am, or a small waterfall, Eunseon Pokpo, which is between Donghak-sa and Deungun-am.

Gap-sa's main hall contains three gleaming Buddha statues, while a smaller shrine houses three shamanist deities – Chilseong, Sansin and Dokseong. From Gap-sa, it's another 15 minutes to the bus stop. The hike is slightly more difficult going in the other direction.

The **information centre** (☎042 823 3944; ⏲9am-6pm) at the Donghak-sa entrance has trail maps (in English) and bus schedules (in Korean).

Sleeping & Eating

There are several motels, hotels and pensions near Donghak-sa and Gap-sa. Because of the comparatively high room cost (₩200,000 or more), pensions are better suited for groups of travellers.

★ **Mushroom** KOREAN $$
(머쉬룸; ☎042 825 1375; 145 Donghaksa 2-ro, Banpo-myeon; dishes from ₩8000; ⏲10am-9pm) The best restaurant at the Donghak-sa entrance is styled after its namesake – you can't miss it. Naturally, it specialises in local mushroom dishes. For groups, there's *beoseot jeongol* (버섯전골, mushroom hotpot; ₩60,000); solo diners can try the delicious *beoseot deopbap* (버섯덮밥, sautéed mushrooms over rice; ₩10,000). Seating is on plush sofas around a blazing hearth.

Getting There & Away

TO/FROM DONGHAK-SA

From Daejeon, take bus 107 (₩2700, 25 minutes, every 20 minutes) from the Yuseong Spa station, Exit 5 bus stop.

From Gongju city bus terminal, take bus 350 (₩1500, 30 minutes, 9.15am, 10.45am and 4.45pm). Donghak-sa buses terminate at a stop near a convenience store and the park entrance. Bus 48 runs from Gyeryong KTX station (₩1400, one hour, every 75 minutes). Get off at the roundabout near two convenience stores and walk about 25 minutes or catch bus 107 to the park entrance.

TO/FROM GAP-SA

From Daejeon, seven buses daily (numbers 340, 341 and 342) run to Gap-sa from the bus stop outside Exit 6 at Yuseong Spa station (₩2700, one hour). The first bus leaves at Yuseong Spa station at 8am.

From Gongju city bus terminal, take bus 320 (₩1500, 40 minutes, every 30 to 90 minutes).

Buses bound for Gap-sa terminate at a bus stop near the park entrance.

Geumsan

041 / POP 55,400

The centre of the Korean ginseng business is Geumsan county (금산군), which despite its diminutive size handles 80% of the country's ginseng trade. There are hundreds of stores, from mum-and-dad operations to wholesalers, and you'll find ginseng sold raw *(susam)* as a potent extract, and in soap, tea and candy.

Ginseng (literally 'man root') is the Chinese name for this stumpish, woody-coloured root; use your imagination and you too might see the shape of a body, complete with limbs and a head-shaped tip. To the Koreans it's *insam* (인삼), and they have been cultivating it for more than 1500 years. It's credited with myriad health benefits, from relieving pain and fatigue to curing cancer and improving sexual stamina.

In October, Geumsan hosts a 10-day Insam Festival, with tours and activities to show how ginseng is grown, harvested, processed and served.

Eating & Drinking

Street vendors make fresh *insam twigim* (인삼튀김; batter-fried ginseng) for around ₩1500.

Geumsan Insamju is a locally produced liquor. Made from five-year-old ginseng, rice malt and water, this 43% alcohol drink is claimed by some to not cause hangovers.

Matkkal KOREAN **$$**
(맛깔; dishes from ₩9000; 10am-9.30pm) The bottles of giant ginseng near the front door may look like something from a mad scientist's lab, but they are a reminder of the house speciality: everything here is made with ginseng, and it's one of the best places in town to eat the local root. Most travellers will be satisfied with the ginseng chicken soup (*samgyetang*; 삼계탕). It's on the 2nd floor of the Susam Market building, which houses the ginseng market.

Shopping

If you're buying ginseng, the prized variety is *hongsam* (홍삼, red ginseng), which is four to six years old and has been steamed and dried to concentrate its medicinal properties.

Geumsan Ginseng Market MARKET
(금산인삼약초시장; 8am-6pm) The country's leading ginseng market is surprising low-tech and wonderfully aromatic. Heaps of fresh ginseng are on display in plastic trays and open cardboard boxes. Stop by any of the stalls, run mostly by grandmotherly types, and you can expect an aggressive sales pitch.

The Herbal Medicine Market in the next-door building contains a panoply of consumer products thought to bring health benefits. In addition to a bewildering array of roots, shoots and extracts, there's a good supply of *phellinus linteus*, a medical mushroom that's boiled into a tea.

From the bus-terminal entrance, walk left along the canal. Turn right at the hospital (look for the green cross), cross the bridge and turn left at the first street.

Getting There & Away

Take an intercity bus from Daejeon Terminal Complex (₩4100, one hour, every 15 minutes) or Seoul Express Bus Terminal (₩11,700, 2¾ hours, every two hours).

Gongju

041 / POP 112,100

Gongju (공주) was the capital of the Baekje Kingdom from AD 475 to 538 and there are a handful of sights here that draw on that legacy; the most notable is the Tomb of King Muryeong. All are clustered within walking distance in the old city south of the river.

Sights

Tomb of King Muryeong ARCHAEOLOGICAL SITE
(백제 무령왕릉; 041 856 0331; 37 Wangreung-ro; adult/youth/child ₩1500/1000/700; 9am-6pm Mar-Oct, to 5pm Nov-Feb) The tomb of King Muryeong, the 25th Baekje king, was discovered – miraculously intact and completely by accident – in 1971. The tomb and the six others in the vicinity aren't open to the public. Instead, an on-site museum has models of two of them that you can enter, as well as English-language information about the history of the Baekje dynasty. The museum is a 20-minute walk from the stone arch in front of Gongsan-seong (p288).

At the entrance to the site, the **Ungjin Baekje Historical Museum** (웅진백제역사관; 041 856 0331; 9am-6pm) FREE has more historical info and a tourist information centre (9am-6pm).

WORTH A TRIP

MAGOK-SA

Just 25km from Gongju, **Magok-sa** (마곡사; ☎041 841 6220; www.magoksa.or.kr; 966 Magoksa-ro, Sagok-myeon; adult/youth/child ₩2000/1500/1000; ⏲sunrise-sunset) makes for a pleasant half-day trip. The utterly serene temple enjoys a pastoral setting beside a river, and see surprisingly few visitors.

Magok-sa has had its buildings restored and reconstructed through the years, but unlike most temples, its extant buildings are being allowed to age gracefully, and there are several atmospheric halls, stumpy pagodas and pavilions. The elaborate entry gates feature colourful statues of various deities and bodhisattvas. Cross the 'mind-washing bridge' to reach the main hall, behind which stands a rare two-storey prayer hall, Daeungbojeon. The temple is located in a pretty setting 24km outside Gongju.

From Magok-sa, three hiking trails head up the nearby hills (there's a signboard with a map, in Korean only), passing small hermitages. The longest trail (10km, 4½ hours) hits the two peaks, **Nabal-bong** (나발봉; 417m) and **Hwarin-bong** (활인봉; 423m).

A templestay can be arranged for ₩50,000, or there is a motel in the small tourist village, as well as a few restaurants serving typical country fare (₩8000 to ₩25,000): *sanchae bibimbap* (산채비빔밥, bibimbap with mountain vegetables), *pyogo jjigae jeongsik* (표고찌개정식, shiitake mushroom stew with side dishes) and *tokkitang* (토끼탕, spicy rabbit soup).

To see the actual artefacts recovered from the tombs, visit the **Gongju National Museum** (국립공주박물관; ☎041 850 6300; http://gongju.museum.go.kr; 34 Gwangwangdanji-gil; ⏲10am-6pm Tue-Fri, to 7pm Sat & Sun) FREE.

Gongsan-seong FORTRESS
(공산성; 280 Ungjin-ro; adult/youth/child ₩1200/800/600; ⏲9am-6pm Mar-Oct, to 5pm Nov-Feb) This stunning hilltop fortress is a reminder of a time when Gongju (then called Ungjin) was Baekje's capital. After entering through the grand stone Geumseoru West Gate, you can walk along the fortress' perimeter and on its wall. Along the way you'll pass numerous pavilions, including Gongbungnu and Gwangbongnu, rebuilt according to archaeological evidence of their original structures. The best views are in the northwest section overlooking the river. In the evening the fortress is lit by floodlights.

Notable structures inside the Gongsan-seong complex include Imnyu-gak, a banquet hall originally built in AD 500 (the building seen today is a replica); the Manharu Pavilion overlooking Gongju's central river Geum-gang, a building that once served twin purposes of defence and recreation; the pavilion Ssangsu-jeong, named for a pair of trees that King Injo used to lean against whilst contemplating the fate of his kingdom; and Yeongeun-sa, a temple first constructed in the 15th century that once served as a boarding house for warrior monks.

A changing-of-the-guards ceremony takes place hourly between 11am and 5pm on weekends during April, May, September, October and November at the main entrance gate, where a stone arch stands opposite.

Festivals & Events

Baekje Cultural Festival CULTURAL
(백제문화제; www.baekje.org) Gongju and Buyeo together host this extravagant festival in September and October, with huge parades, games, traditional music and dancing, and a memorial ceremony for the erstwhile Baekje kings.

Sleeping

Kum-Kang Tourist Hotel HOTEL $
(금강관광호텔; ☎041 852 1071; www.hotel-kumkang.com; 16-11 Jeonmak 2-gil; r incl breakfast ₩35,000-50,000; ❄@📶) This hotel has neat rooms with large bathrooms and is a class above the usual love motels. It's located on the northern side of the river near the express bus terminal.

I-Motel MOTEL $$
(아이 모텔; ☎041 853 1130; 6-5 Minari 3-gil; d ₩40,000; ❄@) One of six motels clustered opposite the fortress, it's close to the sights and great food. The rooms are a little worn, but are good value for people looking for a place to crash who don't want to pay the high weekend rates at nearby properties.

Gongju

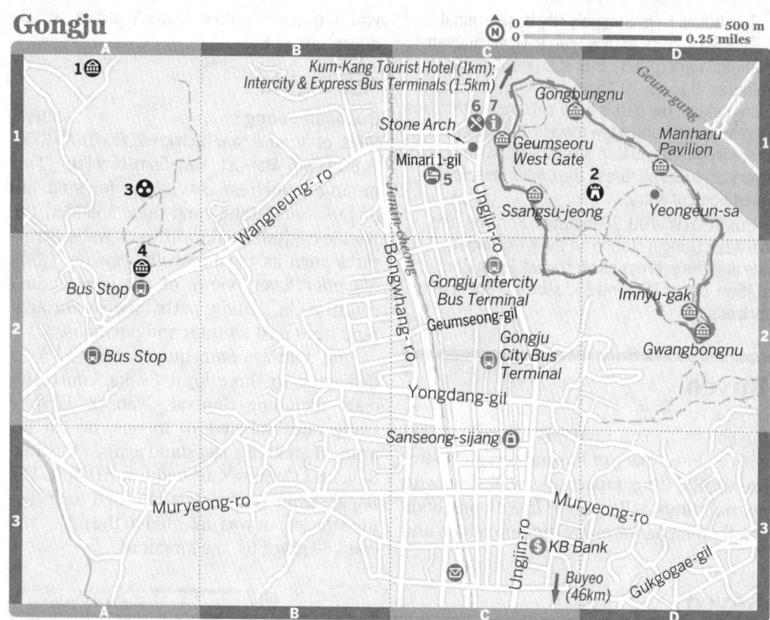

Gongju Hanok Village GUESTHOUSE $$
(공주한옥마을; ☎041 840 8900; http://hanok.gongju.go.kr; 12 Gwangwangdanji-gil; r from ₩50,000; P ❄) This busy *hanok* (traditional wooden homes) village is geared for families looking for an infusion of local history. Everything is rather tidy, so it's not exactly atmospheric of old Korea, but you do get the smell of wood smoke from the traditional *ondol* (underfloor heating).

Eating

Marron Village KOREAN $
(베이커리 밤마을; ☎041 853 3489; from ₩2500; ⏲9am-9pm) This bakery serves an outstanding piece of pastry called chestnut pie, a puff ball filled with sliced chestnut.

★ **Gomanaru** KOREAN $$
(고마나루; ☎041 857 9999; www.gomanaru.co.kr; 5-9 Baekmigoeul-gil; meals ₩9000-25,000; ⏲11am-9pm, last serving 8pm) This restaurant serves the prettiest *ssambap* (assorted ingredients with rice and lettuce wraps) around, with a fragrant array of leaves and handfuls of colourful edible flowers. Solo diners can get a bibimbap (rice, egg, meat and veg with chilli sauce) that looks like a bouquet. Grab a seat by the window for views of Gongsan-seong lit up at night.

Gongju

Sights
1 Gongju National Museum A1
2 Gongsan-seong D1
3 Tomb of King Muryeong A1
4 Ungjin Baekje Historical Museum A2

Sleeping
5 I-Motel C1

Eating
Gomanaru .... (see 6)
6 Marron Village C1

Information
Gongju Museum Tourist Information .... (see 4)
7 Gongsan-seong Tourist Information Centre C1

Information

Gongsan-seong Tourist Information Centre
(☎041 856 7700; ⏲9am-6pm)

Getting There & Away

The largest intercity and express bus terminals are together in the same building north of the river. The old intercity bus terminal south of Gongsan-seong has buses to Seoul and Daejeon.

Two buses from Gongju's city bus terminal (공주 시내 버스 터미널) run to Gyeryongsan National Park (p285). Bus 350 (₩1500, 30 minutes, 9.15am, 10.45am and 4.45pm) runs to Donghak-sa, the park's busy entrance with scads of restaurants and a few motels. Bus 320 runs more frequently to Gap-sa (₩1500, 40 minutes, every 30 to 90 minutes), the park's less developed point of entry.

Bus 200 (₩1400, 30 minutes, 12 daily) runs between Gongju station on the KTX Honam line and the express bus terminal. From Gongju station, buses 200 and 250 stop in front of the fortress.

Buyeo

041 / POP 72,000

Buyeo (부여) is a pretty, countryside town with a slower pace of life and terrific historical sights; it's compact and walkable, with no buildings taller than five floors high. Stroll green parks, enjoy top-notch food and you'll quickly notice Korea's urban tussle doesn't exist here.

Sights

Busosan-seong FORTRESS

(부소산성; adult/youth/child ₩2000/1100/1000; 8am-6pm Mar-Oct, 9am-5pm Nov-Feb) This mountain fortress covers the forested hill of Buso-san (106m) and once shielded the Baekje capital of Sabi within its walls. Structures such as the Banwollu Pavilion (반월루) offer lovely views of the surrounding countryside. Sandy paths weave through pine trees past temples and pavilions.

One temple, Samchung-sa (삼충사), is dedicated to three loyal Baekje court officials, including General Gyebaek. Despite being outnumbered 10 to one, he led his army of 5000 in a last stand against the final Silla and Chinese onslaught in AD 660. The Baekje army dauntlessly repulsed four enemy attacks but was defeated in the fifth – the coup de grâce for the kingdom.

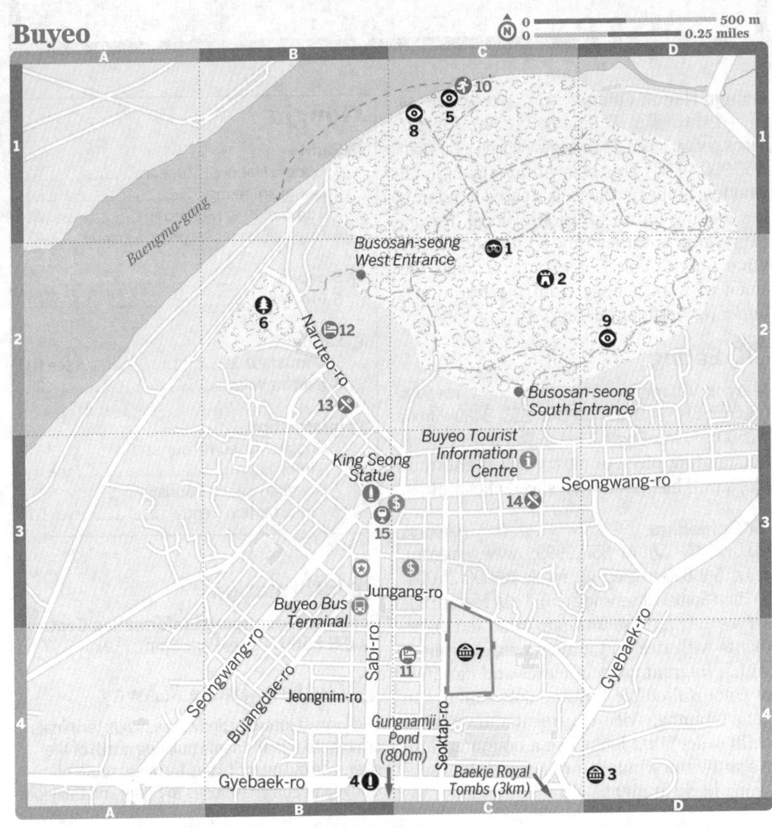

In response, it is said, 3000 court ladies flung themselves off a cliff on the northern side of the fortress into the river Baengma-gang, rather than submit to the conquering armies. The rock where they jumped is now called Nakhwa-am (낙화암), 'falling flowers rock', in their honour.

From Nakhwa-am, there's a rocky and somewhat-steep path down to the tiny temple at the bottom of the cliff, Goran-sa (고란사).

Buyeo National Museum MUSEUM
(국립부여박물관; ☎041 833 8562; http://buyeo.museum.go.kr; 5 Geumseong-ro; ⏰10am-6pm Tue-Sun) FREE This museum houses one of the best collections of Baekje artefacts, and has extensive English captions, making it a good place to get a primer on pre-Baekje and Baekje culture. The highlight is a glittering Baekje-era incense burner. Weighing 12kg, the burner and its pedestal are covered with incredibly intricate and well-preserved metalwork, crested with the legendary *bonghwang* bird.

Gungnamji Pond POND
(궁남지) In July this pond explodes with colour as thousands of lotus flowers bloom. The Buyeo SeoDong Lotus Festival (p292) that month also transforms the surrounding park into a busy place with activities and exhibits around the pond. It's located in Seodong Park (서동공원), which is in the south end of town and close to the General Gyebaek statue.

Baekje Royal Tombs ARCHAEOLOGICAL SITE
(백제왕릉; 16-1 Neungsan-ri; adult/youth/child ₩1000/600/400; ⏰8am-6pm Mar-Oct, to 5pm Nov-Feb; 🚌701 or 702) Buyeo has seven royal tombs, dating from AD 538 to 660. They're sealed for protection, but there's a re-creation of the most impressive one, which is painted with the four celestial creatures (dragon, tiger, tortoise and phoenix) that guard the compass points. There's also a small museum with a model of the oldest tomb, believed to be that of King Seong.

The tombs are on a hillside 3km east of Buyeo, a five-minute bus ride (₩1400, every 15 minutes) from Busosan-seong.

Baekje Cultural Land CULTURAL CENTRE
(백제문화단지; ☎041 635 7740; www.bhm.or.kr; 374 Baekjemun-ro; adult/youth/child ₩4000/3000/2000; ⏰9am-6pm Mar-Oct, to 5pm Nov-Feb, closed Mon; 🚌403, 404 or 405) This 'historical theme park' imagines what the Baekje palace and attendant village might have looked like, with structures you can enter (and plenty of room for kids to run around). There's a history museum too, with English signage. A taxi ride from the town centre costs around ₩8000.

Jeongnimsaji HISTORIC BUILDING
(정림사지; www.jeongnimsaji.or.kr; 83 Jeongnim-ro; adult/youth ₩1500/900; ⏰9am-6pm Mar-Oct, to 5pm Nov-Feb) All that remains here of the Baekje-era temple Jeongnim-sa is a 8.3m five-storey stone pagoda – though this alone is certainly impressive. There's also a small museum on Baekje culture, but it's all in Korean.

Activities

Buyeo Cruise CRUISE
(부여 유람선; ☎041 835 4690; one way/return ₩5000/7000) The ferry between Goran-sa (p291) and Gudurae Sculpture Park (구드래조각공원) glides for 10 minutes along the river Geum-gang, providing nice views of the landscape. There is no fixed schedule; ferries depart when at least seven passengers are on board, which can be quite a wait if it's not peak season.

Passengers can begin the tour at the pier behind Goran-sa or the one at Gudurae Sculpture Park.

Buyeo

Sights

1 Banwollu Pavilion ... C2
2 Busosan-seong ... C2
3 Buyeo National Museum ... D4
4 General Gyebaek Statue ... B4
5 Goran-sa ... C1
6 Gudurae Sculpture Park ... B2
7 Jeongnimsaji ... C4
8 Nakhwa-am ... C1
9 Samchung-sa ... D2

Activities, Courses & Tours

10 Buyeo Cruise ... C1

Sleeping

11 Arirang Motel ... C4
12 Samjeong Buyeo Youth Hostel ... B2

Eating

Gomaru Gamjatang ... (see 11)
13 Gudurae Dolssambap ... B2
14 House of Baekje ... C3

Drinking & Nightlife

15 Bonggu ... B3

Festivals & Events

★ **Buyeo SeoDong Lotus Festival** CULTURAL (부여서동연꽃축제; 041 830 2211; http://lotusfestival.kr) Buyeo comes alive with cultural shows, music performances and dazzling light shows centred around blooming lotus flowers in Gungnamji pond (p291). The festival usually runs in early July. Check the website for exact dates.

Sleeping

Samjeong Buyeo Youth Hostel HOSTEL $ (삼정부여유스호스텔; 041 835 3101; www.buyeoyh.co.kr; 50 Naruteo-ro; dm/f ₩16,000/58,000;) You're as likely to stumble upon a bunch of kids on a field trip as you are a wedding party at this airy hostel that feels more like a hotel. Dorm rooms have two double bunks and good bathrooms. Family rooms, good for four to eight people, have twin beds.

Arirang Motel MOTEL $$ (아리랑 모텔; 041 832 5656; www.arirangmotel.com; 55-1 Cheongrim-ro; d from ₩40,000;) This motel looks as generic as its neighbours, but the rooms are modern and low on love-motel vibes. Close to the market opposite the bus terminal, it's one the tallest buildings in the area.

Lotte Buyeo Resort HOTEL $$$ (롯데부여리조트; 041 939 1000; www.lottebuyeoresort.com; 400 Baekjemun-ro; r from ₩270,000;) This high-end condo-style hotel by conglomerate Lotte is a hunk of gleaming glass and concrete complete with ultraplush and modern rooms on par with the best in Seoul. It's located opposite Baekje Cultural Land.

Eating

★ **Gudurae Dolssambap** KOREAN $$ (구드래돌쌈밥; 041 836 9259; 31 Naruteo-ro; meals ₩7000-22,000; 11am-9pm;) This popular restaurant with an eclectic interior serves delicious *ssambap* (rice and side dishes with lettuce wraps), with fragrant leaves and a whole host of options. The *dolssambap* (hotpot rice and lettuce wraps), served with succulent braised pork, is particularly recommended. Look for the *jangseung* (totem poles with faces) out front.

House of Baekje KOREAN $$ (백제의집; 041 834 1212; 248 Seongwang-ro; meals ₩10,000-20,000; 10am-9pm) Enjoy the house specialities – grilled beef or pork served with *ssam* (lettuce wraps) and *yeonnipbap* (연잎밥, sticky rice steamed with pine nuts inside a lotus leaf) – amid Bruce Lee posters and video cassettes. Solo dinners usually order soybean stew which comes with plenty of side dishes, lettuce and *yeonnipbap*.

Gomaru Gamjatang KOREAN $$ (고마루 감자탕; 041 837 1577; 47-14 Cheongrim-ro; dishes from ₩7000; 24 hours) The speciality here is *gamjatang*, a classic Korean dish. This hearty pork-bone stew has a rich, savoury broth that's a little spicy. Gomaru Gamjatang is open all night, and your only option in Buyeo for late-evening drinks. It's close to the Arirang Motel.

Drinking & Nightlife

Bonggu BAR (봉구; 041 835 0925; drinks from ₩3500; 6pm-2am Mon-Sat, 8pm-midnight Sun) At this casual beer bar the draught flows and conversations become spirited. Like at many bars in Korea, customers here are expected to order some food along with their drinks. Try the fried cheese sticks. From the bus terminal, cross the street and walk left. It's near the roundabout.

Information

Buyeo Police Station (부여경찰서)

KB Bank (041 834 4323; 9am-4pm)

KEB Hana Bank (041 832 1111; 9am-4p

Tourist Information Centre (041 830 2880; 9am-6pm) With English-speaking staff. Located beside the entrance to Busosan-seong (p290).

Getting There & Away

Most travellers to Buyeo arrive by bus and get off at the town's intercity bus terminal (부여 시외 버스터미널). From Seoul and Daejeon, there are direct connections. From most other parts of the country, a transfer is required at a regional centre, such as Gongju or Cheongju.

Boryeong

041 / POP 106,700

Boryeong (보령) is the gateway to the mudflats of Daecheon Beach and a strip dripping with Las Vegas–style neon, as well as the harbour in Daecheon-hang (2km down the road), from where ferries sail to a dozen islands. Few people stay in Boryeong

proper, and instead travel 10km down the road to Daecheon Beach for what usually amounts to a woozy weekend of shellfish, *soju* (local vodka) and song.

The Boryeong Mud Festival is the big event here. Usually held in July, it's been recognised as Korea's top international festival, with more than a million attendees.

Navigating the Daecheon beachfront is easy. At the southern end of the strip, you'll find Citizen's Tower Plaza. Mud Plaza, a wide open space where many festival events take place, is about 1km north. In between, there are dozens of restaurants, motels and *noraebang* (karaoke rooms) on or near the main drag.

Sights

Daecheon Beach BEACH
(대천해수욕장; P) This popular strip of almost golden-hued sand runs for 3.5km and is about 100m wide during low tide. The main hub of activity is at its southern end, near the Citizen's Tower Plaza, but in summer the entire stretch gets overrun with beachgoers, especially during the bacchanalian Boryeong Mud Festival. There's also waterskiing, canoeing, windsurfing, horse-and-carriage rides and speedboat, banana-boat and jet-ski rides.

Sleeping

Most of the larger, modern hotels are around the north end of Daecheon Beach between Mud Plaza and Fountain Plaza (분수광장), while the older establishments are near Citizen's Tower Plaza. Prices are an additional ₩10,000 to ₩70,000 on weekends and easily double or triple in summer.

Motel Coconuts MOTEL $$
(모텔코코넛; ☎041 934 6595; 7 Haesuyokjang 2-gil; r ₩40,000; ❄📶) The Coconuts' updated rooms are attractive and though a teeny bit tiny, they're big enough for two people. Another positive feature is the motel's location: it's close to the beach, but not too close to be bothered by the noise or neon. It's around the corner from the Lotteria near Citizen's Tower Plaza.

Singung Motel MOTEL $$
(신궁 모텔; ☎041 931 0900; 32 Haesuyokjang 6-gil; r ₩40,000-50,000; ❄@) Only the higher floors have sea views, but this motel is quiet yet close to the main strip. Rooms are small, clean and comfortable. Prices are higher on weekends.

Mudrin Hotel HOTEL $$$
(호텔머드린; ☎041 934 1111; www.mudrin.com; 28 Haesuyokjang 8-gil; d from ₩150,000; ⊖❄@📶) Mudrin has big picture windows overlooking the beach, soft white linens and a 24-hour front desk with staff who speak some English. Still, the walls are a bit thin and you can hear noise from the hallways. The hotel is in the middle of the strip, close to Mud Plaza.

Eating

★**Korea's Best Seafood Hotpot** KOREAN $$
(팔도강산 해물뚝배기; ☎041 933 6388; 891 Daehae-ro; dishes from ₩10,000; ⊙8am-8.30pm Mon-Fri, 7.30am-9pm Sat & Sun) Seafood soup

MUD, GLORIOUS MUD

The 10-day **Boryeong Mud Festival** (www.mudfestival.or.kr), held every July, began in 1998 as a way of promoting the health benefits of the local mud, rich in germanium and other minerals. Now it attracts more than a million attendees, and has developed a reputation for the unabashed, alcohol-fuelled frolics of expats, Korean students and international travellers. Daecheon Beach is the principal venue.

After being baptised in a vat of the oozing grey stuff, participants can enter the 'mud prison' and get doused with buckets of warmed mud. There's a mud superslide, a mud rain tunnel and a number of muddy pools where groups run, splash and generally get covered in mud. The festival grounds are just above the beach, where every evening there's a concert or rave and it's easy to zip out to the ocean for a quick swim or de-mudding. The festival is bookended by parades and fireworks.

Many English-speaking volunteers are on hand and there are free lockers, a campsite and basic clean-up facilities, making this one of the most foreigner-friendly events in Korea. Accommodation is booked up months in advance, even in Boryeong, so many come for the day or on tours.

served in a hotpot (해물뚝배기) is the popular dish here. Boil the soup on the table burner and ladle out servings brimming with shellfish, shrimp and crab (₩22,000 for two people). An economical option for solo travellers is the savoury kimchi stew. It's close to Motel Coconuts (p293).

Grilled Shellfish KOREAN $$$
(조은 조개구이; ☎041 936 9289; 50 Haesuyukjang 4-gil; sets from ₩30,000; ⏰noon-5am) One of the busiest restaurants on the beach strip serving grilled shellfish. It's open late, so come for the seafood – typically ordered as a combination platter, or set – and stay for the sunrise.

Sets range in price from ₩30,000 to ₩120,000 or more depending on the quantity and quality of seafood. Other menu items, like stews, noodles or rice, are generally extra.

Drinking & Nightlife

Babeans CAFE
(☎041 934 4030; drinks from ₩2800; ⏰10am-8am) There's fine espresso here, though the best feature of this coffee shop is the sea view from the 3rd-floor outdoor patio.

Information

The **tourist information centre** (☎041 932 2023; ⏰9am-6pm) is inside Daecheon train station. There's a small kiosk near Citizen's Tower Plaza at Daecheon Beach.

Getting There & Around

BUS

Buses 100 and 101 (₩1400, every 10 minutes) run from Boryeong bus terminal and Daecheon train station to Daecheon Beach and on to the ferry terminal at Daecheon-hang. For Citizen's Tower Plaza, get off at the intersection where the access road meets the main strip. A taxi from the bus terminal to the beach will cost about ₩11,000.

Departures from Boryeong

DESTINATION	PRICE (₩)	TIME (HR)	FREQUENCY
Buyeo	5200	¾	8 daily
Daejeon	12,000	2	hourly
Gongju	7700	1¾	17 times daily
Seoul	15,900	2	every 20-60 min
Taean	7100	1½	7 times daily

TRAIN

Daecheon station, located in Boryeong, is across a plaza from the Boryeong bus terminal. Regular *Saemaul* (₩17,400, 2½ hours, six daily) and *Mugunghwa* (₩11,700, 2¾ hours, nine daily) trains run between Daecheon station and Yongsan station in Seoul.

FERRY

Daecheon Ferry Terminal (대천 연안 여객선 터미널; ☎041 934 8896; www.shinhanhewoon.com; adult/child one way ₩9900/4700) services nearby islands. Ferry schedules are subject to change due to the weather, season and tides. Port staff are helpful, but few people speak English and detailed schedule information is available only in Korean.

Sapsido and Yeongmok-hang (on the island Anmyeondo in Taeanhaean National Marine Park) are popular destinations. Other ferries (adult ₩4500 to ₩18,000) run to remote islands – Hojado, Wonsando, Hodo, Nokdo and Oeyeondo – where few international travellers have ventured.

Daecheon Ferry Terminal is at the harbour in Daecheon-hang, a 20-minute ride from Boryeong on bus 100 or 101. A taxi to the ferry terminal from Daecheon Beach costs ₩5000.

Sapsido

☎041

If you like undeveloped beaches and the salty smell of fish, skip out to Sapisdo (삽시도), 13km from Daecheon. There isn't much to do here except hit the sand, wander the roads, hike a coastal trail and admire the sunset if you stay the night. You'll see residents mending nets, collecting shellfish at low tide or working in rice paddies. The pace speeds up in summer with more than 50 *minbak* (private homes with rooms for rent) and pensions drawing visitors from the mainland.

Sights & Activities

A good three-hour hike, about 8km, runs along the southwestern coast, roughly from Jinneomeo Beach to the Bamseom ferry terminal. Some English-language signage is on the trail. The large island map at each ferry terminal shows some trail details.

Jinneomeo Beach BEACH
(진너머 해수욕장) Of the many island beaches, this is one of the cleanest ones: with striking ocean views, the least amount of rubbish and a half dozen nearby pensions.

Sapsido

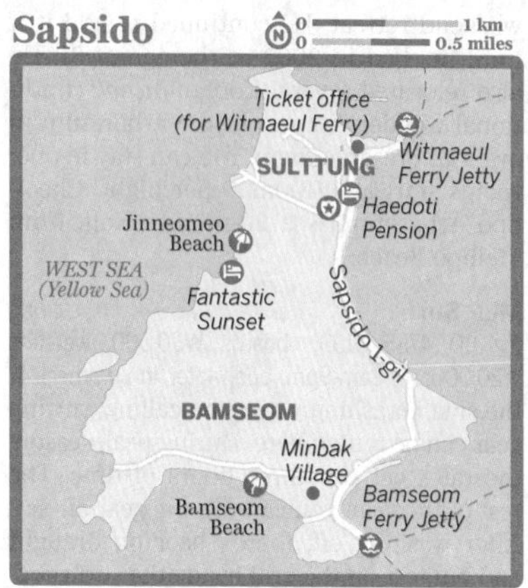

Bamseom Beach BEACH
(밤섬 해수욕장) The largest of Sapsido's beaches is Banseom Beach, a broad stretch of golden sand on the island's southern coast. To find it, follow the road to the left of the *minbak* village at Witmaeul marina.

Sleeping & Eating

There are no shops on the island. Either arrange meals at your *minbak* or bring provisions with you.

Fantastic Sunset PENSION $$
(환상의 노을; ☎010 4024 2001; www.sabsido.kr; 49-37 Sapsido 1-gil; r ₩80,000-100,000) Steps away from Jinneomeo Beach (p294), this pension has some nice ocean views. Most rooms have *ondol* (traditional, sleep-on-a-floor-mattress) sleeping and a kitchenette. The on-site restaurant serves food during the day. At night, it's a bar equipped with a guitar and drum kit.

Haedoti Pension GUESTHOUSE $$
(해돋이펜션; ☎041 935 1617; 168-28 Sapsido 1-gil; r from ₩50,000; ❄) This red-brick *minbak* (private home with rooms for rent) has rooms that are of motel standard, equipped with a fridge and kitchenette. Out front is a homey dining area, where the menu depends on the catch of the day (meals ₩7000 to ₩25,000). It's centrally located on the island's main road and next to a police station.

Getting There & Away

Ferries run from Daecheon Ferry Terminal to Sapsido (₩10,800, 7.40am, 1pm and 4pm) and make three return trips (₩9900, 8.35am, 1.55pm and 5.40pm). The trip takes 40 minutes, longer if the ferry is rerouted to other islands on the way. Daecheon Ferry Terminal is at the harbour Daecheon-hang, a 20-minute bus ride from Boryeong.

Ferries go to one of two jetties on Sapsido: Witmaeul jetty (윗마을 선착장) in Sulttung village or Bamseom jetty (밤섬 선착장) in Minbak village, depending on the tides; check before you board and check your return. Note: few people in the area speak English and ferry schedules are in Korean only.

Return tickets to the mainland can only be purchased on Sapsido. The Witmaeul ticket office is in a small, nondescript building about five minutes on foot from the Witmaeul jetty. The Bamseom ticket office is next to the jetty.

Taeanhaean National Marine Park

☎041

Beautiful Taeanhaean National Marine Park (태안해안국립공원) is an extraordinary preserve offering expansive beaches and a panoply of twisting hiking trails alongside remote villages, lush rice paddies and rugged coastlines so inspiring that even the most dedicated curmudgeon will pause to wonder at the beauty of it all. The park covers 327 sq km of land and sea, with 130 islands and islets, and more than 30 beaches.

Taean-gun is the biggest municipality in the area and a major transport hub. Mallipo Beach, a fun resort town with a small surf scene, is 17km to the west. To the south is Anmyeondo, the park's largest island (and Korea's sixth largest). Here you'll find popular Kkotki Beach. Yeongmok-hang, the island's main harbour with ferries connecting with Daecheon, is on the southern tip of the island.

Anmyeondo

Of the many beaches on Anmyeondo, one of the best is Kkotji Beach (꽃지해수욕장), a gentle 3.2km-long stretch that's a glorious 300m wide at low tide and popular with photographers at sunset. Snack vendors sell fried prawns, crabs and corn dogs around the car park.

There's a pension village a short walk back from the beach.

You can get to Anmyeon-eup (the island's main village) by bus from Seoul (₩11,000, 2¾ hours, hourly) and Daejeon (₩10,300, three hours, three daily).

The most picturesque journey is a ferry ride (₩8700, 7.20am, 1.30pm and 5pm) from Daecheon Ferry Terminal (p294) bound for Yeongmok-hang (영목항), which is at the southern tip of Anmyeondo. The ride takes 45 minutes and usually makes a couple of stops before landing at Yeongmok-hang.

After disembarking at Yeongmok-hang, turn right and then fork left for the two-minute uphill walk to the bus stop. The bus for Anmyeon-eup (₩2100, 40 minutes, hourly) takes a rugged, circuitous route along backcountry roads between rice paddies and rustic farmhouses.

Taean-gun

Sights & Activties

Mallipo Beach BEACH

(만리포; P) Though Mallipo is seeing more and more development every year, it's still a fine stretch of sand, a gentle crescent bookended by piney headlands. It's a 15-minute walk from here to the quieter Cheollipo Beach.

Buses run from a small terminal near the beach to Taean bus terminal (₩2000, 20 minutes, seven daily). There are three daily buses to Seoul (₩11,000, three hours, 7.10am, 8.25am and 12.25pm). A taxi from Mallipo Beach to Taean bus terminal costs ₩22,000.

Cheollipo Arboretum GARDENS

(천리포수목원; 041 672 9982; www.chollipo.org; 187 Cheollipo 1-gil; Nov-Mar ₩6000, Apr-Oct ₩9000; 9am-6pm Apr-Oct, to 5pm Nov-Mar) The Cheollipo Arboretum is among Asia's top botanical institutions, with a collection of more than 13,000 species from over 60 countries, laid out with diligent care across 64 hectares of lush coastal property. Only a fraction of it is open to the public, but even that is spectacular – particularly in spring when the magnolias bloom.

The arboretum was founded and built by a man without formal training: American Carl Ferris Miller was a banker in Seoul when he bought his first plot of farmland in Cheollipo in the 1970s, intending it as a weekend retreat. He continued to add it it until he died in 2002 at the age of 81. He also relocated several Korean *hanok* (traditional wooden homes) to the arboretum in order to preserve them. You can stay in one; rooms start at ₩100,000 per night. Cheollipo Arboretum is a 20-minute walk from Mallipo Beach.

MLP Surf SURFING

(010 4785 5199; boards ₩30,000, wetsuits ₩20,000; 8am-9pm, open later in summer) If the small crashing waves are calling, surfing gear can be rented here. During peak season, the rates get you three hours of time. The rest of the year, you can use the gear all day. After washing off, there's beer on draught and burgers on the grill inside the surf shop.

Sleeping

★Pinocchio Pension COTTAGE $$

(피노키오 펜션; 041 672 3824; www.pinocchiopension.com; 184 Mallipo 2-gil; r from ₩130,000;) Comfortable cottages, with fridges, facing the sea. Find it by walking past the motels to the northern end of Mallipo Beach, stopping only when you see a wooden terrace and Pinocchio on your right. Call for better rates; the owners speak some English.

Eating & Drinking

Seafood is king here. Grilled clams and in-season blue crab are local specialities. Taean sea salt, especially the sun-dried version covered with pine-tree pollen, is a prized ingredient.

Black Brunch Cafe CAFE

(010 3887 4198; 10 Seohye-ro; 7am-9pm, closed 2nd & 4th Tue) This humble coffee shop serves the best espresso on Mallipo Beach.

Getting There & Around

Taean-gun is served by buses from Seoul (₩9000, 2¼ hours, every 30 minutes) and Daejeon (₩9200, 2¾ hours, hourly). From Taean, there are buses to Boryeong (₩12,000, 2½ hours, seven daily) and Daejeon (₩9200, 2½ hours, 11 daily).

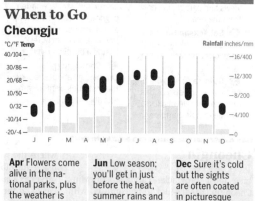

Chungcheongbuk-do

Includes ➡

Best Places to Eat

- Doljip Sikdang (p307)
- Menmusha (p300)
- Sundubu Sikdang (p306)
- Gimbap Heaven (p307)

Best Places to Stay

- Birosanjang (p301)
- Business Y Hotel (p300)
- Factory G. ssang (p306)
- Danyang Hotel Edelweiss (p306)
- Lake Hills Hotel Songnisan (p301)

Why Go?

The only landlocked province in the South, Chungcheongbuk-do (충청북도) – or Chungbuk as it's known informally – is largely mountainous and agricultural (two things that don't mix well, so you'll see all available scraps of land farmed). The province is kind of sleepy and its major cities are hardly compelling, though bibliophiles must make a pilgrimage to Cheongju, where in 1377 Buddhist monks printed the world's oldest extant book with movable metal type.

The province's charms are better appreciated in its smaller towns and three national parks, which are home to an assortment of intriguing and historic Buddhist sites. You can climb the azalea-covered peaks of Sobaek-san, descend into the other-worldly caverns of Gosu Donggul, or simply savour the views along the river and at nearby Chungju-ho. Then there's Guin-sa, a Buddhist temple ensconced in a steep valley, as imposing as the mountain slopes on either side of it.

When to Go

Cheongju

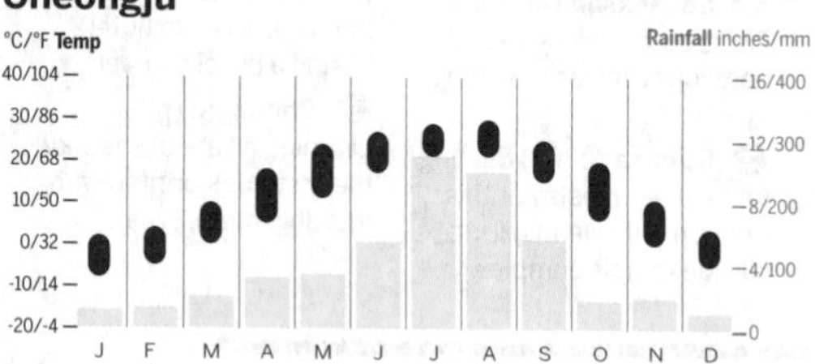

Apr Flowers come alive in the national parks, plus the weather is mercifully cool for hiking.

Jun Low season; you'll get in just before the heat, summer rains and price hikes.

Dec Sure it's cold but the sights are often coated in picturesque sheets of snow.

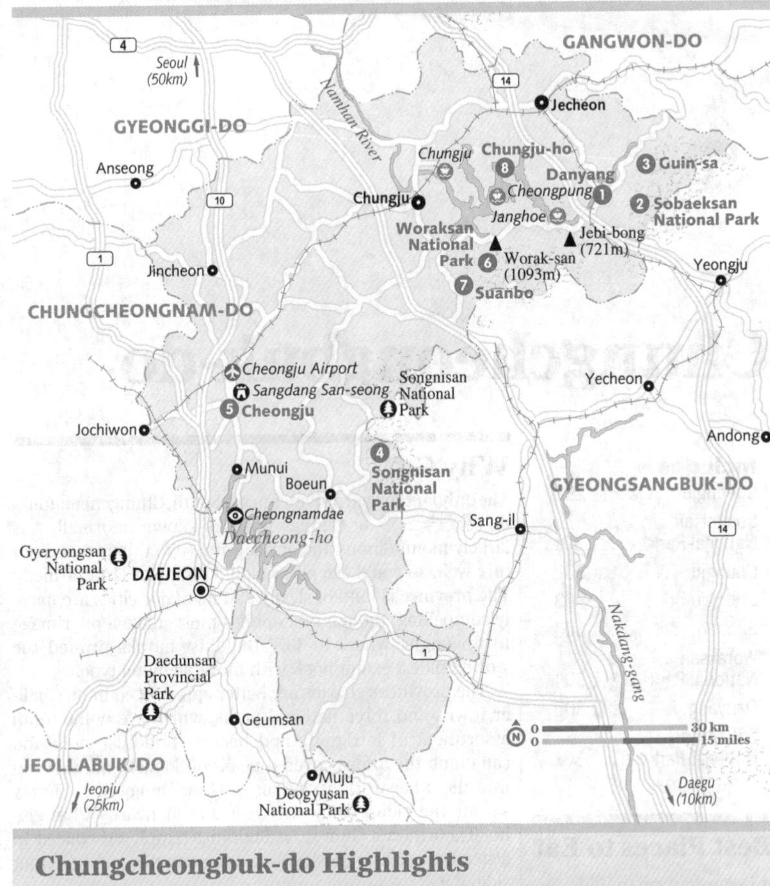

Chungcheongbuk-do Highlights

1. **Danyang** (p305) Waking up to glorious mountain views and paragliding down from the peaks.
2. **Sobaeksan National Park** (p307) Hiking past the gorgeous azaleas blooming in May.
3. **Guin-sa** (p307) Signing up for a templestay at this modern but awe-inspiring hillside temple complex.
4. **Songnisan National Park** (p301) Admiring a unique five-storey wooden pagoda before overnighting at a charming *yeogwan* (small family-run hotel) beside a burbling river.
5. **Cheongju** (p298) Learning all about the *Jikji*, the first book printed with movable metal type.
6. **Woraksan National Park** (p304) Meditating on ancient Buddhist carvings and the evocative ruins of Mireuksaji.
7. **Suanbo** (p303) Soothing away your stresses at an *oncheon* (hot-spring spa).
8. **Chungju-ho** (p303) Photographing the stunning scenery on a lake cruise.

Cheongju

043 / POP 668,000

Like most provincial capitals, sprawling Cheongju (청주) – not to be confused with nearby Chungju – is not terribly captivating. Its primary claim to fame is as the place where the world's oldest book was printed using movable metal type. The town also serves as a launchpad to Songnisan National Park and the presidential villa Cheongnamdae. Once you've seen these, there's really no need to hang around.

OFF THE BEATEN TRACK

PRESIDENTIAL VILLA

Once the holiday home of South Korean presidents, **Cheongnamdae** (청남대; ☎043 220 5677; http://chnam.cb21.net; 646 Cheongnamdae-gil, Sangdang-gu; adult/child incl return shuttle bus ₩8000/7000; ⊙9am-6.30pm Tue-Sun) is no Camp David, but it's a beautiful lakeside park, with 185 hectares of well-manicured grounds and 2.3km of paths along the lakefront and across the gently rolling hills. You can linger in the Chogajeong Pavilion where President Kim Dae-jung liked to sit, or look over the golf course that President Roh Tae-woo favoured but President Kim Young-sam disapproved of (too many associations with corruption).

Cheongnamdae was built in 1983 by President Chun Doo-hwan (whose takeover of power sparked the Gwangju Uprising in 1980). Twenty years later, the much-loved President Roh Moo-Hyun opened it to the public.

The parkland is more attractive than the surprisingly modest two-storey villa, with trails around the compound and a musical fountain (ABBA features on the soundtrack). Where the bus stops, there's a building with a hagiographic exhibition (mostly Korean) on all the presidents, as well as displays of items used by the presidents in residence (polo mallets, Colgate shaving cream, cutlery).

Take local bus 311 (₩1300, 50 minutes, 15km, hourly) from outside Cheongju's intercity bus terminal to the final stop at Munui. Walk out of Munui's small bus depot and turn left. In a few minutes you'll reach the car park and ticket office for the shuttle bus (15 minutes, every 30 minutes), which runs 9am to 4.30pm from February to November, and to 3.30pm December and January.

Sights

Early Printing Museum MUSEUM
(고인쇄박물관; ☎043 269 0556; 866 Uncheon-dong; ⊙9am-6pm Tue-Sun) FREE This small museum tells you everything about the *Jikji,* the oldest book in the world printed with movable metal type. Unfortunately the book is not here – it's in the National Library of France. There is, however, a copy of the book as well as exhibits of many early Korean books, including handwritten sutras and books printed using woodblocks, with extensive information in English. You'll love the interactive set where you can see yourself being rained upon by *hanja* (Chinese characters).

Look out for Korea's oldest printed document, the *Dharani Sutra,* dating back to at least AD 751. It's accompanied by the woodblocks used in its creation.

The museum stands beside the site of Heungdeok-sa, where the Jikji was printed and where you can find a replica temple on the site where the original stood. Don't overlook climbing the wooded hill behind and above the museum for fabulous walks in the trees. To reach the museum, catch bus 831 or 832 (₩1300, 15 minutes) from the bus stop opposite the tourist information centre. Get off at the bus stop beside the pedestrian bridge with green and yellow arches. The museum is about 50m ahead on the left.

Sangdang San-seong FORTRESS
(상당산성; 70 Seongnae-ro, Sangdang-gu) FREE This large fortress is 4km northeast of Cheongju, on the slopes of the mountain Uam-san. Originally built in the 1590s and renovated in the 18th century, it has walls up to 4m in height that stretch 4.2km around wooded hillsides, offering superb views of farms, mountains and the city. Its size makes it easy to imagine that it once housed three temples and several thousand soldiers and monks. Today, Korean families decamp to the fields outside the south gate for family picnics.

A hike around the top of the wall takes about 1½ hours along a route that is completely exposed and can be steep in parts. The easier direction to follow is anticlockwise. From the bus stop, walk back along the road and look on the left for a paved path that ascends to the top of the wall. Along the walk, there are hardly any signs or resting places, and no food stalls, vending machines or toilets – so bring your own water and a sun hat. If you're up for a challenge, follow the path beside the pond and up the steep hill on the right to do a clockwise circuit. There are restaurants and shops near the bus stop.

Hop on bus 717, 832 or 913 from outside the intercity bus terminal to the Cheongju Stadium (청주체육관) bus stop, which is just after the five-storey **golden pavilion** (Sajik-daero). Transfer to bus 862 (₩1150, 30

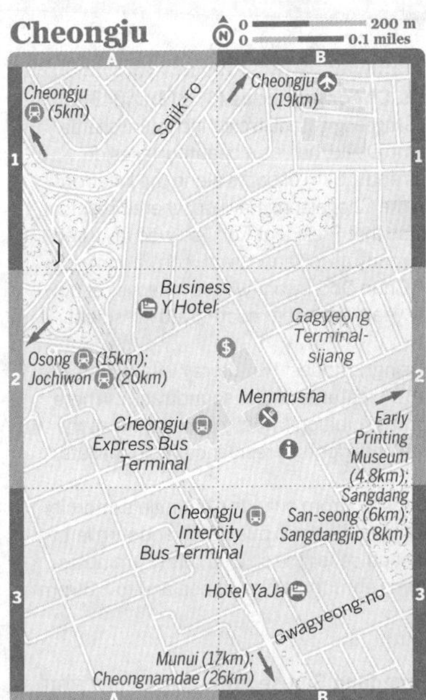

minutes, hourly), which runs to the fortress. The last bus back to Cheongju from Sangdang San-seong leaves at 9.50pm.

Festivals & Events

Jikji Festival CULTURAL
(www.jikjifestival.com) Cheongju hosts the Jikji Festival every September with a demonstration of ancient printing techniques, exhibitions of old printed books, and traditional music and drama performances.

Sleeping & Eating

★ Business Y Hotel HOTEL $
(043 908 6677; 49 Pungnyeon-ro; r incl breakfast ₩50,000-80,000;) Truly excellent service, free popcorn and coffee in the lobby, free laundry and lovely sunset views over the hills (if you have a west-facing room) are just some of the pluses of this excellent hotel. The standard double rooms are modish and contemporary, with huge flat-screen TVs, faultless wi-fi and comfy beds. The hotel has a lift. What struck us the most was the professionalism of the staff, who were always at hand to help.

Hotel YaJa MOTEL $$
(043 238 3216; 8 Gyeongsan-ro 5beon-gil; d/tw from ₩45,000/55,000;) This slick, quiet love motel is convenient for the bus station but offers plenty of little pluses to keep you lingering in the comfy beds or deep spa – including a late 3pm checkout, PCs, wall-mounted mini clothes-washer, and complimentary popcorn, ramen, coffee and hot ginseng. Prices rise ₩5000 to ₩10,000 on Friday and Saturday. Look for the arched brick facade.

Menmusha NOODLES $$
(麵武士, 멘무샤; www.menmusha.co.kr; 2nd fl, Lotte Mall, Pungsan-ro; mains from ₩7000; 10am-10pm) The name means 'Noodle Samurai' and the noodles here sure pack a punch. It's a popular choice and there's a handy full-colour photo menu to help you navigate through the selection, which amazingly resembles the delicious bowls and dishes ferried to your table by efficient staff. Each dish gets a chilli rating for spiciness; the *tantanmen* (탄탄멘) does the trick.

Information

Tourist Information Centre (043 233 8431; 14 Pungsan-ro; 9am-6pm) Outside the intercity bus terminal.

Getting There & Around

AIR

18km from the city, **Cheongju International Airport** (043 210 6110; www.airport.co.kr) has flights to Jeju-do, China, Japan and Taipei, with seasonal flights to Bangkok. Take bus 747 from outside the intercity bus terminal (₩1300, one hour, every 25 minutes). A taxi costs in the region of ₩15,000 to ₩20,000.

BUS

The **Express Bus Terminal** (청주고속버스터미널; Gagyeong-dong) and the **Intercity Bus Terminal** (청주시외버스터미널; 6 Pungsan-ro) are opposite each other in the west of town.

Express Bus Terminal

DESTINATION	PRICE (₩)	DURATION (HR)	FREQUENCY
Busan	17,400-25,600	3½	every 90min
Dong Daegu	11,300-16,500	2½	hourly
Dong-Seoul	9800	1¾	every 40min
Seoul	7700-8100	1¾	every 10-15min

Intercity Bus Terminal

DESTINATION	PRICE (₩)	DURATION (HR)	FREQUENCY
Chuncheon	14,400	3	every 20-40min
Chungju	8800	2	every 20min
Daejeon	7400	1-2	every 15min
Danyang	17,200	4	6 daily

TRAIN

Cheongju Station (청주역; ☎043 232 7788; Gangseo 1-dong) connects primarily with Daejeon (₩3100, 42 minutes, eight daily). Or you can travel to Jochiwon station (조치원역) for a Korea Train Express (KTX; the fastest trains) connection to Seoul (₩12,500, 80 minutes, six per day); *Mugunghwa* (limited-stop express trains) also run from Jochiwon station (₩8400, 1½ to two hours, at least hourly).

To/from the intercity bus terminal, take bus 717 for Cheongju station (20 minutes), or 502 for Jochiwon (one hour). You can also get a fast KTX train to/from Cheongju from Osong station (오송역), about 10km southwest of Cheongju centre.

From Osong station there are trains to Seoul (₩18,500, 50 minutes, every 20 minutes) and Daejeon (₩8400, 15 minutes, every six to 25 minutes). Three *Mugunghwa* trains (₩2700, 35 minutes) also run daily to Daejeon. Buses 500, 511 and 519 run between the intercity bus terminal and Osong station (one hour).

Songnisan National Park

☎043

The **Songnisan National Park** (속리산국립공원; ☎043 542 5267; http://english.knps.or.kr; adult/youth/child ₩4000/2000/1000; ⏲6am-7pm) has easy hikes and year-round beauty amongst craggy cliffs. It's atmospheric and misty in winter and alive with cherry blossoms and azaleas in spring. The mountain's name has a mystical, Buddhist meaning: 'Remote from the Ordinary World Mountain'.

After passing through the temple of Beopju-sa (p301), you'll find hiking trails leading to a series of 1000m-high peaks, including the popular and relatively easy 6km climb up Munjangdae (1033m). Back in 1464 King Sejo was carried up in a palanquin; using your own feet, it's three hours up and two hours down. You can also return via Sinseondae, further south via Biro-bong or, for the truly gung-ho, push on to the highest peak Cheonhwang-bong (1058m).

When planning your trip, note that Songnisan is sometimes spelled Sokrisan.

Beopju-sa BUDDHIST SITE

(법주사; ☎043 543 3615; www.beopjusa.org; 405 Beopjusa-ro, Boeun-gun) This temple originally dates to AD 553 and lies about 1km from the entrance to Songnisan National Park. Composed of a galaxy of halls, the temple is presided over by a glittering and resplendent 33m-high gold-plated Maitreya Buddha statue – of modern construction – and a far more interesting and unique (to Korea) five-storey wooden pagoda, the Palsangjeon (팔상전), which you can enter. Other halls include the main Great Treasure Hall and myriad other side shrines, including one dedicated to a male-looking Avalokitesvara.

You will also find a weather-worn Silla-era bodhisattva statue, a lotus-shaped fountain and an enormous iron cauldron, once used for cooking for up to 3000 monks. Templestays are offered (per person ₩70,000, cash only) here, which is a splendid idea if you wish to discover more about Buddhism and the beauty of the setting. When you want to rest your feet, do so in the Chahyang tea house.

Sleeping

Eorae Motel MOTEL $

(어래모텔; ☎043 543 3882; r ₩30,000; ❄) The closest budget option to the park entrance, just before the bridge and above a restaurant of the same name. Rooms are clean and adequate, if simple, with wood laminate floors and *ondol* (heated-floor) rooms available. Some have mountain views.

★**Birosanjang** GUESTHOUSE $$

(비로산장; ☎043 543 4782; r without bathroom ₩50,000 to ₩80,000) If only every national park had this – a homey, delightful *yeogwan* (small family-run hotel) beside a gurgling river in the middle of the park. There's nothing fancy, just nine *ondol* (heated-floor) rooms. It's on the trail between Beopju-sa and Sinseon-dae, so don't lug a heavy backpack in. The local police station will help keep your luggage. Reservations recommended. Try the refreshing *makgeolli* (fermented rice wine).

Lake Hills Hotel Songnisan HOTEL $$$

(레이크힐스호텔속리산; ☎043 542 5281; www.lakehills.co.kr; r ₩150,000; ❄📶) This is the smartest hotel in the area, near the park entrance and run by helpful and efficient staff. Rooms are perfectly adequate and comfortable, with balconies; rooms at the rear face the woods. There's a restaurant and a supermarket here as well.

Songnisan National Park

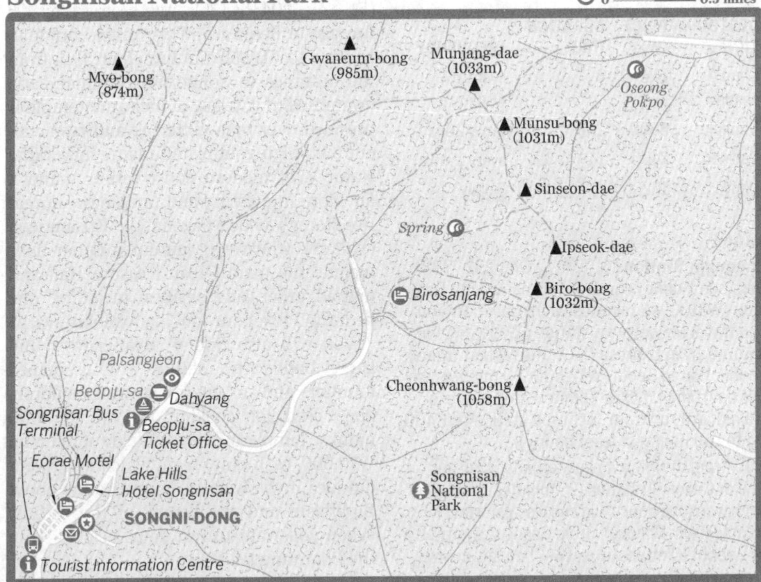

Low-season prices usually dip to around ₩80,000 for a double, making this a very good value choice.

Drinking & Nightlife

Dahyang TEAHOUSE
(다향; coffee from ₩4000; 10am-6pm, shorter hours in winter;) Near the entrance to Beopju-sa, this delightful teahouse is adorned with Buddhist pictures and immersed in tranquillity. Sit down for an Americano, a latte, a chrysanthemum tea, a Job's tears tea or a jujube tea, and *relax*. Look for the name in *hanja* on the sign: 茶香.

Information

There is a **tourist information centre** (043 542 5267; Beopjusa-ro; 9am-6pm) diagonally across the road from the bus terminal. The **Beopju-sa ticket office** (043 543 3615; Beopjusa-ro) also provides information.

Getting There & Away

Buses leave Cheongju's intercity bus terminal (₩8600, two hours, every 30 minutes) for **Songnisan Bus Terminal** (속리산터미널; Beopjusa-ro). There are also direct buses to the park from Dong-Seoul (₩16,300 to ₩16,900, 3½ hours) and Daejeon (₩7900, 1¾ hours), or via Cheongju from Seoul Gangnam (₩16,300, four hours).

Note that Songnisan is sometimes spelled Sokrisan. When buying tickets for your return journey, you may need to use the ticket machines if there's no one in the ticket office, but there is usually someone there to help. If arriving during a festival such as Buddha's Birthday, prepare for big crowds and the possibility of standing on the bus the whole way.

Chungju

043 / POP 202,000

Chungju (충주) might be the town where UN Secretary-General Ban Ki-moon grew up, but there are really only three reasons to come to here: to get the bus to the Chungju-ho ferries or Woraksan National Park, because you really, *really* like apples (there's an Apple Festival every October), or to attend the **World Martial Arts Festival** (043 852 7955; www.martialarts.or.kr).

Every year, between August and October, Chungju hosts a week-long World Martial Arts Festival, alongside a cultural festival with food stalls, music and dance. More than 2000 martial-arts exponents from 30 countries come to demonstrate their amazing and varied skills.

It's a chance to see both traditional Korean martial arts, such as *hapkido* and *taekyeon*, and a slew of snappy moves such

as Chinese *wushu*, Malaysian *silat*, Brazilian *capoeira*, Indian *kalan* and Uzbekistan *kurash*.

If you find yourself in need of a bed in Chungju, the **Titanic** (타이타닉모텔; ☎043 842 5858; 168-2 Bongbang-dong; r from ₩30,000; ❄@) has decent, if dated, rooms with all the usual love-motel trimmings. Look for the *Titanic* movie poster outside on the white, castle-inspired building.

Getting There & Away

BUS

The **bus terminal** (충주 버스 터미널; Bonggye 1-gil) is centrally located, around 1km from the train station.

Departures from Chungju

DESTINATION	PRICE (₩)	DURATION (HR)	FREQUENCY
Busan	29,000	4½	5 daily
Cheongju	8800	2	every 20min
Daejeon	10,100	2½	hourly
Danyang	8500	1¾	8 daily
Dong-Seoul	7800-10,900	2	every 20min
Gyeongju	25,600	5	2 daily

TRAIN

Chungju receives only one direct (evening) train from Seoul (₩13,400, 2½ hours). Alternatively, take a train from Seoul to Jochiwon station (조치원역; ₩8400 to ₩12,500, 1½ hours, every 30 minutes) and change for Chungju (₩5200, 70 minutes, eight daily).

Chungju-ho

Man-made Chungju-ho (충주호; Chungju Lake) is the largest lake in the country, formed when the valleys around Chungju were flooded after the construction of the Chungju Dam, which was completed in 1985. It's a highly scenic area, with mountains rising above the placid waters, including vistas of Woraksan National Park (p304). The lake is accessed by ferry on cruises that mostly leave from the Chungju Dam ferry terminal.

Sights & Activities

Cheongpung Cultural Heritage Complex HISTORIC SITE

(청풍문화재단지; ☎043 641 4301; Munhwajae-gil; adult/child ₩3000/1000; ⏲9am-7pm Jul-Aug, to 6pm Mar-Jun & Sep-Oct; P) When the area around here was flooded to create the Chungju dam and lake, a number of villages were submerged and the residents resettled.

In order to preserve some of the rich heritage, 43 cultural properties, several private residences and more than a thousand artefacts were relocated here from Cheongpung, a historic port during the Joseon dynasty. You can take the ferry to Cheongpung, get off and walk up the hill to the complex, or drive here over the bridge from either Chungju or Danyang.

Chungju-ho Cruise CRUISE

(☎043 851 5771; www.chungjuho.com; Jideung-ro; adult/child one way ₩17,000/8500, return ₩25,000/17,000) This cruise across the lake is a very scenic way to make your way from Chungju towards Danyang via Janghoe (or vice versa). The cruises can get very busy on weekends and in high season. There's a pre-recorded sightseeing commentary (Korean only), so it's not the most relaxing experience, though the placid scenery is beautiful.

There are numerous routes but the most popular cruise (fast boat 1½ hours, ferry 2¼ hours) is from Chungju Dam to Janghoe via Cheongpung (and in reverse); the rocky cliffs are most dramatic between the later stops. Ferries are irregular in the low season but pretty much leave every hour in summer.

Getting There & Around

Ferries ply the waters between the Chungju Dam ferry terminal and Janghoe, 30km to the east. From here, you can continue to Danyang by bus.

Ferries depart hourly in summer and every other hour in winter, though departures are subject to weather conditions, water levels and passenger volume, so ask at the tourist information centre in **Chungju** (충주관광안내소; ☎043 842 0531; Bonggye 1-gil) or Danyang (p307) before you head to the terminal.

To get to the Chungju Dam ferry terminal (충주댐 선착장) take any bus from opposite the Chungju bus terminal to City Hall (시청; seven minutes) and swap to bus 301 (₩1300, 25 minutes, six daily). A taxi will cost around ₩15,000.

Suanbo

☎043 / POP 3511

Surrounded by delightful mountain scenery, the tiny one-horse (but three-church) town of Suanbo (수안보) is known for its hot springs and has *jjimjilbang* (saunas),

restaurants and motels clustered snugly across several streets. It's not a pretty place in itself, but it's a quiet spot off-season and puts on a lovely neon light show come evening. It also makes for a very handy base for exploring Woraksan National Park. The name of the town literally means 'Fort Where the Water is Peaceful'.

Sleeping & Eating

Suanbo Sangnok Hotel HOTEL $$
(수안보상록호텔; ☎043 845 3500; www.sangnokhotel.co.kr; 22, Jujeongsan-ro; r/ste ₩130,000/240,000;) This tourist hotel is a pretty sound choice, with carpeted, smart rooms and a pond in the lobby swimming with *koi*. The hotel has an *oncheon* (hot-spring spa; nonguests/guests ₩9000/6000), a branch of Caffe Bene, and a restaurant serving both Korean and western food. If you go for the American breakfast (₩12,000), you may be put in the VIP room, possibly all by yourself.

Hanwha Resort Suanbo RESORT $$$
(한화리조트 수안보; ☎043 846 8211; www.hanwharesort.co.kr; 321-36 Suanbo-ro; r ₩362,000;) The main reason to stay at this 71-room resort is for access to its on-site hot springs, the only open-air bath in Suanbo. The pool is small but has a beautiful view over the valley. The hotel itself is clean and rooms are comfortable, with kitchenettes and living areas. The resort is closed outside the ski season. It's a short walk from town.

Sikgu KOREAN $
(식구, 食口; 23 Multang 2-gil; mains from ₩7,000) Run by a sweet Catholic woman, this restaurant serves up a delicious kimchi (pickled vegetable) stew in a clay pot, loaded with tofu and chunks of pork. There's also sausage hotpot or grilled pork belly seasoned with red chilli. Walk towards the church on the main road from Korea Post and it's over the bridge on the first major turning to your left.

Look out for the *hanja* characters 食口 in blue on a white cube on the roof.

Information

There is no ATM that takes foreign cards in Suanbo, so come armed with cash.

There's a **tourist information centre** (☎043 845 7829; ⏲9am-6pm) near the town entrance, but the staff speak very minimal English.

Getting There & Away

The most convenient way to arrive in Suanbo is on the quick and comfortable intercity bus (₩2500, 30 minutes), which leaves from platform 9 of the Chungju bus terminal (p303). Alternatively, catch bus 240, 241, 242, 243, 244, 245 or 246 (₩1300, 40 minutes, every 40 minutes) to Suanbo from in front of the Himart building a short walk to the right of the terminal as you exit. It will drop you off on the main road running through Suanbo.

Buses to Woraksan National Park (₩1400, 30 minutes, every two hours) also pass through Suanbo.

Woraksan National Park

Spread across two serene valleys, spectacular Woraksan National Park (월악산국립공원) offers fine hiking through picturesque forests, with sublime waterfalls, ancient Buddhist statues and carvings and, if you climb high enough, views that extend all the way to Chungju-ho. Worak-san (Moon Crags Mountain) is also home to the endangered long-tailed goral, a species of wild goat.

A road conveniently runs through the park; the bus that plies it stops at the villages of Mireuk-ri in the south, Deokju in the middle and Songgye-ri in the north.

Sights & Activities

The most popular of Woraksan's hiking routes starts from Deokju. A gentle path leads past Deokjusan-seong (Deokju), a late Silla-era fortress that has been partly restored, up to Deokju-sa temple. The trail continues for 1.5km to Ma-aebul (Rock-cut Buddha), a rock face with a standing bas-relief Buddha image carved out of it, then it's pretty tough going for 3.4km more to the summit of Yeong-bong (1097m). Allow about 3½ hours to get from Deokju-sa to Yeong-bong. You can also approach Yeong-bong from Songgye-ri (three hours, 4.3km).

Mireuksaji BUDDHIST SITE
This stone Buddhist temple near Mireuk-ri dates to the late Silla or early Goryeo period and contains a five-storey stone pagoda in front of a tall standing and hatted stone statue of Buddha, open to the elements as the wooden hall that housed him has long gone. A new temple stands not far away.

Deokju-sa BUDDHIST SITE
(덕주사, Deokju) This temple, near Deokjusan-seong, is a rebuilding of the orig-

Woraksan National Park

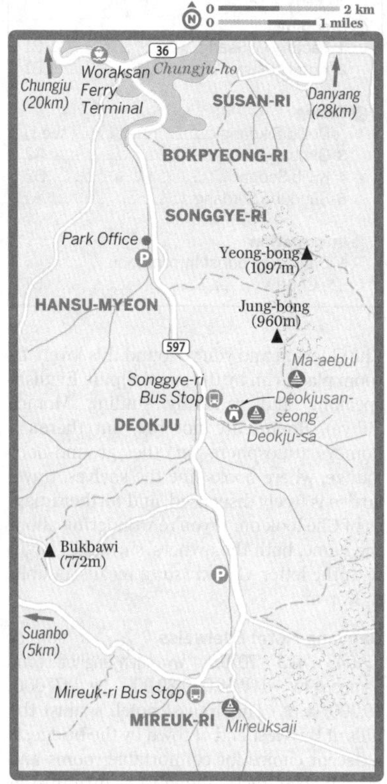

inal which was built at the end of the 6th century and stood a few kilometres distant (legend says it was established by Princess Deokju, last princess of the Silla Kingdom).

Getting There & Away

Bus 246 (₩4600, one hour, six daily) leaves from outside Chungju's bus terminal for the Mireuk-ri bus stop (미륵리). It can also be picked up on Suanbo's main street (₩1300, 30 minutes). Bus 222 (₩4600, 45 minutes, five daily) from Chungju's bus terminal goes directly to the Songgye-ri bus stop (송계리). Bus stops and place names in the park are not well signposted, so ask the bus driver to alert you for your stop.

Boats use the Woraksan Ferry Terminal for tours of Chungju-ho.

Danyang

☎043 / POP 37,000

A little gem of a resort town, Danyang (단양) is cosied right up against the mountains of Sobaeksan National Park, at a bend in the river Namhan-gang. This is small-town Korea at its most charming: you can stay at a riverfront motel and explore limestone caves, hiking trails and a one-of-a-kind Buddhist temple, basking in wooded mountain views wherever you go and paragliding down from peaks above town. It's a great place to dawdle for a couple of days and just stay put. The name of the town means 'Cinnabar Sun': indeed, when the sun goes down over the hills and the river, have your camera handy for photogenic shots.

Sights

Gosu Donggul CAVE

(고수동굴; ☎043 422 3072; adult/youth/child ₩5000/3000/2000; 9am-5.30pm Apr-Oct, to 5pm Nov-Mar) This stunning limestone cave is a rabbit warren of metal catwalks and spiral staircases running through 1.7km of dense, narrow grottoes. It's quite an intimate experience, where you can get up close with the rock formations. Unlike garishly lit caves, Gosu Donggul feels old and drippy – perhaps not as old as its 150,000 years, but certainly authentic.

Walkways are narrow, so it's definitely not for the claustrophobic.

The cave is a 15-minute walk across the Gosu bridge from Danyang, or catch bus 170 from the bus terminal.

Cross the bridge to the tourist information centre and follow the road to the right to a busy tourist village. The cave entrance is tucked away up a stone staircase behind the village. At the village you can refresh yourself with a cup (or jar) of local drinks such as *omija* (five-flavour berry), *kkul* (꿀; honey) or *ma* (마; yam).

Activities

Paragliding is big in Danyang. Prices are generally fixed at ₩80,000, plus ₩20,000 for video of your glide. Ask at Factory G. Ssang (p306) guesthouse, which is affiliated with various companies; head up to mountain-top Cafe Sann (p307), which offers paragliding, as well as coffee or contact **Dansim Mugung** (단심무궁 패러글라이딩; ☎010 9072 4553; http://cafe.daum.net/dypara).

Riverside Walkway HIKING

Head to the bridge over the river by the Danyang Hotel Edelweiss to find this 1.5km-long wooden walkway hugging the cliff-face. Time your hike either for first thing in the

Danyang

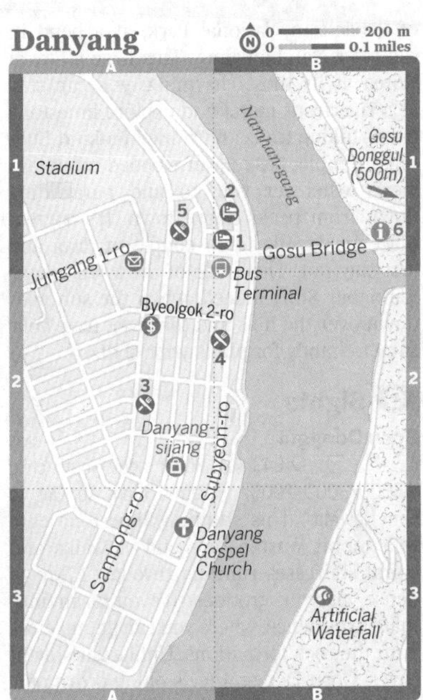

Danyang

Sleeping
1 Factory G. Ssang B1
2 Hotel Luxury B1

Eating
Doljip Sikdang .... (see 1)
3 Gimbap Heaven A2
4 Kujib Ssogari B2
5 Sundubu Sikdang A1

Information
6 Danyang Tourist Information Centre B1

morning as the sun comes up or as dusk approaches in late afternoon. It's a delightful walk with gorgeous views over the river. Keep to the right as you tramp.

Aquaworld AMUSEMENT PARK
(아쿠아월드; ☎043 420 8370; 187-17 Sambong-ro; adult/child Mon-Fri ₩29,000/22,000, Sat & Sun ₩33,000/29,000, sauna ₩10,000/8000; ⏰10am-6pm Mon-Thu, 9am-9pm Fri & Sat, 9am-7pm Sun) Swimming at this indoor water park at Daemyung Resort is a tamer option than the caving or paragliding that usually draws visitors to Danyang. You can also drop by its sauna, which has mineral baths, or jade, charcoal and amethyst saunas.

Festivals & Events

Royal Azalea Festival CULTURAL
Danyang's annual highlight is this 10-day festival in May. Hikers come to see the flowers bloom on Sobaek-san, while the riverside comes alive with concerts, fireworks, food stalls and a funfair.

Sleeping

★ Factory G. Ssang GUESTHOUSE $$
(☎010 8668 0346; s/d/tr ₩30,000/40,000/50,000) Look for the huge mural of Che Guevara and you've found this lovely 11-room place, run by the ever-helpful, English-speaking and radiantly smiling Monica (Jihye). Rooms are not big, but there's a homey atmosphere in the ground-floor lounge, where books line the shelves, travel advice is freely dispensed, and further images of Che look on. If you're wondering about the name, both the owners' surnames begin with the letter 'G' and *ssang* means 'double' in Korean.

Danyang Hotel Edelweiss HOTEL $$
(☎043 423 7070; www.danyanghotel.com; Sambong-ro; d ₩66,000-89,000, tw ₩77,000-99,000; ❄📶) This tourist hotel, against the hills at the west end of town by the bridge, is a decent choice for comfortable rooms and overall cleanliness, though the furniture in the common areas is superkitsch. Staff are generally helpful and you can jump onto any bus heading east to get into town proper.

Hotel Luxury MOTEL $$
(럭셔리 호텔; ☎043 421 9911; www.hotel-luxury.co.kr; r/ste ₩50,000/60,000; P❄@) A so-so, reasonably slick riverside love motel, with stylish rooms decorated with darkened mirrors and bold colours, but suffering from poor service. Rooms cost an extra ₩20,000 on weekends. Enter via the car park to reach reception.

Eating

Sundubu Sikdang KOREAN $
(순두부 식당; mains from ₩7000; ⏰6am-5pm) This traditional style place specialises in soft tofu, served up spicy and sizzling away in a stone pot. The trademark *sundubu* (₩7000) is delicious and needs a spoon to make its way to your mouth, though the matriarch is not a bundle of smiles. *Soju* is ₩4000.

Gimbap Heaven KOREAN $
(김밥천국; meals ₩2500-6000; ⏰6am-8pm) Scrounge up dirt-cheap eats in this small chain restaurant. There's a range of *ramyeon* (instant noodles in soup) and *udong* (thick white noodle broth), served with kimchi. It also serves pork cutlets, assorted rice dishes and of course, half-a-dozen variations of *gimbap* (Korean sushi). It has a bold red and white sign, opposite Paris Baguette, with a supermarket on the corner.

★**Doljip Sikdang** KOREAN $$
(돌집식당; meals ₩7000-15,000) This busy and very popular restaurant has private dining rooms and serves elaborate *jeongsik* (a spread of banquet dishes all served at once), with main-course options such as *suyuk* (수육; boiled beef slices) and locally grown *maneul* (마늘쌈정식; garlic wrap) or *beoseot jjigae* (버섯찌개; mushroom stew). Lighter options are *doenjang sotbap* (된장솥밥; clay-pot rice with fermented-bean paste, jujube and vegetables) or *dolsot bibimbap* (bibimbap in a stone hotpot).

Kujib Ssogari KOREAN $$$
(그집쏘가리; ☎043 423 2111; meals ₩10,000-85,000) This riverfront restaurant serves the mandarin fish *ssogari* raw (쏘가리회; *ssogari hoe*) or as a spicy soup (쏘가리매운탕; *ssogari maeuntang*). A milder option is the catfish bulgogi (메기불고기; *megi* bulgogi).

Drinking & Nightlife

Cafe Sann CAFE
(카페산; ☎010 5556 5679; https://cafesanndy.modoo.at; 196-86 Dusan-gil; ⏰9.30am-7.30pm Mon-Fri, from 8.30am Sat & Sun; 📶) With plunging views from a mountain (Du-san) 600m up on the far side of the river, this cafe pretty much has the monopoly on views in town. The cafe also offers paragliding (₩100,000) from the terrace, so once you've finished your cappuccino you can descend in breathtaking style.

Information

The **tourist office** (☎043 422 1146; ⏰9am-6pm) is inconveniently located on the far side of the bridge facing the bus terminal. Staff are helpful and speak English.

Getting There & Around

BUS

The **bus terminal** (☎043 421 8800) complex is in front of the bridge. Local buses don't have numbers, only signs (in Korean) indicating the destination at the front of the bus. Each platform of the bus terminal also has the name of the bus destination written in Korean.

Departures from Danyang

DESTINATION	PRICE (₩)	DURATION (HR)	FREQUENCY
Chungju	17,300	2	2 daily
Dong-Seoul	13,300	3½	every hour
Guin-sa	3300	½	hourly
Wonju	7200	1½	every 20min

FERRY

The closest ferry terminal for the Chungju-ho ferry is at Janghoe. After you exit the terminal, turn right at the main road and walk down for about 100m. Beside the trail entrance to Worak-san National Park is the waiting point for the bus to Danyang (₩2300, 30 minutes, 21km, every 2½ hours). It's marked with a circular red sign that reads '단양버스정류소'.

TRAIN

The train station is in old Danyang, about 3km from the main town. Eight trains run daily from Seoul's Cheongnyangni station (₩10,600 to ₩15,800, two hours); only two of the services are KTX, the others are *Mugunghwa*. A taxi into town costs ₩6000, the local bus ₩1300.

Sobaeksan National Park

☎043

The third-largest national park in South Korea, Sobaeksan National Park (소백산국립공원) encompasses daintily named Sobaek-san (Little White Mountain), one of the highest peaks in the country. The views here are quite astonishing, so get your hiking boots on and explore the landscape – try to come either in May, when the azaleas are in full bloom, or for the copper shades of autumn.

The 30-odd buildings of the stately (though largely modern) Buddhist temple complex of **Guin-sa** (구인사; ☎043 420 7425; 73 Guinsa-gil) FREE, are wedged beautifully into a valley, between steep, forested slopes. Erected on a considerable incline, the temple halls are connected with elevated walkways; you may hear monks chanting as you climb towards the opulent three-storey hall (대조사전) at the top, dedicated to the temple's founder. It's worth the short hike just for the views of the temples and mountains vanishing into the horizon. The name means 'Protect Benevolence Temple'.

Sobaeksan National Park

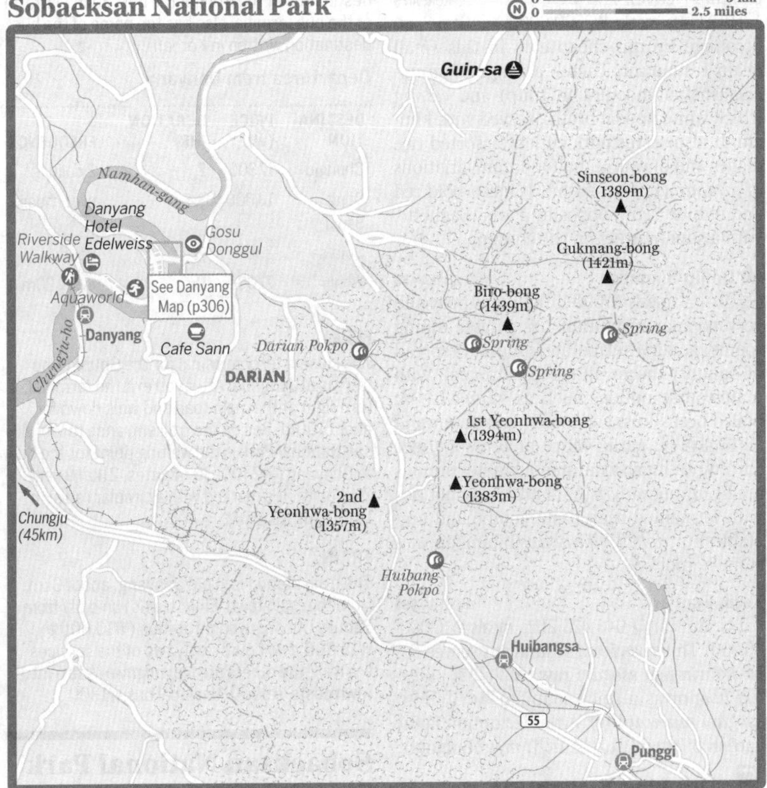

The temple is the headquarters of the Cheontae order of Korean Buddhism, which was reestablished by Sangwol Wongak in 1945. The presiding deity here is the Goddess of Mercy, who is worshipped in her namesake hall where she manifests herself in a figure of carved, pale green stone. From the main hall, it's a further steep climb up stone and concrete steps through the trees for 30 minutes to the founder's tomb atop the hill, where you will also find the One Mind/Heart Pine Tree (一心松); be quiet and respectful if hiking up here as many monks and nuns make the climb on a regular basis. Continue along the dirt path – watching out for the tree roots – to come upon a magnificent view of the hills and valleys beyond.

The communal kitchen serves free vegetarian meals (6am to 7.30am, 11.30am to 1.30pm and 6.30pm to 9.30pm). Leave a donation if you wish, to show your gratitude: it will be well received. There is a popular templestay here if you'd like to immerse yourself in quietude and the mysteries of the Buddhist way.

There's also a delightful and very handy *minbak* (private homes with rooms for rent) village at Darian; they are spread out so it doesn't feel too crowded or noisy. Rooms cost from ₩40,000, and campsites are also available (₩12,000). There's another campsite (₩2000) at Samga; take the bus (₩1300, every 30 minutes) heading to Yeongju (영주).

Getting There & Away

Buses (₩1300, 10 minutes, hourly) leave from the stop outside Danyang's bus terminal for Darian (다리안). Direct buses to Guin-sa (₩3300, 30 minutes, hourly) head from Danyang's bus terminal to the temple entrance. It's hardly worth getting out at the tourist village (the penultimate stop) for the hourly free shuttle bus, as it only shuttles you a short distance to the centre of Guin-sa. From Guin-sa, there are hourly buses to Dong-Seoul (₩16,700, three hours).

North Korea

POP 24.6 MILLION

Includes ➡

Why Go?

There is quite simply nowhere on earth like North Korea. Now on its third hereditary ruler, this nominally communist state has defied all expectations and survived the collapse of the Soviet Union to become a nuclear power. A visit to North Korea offers a glimpse of the world's most isolated nation, where the internet and much of the 21st century remain relatively unknown, and millions live their lives in the shadow of an all-encompassing personality cult.

The compromises required to travel here are significant. You'll be accompanied by two state-employed guides at all times and hear a one-sided account of history while being bussed from sight to sight. Those who can't accept this might be better off staying away – but those who can will undertake a fascinating journey into another, unsettling world.

Best Places to Eat

- ➡ Pyongyang Number One Duck Barbeque (p317)
- ➡ Lamb Barbecue Restaurant (p317)
- ➡ Chongryu Hotpot Restaurant (p317)
- ➡ Italian Restaurant (p317)
- ➡ Okryu (p317)

Best Places to Stay

- ➡ Minsok Folk Hotel (p319)
- ➡ Masik-Ryong Hotel (p320)
- ➡ Yanggakdo Hotel (p316)
- ➡ Imperial Hotel (p324)

When to Go

Pyongyang

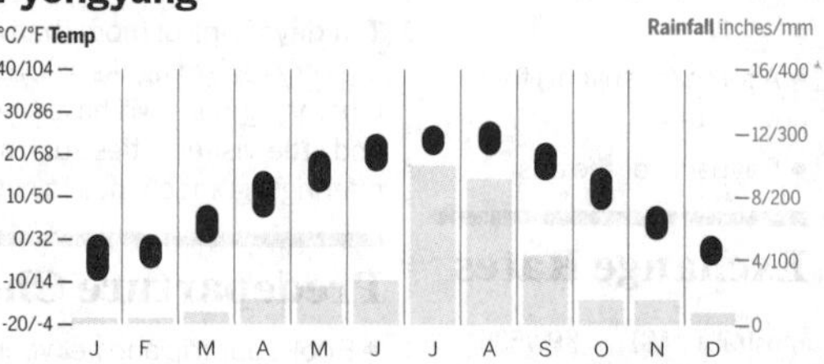

Feb Annual celebrations to mark the birth of Kim Jong-il get underway.

Apr Clear skies and the 15 April national holiday make this a great time to visit.

Sep & Oct These months offer some of the best travel conditions, as well as Pyongyang's Mass Games.

Fast Facts

Area 120,540 sq km

Capital Pyongyang

Connectivity North Korea's country code is 850. The only way to get online or use your phone is to purchase a local SIM card.

Time: GMT/UTC plus nine hours

AT A GLANCE

- Locals use North Korean won (KPW) but travellers must use Chinese RMB, euros or US dollars.
- The local language is Korean.
- Visas are needed by everyone and are normally issued the day before you travel by the North Korean embassy in Běijīng. Individual visas can usually be issued at any North Korean embassy around the world

What to Take

- Cash for tips, drinks and souvenirs
- Small change in $, € or ¥
- Asian two-pin plug adaptor
- A torch (flashlight) for power cuts
- Daypack for the bus

Exchange Rates

Australia	A$1	KPW685
China	¥1	KPW140
Euro zone	€1	KPW1055
Japan	¥100	KPW820
UK	UK£1	KPW1205
USA	US$1	KPW900

Tours

North Korean tours are all ultimately arranged by the national travel agency, Korean International Travel Company (KITC), though they are best purchased through international agencies specialising in travel to the Democratic People's Republic of Korea (DPRK). Specialists include the following:

Regent Holidays (☎+44 2037-335-294; www.regent-holidays.co.uk) In UK.

Young Pioneer Tours (www.youngpioneertours.com) In China.

Lupine Travel (☎+44 1942-497209; www.lupinetravel.co.uk) In UK.

New Korea Tours (☎+1 203-613-5283; www.newkoreatours.com) In US.

KTG Tours (☎+86 24-2284 3816; www.north-korea-travel.com) In China.

Koryo Tours (p333) In China.

Juche Travel Services (p333) In UK.

SET YOUR BUDGET

The cost of a trip to North Korea is considerable. Visitors have to pay to hire their guides and for food and hotels in advance as part of an all-inclusive tour. The only real way to cut costs is to join a large group and share the expenses between many travellers. It's difficult to travel to North Korea for much less than €1000 per person for five days, though competition between the various Běijīng-based travel agencies is currently fierce.

Itineraries

Five days The standard tour of North Korea gives you a couple of days visiting the extraordinary monuments of Pyongyang, a day trip to Kaesong and the Demilitarized Zone (DMZ) and sometimes a visit to the mountains at Myohyangsan.

Ten days Trips of more than a week can be exhausting, but are very rewarding. As well as doing everything in the five-day itinerary, groups will have the opportunity to visit truly remote and little-visited cities such as Nampo, Wonsan or Hamhung, offering a great chance to get closer to real life in North Korea.

Predeparture Checklist

- Book your trip and get your visa through a travel agency
- Download LP's Korea e-book to your tablet/smartphone (hard copies will be confiscated)
- Buy travel insurance that covers North Korea
- Apply for a dual-entry Chinese visa if needed. See Visas (p333)

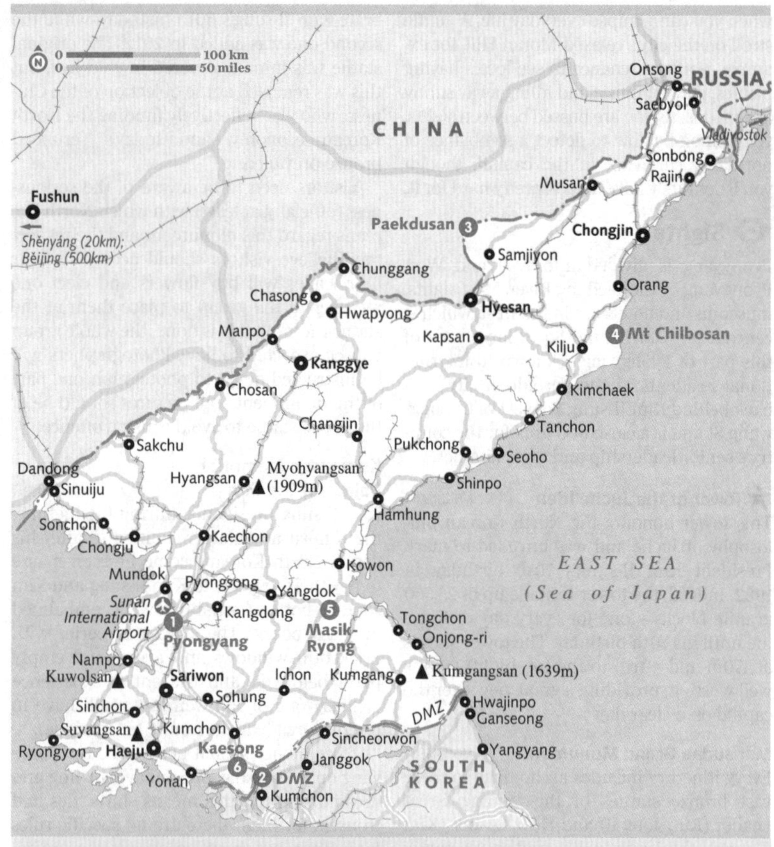

North Korea Highlights

1. **Pyongyang** (p311) Marvelling at the architecture, monuments and general totalitarian weirdness of North Korea's showcase capital city.
2. **DMZ** (p319) Experiencing the full force of Cold War tensions during a visit to Panmunjom in the Demilitarized Zone, where an uneasy armistice holds.
3. **Paekdusan** (p322) Exploring the remote far north and Korea's highest peak, famous crater lake and holy mountain, Mt Paekdu.
4. **Mt Chilbosan** (p323) Enjoying pristine mountain walks and some lovely beaches along the coast around this gorgeous and little-visited corner of the country.
5. **Masik-Ryong** (p320) Skiing down the mountainside at North Korea's showcase winter resort just outside Wonsan.
6. **Kaesong** (p318) Discovering no fewer than 12 Unesco World Heritage sites in this ancient Korean city just a short drive from South Korea.

PYONGYANG

☎02 / POP 3.25 MILLION

An ideological statement forged in concrete, bronze and marble, Pyongyang (평양, Flat Land) is the ultimate totalitarian metropolis, built almost entirely from scratch following its destruction in the Korean War. Every visit to North Korea focuses heavily and enthusiastically on the capital's monuments, towers, statues and buildings that glorify Kim Il-sung, Kim Jong-il and the Juche philosophy (North Korea's founding philosophy of self-reliance and self-determination).

While these bombastic statement pieces are all impressive, the real delights of Pyongyang are to be had in the quieter moments

when you can glimpse everyday life. A gentle stroll on the city's relaxed Moran Hill, for example, is a great chance to see locals having picnics, playing music and idling away sunny afternoons. As you are bussed between sights, you'll often be able to detect a semblance of normality surviving in the capital, though you'll definitely have to look pretty hard for it.

Sights

Pyongyang is divided into East and West Pyongyang by the Taedong River. Most sights, museums and hotels are in the west, which is centred on Kim Il-sung Sq. A large area of this part of Pyongyang – known to international residents as the 'forbidden city' – is back behind Kim Il-sung Sq west of Changgwang St and is a closed-off area for the country's senior leadership and their families.

★Tower of the Juche Idea MONUMENT

This tower honours the North Korean philosophy of Juche and was unveiled to mark President Kim Il-sung's 70th birthday in 1982. Indeed, the tower is made up of 25,550 granite blocks – one for every day of Kim's life until his 70th birthday. The tower stands at 170m and a trip to the top by lift (€5) is well worth it, providing a great view over the capital on a clear day.

Mansudae Grand Monument MONUMENT

Every itinerary includes an homage to these vast bronze statues of the smiling Great Leader (Kim Jong-il) and Dear Leader (Kim Il-sung), the latter in his trademark parka. The first statue was unveiled in 1972 to celebrate Kim Il-sung's 60th birthday, while the second one was added in 2012. The original statue was initially covered in gold leaf, but this was removed at the objection of the Chinese, who were effectively funding the North Korean economy, and today's scrubbed bronze prevailed.

Visitors need to be aware of the seriousness (officially, at least) with which North Koreans regard this monument and the respect they believe visitors should accord it. Your tour leader will buy flowers and elect one member of the group to place them at the statues' feet. As this is done, the whole group will be expected to bow. Photographers will be instructed never to photograph one part of the monument – all pictures should be of the entire statue to avoid causing offence.

Kumsusan Memorial Palace of the Sun MONUMENT

Kim Il-sung's residence during his lifetime, the Kumsusan Palace remained so after his death. North Koreans come here en masse to pay their respects to Kim Il-sung and Kim Jong-il, both of whom now lie embalmed in glass boxes. The palace is eerie, with bricked-in windows and a vast and empty plaza before it, and the entire experience is easily one of the weirdest you'll have in North Korea (which is quite an accolade).

To come here you'll need to be in Pyongyang on a Thursday or Sunday morning and dressed smartly (this means shirts, ties and trousers for men; there are no specific rules for women, but shorts or low-cut tops are no-go). You'll have to go through airport-style

CHILDREN & TOUR GROUPS

Children, who are generally doted upon in North Korean society, feature frequently on tours of the country, and trips to the Democratic People's Republic of Korea (DPRK; North Korea) will involve seeing schoolchildren perform musical or dance routines and will sometimes include visits to kindergartens or schools. Lonely Planet does not endorse these as there is simply no way to tell how voluntary the children's participation in such events is and under what circumstances they train for the shows. If you're uncomfortable with seeing children perform under such conditions, talk to your tour leader, who will be able to talk to the guides and arrange for you to skip parts of the itinerary featuring children. This particularly applies to events in which tour groups interact with children; in some cases we've seen tourists being encouraged to pick up and pose for photos with infants, something that would not be considered acceptable in most countries today.

It's also worth considering the fact that the Mass Games (p318), the enormous gymnastic-dance-propaganda displays that take place annually in Pyongyang during the late summer, are essentially a performance by children as young as five years old. Lonely Planet makes no claim that these children are being mistreated, but wants to encourage visitors to North Korea to think through these issues and be aware of their contentious nature before attending such events.

security – you're allowed to take nothing with you – and pass along kilometres of slow red moving sidewalks and then be dusted off by both automatic shoe cleaners and a giant clothes-dusting machine to ensure no dirt is trampled into either viewing hall. Items on display include the train carriage where Kim Jong-il died, the Dear Leader's boat and a collection of his medals and cars.

Triumphal Arch MONUMENT

Your guides will tell you proudly that the Triumphal Arch is 6m higher than its cousin in Paris, making it the largest of its kind in the world. The arch marks the site where Kim Il-sung first addressed the liberated Koreans after the end of Japanese occupation in 1945. The translation you hear will omit the fact that the Soviets liberated Pyongyang, not the partisans, who themselves gave full credit to the Soviets at the time.

Kim Il-sung Square SQUARE

Pyongyang's central square is where North Korea's massive military parades normally take place. The plaza is ringed by austere-looking buildings: most impressive of these is the Grand People's Study House, the country's largest library. Other buildings on the square include the Korean National Art Gallery and the Korean Central History Museum. There's a great view from the riverbank across the Taedong to the Tower of the Juche Idea.

Victorious Fatherland Liberation War Museum MUSEUM

Perhaps the most interesting museum in Pyongyang, this mouthful of an institution opened its current home in 2013 to mark the 60th anniversary of the end of the Korean War. Outside you'll see war-damaged tanks, weapons and aircraft used by both sides in the conflict, while inside there are dozens of exhibits and a 360-degree diorama of the Battle of Daejon. In the foyer look out for the statue of a young Kim Il-sung; his grandson looks exactly like him.

Monument to the Foundation of the Workers' Party MONUMENT

This startlingly bombastic monument has starred on the cover of more books about North Korea than almost any other. The three hands portrayed represent the worker (holding a hammer), the peasant (holding a scythe) and the intellectual (holding a writing brush). It's an enjoyable visit, not least because you're in the middle of the city and curious locals often pass by.

Ryugyong Hotel LANDMARK

Three decades after construction began on this extraordinary hotel in 1987, it still has not been completed. Planned as a prestige project but abandoned following the collapse of the USSR, its haunting skeleton sat on the Pyongyang skyline for years as an unavoidable symbol of North Korea's economic failure. In 2008 work began on the hotel again when it was clad in glass, and so while it looks far better than before, it sadly remains empty inside and cannot be visited.

Chollima Statue MONUMENT

This impressive statue portrays Chollima, the Korean Pegasus. It's an interesting example of how the North Korean state has incorporated traditional Korean myths into its cult. According to legend, Chollima could cover hundreds of kilometres a day and was untameable. Kim Il-sung appropriated the myth in the period of reconstruction following the Korean War – so that the zeal of the North Korean workers to rebuild their shattered nation and construct monuments to the leadership became known as 'Chollima Speed'.

Moran Hill PARK

This is Pyongyang's top recreation ground: couples wander, families picnic and there are people playing guitars and sometimes even dancing in an incongruously relaxed area of the capital. It's particularly busy on a Sunday and a lovely place to stroll and absorb something of daily life away from politics and propaganda.

Korean Revolution Museum MUSEUM

Despite the museum's rather misleading name, its main function is to document the death of Kim Il-sung (including a film of the extraordinary public reaction to it) and the succession of Kim Jong-il during the turbulent 1990s. One of the more bizarre items on display is a tin of Nivea hand cream that the Dear Leader thoughtfully gifted to factory workers with sore hands. There is also a display of the various Kim regime loyalty badges worn by locals.

Party Founding Museum MUSEUM

Located on the southern slope of Haebang Hill is this museum that originally housed the Central Committee of the Korean Workers' Party, as well as Kim Il-sung's office, from where he 'led the building of a new democratic Korea'. Next door is the Great Leader's conspicuously modest residence,

Pyongyang

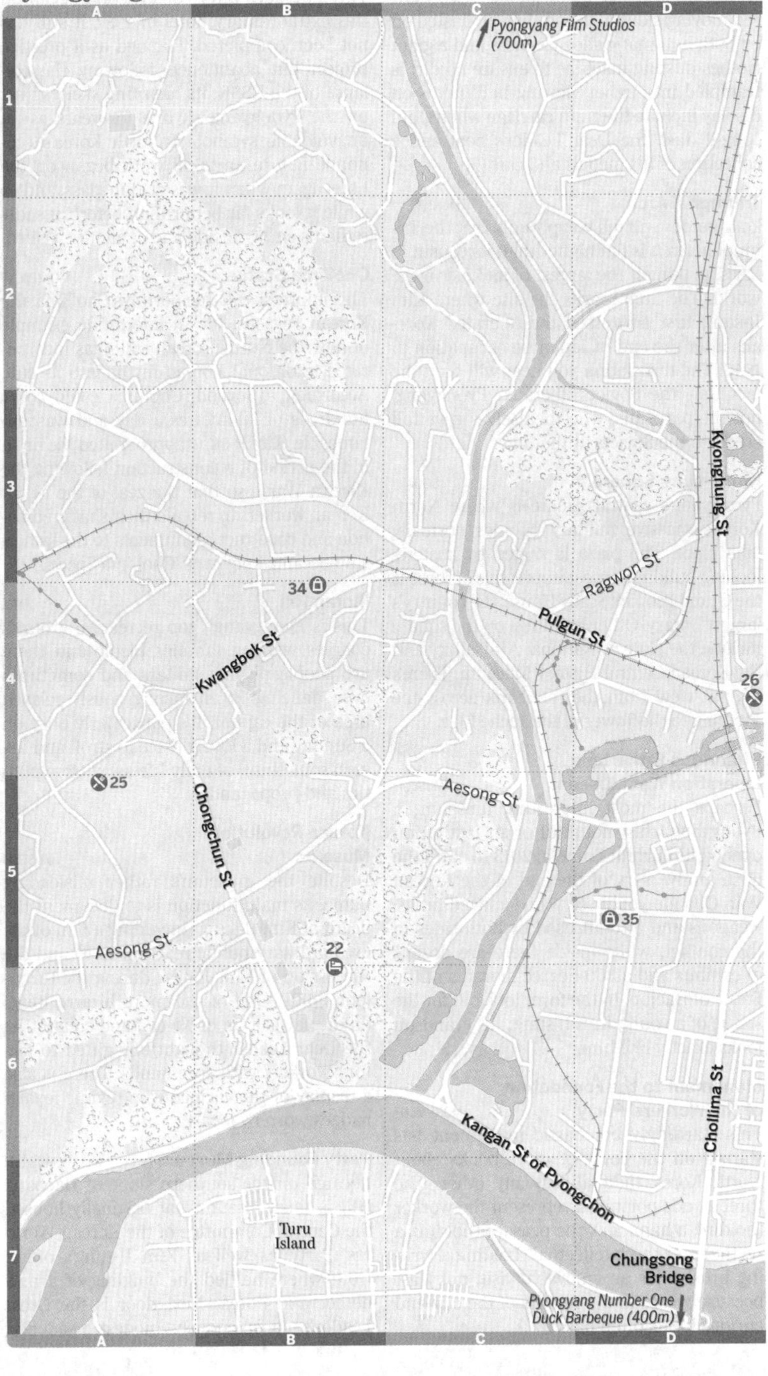

A B C D

1 2 3 4 5 6 7

Pyongyang Film Studios (700m)

Kyonghung St

Ragwon St

Pulgun St

34

Kwangbok St

26

25

Aesong St

Chongchun St

35

Aesong St

22

Chollima St

Kangan St of Pyongchon

Turu Island

Chungsong Bridge

Pyongyang Number One Duck Barbeque (400m)

A B C D

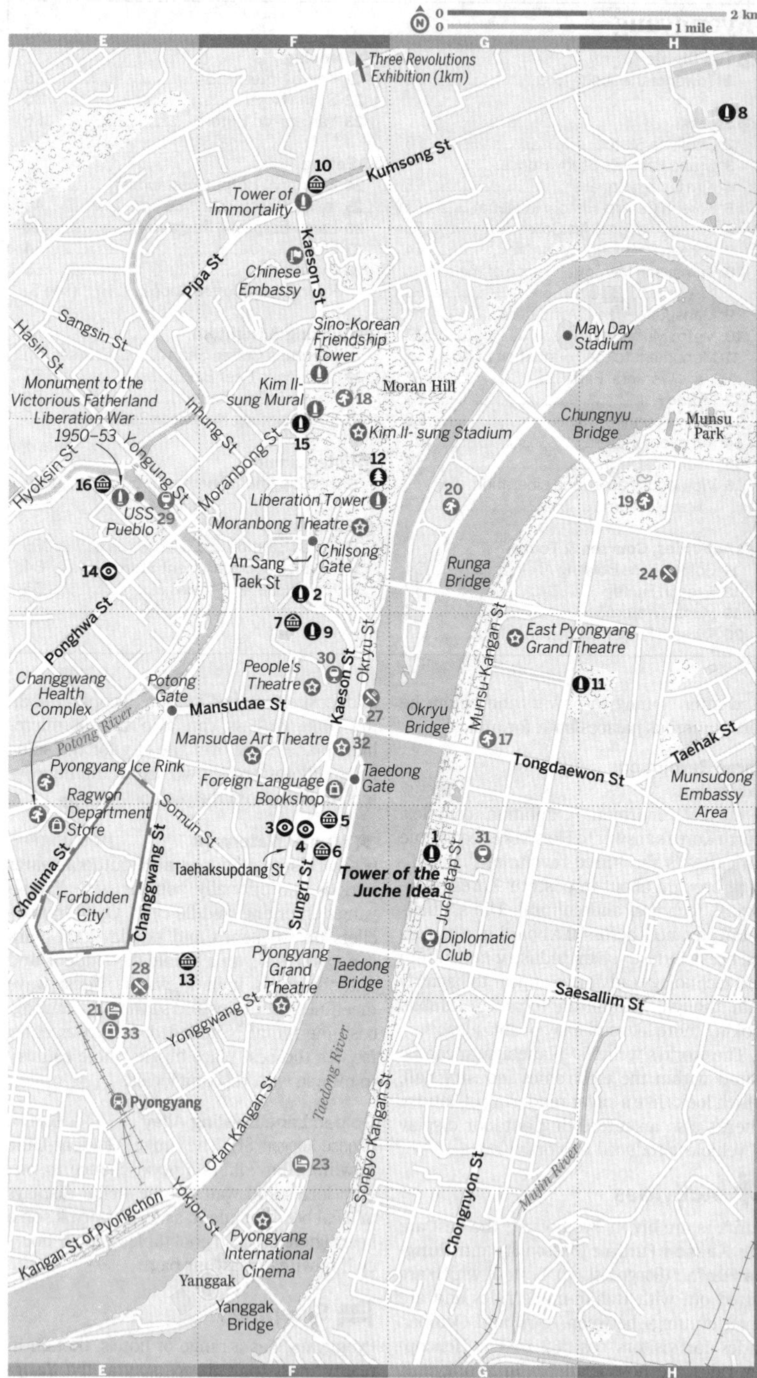

0 2 km
0 1 mile
Three Revolutions Exhibition (1km)
Kumsong St
Tower of Immortality
Kaeson St
Chinese Embassy
Pipa St
Sangsin St
Hasin St
Sino-Korean Friendship Tower
May Day Stadium
Monument to the Victorious Fatherland Liberation War 1950–53
Kim Il-sung Mural
Moran Hill
Inhung St
Moranbong St
Kim Il- sung Stadium
Chungnyu Bridge
Munsu Park
Hyoksin St
Yongung St
Liberation Tower
USS Pueblo
Moranbong Theatre
Chilsong Gate
An Sang Taek St
Runga Bridge
Ponghwa St
Okryu St
Munsu-Kangan St
East Pyongyang Grand Theatre
People's Theatre
Changgwang Health Complex
Potong Gate
Mansudae St
Okryu Bridge
Potong River
Mansudae Art Theatre
Tongdaewon St
Taehak St
Munsudong Embassy Area
Pyongyang Ice Rink
Foreign Language Bookshop
Taedong Gate
Ragwon Department Store
Somun St
Changgwang St
Chollima St
Taehaksupdang St
Sungri St
Tower of the Juche Idea
Juchetap St
'Forbidden City'
Diplomatic Club
Pyongyang Grand Theatre
Taedong Bridge
Saesallim St
Yonggwang St
Taedong River
Pyongyang
Otan Kangan St
Songyo Kangan St
Chongnyon St
Mujin River
Yokjon St
Kangan St of Pyongchon
Pyongyang International Cinema
Yanggak
Yanggak Bridge

Pyongyang

Top Sights
1 Tower of the Juche Idea G5

Sights
2 Chollima Statue F3
3 Grand People's Study House F5
4 Kim Il-sung Square F5
5 Korean Central History Museum F5
6 Korean National Art Gallery F5
7 Korean Revolution Museum F4
8 Kumsusan Memorial Palace of the Sun H1
9 Mansudae Grand Monument F4
10 Metro Museum F1
11 Monument to the Foundation of the Workers' Party H4
12 Moran Hill F3
13 Party Founding Museum E5
14 Ryugyong Hotel E3
15 Triumphal Arch F3
16 Victorious Fatherland Liberation War Museum E3

Activities, Courses & Tours
17 Golden Lane Bowling Alley G4
18 Kaeson Funfair F2
19 Munsu Waterpark H3
20 Rungna Funfair G3

Sleeping
21 Koryo Hotel E6
22 Sosan Hotel B6
23 Yanggakdo Hotel F6

Eating
24 Chongryu Hotpot Restaurant H3
25 Italian Restaurant A5
26 Lamb Barbecue Restaurant D4
27 Okryu F4
28 Pyulmori E5
Ryongwang Coffee Shop .... (see 5)

Drinking & Nightlife
Kumrung Coffee Shop .... (see 17)
29 Mansugyo Beer Bar E3
30 Pauläner Brauhaus F4
31 Taedonggang No 3 Beer Bar G5

Entertainment
32 Taedongmun Cinema F4

Shopping
33 Korea Stamp E6
34 Kwangbok Department Store B4
35 Mansudae Art Studio D5

used after coming to power (and before he had numerous palaces built for him).

Three Revolutions Exhibition MUSEUM
A surreal, enormous exhibition complex, North Korea's answer to Florida's Epcot theme park details the 'three revolutions' Kim Il-sung brought about in postwar Korea: ideological, technical and cultural. The six halls detail advances across the board in electronics, heavy industry, light industry, agriculture and technology (advances appear to be fairly slim, though, with all the technical exhibits looking more like a display of antiques).

The world's weirdest planetarium can be found within the electronics industry hall, which looks like a silver rendering of Saturn. There's also an interesting outdoor display of vehicles produced in North Korea.

Activities

Funfairs are big in Pyongyang; the best are the **Kaeson Funfair** (Kaeson St) and **Rungna Funfair** (Rungna Island), both of which are kitted out with Italian-made rides and are open evenings between April and October. Rides for visitors cost €2 to €5. Helicopter rides are now available in Pyongyang, and cost €180 per person. People weighing 90kg or less can also take a microlight plane flight over the city for the same price. Photos are allowed from the helicopters, but not from the plane.

★ **Munsu Waterpark** AMUSEMENT PARK
(€10) This vast indoor and outdoor water park is exceptionally popular with Pyongyang's emerging middle class. Open to travellers on weekends and holidays, the park can easily take up a whole day. Indoor and outdoor pools include water slides, wave machines, fountains and saunas. Swimming-costume rental is included with your entry fee. It's the best place in the whole country to mingle with relaxing locals.

Golden Lane Bowling Alley BOWLING
(Munsu-Kangan St) The huge Golden Lane Bowling Alley offers a good chance to mix with locals and watch some stellar displays of local bowling talent, as well as drink some beer. There are also pool tables and air hockey if bowling isn't your bag.

Sleeping

Pyongyang has a range of hotels, though in reality most tour groups stay at the **Yang-**

gakdo Hotel (☎02-381 2134; Yanggak Island; ❄✉), situated in the centre of the city on its own island. Budget tours tend to stay at the **Sosan Hotel** (Chongchun St). In general visitors have little say in where they bed down.

Eating

Pyongyang has by far the best restaurants in North Korea, though that's not saying a huge amount. Most restaurants used by tour groups will be run by the Korea International Travel Company (KITC) and therefore the exclusive preserve of international visitors and the local elite. If possible, do be sure to try the local speciality of cold noodles.

★Pyongyang Number One Duck Barbeque KOREAN
Pyongyang Number One Duck Barbeque is one of the best places in town and will often be where groups go on their last evening. Here you'll be served delicious strips of duck meat you cook at your table.

★Lamb Barbecue Restaurant KOREAN
The Lamb Barbecue Restaurant has some of the friendliest and most boisterous staff in the country. Once the delicious lamb barbecue has been served at your table the waitresses will burst into song and encourage diners to dance with them.

Chongryu Hotpot Restaurant KOREAN
(Sanwon St) The Chongryu Hotpot Restaurant is nearly always on the itinerary. It's a pleasant place where you make your own hotpot dish on little individual gas stoves. There's a second branch of this restaurant housed in a boat-shaped restaurant overlooking the Potong River, by the ice-skating rink.

Italian Restaurant PIZZA
(Kwangbok St) Pyongyang's imaginatively named first pizza joint caused a sensation when it opened in 2009 after Kim Jong-il reportedly sent a team of chefs to Italy to learn how to make the perfect pizza. The results are pretty decent, although if you don't fancy pizza, there's a full range of pasta dishes, as well as the ubiquitous after-dinner karaoke.

Okryu KOREAN
Okryu, the most famous restaurant in North Korea, is a faux-traditional structure on the riverside that's famed for its cold noodles and very popular with locals. For this reason it's not usually on the schedule for groups, but you may get lucky. The restaurant is divided into a cold-noodles section and a turtle-soup section. Locals call this place 'Ongnyugwan'.

Ryongwang Coffee Shop CAFE
Right in the centre of the city, just off Kim Il-sung Sq, is this joint-venture project set up by Austrian investors in partnership with North Koreans. It's a great option for coffee and cake between sights.

Pyulmori CAFE
(Changwang St) Pyulmori is an innovative project run by a charity supplying food to local orphanages and is made up of a restaurant, coffee shop and bar. You can get decent food, coffee and excellent cake here, and in the evenings it's a popular bar and something of an expat hang-out (this being a relative term in North Korea, of course).

Drinking & Nightlife

Nightlife in Pyongyang is almost nonexistent, although hotel bars can be busy and fun, especially in the summer months, when there are plenty of tour groups in town. Diplomatic and NGO presence here means that there are some clubs too, but these are usually inaccessible to tourists. Ask your guides nicely if you'd like a night out on the town, as they'll have to accompany you on top of their already gruelling schedules.

★Kumrung Coffee Shop COFFEE
This rather-stylish place in East Pyongyang is a good place for a relaxing drink and a pastry. The low-lit space is presided over by an all-female team who pride themselves in their excellent brews. It's certainly one of the very few places in North Korea where you can get a cold-brew coffee or a real cappuccino.

★Mansugyo Beer Bar BAR
(Yongung St) This regularly visited beer bar is a great way to socialise with locals who come here in droves after work. You'll find a boisterous crowd standing around tables drinking one of seven types of locally produced beer and sharing snacks such as nuts, eggs and fish.

Taedonggang No 3 Beer Bar BAR
This bar near the Juche Tower has seven different types of beer on tap, plus cocktails and meals. It's a good chance to see how the middle-class North Koreans spend their time, and its quiet gentility is a world away from typical North Korean bars, which tend to be full of people drinking beer while standing around tables.

Pauläner Brauhaus BEER HALL
(Haemaji Shopping Centre, Sungri St) Inside the Haemaji Shopping Centre you'll find this German-run venture where beer is served up to locals and visitors to the capital. Brews are pricey here and not necessarily any better than in a normal bar, but it's unusual to be sitting in a genuine international bar in North Korea. It's popular with tour groups.

☆ Entertainment

Mass Games LIVE PERFORMANCE
(Aug-Oct) The long-running Arirang Mass Games, the story of Korea's history performed by over 100,000 incredibly well-coordinated schoolchildren, was finally retired in 2012 and a new show started at the May Day Stadium in 2018. Tickets are steeply priced – starting at €80 for a 'third-class' ticket and rising to €300 for VIP tickets.

Taedongmun Cinema CINEMA
(Sungri St) Dating from 1955, this famous cinema with a notable neoclassical facade has two screens and is considered Pyongyang's most prestigious movie theatre. If you're lucky you may be taken here to see a North Korean film, a fascinating experience as locals often shout and stamp their feet during particularly significant scenes.

Shopping

Kwangbok Department Store DEPARTMENT STORE
(Kwangbok St; Tue-Sun) Notable as the venue for Kim Jong-il's final public appearance, this multistorey department store stocks a good range of mostly imported goods, but also a good amount of local produce. You can roam freely inside, change money at the market rate and see what the middle class are spending their money on. Some great street snacks are sold in the food court on the top floor, while the ground-floor supermarket is the best stocked in the city.

Mansudae Art Studio ART
(Saemaul St) Art is another popular purchase in Pyongyang. Mansudae is a centralised art studio employing thousands of painters, embroiderers and sculptors. There's a large selection of socialist-realist art available, as well as more traditional landscape paintings.

Korea Stamp GIFTS & SOUVENIRS
(Changgwang St) Next door to the **Koryo Hotel** (02-381 4397; Changgwang St;) is Korea Stamp, a good place to buy North Korean stamps, which are generally spectacular propaganda pieces. T-shirts and postcards are also on sale.

AROUND NORTH KOREA

Kaesong

POP 338,000

Though just a few miles from the DMZ and the world's most concentrated build-up of military forces, Kaesong (개성) is a fairly relaxed place just off the Reunification Hwy from Pyongyang. The city may boast an impressive 12 Unesco World Heritage sites, but is dominated by massive statues of Kim Il-sung and Kim Jong-il atop a large hill.

Once the capital of the Koryo dynasty, Kaesong has an interesting old quarter as well as the country's most atmospheric hotel, but tours rarely spend much time here. Having seen the DMZ, you'll usually be billeted at the hotel for the night before returning to Pyongyang, although a fascinating walk through the town with your guides to the top of the hill is usually possible.

Sights

Within the city are a number of tourist sights that include the Sonjuk Bridge, a tiny clapper bridge built in 1216 and, opposite, the Songin Monument, which honours neo-Confucian hero Chong Mong-ju. There is also the Nammun, the south gate of the old walled city, which dates from the 14th century and houses an old Buddhist bell, and the Sungyang Seowon, a Confucian academy.

★ **Tomb of King Kongmin** TOMB
The 31st Koryo king, Kongmin reigned between 1352 and 1374 and his tomb is the best preserved and most elaborate in the country. It is richly decorated with traditional granite facing and statuary, including sheep statues (in honour of his Mongolian wife, whom the king was forced to marry by his Mongolian overlords) and plenty of vaguely Aztec-looking altars. It's a very secluded site, about 13km west of Kaesong, and is part of the city's Unesco World Heritage listing.

Songgyungwan Neo-Confucian College MUSEUM
This well-preserved college, originally built in AD 992 and rebuilt after being destroyed in the 1592 Japanese invasion, today hosts the Koryo Museum, which contains celadon (green-tinged) pottery and other Buddhist

relics. The buildings surround a wide courtyard dotted with ancient trees, and there are also two good souvenir shops, one selling ginseng and the other selling commemorative stamps and souvenirs. The complex is one of Kaesong's 12 Unesco World Heritage–listed sites. It's a short drive northeast of town.

Chanamsan HILL

The largest hill in Kaesong is unsurprisingly topped by two giant statues of Kim Il-sung and Kim Jong-il. Groups often walk up here to pay their respects to the leaders and for the great city views.

Sleeping

★Minsok Folk Hotel HOTEL

If you stay over in Kaesong, you'll normally be based at this wonderful hotel consisting of 20 traditional Korean *yeogwan* (small, well-equipped en suite rooms), all off small courtyards, and featuring a charming stream running through it. There's no electricity during the day, but there's usually light in the evening and hot water.

It's basic (the rice-husk pillows are distinctly hard!) but fascinating and far more atmospheric than anywhere else you'll stay in the country. There are a couple of rooms with beds for those who are infirm or have back problems – request ahead.

Nampo

POP 455,000

On the Taedong delta, 55km southwest of Pyongyang, is Nampo (남포), North Korea's most important port and centre of industry. Nampo made its name as the 'birthplace of the Chollima movement' after the workers at the local steel plant supposedly 'took the lead in bringing about an upswing in socialist construction', according to local tourist pamphlets.

Sadly there's nothing much to see in the town itself, though it makes for an interesting glimpse at provincial life. The big attraction here – according to North Korean tour guides, anyway – is the West Sea Barrage, built across an 8km estuary of the Taedong River, to solve the area's irrigation and drinking-water problems. The impressive structure, built during the early 1980s, is nevertheless a rather dull visit – in every way a classic piece of socialist tourism. There are some decent beaches about 20km from Nampo, which you may be lucky enough to visit if you come this way.

Sinchon

Small, nondescript Sinchon (신천) is often visited on trips between Nampo and Kaesong. You're here to visit the Sinchon Museum, which details the atrocities allegedly carried out here against civilians by the US during the Korean War. That atrocities were committed here and in other places is not in question (both sides frequently violated the Geneva Convention), but the typically hyperbolic portrayal of these sad events does little to restore the dignity of those who suffered.

Since a new building opened in 2015, the depictions of the purported American crimes have become even more gruesomely far-fetched and a new 'revenge-pledging place' has been added to the mix – here North Korean groups angrily pledge vengeance for supposed US war crimes.

On arrival you'll be given an anti-American lecture, followed by a tour of various exhibits depicting the extraordinary, elaborate American brutality – the outlandishness of the presentation here arguably only serves to undermine the real suffering that occurred.

Following the museum, the standard tour includes laying a wreath at a memorial next door and then travelling to the site of two barns, where mothers and children were allegedly burned alive by the US army.

There is no hotel in Sinchon, but from here it's a three-hour drive to Kaesong, or it's possible to stay at the 8th March Hotel in the nearby small town of Sariwon.

Panmunjom & the DMZ

The sad sight of a divided nation remains one of the most poignant aspects of any trip to North Korea. Even if you're just in North Korea for a couple of days, almost every tour includes a trip to the DMZ (Panmunjom). Seeing the situation from the North – facing off against US and South Korean troops to the south – is a unique chance to witness things from an alternative perspective.

The eerily quiet drive from Pyongyang down the six-lane Reunification Hwy – the road is deserted save for military checkpoints – gives you a sense of what to expect. Just before you exit to the DMZ, the sign saying 'Seoul 70km' is a reminder of just how close and yet how far normality is.

There are several aspects to a DMZ visit. Your first stop will be at a Korean People's Army (KPA) post just outside the DMZ. Here

a soldier will show you a model of the entire site, pointing out South Korean as well as North Korean headquarters and watchtowers. Then you'll be marched (single file!) through an antitank barrier to rejoin your bus, and you'll be driven down a long concrete corridor. Look out for the tank traps either side – huge slabs of concrete ready to be dropped into the road at any minute in the event of a land invasion.

The next stop is the Armistice Talks Hall, about 1km into the DMZ. Here negotiations were held between the two sides from 1951 until the final armistice, which was signed here on 27 July 1953. You'll see two copies of the agreement on display in glass cases, along with the original North Korean and UN flags. Next door there's an exhibition of photos from the war. Outside, a plaque in red script best sums up the North Korean version of the ceasefire. It reads: 'It was here on July 27, 1953 that the American imperialists got down on their knees before the heroic Chosun people to sign the ceasefire for the war they had provoked June 25, 1950.'

From here you'll reboard the bus and drive to the Demarcation Line itself, and you'll be reminded in more than usually severe language about sticking together 'for your own safety'. The site consists of two sinister-looking headquarters staring at each other across the line (the North Korean one is built to be the bigger of the two) and several huts built over the line for meetings. Amazingly, you can cross a few metres into South Korea within the huts, but the doors out to the south are closed and guarded by two soldiers.

Being at the centre of the biggest military face-off on earth is rather like being in the eye of a storm – tension is in the air, but it appears so peaceful that it makes the very idea of imminent combat seem ridiculous. South Korean and American soldiers eyeball their northern counterparts as they have done every day since 1953. Do not be fooled by the prevailing air of calm, though: any attempt to even approach the border will result in your being shot at, possibly from both sides. In the 1980s, however, a Soviet tourist found a unique way to flee the communist bloc, defecting amid gunfire from both sides. In recent years, North Korean soldiers have made the dash successfully in 2012, 2015, 2016 and 2017.

The other interesting sight at the DMZ is the Concrete Wall, a US-constructed antitank barrier that runs the length of the 248km border. It has been hijacked as an emotive propaganda weapon by the North, which since 1989 has been comparing it with the Berlin Wall. Indeed, the issue has proved an emotive one in the South as well, where students have demanded it be dismantled. You will inspect the wall with binoculars and be shown a particularly bizarre North Korean propaganda video.

Wonsan

POP 300,000

This port city on the East Sea is not a big tourist draw, but makes for an interesting stop en route to Kumgang Region from Pyongyang. Wonsan (원산) is an important port, a centre of learning with 10 universities and a popular holiday resort for North Koreans, with lovely sandy beaches at nearby Lake Sijung and Lake Tongjong. Kim Jong-un is known to have a house on the peninsula here, where Dennis Rodman visited him in 2013.

Just outside Wonsan is the Masik-Ryong Ski Resort, a pet project of Kim Jong-un that was completed in record time by the army in 2016. With several runs (one over 5km long), bunny slopes, skidoos, skating and the very impressive and luxurious **Masik-Ryong Hotel** (@ 🏊), this is truly unlike anything else in North Korea.

In the nonwinter months it's possible to visit the area to stay in the hotel, but the real highlight is hitting the powder with locals. Access to the slopes costs US$40 per day; all equipment, including snowboards, can be rented.

Hamhung

North Korea's massively industrial second city, Hamhung (함흥) has been open to tour groups since 2012 and is a fascinating place to get a look at a real North Korean city, far away from the glittering capital. Here, locals will look astounded to see you and you'll almost certainly be the only foreigners in town. Tours of Hamhung generally include visiting a fertiliser factory, the city's main theatre and a nearby collective farm.

Bucolic it isn't, however, with suburbs made up of factory after factory and bad air pollution from all the industry. But even by North Korean standards, this is definitely getting off the beaten path.

Some way outside of Hamhung is the Tongbong Cooperative Farm, which produces mainly rice. While you're unlikely to see any

actual farming (except from a distance), you'll visit a kindergarten and a gift shop and see the inside of a collective-farm worker's home. This is the best farm to visit in the country, with an impressive collection of tractors.

The kindergarten visit is optional and involves attending a classroom where children are learning from a teacher, and then a chat with the teacher while the children play outside. It is important to note that the welfare of the children is impossible to verify and travellers should be very mindful when choosing whether to participate in activities that involve minors.

There are two hotels where visitors are normally put up: the Sin Hung San Hotel, centrally located on Hamhung's main thoroughfare, and the more comfortable Majon Beach Guesthouse, some way out of town. The latter is far more commonly used.

Myohyangsan

A trip to this pretty resort area, just 150km north of Pyongyang, provides a chance to experience the pristine North Korean countryside, along with an inevitable slice of personality cult. Myohyangsan (묘향산) means 'Mountain of Mysterious Fragrance' and it's certainly no misnomer. The scenery is quite wonderful and in summer the area is awash with flowers. The nearby Sangwon Valley is the most common place for a hike.

Sights

★International Friendship Exhibition MUSEUM

This exhibition hosts a massive display of gifts given to Kim Il-sung, Kim Jong-il and Kim Jong-un. Housed in a mountainside vault that is vaguely reminiscent of a Bond villain's hideout, on display is everything from Kim family transportation to glassware and wax figurines.

A member of your group may be honoured with the task of opening the vast doors that lead into the exhibit – after putting on ceremonial gloves to protect the polished doorknob, naturally.

Kim Il-sung's gifts are very impressive. Particularly noteworthy is the beautiful armoured train carriage presented to him by Mao Zedong and a limousine sent by that great man of the people, Josef Stalin. The exhibits are arranged geographically, although you will thankfully only be shown the highlights of the 100,000-plus gifts that are spread over 120 rooms. Gifts from heads of state are displayed on red cloth, those from

IS NORTH KOREA SAFE?

The Democratic People's Republic of Korea (DPRK; North Korea) is a police state with a human-rights record that is considered among the worst on earth. Concentration camps, executions, state-orchestrated terror and mass control by a vast propaganda machine are a daily reality for millions here. The revenue from your trip will go entirely to the state, and given the cost of just one traveller's tour, this totals a sizeable amount. So should you visit, and is it morally acceptable to do so?

The case against is strong. On the other hand, those who argue that you should visit point out that tourism is one of the few ways of encouraging openness in the DPRK, of letting people see that the outside world is interested and, more importantly, friendly – not an insignificant fact for a population brought up on a relentless diet of anti-US propaganda.

Though North Korea isn't a dangerous destination, several chilling cases in recent years have demonstrated the foolhardiness of breaking local laws, or staging any form of political protest or religious devotion.

Spare a thought for your guides – despite being official representatives of the regime, they're the ones who are vulnerable should you decide to speak your mind or insult the leadership. Likewise, escaping the group, disobeying photography instructions or otherwise stirring up trouble is dangerous for everyone involved, but particularly for your guides.

Always take your lead from the guides. Ask before taking photographs, keep conversations nonpolitical and accept that you're unable to freely mix with locals.

The obligation to be with your guides at all times outside the hotel is a serious one. Individual exploration is totally impossible and often leads to frustration for seasoned travellers unused to the confines of group travel. However, it's important for travellers to accept and conform to the rules, as travellers to North Korea who do not abide by the rules and laws of the country are putting themselves in serious danger.

other officials on blue and gifts from individuals on brown. The undeniable highlight is a stuffed caiman (small reptile related to the alligator) holding a tray of wooden cups, presented to the Great Leader by the Sandinistas, a Nicaraguan socialist political party.

The tone of the visit is very strict and sombre, so avoid the very real temptation to ice-skate across the overpolished floor in your foot covers. The most reverential and surreal part of the exhibit is the final room, in which there is a grinning life-sized waxwork of the Great Leader, to which you will be expected to bow your head before leaving respectfully.

Next is Kim Jong-il's similarly spectacular warehouse, where gifts given to him have been housed in a vault built into the cave wall. Kim Jong-il's gifts include those from Hyundai and CNN, as well as a good-luck note from Jimmy Carter and a basketball from former US Secretary of State Madeleine Albright. Indeed, some parts of the exhibit look like any upmarket electronics showroom – row after row of wide-screen TVs and stereo equipment donated by industrialists. There's also a rendering of the Dear Leader in wax here. In recent years gifts to Kim Jong-un have been added to this section of the IFE.

Pyohon Temple TEMPLE

The most historically important Buddhist temple in western North Korea, the Pyohon Temple complex dates back to 1044, with numerous renovations over the centuries. It features several small pagodas and a large hall housing images of Buddha, as well as a museum that sports a collection of woodblocks from the Buddhist scriptures, the *Tripitaka Koreana*. It's just a short walk from the International Friendship Exhibition (p321), at the entrance to Sangwon Valley.

Ryongmun Big Cave CAVE

It's common for tours to visit this 6km-long limestone cave either prior to or after a visit to Myohyangsan. It has some enormous caverns and a large number of stalactites. Sights include the Pool of the Anti-Imperialist People's Struggle, the Juche Cavern and the Mountain Peak of the Great Leader.

Sleeping

There are two choices here, but nearly everyone stays at the **Chongchon Hotel** (Hyangsan). The pyramidal Hyangsan Hotel has been redone to be 'seven-star', though it's really just enormously expensive, and very rarely used for tour groups.

Kumgang Region

South of the port city of Wonsan on the east of the Korean Peninsula, the most dramatic scenery in the entire country begins to rise in the Kumgang Mountains. This picturesque, bucolic area is divided into the Inner, Outer and Sea Kumgang Regions and is often visited on tours. The area is classical East Asian landscape dotted with Buddhist temples and hermitages, waterfalls and mineral springs, all set against a background of gentle mountain peaks, including Pirobong (1639m) – the highest peak in the area.

If your time here is limited, the best places to visit in the Outer Kumgang Region are the Samil Lagoon and the Manmulsang Area, where the scenery is breathtaking.

While in the Inner Kumgang Region, it's worth visiting the Pyohon Temple, an impressively reconstructed temple founded in AD 670 and one of old Korea's most important Zen monasteries.

Paekdusan

Apart from being the country's highest mountain at 2744m (9000ft), and an amazing geological phenomenon (an extinct volcano with a vast crater lake at its centre), Paekdusan (백두산, Mt Paekdu) is also of huge mythical importance to Koreans.

The natural beauty of this extinct volcano, now containing one of the world's deepest lakes, is made more magical by the mythology that surrounds the lake, both ancient and modern. The legend runs that Hwanung, the Lord of Heaven, descended onto the mountain in 2333 BC, and from here formed the nation of Choson – 'The Land of Morning Calm', or ancient Korea. It therefore only seems right and proper that, four millenniums later, Kim Jong-il was born at a Secret Camp nearby 'and flying white horses were seen in the sky', according to official sources. In all likelihood, Kim Jong-il was born in Khabarovsk, Russia, where his father was in exile at the time, but this story contributes to the all-important Kim myth that has contributed to the family's continued cult of personality.

Set in a huge clearing in the woods with views to Paekdusan and overlooking a large lake, the Samjiyon Grand Monument must be North Korea's most impressive paean to the leadership outside Pyongyang. The monument commemorates the battle of

Pochombo, where anti-Japanese forces first moved from guerrilla tactics to conventional warfare and took the town of the same name. The centrepiece is a 15m-high statue of a 27-year-old Kim Il-sung, as well as a smaller version of Pyongyang's Juche Tower and several large sculptures of various revolutionary scenes.

Trips here are strictly organised as this is a sensitive border region and a military zone. Having arrived at the military station at the bottom of the mountain, you'll be checked in, then will take the funicular railway up the side of the mountain. From here it's a 10-minute hike up to the mountain's highest point, past some superb views down into the crater lake. You can either walk down to the shore of Lake Chon (an easy hike down, but somewhat tougher coming back up!) or take the cable car (€7 per person return) for the easier option. Bring warm clothing; it can be freezing at any time of year, with snow on the ground year-round.

Revisionist history aside, the reason to visit Paekdusan is the natural beauty of the area – vast tracts of virgin forest, abundant wildlife, lonely granite crags, fresh springs, gushing streams and dramatic waterfalls – and, for those able to make the steep and treacherous climb, the astounding Jong-il Peak. It is accessible only from around late June to mid-September (due to weather conditions).

Chilbosan

The area around Chilbosan (칠보산, Mt Chilbo) is one of the most beautiful places in North Korea. It's also incredibly remote – the only way to get here in reasonable time is to charter a flight from Pyongyang to Orang airport, from where Chilbosan is a three-hour drive down a rather Mediterranean-looking coastline of high, jagged cliffs, small fishing villages and sandy beaches.

There's little to do here save enjoy the spectacular scenery, and you'll usually be driven around the attractive valleys, peaks and viewpoints of Chilbosan, including a stop at various beaches and the Kaesim Buddhist Temple, which dates from the 9th century. The unusual Mt Chilbo Homestay Program is another reason to visit – this is a unique accommodation option that allows you to stay with a local family (more or less).

This World Tourism Organization-pioneered project is some way from what you might imagine of a 'homestay' – a purpose-built village of large traditional and modern-style houses where one family lives in part of the house, and guests in the other. There's a restaurant, a shop and a nearby beach with another squid-barbecue restaurant on it.

While it does feel rather contrived, it's still one of the best opportunities in the country to meet and talk with North Koreans, though the main problem is communicating, unless you speak some Korean or Chinese.

Chongjin

Jump at the chance to visit Chongjin (청진), North Korea's third-largest city and a great spot to see how North Koreans really live. This huge industrial centre and port is a world away from gleaming Pyongyang, and despite a few attempts to mimic the capital's socialist grandeur around the city centre, it's a poor, ugly and polluted place. Coming here is fascinating, though – most locals have never seen international visitors and this is about as 'real' an experience of the country as you'll ever get.

The rules about photography are very strict here; your guides will become far more stern and you'll see little of Chongjin save what you glimpse out of the bus as it races through the city's deserted yet apparently endless avenues at high speed.

You'll visit the obligatory statues of Kim Il-sung and Kim Jong-il on the city's main square, as well as the fairly grotesque Revolutionary Museum next door, and an 'e-library' full of occasionally working computers that are theoretically linked to the national intranet. Tourists always stay at the Chongjin Tourist Hotel, the one hotel in the city that's open to visitors.

Rajin-Sonbong

This eccentric corner of North Korea, right on the border with China and Russia, has been designated a 'free-trade zone' since 1991. The two towns of Rajin (라진) and Sonbong (선봉), usually referred to collectively as Rason, are both unremarkable industrial ports surrounded by attractive hills, wetlands and forest. Rajin-Sonbong's rocky cliffs, lakes and sandy coastline are uniquely beautiful, but it feels like the end of the world and very few tourists make it here.

Tours here usually take in the fascinating Rajin Market, the only one in the country tourists are allowed to visit and shop at, the Rajin City Port and the Taehung Trading Corporation, a large seafood-processing plant and mushroom wine factory.

There are around 30 hotels in and around the twin towns. These include the Chinese-owned five-star Imperial Hotel (the fanciest in the country), which is right on the beach but some way from either town.

UNDERSTAND NORTH KOREA

North Korea Today

Since taking the reins in 2012, Kim Jong-un has made an enormous impact both at home and internationally. Initially dismissed by many as immature and lacking the strategic vision for leading a country such as North Korea, Kim Jong-un effectively silenced his critics soon after he came to power with a wave of brutal repression aimed at North Korea's elite, followed by shameless brinkmanship on the world stage, which culminated in a series of unprecedented diplomatic summits, the most significant of which was his face-to-face meeting with US President Donald Trump in Singapore on 12 June 2018. The summit, at which the leaders appeared to enjoy a good personal rapport, did not result in any significant agreement, but was hailed by many commentators as a massive victory for Kim Jong-un, whose father and grandfather had both pursued a meeting with a sitting US president to no avail.

It was a combination of calculated nuclear testing and the simultaneous playing-off of major powers against each other that forced the world to refocus on the danger North Korea presented to regional stability – and potentially to world peace. After a year of fever-pitch rhetoric and the threat of imminent war in 2017, Kim Jong-un dramatically changed tack in 2018 and instead pursued diplomatic encounters with Chinese President Xi Jinping, his South Korean counterpart Moon Jae-in, US Secretary of State Mike Pompeo and, finally, US President Donald Trump.

South Korean president Moon Jae-in and Kim Jong-un demonstrated a surprising personal chemistry during their two meetings, which suggested to many that there might finally be some progress on officially ending the Korean War and beginning the process of de-armament and denuclearisation on the Korean Peninsula. The latter, the key US demand for lifting sanctions on North Korea, is unlikely to happen without some fairly major concessions and guarantees, not least as North Korea knows that its nuclear weapons are all that presently prevent it from being invaded. While at the time of writing North Korea hadn't tested its weapons since 2017, it also had yet to make any serious moves to dismantle its stockpile; this was the main focus of the Singapore summit, which ended with a vague pledge to denuclearise the Korean Peninsula, although this was short on detail and committed neither side to any concrete measures.

Other analysts argue that the increasingly tough sanctions imposed on North Korea by the rest of the world in recent years are what forced Kim Jong-un to the negotiating table, as the relative economic prosperity that the country had enjoyed with the introduction of private markets and the availability of more consumer goods has been under threat as import sources dry up. While Kim Jong-un's rule has never faced any serious challenge domestically, it's unlikely that the North Korean government wants to risk going back to the years of bleak austerity, particularly as Kim Jong-un's rise to power has been accompanied by huge building sprees in Pyongyang and elsewhere, and a popular refocusing of the country's resources on the people rather than simply on the army, as was the case under his father, Kim Jong-il.

Indeed, Kim Jong-un's avuncular manner and smiling face and the speeches he's given seem to have massively boosted his popularity at home. With an appearance and manner reminiscent of his grandfather (North Korea's founder, Kim Il-sung), Kim Jong-un has arguably earned the respect of a nation that has grown up with enormous reverence for the late Great Leader.

That's not to say that factionalism, real or imagined, has not played a role in North Korea's tiny and secluded elite. Shortly after assuming power, Kim Jong-un very publicly purged his uncle, whom many North Korea watchers had assumed was the power behind the throne. Jang Sung-taek was arrested, paraded on national television and described by state media as 'worse than a dog' before being publicly executed. In 2018, just days before his meeting with Donald Trump, Kim Jong-un sacked three of his highest-ranking military officers and replaced them with loyalists – a move that analysts concluded was to ensure he had a free hand in negotiations with the US without worrying about a mutiny at home should greater concessions than planned be made.

While Pyongyang's politics may have changed forever with the ascent of the young Kim, for the vast majority of North Koreans, life has changed little in decades. While the terrifying famine and unspeakable sufferings of the 1990s may now be a distant memory, the effects they had in breaking the social contract between the loyal people and their authoritarian leaders endures. The system, which has morphed from communist to feudalist and on to black-market capitalist, has created a society in which almost anything can be had for the right price. Non-governmental organisation Transparency International has repeatedly ranked North Korea as the most corrupt nation on earth on its Global Corruption Barometer.

For most people, day-to-day life remains incredibly hard. Fear of arrest or denouncement is never far away; food is never plentiful; consumer goods remain unimaginable luxuries for most; propaganda is ubiquitous and relentless; electricity is scant; work is demanding and often weeks on end will be spent doing back-breaking manual agricultural work, even for those with comfortable desk jobs.

Against all odds though, North Korea has survived for a quarter of a century since the end of the Cold War, and the Kim regime retains a fierce grip on the country. After 60 years of total repression of all opposition, it appears there are simply no surviving networks of dissent. How long the status quo can go on remains a mystery, but the fact that North Korea is now on its third hereditary leader and has survived devastating famine, complete international isolation and recurring energy crises suggests that the quick dissolution of North Korea is far from inevitable.

History

Division of the Peninsula

The Japanese occupation of the Korean Peninsula between 1910 and 1945 was one of the darkest periods in Korean history. The occupation forces press-ganged many Korean citizens – particularly in the north – into slave-labour teams to build factories, mines and heavy industry. Moreover, the use of Korean girls and women as 'comfort women' – a euphemism for enforced prostitution – for Japanese soldiers remains a huge cause of resentment and controversy in both Koreas.

Most of the guerrilla warfare conducted against the Japanese police and army took place in the northern provinces of Korea and neighbouring Manchuria, and northerners are still proud of having carried a disproportionate burden in the struggle against Japan. In fact, some modern North Korean history books would have you believe that Kim Il-sung defeated the Japanese nearly single-handedly (with a bit of help from loyal comrades and his infant son).

While his feats have certainly been exaggerated, Kim Il-sung was a strong resistance leader, although not strong enough to rid Korea of the Japanese. This task was left to the Chinese Red Army, which in the closing days of WWII entered Manchuria and northern Korea as the Japanese forces retreated. The USA, recognising the strategic importance of the peninsula and wishing for it not to be left in Soviet hands, similarly began to move troops to the country's south. Despite an agreement at Yalta to give joint custodianship of Korea to the USSR, the USA and China, no concrete plans had been made to this end,

THE GENERAL SHERMAN & USS PUEBLO

During the 'hermit kingdom' phase of the Joseon dynasty (1392–1897), one of Korea's first encounters with Westerners was the ill-fated attempt of the American ship the *General Sherman* to sail up the Taedong River to Pyongyang in 1866. It arrogantly ignored warnings to turn around and leave, and insisted on establishing trade relations. When it ran aground on a sandbar just below Pyongyang, locals burnt it and killed all those on board, including a Welsh missionary and the Chinese and Malay crew. An American military expedition later pressed the Seoul government for reparations for the loss, but otherwise the incident was virtually forgotten in South Korea. However, North Koreans have always regarded it with great pride as being their first of many battles with, and victories over, American imperialists. This early US–Korean conflict was echoed in the capture of an American spy ship, the USS *Pueblo,* off the coast of North Korea in 1968. Today the *Pueblo* can be found on proud display in central Pyongyang, where it's visited by locals and tour groups alike.

and the US State Department assigned the division of the country to two young officers: working from a *National Geographic* map, they divided Korea across the 38th parallel.

American forces quickly took possession of the southern half of the country, while the Soviets established themselves in the north, with both sides stopping at the largely arbitrary dividing line. The intention to have democratic elections across the whole peninsula soon became hostage to Cold War tensions, and after the North refused to allow UN inspectors to cross the 38th parallel, the Republic of Korea was proclaimed in the South on 15 August 1948. The North proclaimed the Democratic People's Republic (DPRK) just three weeks later on 9 September 1948.

The Korean War

Stalin, it is rumoured, personally chose the 33-year-old Kim Il-sung to lead the new DPRK. The ambitious and fiercely nationalistic Kim was an unknown quantity, although Stalin is said to have favoured him due to his youth. He would have had no idea that Kim would outlive not only him and Mao Zedong, but communism itself, to become the one of the world's longest-serving heads of state. As soon as Kim had assumed the leadership of North Korea, he applied to Stalin to sanction an invasion of the South. The 'Man of Steel' refused Kim twice in 1949, but – perhaps bolstered by Mao's victory over the nationalists in China the same year, and the USSR's own A-bomb project – he gave Kim the green light a year later.

The brutal and pointless Korean War of 1950–53 saw a powerful North Korean advance into the South, where it almost drove US forces into the sea, followed by a similarly strong counterattack by the US and the UN, which managed to occupy most of North Korea. As the situation began to look bleak for the North, Kim advocated retreating to the hills and waging guerrilla warfare against the South, unaware that China's Mao Zedong had decided to covertly help the North by sending in the People's Liberation Army in the guise of 'volunteers'. Once the PLA moved in, the North pushed the front down to the original 38th parallel and, with two million dead, the original stalemate was more or less retained. The armistice agreement obliged both sides to withdraw 2km from the ceasefire line, thus creating the Demilitarized Zone (DMZ), still in existence today.

Rebuilding the Country

Despite the Chinese having alienated Kim by taking control of the war – Chinese commander Peng Dehuai apparently treated Kim as a subordinate, much to the future Great Leader's anger – the Chinese remained in North Korea and helped with the massive task of rebuilding a nation all but razed to the ground by bombing.

Simultaneously, following his ill-fated attempt to reunite the nation, Kim Il-sung began a process of political consolidation and brutal repression. He executed his foreign minister and those he believed a threat to him in an attempt to take overall control of the Korean Workers' Party. Following Khrushchev's 1956 denunciation of Stalin's personality cult, Central Committee member Yun Kong-hum stood up at one of its meetings and denounced Kim for similar crimes. Yun was never heard from again, and his disappearance was the death knell for North Korean democracy.

Unlike many communist leaders, Kim's personality cult was generated almost immediately – the sobriquet *suryong* or 'Great Leader' was employed in everyday conversation in the North by the 1960s – and the initial lip service paid to democracy and multiparty elections was soon forgotten.

The first decade under Kim Il-sung saw vast material improvements in the lives of workers and peasants. Literacy and full health care were soon followed by access to higher education and the full militarisation of the state. However, by the 1970s North Korea slipped into recession, from which it has never recovered. During this time, in which Kim Il-sung had been raised to a divine figure in North Korean society, his son Kim Jong-il, referred to only as the 'party centre' in official-speak, began to emerge from the nebulous mass of Kim's entourage.

At the 1980 party congress Kim Jong-il was awarded several important public posts, including a seat in the politburo, and even given the honorific title 'Dear Leader'. Kim Jong-il was designated hereditary successor to the Great Leader and in 1991 was made supreme commander of the Korean army, despite never having served a day in it. From 1989 until 1994, father and son were almost always pictured together, praised in tandem and generally shown to be working in close proximity, preparing the North Korean people for a hereditary dynasty far

more in keeping with Confucianism than communism.

Beyond Perestroika

It was during the late 1980s, as communism shattered throughout Eastern Europe, that North Korea's development began to differ strongly from that of other socialist nations. Its greatest sponsor, the Soviet Union, disintegrated in 1991, leaving the North at a loss for the subsidies it ironically needed to maintain its facade of self-sufficiency.

North Korea, having always played China and the USSR off against one another, turned to the Chinese, who have acted as the DPRK's greatest ally and benefactor ever since. While China's increasingly close relationship to the South and Japan also makes its reluctant support for the Kim regime all the more incongruous, China has remained the North's one trusted ally ever since, even if it's had to condemn Pyongyang on the world stage for rocket launches, nuclear tests and other breaches of international law.

The regime's strategy did pay off in 1994, however, when North Korea negotiated an agreement with the Clinton administration in which it agreed to cancel its controversial nuclear program in return for US energy supplies in the short term. This was to be followed by an international consortium constructing two light-water reactors for North Korean energy needs in the long term.

Midway through negotiations, Kim Il-sung suffered a massive heart attack and died. He had spent the day personally inspecting the accommodation being prepared for the planned visit of South Korean president Kim Young-sam. This summit between the two leaders would have been the first-ever meeting between the heads of state of the two nations, as Kim Il-sung's stance towards the South had noticeably changed in the last year of his life. The reaction to Kim Il-sung's death inside North Korea was a form of mass hysteria: the entire country came out en masse to mourn the president, with crowds frequently being driven into frenzied wailing and screaming by the state television channel.

Kim's death rendered the North weaker and even less predictable than before. Optimistic Korea watchers, including many within South Korea's government, expected the collapse of the regime to be imminent without its charismatic leader. In a move that was to further derail the reunification process, Kim Young-sam's government in Seoul did not therefore send condolences for Kim's death to the North – something even then US President Bill Clinton felt obliged to do. This slight to a man considered by North Koreans to be, quite literally, a living god was a miscalculation that set back any progress another five years.

While the expected collapse did not occur, neither did any visible sign of succession by the Dear Leader. North Korea was more mysterious than ever, and in the three years following Kim Il-sung's death, speculation was rampant that a military faction had taken control in Pyongyang and that continuing power struggles between them and Kim Jong-il meant there was no overall leader.

After a three-year mourning period Kim Jong-il finally assumed the mantle of power in October 1997, when he was elected Supreme Leader of North Korea and Leader of the Workers' Party of Korea. Surprisingly, the presidency rested with the late Kim Il-sung, who was declared North Korea's 'eternal' president, making him the world's only deceased head of state. However, the backdrop to Kim Jong-il's succession was horrific. While the North Korean economy had been contracting since the collapse of vital Soviet supplies and subsidies to the DPRK's ailing industrial infrastructure in the early 1990s, terrible floods in 1995 led quickly to disaster. Breaking with a strict tradition of self-reliance (one that had never reflected reality – aid had long been received secretly from both communist allies and even the South two months previously), the North appealed to the UN and the world community for urgent food aid.

So desperate was the state that it even acceded to UN demands for access to the whole country for its own field workers, something that would have previously been unthinkable in North Korea's staunchly secretive military climate. Aid workers were horrified by what they saw – malnutrition everywhere and the beginnings of starvation, which led over the next few years to deaths estimated anywhere from hundreds of thousands to 3.5 million people.

Axis of Evil

Kim Jong-il's pragmatism and relative openness to change came to the fore in the years following the devastation of the famine, and a series of initiatives to promote reconciliation with both the South and the US were implemented. These reached their height with a swiftly convened Pyongyang summit

between the South's Kim Dae-jung and Kim Jong-il in June 2000. It was the first-ever meeting on such a level between the two countries. The two leaders, their countries ready at any second to launch Armageddon against one another, held hands in the limousine from the airport to the guesthouse in an unprecedented gesture of solidarity. The summit paved the way for US Secretary of State Madeleine Albright's visit to Pyongyang later the same year. Kim Jong-il's aim was to have his country legitimised through a visit from the US president himself. However, as Clinton's second term ended and George W Bush assumed office in 2001, the international climate swiftly changed.

In his 2002 State of the Union address, President Bush labelled the North (along with Iran and Iraq) part of an 'Axis of Evil', a phrase that came to haunt Kim Jong-il in his final years. This speech launched a new era of acrimonious relations between the two countries, exemplified the following year by North Korea's resuming its nuclear program, claiming it had no choice due to American oil supplies being stopped and the two promised light-water reactors remaining incomplete. Frustrated at being ignored by the US throughout the Bush presidency, North Korea test-launched several missiles in July 2006, followed by the detonation of a nuclear device on its own soil three months later.

An Uncertain Future

Kim Jong-il appeared to suffer a serious stroke in 2008, following which he lost a great deal of weight and became visibly frail. Shortly afterwards he began promoting his third son, Kim Jong-un, to whom great feats were accorded and who was soon accompanying the Dear Leader on public appearances. Kim Jong-il died from a heart attack on his private train on 17 December 2011, with the announcement of his passing causing similarly dramatic scenes of public hysteria to that of Kim Il-sung's death in 1994. An enormous state funeral was presided over by Kim Jong-un, who as predicted went on to succeed his father.

Almost nothing was known about Kim Jong-un either domestically or internationally, but since taking over the running of the country he has proven himself to be a formidable figure, quickly dispatching anyone who threatens his position with swift brutality, while simultaneously cultivating an avuncular personality cult among a people who had virtually no idea who he was just a decade ago. Having learned all about brinkmanship during his father's last years, Kim Jong-un has tested his growing nuclear arsenal with disturbing alacrity, launching dozens of short- and medium-range missiles and intercontinental ballistic missiles between 2013 and 2017. While these tests have left the North Korean government a pariah internationally, many observers have pointed out that North Korea's safety from invasion is almost certainly guaranteed as a result.

The Culture

The National Psyche

To say the North Korean national psyche is different to that of its southern cousin is an extraordinary understatement. While North Korean individuals are generally exceptionally polite, if rather shy at first, their psyche as a nation is one defined by a state-promulgated obsession with the country's victimisation by the forces of American and Japanese imperialism and most notable for its refusal to move on in any way from the Korean War. Of course, the Korean War was horrific and its legacy of a divided nation is the source of great sorrow for people on both sides of the DMZ, but the North's propaganda about how the war was everyone's fault but North Korea's is quite extraordinary. One of the key ingredients to a pleasant trip here is understanding that this persecution complex is inculcated from birth and that it's borne of ignorance rather than wilful rewriting of history on the part of individuals.

The North Koreans are also a fiercely nationalistic and proud people, again largely due to endless nationalist propaganda fed to them since birth. Even more significant is the cult of Kim Il-sung (the Great Leader) and Kim Jong-il (the Dear Leader), which pervades everyday life to a degree that most people will find hard to believe. There are no Kim Il-sung jokes, there is no questioning of the cult and almost no resistance to it.

While North Koreans will always be polite to visitors, there remains a large amount of antipathy towards the USA and Japan. Both due to propaganda and the very real international isolation they feel, North Koreans have a sense of being hemmed in on all sides – threatened particularly by the South and the USA, but also by Japan. The changes over the past two decades in China and

Russia have also been cause for concern: these two big siblings who guaranteed survival and independence have both sought rapprochement with the South.

On a personal level, Koreans are typically very good-humoured and hospitable, yet remain extremely socially conservative after centuries of Confucianism and decades of communism. By all means, smile and say 'hello' to people you see on the street – North Koreans have been instructed to give visitors a warm welcome – but don't take photos of people without their permission; it may be far more relaxing for both of you to simply leave the camera in its bag. Similarly, giving gifts to ordinary people could result in unpleasant consequences for them, so ask your guide what is appropriate in any given situation.

Children tend to be remarkably forthcoming and will wave back and smile ecstatically when they see a visiting tour group. Some older children are even able to manage a few phrases in English. Personal relationships with North Koreans who are not your tour guides or business colleagues will be impossible. Men should bear in mind that any physical contact with a Korean woman will be seen as unusual, so while shaking hands is perfectly acceptable, do not greet a Korean woman with a kiss in the European manner. Women should also greet all North Koreans with a handshake, although receiving a kiss from a foreign woman is less of a taboo. North Korea is still a patriarchal society and despite the equality of women on an ideological level, this is not the case in day-to-day life.

Lifestyle

Trying to give a sense of day-to-day North Korean life is a challenge indeed. It's difficult to overstate the ramifications of half a century of isolation from the outside world. Facts meld with rumour about the real situation in the country, but certain things are doubtless true: power cuts are regular and shortages of food and consumer goods remain facts of everyday life. But some things do appear to have eased under Kim Jong-un, such as electricity supply. Once plunged into darkness in most places as soon as the sun went down, North Korea today has a growing number of individual Chinese-made solar panels that store energy for light and TV in the evening.

All people are divided up by *taedo* – a uniquely North Korean caste system whereby people are divided into loyal, neutral or hostile categories in relation to the regime. The hostile are deprived of everything and often end up in forced-labour camps in entire family groups, maybe for nothing more than having South Korean relatives, or for one family member having been caught crossing into China. The neutral have little or nothing but are not persecuted, while the loyal enjoy everything from Pyongyang residency and desk jobs to Party membership and the privileges of the elite. At the top of the tree, the Kim family and its courtiers enjoy great wealth and luxury, although evidence of this is hard to produce – the North Korean elite is also obsessed with secrecy.

North Korea is predictably austere. The six-day week (which, even for office workers, includes regular stints of back-breaking labour in the rice fields) makes for an exhausted populace. In turn, Sundays become a real event and Koreans visibly beam as they relax, go on picnics, sing songs and drink in small groups all over the country. A glance at the showcase shops and department stores in Pyongyang confirms that there is only a small number of imported goods – highly priced and of variable quality – available to the general population.

While in the 20 years following the Korean War it could genuinely be claimed that Kim Il-sung's government increased the standard of living in the North, bringing literacy and health care to every part of the country, the regression since the collapse of communism throughout the world has been spectacular. Most people are now just as materially poor as their grandparents were in the early 1950s.

Population

With around 25 million people, North Korea is conspicuous for its ethnic homogeneity, a result of the country's long history of isolation and even xenophobia, dating back to the 'hermit kingdom' days, which only ended in the early 20th century. The number of foreigners living in North Korea is very small and all of them are either diplomats or temporary residents working in the aid or construction industries. All of the three million inhabitants of Pyongyang are from backgrounds deemed to be loyal to the Kim regime. With a complete lack of free movement in the country (all citizens need special permission to leave their town of residence), no visitor is likely to see those termed 'hostile' – and anyway, most people in this unfortunate category are in hard-labour camps kilometres from anywhere. All North Korean adults have been

obliged to wear a 'loyalty' badge since 1970 featuring Kim Il-sung's portrait (and more recently, that of Kim Jong-il). You can be pretty certain that anyone without one is a visitor.

Sport

Soccer is the national sport, and seeing an international match in Pyongyang is sometimes possible. Volleyball is the game you're most likely to see locals playing though, as both sexes are allowed to play together, making it popular among work groups.

The North's greatest sporting moment came at the 1966 World Cup in England, when it thrashed tournament favourites Italy, stunning the world. It subsequently was knocked out by Portugal in the quarter-finals. The story of the team is told in a strangely touching documentary – one of the few ever to be made by western crews in the DPRK – called *The Game of Their Lives* (2005).

Weightlifting and martial arts are the other sporting fields in which North Korea has had an international impact, winning multiple Olympic medals in both London (2012) and Rio de Janeiro (2016).

Religion

In North Korea traditional religion is regarded, in accordance with Marxist theory, as an expression of a 'feudal mentality' and has effectively been banned since the 1950s. However, as the Kim family became more and more deified in the 1990s, official propaganda against organised religion accordingly stopped, and one guide on a recent visit told us that Juche – North Korea's founding philosophy of self-reliance and self-determination – was a religion and that one could not follow both it and Buddhism.

Despite the effective ban on traditional religion, a number of Buddhist temples are on show to tourists, although they're showpieces – you won't see locals or any real Buddhist community. In recent years several churches and a mosque have been built in Pyongyang, catering to the capital's diplomatic community.

TRADITIONAL RELIGIONS

The northern version of Korean shamanism was individualistic and ecstatic, while the southern style was hereditary and based on regularly scheduled community rituals. As far as is known, no shamanist activity is now practised in North Korea. Many northern shamans were transplanted to the South, chased out along with their Christian enemies, and the popularity of the services they offer (fortune telling, for instance) has endured there. Together with the near destruction of southern shamanism by South Korea's relentless modernisation, there's the curious situation where the actual practice of North Korean shamanism can be witnessed only in South Korea.

Northern Korea held many important centres of Korean Buddhism from the 3rd century through the Japanese occupation period. The Kumgang Region and Myohyangsan mountain areas, in particular, hosted large Zen-oriented (Jogye) temple complexes left over from the Koryo dynasty. Under the communists, Buddhism in the North (along with Confucianism and shamanism) suffered a fate identical to that of Christianity.

Some historically important Buddhist temples and shrines still exist, mostly in rural or mountainous areas. The most prominent among them are Pyohon Temple at Kumgang Region, Pyohon Temple at Myohyangsan and the Confucian Shrine in the Songgyungwan Neo-Confucian College, just outside Kaesong.

Arts

North Korean film enjoys something of a cult following with movie buffs, mainly as cinema was a lifelong passion for Kim Jong-il and the industry was relatively well financed for decades. Perhaps the most famous North Korean film is Shin Sang-ok's *Pulgasari* (1985), a curious socialist version of *Godzilla* made by the kidnapped South Korean director, who escaped back to the South in 1986. Since his escape and subsequent 'non-person' status in the DPRK, his involvement in the film is no longer credited by the North Koreans.

Separating truth from myth is particularly hard with the film industry in North Korea – despite claims that scores of films are produced annually, the reality is probably far less impressive. Cinema visits are sometimes included on tours, when local films are shown with English subtitles, and are a fascinating experience. You can also request a visit to the Pyongyang Film Studios when booking your tour – and you may even be lucky enough to see a political-propaganda piece in production.

North Korean literature has not profited from the Kim dynasty, which has done nothing to encourage original writing. Despite an initial artistic debate in the 1950s,

all non-party-controlled forms of expression were quickly repressed. Bookshops stock an unimaginably restrictive selection of works, focusing heavily on the writings of Kim Il-sung and Kim Jong-il.

Tourists with an interest in traditional arts can request visits to performances of traditional Korean music, singing and dance, though these are rarely available. More feasible is a visit to a revolutionary opera or a classical-music concert in Pyongyang.

Environment

North Korea is spookily litter-free, with streets cleaned daily and no graffiti save that scratched onto the window panes of the Pyongyang Metro (explained by the fact that carriages were bought from Berlin after German reunification). However, the country's cities are polluted and there is little or no environmental consciousness.

The varying climatic regions on the northern half of the Korean Peninsula have created environments that are home to sub-arctic, alpine and subtropical plant and tree species. Most of the country's fauna is contained within the limited nature reserves around the mountainous regions, as most of the lower plains have been converted to arable agricultural land. An energetic reforestation program was carried out after the Korean War to replace many of the forests that were destroyed by the incessant bombing campaigns, a notable exception being the area to the north of the DMZ, where defoliants are used to remove vegetation for security purposes. The comparatively low population has resulted in the preservation of most mountainous regions.

Areas of particular biodiversity are the DMZ, the wetlands of the Tumen River and the Paekdusan and Chilbosan mountains in the far north. For those interested in tours with a greater emphasis on nature, it is possible to organise an itinerary with your travel company, though any hopes of a truly nature-focused tour are likely to be dashed by the ubiquitous revolutionary sights that always take priority over hikes.

Two particular flora species have attracted enormous attention from the North Koreans, and neither of them are native. In 1965 Indonesia's then-president Sukarno named a newly developed orchid after Kim Il-sung – *kimilsungia* – with popular acclaim overcoming Kim's modest reluctance to accept such an honour. Kim Jong-il was presented with his namesake, *kimjongilia,* a begonia developed by a Japanese horticulturist, on his 46th birthday. The blooming of either flower is announced annually as a tribute to the two leaders and visitors will notice their omnipresence at official tourist sites.

Environmental Issues

The main challenges to the environment in North Korea are from problems that aren't obviously visible at first glance. The devastating floods and economic slowdown during the 1990s wreaked havoc not only on property and agricultural land, but also on the environment. Fields were stripped of their topsoil, which, combined with fertiliser shortages, forced authorities to expand the arable land under cultivation. Unsustainable and unstable hillside areas, riverbanks and road edges were brought under cultivation, further exacerbating erosion, deforestation, fertiliser contamination of the land and rivers and the vulnerability of crops. Recovery is underway, but frequent food shortages since the 1990s have meant that poor farming practices recur again and again.

SURVIVAL GUIDE

Directory A–Z

ACCOMMODATION

All accommodation in North Korea is in state-run hotels, which are all of a passable standard, even if the wallpaper is peeling and the plumbing ancient. You won't usually have any control over where you stay unless you organise your own private group tour, but you can always make requests. All hotels have the basics: a restaurant, a shop, and some form of entertainment, from karaoke to a bar.

CHILDREN

It is possible to take children to North Korea, though you will have to book a private tour, as most group tours will not take minors.

CUSTOMS REGULATIONS

North Korean customs procedures vary in severity from general polite enquiries to thorough goings-over. You will normally have to present all books on arrival for inspection, and the Lonely Planet *Korea* guide and other books about the country will usually be confiscated, although it's not always common for bags to be searched. All electronic goods, including cameras, laptops, e-readers, tablets and phones, will also need to be presented. Cameras of almost any size and nonprofessional video recorders are fine, though

huge zoom lenses and enormous tripods are not allowed.

EMBASSIES & CONSULATES

North Korea now enjoys diplomatic relations with many countries, although very few maintain embassies in Pyongyang. North Korean embassies abroad can all process visa applications, but most travellers will have theirs processed at the North Korean embassy in Běijīng by their tour agency the day before they travel; see the Visas section for more information

The UK Embassy represents the interests of Australians, New Zealanders and citizens of the Republic of Ireland, while the Swedish legation looks after US and Canadian citizens as well as EU citizens whose own country does not have representation in Pyongyang. All embassies are in the Munsudong diplomatic compound.

Chinese Embassy (02-381 3116; http://kp.china-embassy.org/eng/)

German Embassy (02-381 7385; fax 02-381 7397)

Indian Embassy (02-381 7274/15; http://eoi.gov.in/PyongYang/)

Russian Embassy (02-381 3101/02; www.rusembdprk.ru/en/)

Swedish Embassy (02-381 7485; www.swedenabroad.se/en/embassies/north-korea-pyongyang/)

UK Embassy (02-381 7982, 02-382 7980; www.gov.uk/world/organisations/british-embassy-pyonyang)

INTERNET ACCESS

With the exception of the flagship Masik-Ryong Hotel (p320) near Wonsan, where cable internet is available in the rooms, there is no internet access available in hotels. The only way to get online in North Korea currently is by purchasing a KoryoLink SIM card, which costs €215 plus data. The cards are designed for international residents rather than tourists, but they are available to short-term visitors: the best place to buy one is at the airport on arrival.

LEGAL MATTERS

While most travellers will not run into legal problems in North Korea, a number of cases in the past few years have highlighted the devastating ramifications that this can have, most particularly in the case of the young American tourist Otto Warmbier. He died shortly after his release from a North Korean prison in 2017, having been arrested for allegedly stealing a propaganda poster from the Yanggakdo Hotel in Pyongyang.

Usually, tourists who break the law in North Korea are deported immediately, though the growing trend in the past decade has been to use prisoners for international leverage. Only the truly reckless and foolhardy would travel to DPRK with the intention of proselytising or protesting against the regime.

MONEY

The unit of currency is the North Korean won (KPW), though most travellers will never even see them. Visitors can pay for everything with euros, Chinese RMB or US dollars. Credit cards and travellers cheques are completely useless and there are no ATMs. It's officially illegal to take North Korean won out of the country.

Tipping

You'll be accompanied by two state-employed guides at all times. Tipping is expected by your two guides and driver and is generally calculated at €10 per driver or per guide per day, meaning that you should plan for €30 per day in total. Tips will be given collectively on your final morning in North Korea. Elsewhere tipping is not expected anywhere in the country.

PHOTOGRAPHY

Always ask before taking photos and obey the reply. North Koreans, acutely aware of the political power of an image in the western press, are especially sensitive about visitors taking photos of them without their permission. Your guides are familiar with the issue of tourists taking photos that end up in anti-DPRK news content, and it's quite normal for customs officers to give your pictures a quick look-through at the border – they will ask you to delete any offending content. Taking photographs from the bus is officially banned, though in practice travellers do get away with it if they are discreet and are not photographing sensitive objects. Avoid taking photos of soldiers or any military facilities (including train stations) at any time, unless told otherwise by your guides (the DMZ is generally an exception to that rule). The safest and recommended practice is to only take photographs when granted express permission by your guides.

POST

Like all other means of communication in North Korea, the post is monitored. It is, however, generally reliable and the colourful North Korean stamps, featuring everything from tributes to the Great Leader to Princess Diana commemoratives, make great souvenirs.

TAP WATER

It is not recommended to drink tap water in North Korea. Bottled water is available at all hotels.

TELEPHONE

Mobile phones – once banned – are now ubiquitous in Pyongyang and several other cities, and visitors are welcome to bring their smartphones with them into the country. International SIM cards will not roam here, though it is possible to

purchase a KoryoLink SIM card for the considerable cost of €215. KoryoLink 3G services allow access to the internet, but a virtual private network (VPN; which must be downloaded before arriving in North Korea or China) is necessary to get past the firewall, which is as strict as China's. Data is expensive, but the network works well in much of the country.

Do note, however, that you will only be able to call internationally and to other KoryoLink visitor numbers in North Korea – it's impossible to call locals, whose phones connect to a ring-fenced network.

TIME

The time in North Korea is GMT/UTC plus nine hours, exactly the same as in South Korea. Previously clocks in North Korea were set 30 minutes earlier to those in the South, with the change to Pyongyang time coming after the summit between Kim Jong-un and Moon Jae-in in early 2018.

You will also see years such as Juche 8 (1919) or Juche 99 (2011). Three years after the death of Kim Il-sung, the state adopted a new system of recording years, starting from Juche 1 (1912) when Kim No 1 was born. Despite the wide use of these dates internally, they are always clarified with 'normal' years.

TOILETS

In Pyongyang and around frequently visited tourist sites, toilet facilities are basic and smelly, usually with squat toilets. There are regular cuts in the water supply outside Pyongyang, and often a bucket of water will be left in your hotel room or a public toilet for this eventuality. Toilet paper is supplied in hotels but it's always a good idea to carry tissues for emergencies, especially as diarrhoea is a common problem for visitors. Hand sanitiser is also a handy thing to bring with you, as soap is nearly as scarce as running water in public toilets.

VISAS

People of all nationalities need a visa to visit North Korea. At present North Korea bans only citizens of South Korea and Malaysia from visiting, while since 2017 the US government has banned all its citizens from travelling to the DPRK.

Restrictions have relaxed somewhat for visa applicants, and you currently just have to supply the name of your employer and your job. If you work in the media, human rights or any other potentially controversial professions, you might not be offered a visa. Each visa needs approval from Pyongyang, so apply at least one month before you travel. Your travel agency will normally handle the application for you, and in most cases the visa is a formality if you travel with an established agency.

Tour groups usually have visas issued in Běijīng the day before travel, so don't worry about leaving home without one in your passport. It does mean that you need to spend 24 hours in Běijīng before going on to Pyongyang, but you won't have to go to the embassy yourself in most cases. Individual visas can usually be issued at any North Korean embassy around the world.

The embassy visa charges (€50 in Běijīng) are included in some, but not all, tour packages. North Korean visas are not put into passports, but are separate documents taken from you when you exit the country. If you want a souvenir, ask if you can make a photocopy or take a photo (and obey your guides if they say no). No stamp of any kind will be made in your passport.

Bear in mind that in most cases you will need to travel through China to enter and leave North Korea. This means that you'll either need to get a dual-entry visa for China, or – much simpler –

SPECIALIST TOURS

While the day-to-day realities and restrictions of travel in Democratic People's Republic of Korea (DPRK; North Korea) remain similar no matter who you travel with, one option for seeing and doing something rather different is to take a specialist tour of the country. These are offered by many tour operators and range from sporting trips – where teams travel together to DPRK and play matches with their North Korean counterparts – to train tours, which allow travellers to make the journey by rail from Pyongyang to the northern city of Chongjin, the only chance at present to see much of this part of the country. Also on offer are architecture tours, marathon tours (allowing participants to take part in the mid-April Pyongyang Marathon), cycling tours, aviation tours and golf tours. **Koryo Tours** (☎+86 10-6416-7544; www.koryotours.com) offers the widest range of specialist tours.

Juche Travel Services (☎+44 7754 670186; www.juchetravelservices.com) organises stints of two to three weeks for visiting volunteers to teach English in North Korea. Despite being unpaid positions, there's still a considerable price tag attached. While this is very far from being an organised tour, volunteers still live in hotels and have their movements as restricted as tourists do, so unless you get a job as a diplomat or NGO worker in North Korea, your chances to experience the country as a local remain thin.

THE MYSTERY UNDERGROUND

Visiting the Pyongyang metro has traditionally involved a one-stop trip between Puhung (Rehabilitation) and Yonggwang (Glory) stations, the two most elaborately decorated of the network's 17 stations. But in recent years a longer trip has become possible, allowing you to pass through several stations – which quashes the rumours that power cuts and repairs meant that the rest of the system no longer worked on a daily basis, and that the 'passengers' tourists see on the network are employed to make the system look functional. Some tours offer the chance to travel the entire length of the Pyongyang metro along its two lines.

The entire system's construction was, inevitably, overseen by the Great Leader (Kim Il-sung), who offered his so-called 'on-the-spot guidance' – which generally consisted of a few common-sense suggestions, all of which were hastily written down by everyone around him in their notepads. Indeed, the Metro Museum, next to the Tower of Immortality, covers almost exclusively the role of the two leaders in the construction of the metro and gives almost no technical information, although there is a very cool diorama. Rumours of a parallel metro system connecting government offices and military installations have persisted for years, although as with most rumours about North Korea, no evidence of its existence has ever been produced.

use the 144-hour visa-free transit scheme, for which you simply need to show an onward air ticket out of China within that time period.

Getting There & Away

Běijīng is the only real transport hub for entering North Korea, offering regular trains and flights to Pyongyang. The only other cities with regular air connections to Pyongyang are Vladivostok in Russia and Shěnyáng in northern China. As tourists are often obliged to pick up their visas in Běijīng anyway, other routes would generally be impossible even if there were more transport options.

AIR

Pyongyang's Sunan International Airport (airport code: FNJ) is the only airport in the country open to flights from abroad. It was given a full refit in 2015 and now looks much like any small airport anywhere in the world, even though it receives just a tiny number of flights.

TRAIN

There are four weekly overnight trains in either direction between Běijīng and Pyongyang. The journey takes around 24 hours, though delays are not uncommon. Trains run on Monday, Wednesday, Thursday and Saturday. On each day, train No 27 leaves Běijīng at 5.25pm and arrives at Pyongyang the next day at 7.30pm. Going the other way, train No 26 departs from Pyongyang at 10.10am, arriving in Běijīng at 8.34am the next morning. In contrast to the plane, it's possible to pick up your train tickets to Pyongyang without a DPRK visa.

The North Korean train is actually two carriages attached to the main Běijīng–Dāndōng train, which are detached at Dāndōng (Chinese side) and then taken across the Yalu River Bridge to Sinuiju (Korean side), where more carriages are added for local people. You'll remain in the same carriage for the entire journey, however, and can mingle with locals in the dining car on both legs of the trip. Accommodation is in four-berth compartments, though sometimes two-berth compartments are available. Trains usually spend about four hours at the border – two hours at Dāndōng and two hours at Sinuiju – for customs and immigration.

Food is available from the restaurant car on both legs of the journey. Make sure you have some small-denomination euro or Chinese RMB notes to pay for meals (€5) from the North Korean buffet car, as this is not usually included in tours. There are no facilities for changing money at Sinuiju or on the train.

Your guide will meet you on arrival at Pyongyang train station and accompany you to your hotel. Be very discreet taking pictures from the train in North Korea. While you'll get some great opportunities to snap everyday DPRK scenes, do not take pictures in stations as these are considered to be military sites.

As well as the service to Běijīng there's an irregular (approximately twice monthly) train in both directions between Moscow and Pyongyang, which travels via Hamhung and Chongjin before crossing the Russian–North Korean border at Tumangang and joining the Trans-Siberian main line at Ussuriysk. The trip takes eight days, and in 2018 was opened to visitors travelling with Koryo Tours (p333).

Getting Around

All transport within North Korea will be arranged for you by the authorities, so there's no need to worry about the practicalities of getting around once you're in the country.

Understand Korea

Korea Today

Plagued with high youth unemployment, growing social-welfare liabilities, old-age poverty and a rapidly declining birth rate, South Korea today faces multiple challenges. Relations with China and Japan have been uncertain, yet the South Korean economy is the world's 11th largest and a dramatic rapprochement between North and South Korea promises – but does not guarantee – to replace decades of hostility.

Best on Film

Chingu (Friend; 친구; 2001) Directed by Kwak Kyung-taek; gritty, disturbing and compelling Busan drama.

The Host (괴물; 2006) Directed by Bong Joon-ho; classic monster movie juggles humour, poignancy and heart-stopping action.

Train to Busan (부산행; 2016) Just when you thought it was good to go 1st class: rail-roading apocalyptic zombie horror, directed by Yeon Sang-ho.

Ode to my Father (국제시장; 2014) Directed by Yoon Je-kyoon, about a boy who survives the Korean War, grows up in hardship and works around the world.

Best in Print

I'll Be Right There (Shin Kyung-sook; 2014) A city wracked by pro-democracy protests in the 1980s is elegantly evoked by this award-winning Korean author.

Three Generations (Yom Sang-seop; 2005) Originally published in newspaper serialisations in the 1930s, this epic-scale novel focuses on the travails of a family under colonisation.

The Vegetarian (Han Kang; 2007) Three-part drama narrating the devastating effects of a young woman's decision to abstain from eating meat.

Foes or friends in the North?

South Korea is today, by any measure, one of the world's star performers. Its top companies, such as Samsung, LG and Hyundai, make products the world wants. South Korea is now possibly the most wired nation on earth. The talented younger generation has created such a dynamic pop culture that *hallyu* (the Korean Wave) has swept the globe.

The single anachronism in South Korea's progress, however, remains its fractious relations with North Korea. The North successfully tested nuclear bombs in underground detonations, first in 2006, again in 2009 and 2013, twice in 2016 and once again in 2017. In parallel, North Korea busily built and tested intercontinental ballistic missiles (ICBMs) that it claims can reach the USA.

Possibly the single most significant international event in this fractious timeline – though at the time of writing the final effects of this were yet to be fully ascertained – was the aggressive stance of US President Donald Trump to Kim Jong-un's belligerent rhetoric, often delivered in soundbite tweets from his Twitter account. For a while in 2018 it seemed as though brinkmanship from both sides may lead to war, but there were already signs from Kim's conciliatory New Year speech of the same year that he was seeking a rapprochement with South Korea.

North Korea sent teams to the Winter Olympics in Pyeongchang and in April Kim met with South Korean President Moon Jae-in and signed the Panmunjom Declaration aiming towards a full peace treaty between the two countries. This paved the way for Donald Trump and Kim Jong-un's high-profile Singapore summit in June 2018 to sign a joint statement, with the US agreeing to security guarantees for North Korea in return for

the denuclearisation of the Korean Peninsula. Where this will eventually lead is unknown, but the steps were unprecedented.

Rocky Relations

The supposed lack of a sincere apology for Japan's past actions in Korea is not the only issue the Republic of Korea (ROK; South Korea) has with its neighbour across the East Sea. Japan calls this same body of water the Sea of Japan and lays claim to a group of islets it calls Takeshima (Bamboo Island) and which Koreans term Dokdo (Solitary Island); the islet cluster is called Liancourt Rocks internationally. The rocks are closer to Korean territory than Japanese and only house two permanent inhabitants (Koreans). They have been squabbled over for decades as a point of pride as much as for their rich fishing grounds and possible reserves of natural gas.

Even though territorial disputes are also a small part of the diplomatic dance between South Korea and China, relations between the two are generally rosier than they are between Korea and Japan. However, the deployment of the US-made anti-ballistic missile system Terminal High Altitude Area Defense (THAAD) in South Korea in 2017, created a rapid frosting of relations with Beijing, which feared the system's radar capabilities could be used against it. As China is South Korea's largest trading partner, the effects of this souring of relations hit South Korea's economy hard, including tourism (with a big drop-off in Chinese visitors) and manufacturing. At the time of writing, the 2018 détente between South Korea and the Democratic People's Republic of Korea (DPRK; North Korea) was set to reshape the entire strategic nature of South Korea–North Korea–China–US relations, potentially for the better: watch this space.

Low Birth Rate Blues

With South Korea recording its lowest ever birth rate in 2017 (exceeding even Japan's notoriously low birth rate) – and the lowest fertility rate recorded in South Korea for females, at 1.05 children born to women of child-bearing age – the nation faces a demographic time-bomb.

Young people are postponing marriage until later and having fewer children within marriage. With only 357,700 babies being born in 2017– the first time the number has fallen below 400,000 – the country is not producing nearly enough babies to stop its population from dropping (women need to be having 2.1 babies each to keep the population stable). South Korea is consequently ageing faster than any other developed nation and now has more elderly people than young. The effects of this greying of the

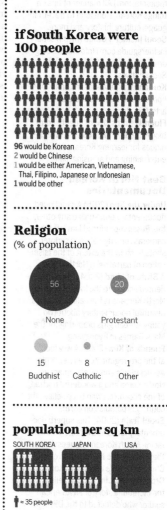

AREA: 100,210 SQ KM (SOUTH KOREA); 120,540 SQ KM (NORTH KOREA)

GDP: US$1.54 TRILLION (SOUTH KOREA)

INFLATION: 1.94% (SOUTH KOREA)

POPULATION: 51.16 MILLION (SOUTH KOREA); 24.6 MILLION (NORTH KOREA)

if South Korea were 100 people

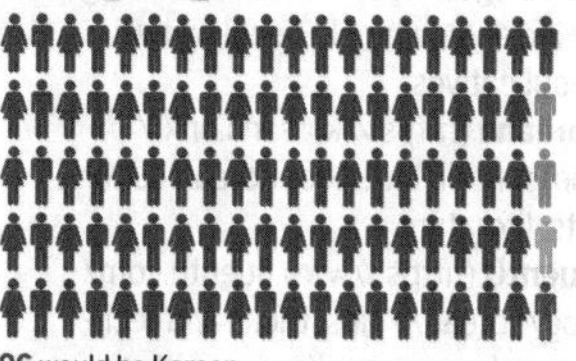

96 would be Korean
2 would be Chinese
1 would be either American, Vietnamese, Thai, Filipino, Japanese or Indonesian
1 would be other

Religion

(% of population)

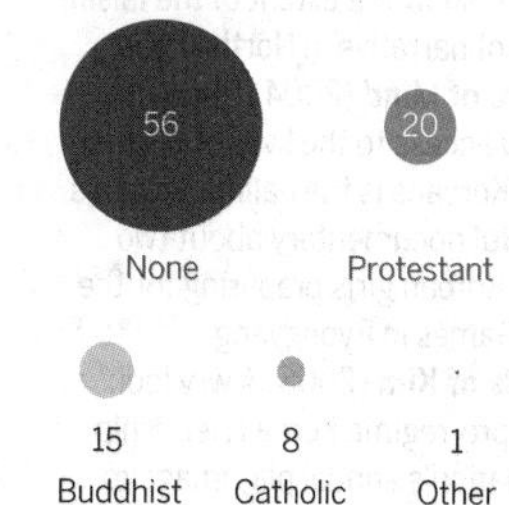

population per sq km

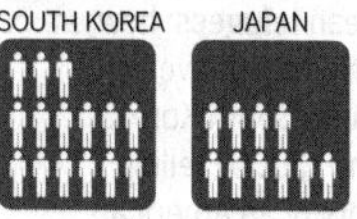

≈ 35 people

A Geek in Korea (Daniel Tudor; 2014) Fully illustrated and ranging from religion and traditional martial arts to K-Pop, Samsung and the *hallyu* pop-culture wave.

Best Blogs

Ask A Korean (http://askakorean.blogspot.co.uk) Go on, ask him. You may be surprised by the answer.

Inspire Me Korea (http://blog.inspiremekorea.com) All manner of tips on things Korean, from food to travel, language, culture, history and more.

Seoul Insider's Guide (http://seoulinsidersguide.com) Informative blog on life and culture in Seoul by two Seoul natives.

Koreana (https://koreana.or.kr/home/homeIndex.do) Korean culture, arts, literature.

FluentU (https://www.fluentu.com/blog/korean/) Tips, tricks and techniques for learning Korean, with an entertaining and amusing slant.

Best North Korean Documentaries

Under the Sun (2015) A sanctioned documentary quite unlike any other, this Russian-produced film left the cameras running between scripted shots to show the extent of the falsification of narrative in North Korea.

A State of Mind (2004) Unprecedented access to the lives of normal North Koreans is the hallmark of this beautiful documentary about two young Korean girls preparing for the Mass Games in Pyongyang.

Friends of Kim (2006) A wry look at the pro-regime Korea Friendship Association's annual pilgrimage to North Korea and a wonderful portrait of the eccentrics who truly believe the country is paradise on earth.

Seoul Train (2004) This superb documentary looks at the huge problems facing North Korean refugees: how they escape the North, survive in China and make it to South Korea.

Crossing the Line (2006) Telling the incredible story of an American soldier who defected to the DPRK in the 1960s and continues to live there today, this bittersweet film provides haunting insight into life in the North.

population are enormous, ranging from mushrooming health-care costs to decreasing productivity, huge poverty among the elderly, a growing burden on the young and increased suicide among older people (often, tragically, as they wish to avoid heaping pressure on their children).

Impeachment & Replacement

After revelations of corrupt links between former president Park Geun-hye – South Korea's first female leader – and Choi Soon-sil, a woman with no official position who embezzled vast amounts of money through her friendship with Park, the president was impeached in March 2017, and arrested, tried and finally imprisoned in 2018. The impeachment process was accompanied by huge demonstrations against Park known as the Candlelight Revolution, matched in later stages by equally large counterprotests in support of the beleaguered president, dividing the nation. Park Geun-hye was provisionally replaced as president by former Justice Minister Hwang Kyo-ahn until the election of Moon Jae-in in May 2017.

History

Koreans can trace a continuous history on the same territory reaching back thousands of years. The present politically divided peninsula is mirrored by distant eras such as the Three Kingdoms period (57 BC–AD 668), when the kingdoms of Goguryeo, Silla and Baekje jockeyed for control of territory that stretched deep into Manchuria. Korea's relationship with powerful neighbours China and Japan has also long defined the country's fortunes, while ties to the West have added further complexity to national self-understanding.

The First Korean

The imagined beginning of the Korean nation was the 3rd millennium BC, when a legendary king named Dangun founded old Joseon. Joseon (also spelled Choson) remains the name of the country in North Korea (and the name used by China to describe it: Cháoxiǎn), but South Koreans use the term Daehanminguk (Hánguó in Chinese), a name dating from the 1890s.

Real or not, Dangun has been a continuous presence from his time to the present; a kingly vessel filled by different people at different times who drew their legitimacy from this eternal lineage. Under its first president, for example, South Korea used a calendar in which Dangun's birth constituted year one – setting the date at 2333 BC. The two Koreas can't agree on many things, including what to call their country, but they can agree on Dangun.

Bronze Age (c 10,000 BC) people on the Korean Peninsula built dolmen or stone burial chambers such as those found on the island of Ganghwado.

Unfortunately there is no written history of Korea until a couple of centuries BC, and that history was chronicled by Chinese scribes. But there is archaeological evidence that humans have inhabited this peninsula for thousands of years, and that an advanced people were here seven or eight thousand years ago. These Neolithic people practised agriculture in a settled communal life and are widely supposed to have had family clans as their basic social grouping. Nationalist historians also trace many Korean social and cultural traits back to these Neolithic people.

The Three Kingdoms

Around the time of Christ, three kingdoms emerged on the Korean Peninsula: Baekje (also spelled Paekche), Goguryeo (Koguryŏ) and Silla (Shilla).

The Korean Peninsula is divided by a major mountain range about three-quarters of the way down at the 37th parallel. This southwest extension of mountains framed Baekje's historic territory, just as it did the Silla kingdom to the east. Goguryeo, however, ranged over a wild region

TIMELINE

2333 BC

Dongguk Tonggam, a chronicle of early Korean history compiled in the 15th century, gives this date for the founding of Gojoseon by the mythical leader Dangun.

c 57 BC

Start of the Three Kingdoms period in which the ancient kingdoms of Goguryeo, Baekje and Silla rule over the Korean Peninsula and parts of Manchuria.

AD 372

Chinese monk Sundo brings Buddhism to Goguryeo, where it blends with local shamanism. It takes two centuries for the religion to spread throughout the peninsula.

The common Korean custom of father-to-son royal succession is said to have begun with Baekje king Geun Chogo. His grandson inaugurated another long tradition by adopting Buddhism as the state religion in AD 384.

consisting of northeastern Korea and eastern Manchuria, giving rise to contemporary dreams of a 'greater Korea' in territories that now happen to be part of China and Russia. While South Korea identifies itself with the glories of the Silla kingdom, which it says unified the peninsula in AD 668, the North identifies with Goguryeo and says the country wasn't truly unified until the founding of the Goguryeo dynasty.

Central Kingdom

Baekje was a centralised, aristocratic state melding Chinese and indigenous influences. By the 3rd century AD, Baekje was strong enough to demolish its rivals and occupy what today is the core area of Korea, around Seoul. The kingdom controlled much of western Korea up to Pyongyang and, if you believe certain controversial records, coastal regions of northeastern China too.

By the time Baekje moved its capital to Chungnam, however, its influence was under siege. Its centre of power, Hanseong (in the modern-day Seoul region), had fallen to Goguryeo from the north, and in 475 Baekje had to relocate its capital to Gongju (then known as Ungjin), where the mountains provided a bulwark and offered some protection.

The dynasty thrived anew, nurturing relations with Japan and China, and in 538 King Seong moved the capital further south to Buyeo (then known as Sabi). Unfortunately his Silla allies betrayed him, killing him in battle. Baekje fell into decline and was finally vanquished in 660 by a combined army from Silla and China's Tang dynasty, though pockets of resistance held out for some years.

Northern Kingdom

Goguryeo conquered a large swath of territory by AD 312 and expanded in all directions, especially towards the Taedong River, which runs through Pyongyang, in the south. By the 5th century Goguryeo was in the ascendancy on the peninsula, and under warrior kings such as Gwanggaeto the Great (AD 391–412) and his son Jangsu (AD 413–419), it was also in control of huge chunks of Manchuria.

Southern Kingdom

Silla emerged victorious on the peninsula in 668. However, a consequence of this was that the country had come under the long-term sway of the great Tang dynasty (618–907) in China. Chinese statecraft, Buddhist and Confucian philosophy, Confucian practices of educating the young, and the Chinese written language became entrenched.

Silla sent many students to Tang schools and acquired a level of civilisation high enough to merit the Chinese designation of 'flourishing land in the East'. Its capital at Gyeongju was renowned as the 'city of gold', where the aristocracy pursued a high culture and extravagant pleasures.

427

King Jangsu, the 20th monarch of the Goguryeo dynasty, moves his capital south from the present-day Chinese–Korean border to Pyongyang on the banks of the Taedong River.

668

Having allied his kingdom with China's Tang dynasty, Munmu of Silla defeats Goguryeo to become the first ruler of a unified southern Korean Peninsula.

918

The Goryeo dynasty is established by King Taejo. It rules Korea until 1392, during which time the territory under its rule expands to the whole Korean Peninsula.

1231

As part of a general campaign to conquer China, Mongols invade the Korean Peninsula, forcing the Goryeo royal court to regroup on the island of Ganghwado.

Chinese historians wrote that elite officials possessed thousands of slaves, with similar numbers of horses, cattle and pigs. Their wives wore solid-gold tiaras and earrings of delicate and intricate filigree. Scholars studied the Confucian and Buddhist classics and developed advanced methods for astronomy and calendrical science. 'Pure Land' Buddhism, a simple doctrine, united the mass of common people who could become adherents through the repetition of simple chants.

Artists from Goguryeo and Baekje also perfected a mural art found on the walls of tombs and took it to Japan, where it deeply influenced that country's temple and burial art. However, it was the blossoming of Silla that still astounds contemporary visitors to Korea and makes its ancient capital at Gyeongju one of the most fascinating tourist destinations in East Asia.

Based on primary sources, the superbly illustrated *Joseon Royal Court Culture* by Shin Myung-ho (2004) details the unique Confucian royal-court lifestyle.

Silla vs Balhae

Despite Silla's military strength and prowess, broad territories of the old Goguryeo kingdom remained unconquered and a section of the Goguryeo elite established a successor state known as Balhae (Parhae), above and below the Amnok and Tuman boundaries that now form the border between China, Russia and Korea. Balhae's continuing strength forced Silla to build a northern wall in 721 and kept Silla forces permanently below a line running from present-day Pyongyang in the east to the west coast.

KING SEJONG'S GIFT

Hangeul is a phonetic script: concise, elegant and considered one of the most scientific in the world in rendering sounds. It was developed in 1443, during the reign of Korea's greatest king, Sejong, as a way of increasing literacy – it is vastly simpler and easier to learn than Chinese characters (which reflect sound poorly and can have upwards of 50 strokes for just one character). But the Confucian elite wanted to maintain a supremacy and opposed *the wide use of hangeul*, hoping to keep the government exams as difficult as possible so only aristocratic children had the time and money to pass.

Hangeul didn't come into general use until after 1945, and then only in North Korea. South Korea used a Sino-Korean script requiring the mastery of thousands of Chinese characters until the 1990s, but as Korean is not a tonal language like Chinese and therefore has more syllabic variety, the usefulness of Chinese characters in Korean was questionable (although tonal languages like Vietnamese, which also used Chinese characters, eventually replaced them with a romanised alphabet). Today, though, Chinese characters (*hanja*; 漢字) have mostly disappeared from Korea's public space, to the consternation of Chinese and Japanese travellers who used to be able to read all the street and commercial signs. *Hanja* are, however, making a reappearance at tourists sights, due to the growth in Chinese tourism, and you will see old temples, Confucian academies and pagodas inscribed with *hanja*, in their full and traditional form (rather than in the more recent simplified Chinese variant).

King Sejong's face, meanwhile, is etched on the ₩10,000 note.

1251

Monks at Jeondeung-sa, Ganghwado, complete the second *Tripitaka Koreana*, 80,000 woodblocks of Buddhist scriptures; the first having been destroyed in the 1231 Mongol invasion.

1377

Monks at Cheongju's Heungdeok-sa temple beat Johannes Gutenberg by 78 years by creating the *Jikji*, the world's first book printed using moveable metal type.

1392

Having had King Gongyang and his family murdered, General Yi Seong-gye names himself King Taejo and establishes the Joseon dynasty that will rule Korea for the next 500 years.

1394

King Taejo employs geomancy, or feng shui (*pungsu* in Korean), to select Hanyang (Seoul) as Joseon's capital. He also adopts Neo-Confucianism as the country's religion.

Bulguk-sa (Pulguk-sa) temple and the nearby Seokguram Grotto in Gyeongju are both on the Unesco World Cultural Heritage list; the latter dates to around AD 750 and is home to some of the world's finest Buddhist sculptures (though you must admire them from a distance).

Like Silla, Balhae continued to be influenced deeply by the Chinese civilisation of the Tang dynasty, sending students to the capital at Cháng'ān (present-day Xī'ān in Shaanxi province), on which it modelled its own capital city (the Japanese also modelled Kyoto on Cháng'ān).

Unification Under Goryeo

A formidable military leader named Wang Geon had defeated Silla as well as some Baekje remnants by 930 and established a flourishing dynasty, Goryeo, from which came the name Korea. Korea was now fully unified with more or less the boundaries that it retains today. Wang was a magnanimous unifier. Regarding himself as the proper lineal king of Goguryeo, he embraced that kingdom's survivors, took a Silla princess as his wife and treated Silla aristocracy with unprecedented generosity. His dynasty ruled for nearly 500 years and in its heyday was among the most advanced civilisations in the world. Among its cultural achievements was the *Jikji*, a Buddhist text and the oldest surviving book printed with metal moveable type, dating to 1377 and predating the Gutenberg Bible by 78 years; a great flourishing in ceramics, especially celadon; and the *Tripitaka Koreana*, one of the world's largest libraries of Buddhist scriptures, held today at the temple of Haein-sa.

Goryeo Culture

In 1971 the tomb of King Muryeong, the longest-ruling Baekje king, was discovered in Gongju. It contained a wealth of funerary objects that had not seen the light of day in 1500 years, including remains of the king and queen's wooden coffins, golden diadem ornaments, jewellery, clothing accessories and the king's sword.

With its capital at Kaesong, the Goryeo dynasty's composite elite also forged a tradition of aristocratic continuity that lasted down to the modern era. By the 13th century there were two government groupings: civil officials and military officials. At that time the military people were stronger, but thereafter both were known as *yangban* (the two orders), which became the Korean term for aristocracy. Below the hereditary aristocracy were common people such as peasants and merchants. Below them were outcast groups of butchers, tanners and entertainers, who were called *cheonmin* and who lived a caste-like existence, often in separated and ostracised villages, and whose status fell upon their children as well. Likewise, slavery was hereditary (matrilineally), with slaves making up as much as 30% of Goryeo society.

The Goryeo aristocracy admired and interacted with the splendid Chinese civilisation that emerged during the contemporaneous Song dynasty (960–1279). Official delegations and ordinary merchants took Korean gold, silver and ginseng to China in exchange for silk, porcelain and woodblock books. Finely crafted Song porcelain stimulated Korean artisans to produce an even finer type of inlaid celadon pottery – unmatched in the world before or since for the pristine clarity of its blue-green glaze and the delicate art of its inlaid portraits.

1400

Yi Bang-won is crowned King Taejong and he sets about creating a stronger central government and an absolute monarchy. Private armies are banned and many relatives and rivals are killed.

1418

Following King Taejong's abdication, his third son becomes King Sejong, later to be known as Sejong the Great. His father continues to wield power until his death in 1422.

1446

Sejong the Great oversees the invention of *hangeul*, Korea's unique script, which is announced to the public in the document known as the *Hunminjeongeum*.

1592

Seoul falls to Japan during the Imjin War. Korean forces use metal-covered 'turtle boats' to win several decisive naval battles in a successful quest to expel the invaders.

Buddhism was the state religion, but it coexisted with Confucianism throughout the Goryeo period. Buddhist priests systematised religious practice by rendering the Korean version of the Buddhist canon into mammoth woodblock print editions, known as the *Tripitaka*. The first was completed in 1087 after a lifetime of work, but was lost. Another – the *Tripitaka Koreana* – was completed in 1251.

The Rise of the Mongols

This high point of Goryeo culture coincided with internal disorder and the rise of the Mongols, whose power swept most of the known world during the 13th century. Korea was no exception, as Kublai Khan's forces invaded and demolished Goryeo's army in 1231, forcing the government to retreat to the island of Ganghwado, a ploy that exploited the Mongol horsemen's fear of water.

After a more devastating invasion in 1254, in which countless people died and around 200,000 people were taken captive, Goryeo succumbed to Mongol domination and its kings came to intermarry with Mongol princesses. The Mongols then enlisted thousands of Koreans in ill-fated invasions of Japan in 1274 and 1281, using craft made by Korea's great shipwrights. The Kamakura Shogunate turned back both invasions with help, as legend has it, from opportune typhoons known as *kamikaze* (divine wind).

Joseon: The Last Dynasty

The overthrow of the Mongols by the Ming dynasty in China (1316–1644) gave an opportunity to rising groups of Korean military men to contest for power. One of them, Yi Seong-gye, grabbed the bull by the horns and overthrew Goryeo leaders, thus becoming the founder of Korea's longest and last dynasty (1392–1910). The new state was named Joseon, harking back to the old Joseon kingdom 15 centuries earlier, and its capital was built at Seoul.

General Yi announced the new dynasty by mobilising some 200,000 labourers to surround the new capital with a great wall that was completed in 1396. Around 70% of it still stands today, including Sungnyemun (Namdaemun; the Great South Gate) and the Heunginjimun (Dongdaemun; the Great East Gate).

The deep Buddhist influence on the previous dynasty led the literati to urge the king to uproot Buddhist economic and political influence, which led to exile in the mountains for monks and their disciples – this is one of the reasons why many of Korea's Buddhist temples are located in mountain areas.

Influential literati in the Joseon dynasty were ideologues who wanted to restore Korean society to its proper path as they saw it, by using the

The Balhae bequeathed a lasting invention to the Korean people: sleeping on *ondol* floors. This system, which uses flues from a central hearth to heat the floors of each room, is still in wide use in contemporary Korea, with the stone flues covered by waxed and polished rice paper.

1666

Dutchman Hendrick Hamel, held prisoner in the country for 13 years after being shipwrecked off Jeju-do, writes the first Western account of the Joseon dynasty.

1796

King Jeongjo moves the royal court to Suwon and builds the Hwaseong fortress (now a World Heritage site) to protect the new palace.

1800

Sunjo succeeds his father as the 23rd king of the Joseon dynasty and reigns for 34 years, during which time Korean Catholics are increasingly persecuted.

1849

Following the 24th king's death, the Andong Kims track down the great-grandson of King Yeongjo, living in poverty on Ganghwa-do. The illiterate and easily manipulated 18-year-old is crowned King Cheoljong.

virtues to discipline the passions and the interests. Over many decades the literati thus accomplished a deep Confucianisation of Joseon society. The reforming came in the name of Neo-Confucianism and Chu Hsi, the Chinese progenitor of this doctrine. The result was that much of what we now see as 'Korean culture' or 'tradition' arose from major social reorganisation by self-conscious 15th-century ideologues. Foreign observers declared that Korea was 'more Confucian than China'.

Korea & China: A Special Relationship

General Yi Seong-gye founded his dynasty when he refused to send his troops into battle against a Chinese army, instead using them to overthrow his own government and make himself king. Not surprisingly, he received the blessing and support of the Chinese emperor, and Korea became a 'tributary' country to China – but more than that, it became the ideal tributary state, modelling itself on Chinese culture and statecraft.

From 1637 until the end of the practice in 1881, Korea sent a total of 435 special embassies and missions to China. The emperor sent gifts in return, but the lavish hospitality provided to the Chinese emissaries when they came to Seoul could take up 15% of the government's revenue.

Most of the time China left Korea alone to run its own affairs, and Korea was content to look up to China as the centre of the only world civilisation that mattered. This policy was known as *sadae* (serving the great). Because of this special relationship, when Japan attacked in the 1590s, Chinese troops were sent to help repel them. In just one battle, as many as 30,000 Chinese soldiers died.

It isn't clear what the common people thought about China until the modern period, nor were they asked. The vast majority were illiterate in a country that marked its elite according to their literacy – in Chinese. The aristocrats were enthusiastic Confucianists, adopting Chinese painting, poetry, music, statecraft and philosophy. The complicated Chinese script was used for virtually all government and cultural activities throughout the Joseon period, even though the native alphabet, *hangeul,* was an outstanding cultural achievement and possessed astonishing versatility.

Chihwaseon (2002), which won a prize for director Im Kwon-taek at Cannes, is a visually stunning film based on the true story of a talented, nonconformist painter who lived at the end of the Joseon dynasty.

Royal Pomp & Ceremony

Many of the premier cultural attractions in Korea today, such as Seoul's palaces, are imperial relics of the long-lived Joseon dynasty. They are windows into a time in Korea's history when absolute monarchs ruled. Pomp and ritual became an essential aspect of royal power, with attention to ritual and protocol developed into an art form. Koreans appeared to break sharply with this royal system in the 20th century, but when you look at the ruling system in North Korea, or the families that run most of

1864

The 11-year-old Gojong, son of the shrewd courtier Yi Ha-eung (later called the Daewongun or 'Prince of the Great Court'), is crowned Joseon's 26th ruler.

1866

French forces invade Ganghwado, ostensibly in retaliation for the execution of French Catholic priests who had been illicitly proselytising in Korea. They are forced to retreat after six weeks.

1871

Ganghwado witnesses another international tussle as a US diplomatic mission is rebuffed, leading to an armed conflict on the island that leaves 243 Koreans and three Americans dead.

1876

The Japanese prevail in getting Korea to sign the Treaty of Ganghwa, formally opening up three of the nation's ports – Busan, Incheon and Wonsan – to international trade.

South Korea's major corporations, you can see the family and hereditary principles of the old system continuing in modern form.

In these more democratic times it is difficult to imagine the wealth, power and status of Joseon kings. The main palace, Gyeongbokgung (경복궁), contained 800 buildings and more than 200 gates – in 1900, for example, palace costs accounted for 10% of all government expenditures. In the royal household were 400 eunuchs, 500 ladies-in-waiting, 800 other court ladies and 70 *gisaeng* (female entertainers who were expert singers and dancers). Only women and eunuchs were allowed to live inside the palace – male servants, guards, officials and visitors had to leave at sunset.

Most of the women lived like nuns and never left the palace. A *yangban* woman had to be married for years before daring to move in the outer world of society, and then only in a cocoon of clothing inside a cloistered sedan chair, carried by her slaves. In the late 19th century foreigners witnessed these cloistered upper-class women, clothed and swaddled from head to toe, wearing a green mantle like the Middle Eastern chador over their heads and bringing the folds across the face, leaving only the eyes exposed. They would come out after the nightly curfew, after the bells rang and the city gates were closed against tigers, and find a bit of freedom in the darkness.

Lives of the Eunuchs

The only 'male' staff allowed to live inside the palaces, eunuchs (내시; *naesi*) were privy to all the secrets of the state and had considerable influence because they waited upon the king and were around the royal family 24 hours a day. All access to the king was through them, as they were the royal bodyguards and responsible for the safety of their master. This was an easy way to earn money and they usually exploited it to the full. These bodyguard eunuchs, toughened by a harsh training regime of martial arts, were also personal servants to the king and even nursemaids to the royal children. They played so many roles that life must have been very stressful for them, particularly as any mistake could lead to horrific physical punishments.

Although often illiterate and uneducated, a few became important advisers to the king, attaining high government positions and amassing great wealth. Most were from poor families and their greed for money was a national scandal. Eunuchs were supposed to serve the king with total devotion, like monks serving the Buddha, never thinking about mundane matters like money or status.

Surprisingly, eunuchs were usually married and adopted young eunuch boys who they brought up to follow in their footsteps. The eunuch in charge of the king's health would pass on his medical knowledge to his 'son'. Under the Confucian system, eunuchs had to get married. The system continued

Best North Korea Books

Nothing to Envy: Ordinary Lives in North Korea *(Barbara Demick; 2009)* Award-winning account of life in Chongjin, a bleak town near the border with China.

In Order to Live: A North Korean Girl's Journey to Freedom *(Yeonmi Park; 2015)* Eviscerating narration of one young girl's escape from North Korea.

Aquariums of Pyongyang: 10 years in the North Korean Gulag *(Kang Chol-hwan; 2006)* Harrowing tale of a defector who survived a decade in the notorious Yodok camp.

Without You, There Is No Us *(Suki Kim; 2015)* An account of Kim's stint teaching at an elite Pyongyang all-male university.

1882

A military insurrection, supported by the Daewongun, seeks to overthrow King Gojong and reform-minded Queen Myeongseong. They escape Seoul in disguise, returning when support arrives from China.

1884

Progressive forces, backed by Japan, attempt a coup at the royal palace. Again Queen Min calls on the Chinese for help and the revolt is suppressed after three days.

1894

Peasants rise up in the Donghak Rebellion. The rebels are defeated but the Joseon court responds with the Gabo Reform, abolishing slavery, among other sweeping changes.

1895

Queen Min is assassinated at Gyeongbokgung palace. Posthumously named Empress Myeongseong, Min is considered a heroine for her reforms and attempts to maintain Korea's independence.

until 1910 when the country's new Japanese rulers summoned all the eunuchs to Deoksugung and dismissed them from government service.

Korea & Japan

In 1592, 150,000 well-armed Japanese troops, divided into nine armies, rampaged throughout Korea, looting, raping and killing. Palaces and temples were burned to the ground and priceless cultural treasures were destroyed or stolen. Entire villages of ceramic potters were shipped back to Japan, along with thousands of ears clipped from dead Koreans, which were piled into a mound in Japan, covered over and retained into modern times as a memorial to this war.

A series of brilliant naval victories by Admiral Yi Sun-sin helped to turn the tide against the Japanese. Based in Yeosu, Yi perfected the *geobukseon* (거북선; turtle ship), a warship protected with iron sheets and spikes against the Japanese 'grapple and board' naval tactics. The standard Korean warship was the flat-bottomed, double-decked *panokseon* (판옥선), powered by two sails and hard-working oarsmen. It was strong-

DONGHAK DEMANDS

The Donghak Rebellion, which had been building for decades, erupted in 1894 in Jeolla province, attracting large numbers of peasants and low-born groups of people. The rebels were only armed with primitive, homemade weapons, but they defeated the government army. The rebellion then spread to neighbouring provinces, and when King Gojong called in Chinese troops, Japanese troops took advantage of the uproar to march into Seoul. The rebels were defeated and their leaders (including Jeon Bong-jun, who was known as the 'Green Pea General' because of his small size) were executed by Japanese firing squads.

The demands of the rebels revealed their many grievances against the Joseon social system:

- Slaves should be freed.
- The low-born should be treated fairly.
- Land should be redistributed.
- Taxes on fish and salt should be scrapped.
- No unauthorised taxes should be levied and any corrupt *yangban* (aristocrat) should be severely punished.
- All debts should be cancelled.
- Regional favouritism and factions should be abolished.
- Widows should be allowed to remarry.
- Traitors who supported foreign interference should be punished.

1897

As an independence movement grows in Korea, King Gojong declares the founding of the Korean Empire, formalising the end of the country's ties to China.

1900

Korea's modernisation continues with the opening of a railroad between the port of Incheon and Seoul. In the capital an electricity company provides public lighting and a streetcar system.

1905

Treaty of Portsmouth ends the Russo–Japanese war over Manchuria and Korea. Russia recognises Korea as part of Japan's sphere of influence, further imperilling Korea's attempts to become independent.

1907

Having angered Japan by trying to drum up international support for his sovereignty over Korea, Gojong is forced to abdicate in favour of his son, Sunjong.

er and more manoeuvrable than the Japanese warships and had more cannons. With these advantages, clever tactics and an intimate knowledge of the complex patterns of tides and currents around the numerous islands and narrow channels off the southern coast, Admiral Yi was able to sink hundreds of Japanese ships and thwart Japan's ambition to seize Korea and use it as a base for the conquest of China.

Ming troops also arrived from China and by 1597 the Japanese were forced to withdraw. Stout resistance on land and sea thwarted Japanese ambitions to dominate Asia, but only at the cost of massive destruction and economic dislocation in Korea.

Men wearing a topknot were widespread during Korea's pleasant relations with China's Ming dynasty, but later it became a symbol of 'Ming loyalists' in Korea after that dynasty fell. In 1895 King Gojong had his topknot cut off, but conservatives didn't follow his example or share his enthusiasm for reforms.

Japanese Takeover

Japan's ambitions to seize Korea resurfaced at the end of the 19th century, when the country began to rapidly transform into Asia's first modern industrialised power. Seizing on the Donghak peasant rebellion in Korea, Japan instigated war with China, defeating it in 1895. After another decade of imperial rivalry over control of the peninsula, Japan smashed Russia in lightning naval and land attacks, stunning the Western world, which had previously viewed Asians as people to be subjugated rather than feared as economic and military rivals.

Japan was now in a secure position to realise its territorial ambitions with regard to Korea, which became a Japanese protectorate in 1905. Following King Gojong's abdication in 1907, Korea became a full colony of Japan in 1910, with the acquiescence of all the great powers, even though progressive calls were beginning to emerge to dismantle the entire colonial system. Furthermore, Korea had most of the prerequisites for nationhood long before most other countries in colonised areas of the world: common ethnicity, language and culture, and well-recognised national boundaries since the 10th century.

Colonisation

Once fully in control, Japan tried to destroy the Korean sense of national identity. A Japanese ruling elite replaced the Korean *yangban* scholar-officials; Japanese modern education replaced the Confucian classics; Japanese capital and expertise were built up in place of the Korean versions – Japanese talent for Korean talent; and eventually even the Korean language was replaced with Japanese.

Few Koreans thanked the Japanese for these substitutions, or credited Japan with any social improvements. Instead they saw Japan as snatching away the ancient regime, Korea's sovereignty and independence, its indigenous if incipient modernisation and, above all, its national dignity. Most Koreans never saw Japanese rule as anything but illegitimate and humiliating. The very closeness of the two nations – in geography, in common

Historic Bastions

- *Mongchon-toseong, Seoul*
- *Old City Wall, Seoul*
- *Hwaseong, Suwon*
- *Namhansanseong*
- *Banwolseong, Gyeongju*

1909

Independence activist An Jung-geun assassinates Hirobumi Ito, Korea's ex-resident-general, at the train station in Harbin, Manchuria. Japan uses the incident to move towards annexation of the Korean Peninsula.

1910

Emperor Sunjong refuses to sign the Japan–Korea Annexation Treaty, but Japan effectively annexes Korea in August. Terauchi Masatake is the first Japanese governor general of Korea.

1919

The March 1st Movement sees millions of Koreans in nonviolent nationwide protests against Japanese rule. A declaration of independence is read out in Seoul's Tapgol Park.

1926

Emperor Sunjong dies. His half-brother, Crown Prince Euimin, who had married into a branch of the Japanese royal family, is proclaimed King Ri of Korea by the Japanese.

Hendrick Hamel's fascinating account of his 13 years in Korea, after he and 36 other sailors were shipwrecked on Jeju-do in 1653, is available in Gari Ledyard's *The Dutch Come to Korea*, with full scholarly annotation.

Chinese civilisational influences and in levels of development until the 19th century – made Japanese dominance all the more galling to Koreans and gave a peculiar hate/respect dynamic to their relationship.

During colonisation there were instances when Koreans fought back. The South Korean national holiday on 1 March honours the day in 1919 when the death of ex-king Gojong and the unveiling of a Korean declaration of independence sparked massive pro-independence demonstrations throughout the country. The protests were ruthlessly suppressed, but still lasted for months. When it was over, the Japanese claimed that 500 were killed, 1400 injured and 12,000 arrested, but Korean estimates put the casualties at 10 times those figures.

Collaborating with Japan

A certain amount of Korean collaboration with the Japanese was unavoidable given the ruthless nature of the regime under the Japanese colonialists. Also in the last decade of colonial rule, when Japan's expansion across Asia caused a shortage of experts and professionals throughout the empire, educated and ambitious Koreans were further co-opted.

The burst of consumerism that came to the world in the 1920s meant that Koreans shopped in Japanese department stores, banked at Japanese banks, drank Japanese beer, travelled on the Japanese-run railway and often dreamed of attending a Tokyo university.

Ambitious Koreans found new careers opening up to them just at the most oppressive point in this colony's history, as Koreans were commanded to change their names and not speak Korean, and millions were used as mobile human fodder by the Japanese. Koreans constituted almost half of the hated National Police, and young Korean officers (including Park Chung-hee, who seized power in 1961, and Kim Jae-gyu, who, as intelligence chief, assassinated Park in 1979) joined the aggressive Japanese army in Manchuria. Pro-Japanese *yangban* were rewarded with special titles, and some of Korea's greatest early nationalists, such as Yi Gwang-su, were forced into public support of Japan's empire.

The Dongnimmun (독립문; Independence Gate), built in Seoul in 1897 by the Independence Club, stands where envoys from Chinese emperors used to be officially welcomed to the city.

The issue of this collaboration was never punished or fully and frankly debated in South Korea, leaving the problem to fester until 2004, when the government finally launched an official investigation into collaboration – along with estimates that upwards of 90% of the pre-1990 South Korea elite had ties to collaborationist families or individuals.

The colonial government implemented policies that developed industries and modernised the administration, but always in the interests of Japan. Modern textile, steel and chemical industries emerged, along with new railroads, highways and ports. Koreans never thanked Japan for any of this, but it did leave Korea much more developed in 1945 than other countries under colonial rule, such as Vietnam under the French.

1929

A nationwide student uprising in November leads to the strengthening of Japanese military rule in 1931, after which freedom of the press and expression are curbed.

1945

With the Allied victory in WWII, Korea is liberated from Japan and divided into two protectorates – the Soviets handling the North and the US the South.

1947

Between 1947 and 1953 as many as 30,000 islanders on Jeju-do are massacred by right-wing government forces in events collectively labelled the 'April 3 Incident'.

1948

The Republic of Korea (ROK) is founded in the southern part of the peninsula, with Seoul designated the capital city. The Democratic People's Republic of Korea (DPRK, or North Korea) is also founded.

WWII & After

By 1940 the Japanese owned 40% of the land and there were 700,000 Japanese living and working in Korea – an enormous number compared to most other countries. But among large landowners, many were as likely to be Korean as Japanese – most peasants were tenant farmers working their land. Upwards of three million Korean men and women were uprooted from their homes and sent to work as miners, farm labourers, factory workers and soldiers abroad, mainly in Japan and Manchukuo, the Japanese colony in northeast China.

More than 130,000 Korean miners in Japan – men and women – worked 12-hour days, were paid wages well under what Japanese miners earned, were poorly fed and were subjected to brutal, club-wielding overseers. The worst aspect of this massive mobilisation, however, came in the form of 'comfort women' – the hundreds of thousands of young Korean women who were forced to work as sex slaves for the Japanese armed forces.

THE HOUSE OF SHARING

An hour's journey southeast of Seoul, in bucolic countryside, is the **House of Sharing** (나눔의 집; http://nanum.org; 65 Wondang-ri, Gwangju-si, Gyeonggi-do; ₩5000; ⏲10am-5pm Tue-Sun), a very special retirement home and museum. Here live a handful of women, now in their 90s, who were forced to work in Japanese military brothels across Asia before and during WWII. 'Comfort women' is the euphemism coined by the Japanese military for these women, 70% of whom were Korean. A study by the UN has put the number of women involved at around 210,000 (the Japanese government claims the figure was 50,000).

At the House of Sharing they prefer the respectful term *halmoni*, which means grandmother. In the museum here you can learn more about the atrocious conditions and experiences these women were forced to endure. Most of them were aged between 13 and 16, and had to service between 30 and 40 soldiers a day.

'We must record these things that were forced upon us.' These words by Kim Hak Soon, one of the first Korean *halmoni* to testify about her experiences, introduces the museum exhibition which includes a display of the artworks created by the *halmoni* that reflect their feelings and experiences. Video documentaries about the *halmoni* are screened and discussions are held about their plight and the ongoing sexual trafficking of women around the world. The overall picture painted by the guides of these frail, sometimes crotchety women, is of pillars of strength who after a lifetime of shame and sorrow have chosen to spend their twilight years as campaigners for social justice.

It's a heavy-going experience but one not without a sense of hope – both for the resilience of the human spirit and the prospect for reconciliation. The greatest number of visitors to the House come from Japan and every year a Peace Road Program brings Korean and Japanese students together to help further understanding of their countries' painfully entwined history and how they might be better neighbours in the future.

25 June 1950

North Korea stages a surprise invasion of the South over the 38th-parallel border, triggering the Korean War. By the end of the month, it occupies Seoul.

Septemer 1950

UN troops led by US General MacArthur mount a daring counterattack in the Battle of Incheon. By 25 September Seoul is recaptured by South Korean forces.

1953

The armistice ending the Korean War is signed by the US and North Korea, but not South Korea. The Demilitarized Zone (DMZ) is established around the 38th parallel.

1960

Popular protest ousts President Rhee Syngman. Attempts at democratic rule fail – a military coup topples the unstable elected government and installs General Park Chung-hee into power in 1961.

ROOTS OF GENDER INEQUALITY

Park Geun-hye made women's rights one of the cornerstones of her campaign to become South Korea's first female president in 2012. She promised a 'women's revolution' for the country, which ranks 15th on the UN Development Programme's Gender Inequality Index. Women here can expect to make an average of 32% less than a man in the same job.

The roots of such inequality stretch way back to the 15th century, when the Joseon dynasty established new reforms and laws that led to a radical change in women's social position and an expropriation of women's property. Where many women were prominent in Goryeo society, they were now relegated to domestic chores of child-rearing and housekeeping, as so-called 'inside people'.

From then on, the latticework of Korean society was constituted by patrilineal descent. The nails in the latticework, the proof of its importance and existence over time, were the written genealogies that positioned families in the hierarchy of property and prestige. In succeeding centuries a person's genealogy would be the best predictor of his or her life chances – it became one of Korea's most lasting characteristics. Since only male offspring could prolong the family and clan lines, and were the only names registered in the genealogical tables, the birth of a son was greeted with great fanfare.

Such historical influences remain strong in both Koreas today, where first sons and their families often live with the male's parents, and all stops are pulled out to father a boy.

It was Korea's darkest hour, but Korean guerrilla groups continued to fight Japan in Manchukuo – they were allied with Chinese guerrillas, but Koreans still constituted by far the largest ethnic group. This is where we find Kim Il-sung, who began fighting the Japanese around the time they proclaimed the puppet state of Manchukuo in 1932 and continued into the early 1940s. After murderous counterinsurgency campaigns (participated in by many Koreans), the guerrillas numbered only about 200. In 1945 they returned to northern Korea and constituted the ruling elite from that point down to the present.

War Diary of Admiral Yi Sun-sin, edited by Sohn Pow-key (1977), is a straightforward and fascinating account by Korea's greatest admiral of the battles, floggings and court intrigues that were his daily preoccupations.

Mutual Animosity

Japan's surrender to the Allies in 1945 opened a new chapter in the stormy relationship between the two countries. Thanks to munificent American support, Japan began growing rapidly in the early 1950s and South Korea got going in the mid-1960s. Today companies in both countries battle each other to produce the best ships, cars, steel products, computer chips, smartphones, flat-screen TVs and other electronic equipment. The new rivalry is a never-ending competition for world markets.

Several generations have passed since the end of WWII, and Japan and South Korea are both democracies and natural trading partners and allies. However, a high degree of mistrust and mutual animosity remains

1963

Following pressure from the US, civilian rule is restored. However, the Democratic Republican Party, a political vehicle for Park, wins the general election.

1967

Even with rigged elections, and the economic revitalisation of the country well underway, Park only just manages to be reelected president.

1968

In January North Korean agents are halted just 800m from the presidential Blue House, foiling a daring assassination attempt on Park Chung-hee.

1971

The constitution is amended so Park can run for a third term of office. He wins against Kim Dae-jung. The following year Park dissolves parliament and suspends the constitution.

between the countries. Sticking points include perceptions of what happened during the colonisation period and territorial issues over the islands of Dokdo/Takehima. A survey by a Tokyo think tank in 2015 found that 52.4% of Japanese have a negative impression of Korea, while 72.5% of Koreans feel the same about Japan. In South Korea, one survey found that Japan's current right-wing prime minister, Shinzo Abe, is less popular than the North Korean leader, Kim Jong-un.

The Korean War

The 38th Parallel

In the immediate aftermath of the obliteration of Nagasaki, three Americans in the War Department (including Dean Rusk, later Secretary of State) drew a fateful line at the 38th parallel in Korea. The line was supposed to demarcate the areas in which American and Soviet forces would receive the Japanese surrender, but Rusk later acknowledged that he did not trust the Russians and wanted to get the nerve centre of the country, Seoul, into the American zone. He consulted no Koreans, no allies and not even the president in making this decision. But it followed on from three years of State Department planning in which an American occupation of part or all of Korea was seen as crucial to the postwar security of Japan and the Pacific. The US then set up a three-year military government in southern Korea that deeply shaped postwar Korean history.

The Soviets came in with fewer concrete plans for Korea and moved more slowly than the Americans in setting up an administration. They thought Kim Il-sung would be good as a defence minister in a new government, but sought to get him and other communists to work together with Christian nationalist figures such as Jo Man-sik. Soon, however, the Cold War rivalry overshadowed everything in Korea, as the Americans turned to Rhee Syngman (an elderly patriot who had lived in the US for 35 years) and the Russians to Kim Il-sung.

By 1948 Rhee and Kim had established separate republics and by the end of the year, Soviet troops had withdrawn, never to return again. American combat troops departed in June 1949, leaving behind a 500-man military advisory group. For the first time in its short history since 1945, South Korea had operational control of its own military forces. Within a year war had broken out and the US took back that control and has never relinquished it.

The War Begins

In 1949 both sides sought external support to mount a war against the other side, and the North succeeded where the South failed. Its greatest strength came from tens of thousands of Koreans who had been sent to fight in China's civil war, and who returned to North Korea in 1949 and 1950. Kim

Isabella Bird Bishop visited Gyeongbokgung in 1895 and noted: 'What with 800 troops, 1500 attendants and officials of all descriptions, courtiers and ministers and their attendants, secretaries, messengers and hangers-on, the vast enclosure of the palace seemed as crowded and populated as the city itself'.

1972
The new constitution, which includes no limits on reelection, turns Park's presidency into a virtual dictatorship. He's reelected with no opposition in both 1972 and 1978.

1979
After surviving a couple of assassination attempts (one of which killed his wife), Park is shot dead by the trusted head of his own Central Intelligence Agency.

1980
The military brutally suppresses a pro-democracy uprising in the southern city of Gwangju, killing at least 154 civilians and wounding or arresting more than 4000 others.

1987
Following sweeping national protests, with the strongest concentration in Seoul, Korea's last military dictatorship (under Chun Doo-hwan) steps down to allow democratic elections.

Korea, by Angus Hamilton (1904), is a rare and lively description of life in Korea under the last dynasty.

Il-sung also played Stalin off against Mao Zedong to get military aid and a critical independent space for himself, so that when he invaded he could count on one or both powers to bail him out if things went badly. After years of guerrilla war in the South (fought almost entirely by southerners) and much border fighting in 1949, Kim launched a surprise invasion on 25 June 1950, when he peeled several divisions off in the midst of summer war games; many high officers were unaware of the war plan. Seoul fell in three days, and soon North Korea was at war with the US.

The Americans responded by getting the UN to condemn the attack and gaining commitments from 16 other countries, although Americans almost always bore the brunt of the fighting, and only British and Turkish combat forces had a substantial role. The war went badly for the UN at first and its troops were soon pushed far back into a small pocket around Busan (Pusan). But following a daring landing at Incheon (Inchon) under the command of General Douglas MacArthur, North Korean forces were pushed back above the 38th parallel.

Creating the DMZ

The question then became whether the war was over. South Korea's sovereignty had been restored and UN leaders wanted to call it a victory. But for the previous year, high officials in the Truman administration had been debating a more 'positive' strategy than containment, namely 'rollback' or liberation, and so Truman decided to march north to overthrow Kim's regime. Kim's long-time relations with Chinese communists bailed his chestnuts out of the fire when Mao committed a huge number of soldiers, but now the US was at war with China.

By the start of 1951, US forces were pushed back below the 38th parallel, and the communists were about to launch an offensive that would retake Seoul. This shook America and its allies to the core, Truman declared a national emergency and WWIII seemed to be at the doorstep. But Mao did not want general war with the US and did not try to push the UN forces off the peninsula. By spring 1951 the fighting had stabilised roughly along the lines where the war ended. Truce talks began, dragging on for two years amid massive trench warfare along the lines. These battles created the Demilitarized Zone (DMZ).

US Academic Bruce Cumings' *The Korean War: A Modern History* (2010) and UK journalist Max Hastings' *The Korean War* (1988) are two takes on this pivotal conflict, analysing its causes, progress and repercussions.

At the end of the war, Korea lay in ruins. Seoul had changed hands no less than four times and was badly damaged, but many prewar buildings remained sufficiently intact to rebuild them much as they were. The US Air Force pounded the North for three years until all of its cities were destroyed and some were completely demolished, leaving the urban population to live, work and go to school underground, like cavemen. Millions of Koreans died (probably three million, two-thirds of them in the North), millions more were left homeless, industries were destroyed and

1988

Seoul hosts the Summer Olympic Games, bulldozing and/or concealing slums to build a huge Olympic park south of the Han River and a major expressway.

1991

Following two years of talks, an Agreement of Reconciliation is signed between Seoul and Pyongyang. One of the aims is to make the Korean Peninsula nuclear-free.

1992

The first civilian to hold the office since 1960, Kim Young-sam, is elected president. During his five-year term he presides over a massive anti-corruption campaign.

1994

During nuclear-program negotiations with the US, and prior to what would have been a historic summit with Kim Young-sam, North Korea's Kim Il-sung dies of a heart attack.

the entire country was massively demoralised because the bloodletting had only restored the status quo. Of the UN troops, 37,000 were killed (about 35,000 of them Americans) and 120,000 were wounded.

Postwar Recovery

The 1950s was a time of depressing stagnation for the South, but rapid industrial growth for the North. Then, over the next 30 years, both Koreas underwent rapid industrial growth. The North's growth was as fast as any in the world from the mid-1950s into the mid-1970s, and even in the early 1980s its per-capita GNP was about the same as the South's. But then the South began to build an enormous lead that soon became insurmountable and by the 1990s huge economic disparities had emerged. The North experienced depressing stagnation that led finally to famine and massive death, while the South emerged as a major global economic power.

RISE OF THE JAEBEOL

Much of the credit for what came to be known as the 'Miracle on the Han' (after the Han River running through Seoul) belongs to Korea's industrial conglomerates or *jaebeol* (also spelt *chaebol;* 재벌). Although their origins as family-owned business organisations stretch back to the days of Japanese colonisation, it was in the 1960s that the *jaebeol* came into their own. In 1963 the key companies came together to form the Federation of Korean Industries to promote their interest and support President Park Chung-hee's drive for economic development.

Operating under a motto of 'if it doesn't work, make it work' Hyundai, in particular, made huge strides for Korea – for example, building the 400km-long Gyeongbu Expressway connecting Seoul to Busan in less than 2½ years, and building a successful shipyard from scratch as a new business. In contrast to this gung-ho approach, Samsung had a reputation for reviewing all the options before making a choice – something that served it equally well as it became the country's largest *jaebeol,* its revenue accounting for around 15% of South Korea's GDP.

This great triumph came at enormous cost, as South Koreans worked the longest hours in the industrial world for decades and suffered under one military dictatorship after another. Corrupt, autocratic rulers censored the media, imprisoned and tortured political opponents, manipulated elections and continually changed the country's constitution to suit themselves. Washington backed them up (except for a brief moment in the 1960s) and never did more than issue tepid protests at their authoritarian rule. Student protests and less frequent trade-union street protests were often violent, as were the police or military forces sent to suppress them. But slowly a democratisation movement built strength across the society.

1996

Two ex-presidents, Chun Doo-hwan and Roh Tae-woo, are put on trial and jailed for corruption charges. A year later they are both pardoned by President-elect Kim Dae-jung.

1997

Long-time democracy champion Kim Dae-jung is elected president in the midst of a region-wide economic crisis. The International Monetary Fund offers the country a $57-million bailout.

1998

Kim Jong-il takes full power on the 50th anniversary of the founding of North Korea, at the same time as his deceased father is proclaimed the country's 'eternal leader'.

2000

In June Kim Dae-jung and Kim Jong-il meet in Pyongyang at the first-ever summit of the two countries. Kim Dae-jung is awarded the Nobel Peace Prize.

Dictatorship & Massacre

Samurai Invasion, by Stephen Turnbull (2002), is a detailed account of the Japanese invasions of Korea in the 1590s.

When the Korean War ended in 1953, Rhee Syngman continued his dictatorial rule until 1961, when he and his wife fled to Hawaii following widespread demonstrations against him that included university professors demonstrating in the streets of Seoul. Ordinary people were finally free to take revenge against hated policemen who had served the Japanese. Following a military coup later in 1961, Park Chung-hee ruled with an iron fist until the Kennedy administration demanded that he hold elections. He narrowly won three of them in 1963, 1967 and 1971, partly by spreading enormous amounts of money around (peasants would get envelopes full of cash for voting).

In spite of this, the democracy activist Kim Dae-jung nearly beat him in 1971, garnering 46% of the vote. That led Park to declare martial law and make himself president for life. Amid massive demonstrations in 1979, his own intelligence chief, Kim Jae-gyu, shot him dead over dinner one night, in an episode never fully explained. This was followed by five months of democratic discussion until Chun Doo-hwan, a protégé of Park, moved to take full power.

In response the citizens of Gwangju took to the streets on 18 May 1980, in an incident now known as the May 18 Democratic Uprising. The army was ordered to move in, on the pretext of quelling a communist uprising. The soldiers had no bullets, but used bayonets to murder dozens of unarmed protesters and passers-by. Outraged residents broke into armouries and police stations and used seized weapons and ammunition to drive the troops from their city.

For over a week pro-democracy citizen groups were in control, but the brutal military response came nine days later, on 27 May, when soldiers armed with loaded rifles, supported by helicopters and tanks, retook the city. Most of the protest leaders were labelled communists and summarily shot. At least 154 civilians were killed, with another 74 missing, presumed dead. An additional 4141 were wounded and more than 3000 were arrested, many of whom were tortured.

The fascinating *Times Past in Korea: An Illustrated Collection of Encounters, Customs and Daily Life Recorded by Foreign Visitors* (2003) was compiled by Martin Uden, former British ambassador to South Korea.

The Return of Democracy

Finally, in 1992, a civilian, Kim Young-sam, won the presidential election and began to build a real democracy. Although a charter member of the old ruling groups, Kim had resigned his National Assembly seat in the 1960s when Rhee tried to amend the constitution and had since been a thorn in the side of the military governments along with Kim Dae-jung. Among his first acts as president were to launch an anticorruption crusade, free thousands of political prisoners and put Chun Doo-hwan on trial.

The former president's conviction of treason and monumental corruption was a great victory for the democratic movement. One of the

2002
Human-rights lawyer Roh Moo-hyun becomes South Korea's 16th president and continues the 'Sunshine Policy' of engagement with the North. South Korea and Japan cohost soccer's World Cup.

2003
North Korea withdraws from the Nuclear Non-Proliferation Treaty. The first round of the so-called 'six-party talks' between North and South Korea, China, Japan, Russia and the US begin.

2005
The death of King Gojong's 74-year-old grandson, Lee Gu, in Tokyo ends the Joseon dynasty's bloodline and any possibility of the return of a monarchy in Korea.

2006
In October North Korea claims to have successfully conducted an underground nuclear test explosion. By the end of the month North Korea rejoins the six-party disarmament talks.

strongest labour movements in the world soon emerged and when former dissident Kim Dae-jung was elected at the end of 1997, all the protests and suffering and killing seemed finally to have effected change.

Kim was ideally poised to solve the deep economic downturn that hit Korea in 1997, as part of the Asian financial crisis. The International Monetary Fund (IMF) demanded reforms of the *jaebeol* as the price for its $57-million bailout, and Kim had long called for a restructure of the conglomerates and their cronyism with the banks and the government. By 1999 the economy was growing again.

Sunshine Policy

In 1998 Kim also began to roll out a 'Sunshine Policy' aimed at reconciliation with North Korea, if not reunification. Within a year Pyongyang had responded, various economic and cultural exchanges began and, in June 2000, the two presidents met at a summit for the first time since 1945. Seen by critics as appeasement of the North, this engagement policy was predicated on the realist principles that the North was not going to collapse and so had to be dealt with as it was, and that the North would not object to the continued presence of US troops in the South during the long process of reconciliation if the US normalised relations with the North – something Kim Jong-il acknowledged in his historic summit meeting with Kim Dae-jung in June 2000.

Between 2000 and 2008, when Lee Myung-bak's administration suspended the policy, tens of thousands of South Koreans were able to visit the North, some for heartbreakingly brief meetings with relatives they hadn't seen for half a century. Big southern firms established joint ventures using northern labour in a purpose-built industrial complex at Kaesong. In 2000 Kim Dae-jung was awarded the Nobel Peace Prize for implementing the Sunshine Policy.

After Kim

When President Kim retired after his five-year term his party selected a virtual unknown, Roh Moo-hyun, a self-taught lawyer who had defended many dissidents in the darkest periods of the 1980s. To the surprise of many, including officials in Washington, he narrowly won the 2002 election and represented the rise to power of a generation that had nothing to do with the political system that emerged in 1945 (even Kim Dae-jung had been active in the 1940s). That generation was mostly middle-aged, having gone to school in the 1980s with indelible images of conflict on their campuses and American backing for Chun Doo-hwan. The result was a growing estrangement between Seoul and Washington, for the first time in the relationship.

Sourcebook of Korean Civilisation (1993), edited by Peter H Lee, has a wide selection of original historical documents and materials, in translation and with commentary.

2007
Former South Korean foreign minister Ban Ki-moon becomes the eighth UN Secretary General. Lee Myung-bak, ex-CEO of Hyundai Engineering and Construction and Seoul mayor, becomes South Korea's 17th president.

2008
President Lee faces his first major domestic challenge as 20,000 people take to Seoul's streets to protest a government plan to resume US beef imports.

2009
The nation mourns as former president Roh Moo-hyun, under investigation for corruption, commits suicide in May. Another former premier, Kim Dae-jung, succumbs to natural causes in August.

2010
Seoul hosts the G20 Economic Summit and becomes World Design Capital, but its centrepiece – Dongdaemun Design Plaza & Park, by architect Zaha Hadid – remains uncompleted.

The Dawn of Modern Korea (Andrei Lankov; 2007) is a fascinating, accessible look at Korea in the early 20th century and the cultural and social impacts of Westernisation as King Gojong tried to modernise his tradition-bound hermit kingdom.

Roh continued Kim's policy of engagement with the North, but his mismanagement of the economy and the decision to send South Korean troops to Iraq saw his public support plummet. The opposition tried to impeach Roh when, ahead of national parliamentary elections in 2004, he voiced support for the new Uri Party – a technical violation of a constitutional provision for the president to remain impartial. The impeachment failed, but Roh's popularity continued to slip and the Uri Party, suffering several defeats by association with the president, chose to distance itself from him by reforming as the Democratic Party.

The end result was a swing to the right that saw Lee Myung-bak of the Grand National Party elected president in 2007, and Roh retire to the village of Bongha, his birthplace in Gyeongsangnam-do. Eighteen months later, as a corruption investigation zeroed in on his family and former aides, Roh committed suicide by jumping off a cliff behind the village. The national shock at this turn of events rebounded on President Lee, who was already suffering public rebuke for opening Korea to imports of US beef.

Changes of Guard

President Lee served out his five-year term of office, to be replaced in the December 2012 national election by Park Geun-hye, South Korea's first female president and the daughter of former dictator Park Chung-hee. Born

TAMING KOREA'S UNRULY PARLIAMENT

In 2009 *Foreign Policy* magazine cited South Korea's National Assembly as one of the most unruly parliaments in the world, where debates often get out of hand and even resort to violence. Such were the scenes in 2004 when then-President Roh Moo-hyun was being impeached. In 2008 angry opposition lawmakers reached for sledgehammers and electric saws to break into a locked committee room where the governing Grand National Party (now renamed Saenuri, or New Frontier Party) was attempting to rush though a free-trade bill. This was followed by a 12-day sit-in before the matter was resolved. Fist fights again broke out during the heated debate over media privatisation in July 2009. And in 2011, during a vote to ratify the nation's free-trade agreement with the US, an opposition lawmaker exploded a tear-gas canister in the chamber.

In December 2014 no such scenes accompanied the passing of the 2015 budget – the first time since 2002 that the budget had been passed within the constitutional deadline of 30 days before its implementation at the start of January. However, it wasn't exactly that politicians had mended their brawling ways. The deadline for budget approval was met because of new legislation mandating that the budget bill is automatically forwarded to a plenary session by 30 November. Speaking to the *Korea Herald*, Myongji University professor of politics Chung Jin-min said that the law attempted to create a 'culture of handshaking' among lawmakers.

2011

Independent candidate and former human-rights lawyer Park Won-soon is elected Seoul's mayor. He puts the brakes on major construction projects, focusing instead on welfare spending.

2012

Park Geun-hye, daughter of South Korea's former dictator Park Chung-hee, wins the presidential election for the right-of-centre Saenuri Party and becomes the country's first female leader.

2013

Tensions between North and South Korea ratchet up as Pyongyang carries out an underground nuclear-bomb test and, in response to subsequent UN sanctions, says it's scrapping the 1953 truce.

2014

Protestors are arrested as a candlelight vigil in Seoul turns into angry demands for the Park Geun-hye government to resign over the Sewol ferry disaster.

in 1952, Park had served as the country's first lady in the 1970s, following the assassination of her mother in 1974 and before the killing of her father in 1979. She publicly apologised for the suffering of pro-democracy activists under her father's dictatorial regime and was first elected as an MP in 1998. Quite apart from her political stance, Park was not married, which in South Korea's conservative society elevated the significance of her presidential election win even more.

In October 2011 Park Won-soon, a former human-rights lawyer and independent candidate, was elected Seoul's mayor, ending a decade of right-wing political domination of the capital. In February 2012 Park affiliated himself with the Democratic Union Party (DUP) and in 2014 won a second term of office in the most powerful post in South Korea after the president. That same year the DUP merged with the New Political Vision Party to form the New Politics Alliance for Democracy (NPAD), but performed poorly in by-elections in 2015.

Other succession issues dominated the Korean Peninsula. North of the border, Kim Jong-un was hailed the 'great successor' following the death of his father, Kim Jong-il, in December 2011. At the time little was known about Kim Jnr, the third in the family dynasty that has ruled the repressive single-party state since 1948 – even his birthday (1982–1984?) was unclear, though it was known he had been educated in Switzerland, a period that saw him develop a strong fondness for Nike trainers (according to his classmates). North Korea analysts scrambled to interpret scraps of news from the secretive country, such as the public appearances of Ri Sol-ju, officially acknowledged as Kim's wife, and the public execution of Kim's uncle, Jang Sung-taek, who had previously been believed to be pulling the strings of power behind the scenes.

Downfall of Park Geun-hye

In April 2015, South Korean President Park suffered a further setback when the prime minister, Lee Wan-koo, tendered his resignation after just two months in the job following bribery accusations by a business tycoon who had recently committed suicide, leaving a letter detailing alleged corruption. Lee was the fifth of Park's prime ministers since 2013 and charges against him followed hard on his declaration of an 'all-out war' on corruption by the government.

All this was mere a mere softening up for the final, inglorious demise of Park Geun-hye, when she was impeached and removed from office in 2017 for abuse of power and corruption and finally sentenced to 24 years in prison in 2018. Park was succeeded by Moon Jae-in of the Democratic Party, a former human-rights lawyer, whose early presidential tenure was most notably marked by a warming of relations with North Korea in 2018.

Korea: The Impossible Country, by Daniel Tudor (2012), is a good primer on modern life and times in Korea, including aspects of the country's history and politics.

2017

Park Geun-hye is forced to step down as South Korean president after she is impeached for corruption and abuse of power.

2018

South Korean President Moon Jae-in meets with North Korean leader Kim Jong-un to sign the Panmunjom Declaration, which seeks a formal conclusion to the Korean War.

2018

US President Donald Trump and North Korean leader Kim Jong-un meet at a summit in Singapore and sign a joint declaration, pledging to denuclearise the Korean Peninsula.

The Korean People

Once divided strictly along nearly inescapable social-class lines, South Koreans today are comparatively better off in terms of economic opportunities and are more individualistic in their world view. Nuclear rather than extended families have become the norm, and birth rates are among the lowest in the developed world. Still, there linger strong traces of Korea's particular identity; remnants of its Confucian past coexist alongside 'imported' spiritual beliefs and a striking devotion to displays of material success.

The Main Belief Systems

Confucianism

The state religion of the Joseon dynasty, Confucianism (*Yugyo*, 유교) lives on as a kind of ethical bedrock in the minds of most Koreans.

The Chinese philosopher Confucius (552–479 BC), known in Korean as Gongja (공자), devised a system of ethics that emphasised devotion to parents and family, loyalty to friends and dedication to education. He also urged that respect and deference be given to those in positions of authority. These ideas led to the system of civil-service examinations *(gwageo)*, where one could gain position through ability and merit rather than from noble birth or connections. Confucius preached against corruption and excessive taxation, and was the first teacher to open a school to all students solely on the basis of their willingness to learn.

As Confucianism trickled into Korea it evolved into Neo-Confucianism, which combined the sage's original ethical and political ideas with the quasi-religious practice of ancestor worship and the idea of the eldest male as spiritual head of the family.

Korean Buddhism operates a templestay (http://eng.templestay.com) program at facilities across the country. Many Koreans as well as international visitors take part in these programs, regardless of whether they are Buddhist or not, as a chance to escape societal pressures and clear their minds.

Buddhism

When first introduced during the Koguryo dynasty in AD 370, Buddhism coexisted with shamanism. Many Buddhist temples have a *samseong-gak* (three-spirit hall) on their grounds, which houses shamanist deities such as the Mountain God.

Buddhism was persecuted during the Joseon period, when temples were tolerated only in remote mountains. The religion suffered another sharp decline after WWII as Koreans pursued worldly goals. But South Korea's success in achieving developed-nation status, coupled with a growing interest in spiritual values, is encouraging a Buddhist revival. Temple visits have increased and large sums of money are flowing into temple reconstruction. According to 2015 data from Statistics Korea, 7.7 million Koreans (15% of the population) claim to be Buddhist.

FORTUNE-TELLING

These days most people visit street-tent fortune tellers for a bit of fun, but no doubt some take it seriously. For a *saju* (reading of your future), inform the fortune-teller of the hour, day, date and year of your birth; another option is *gunghap* (a love-life reading), when a couple give their birth details and the fortune-teller pronounces how compatible they are. Expect to pay ₩10,000 for *saju* and double that for *gunghap*. If you don't speak the language, you'll need someone to translate.

Entrance to the Gangnam subway station, Seoul, South Korea

Christianity

Korea's first exposure to Christianity was in the late 18th century. It came via the Jesuits from the Chinese Imperial court when a Korean aristocrat was baptised in Beijing in 1784. The Catholic faith took hold and spread so quickly that it was perceived as a threat by the Korean government and was vigorously suppressed, creating the country's first Christian martyrs.

Christianity got a second chance in the 1880s with the arrival of American Protestant missionaries who founded schools and hospitals, and gained many followers. Today, about 13.5 million Koreans (26% of the population) claim some sort of affiliation with a Christian church.

Shamanism

Historically, shamanism influenced Korean spirituality. It's not a religion but it does involve communication with spirits through intermediaries known as *mudang* (female shamans). Although not widely practised today, shamanist ceremonies are held to cure illness, ward off financial problems or guide a deceased family member safely into the spirit world.

Ceremonies involve contacting spirits who are attracted by lavish offerings of food and drink. Drums beat and the *mudang* dances herself into a frenzied state that allows her to communicate with the spirits and be possessed by them. Resentments felt by the dead can plague the living and cause all sorts of misfortune, so their spirits need placating. For shamanists, death does not end relationships. It simply takes another form.

On Inwangsan, in northwestern Seoul, ceremonies take place in or near the historic Inwangsan Guksadang shrine.

About 90% of Korean Buddhist temples belong to the Jogye sect (www.korean buddhism.net). The Buddha's birthday is a national holiday, and celebrations includes an extravagant lantern parade in Seoul.

Competitive Lives

Koreans don't think much of happiness. It's not a state of mind that people generally aspire to. When discussing the human condition, *stress* is a much more descriptive word. People here, it seems, are in a

continual state of stress or are seeking ways to escape it through faddish elixirs. Much of that stress comes from the way life is manifest: it's a zero-sum game. From corporate manoeuvres to primary-school maths class, everything is competitive.

Take, for example, the country's hypercompetitive education system. To get into a top Korean university, high-school students go through a gruelling examination process, spending 14 hours a day or more memorising reams of data for the annual college-entrance test. But that's only part of the story. A good number of students give up the game, feign studying or simply sleep in class because the race to the top is no longer a reflection of one's abilities or willpower. Vast amounts of money for pri-

KOREA'S SPORTING CULTURE

Baseball rules as the most popular spectator sport – the Korean Baseball Organization (KBO) reported 8.4m spectators during the league's 2017 season. Among the young, soccer is a popular game to play, or to watch on TV if the match involves the Korean national team in a World Cup match. Interest in soccer peaked with Park Ji-sung, the most decorated player in Asian history. Since his retirement in 2014, Park has served as a Global Ambassador for Manchester United.

Baseball

There are 10 professional teams in the KBO, all sponsored by *jaebeol* (business conglomerates). Five teams are based in or around Seoul. The LG Twins and Doosan Bears share Jamsil stadium in Seoul. The other five teams play in Korea's largest cities and regions. The season runs from April to October and each team plays 144 games. Since 2014, teams have been allowed to sign up to three foreign players (in the past, two players), a strategy designed to increase the calibre of play. Salary caps and mandatory one-year contracts for foreign players were abolished by the league in the same year.

Soccer

There are two divisions in Korean professional soccer: 12 teams play in the top-tier K-League 1, and 10 teams in the second-division K-League 2. Matches are played between March and November. The Korean national team's greatest accomplishment was finishing fourth in the 2002 World Cup.

Basketball

Ten teams play in the Korean Basketball League (KBL). Each team plays 54 games during the regular season, October to March. Two foreign players (usually Americans) are allowed on each team; in 2018 the KBL imposed new height limits for foreign players, stating that one player cannot not be taller than 2m and one may be no taller than 1.86m. David Simon, an American centre player for Anyang KGC and the number-one scorer in the league during the 2017–2018 season, was expelled for standing 2.02m, along with several other players.

Taekwondo

By some accounts taekwondo is the world's most popular martial art (measured by number of participants). This is despite only having been cobbled together at the end of WWII by fighters who wanted a sport that, on the surface at least, was unrelated to anything Japanese. Bits were taken from (ahem) karate and blended with lesser-known Korean fighting skills such as *taekyon*, which relies primarily on leg thrusts. By the mid-1950s the name 'taekwondo' was born.

Today, taekwondo thrives as a sport that most boys practice as primary-school students. It is also part of the physical training program that young men complete as part of their compulsory military service. Taekwondo in Korea is not a popular spectator sport. Matches are not broadcast on TV and few tournaments draw popular attention outside the Olympics. In 2014, the World Taekwondo Federation opened a training facility and museum in Deogyusan National Park in Muju-gun.

THE CONFUCIAN MINDSET

Not everyone follows the rules, but Confucianism does continue to shape the Korean paradigm. Some of the key principles and practices:

➡ Public, symbolic displays of obedience and respect towards seniors (parents, teachers, the boss, older brothers and sisters) are crucial. Expect a penalty if you step out of line.

➡ Seniors get obedience, but it's not a free ride. Older sisters help out younger siblings with tuition fees, and the boss always pays for lunch.

➡ Education is the mark of a civilised person. A high-school graduate, despite having built a successful business, still feels shame at their lack of scholastic credentials.

➡ Obvious displays of one's social status, from brand names worn by middle-school children to overzealous criticisms by an airline executive about the way a steward presents a bag of nuts, are paramount. Every action reflects on the family, company and country.

➡ Everything on earth is in a hierarchy. Never, ever, forget who is senior and who is junior to you.

➡ Families are more important than individuals. Everyone's purpose in life is to improve the family's reputation and wealth. No one should choose a career or marry someone against their parents' wishes – a bad choice could bring about family ruin.

➡ Loyalty is important. A loyal liar is virtuous.

vate education are required to be competitive at school. As a result, higher education is no longer a social leveller, it exacerbates social divisions.

To stay competitive, Korean fanaticism extends to health. The millions of hikers who stream into the mountains at weekends are not only enjoying nature but also keeping fit. Thousands of health foods and drinks are sold in markets and pharmacies, which stock traditional as well as Western medicines. Nearly every food claims to be a 'well-being' product or an aphrodisiac – 'good for stamina' is the local phrase.

Contemporary & Traditional Culture

Driven by the latest technology and fast-evolving trends, Korea can sometimes seem like one of the most cutting-edge countries on the planet. People tune into their favourite TV shows via their smartphones. In PC *bang* (computer-game rooms) millions of diehard fans battle at online computer games.

General fashions too tend to be international and up to the moment. However, it's not uncommon to see some people wearing *hanbok*, the striking traditional clothing that follows the Confucian principle of unadorned modesty. Women wear a loose-fitting short blouse with long sleeves and a voluminous long skirt, while men wear a jacket and baggy trousers.

Today *hanbok* is worn mostly at weddings or special events, and even then it may be a more comfortable 'updated' version. Everyday *hanbok* is reasonably priced, but formal styles, made of colourful silk and intricately embroidered, are objects of wonder and cost a fortune.

Koreans give their family name first followed by their birth name, which is typically two syllables, eg Lee Myong-bak. There are fewer than 300 Korean family names, with Kim, Lee, Park and Jeong accounting for 46% of the total.

Multiculturalism

Korea is a monocultural society. As of 2016, *foreigners* (the local name given to foreign nationals) numbered two million or 3.9% of the population. Foreign residents tend to congregate in pockets, such as international tradespeople working in the shipbuilding industry on Geojedo, though none qualify as a distinct cultural community.

Much like a foreigner among any homogenous group of people, you can expect to get stared at in public. This can be more intense depending on how melanin-rich your skin is, and often lingers most unabashedly from people of older generations.

In the Korean Kitchen

Koreans love eating out and dining options range from casual bites at a market stall to elaborate multicourse meals at lavish restaurants. Booking ahead is rarely needed except in top-end restaurants, which can require booking weeks in advance. The main course is nearly always served with *bap* (boiled rice), soup, kimchi (pickled vegetables) and a procession of *banchan* (side dishes).

Restaurant Types & Typical Dishes

Barbecue

Perhaps the most recognisable of Korean restaurants, these are often boisterous establishments where every table has its own small grill and the main selling point is the quality of the meat and the marinade. The menu typically consists of a mind-boggling array of meat cuts. Beef, usually local, is highly prized and more expensive; pork is more afforda-

Above Bibimbap, a dish of rice, meat and vegetables, is a speciality of Jeonju, South Korea.

ble. Bulgogi is thin slices of meat, marinated in sweetened soy sauce, while *galbi* are short ribs, similarly flavoured. These terms usually refer to beef but can also be used for pork *(dwaeji)*. Another popular cut is *samgyeopsal* (streaky pork belly).

Diners cook their own meat on the grill, though servers will assist foreign customers. Grilled meats are often eaten wrapped in *ssam* (vegetable leaves) with slices of fresh garlic, green pepper, kimchi and a daub of spicy *ssamjang* (soybean and red-pepper sauce). The vegetables used for *ssam* are lettuce, perilla (similar to shiso leaf, and what Koreans call wild sesame), crown daisy and seaweed. Rounding off the meal – or just something to munch on while the meat is cooking – are dishes such as *bossam* (steamed pork and kimchi), *pajeon* (green-onion pancake) or *jjigae* (stew). Expect to pay ₩12,000 to ₩50,000 per person.

All-seafood barbecues (sometimes called grilled seafood) on the coast focus on oily fish such as mackerel, but also include flounder and squid, served with an array of *banchan*. Expect to pay ₩10,000 to ₩20,000 per person.

Seoul is the best place to take cookery courses in English. A great online resource is Maangchi's recipe archive (www.maangchi.com/recipes), which includes demonstration videos.

Soups, Stews, Jeongol & Jjim

Many Korean dishes are served as boiling or sizzling hot off the stove. Besides the soup that accompanies every meal, there are many hearty, piquant main-course soups called *tang* or *guk*. Soup restaurants usually specialise in just a few dishes.

Samgyetang is a ginseng chicken soup, infused with jujube, ginger and other herbs. It's not spicy and is very easy on the palate – the idea is to savour the hint of ginseng and the quality of the chicken. Though it originated as court cuisine, it is now enjoyed as a summer tonic.

A stouter alternative is *gamjatang*, a spicy peasant soup with meaty bones and potatoes. Other meat broths are delicate, even bland, such as *galbitang* (beef-rib soup) or *seolleongtang* (beef and rice soup). *Haejangguk* (hangover soup), to dispel the night's excesses, is made from a *doenjang* (fermented soybean paste) base, with bean sprouts, vegetables and sometimes cow's blood.

Jjigae are stews for everyday eating, often orangey, spicy and served in a stone hotpot. The main ingredient is usually *dubu* (tofu), *doenjang* or kimchi, with vegetables and meat or fish. *Budae jjigae* ('army stew') was concocted during the Korean War using leftover hot dogs, Spam and macaroni scrounged from American bases.

LOCAL SPECIALITIES

- *jjimdak* (simmered chicken) – Andong
- *ureok* (rockfish) – Busan
- *dakgalbi* (spicy chicken grilled with vegetables and rice cakes) – Chuncheon
- *maneul* (garlic) – Danyang
- *sundubu* (soft or uncurdled tofu) – Gangneung
- *oritang* (duck soup); *tteokgalbi* (grilled patties of ground beef) – Gwangju
- *okdomgui* (grilled, semidried fish); *jeonbok-juk* (abalone rice porridge); *heukdwaeji* (black-pig pork) – Jeju-do
- bibimbap – Jeonju
- *ojing-eo* (squid) served *sundae* (sausage) style – Sokcho
- *galbi* (beef ribs) – Suwon
- *chungmu gimbap* (rice, dried seaweed and kimchi) – Tongyeong
- *gatkimchi* (leafy mustard kimchi) – Yeosu

In 2012, Jeonju in Jeollabuk-do was recognised as a Unesco City of Gastronomy for safeguarding its culinary heritage. One visit to its hugely popular street-food stalls and you can see and taste why.

Jeongol is a more elaborate stew, often translated as a casserole or hotpot. Raw ingredients are arranged in a shallow pan at the table, then topped with a spicy broth and brought to a boil. *Jjim* are dishes where the main ingredient is marinated in sauce, then simmered in a broth or steamed until the liquid is reduced. It's a popular (and extremely spicy) serving style for prawns, crab and fish. Soup and stew meals cost ₩6000 to ₩20,000 per person. *Jeongol* and *jjim* are rarely served in individual portions, unlike *jjigae*.

Fish & Seafood

Hoe (raw fish) is extremely popular in coastal towns, despite the high prices. *Modeumhoe* or *saengseonhoe* is raw fish served with *ssam* or *ganjang* (soy sauce) with wasabi, usually with a pot of spicy *maeuntang* (fish soup) to complete the meal. *Chobap* is raw fish served over vinegar rice. Restaurants near the coast also serve squid, barbecued shellfish, octopus and crab. More gung-ho eaters can try *sannakji* (raw octopus, not live but wriggling from postmortem spasms) or *hongeo* (ray, served raw and fermented, or steamed in *jjim* – neither of which masks its pungent ammonia smell). A seafood meal costs from ₩15,000 per person.

Jeongsik

Often translated as a set menu or table d'hôte, this is a spread of banquet dishes all served at once: fish, meat, soup, *dubu jjigae* (tofu stew), rice, noodles, shellfish and a flock of *banchan*. It's a delightful way to sample a wide range of Korean food in one sitting. *Hanjeongsik* (Korean *jeongsik*) may denote a traditional royal banquet spread of 12 dishes, served on *bangjja* (bronze) tableware. Expect to pay from ₩20,000 for a basic *jeongsik* to more than ₩100,000 for a high-end version.

Everyday Eats

Not every meal in Korea is a *banchan* or meat extravaganza. For casual dining, look for one-dish rice or noodle dishes. Bibimbap is a perennial favourite: a tasty mixture of vegetables, sometimes meat and a fried egg on top of rice. The ingredients are laid out in a deep bowl according to the five primary colours of Korean food – white, yellow, green, red and black – which represent the five elements. Just stir everything up (go easy on the red *gochujang* if you don't want it too spicy) and eat. A variant is *dolsot bibimbap*, served in a stone hotpot; the highlight of this is *nurungji*, the crusty rice at the bottom. Vegetarians can order bibimbap without meat or egg.

As in much of East Asia, noodle joints are plentiful. A common dish is *naengmyeon*, buckwheat noodles served in an icy beef broth, garnished with vegetables, Korean pear, cucumber and half a boiled egg. You can add *gochujang, sikcho* (vinegar) or *gyeoja* (mustard) to taste. *Naengmyeon* is especially popular in summer. Sometimes it's served with a small

SAUCY SIDE DISHES

It's not a Korean meal unless there's kimchi (pickled vegetables) and *banchan* (side dishes). *Banchan* creates balance with saltiness, spiciness, temperature and colour. The number of *banchan* varies greatly, from three in an ordinary meal to 12 in traditional royal cuisine, to an incredible 20 or more in *jeongsik* (set menu or table d'hôte).

Besides the archetypal cabbage kimchi, it's common to see radish or cucumber kimchi, and dishes with spinach, seaweed, bean sprouts, tofu, *jeon* (savoury pancakes made with wheat flour), *bindaetteok* (savoury pancakes made with mung-bean flour), small clams, anchovies – just about anything the chefs can concoct. You don't have to eat it all, though if you like a particular dish, you can ask for free refills (within reason).

Hoe (raw fish) is a popular dish, particularly along the ooast

bowl of meat broth, piping hot, that you can drink with your meal (but it's not for pouring onto the noodles).

Japchae are clear 'glass' noodles stir-fried in sesame oil with strips of egg, meat and vegetables. A Koreanised Chinese dish is *jajangmyeon,* wheat noodles in a black-bean sauce with meat and vegetables. *Gimbap* joints often serve *ramyeon* (instant noodles) in spicy soup.

Gimbap are colourful rolls of *bap* (rice) flavoured with sesame oil and rolled in *gim* (dried seaweed). Circular *gimbap* contains strips of vegetables, egg and meat. *Samgak* (triangular) *gimbap* is topped with a savoury fish, meat or vegetable mixture. Just don't call it sushi – the rice does not have vinegar added and it is not topped with raw fish.

Mandu are dumplings filled with meat, vegetables and herbs. Fried, steamed or served in soup, they make a tasty snack or light meal. Savoury pancakes, often served as a side dish, can also be ordered as a meal. *Bindaetteok* are made with mung-bean flour and are heavier on the batter, while *jeon* are made with wheat flour. Common fillings are kimchi, spring onion *(pajeon)* and seafood *(haemul pajeon)*.

Some eateries specialise in *juk* (rice porridge). Savoury versions are cooked with ginseng chicken, mushroom or seafood, sweet ones with pumpkin and red bean. The thick, black rice porridge is sesame. *Juk* is considered a healthy meal, good for older people, babies or anyone who's ill.

Rice and noodle dishes cost ₩6000 to ₩10,000 each, a meal-sized *jeon* is ₩7000 to ₩10,000, and *gimbap* or *mandu* meals cost ₩3000 to ₩7000.

A helpful guide to the dizzying range of meat choices at a barbecue restaurant is Kimchimari's Know Your Beef Cut! (http://kimchimari.com/2012/01/28/know-your-beef-cut)

Say Kimchi

It appears at every meal (including breakfast) and often as an ingredient in the main course too. What began as a pickling method to preserve

South Koreans eat 1.5 million tonnes of kimchi every year. When the country's first astronaut went into space in 2008, he took a specially engineered 'space kimchi' with him.

vegetables through Korea's harsh winters has become a cornerstone of its cuisine. With its lurid reddish hues and limp texture, kimchi doesn't look that appealing, but just one bite packs a wallop of flavours: sour, spicy, with a sharp tang that often lingers through the meal.

The most common type is *baechu* kimchi, made from Chinese cabbage, but there are more than 180 varieties, made with radish, cucumber, eggplant, leek, mustard leaf and pumpkin flower, among others. Some are meant to be eaten in tiny morsels while others, such as *bossam* kimchi, are flavour-packed packages containing vegetables, pork or seafood.

To make kimchi, vegetables are salted to lock in the original flavour, then seasoned with garlic, red-pepper powder, green onions, ginger, fish sauce and other spices, and left in earthenware jars to ferment for hours, days or even years. Kimchi can be made all year round using seasonal vegetables, but traditionally it is made in November. Many regions, restaurants and families have their own recipes, jealously guarded and handed down through the generations. High in fibre and low in calories, kimchi is said to lower cholesterol, fight cancer, supercharge gut health and prevent flu viruses.

Desserts

While desserts are not traditional in Korean dining, sometimes at the end of a meal you'll be served fruit or *sujeonggwa,* a cold drink made from cinnamon and ginger.

The classic summer dessert is *patbingsu,* a bowl heaped with shaved ice, *tteok* (rice cakes) and sweet red-bean topping with a splash of condensed milk. Modern toppings include strawberries, green-tea powder and fresh or canned fruit. It costs ₩2500 to ₩7000 at cafes.

Bakeries and street vendors sell bite-sized *hangwa* (Korean sweets) such as *dasik* (traditional cookies), and *tteok* flavoured with nuts, seeds and dried fruit. Look out for *hotteok* (Korean doughnuts) and *bungeoppang* (red-bean waffles).

Vegetarians & Vegans

Although Korean cuisine uses lots of vegetables, much of it is pickled or cooked with meat or seafood. *Dubu jjigae* may be made from beef or seafood stock, and *beoseot deopbap* (mushrooms on rice) may contain a little pork. Even kimchi is often made with fish sauce. The only assuredly meat-free meals are those served at Buddhist temples or restaurants. Seoul Veggie Club (www.facebook.com/groups/seoulveggieclub) and www.happycow.net are good resources.

The safest approach is to ask about ingredients or order something such as bibimbap without the ingredients you don't eat. Be as specific about your requirements as you can be – for instance, saying 'no meat' may not suffice to omit seafood. A useful phrase: 저는 채식주의자입니다 (*jeoneun chaesigjuuija imnida*; 'I am a vegetarian'), or simply say '*chaesigjuuija*' and point to yourself.

Food Sites

- *American foodie's Seoul food blog (www.seouleats.com)*
- *Guide to Korean food and cooking (http://english.visitkorea.or.kr)*
- *Korean food and pop-up restaurant journal (www.zenkimchi.com)*
- *Frank Seoul food blog (www.afatgirlsfoodguide.com)*

Drinks

Tea is a staple and the term is also used to describe drinks brewed without tea leaves. The most common leaf tea is *nokcha* (green tea), grown on plantations in Jeju-do and Jeollanam-do. Black tea is harder to find. Nonleaf teas include the ubiquitous *boricha* (barley tea), *daechucha* (red-date tea), *omijacha* (five-flavour berry tea), *yujacha* (citron tea) and *insamcha* (ginseng tea).

Koreans have taken to *keopi* (coffee) in a big way in recent decades. Aside from the ever-present vending machines which churn out an overly sweet three-in-one (coffee, cream and sugar) instant coffee mix (₩300), the number of gourmet coffee shops has multiplied by about 10

since 2006 – from Korean chains such as Angel-in-us Coffee and Hollys, to home-grown speciality roasters and slow-brewers, to foreign imports like Starbucks (with the world's fourth-highest concentration per capita). In Seoul, expect to pay from ₩4000 for coffee at a chain outlet to ₩10,000 for a speciality brew.

Every restaurant serves *mul* (water) or tea. Most serve alcohol, but not usually soft drinks. Some unusual Korean canned soft drinks, readily available from convenience stores, are grape juice with whole grapes inside and *sikhye,* rice punch containing rice grains.

Bosintang (dog-meat soup) is said to make men more virile and it's eaten on the hottest days of the year. It's less popular with the younger generation and there are growing concerns about animal protection.

Alcoholic Drinks

Drinking, and drinking heavily, is the mainstay of Korean socialising, and an evening out can quickly turn into a blur of bar-hopping. The most common poison of choice is *soju,* the mere mention of which tends to elicit looks of dismay from foreigners who have overindulged before. The stuff is, to put it bluntly, ethanol mixed with water and flavouring. If you think that it goes down easy, remember it can also leave you with a killer hangover.

The cheaper varieties (sold in convenience stores for as little as ₩1500) have all the subtlety of really awful moonshine, while those distilled from grain (₩7000 and up) offer a far more delicate flavour. The

STREET FOOD

Korean street food runs the gamut from snacks to full meals. Expect to pay ₩500 to ₩2000 per serve, although some meals at *pojangmacha* (street tent bars) cost up to ₩15,000 per dish.

- *bungeoppang* (red-bean waffles) – fish-shaped sweet cakes with a golden-brown, waffle-like exterior and a hot, sweet, red-bean-paste interior.
- *dakkochi* (grilled chicken skewers) – skewers of chicken and spring onion with a smoky charred flavour under a sticky, tangy barbecue sauce.
- *gyeranppang* (egg muffins) – literally egg bread, *gyeranppang* is a golden oblong muffin with a still-moist whole egg baked on top with a dusting of parsley.
- *haemul pajeon* (seafood pancakes) – these savoury seafood pancakes are a full meal on the go. Lots of squid and sometimes prawns or mussels are fried in a batter with lashings of leeks.
- *hotteok* (Korean doughnuts) – spiced, plump pancakes filled with a mixture of sunflower seeds, cinnamon and brown sugar. Other fillings include black sesame seeds, peanuts, red beans and honey.
- *jjinppang* (steamed buns) – soft fluffy buns with various fillings, but usually coarse red-bean paste, pork or kimchi.
- *mandu* (dumplings) – fried or steamed Korean dumplings, often including a tofu or vermicelli-noodle filling. *Kogi mandu* are stuffed with a gingery minced pork and spring onions. *Kimchi mandu* adds spicy kimchi.
- *odeng* (fish cake skewers) – flat fish cakes on a skewer, either long or folded over. They jut from vats of broth, which is a seafood and spring-onion soup that Koreans say cures hangovers.
- *sundae* (blood sausage) – slices of black sausage eaten with toothpicks or chopsticks.
- *tteokbokki* (spicy rice cakes) – chewy rice cakes that resemble penne pasta in pans of spicy, saucy *gochujang* (hot red-pepper paste). Variations add slices of fish cakes, boiled eggs or *ramyeon* (ramen or wheat noodles).
- *twigim* (Korean-style tempura) – various batter-fried (like Japanese tempura but more substantial) ingredients such as squid, a hash of vegetables, sweet potatoes and even boiled eggs.

LINGXIAO XIE / GETTY IMAGES ©

Korean barbecue (p362), including *samgyeopsal* (streaky pork belly)

cheap stuff has an alcohol content of 20% to 35%, while the good stuff goes up to 45%. The latter includes Andong *soju* and white *soju*, available in Gyeongsangbuk-do and Gyeongsangnam-do respectively.

Makgeolli is a traditional farmer's brew made from unrefined, fermented rice wine. Much lower in alcohol content than *soju*, it has a cloudy appearance and a sweetish yoghurt flavour. It has gained popularity and credibility in recent years with artisanal *makgeolli* bars in Seoul serving quality drops minus the dreaded aspartame found in many commercial varieties. In Seoul, Makgeolli Mamas & Papas (http://mmpkorea.wordpress.com) and Makgeolli Makers (www.facebook.com/makgeollimakers) are a community of *makgeolli* lovers and educators who run *makgeolli*-making courses. The cheaper sort served in bottles at convenience stores, bars and clubs is made for sharing, often with flavours such as berry to make it more palatable. It's traditional to slug down *makgeolli* with a side of *pajeon* (green-onion pancake) on rainy days.

Dongdongju is similar to *makgeolli*, with rice grains floating in it. Both are popular tipples in national parks, where it's practically ritual to swig down a bowl or two after (or during) an arduous hike. They cost ₩1000 to ₩2500 in supermarkets, double that in restaurants and bars.

Sweeter on the palate are a host of traditional spirits, brewed or distilled from grains, fruits and roots. *Bokbunjaju* is made from wild raspberries, *meoruju* from wild fruit, *maesilju* from green plums and *insamju* from ginseng.

Maekju (beer) is the least exciting of all Korean alcohol. Local brands, all lagers, are the rather bland Cass, Hite and OB. Interesting microbreweries have taken off, no longer just in Seoul but also in cities from Daegu to Jeju-si, and imported beers are increasingly available. Local beers cost ₩2000 to ₩6000 in a restaurant or bar. Koreans like to give names to pairing beer with other food and drink. The most famous combo in recent years is fried chicken with beer, known as *chimek*; but you'll also

Cooking at Home

Growing Up in a Korean Kitchen by Hisoo Shin Hepinstall

Eating Korean by Cecilia Hae-Jin Lee

A Korean Mother's Cooking Notes by Sun-Young Chang

find clubs concocting a near-lethal *poktanju* of a shot of soju dropped into beer.

During an evening of drinking, Koreans usually order *anju* (bar snacks; obligatory in some bars), which traditionally meant kimchi, *dotorimuk* (acorn jelly) or *dubu kimchi* (tofu kimchi). Nowadays you're more likely to get heaped plates of oil-soaked food – fried chicken, French fries or vegetable *twigim* (fritters). Chain bars that serve just beer and French fries have taken off in university areas. A *hof*, a term inspired by German beer halls, is any watering hole that serves primarily Korean beer, with the requisite plate of fried chicken and other *anju*.

Koreans drink so much *soju* that the brand Jinro Soju has been the top-selling brand of spirits worldwide for over a decade.

Dining & Drinking Etiquette

From casual eateries to high-end restaurants, you're as likely to encounter traditional floor seating as western-style chair seating. If it's the former, remove your shoes at the door and sit on floor cushions (stack a few for more comfort). The menu is often posted on the wall. Main courses come with rice, soup, kimchi and *banchan* (usually included in the price). Don't worry about not finishing the *banchan* as no one is expected to eat everything.

Meals are eaten communally and rarely, if ever, alone. Lone travellers may encounter a quizzical '*Honja*?' ('Alone?'). Occasionally a restaurant may turn away solo diners because they only serve meals in portions for two (especially for *jeongsik* and barbecue).

If the table is not set, there will be an oblong box or hidden drawer containing metal chopsticks and long-handled spoons, as well as metal cups and a bottle of water or tea. The spoon is for rice, soup and any dish with liquids; chopsticks are for everything else. Don't touch food with your fingers, except when handling *ssam*. Remember not to let the chopsticks or spoon stick up from your rice bowl – this is taboo, only done with food that is offered to deceased ancestors.

Koreans eat out – a lot – and love to sit and sup on a main course for several hours (and over several bottles of *soju*). Seniors or elders begin eating first. Dining companions usually pour drinks for each other – traditionally, never for themselves. It's polite to use both hands when pouring or receiving a drink.

To call a server, say '*Yogiyo*', which if translated seems rude (it means 'here') but is a bona fide way of hailing attention. Tipping is not expected, though high-end restaurants often add a 10% service charge.

Food Glossary

Fish & Seafood Dishes

chobap	초밥	raw fish on rice
garibi	가리비	scallops
gwang-eohoe	광어회	raw halibut
jangeogui	장어구이	grilled eel
kijogae	키조개	razor clam
kkotgejjim	꽃게찜	steamed blue crab
modeumhoe	모듬회	mixed raw-fish platter
nakji	낙지	octopus
odeng	오뎅	processed seafood cakes
ojingeo	오징어	squid
saengseongui	생선구이	grilled fish
saeugui	새우구이	grilled prawns

Kimchi

baechu kimchi	배추김치	cabbage kimchi; the classic spicy version
kkakdugi	깍두기	cubed radish kimchi
mul kimchi	물김치	cold kimchi soup

Meat Dishes

bossam	보쌈	steamed pork with kimchi, cabbage and lettuce wrap
bulgogi	불고기	barbecued beef slices and lettuce wrap
dakgalbi	닭갈비	spicy chicken pieces grilled with vegetables and rice cakes
dwaeji galbi	돼지갈비	pork ribs
galbi	갈비	beef ribs
heukdwaeji	흑돼지	black pig
jjimdak	찜닭	spicy chicken pieces with noodles
metdwaejigogi	멧돼지고기	wild pig
neobiani/ tteokgalbi	너비아니/ 떡갈비	large minced-meat patty
samgyeopsal	삼겹살	barbecued (bacon-like) streaky pork belly
tangsuyuk	탕수육	Chinese-style sweet-and-sour pork
tongdakgui	통닭구이	roasted chicken
yukhoe	육회	seasoned raw beef

Noodles

bibim naengmyeon	비빔냉면	cold buckwheat noodles with vegetables, meat and sauce
bibimguksu	비빔국수	noodles with vegetables, meat and sauce
jajangmyeon	자장면	noodles in Chinese-style black-bean sauce
japchae	잡채	stir-fried 'glass' noodles and vegetables
kalguksu	칼국수	wheat noodles in clam-and-vegetable broth
kongguksu	콩국수	wheat noodles in cold soybean soup
makguksu	막국수	cold buckwheat noodles with vegetables
mulnaengmyeon	물냉면	buckwheat noodles in cold broth
ramyeon	라면	instant noodles in soup

Rice Dishes

bap	밥	boiled rice
bibimbap	비빔밥	rice topped with egg, meat, vegetables and sauce
bokkeumbap	볶음밥	Chinese-style fried rice
boribap	보리밥	boiled rice with steamed barley
chamchi gimbap	참치김밥	tuna *gimbap*
chijeu gimbap	치즈김밥	cheese *gimbap*
daetongbap	대통밥	rice cooked in bamboo stem
dolsot bibimbap	돌솥비빔밥	bibimbap in stone hotpot
dolsotbap	돌솥밥	hotpot rice
dolssambap	돌쌈밥	hotpot rice and lettuce wraps
gimbap	김밥	rice flavoured with sesame oil and rolled in dried seaweed
gulbap	굴밥	oyster rice

hoedeopbap	회덮밥	bibimbap with raw fish
honghapbap	홍합밥	mussel rice
jeonbokjuk	전복죽	rice porridge with abalone
juk	죽	rice porridge
modeum gimbap	모듬김밥	assorted *gimbap*
pyogo deopbap	표고덮밥	mushroom rice
sanchae bibimbap	산채비빔밥	bibimbap with mountain vegetables
sinseollo	신선로	meat, fish and vegetables cooked in broth
ssambap	쌈밥	assorted ingredients with rice and wraps

Snacks

beondegi	번데기	boiled silkworm larvae
bungeoppang	붕어빵	fish-shaped waffle with red-bean paste
dakkochi	닭꼬치	spicy grilled chicken on skewers
gukhwappang	국화빵	flower-shaped waffle with red-bean paste
hotteok	호떡	wheat pancake with sweet filling
jjinppang	찐빵	giant steamed bun with sweet-bean paste
norang goguma	노랑고구마	sweet potato strips
nurungji	누룽지	crunchy burnt-rice cracker, often at the bottom of *dolsot bibimbap*
patbingsu	팥빙수	shaved-iced dessert with *tteok* and red-bean topping
tteok	떡	rice cake
tteokbokki	떡볶이	pressed rice cakes and vegetables in a spicy sauce

Soups

bosintang	보신탕	dog-meat soup
dakbaeksuk	닭백숙	chicken in medicinal herb soup
dakdoritang	닭도리탕	spicy chicken and potato soup
galbitang	갈비탕	beef-rib soup
gamjatang	감자탕	meaty bones and potato soup
haejangguk	해장국	'hangover soup'
haemultang	해물탕	spicy assorted seafood soup
kkorigomtang	꼬리곰탕	oxtail soup
maeuntang	매운탕	spicy fish soup
manduguk	만두국	soup with meat-filled dumplings
oritang	오리탕	duck soup
samgyetang	삼계탕	ginseng chicken soup
seolleongtang	설렁탕	beef and rice soup

Stews

budae jjigae	부대찌개	'army stew' with hot dogs, Spam and vegetables
dakjjim	닭찜	braised chicken
doenjang jjigae	된장찌개	soybean-paste stew
dubu jjigae	두부찌개	tofu stew
galbijjim	갈비찜	braised beef ribs

gopchang jeongol	곱창전골	tripe hotpot
kimchi jjigae	김치찌개	kimchi stew

Other

bindaetteok	빈대떡	mung-bean pancake
donkkaseu	돈까스	pork cutlet with rice and salad
dotorimuk	도토리묵	acorn jelly
gujeolpan	구절판	eight snacks and wraps
hanjeongsik	한정식	Korean-style banquet
jeongsik	정식	set menu or table d'hôte, with lots of side dishes
mandu	만두	filled dumplings
omeuraiseu	오므라이스	omelette filled with rice
pajeon	파전	green-onion pancake
sujebi	수제비	dough flakes in shellfish broth
sundae	순대	noodle and vegetable sausage
sundubu	순두부	uncurdled tofu
twigim	튀김	seafood or vegetables fried in batter

Nonalcoholic Drinks

boricha	보리차	barley tea
cha	차	tea
daechucha	대추차	red-date tea
hongcha	홍차	black tea
juseu	주스	juice
keopi	커피	coffee
dikapein keopi	디카페인커피	decaffeinated coffee
mul	물	water
nokcha	녹차	green tea
omijacha	오미자차	five-flavour berry tea
saengsu	생수	mineral spring water
seoltang neo-eoseo/ ppaego	설탕넣어서/ 빼고	with/without sugar
sikhye	식혜	rice punch
sujeonggwa	수정과	cinnamon and ginger punch
uyu	우유	milk
uyu neo-eoseo/ppaego	우유넣어서/ 빼고	with/without milk
yujacha	유자차	citron tea

Alcoholic Drinks

bokbunjaju	복분자주	wild-berry liquor
dongdongju/makgeolli	동동주/막걸리	fermented rice wine
maekju	맥주	beer
maesilju	매실주	green-plum liquor
soju	소주	local vodka

Architecture & the Arts

Historically, Korea was a land of scholar artists, meditative monks and whirling shamans, all of whom have left a mark on the country's artistic traditions. See it in the elegant brush strokes of a calligraphic scroll, the serene expression on a Buddhist statue or in an impassioned folk dance. Contemporary Korea, meanwhile, punches above its weight in cinema and pop culture, and is rediscovering its artistic heritage too. Its built space includes monumental palaces, charming early-20th-century *hanok* (traditional wooden homes) and dramatic structures of glass and steel.

The Arts

Traditional Visual Arts

Traditional visual arts in Korea were heavily influenced first by China and Buddhism and then, in the Joseon period, by Neo-Confucian ideals. Typical styles include landscape and ink-brush painting, religious statuary, calligraphy, ceramics and ornate metal craft (such as incense burners). In painting, particular attention is paid to the brush stroke, which varies in thickness and tone. The painting is meant to surround the viewer and there is no fixed viewpoint. The National Museum of Korea in Seoul has the best collection of traditional art. Cast-iron Buddhist statues and murals depicting scenes from Buddha's life can be found in temples and museums around the country.

Of all the traditional arts, Korea is especially known for its ceramics. Originally using techniques brought over from China, Korean pottery came into its own in the 12th century with the production of Goryeo celadon. The beautiful, jade-coloured works were highly prized in trade on the Silk Road, and today earn thousands of dollars at auction. Another noteworthy style is *buncheong* (less refined pottery than celadon), which came into vogue in the early years of the Joseon dynasty. In bold shapes, dipped in white glaze and decorated with sgraffito and incising, *buncheong* ware has a vibrant, earthy quality and still looks modern today.

The Leeum Samsung Museum of Art in Seoul has an outstanding and informative display of traditional ceramics. You can also go right to the source, to the ancient celadon kilns in Gangjin, home to the Gangjin Celadon Museum.

Literary Anthologies

Land of Exile: Contemporary Korean Fiction (2014)

Modern Korean Fiction (2005)

Words of Farewell: Stories by Korean Women Writers (1993)

Anthology of Korean Literature: From Early Times to the 19th Century (1981)

Modern & Contemporary Visual Arts

The most important movement of the modern era was the *dansaekhwa* (monochrome paintings) of the 1970s. Though similar in many ways to abstract expressionism, *dansaekhwa* is noted for its tactile nature and use of traditional Korean materials, such as *hanji* (mulberry paper). There's been a recent resurgence of interest in the movement, with exhibitions featuring key artists such as Chung Sang-hwa, Yun Hyong-keun, Ha Chong-hyun and Lee Ufan popping up in New York, Los Angeles and cities across Asia.

However, the most famous Korean artist is, hands down, Nam June Paik (1932–2006; www.paikstudios.com). Paik, who eventually settled in the US, is considered the founder of video art, though he was essentially a multimedia artist. He used sound, circuits and performance to make insightful and playful cultural critiques. One of his larger creations, *The More the Better*, is an 18m tower with 1000 monitors on display at the National Museum of Contemporary Art inside Seoul Grand Park.

While Seoul is still far and away the centre of the arts scene, Gwangju, home to the Gwangju Biennale and the Asian Culture Centre, is a burgeoning hub. The Arario Museum earned Jeju-si a star on the country's art map.

Mural Villages

Daldongne (moon village) is the euphemistic term for the shanty towns that appeared on urban hillsides during the postwar reconstruction years – built by those who had been left out of reconstruction. Considered eyesores by some, memories of humbler times by others, many *daldongne* were slated for demolition. However, a decade ago, local municipalities, residents and artists hit upon an idea: decorating the villages with murals. Today there are around a dozen 'mural villages' scattered around Korea and they've become big tourist draws. Look for them in Seoul (Ihwa-dong), Suwon, Tongyeong and Jeonju. Many artists have since settled in the neighbourhoods, bringing with them galleries and cafes.

Performing Arts

Pansori is an impassioned, operatic form of storytelling that's been around for centuries (and was named a Masterpiece of Intangible Heritage by Unesco in 2013). It's usually performed by a single woman, who flicks her fan at dramatic moments, singing to the beat of a male drummer. *Changgeuk* is an opera performed by a larger cast.

Samulnori is a lively folk style combining music and dance, originally played by travelling entertainers. It died out during Japanese colonial rule but was reinvented in the 1970s to mean musicians playing four traditional percussion instruments. *Samulnori* troops sometimes play overseas and the style has influenced contemporary productions such as the incredibly popular show *Nanta*. Other forms of folk performance include *talchum* (mask dance) and solo, improvisational *salpuri* (shamanist dance).

KOREAN SOAPS CLEAN UP IN ASIA

Psy – the rapper whose 'Gangnam Style' music video was a YouTube sensation in 2012 – may have been the first emissary of Korean pop culture to become a universal household name; however, Korean stars have been making waves around Asia since the early 2000s.

It started with the soap opera *Winter Sonata* (2002), whose star Bae Yong-joon made Japanese housewives swoon when the show later aired in Japan. The drama *My Love from a Star* (2013–14), about the budding romance of an alien stranded on earth and an ice-queen actress, was a sensation in China, notably bumping up sales of fried chicken (the main character's favourite snack); an American remake is in the works.

On free-to-air television, 2017's number-one prime-time show was the legal thriller *Defendant*, in which a Seoul prosecutor is accused, wrongfully charged and faced with a death sentence for allegedly killing his wife. On cable, prime-time romantic comedy *Strong Woman Do Bong Soon*, about a woman with superhuman strength who becomes wrapped up in a murder case and shacks up with her long-time crush and CEO boss, took the top spot.

YEONGSIK IM / SHUTTERSTOCK ©

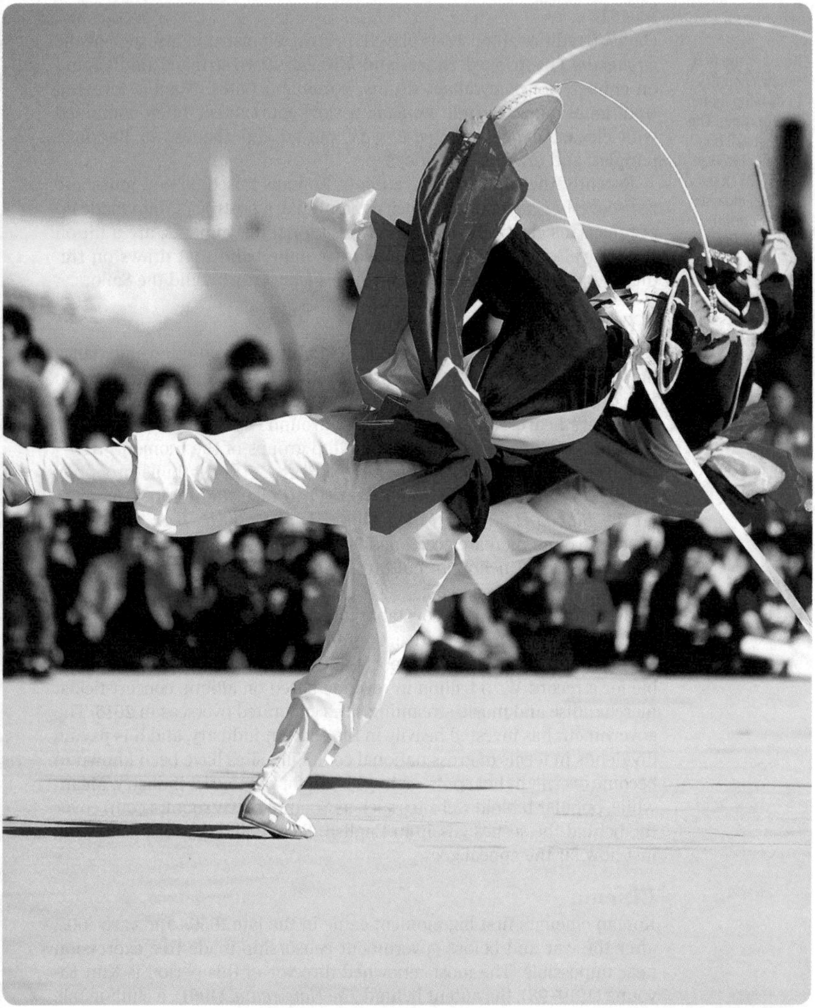

Top *Samulnori* combines music and dance, and originated from travelling entertainers.

Bottom *Pansori* is traditionally performed by a woman using a fan to accompany a man beating a drum.

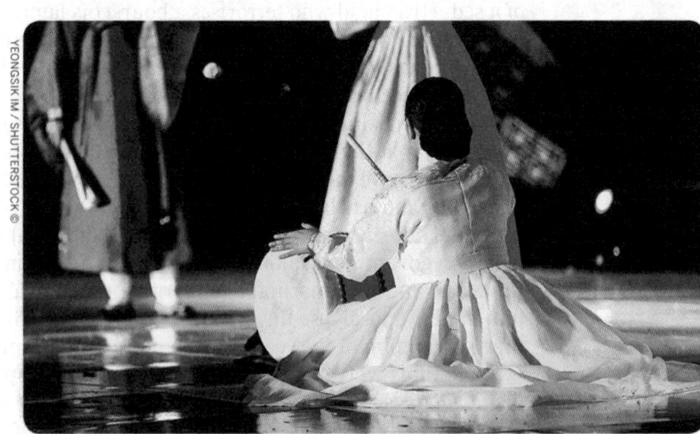

Korea is the first known country to develop metal type printing. The oldest existing artefact is the *Jikji* (1377), but records indicate that printing began at least a century earlier. Learn all about it at the Early Printing Museum in Cheongju.

Music

Gugak (traditional music) is played on stringed instruments, such as the *gayageum* (12-stringed zither) and *haegeum* (two-stringed fiddle), and on chimes, gongs, cymbals, drums, horns and flutes. Notable forms of traditional music include *jeongak*, a slow court music often combined with elegant dances; *bulgyo eumak*, played and chanted in Buddhist temples; and *arirang*, folk songs.

Recently, the younger generation of Koreans raised on pop music are rediscovering *gugak*. Bands such as Jambinai, a postrock group made up of musicians classically trained on traditional instruments, are a hit on the festival circuit. Another noteworthy indie band that draws on traditional music – this time folk music – is Danpyunsun and the Sailors.

K-Pop & Cultural Exports

K-Pop, with its catchy blend of pop R&B, hip-hop and electronic dance music (EDM) – complete with synchronised dance moves – shows no sign of fading away. As soon as critics declare it over, new groups emerge to capture hearts (and endorsements) around Asia, and more recently, the United States. In 2018 one of the top groups of the moment, BTS – which stands for '*bangtan sonyeondan*' (방탄소년단) or 'bulletproof boy scouts' – became the first-ever K-Pop act to take the number-one spot on the *Billboard* 200 with their album *Love Yourself: Tear*. The group of seven young men are acclaimed for speaking out on subjects that are especially taboo in Korean culture, such LGBTQ rights, mental health and the pressure to succeed.

But it's not just about covetable hairstyles and infectious tunes. According to the Korea Creative Content Agency, an arm of the South Korean Ministry of Culture, Sports and Tourism, K-Pop was responsible for a record ₩5.3 trillion in revenue based on album, concert-ticket, merchandise and music-streaming sales generated overseas in 2016. The government has invested heavily in the content industry, and it is paying dividends in terms of gross national cool. Film sites have been known to become overnight hot spots – a huge boon for the tourist industry. Meanwhile, popular tabloid websites such as Soompi (www.soompi.com) cover the behind-the-scenes gossip in English, French and Spanish – showing just how far the appeal goes.

Cinema

Korean cinema's first big moment came in the late 1950s and early '60s, after the war and before government censorship made free expression near impossible. The most renowned director of this period is Kim Ki-young (1919–98), the auteur behind *The Housemaid* (1961), a chilling tale of a seductive maid who terrorises a bourgeois family.

However, no director did more to put Korean cinema on the map than Im Kwon-taek (1936–). The prolific film-maker (102 titles and counting) won best director at Cannes in 2002 for *Chihwaseon* – about influential 19th-century painter Jang Seung-up – and was awarded an honorary Golden Bear at the Berlin Film Festival in 2005. He is also considered to have helped pave the way for the art-house movement that took off in the mid-1990s and has been going on ever since.

Today, Korean cinema is embraced by both local audiences (thanks partly to government quotas that mandate a certain amount of screen time for domestic films) and the international festival circuit. Yeon Sang-ho's zombie apocalypse thriller *Train to Busan* (2016) set a record as the first Korean film of the year to reach more than 10 million theatregoers.

Some films worth watching include the jaw-dropping action-revenge flick *Oldboy* (Park Chan-Wook; 2003); the critically acclaimed monster

epic *The Host* (Bong Joon-ho; 2006); the controversial, and hypersexual, *Pieta* (Kim Ki-duk; 2012), a Golden Lion winner at Venice; and anything by low-budget, shoe-gazer Hong Sang-soo – his 2017 *On the Beach at Night Alone* won a handful of awards.

Literature

The watershed moment for Korean literature occurred with the introduction of the *hangeul* writing system in the 15th century, which exponentially increased who could create and consume literature. Previously, all texts were penned in classical Chinese (which continued to be used by the predominantly male elite until the Japanese occupation). Newly in translation, the 18th-century *Memoirs of Lady Hyegyong*, penned by the lady herself, provides a fascinating inside look at the downfall of her famous husband, Prince Sado.

The modern period brought an increased proliferation of voices, including the experimental (read: Yi Sang's *Wings*; 1936). It also brought a crisis of language: the Japanese occupation (1910–45) mandated that Japanese be taught in schools. Consequently the generation of writers born after WWII are known as the *hangeul* generation, meaning they were raised neither on classical Chinese nor Japanese but rather in their own native tongue. Important authors include Cho Se-hui, whose novel *The Dwarf* (1978) recounts the daunting social costs of rapid industrialisation on the working poor during the 1970s, and Choe In-ho, whose award-winning *Deep Blue Night* (1982) tells the story of two wayward Koreans tearing through California. Kim Young-ha, author of the existentialist, urbane *I Have the Right to Destroy Myself* (1996) is considered one of the leading voices among contemporary writers. His works are just now coming out in translation.

More and more women are breaking into the literary world long dominated by men and, with translation, onto the international stage. Works to read include Park Wan-suh's plain-talking, semiautobiographical portrait of a family torn by the Korean War, *Who Ate Up All the Shinga* (1992); Shin Kyung-sook's melancholy meditation on modern families, *Please Look After Mom* (2011); and Yun Ko Eun's *Table for One* (2018), an exploration of solitude and social awkwardness in a culture that prioritises community and family.

Architecture

Temples & Palaces

Traditional Korean buildings are made from stone and wood, with construction techniques originally imported from China, and emphasise a harmony with the natural environment. Sturdy wooden beams – set on a stone foundation and often joined with notches instead of nails – support heavy, sloping roofs. Location is determined by principles of Chinese geomancy (feng shui). Korea's best-known architectural innovation is the *ondol*, the radiant floor-heating system that makes use of flues under the floor. Archaeological records show that this ingenious invention is likely a thousand years old, and originated in the harsh climes of what is now North Korea.

During the Joseon period, palace design became increasingly influenced by Neo-Confucian principles of geometry and restraint. Meanwhile, Buddhist temples, whose reconstruction was often sponsored by merchants, reflected the tastes of this increasingly wealthy demographic. Lavish decoration, such as colourful painted ceilings and intricate latticework, became popular.

Centuries of war and invasion mean that Korea has few truly old structures, though reconstructed temples and palaces are often faithful

Traditional folk art includes *jangseung* (wooden shamanist guardian posts) and the *dolharubang* (grandfather stones) of Jeju-do.

HANOK: SAVING KOREA'S TRADITIONAL HOMES

Hanok are traditional one-storey, wooden homes insulated with mud and straw and topped with clay-tiled roofs. Unlike the ostentatious manor homes of Europe, even an aristocrat's lavish *hanok* was designed to blend with nature; they are typically left unpainted, their brown and tan earth tones giving off a warm, intimate feel. All rooms look onto a courtyard (*madang*). Life was lived on the floor and people sat and slept on mats rather than chairs and beds.

Few people live in *hanok* today – there are less than 10,000 around the country, compared to 800,000 nearly 40 years ago. While colonisation by the Japanese destroyed Korea's monumental palaces and fortresses, modern development doomed the *hanok*, which were written off as dirty, old and rundown, apt for demolition.

Scheming contractors and perhaps well-intended, but ultimately ineffective government measures didn't help. In the Bukchon neighbourhood of Seoul, for example, which has been a preservation zone since 1977 (and is the only such zone in the country), only one-third of the *hanok* are original; the rest have been scrapped and rebuilt. (For more about preservation issues in Bukchon, see www.kahoidong.com).

However, it seems that the tides are starting to turn: over the last decade, there's been a proliferation of guesthouses, restaurants and coffee shops setting up inside former homes. As vessels of Korean culture, *hanok* are a way to authentically experience analogue life in an increasingly digital society.

K-Indie is the artist-driven alternative to K-Pop. Hunt for new underground bands at Korean Indie (www.koreanindie.com) and their shows at Korea Gig Guide (www.koreagigguide.com). Don't miss the July music festivals Pentaport Rock Festival (www.pentaportrock.com) – Korea's answer to Glastonbury – and Ansan Valley Rock Festival (www.valleyrockfestival.com).

replicas (Joseon-dynasty civil servants were meticulous record keepers). Meanwhile, the oldest structures you'll likely come across are granite pagodas in temple courtyards, some of which date to the Silla period.

Post WWII & Contemporary Architecture

The Korean War reduced the peninsula to the worst kind of blank slate, and hurried reconstruction resulted largely in a landscape of drab concrete towers. There are some notable exceptions: the most prominent architect of the reconstruction era was Kim Swoo-geun (1931–86), who along with his contemporary, Kim Joong-eop (1922–88), laid the foundation for a modern Korean aesthetic. Among Kim Swoo-geun's most notable structures is the Seoul Olympic Stadium, with curves said to be inspired by traditional pottery.

As Korea becomes richer, design is becoming more and more prominent, especially in cities like Seoul and Busan. Spurred on by its winning bid to be the World Design Capital in 2010, Seoul went on a construction spree, hiring world-renowned architects such as Zaha Hadid for the Dongdaemun Design Park (2013). Of Korea's contemporary home-grown architects, Seung H-Sang is the biggest name; a protege of Kim Swoo-geun, Seung was named Seoul's official architect in 2014. He also worked on Paju Book City in Gyeonggi-do. In 2017 Seoul's Lotte World Tower was completed, making it the tallest skyscraper in Korea and fifth tallest in the world.

The Natural Environment

At 96,920 sq km, South Korea is a similar size to Portugal. Bordered only by North Korea, the country has 2413km of coastline along three seas – the West Sea (also known as the Yellow Sea), the East Sea (Sea of Japan) and the South Sea (East China Sea). Its overall length from north to south (including Jeju-do) is 500km, while the narrowest point is 220km wide.

The largest of some 3400 islands is 1847-sq-m Jeju-do, a volcanic landmass with spectacular craters and lava tubes. Off the east coast is Ulleungdo, another scenic volcanic island. Korea is not in an earthquake zone, but there are dozens of mineral-laden *oncheon* (hot springs) that bubble up through the ground, some of which have been developed into health spas.

Forested mountains cover 70% of the land, although they are not very high – Halla-san (1950m) on Jeju-do is the highest peak. Many mountains are granite with dramatic cliffs and pinnacles, but there are also impressive limestone caves to visit. The 521km Nakdong-gang and 514km Han River are the country's longest. They, like most other larger rivers, have been dammed, creating scenic artificial lakes.

The plains and shallow valleys are still dominated by irrigated rice fields that are interspersed with small orchards, greenhouses growing vegetables, and barns housing cows, pigs and chickens. In the south are green-tea plantations and on Jeju-do citrus fruit is grown.

The hundreds of sparsely populated islands scattered off the western and southern coasts of the peninsula have relaxed atmospheres; a few have attractive sandy beaches. Here you can go way off the beaten track to islands where the inhabitants have never seen a foreigner.

Korea's largest environmental nongovernment organisation is Korea Federation for Environmental Movements (KFEM; www.kfem.or.kr), which has around 80,000 members and 31 branch offices across the country.

Animals

Korea's forested mountains used to be crowded with Siberian tigers, Amur leopards, bears, deer, goral antelopes, grey wolves and red foxes. Unfortunately these wild animals are now extinct or extremely rare in Korea.

WHAT CAN YOU DO?

Responsible travellers can do their bit for Korea's environment by keeping in mind the following:

- Use the country's excellent public-transport system or rent a bicycle where you can.
- Place your rubbish in the appropriate recycling bins for paper, cans and plastic.
- Refuse unnecessary packaging in shops – carry your own shopping bag.
- Patronise organic and vegetarian restaurants and businesses that have a seal of approval from Lifestyles of Health & Sustainability (LOHAS; http://korealohas.or.kr).

Birds Korea (www.birdskorea.org) is a conservation NGO with an online bird-ID guide.

Small efforts are being made to build up the number of wild animals in the country – goral antelopes have been released into Woraksan National Park and there's an ongoing project to protect the tiny population of Asiatic black bears (known in Korea as moon bears) in Jirisan National Park. In Seoul, small populations of roe deer and elk live on Bukak-san and in Seoul Forest Park.

Jindo is home to a special breed of Korean hunting dog, Jindogae. Brave, intelligent, loyal and cute as any canine on the planet, the breed can be a challenge to train and control, but they possess an uncanny sense of direction – one dog was taken to Daejeon but somehow made its way back to the island, a journey of hundreds of kilometres. Being hunting dogs, they are an active, outdoor breed that is not suited to an urban environment. Any other breed of dog found on Jindo is immediately deported to the mainland in order to maintain the breed's purity.

Magpies, pigeons and sparrows account for most of the birds in towns and cities, but egrets, herons and swallows are common in the countryside, and raptors, woodpeckers and pheasants can also be seen. Although many are visiting migrants, more than 500 bird species have been sighted, and Korea has a growing reputation among birders keen to see Steller's sea eagles, red-crowned cranes, black-faced spoonbills and other rarities.

Plants

Jeju-do World Heritage Sites

Hallasan National Park

Seong-san Ilchul-bong

Geomunoreum Lava Tube System

Northern parts of South Korea are the coldest and the flora is alpine: beech, birch, fir, larch and pine. Further south, deciduous trees are more common. The south coast and Jeju-do are the warmest and wettest areas, so the vegetation is lush. Cherry trees blossom in early spring followed by azaleas and camellias.

Korea's mountainsides are a pharmacy and salad bar of health-giving edible leaves, ferns, roots, nuts and fungi. Many of these wild mountain vegetables end up in restaurant side dishes and *sanchae bibimbap* (a meal of rice, egg, meat and mountain vegetables). Wild ginseng is the most expensive and sought-after plant.

National & Provincial Parks

With an abundance of river valleys, waterfalls and rocky outcrops, plus brightly painted wooden Buddhist temples and hermitages gracing many mountains, it's not surprising that many visitors rate Korea's national and provincial parks as its top attractions.

Since the first national park, Jirisan, was established in 1967 it has been joined by 19 others covering 3.7% of the country. For more details see Korea National Parks (http://english.knps.or.kr). There are also 22 smaller provincial parks (covering 747 sq km) and 29 county parks (covering 307 sq km). All the parks have well-marked hiking trails; some have been so popular that they've had to be closed to protect them from serious erosion.

Beautiful Wildflowers in Korea (2002), published by the Korea Plant Conservation Society, has photos of 200 native flowers and will encourage you to stop and ID flowers on your travels.

The parks can be enjoyed in every season. In spring cherry blossoms, azaleas and other flowers are a delight; in summer the hillsides and river valleys provide a cool escape from the heat and humidity of the cities; during the summer monsoon, the waterfalls are particularly impressive; in autumn red leaves and clear blue skies provide a fantastic sight; and in winter snow and ice turn the parks into a white wonderland, although crampons and proper clothing are needed for any serious hikes. Korean winters can be arctic, especially if you're high up in the mountains.

All the parks have tourist villages near the main entrances with restaurants, market stalls, souvenir and food shops, and budget accommodation where big groups can squeeze into a small room. Camping grounds (₩6000 to ₩7000 per person per day) and mountain shelters

(₩10,000 to ₩13,000 for a bunk) are cheap, and while some have modern facilities, most are very basic.

With an average of five million visitors a year, Bukhansan National Park, located on Seoul's doorstep, has qualified for a Guinness World Record as the national park with the highest number of visitors per square foot in the world.

Environmental Issues

South Korea's economic growth since 1960 has transformed the country from an agricultural to an industrial society. Sprawling apartment-block cities and huge industrial complexes have been constructed, rivers have been dammed and freeways have been bulldozed through the countryside. Authoritarian governments stamped on any opposition to development projects and the environmental effects of the projects were ignored.

Fortunately the 70% of Korea that is mountainous and forested is still largely undeveloped, and the hundreds of offshore islands are also unspoilt. For a developed country Korea is surprisingly green, as 90% of the population is packed into high-rise city apartments.

Nowadays politics is more democratic, politicians win votes by promising green policies and environmental groups are no longer ignored by the media. Unpopular construction projects can face fierce opposition. Among the country's most contentious environmental flashpoints are what to do with nuclear waste and land reclamation.

Energy Reform

Shortly after being elected into office in 2017, South Korea president Moon Jae-in unveiled plans for energy-policy reform that would move the country away from coal and nuclear sources. They will be replaced with gas-fired and renewable resources – coal power will drop from 40% to 21% of electricity generation and nuclear-fired power will decrease from 30% to 22% by 2030.

To reach this ambitious goal, the country plans to increase its capacity of renewable energy from 11.3 gigawatts to 58.5G gigawatts over the next 12 years. Solar and wind power capacity will also see an uptick – the plan calls for the addition of 30.8 gigawatts for the former and 16.5 gigawatts for the latter. The Korea Gas Corporation will soon begin construction

JEJU'S ENVIRONMENTAL INITIATIVES

It's no accident that Jeju was chosen to host the World Conservation Congress in September 2012, a 10-day symposium where experts exchanged ideas for tackling pressing environmental issues including climate change, biodiversity and green growth. South Korea's largest island, recognised by Unesco for its extraordinary ecosystem and natural features, is through various schemes pushing ahead with its aim to be crowned, in the words of Korea's environment minister Yoo Young-sook, as the 'environment capital of the world'.

A trust has been set up to protect *gotjawal* (forests on rocky terrain), which cover around 12% of the island. Considered the 'lungs of Jeju', they are not only an essential part of the island's groundwater supply system but also a species-rich biosphere. Five of Jeju's wetland regions are also listed under the Ramsar Convention as being of 'international importance'. In 2015, Jeju's Governor Won Hee-ryong declared that he would push skyrocketing Chinese investment in property development on the island towards renewable energy. You will already find 50% of South Korea's electric cars on Jeju, and in 2018 20 electric buses were introduced on the island.

Along the northeast coast of Jeju, giant wind farms form part of the island's Smart Grid Testbed (www.smartgrid.or.kr) – an attempt to use information technology to transmit power and cut down on CO^2 emissions. The long-term plan is to make Jeju carbon-free and self-sustainable by 2030 through renewable energy resources. Already the island of Gapado off Jeju's southwest coast is carbon-free: its power comes from wind farms and solar panels, its cars have been replaced with electric vehicles and its water comes from a desalination plant.

KUYSANG CHO / SHUTTERSTOCK ©

Top World Heritage–listed Hallasan National Park (p257) surrounds Korea's highest mountain, Halla-san.

Bottom With more than 500 bird species, Korea is growing birdwatching destination.

A DMZ NATIONAL PARK?

The dearth of human intervention in the Demilitarized Zone (DMZ) for more than 50 years has made it something of an environmental haven. The zone is home to 5097 wild plants and animals, including 106 endangered species such as the Siberian musk deer, the Amur goral (a mountain goat that resembles an antelope), a third of the world's remaining red-crowned cranes and half the remaining white-naped cranes. Environmentalists hope that the day the two Koreas cease hostilities, the DMZ will be preserved as a nature reserve, a plan that has the support of the South Korean government. As a first step towards this goal, trekking and cycling paths are being created within the Civilian Control Zone, a buffer zone that runs along the southern border of the DMZ.

of South Korea's fifth liquefied-natural-gas-import terminal at Dangjin Port, with goals of being fully operational by the year 2031.

Caves, by Kyung Sik Woo (2005), is a lavishly illustrated book on Korean caves by a geological expert and cave enthusiast.

Land Reclamation

Reclaiming the mudflats off Korea's west coast for farming and construction has become a highly emotive and divisive issue. According to the Korean Federation for Environmental Movements (KFEM), since 1990 more than 140,000 hectares of coastal wetlands have been reclaimed or are in the process of being reclaimed.

The environmental impact that such projects can have is seen at Saemangeum in Jeollabuk-do, where in 2006 a 33km sea wall was built to reclaim 40,000 hectares of mudflats. Opponents, who battled hard against the project during its construction, stressed the importance of the mudflats as a fish and shellfish breeding area and as a vital feeding ground for more than 100,000 migrant birds, including black-faced spoonbills and 12 other threatened species.

In response to the Saemangeum protests, the government declared 60 sq km of wetlands at the Han River estuary in Gyeonggi-do a protected area. Ten smaller wetland areas (covering a total of 45 sq km) had already been protected. The Ministry of Environment has since increased the number of protected wetlands, and with Sumeunmulbaengdui on Jeju-do and the Hanbando Wetland in Gangwon-do in May 2015, Korea's list of Ramsar Wetlands stands at 21. In one of these wetlands, Suncheon-man – the winter nesting ground of five endangered species of crane – the cancellation of a land-reclamation project in favour of the area's promotion as an ecotourism destination is a positive sign for the future.

Green Korea?

In June 2015 South Korea announced it would aim to cut greenhouse-gas emissions by 37% by 2030. This was another step in the strategy mapped out in 2008 to create jobs using green technology and clean energy. The government reached a milestone in 2012 by completing the 'Four Rivers Project', which saw the clean-up of four major rivers (the Han, Nakdong, Geum and Yeongsan) and their surroundings to reduce flooding by building water-treatment facilities, banks and 20 new dams. It also included a 1757km bicycle route running alongside the four rivers. The project was such a success that both Turkey and Paraguay looked to it as a model for cleaning their own waterways.

Green Korea (www.greenkorea.org) is a pressure group with practical ideas such as Buy Nothing Day, Car Free Day (22 September in Seoul) and Save Paper Day.

Among the other 'ecofriendly' success stories on the government's green agenda was the construction of a 20-mile solar-panel-covered bicycle lane between Daejeon and Sejong, south of Seoul; and converting all of Seoul's 8750-plus buses to low-polluting natural-gas, full-hybrid or fuel-cell electric vehicles. Ongoing work includes more high-speed railway

MOON BEARS: A GLIMMER OF HOPE

According to legend the Korean nation was born from a bear – one of the reasons why Asiatic black bears (also called moon bears because of the crescent moon of white fur on their chests) are accorded the status of a national treasure and a protected species. However, by the late 20th century the hunting of bears for their meat and use in traditional medicine had contributed to them being thought extinct in the wild in South Korea.

Then in 2001, video footage proved that up to six wild bears were living in a remote part of Jirisan National Park. Soon after, the park established a project with the aim of building up a self-sustaining group of 50 wild bears in Jirisan (as of 2010 it was believed there were 19 bears). However, according to Moonbears.org, one of several Korean groups campaigning for protection of the animal, even these few are threatened by poaching. This is despite the fact that well over 1000 bears were bred at farms across the country for the lucrative bear-meat and gall-bladder trade. The conditions that the bears were kept in were often horrific.

Moonbears.org, Bear Necessity Korea, Green Korea and other pressure groups had long campaigned for the government to ban such farms. A landmark agreement was reached between the government and the Farmers Association of South Korea in 2014, resulting in a voluntary exit plan for farmers and encouraging them to have their captive bears sterilised in order to stop the breeding of new bears for the industry. In early 2017 the plan was completed.

lines; the provision of energy-saving 'green homes'; and energy-recycling projects including the production of gas from garbage.

Many of these policies were given the thumbs up from the UN Environment Program but local environmental groups felt the Four Rivers Project opened the door to reviving a plan for a grand canal between Seoul and Busan.

Field Guide to the Birds of Korea, by Lee, Koo & Park (2000), is the standard bird guide, but doesn't include all feathered visitors.

Despite commitments to preserve wetland and coastal areas, Seoul is also building two more tidal power plants along the west coast, in addition to the two already in operation there: Uldolmok in Jeollanam-do and Sihwa Lake in Gyeonggi-do, which is the largest in the world. Incheon Tidal Power Station began construction in 2017 and Garorim Bay Tidal Power Station is still in the proposal stage.

Survival Guide

Directory A–Z

Accessible Travel

Facilities for travellers with disabilities in Seoul and some other cities are far from perfect but are improving. Most Seoul subway stations have stair lifts, elevators and toilets with wheelchair access and handrails, while buses have ramps to aid wheelchair access. Tourist attractions, especially government-run ones, offer generous discounts or even free entry for people with disabilities and a helper. There are also some hotels with accessible rooms. For more information go to http://english.visitkorea.or.kr/enu/GK/GK_EN_2_5_2.jsp.

Download Lonely Planet's free Accessible Travel guides from http://lptravel.to/AccessibleTravel.

Before setting off get in touch with your national support organisation (preferably with the travel officer, if there is one). For general travel advice in Australia contact **Nican** (☎02-6241 1220); in the UK contact **Tourism For All** (www.tourismforall.org.uk; ☎0845 124 9971); in the USA try **Accessible Journeys** (www.accessiblejourneys.com; ☎800-846-4537), an agency specialising in travel for the disabled, or **Mobility International USA** (www.miusa.org; ☎541-343-1284).

PRACTICALITIES

Daily newspapers *Korea Herald* (www.koreaherald.co.kr), *Korea JoongAng Daily* (www.joongangdaily.joins.com) and *Korea Times* (www.koreatimes.co.kr).

Monthly magazines *10 Magazine* (10mag.com), *Groove Korea* (www.groovekorea.com) and *Seoul* (www.seoulselection.com).

TV & Radio KBS World (www.world.kbs.co.kr) for news, features; Arirang (www.arirang.co.kr) an English-language TV and radio; Radio Gugak (www.gugakfm.co.kr) for traditional Korean music; TBS (tbsefm.seoul.kr) for music and news.

DVD Region 3; some with English-language option.

Weights & Measures South Korea uses the metric system, but real estate is often measured in *pyeong* (3.3 sq metres or almost 6ft x 6ft), and some traditional markets still use wooden measuring boxes.

Accommodation

You shouldn't need to worry about where to stay as hotels and motels are so numerous there's usually little need to book ahead.

Outside the big cities and towns – where you'll find regular hotels, motels and hostels – the most common type of accommodation will be *minbak* (private homes with rooms for rent).

Accommodation is normally charged per room, so solo travellers receive little or no discount. Still, it's always worth asking. If you're staying a few days or if it's low season (outside July and August on the coast or outside July, August, October and November in national parks), you can always try for discounts. Some hostels and *hanok* (traditional wooden home) guesthouses include a simple breakfast in their rates; most hotels don't.

Budget and midrange places usually include a value-added tax (VAT) of 10% in their rates. Top-end hotels include this VAT as well as another service charge of 10% in their rates. The Korean government runs a Hotel Tax Refund promotion, refunding the VAT from a select list of hotels – mostly high-end in the major cities. See the list and refund procedure at http://english.visitkorea.or.kr/enu/ACM/AC_ENG_4_2.jsp.

Only staff in Seoul guesthouses and upper-midrange and top-end hotels are likely to speak any English. An extra bed or *yo* (mattress or futon on the floor) is usually available. Check-out time is generally noon. Prices can rise on Friday and Saturday and at peak times (July and August near beaches or national parks, plus October and November near national parks). Many guesthouses are technically private residences and do not have open doors for enquiries, so you need to call ahead if you want to take a peek.

Although some places offer use of a washing machine (and sometimes a dryer), laundry can be a problem – outside Seoul you may find yourself having to wash your clothes in the bathroom and hanging them up in your room to dry, or laying them on the *ondol*-heated floor.

Backpacker & Youth Hostels

The backpacker scene is well established in Seoul, and is starting to become popular elsewhere in Korea. When you find them, these internationally minded hostels are ideal for budget-oriented tourists, and have staff who are friendly and speak English. In Korea the line between a guesthouse and a hostel is often blurred. Both usually offer dormitories (from ₩17,000 per night) and double rooms (from ₩40,000), some of which have private bathrooms, though motels offer better value for private rooms. Communal facilities include toilets, showers, satellite TV, a kitchen and washing machine. Free internet and a simple breakfast is typically provided.

Hostelling International Korea (www.youthhostel.or.kr) runs 70 large, modern youth hostels around the country. The dormitories offer a good deal for solo travellers on a budget, at around ₩20,000 a night. Private and family rooms cost as much as motel rooms and are unlikely to be as good. They also can be rather institutional and inconveniently located, and are sometimes full of noisy children on a school trip. You can buy e-membership through a Youth Hostel Certificate and use it immediately from your phone (annual membership ₩17,000).

SLEEPING PRICE RANGES

The following price ranges refer to a double room with private bathroom.

PRICE INDICATOR	SEOUL	REST OF SOUTH KOREA
$	less than ₩60,000	less than ₩40,000
$$	₩60,000–₩250,000	₩40,000–₩150,000
$$$	more than ₩250,000	more than ₩150,000

Camping & Mountain & Forest Huts

Camping at beaches and in or near some national and provincial parks is possible. The cost is ₩2000 to ₩3000 per person per night but facilities are very basic and they are usually only open in July and August.

Only a few major hikes in Seoraksan and Jirisan National Parks require an overnight stay in a mountain hut or shelter. Huts and camping grounds can be fully booked at weekends and during high season, when there is often also a small price increase.

For more information see http://english.knps.or.kr.

Hanok Guesthouses

Traditional *hanok* are increasingly being turned into guesthouses. Staying in one of these is a unique and memorable experience. Rooms are small and you'll sleep on *yo* (padded quilts and mattresses) on the floor, but underfloor heating systems *(ondol)* keep them snug in winter. At the cheaper *hanok* you'll be sharing the bathroom, but many guesthouses do offer en suite rooms. Rates often include breakfast, and traditional cultural experiences may be offered too.

For more about *hanok* guesthouses across Korea see the Korea Tourism Organization (KTO) site Hanokstay (www.hanokstay.or.kr).

Homestays

These are the best way to experience Korean food, customs and family life at close quarters. Most Korean families sign up to such schemes to meet and make friends with foreigners and to practise their English. Some families offer pick-ups and dinner, and rates are greatly reduced if you stay long-term. The charge for bed and breakfast per night can be as low as ₩30,000 per person. Homestays can be booked online (p388).

Hotels

Luxury hotels are relatively scarce outside major cities and Jeju-do, except for some resorts such as those in Pyeongchang. The lobbies, fitness centres, restaurants and other services are often their strong points – when it comes to room design and facilities, motels tend to offer a better deal. We list rack rates (including service and taxes), but discounts or packages are nearly always available.

Minbak & Pension

Most *minbak* provide simple accommodation (and

BOOK YOUR STAY ONLINE

For more accommodation reviews by Lonely Planet authors, check out http://lonelyplanet.com/hotels/. You'll find independent reviews, as well as recommendations on the best places to stay. Best of all, you can book online.

usually meals) on islands, near ski resorts, in rural areas and near beaches and national parks. Expect to pay ₩40,000 for a room but double that in peak seasons. You sleep on a *yo* on an *ondol*-heated floor, usually with a TV and a heater or fan in the room. Facilities may not include private bathrooms. Lots of people can squeeze into one room – an extra person usually costs ₩10,000. More upmarket *minbak* cost ₩50,000 or more and provide smart, stylish rooms with beds and kitchenettes.

Pension cost from ₩50,000 upwards and can be more luxurious than most *minbak*. They are often simple properties with an equipped kitchen and lots of space, inside and out, for groups of self-catering travellers.

Motels & Love Motels

Motels and love motels are by far the most common form of accommodation across Korea. The rooms are always on the small size but they are packed with facilities: private bathroom, smart TV, phone, fridge, drinking water, air-con and heating, toiletries and even computers. However, staff rarely speak English and motels lack communal areas beyond the lobby, which is not designed for lingering.

Love motels cater for couples seeking some by-the-hour privacy, but they also accept conventional overnight guests. The modern kind are clean, aimed at young guests and are easy to spot by the neon and glitzy casino-like exteriors. If you can cope with the clandestine locations (and possibly intrusive noise from neighbouring rooms), they can be an excellent option; some of the extravagantly decorated rooms are a bargain compared with what you'd pay for similar facilities at a top-end hotel. Some love motels, however, require a late check-in, around 9pm; earlier check-ins cost more.

BOOKING SERVICES

Apart from booking directly with hotel websites, you can also book rooms via the following:

Benikea (www.benikea.com)

Korean Hotel Reservation Center (www.khrc.com)

Lonely Planet (lonelyplanet.com/south korea/hotels)

Homestays can be booked online:

BnB Hero (www.bnbhero.com)

Go Homestay (www.gohomestay.com)

Homestay Korea (www.homestaykorea.com)

Koreastay (www.koreastay.or.kr)

Lex (www.lex.or.kr)

Rental Accommodation

If you want to rent an apartment it's recommended that you see a licensed real-estate agent, who can make navigating the traditional payment system easy. Otherwise. it can be necessary to pay a huge deposit and the whole rental period up front to the landlord. Browse Seoul websites Nicerent (www.nicerent.com) or Seoul Homes (www.seoulhomes.kr) for what's on offer. Real estate is measured in *pyeong* (one *pyeong* is 3.3 sq metres). Backpacker guesthouses and motels sometimes offer reduced rates for long-term tenants.

Go to www.korea4expats.com for useful information on this topic under the 'Moving To Korea' section.

Sauna Dormitories

Saunas and *jjimjilbang* (luxury saunas) usually have a dormitory or napping room. They are not really meant for overnight sleepovers, but they can be used for that purpose. Pay the entry fee (usually under ₩10,000), use the facilities and then head for the dormitory. Don't expect much in the way of bedding, and the pillow may be a block of wood. Be sure that your belongings and locker key are secure while you sleep, as thefts can occur.

Serviced Apartments

Seoul has several serviced-apartment complexes, which can be a good alternative to hotel rooms and the hassle of finding and renting an apartment. They're known locally as residences or suites; prices start at ₩90,000 a day for a studio apartment, with big discounts for month-long stays.

Templestays

Around 100 temples across the country provide overnight accommodation in the form of a Templestay

program (www.templestay.com), most charging ₩50,000 to ₩70,000 per night including all meals. No attempt will be made to try to convert you to Buddhism and they provide a chance not only to experience the life of a monk but also to stay in some incredibly beautiful places. That said, you do learn about Buddhist practices such as meditation and the 108 prostrations; there is usually at least one person who speaks some English. This is an increasingly popular choice of accommodation, with more temples geared towards accepting foreigners, while others will also happily let you stay if you bring along a Korean to help translate.

Yeogwan

'Adequate but shabby' sums up most *yeogwan* (small, family-run hotels), which provide old-fashioned budget rooms, but are only ₩5000 to ₩10,000 cheaper than much better modern motels. Quilts are usually aired rather than washed so you may want to bring sheets with you.

Children

Koreans adore children and make them the centre of attention, so travelling with your offspring here is highly recommended. Expect the locals to be particularly helpful and intrigued. Check out www.travelwithyourkids.com for general advice and a firsthand report on Seoul for kids, which gives the city a thumbs up.

Zoos, funfairs and parks can be found in most cities along with cinemas, DVD rooms, internet rooms, video-game arcades, ten-pin bowling alleys, *noraebang* (karaoke rooms), pool tables and board-game cafes. Children will rarely be more than 100m away from an ice-cream, cake or fast-food outlet. In winter hit the ski slopes, and in summer head for the water parks or beaches.

Only luxury hotels are likely to be able to organise a cot, but you could always ask for a *yo* (traditional floor mattress). Few restaurants have high chairs. Nappy-changing facilities are more common in Seoul toilets than in the provinces.

For general advice pick up a copy of Lonely Planet's *Travel with Children*.

Customs Regulations

Visitors must declare all plants, fresh fruit, vegetables and dairy products that they bring into South Korea. Meat is not allowed in without a certificate. Go to www.customs.go.kr for further information.

Antiques of national importance are not allowed to be exported.

Discount Cards

Korea Pass (www.koreapass.or.kr) A prepaid card, available in denominations from ₩50,000 to ₩500,000. It provides discounts on a range of goods and services, especially those offered by the Lotte department stores, since the pass was taken over by Lotte Card in 2013. It can be bought at Incheon and Gimpo International Airports as well as Lotte Mart and 7-Eleven stores.

Discover Seoul Pass (www.discoverseoulpass.com) A foreigner-only tourist pass that comes with unlimited transport and free admission for 24/48/72 hours (from ₩39,900) to attractions such as Gyeongbokgung and the major palaces, Musical Chef, SMTown coexartium, 63 Square Art Gallery and N Seoul Tower, plus free use of the A'REX train, Seoul City Tour Bus and Seoul Bike, and discounted entry to Lotte World.

Electricity

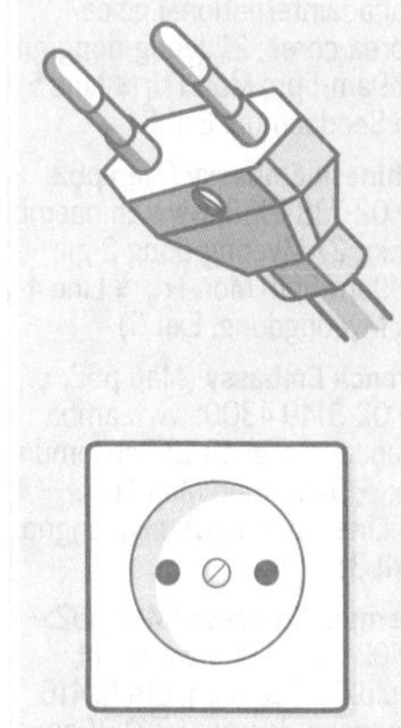

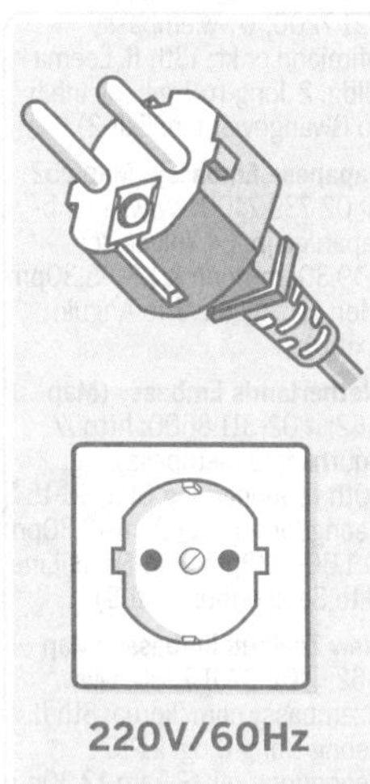

Embassies & Consulates

Most embassies are located in Seoul.

Australian Embassy (Map p52; ☎02-2003 0100; www.southkorea.embassy.gov.au; 19th fl, Kyobo Bldg, 1 Jong-ro;

⏱9am-5pm Mon-Fri; SLine 5 to Gwanghwamun, Exit 4)

Canadian Embassy (Map p62; ☎02-3783 6000; www.canadainternational.gc.ca/korea-coree; 21 Jeong-dong-gil; ⏱9am-5pm Mon-Fri; SLine 5 to Seodaemun, Exit 5)

Chinese Embassy (Map p62; ☎02-738 1038; www.chinaemb.or.kr; 27 Myeong-dong 2-gil; ⏱9am-6pm Mon-Fri; SLine 4 to Myeongdong, Exit 5)

French Embassy (Map p62; ☎02-3149 4300; www.ambafrance-kr.org; 43-12 Seosomun-ro; ⏱9am-noon Mon-Fri; SLine 2 or 5 to Chungjeongno, Exit 3)

German Embassy (Map p62; ☎02-748 4114; www.seoul.diplo.de; Seoul Sq, 8th fl, 416 Hangang-daero; ⏱9-11.30am Mon, Tue & Thu, 2-4.30pm Wed, 8.30-11am Fri; SLine 1 or 4 to Seoul Station, Exit 8)

Irish Embassy (Map p52; ☎02-721 7200; www.embassyofireland.or.kr; 13th fl, Leema Bldg, 2 Jong-ro 1-gil; SLine 5 to Gwanghwamun, Exit 2)

Japanese Embassy (Map p52; ☎02-739 7400; www.kr.emb-japan.go.jp; 64 Yulgok-ro; ⏱9.30am-noon & 1.30-5.30pm Mon-Fri; SLine 3 to Anguk, Exit 6)

Netherlands Embassy (Map p62; ☎02-311 8600; http://southkorea.nlembassy.org; 10th fl, Jeongdong Bldg, 21-15 Jeongdong-gil; ⏱9am-12.30pm & 1.30-5.30pm Mon-Fri; SLine 5 to Seodaemun, Exit 5)

New Zealand Embassy (Map p62; ☎02-3701 7700; www.nzembassy.com/korea; 8th fl, Jeong Dong Bldg, 21-15 Jeongdong-gil; ⏱9am-12.30pm & 1.30-5.30pm Mon-Fri; SLine 5 to Seodaemun, Exit 5)

UK Embassy (Map p62; ☎02-3210 5500; www.gov.uk/world/organisations/british-embassy-seoul; 24 Sejong-daero 19-gil; ⏱9am-12.30pm & 1.30-5pm Mon-Fri; SLine 1 or 2 to City Hall, Exit 3)

US Embassy (Map p52; ☎02-397 4114; https://kr.usembassy.gov; 188 Sejong-daero; ⏱9am-5pm Mon-Fri; SLine 5 to Gwanghwamun, Exit 2)

EATING PRICE RANGES

The following price ranges are for a main dish:

PRICE INDICATOR	SEOUL	REST OF SOUTH KOREA
$	less than ₩12,000	less than ₩7000
$$	₩12,000–₩25,000	₩7000–₩18,000
$$$	more than ₩25,000	more than ₩18,000

Food

In this guide, restaurant listings are by budget then author preference, and are accompanied by the symbols $ (budget), $$ (midrange) or $$$ (top end). For more information about eating and drinking see p362.

Health

The quality of medical care in Seoul is high. You need a doctor's prescription to buy most medications and it may be difficult to find the exact medication you use at home, so take extra. A letter from your physician outlining your medical condition and a list of your medications (using generic names) could be useful.

Insurance

A policy covering theft, loss, medical expenses and compensation for cancellation or delays in your travel arrangements is highly recommended. If items are lost or stolen, make sure you obtain a police report straight away – otherwise your insurer might not pay up. There is a wide variety of policies available, but always check the small print.

Worldwide travel insurance is available at www.lonelyplanet.com/travel-insurance. You can buy, extend and claim online any time – even if you're already on the road.

Internet Access

With the world's fastest connections and one of the highest rates of internet usage, you'll find abundant free internet access, either via a computer or wi-fi in cafes, public streets, guesthouses, hotels and tourist information centres.

➡ Some motels and nearly all hotels provide computers with broadband access.

➡ Major phone companies offer USB dongle devices (known as 'pocket wi-fi' or a 'wi-fi egg') to rent, in the same way as mobile phones, to connect all your devices to the internet from your own portable wi-fi hot spot. If you are travelling outside Seoul or major cities, make sure your device plan covers the whole country. Reliable services are available from Pocket WiFi Korea (www.pocketwifikorea.com) and Package Korea (www.packagekorea.com) and cost from ₩7150 per day. Link Korea (www.linkkorea.co.kr) rents pocket wi-fi devices (US$5 per day) that you can pre-order and pay for online, then pick up at airports or Hongik University station in Seoul.

➡ If you just need internet access on your (unlocked) phone, a Korean SIM geared towards foreigners might be a cheaper option, with one-month plans for 1GB data starting at ₩34,900 with Korea Telecom (www.

roaming.kt.com), widely available from stores aimed at tourists in Itaewon and Hongdae in Seoul, and some convenience stores such as at the entrance to Gimpo Airport subway.

Legal Matters

Most tourists' legal problems involve visa violations or illegal drugs. In the case of visa transgressions, the penalty is normally a fine and possible expulsion from the country. If caught using or selling narcotics, you'll either be deported or spend a few years researching the living conditions in a South Korean prison.

LGBT+ Travellers

Korea has never passed any laws that mention homosexuality, but this shouldn't be taken as a sign of tolerance or acceptance. Attempts to include sexual orientation in antidiscrimination laws by the Democratic Party in 2013 were shot down by conservative religious groups. President Moon – despite being a former human-rights lawyer – said he 'opposed homosexuality' in 2017. Some older Koreans insist that there are no queer people in Korea – even though there are at least several very high-profile ones such as the TV personality and Seoul restaurateur Hong Seok-chun and transgender celebrity Ha Ri-su.

Attitudes are changing, especially among young people – 2018 saw South Korea's first openly gay K-Pop idol (Holland), its first drag parade, and the most internationally successful K-Pop group, BTS, speak about supporting LGBT rights – but virtually all local gays and lesbians choose to stay firmly in the closet. Gay and lesbian travellers who publicise their sexual orientation tend to receive less than positive reactions. However, there are openly gay areas of Seoul where few will blink an eye at displays of affection, and other major cities have gay bars too. Gay and lesbian locals use the English loan words *gei* and *lejeubieon* as the other term in Korean, *ivan*, can mean 'second-class citizen'.

Local resources include:

Chingusai (Between Friends; www.chingusai.net) Korean LGBT human-rights group.

Solidarity for LGBT Human Rights of Korea (Haeng Seong In; ☎02-715-9984; lgbtpride.or.kr) Campaigns for LGBT equality and runs community workshops.

iShap (www.ishap.org) Gay HIV/AIDS awareness project; produces a free Korean guidebook to gay bars and clubs – ask for it at bars such as Barcode in Nagwon-dong in Seoul, and in bars in Busan.

Utopia (www.utopia-asia.com) Check the Korea section for maps and reviews to gay bars, clubs and services.

Money

ATMs that accept foreign cards are common: look for one that has a 'Global' sign or the logo of your credit-card company. ATMs often operate from 7am to 11pm but some are 24-hour. Restrictions on the amount you can withdraw in one transaction can vary but is usually around ₩1,000,000 per day. Lotte ATMs in 7-Eleven stores allow you to select from international banks for the transaction, including Citibank.

Many banks offer a foreign-exchange service. In big cities there are also licensed money changers, which keep longer hours than the banks and provide a faster service, but may only exchange $US cash.

Photography & Video

- All the major camera and video brands are available including the local ones, such as Samsung. Yongsan Electronics Market and Namdaemun Market in Seoul are the cheapest places to buy the latest camera and video equipment.
- Some Koreans are shy, reluctant or even hostile about being photographed, so always ask first.
- Never take photographs inside Buddhist shrines or of shamanist ceremonies without asking permission first, and don't expect Seoul's riot police to be too happy to be snapped either. In and around the Demilitarized Zone (DMZ) there are very strict rules about what can

MEDICAL TOURISM

In image-conscious South Korea, medical tourism is a booming industry, with annual visitor numbers expected to reach nearly one million by 2020. The focus might be on cosmetic surgery – with the highest rate of procedures per capita in the world – but can include anything from cutting-edge cancer treatments to simple check-ups. Health tourism is heavily promoted by the Korea Tourism Organization (www.visitmedicalkorea.com), with specialised information booths (and even festivals) in Seoul, Incheon, Daegu and Busan. Staff keep lists (but not prices) of medical practitioners who speak English, Chinese and other languages and have surgeries that resemble high-end hotel lobbies. Speak with your own doctor and health-insurance company before considering getting anything done; despite the gloss, botched work still happens.

and can't be photographed, as prominently signposted on site.

➡ *Lonely Planet's Guide to Travel Photography* is full of helpful tips for photography while on the road.

Post

For postal rates see Korea Post (www.koreapost.go.kr); post offices are fairly common and have a red/orange sign.

Public Holidays

Eight Korean public holidays are set according to the solar calendar and three according to the lunar calendar, meaning they fall on different days each year. Restaurants, shops and tourist sights stay open during most holidays, but may close over the three-day Lunar New Year and Chuseok (Thanksgiving) holidays. Buddha's Birthday, while not a public holiday, can be a very busy time with accommodation booked out, but is a festive period to visit Buddhist temples. School holidays mean that beaches and resort areas are busy in August.

New Year's Day 1 January

Lunar New Year 5 February 2019, 25 January 2020, 12 February 2021

Independence Movement Day 1 March

Children's Day 5 May

Memorial Day 6 June

Constitution Day 17 July

Liberation Day 15 August

Chuseok 12 September 2019, 30 September 2020, 20 September 2021

National Foundation Day 3 October

Christmas Day 25 December

Safe Travel

With some common sense, South Korea is generally very safe.

➡ Drivers routinely jump red lights late at night, so take care on pedestrian crossings even if they are protected by lights.

➡ Drivers rarely stop for pedestrian crossings unless they are protected by traffic lights.

➡ Motorcyclists often drive along pavements and pedestrian crossings.

➡ In Seoul, you might see police in full riot gear streaming out of blue police buses with their windows covered in protective wire. Student, trade-union, anti-American, environmental, ferry-disaster and other protests occasionally turn violent. Keep well out of the way of any confrontations that may occur.

Smoking

Smoking Nationwide ban on smoking in public enclosed spaces such as bars and restaurants, and also in parks in Seoul, on train platforms and 10m from station exits. Street smoking is not allowed on many tourist streets; smoking booths exist in areas such as Myeongdong, Seoul.

Vaping Increasingly popular, fashionable and accepted in many, but not all, bars and restaurants where smoking is not permitted.

Tap Water

South Korea has some of the cleanest tap water in the world, though most locals and visitors drink filtered or purified water from bottles or dispensers. The practice comes from a belief that bottled water is healthier, and the fear that old pipes can contain heavy metals. Filtered or bottled water is served free in most restaurants, and machines with free purified hot and cold water are available in most motels, guesthouses and shopping-plaza entrances.

Telephone

Most networks in South Korea use the WCDMA 2100MHz network, as well as one of five different 4G LTE bands. Most unlocked recent smartphones will work with a Korean SIM.

➡ Korea's nine provinces and seven largest cities have their own area codes.

➡ The major cities have their own codes – thus Gwangju City's code (☎062) is one digit different to the surrounding province of Jeollanam-do (☎061).

➡ South Korea's country code is ☎82.

GOVERNMENT TRAVEL ADVICE

The following government websites offer travel advisories and information on current hot spots:

Australian Department of Foreign Affairs & Trade (www.smarttraveller.gov.au)

Canadian Department of Foreign Affairs (www.dfait-maeci.gc.ca)

New Zealand Ministry of Foreign Affairs & Trade (www.safetravel.govt.nz)

UK Foreign & Commonwealth Office (www.gov.uk/foreign-travel-advice)

US Department of State (www.travel.state.gov)

FINDING AN ADDRESS

Under an old system of addresses, big cities such as Seoul were divided into districts (*gu*, eg Jongno-gu) with these districts further divided into subdistricts (*dong*, eg Insa-dong). Buildings were then numbered according to their chronology within the subdistrict. It was pretty confusing, so Korea moved over to a new address system of logically numbered buildings on named streets *(gil)*.

However, until the end of 2013 the old address system existed alongside the new one and you will still find that giving a description to a local works better than a new address.

If you have the correct full address (either system), or the telephone number, these can be used by satellite navigation in a taxi or on phones to find your location. For more information on the address changeover including an address converter, see www.juso.go.kr. There is also a free app (search for Juso or 주소 찾아, Korean only).

➡ Do not dial the first zero of the area codes if you are calling from outside Korea.

➡ Phone numbers that begin with a four-figure number starting with 15 do not have an area code.

➡ Korean mobile-phone numbers have three-digit codes, always beginning with 01, eg 011 1234 5678. You'll also come across internet phone numbers (also known as VoIP), which begin with 070. When you make a call from your mobile phone, you always input these initial codes or area codes, even if you're in the city you're trying to reach.

➡ The international access code is ☎001.

Toilets

➡ Korea has plenty of clean, modern and well-signed *hwajangsil* (public toilets; 화장실); inside the subway is a reliable place to find them in Seoul.

➡ Virtually all toilets are free, some are decorated with flowers and artwork, and a few even have music.

➡ Toilet paper is usually outside the cubicles. As always, it's wise to carry a stash of toilet tissue around with you just in case.

➡ Asian-style squat toilets are losing their battle with European-style ones, but there are still a few around. Face the hooded end when you squat.

Tourist Information

➡ In Seoul the excellent **KTO Tourist Information Centre** (Map p62; ☎02-1330; www.visitkorea.or.kr; 2nd fl, 40 Cheonggyecheon-ro; ⏰9am-8pm; 🚻; Ⓢ Line 1 to Jonggak, Exit 5) has stacks of brochures on every region plus helpful, patient and well-informed staff. They can book hotels for you and advise you about almost anything. Chat to them also about the nationwide system of Goodwill Guides (www.hiseoulyh.com/en/youth-goodwill-guide), who are volunteer tour guides.

Many tourist areas throughout the country have their own tourist information centres, so it's not a problem to locate one.

Visas

Many visitors don't need a visa, but if your country is not on the permit-on-arrival list, you will need one.

➡ With a confirmed onward ticket, visitors from the USA, nearly all Western European countries, New Zealand, Australia and around 30 other countries receive 90-day permits on arrival. Visitors from a handful of countries, such as South Africa, receive 30-day permits, while 60-day permits are given to citizens of Italy and Portugal. Canadians receive a six-month permit.

➡ About 30 countries – including India and Nigeria – do not qualify for visa exemptions. Citizens from these countries must apply for a tourist visa, which allows a stay of 90 days.

➡ Visitors cannot extend their stay beyond 90 days except in situations such as a medical emergency. More info is at www.mofat.go.kr and www.moj.go.kr.

➡ Flights direct to Jeju-do are 30 days visa-free for most passport holders.

➡ Holders of a passport from China must apply for a tourist visa but are allowed an exemption of 120 hours (five days) in South Korea if they join a tour group to visit Jeju-do (where they can stay for 15 days) and arrive through certain airports. This list is always increasing but includes the airports Gimpo (Seoul), Incheon (near Seoul), Gimhae (Busan), Daegu (Gyeongsangbuk-do), Yangyang (Gangwon-do) and Cheongju (Chungcheongbuk-do). Other incentives aimed at wooing Chinese tourists include being able to apply online for electronic visas and increased visa-application centres in China.

TAX -FREE SHOPPING

Global Blue (www.globalblue.com; also Global Tax Free or KT Tourist Reward) offers a partial refund (between 5% and 7%) of the 10% value-added tax (VAT) on some items. Spend more than ₩30,000 in any participating shop and the retailer gives you a special receipt, which you must show to a customs officer at Incheon International Airport within three months of purchase.

Go to a Customs Declaration Desk (near the check-in counters; or to kiosks for refunds less than ₩75,000) before checking in your luggage, as the customs officer will want to see the items before stamping your receipt. After you go through immigration, show your stamped receipt at the refund desk corresponding to the brand of the refund service to receive your won refund in cash or by cheque. Some stores now offer immediate tax refunds when you show your passport, or from in-store machines.

➡ An electronic travel authorisation system for visa-free visitors to South Korea was being rolled out at the time of writing. The system is expected to resemble that of the USA's ESTA and Canada's eTA where visitors must provide personal and travel information, and pay a small fee, through an online portal at least 72 hours before flying to obtain a waiver that is valid for years.

➡ As rules are always changing, see www.hikorea.go.kr for more visa information.

Volunteering

Many travellers find that volunteering to teach English can be a fulfilling way to experience the local culture.

The Seoul Global Center (www.global.seoul.go.kr) is a good place to start looking for other volunteer possibilities. More charities and organisations with volunteer opportunities:

Amnesty International (www.amnesty.or.kr) Raises awareness in Korea about international human-rights issues.

Cross-Cultural Awareness Program (CCAP; www.ccap.or.kr) Unesco-run program activities include presenting a class about your culture to Korean young people in a Korean public school, or on a weekend trip to a remote area.

Korea Women's Hot Line (KWHL; www.eng.hotline.or.kr; ☎02-3156 5400) Nationwide organisation that also runs a shelter for abused women.

Korean Federation for Environmental Movement (KFEM; www.kfem.or.kr; ☎02-735 7000) Volunteer on various environmental projects and campaigns.

Korean Unwed Mothers' Families Association (KUMFA; www.facebook.com/groups/kumfa) Provides support to single mothers.

Seoul International Women's Association (www.siwakorea.com) Organises fundraising events to help charities across Korea.

Seoul Volunteer Center (www.volunteer.seoul.go.kr; ☎070-8797 1861) Teach language and culture, take part in environmental clean-ups and help at social-welfare centres.

World Wide Opportunities on Organic Farms (WWOOF; http://wwoofkorea.org; ☎02-723 4458) Welcomes volunteers to farms across Korea who provide labour in exchange for board and lodging.

TRANSLATION & INFORMATION SERVICES

If you need interpretation help or information on practically any topic, any time of the day or night, you can call either of the following:

BBB (☎1588 5644; www.bbbkorea.org)

Tourist Phone Number In Seoul ☎1330 or ☎02 1330 from a mobile phone; outside Seoul dial the provincial or metropolitan code first – so for information on Gangwon-do, dial ☎033 1330.

Work

Although a few other opportunities are available for work (particularly for those with Korean-language skills), the biggest demand is for English teachers.

Native English teachers on a one-year contract can expect to earn around ₩2 million or more a month, with a furnished apartment, return flights, 50% of medical insurance, 10 days paid holiday and a one-month completion bonus included in the package. Income tax is very low (around 4%), although a 4.5% pension contribution (reclaimable by some nationalities) is compulsory.

The best starting point for finding out more about the English-teaching scene is the **Korea Association of Teachers of English** (KATE; www.kate.or.kr).

Transport

GETTING THERE & AWAY

Flights, cars and tours can be booked online at lonelyplanet.com/bookings.

Entering Korea

Entry to South Korea is not complicated or time-consuming for most visitors, who simply receive a stamp in their passport on arrival. A paper slip verifying this entry (which isn't the visa itself) is provided; hold onto this slip as it is requested by some hotels and when leaving the country.

> **DEPARTURE TAX**
>
> Departure tax is included in the price of a ticket.

Air

Airports & Airlines

Most international flights leave from **Incheon International Airport** (Map p113; www.airport.kr; Wi-Fi), connected to Seoul by road (80 minutes) and train (60 minutes), from Terminal 1. Terminal 2 opened in January 2018, with services limited to Air France, Delta, KLM and Korean Air; check for updates. There are also some international flights (mainly to China and Japan) from **Gimpo International Airport** (☎02-1661 2626; www.airport.co.kr), **Gimhae International Airport** (김해 국제 공항; Map p184; ☎051 974 3114; www.airport.co.kr/gimhaeeng/index.do; Ⓜ Busan-Gimhae LRT, Exit Airport) for Busan and **Jeju International Airport** (제주국제공항; ☎1661 2626; www.airport.co.kr/jejueng/main.do). Go to www.airport.co.kr for information on all the airports.

Tickets

Good deals can be found online and with discount agencies.

Prices of flights from Korea can increase 50% in July and August, and special offers are less common during holiday periods. The peak period for outbound flights is early August, when it can be difficult to find a seat.

Sea

International ferries are worth considering if you're travelling around North Asia.

China

Ferries link a dozen Chinese ports with Incheon.

Japan

Regular ferries shuttle between Busan and four cities in Japan: Fukuoka, Shimonoseki, Osaka and Tsushima. Faster services are available on hydrofoils (www.jrbeetle.co.jp/internet/english) from Busan to Fukuoka.

A Korea-Japan Joint Railroad Ticket via Korail (www.letskorail.com) lasts a week. It offers discounts of up to 30% on train fares in Korea and Japan, and on ferry tickets between the two countries from Busan.

Russia

DBS Cruise Ferry Co (www.dbsferry.com) runs the ferry 'Eastern Dream' that makes the trip from Donghae in Gangwon-do to Vladivostok on a regular basis; check the company website for fares and the schedule, which varies by season.

GETTING AROUND

Air

Korean Air and Asiana, the two major domestic airlines, provide flights to and from a dozen local airports, and usually charge identical but reasonable fares – competition is being supplied by a handful of budget airlines. Gimpo International Airport handles nearly all Seoul's domestic flights, but Incheon International Airport also has a handful of domestic flights to Busan, Daegu and Jeju-do. Budget T'way Airlines now runs more domestic fights to Jeju-do, from Gimpo, Daegu

CLIMATE CHANGE & TRAVEL

Every form of transport that relies on carbon-based fuel generates CO_2, the main cause of human-induced climate change. Modern travel is dependent on aeroplanes, which might use less fuel per kilometre per person than most cars but travel much greater distances. The altitude at which aircraft emit gases (including CO_2) and particles also contributes to their climate change impact. Many websites offer 'carbon calculators' that allow people to estimate the carbon emissions generated by their journey and, for those who wish to do so, to offset the impact of the greenhouse gases emitted with contributions to portfolios of climate-friendly initiatives throughout the world. Lonely Planet offsets the carbon footprint of all staff and author travel.

or Gwangju. The longest flight time is just over an hour between Seoul Gimpo and Jeju-do.

Fares are 15% cheaper from Monday to Thursday, when seats are easier to obtain. Flights on public holidays have a surcharge and are often booked out. Students and children receive discounts. Foreigners should always carry their passports on domestic flights for ID purposes.

Bicycle

The Korean government promotes cycling as a green and healthy means of transport. Seoul's metropolitan government has expanded cycling infrastructure in the city, including its own city bike scheme, Seoul Bike (www.bikeseoul.com), which visitors can use. However, poor local driving habits make cycling in Korea a less than pleasurable experience, especially in urban areas.

That said, hiring a bike for short trips in areas with bike paths or little traffic is a good idea. Bicycle hire starts at ₩3000 per hour, with discounts available for a day's hire. You'll have to leave your passport or negotiate some other ID or deposit. Helmets are typically not available and you may need your own bike lock.

Jan Boonstra's website Bicycling in Korea (www.janboonstra.com) has some useful information.

Boat

Korea has an extensive network of ferries that connects hundreds of offshore islands to each other and to the mainland. Services from Incheon's Yeonan Pier connect to a dozen nearby and more distant islands, while other west-coast islands further south can be reached from Daecheon harbour and Gunsan.

ISLAND	MAINLAND PORT(S)
Jeju-do (Jeju-si)	Incheon, Mokpo, Wan-do, Sam-chunpo
Jeju-do (Seongsan-ri)	Jangheung
Ulleungdo	Pohang

Bus

Long-distance buses whiz to every nook and cranny of the country, every 15 minutes between major cities and towns, and at least hourly to small towns, villages, temples, and national and provincial parks. Listed bus frequencies are approximate, as buses don't usually run on a regular timetable and times vary throughout the day. Bus terminals have staff on hand to ensure that everyone boards the right bus, so help is always available. Most buses don't have toilets on board, but on long journeys drivers take a 10-minute rest at a refreshment stop every few hours. When buses aren't busy, locals ignore designated seating and sit where they like.

Express buses link major cities, while intercity buses stop more often and serve smaller cities and towns. The buses are similar, but they use separate (often neighbouring) terminals. Expressways have a special bus lane that operates at weekends and reduces delays due to heavy traffic. Buses always leave on time (or even early) and go to far more places than trains, but are not as comfortable (sometimes overheated) or smooth, so for travelling long distances, trains can be the better option.

Udeung (superior-class express buses) have three seats per row instead of four, but cost 50% more than *ilban* (standard buses). Buses that travel after 10pm have a 10% surcharge and are generally superior class.

Expect to pay around ₩4000 for an hour-long journey on a standard bus.

Buses are so frequent that it's unnecessary to buy a ticket in advance except on weekends and during holiday periods. Buy tickets at the bus terminals. You can check schedules on www.kobus.co.kr and www.hticket.co.kr.

Car & Motorcycle

Driving Licence

Drivers must have a current (issued the year of travel) International Driving Permit, which should be obtained in your home country before arrival in Korea; they are not available in Korea and many motorbike- and car-rental companies will not rent you a vehicle unless you have one.

Car Hire

Not recommended for first-time visitors, but travellers who wish to hire a car must be 21 years or over and must by law have an International Driving Permit (a driving licence from your own country is not acceptable). Rates start at around ₩65,000 per day for a compact car but can be discounted by up to 50%. Insurance costs around ₩10,000 a day, but depends on the level of the excess you choose. It is better to rent a Korean car because in the event of an accident, it is much cheaper to fix, resulting in a lower deductible. Chauffeur service is also an option.

Incheon International Airport has a couple of car-rental agencies. Try **Lotte Rent-a-Car** (www.lotterentacar.net) or **Avis** (Map p113; ☎032-743 3300; www.avis.com; Incheon International Airport). GPS is likely to be in Korean only.

Insurance

Insurance is compulsory for all drivers in Korea. Since the chance of having an accident is higher than in nearly all other developed countries, obtain as much cover as you can, with a low excess.

Road Conditions

Korea has an appalling road-accident record, and foreign drivers in large cities are likely to spend most of their time lost, stuck in traffic jams, looking for a parking space or taking evasive action. Impatient and careless drivers are a major hazard and traffic rules are frequently ignored. Driving in rural areas or on islands such as Jeju-do or Ganghwado can be much smoother but public transport is so good that there's little incentive to sit behind a steering wheel.

Road Rules

- Vehicles drive on the right side of the road.
- The driver and front-seat passenger must wear seatbelts.
- Drunk drivers receive heavy fines, and victims of road accidents are often paid a big sum by drivers wanting to avoid a court case.

Hitching

Accepting a lift anywhere has an element of risk so we don't recommend it. Hitching is not a local custom and there is no particular signal for it. However, Korea is relatively crime-free, so if you get stuck in a rural area, stick out your thumb and the chances are that some kind person will give you a lift. Drivers often go out of their way to help foreigners. Normally bus services are frequent and cheap enough, even in the countryside, to make hitching unnecessary.

Local Transport

Bus

Local city buses provide a frequent and inexpensive service (from ₩1200 a trip, irrespective of how far you travel), and although rural buses provide a less-frequent service, many run on an hourly or half-hourly basis. Put the fare in the glass box next to the driver – make sure you have plenty of ₩1000 notes because the machines only give coins in change.

The main problem with local buses is finding and getting on the right bus – bus timetables, bus-stop names and destination signs on buses are rarely in English,

K-SHUTTLE BUS TOURS

The foreigner-only K-shuttle (www.k-shuttle.com) tour-bus service departs Seoul with a couple of three days, two nights packages (₩428,000), which include accommodation, breakfast, a guide who speaks English, Japanese or Chinese, and admission fees to various tourist sites along the way:

Western Course Stops in Buyeo, Jeonju, Yeosu and Busan before returning to Seoul.

Eastern Course Stops in Gangneung, Pyeonchang, Wonju, Andong, Gyeongju and Busan before returning to Seoul.

It's also possible to use the service to cover one or more sectors of a tour without the package component; for example, the fare from Seoul to Jeonju is ₩42,000, or to Andong ₩70,000.

Reserve your place on the 35-seater coaches at least five days in advance. There is no designated seating.

SUSTAINABLE TRAVEL TO KOREA

Unless you're already based in Asia, a journey to Korea is likely to be by aeroplane. When the train link between North and South Korea resumes it will open the way to the development of a Seoul–London train journey. For now, such a trip remains a distant dream.

The most direct rail route for getting to this side of the world from Europe or Asia is to ride the Trans-Siberian Railway: Lonely Planet's *Trans-Siberian Railway* guide provides the low-down on how to get to Vladivostok, from where it's possible to hop on a ferry to Sokcho. There are also regular ferries to Korea from several ports in China or from Japan.

Once in Korea you can do your bit for the environment by using the country's excellent public-transport system. Seoul's extensive subway and train system is particularly impressive and the city moved all its 8750-plus buses over to low-polluting natural-gas as well as full-hybrid and fuel-cell electric buses. Even the tiny island of Udo near Jeju-do is kitted out with 20 all-electric buses.

and bus drivers usually don't speak English. Writing your destination in big *hangeul* (Korean phonetic alphabet) letters on a piece of paper will be helpful. Local tourist information centres usually have English-speaking staff; these are the best places to find out which local bus goes where, and where to pick it up. The app Naver Map is available in English and has accurate journey-planner information for the whole country.

Metro/Subway

Six cities have a subway system: Seoul, Busan, Daejeon, Daegu, Gwangju and Incheon. The subway (also referred to as the metro) is a cheap and convenient way of getting around these major cities, and since signs and station names are in English as well as Korean, it is foreigner friendly and easy to use.

Taxi

Taxis are numerous almost everywhere and fares are inexpensive. Every taxi has a meter that works on a distance basis but switches to a time basis when the vehicle is stuck in a traffic jam. Tipping is not a local custom and is not expected or necessary.

Ilban (regular taxis) cost around ₩3300 for the first 2km with a 20% surcharge from midnight to 4am, while the pricier *mobeom* (deluxe taxis; black with a yellow top) that exist in some cities cost around ₩5500 for the first 3km but with no late-night surcharge.

Any expressway tolls are added to the fare. In the countryside check the fare first as there are local quirks, such as surcharges or a fixed rate to out-of-the-way places with little prospect of a return fare.

Since few taxi drivers speak English, plan how to communicate with the driver; if you have a mobile phone you can also use the 1330 tourist advice line to help with interpretation. Ask to be dropped off at a nearby landmark if the driver doesn't understand what you're saying or doesn't know where your destination is. It can be useful to write down your destination or a nearby landmark in *hangeul* on a piece of paper.

Train

South Korea has an excellent but not comprehensive train network operated by **Korail** (www.letskorail.com, ☎1544 7788). Trains are clean, comfortable and punctual, and just about every station has a sign in Korean and English. Trains are the best option for long-distance travel.

If you plan to travel by train a lot over a short period consider buying a 'KR pass'; see the website for details.

Classes

The fastest train is the Korea Train Express (KTX). A grade down are *Saemaeul* services, which also only stop in major towns. *Mugunghwa* trains are comfortable and fast but stop more often.

Many trains have a train cafe where you not only buy drinks and snack foods but also surf the internet, play computer games, even sing karaoke. If a train is standing-room only, hanging out in the train cafe for the journey is the best way to go.

Costs

The full range of discounts is complicated and confusing. For fares and schedules see the Korail website (www.letskorail.com). KTX trains are 40% more expensive than *Saemaul* trains (and KTX 1st class is another 40%). *Saemaul* 1st class is 22% more than the standard *Saemaul* fare. *Saemaul* standard fares are 50% more than *Mugunghwa* class. KTX tickets are discounted 7% to 20% if you buy them seven to 30 days before departure. Tickets are discounted 15% from Monday to Friday, and *ipseokpyo* (standing tickets) are discounted 15% to 30% depending on the length of the journey; with a standing ticket, you are allowed to sit on any unoccupied seat.

Children travel for half price any time; over 65-year-olds receive a 30% discount Monday to Friday.

Reservations

The railway ticketing system is computerised and you can buy tickets up to a month in advance online, on the Korail app KorailTalk (from the Apple App Store or Google Play), at train stations and many travel agencies. Seat reservations are sensible and necessary on weekends, holidays and other busy times.

Train Passes

Foreigners can buy a Korail Pass (www.letskorail.com) at overseas travel agencies or online; it offers unlimited rail travel (including KTX services) for one (₩81,000), three (₩113,000), five (₩168,000) or seven (₩195,000) consecutive days; there is also a 'select pass' that allows you to select either two (₩102,000) or four (₩154,000) days within a 10-day window, without having to travel on consecutive days. Children (four to 12 years) receive a 50% discount, and youths (13 to 25 years old) receive a 20% discount.

However, distances in Korea are not great, and trains don't go everywhere, so the pass is unlikely to save you much, if any, money unless you plan to shuttle more frequently than a Lonely Planet researcher back and forth across the country.

T-MONEY CARDS

Bus, subway, taxi and train fares can all be paid using the rechargeable, touch-and-go T-Money Card (http://eng.t-money.co.kr); the card provides a ₩100 discount per trip. The basic card can be bought for a nonrefundable ₩3000 at any subway-station booth, bus kiosks and convenience stores displaying the T-Money logo across the country. Reload it with credit at any of the aforementioned places, and get money refunded that hasn't been used (up to ₩20,000 minus a processing fee of ₩500) at subway machines and participating convenience stores before you leave. A competitor, but less widely accepted and available, card is Cash Bee. Both cards can be used to purchase goods at convenience stores and from vending machines.

T-Money cards are highly recommended because of the convenience but also the discounts offered when transferring to a different bus or train route. In Seoul for example, you can transfer within 30 minutes of one trip and potentially pay only ₩100 for the second leg of the journey.

Language

Korean belongs to the Ural-Altaic language family and is spoken by around 80 million people. The standard language of South Korea is based on the dialect of Seoul.

Korean script, *hangeul*, is simple and accessible, as each character represents a sound of its own. There are a number of competing Romanisation systems in use today for *hangeul*. Since 2000, the government has been changing road signs to reflect the most recent Romanisation system, so you may encounter signs, maps and tourist literature with at least two different Romanisation systems.

Korean pronunciation is pretty straightforward for English speakers, as most sounds are also found in English or have a close approximation. If you follow our coloured pronunciation guides, you should be understood just fine. Korean distinguishes between aspirated consonants (formed by making a puff of air as they're pronounced) and unaspirated ones (pronounced without a puff of air). In our pronunciation guides, aspirated consonants (except for s and h) are followed by an apostrophe ('). Syllables are pronounced with fairly even emphasis in Korean.

BASICS

Hello.	안녕하세요.	an·nyŏng ha·se·yo
Goodbye. (if leaving/ staying)	안녕히 계세요/ 가세요.	an·nyŏng·hi kye·se·yo/ ka·se·yo
Yes.	네.	né
No.	아니요.	a·ni·yo
Excuse me.	실례합니다.	shil·lé ham·ni·da
Sorry.	죄송합니다.	choé·song ham·ni·da
Thank you.	고맙습니다./ 감사합니다.	ko·map·sŭm·ni·da/ kam·sa·ham·ni·da
You're welcome.	천만에요.	ch'ŏn·ma·ne·yo

How are you?
안녕하세요? — an·nyŏng ha·se·yo

Fine, thanks. And you?
네. 안녕하세요? — ne an·nyŏng ha·se·yo

What is your name?
성함을 여쭤봐도 될까요? — sŏng·ha·mŭl yŏ·tchŏ·bwa·do doélk·ka·yo

My name is ...
제 이름은 ...입니다. — che i·rŭ·mŭn ... ·im·ni·da

Do you speak English?
영어 하실 줄 아시나요? — yŏng·ŏ ha·shil·jul a·shi·na·yo

I don't understand.
못 알아 들었어요. — mot a·ra·dŭ·rŏss·ŏ·yo

ACCOMMODATION

Do you have a ... room?	... 룸 있나요?	... rum in·na·yo
single	싱글	shing·gŭl
double	더블	tŏ·bŭl
twin	트윈	t'ŭ·win

How much per ...?	...에 얼마예요?	...·é ŏl·ma·ye·yo
night	하룻밤	ha·rup·pam
person	한 명	han·myŏng
week	일주일	il·chu·il
air-con	냉방	naeng·bang
bathroom	욕실	yok·shil
internet	인터넷	in·t'ŏ·net
toilet	화장실	hwa·jang·shil
window	창문	ch'ang·mun

Is breakfast included?
아침 포함인가요? — a·ch'im p'o·ha·min·ga·yo

KEY PATTERNS

To get by in Korean, mix and match these simple patterns with words of your choice:

When's (the next bus)?
(다음 버스) 언제 있나요? (ta·ŭm bŏ·sŭ) ŏn·jé in·na·yo

Where's (the train/subway station)?
(역) 어디예요? (yŏk) ŏ·di·ye·yo

I'm looking for (a hotel).
(호텔) 찾고 있어요. (ho·t'el) ch'ak·ko iss·ŏ·yo

Do you have (a map)?
(지도) 가지고 계신가요? (chi·do) ka·ji·go kye·shin·ga·yo

Is there (a toilet)?
(화장실) 있나요? (hwa·jang·shil) in·na·yo

I'd like (the menu).
(메뉴) 주세요. (me·nyu) ju·se·yo

I'd like to (hire a car).
(차 빌리고) 싶어요. (ch'a pil·li·go) shi·p'ŏ·yo

Could you please (help me)?
(저를 도와) 주시겠어요? (chŏ·rŭl to·wa) ju·shi·gess·ŏ·yo

How much is (a room)?
(방) 얼마예요? (pang) ŏl·ma·ye·yo

Do I need (a visa)?
(비자) 필요한가요? (pi·ja) p'i·ryo·han·ga·yo

DIRECTIONS

Where's a/the ...?
... 어디 있나요? ... ŏ·di in·na·yo

What's the address?
주소가 뭐예요? chu·so·ga mwŏ·ye·yo

Could you please write it down?
적어 주시겠어요? chŏ·gŏ ju·shi·gess·ŏ·yo

Please show me (on the map).
(지도에서) 어디인지 가르쳐 주세요. (chi·do·e·sŏ) ŏ·di·in·ji ka·rŭ·ch'ŏ ju·se·yo

Turn left/right.
좌회전/우회전 하세요. chwa·hoé·jŏn/u·hoé·jŏn ha·se·yo

Turn at the ...	...에서 도세요.	...·e·sŏ to·se·yo
corner	모퉁이	mo·t'ung·i
pedestrian crossing	횡단 보도	hoéng·dan·bo·do

It's ...	... 있어요.	... iss·ŏ·yo
behind ...	... 뒤에	... dwi·é
in front of ...	... 앞에	... a·p'é
near ...	... 가까이에	... kak·ka·i·é
next to ...	... 옆에	... yŏ·p'é
on the corner	모퉁이에	mo·t'ung·i·é
opposite ...	... 반대 편에	... pan·dae·p'yŏ·né
straight ahead	정면에	chŏng·myŏ·né

EATING & DRINKING

Can we see the menu?
메뉴 볼 수 있나요? me·nyu bol·su in·na·yo

What would you recommend?
추천 해 주시겠어요? ch'u·ch'ŏn hae·ju·shi·gess·ŏ·yo

Do you have any vegetarian dishes?
채식주의 음식 있나요? ch'ae·shik·chu·i ŭm·shik in·na·yo

I'd like ..., please.
... 주세요. ... ju·se·yo

Cheers!
건배! kŏn·bae

That was delicious!
맛있었어요! ma·shiss·ŏss·ŏ·yo

Please bring the bill.
계산서 가져다 주세요. kye·san·sŏ ka·jŏ·da ju·se·yo

I'd like to reserve a table for ...	... 테이블 예약해 주세요.	... t'e·i·bŭl ye·ya·k'ae ju·se·yo
(eight) o'clock	(여덟) 시	(yŏ·dŏl)·shi
(two) people	(두) 명	(tu)·myŏng

Key Words

bar	술집	sul·chip
bottle	병	pyŏng
bowl	사발	sa·bal
breakfast	아침	a·ch'im
chopsticks	젓가락	chŏk·ka·rak
cold	차가운	ch'a·ga·un
dinner	저녁	chŏ·nyŏk
fork	포크	p'o·k'ŭ
glass	잔	chan
hot (warm)	뜨거운	ddŭ·gŏ·un
knife	칼	k'al
lunch	점심	chŏm·shim
market	시장	shi·jang
plate	접시	chŏp·shi
restaurant	식당	shik·tang

Signs

영업 중	Open
휴무	Closed
입구	Entrance
출구	Exit
... 금지	... Prohibited
금연 구역	No Smoking Area
화장실	Toilets
신사용	Men
숙녀용	Women

snack	간식	kan·shik
spicy (hot)	매운	mae·un
spoon	숟가락	suk·ka·rak

Meat & Fish

beef	쇠고기	soé·go·gi
chicken	닭고기	tak·ko·gi
duck	오리	o·ri
fish	생선	saeng·sŏn
herring	청어	ch'ŏng·ŏ
lamb	양고기	yang·go·gi
meat	고기	ko·gi
mussel	홍합	hong·hap
oyster	굴	kul
pork	돼지고기	twae·ji·go·gi
prawn	대하	tae·ha
salmon	연어	yŏ·nŏ
seafood	해물	hae·mul
tuna	참치	ch'am·ch'i
turkey	칠면조	ch'il·myŏn·jo
veal	송아지 고기	song·a·ji go·gi

Fruit & Vegetables

apple	사과	sa·gwa
apricot	살구	sal·gu
bean	콩	k'ong
capsicum	고추	ko·ch'u
carrot	당근	tang·gŭn
corn	옥수수	ok·su·su
cucumber	오이	o·i
eggplant	가지	ka·ji
fruit	과일	kwa·il
legume	콩류	k'ong·nyu
lentil	렌즈콩	ren·jŭ·k'ong
lettuce	양상추	yang·sang·ch'u
mushroom	버섯	pŏ·sŏt
nut	견과류	kyŏn·gwa·ryu
onion	양파	yang·p'a
orange	오렌지	o·ren·ji
pea	완두콩	wan·du·k'ong
peach	복숭아	pok·sung·a
pear	배	pae
plum	자두	cha·du
potato	감자	kam·ja
pumpkin	늙은 호박	nŭl·gŭn ho·bak
spinach	시금치	shi·gŭm·ch'i
strawberry	딸기	ddal·gi
tomato	토마토	t'o·ma·t'o
vegetable	야채	ya·ch'ae
watermelon	수박	su·bak

Other

bread	빵	bbang
cheese	치즈	ch'i·jŭ
egg	계란	kye·ran
honey	꿀	ggul
noodles	국수	kuk·su
rice (cooked)	밥	pap
salt	소금	so·gŭm
soup	수프	su·p'ŭ
sugar	설탕	sŏl·t'ang

Drinks

beer	맥주	maek·chu
coffee	커피	k'ŏ·p'i
juice	주스	jus·sŭ
milk	우유	u·yu
mineral water	생수	saeng·su
red wine	레드 와인	re·dŭ wa·in

Question Words

how	어떻게	ŏt·tŏ·k'é
what (object)	무엇을	mu·ŏ·sŭl
what (subject)	뭐가	mwŏ·ga
when	언제	ŏn·jé
where	어디	ŏ·di
which	어느	ŏ·nŭ
who (object)	누구를	nu·gu·rŭl
who (subject)	누가	nu·ga
why	왜	wae

soft drink	탄산 음료	t'an·san ŭm·nyo
tea	차	ch'a
water	물	mul
white wine	화이트 와인	hwa·i·t'ŭ wa·in

EMERGENCIES

Help!	도와주세요!	to·wa·ju·se·yo
Go away!	저리 가세요!	chŏ·ri ka·se·yo

Call ...!	... 불러주세요!	... pul·lŏ·ju·se·yo
a doctor	의사	ŭi·sa
the police	경찰	kyŏng·ch'al

I'm lost.
길을 잃었어요. ki·rŭl i·rŏss·ŏ·yo

Where's the toilet?
화장실이 어디예요? hwa·jang·shi·ri ŏ·di·ye·yo

I'm sick.
전 아파요. chŏn a·p'a·yo

It hurts here.
여기가 아파요. yŏ·gi·ga a·p'a·yo

I'm allergic to ...
전 ...에 알레르기가 있어요. chŏn ...·é al·le·rŭ·gi·ga iss·ŏ·yo

SHOPPING & SERVICES

I'm just looking.
그냥 구경할게요. kŭ·nyang ku·gyŏng halk·ke·yo

Do you have (tissues)?
(휴지) 있나요? (hyu·ji) in·na·yo

How much is it?
얼마예요? ŏl·ma·ye·yo

Can you write down the price?
가격을 써 주시겠어요? ka·gyŏ·gŭl ssŏ ju·shi·gess·ŏ·yo

Can I look at it?
보여 주시겠어요? po·yŏ ju·shi·gess·ŏ·yo

Do you have any others?
다른 건 없나요? ta·rŭn·gŏn ŏm·na·yo

That's too expensive.
너무 비싸요. nŏ·mu piss·a·yo

Please give me a discount.
깎아 주세요. ggak·ka·ju·se·yo

There's a mistake in the bill.
계산서가 이상해요. kye·san·sŏ i·sang·hae·yo

ATM	현금인출기	hyŏn·gŭ·min·ch'ul·gi
internet cafe	PC방	p'i·shi·bang
post office	우체국	u·ch'e·guk
tourist office	관광안내소	kwan·gwang an·nae·so

TIME & DATES

What time is it?
몇 시예요? myŏs·shi·ye·yo

It's (two) o'clock.
(두) 시요. (tu)·shi·yo

Half past (two).
(두) 시 삼십 분이요. (tu)·shi sam·ship·pu·ni·yo

At what time ...?
몇 시에 ...? myŏs·shi·é ...

At (five) o'clock.
(다섯) 시에. (ta·sŏs)·shi·é

Numbers

Use pure Korean numbers for hours when telling the time, for counting objects and people, and for expressing your age.

1	하나	ha·na
2	둘	tul
3	셋	set
4	넷	net
5	다섯	ta·sŏt
6	여섯	yŏ·sŏt
7	일곱	il·gop
8	여덟	yŏ·dŏl
9	아홉	a·hop
10	열	yŏl

Use Sino-Korean numbers for minutes when telling the time, for dates and months, and for addresses, phone numbers, money and floors of a building.

1	일	il
2	이	i
3	삼	sam
4	사	sa
5	오	o
6	육	yuk
7	칠	ch'il
8	팔	p'al
9	구	ku
10	십	ship

morning	아침	a·ch'im
afternoon	오후	o·hu
evening	저녁	chŏ·nyŏk
yesterday	어제	ŏ·jé
today	오늘	o·nŭl
tomorrow	내일	nae·il

Monday	월요일	wŏ·ryo·il
Tuesday	화요일	hwa·yo·il
Wednesday	수요일	su·yo·il
Thursday	목요일	mo·gyo·il
Friday	금요일	kŭ·myo·il
Saturday	토요일	t'o·yo·il
Sunday	일요일	i·ryo·il

January	일월	i·rwŏl
February	이월	i·wŏl
March	삼월	sa·mwŏl
April	사월	sa·wŏl
May	오월	o·wŏl
June	유월	yu·wŏl
July	칠월	ch'i·rwŏl
August	팔월	p'a·rwŏl
September	구월	ku·wŏl
October	시월	shi·wŏl
November	십일월	shi·bi·rwŏl
December	십이월	shi·bi·wŏl

TRANSPORT

Public Transport

A ... ticket (to Daegu), please.	(대구 가는) ... 표 주세요.	(tae·gu ka·nŭn) ... p'yo chu·se·yo
1st-class	일등석	il·dŭng·sŏk
one-way	편도	p'yŏn·do
return	왕복	wang·bok
standard class	일반석	il·ban·sŏk
standing room	입석	ip·sŏk

When's the ... (bus)?	... (버스) 언제 있나요?	... (bŏ·sŭ) ŏn·jé in·na·yo
first	첫	ch'ŏt
last	마지막	ma·ji·mak
Which ... goes to (Myeongdong)?	어느 ...이/가 (명동)에 가나요?	ŏ·nŭ ...·i/·ga (myŏng·dong)·é ka·na·yo
boat	배	pae
bus	버스	bŏ·sŭ
metro line	지하철 노선	chi·ha·ch'ŏl no·sŏn
train	기차	ki·ch'a

platform	타는 곳	t'a·nŭn·got
ticket machine	표 자판기	p'yo cha·pan·gi
timetable display	시간표	shi·gan·p'yo
transportation card	교통카드	kyo·t'ong k'a·dŭ

At what time does it get to (Busan)?
(부산)에 언제 도착하나요? (pu·san)·é ŏn·jé to·ch'a·k'a·na·yo

Does it stop at (Gyeongju)?
(경주) 가나요? (kyŏng·ju) ka·na·yo

Please tell me when we get to (Daejeon).
(대전)에 도착하면 좀 알려주세요. (tae·jŏn)·é to·ch'a·k'a·myŏn chom al·lyŏ·ju·se·yo

Please take me to (Insa-dong).
(인사동)으로 가 주세요. (in·sa·dong)·ŭ·ro ka·ju·se·yo

Driving & Cycling

I'd like to hire a ...	... 빌리고 싶어요.	... pil·li·go shi·p'ŏ·yo
4WD	사륜구동	sa·ryun·gu·dong
car	차	ch'a

I'd like to hire a bicycle.
자전거 빌리려고요. cha·jŏn·gŏ pil·li·ryŏ·go·yo

Do I need a helmet?
헬멧 써야 하나요? hel·met ssŏ·ya ha·na·yo

Is this the road to (Donghae)?
이게 (동해) 가는 길인가요? i·gé (tong·hae) ka·nŭn ki·rin·ga·yo

(How long) Can I park here?
(얼마 동안) 여기 주차해도 되나요? (ŏl·ma·dong·an) yŏ·gi chu·ch'a·hae·do doé·na·yo

Where's a petrol station?
주유소가 어디있나요? chu·yu·so·ga ŏ·di in·na·yo

I need a mechanic.
자동차정비사가 필요해요. cha·dong·ch'a chŏng·bi·sa·ga p'i·ryo·hae·yo

I'd like my bicycle repaired.
자전거 고치려고요. cha·jŏn·gŏ ko·ch'i·ryŏ·go·yo

GLOSSARY

For more food and drink terms, see the Food Glossary (p369).

ajumma – a married or older woman
~am – hermitage
anju – snacks eaten when drinking alcohol

bang – room
bawi – large rock
~bong – peak
buk~ – north
buncheong – Joseon-era pottery with simple designs

celadon – green-tinged pottery from early 12th century
cha – tea
~cheon – small stream
Chuseok – Thanksgiving Day

dae~ – great, large
dancheong – ornate, multi-coloured eaves that adorn Buddhist temples and other buildings
Dangun – mythical founder of Korea
DEP – Democratic Party
DMZ – the Demilitarized Zone that runs along the 38th parallel of the Korean peninsula, separating North and South
-do – province, also island
-dong – neighbourhood or village
dong~ – east
donggul – cave
DPRK – Democratic People's Republic of Korea (North Korea)
DVD-bang – room for watching DVDs

-eup – town

-ga – section of a long street
~gang – river
geobukseon – 'turtle ships'; iron-clad warships of the late 16th century
gil – small street
-gu – urban district
gugak – traditional Korean music
~gul – cave
-gun – county
~gung – palace
gwageo – Joseon government service exam

hae – sea
haenyeo – traditional female divers of Jeju-do
hagwon – private school where students study after school or work
hallyu – (Korean Wave) increasing global interest in Korean pop culture
hanbok – traditional Korean clothing
hang – harbour
hangul – Korean phonetic alphabet
hanja – Chinese characters
hanji – traditional Korean handmade paper
hanok – traditional Korean one-storey wooden house with a tiled or thatched roof
harubang – lava-rock statues found only on Jeju-do
~ho – lake
hof – local pub

insam – ginseng

jaebeol – huge family-run corporate conglomerate
~jeon – hall of a temple
~jeong – pavilion
jjimjil-bang – upmarket spa and sauna
Juche – North Korean ideology of economic self-reliance

KTO – Korea Tourism Organization
KTX – Korea Train Express; fast 300km/h train service

minbak – private homes with rooms for rent
mudang – female shaman
Mugunghwa – semi-express train
~mun – gate
-myeon – township
~myo – shrine

nam~ – south
~neung – tomb
~no – street
norae-bang – karaoke room
~nyeong – mountain pass

oncheon – hot-spring bath
ondol – underfloor heating system

pansori – traditional Korean solo opera
PC-bang – internet cafe
pension – upmarket accommodation in the countryside or near beaches
pocketball – pool
pokpo – waterfall
pyeong – real-estate measurement equal to 3.3 sq m

~reung – tomb
-ri – village
~ro – street
ROK – Republic of Korea (South Korea)
~ryeong – mountain pass

-sa – temple
Saemaul – luxury express train
samulnori – drum-and-gong dance
~san – mountain
sanjang – mountain hut
sanseong – mountain fortress
seo~ – west
Seon – Korean version of Zen Buddhism
~seong – fortress
seowon – Confucian academy
shamanism – set of traditional beliefs; communication with spirits is done through a *mudang*
~si – city
sijang – market
sijo – short poems about nature and life; popular in the Joseon period
soju – the local firewater; often likened to vodka
ssireum – Korean-style wrestling

taekwondo – Korean martial art
tap – pagoda
tonggeun – commuter-class train

yangban – aristocrat
yeogwan – motel with small en suite
yeoinsuk – small, family-run budget accommodation with shared bathroom
yo – padded quilt that serves as a mattress or futon for sleeping on the floor

Behind the Scenes

SEND US YOUR FEEDBACK

We love to hear from travellers – your comments keep us on our toes and help make our books better. Our well-travelled team reads every word on what you loved or loathed about this book. Although we cannot reply individually to your submissions, we always guarantee that your feedback goes straight to the appropriate authors, in time for the next edition. Each person who sends us information is thanked in the next edition – the most useful submissions are rewarded with a selection of digital PDF chapters.

Visit **lonelyplanet.com/contact** to submit your updates and suggestions or to ask for help. Our award-winning website also features inspirational travel stories, news and discussions.

Note: We may edit, reproduce and incorporate your comments in Lonely Planet products such as guidebooks, websites and digital products, so let us know if you don't want your comments reproduced or your name acknowledged. For a copy of our privacy policy visit lonelyplanet.com/privacy.

OUR READERS

Many thanks to the travellers who used the last edition and wrote to us with helpful hints, useful advice and interesting anecdotes:

Anemieke Drenth, Jennifer Flanagan, Ignacio Gabaldon, John Hutchings, Pierre Japhet, Michelle Josselyn, Mirna Knight, Miroslav Kotaska, Seohyun Lee, Ettore Mazza, Chay Mckenzie, Judson Quicksall, Sofia Riga, Eve Rosenhaft, Federico Saez, Ronald Steenstra, Maciej Swietlik, Tekke Terpstra, Ray VarnBuhler, Mark Vosmek, Lucy Whalley, John Williams, Danielle Wolbers, Andrew Youl, Ken Zumstein

WRITERS' THANKS

Damian Harper

Huge roll call of thanks for everyone who helped me: Lylah Lim, Olivia Buckley, Ju Young Jung, Kang Hui Jeong, Jeon Hyun Yang, Sean Hwang, Lee Jeong Uk, An Hey Jeong, Kim Hye-yong, Son Eun Young, Go Jihye, Kim Eunjung, Lee Hyun Soon, Yang Sa Hyun, Cho Young-chae, Lee Seung Hyun, Kim Jae Woo, Kim Jun-Woo, Kang Dong-hyo, Professor Rosa, Kyeong Min Kim, Elizabeth Lee, Kim In-Seon, Kim Seo Hyeon, Daniel Lee, Jati, Hyo-Jun Yoo, Choi Sung, Rosalinda F Arroyo, Kim Jin Yong, Clint Kwon, Richard Steward, Nervin Alban, Shingo Nagata, 김진경, Jordan Perrigo, Jessica Butler, Bill Moran, Lee Hyo Jeong, Ji Hye Jeong, Spencer Fox, Brother Lee and KS Kim. Thanks, as always to Daisy, Tim and Emma, plus the warmest of thanks to the lovely Korean people who made my journey the happiest of all.

MaSovaida Morgan

Many thanks to everyone who shared their insights and resources before, during and after this eye-opening adventure, especially: Holley LeFever, Janna Gibson, Sangyeob Han, Youngbok Jang, Marike Kotze, Taewoo, Kate and Marianna; Lucia and Mr and Mrs Kim; Mrs Park and Mr Ryu; and Mish, Tracy and Dionne. Thanks also to my co-authors, and to my editor Megan Eaves for the opportunity and unwavering encouragement. Love and gratitude to Ny, Ty and Haj, always.

Thomas O'Malley

Thanks to my esteemed co-writers and editors, to Yoon (ique Universe), to Mr & Mrs Kim for their hospitality and gourmet breakfasts, Leo, Paris Baguette's coffee, all the beers at Magpie Brewing, and most of all, to Ophelia.

Phillip Tang

A huge thanks to Octavio Nájera for making Seoul dance and sing, *ganando como siempre*. Mariah Lee and friends for workshopping Seoul tips and the *dakgalbi* city escape. Thanks to

Félix Barría and Jules Thivent for *makgeolli*, *galbi* and blossom flavoured chips, and Da Sel Lee and Jenny for Korean hospitality. Thank you to Megan Eaves and the co-writers for being patient and great virtual workmates. Thank you Vek Lewis, Fiona Ross and Francisco Vargas for additional virtual support.

Rob Whyte

A hearty thanks to the folks working in the tourist information offices. They're resourceful and incredibly patient. Thanks to Kim Tae-ho and Kim Seoung-ok for their insider knowledge about destinations and local food. On the road, thanks to the many people who took the time to open their Naver maps app and point me in the right direction. In Buyeo, I'm glad I had a chance to talk local history with Yun Yun-su, a knowledgeable tour guide.

ACKNOWLEDGEMENTS

Climate map data adapted from Peel MC, Finlayson BL & McMahon TA (2007) 'Updated World Map of the Köppen-Geiger Climate Classification', Hydrology and Earth System Sciences, 11, 163344.

Cover photograph: Changdeokgung, Seoul, South Korea. Ducoin-ana / Onlyworld / 4Corners ©

THIS BOOK

This 11th edition of Lonely Planet's *Korea* book was curated by Megan Eaves, and researched and written by Damian Harper, MaSovaida Morgan, Thomas O'Malley, Phillip Tang and Rob Whyte. The previous edition was written by Megan Eaves, Trent Holden, Rebecca Milner, Simon Richmond, Phillip Tang and Rob Whyte. This guidebook was produced by the following:

Destination Editor Megan Eaves

Senior Product Editor Kate Chapman

Product Editor Amanda WIlliamson

Senior Cartographer Diana Von Holdt

Book Designer Meri Blazevski

Assisting Editors Pete Cruttenden, Andrea Dobbin, Samantha Forge, Jennifer Hattam, Ali Lemer, Charlotte Orr, Jaeyoon Shin, Simon Williamson

Cartographer Julie Dodkins

Assisting Book Designer Virginia Moreno

Cover Researcher Naomi Parker

Thanks to Jennifer Carey, Grace Dobell, James Hardy, Andi Jones, Victoria Smith, Sam Wheeler

Index

Map Pages **000**
Photo Pages **000**

M

Map Pages **000**
Photo Pages 000

Map Legend

Sights
- Beach
- Bird Sanctuary
- Buddhist
- Castle/Palace
- Christian
- Confucian
- Hindu
- Islamic
- Jain
- Jewish
- Monument
- Museum/Gallery/Historic Building
- Ruin
- Shinto
- Sikh
- Taoist
- Winery/Vineyard
- Zoo/Wildlife Sanctuary
- Other Sight

Activities, Courses & Tours
- Bodysurfing
- Diving
- Canoeing/Kayaking
- Course/Tour
- Sento Hot Baths/Onsen
- Skiing
- Snorkelling
- Surfing
- Swimming/Pool
- Walking
- Windsurfing
- Other Activity

Sleeping
- Sleeping
- Camping

Eating
- Eating

Drinking & Nightlife
- Drinking & Nightlife
- Cafe

Entertainment
- Entertainment

Shopping
- Shopping

Information
- Bank
- Embassy/Consulate
- Hospital/Medical
- Internet
- Police
- Post Office
- Telephone
- Toilet
- Tourist Information
- Other Information

Geographic
- Beach
- Gate
- Hut/Shelter
- Lighthouse
- Lookout
- Mountain/Volcano
- Oasis
- Park
- Pass
- Picnic Area
- Waterfall

Population
- Capital (National)
- Capital (State/Province)
- City/Large Town
- Town/Village

Transport
- Airport
- Border crossing
- Bus
- Cable car/Funicular
- Cycling
- Ferry
- Metro/MRT/MTR station
- Monorail
- Parking
- Petrol station
- Skytrain/Subway station
- Taxi
- Train station/Railway
- Tram
- Underground station
- Other Transport

Note: Not all symbols displayed above appear on the maps in this book

Routes
- Tollway
- Freeway
- Primary
- Secondary
- Tertiary
- Lane
- Unsealed road
- Road under construction
- Plaza/Mall
- Steps
- Tunnel
- Pedestrian overpass
- Walking Tour
- Walking Tour detour
- Path/Walking Trail

Boundaries
- International
- State/Province
- Disputed
- Regional/Suburb
- Marine Park
- Cliff
- Wall

Hydrography
- River, Creek
- Intermittent River
- Canal
- Water
- Dry/Salt/Intermittent Lake
- Reef

Areas
- Airport/Runway
- Beach/Desert
- Cemetery (Christian)
- Cemetery (Other)
- Glacier
- Mudflat
- Park/Forest
- Sight (Building)
- Sportsground
- Swamp/Mangrove

OUR STORY

A beat-up old car, a few dollars in the pocket and a sense of adventure. In 1972 that's all Tony and Maureen Wheeler needed for the trip of a lifetime – across Europe and Asia overland to Australia. It took several months, and at the end – broke but inspired – they sat at their kitchen table writing and stapling together their first travel guide, *Across Asia on the Cheap*. Within a week they'd sold 1500 copies. Lonely Planet was born.

Today, Lonely Planet has offices in Franklin, London, Melbourne, Oakland, Dublin, Běijīng and Delhi, with more than 600 staff and writers. We share Tony's belief that 'a great guidebook should do three things: inform, educate and amuse'.

OUR WRITERS

Damian Harper

Chungcheongbuk-do, Gangwon-do, Gyeongsangbuk-do

With two degrees (one in modern and classical Chinese from SOAS), Damian has been writing for Lonely Planet for over two decades, contributing to titles as diverse as *China*, *Běijīng*, *Shànghǎi*, *Vietnam*, *Thailand*, *Ireland*, *London*, *Mallorca*, *Malaysia, Singapore & Brunei* and *Hong Kong*. A seasoned guidebook writer, Damian has penned articles for numerous newspapers and magazines, including the *Guardian* and the *Daily Telegraph*, and currently makes Surrey, England, his home. A self-taught trumpet novice, his other hobbies include collecting modern first editions, photography and Taekwondo. Follow Damian on Instagram @damian.harper. Damian also wrote the Plan Your Trip (excluding Outdoor Activities), Korea Today and History chapters.

MaSovaida Morgan

Busan & Gyeongsangnam-do, Jeollanam-do

MaSovaida is a Lonely Planet writer and multimedia storyteller whose wanderlust has taken her to more than 35 countries across six continents. Prior to freelancing, she was Lonely Planet's Destination Editor for South America for four years and worked as an editor for newspapers and NGOs in the Middle East and United Kingdom. Follow her on Instagram @MaSovaida. MaSovaida also wrote The Korean People, Architecture & the Arts and The Natural Environment chapters.

Thomas O'Malley

Seoul, Around Seoul

A British writer based in Beijing, Tom is a world-leading connoisseur of cheap eats, dive bars, dark alleyways and hangovers. He has contributed travel stories to everyone from the BBC to *Playboy*, and reviews hotels for the *Telegraph*. Under another guise, he is a comedy scriptwriter. Follow him by walking behind at a distance.

OVER PAGE MORE WRITERS

Published by Lonely Planet Global Limited
CRN 554153
11th edition – February 2019
ISBN 978 1 78657 289 9

10 9 8 7 6 5 4 3 2 1
Printed in Singapore

Phillip Tang

Seoul, Jeju-do

Phillip grew up on a typically Australian diet of pho and fish'n'chips before moving to Mexico City. A degree in Chinese- and Latin-American cultures launched him into travel and then writing about it for Lonely Planet's *Canada*, *China*, *Japan*, *Korea*, *Mexico*, *Peru* and *Vietnam* guides. Writing at hellophillip.com, photos @mrtangtangtang, and tweets @philliptang. Philip also wrote the Outdoor Activities, In the Korean Kitchen, Directory and Transport chapters.

Rob Whyte

Chungcheongnam-do, Jeollabuk-do

Rob is a Korea-based writer, explorer and educator. For almost two decades, he has been travelling the country with a special interest in island getaways, long distance walks on isolated trails and barbecue-pork restaurants. He has written Korea travel and foody content for numerous Lonely Planet publications.

North Korea The writer of our North Korea chapter has chosen to remain anonymous.

Korea's Top 13

1

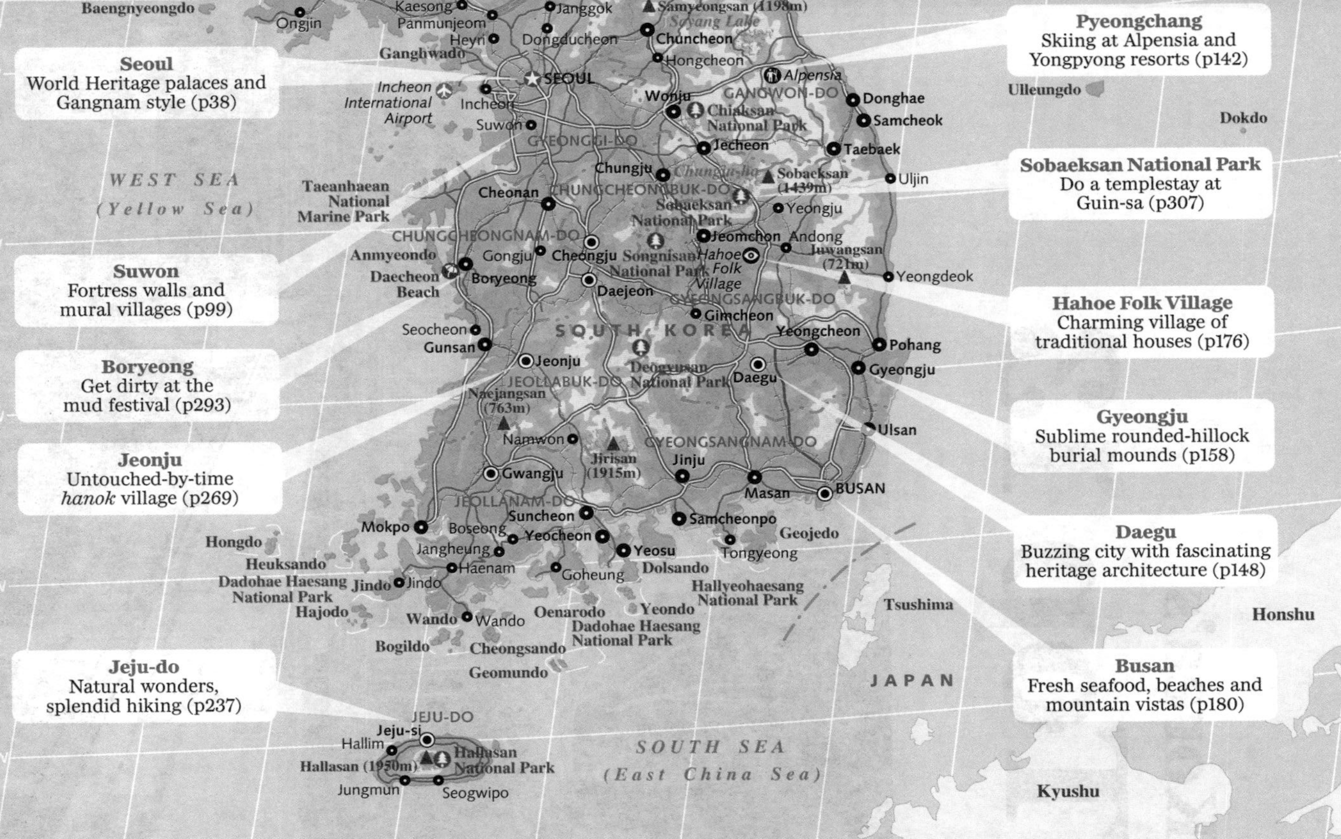

Seoul
World Heritage palaces and Gangnam style (p38)
Suwon
Fortress walls and mural villages (p99)
Boryeong
Get dirty at the mud festival (p293)
Jeonju
Untouched-by-time *hanok* village (p269)
Jeju-do
Natural wonders, splendid hiking (p237)
Pyeongchang
Skiing at Alpensia and Yongpyong resorts (p142)
Sobaeksan National Park
Do a templestay at Guin-sa (p307)
Hahoe Folk Village
Charming village of traditional houses (p176)
Gyeongju
Sublime rounded-hillock burial mounds (p158)
Daegu
Buzzing city with fascinating heritage architecture (p148)
Busan
Fresh seafood, beaches and mountain vistas (p180)
WEST SEA
(Yellow Sea)
SOUTH SEA
(East China Sea)
SOUTH KOREA
JAPAN
SEOUL
BUSAN
Baengnyeongdo
Ongjin
Kaesong
Panmunjeom
Heyri
Ganghwado
Janggok
Dongducheon
Samyeongsan (1198m)
Soyang Lake
Chuncheon
Hongcheon
Alpensia
Incheon International Airport
Incheon
Suwon
GYEONGGI-DO
GANGWON-DO
Wonju
Chiaksan National Park
Donghae
Samcheok
Jecheon
Taebaek
Ulleungdo
Dokdo
Chungju
Sobaeksan (1439m)
Uljin
Taeanhaean National Marine Park
Cheonan
CHUNGCHEONGBUK-DO
Sobaeksan National Park
Yeongju
CHUNGCHEONGNAM-DO
Jeomchon
Andong
Anmyeondo
Gongju
Cheongju
Songnisan National Park
Hahoe Folk Village
Juwangsan (721m)
Daecheon Beach
Boryeong
Yeongdeok
Daejeon
GYEONGSANGBUK-DO
Gimcheon
Seocheon
Yeongcheon
Pohang
Gunsan
Jeonju
Deogyusan National Park
Daegu
Gyeongju
JEOLLABUK-DO
Naejangsan (763m)
Ulsan
Namwon
GYEONGSANGNAM-DO
Jirisan (1915m)
Jinju
Gwangju
Masan
JEOLLANAM-DO
Suncheon
Samcheonpo
Mokpo
Boseong
Geojedo
Hongdo
Yeocheon
Yeosu
Tongyeong
Jangheung
Heuksando
Haenam
Dolsando
Goheung
Dadohae Haesang National Park
Jindo
Hallyeohaesang National Park
Hajodo
Oenarodo
Yeondo
Tsushima
Wando
Honshu
Dadohae Haesang National Park
Bogildo
Cheongsando
Geomundo
JEJU-DO
Jeju-si
Hallim
Hallasan National Park
Hallasan (1950m)
Jungmun
Seogwipo
Kyushu
38°N
37°N
36°N
35°N
34°N
123°E
124°E
125°E
126°E
127°E
128°E
129°E
133°E

Korea

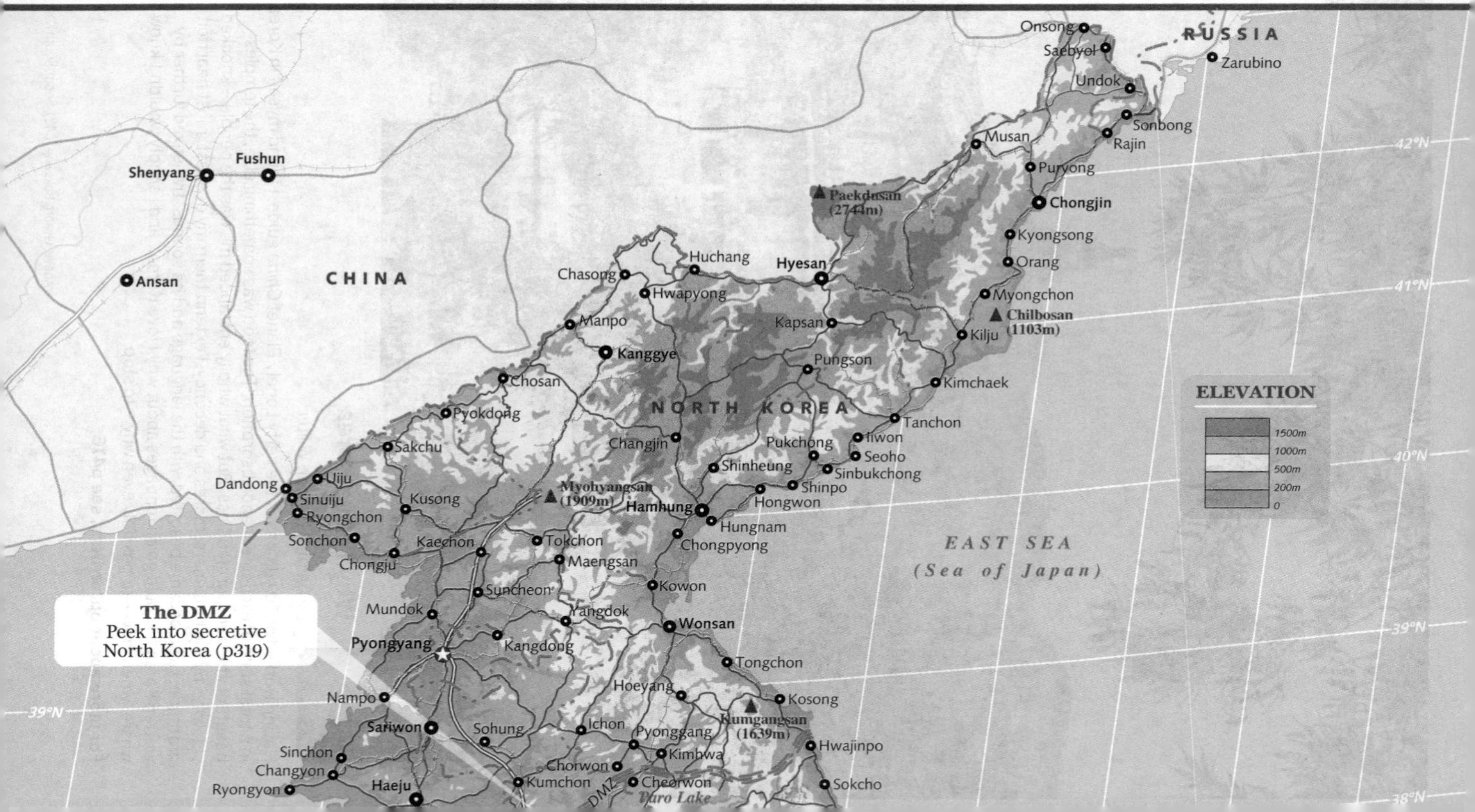

The DMZ
Peek into secretive North Korea (p319)

RUSSIA
Zarubino
Onsong
Saebyol
Undok
Sonbong
Rajin
Musan
Puryong
Chongjin
Kyongsong
Orang
Myongchon
Chilbosan (1103m)
Kilju
Kimchaek
Tanchon
Iiwon
Seoho
Sinbukchong
Pukchong
Shinpo
Hongwon
Shinheung
Hamhung
Hungnam
Chongpyong
Paekdusan (2744m)
Hyesan
Kapsan
Pungson
Huchang
Chasong
Hwapyong
Manpo
Kanggye
Changjin
NORTH KOREA
Chosan
Pyokdong
Sakchu
Uiju
Dandong
Sinuiju
Ryongchon
Sonchon
Chongju
Kusong
Kaechon
Myohyangsan (1909m)
Tokchon
Maengsan
Suncheon
Kowon
Wonsan
Mundok
Yangdok
Kangdong
Pyongyang
Tongchon
Hoeyang
Kosong
Kumgangsan (1639m)
Nampo
Sariwon
Sohung
Ichon
Pyonggang
Kimhwa
Hwajinpo
Sinchon
Changyon
Ryongyon
Haeju
Chorwon
Kumchon
Cheorwon
DMZ
Paro Lake
Sokcho
CHINA
Shenyang
Fushun
Ansan
EAST SEA
(Sea of Japan)
ELEVATION
1500m
1000m
500m
200m
0
42°N
41°N
40°N
39°N
38°N

Why I Love Korea

By Damian Harper, Writer

Having worked on 10 editions of the hefty Lonely Planet *China* guide, I found myself in Korea in a total state of excitement and absorption. The food was something else, the temples beautiful, the transport faultless. But what wholly entranced me was the people – knocked sideways by their manners, mores and decency, I extend them my deepest, most heartfelt gratitude. I also became besotted with the language and its sounds, transfixed further by written Korean. I could go on for pages about why I love Korea...and I simply wouldn't know where, when, how – or possibly even why – to stop.

For more about our writers, see p416

Above: Gyeongbokgung (p42), Seoul, South Korea

Welcome to Korea

Split by a hair-trigger border, the Korean Peninsula offers the traveller a dazzling range of experiences, beautiful landscapes and 5000 years of culture and history.

Welcoming Hospitality

Decorum plays a major role in Koreans' generosity to outsiders, and their instinctive graciousness possesses an endearing quality. Helpfulness abounds, whether it's at a tourist office, asking for directions or finding yourself deep in a conversation with a local. Time-honoured Confucian principles have set a template for strong civic pride in a society that is introspective, perhaps, but also decorous and affirmative. You may pass glorious landscapes and gaze out across dazzling seas but don't forget, half of your travel journey will be about the people, and the Koreans are a joy to be among.

Urban Buzz

Korea might be known as the Land of the Morning Calm, but dive into its capital Seoul, the powerhouse of Asia's third-largest economy, and serenity may be the last thing you'll perceive. This round-the-clock city is constantly in motion, with a work-hard, play-hard mentality that epitomises the nation's indefatigable, can-do spirit. You can hardly turn a corner without stumbling across a helpful tourist information booth, a bustling subway station or a taxi in this multifaceted metropolis where meticulously reconstructed palaces rub shoulders with teeming night markets and dramatically modern architecture.

Idyllic Countryside

South Korea's compact size and superb transport infrastructure mean that tranquillity is within easy reach of urban sprawl. Hike to the summits of craggy mountains – some of which transform into ski slopes come winter – enveloped within densely forested national parks. Get further off the beaten path than you thought possible by sailing to remote islands, where farming and fishing folk welcome you into their homes or simple seafood cafes. Gaze up at the distant stars from serene villages surrounded by rice fields and sleep in rustic *hanok* (traditional wooden house) guesthouses.

Festivals & Food

Rest assured the Republic of Korea (ROK, South Korea) also knows how to rock. A packed calendar of festivals and events means there's almost always a celebration of some sort to attend wherever you are: it might be Boryeong for its mud fest, or Gwangju for its Biennale or its annual salute to that most Korean of foods – kimchi (pickled vegetables). Koreans are proud of their culinary culture and rightly so – there's a tantalising array of dishes, flavours, aromas and textures in the local cuisine, to be washed down with plenty of toasting involving a head-spinning array of alcoholic concoctions.

Contents

UNDERSTAND

SURVIVAL GUIDE

SPECIAL FEATURES

PLAN YOUR TRIP

MARK LIDDELL / GETTY IMAGES ©

KIMCHI P365

CHOONGMIN63 / GETTY IMAGES ©

CHANGNG OF THE GUARD, DEOKSUGUNG (P49), SEOUL, SOUTH KOREA

ON THE ROAD

Korea

North Korea
p309

Seoul
p38

Around Seoul
p93

Gangwon-do
p118

Chungcheongbuk-do
p297

Chungcheongnam-do
p280

Gyeongsangbuk-do
p146

Jeollabuk-do
p267

Busan &
Gyeongsangnam-do
p180

Jeollanam-do
p212

Jeju-do
p237

Damian Harper, MaSovaida Morgan, Thomas O'Malley,
Phillip Tang, Rob Whyte